Botswana

Okavango Delta • Chobe • Northern Kalahari

the Bradt Safari Guide

Chris McIntyre

edition
2

www.bradtguides.com

Bradt Travel Guides Ltd, UK
The Globe Pequot Press Inc, USA

BOTSWANA: OKAVANGO DELTA, CHOBE, NORTHERN KALAHARI

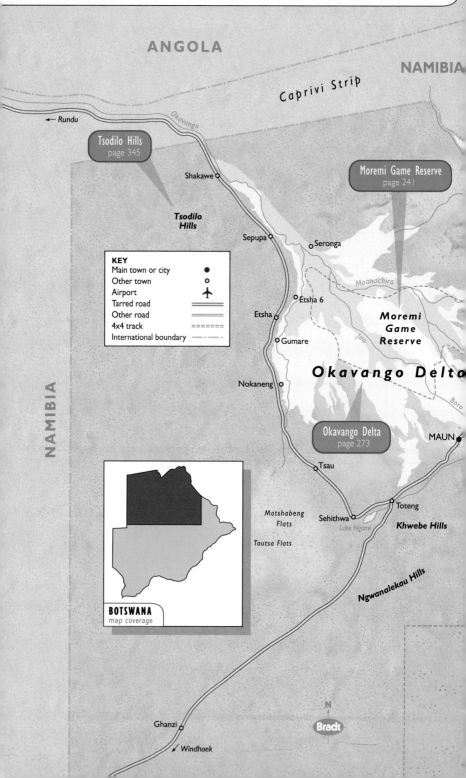

ANGOLA

NAMIBIA

Caprivi Strip

Okavango

← Rundu

Tsodilo Hills
page 345

Shakawe

Tsodilo Hills

Moremi Game Reserve
page 241

Sepupa

Seronga

Moanachira

KEY
Main town or city ●
Other town ○
Airport ✈
Tarred road
Other road
4x4 track
International boundary

Etsha 6

Etsha

Moremi Game Reserve

Gumare

Jao

Okavango Delta

Nokaneng

Boro

Okavango Delta
page 273

MAUN

NAMIBIA

Tsau

Toteng

Motshabeng Flats

Sehithwa

Lake Ngami

Khwebe Hills

Tautsa Flats

BOTSWANA
map coverage

Ngwanalekau Hills

N

Bradt

Ghanzi

↙ Windhoek

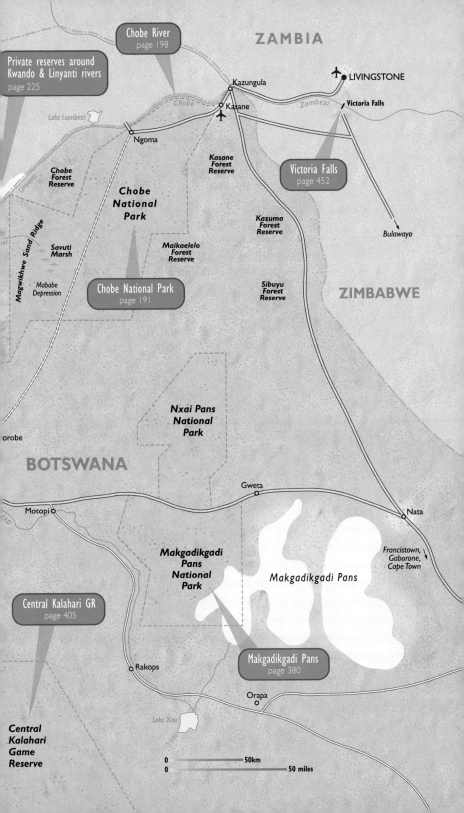

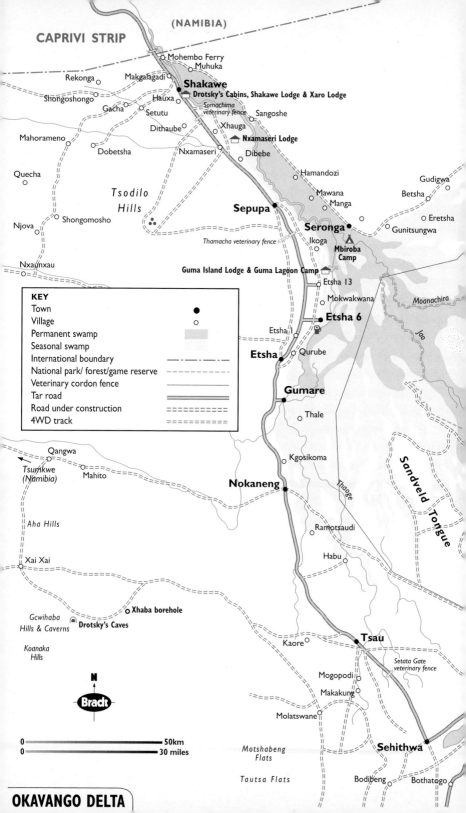

OKAVANGO DELTA

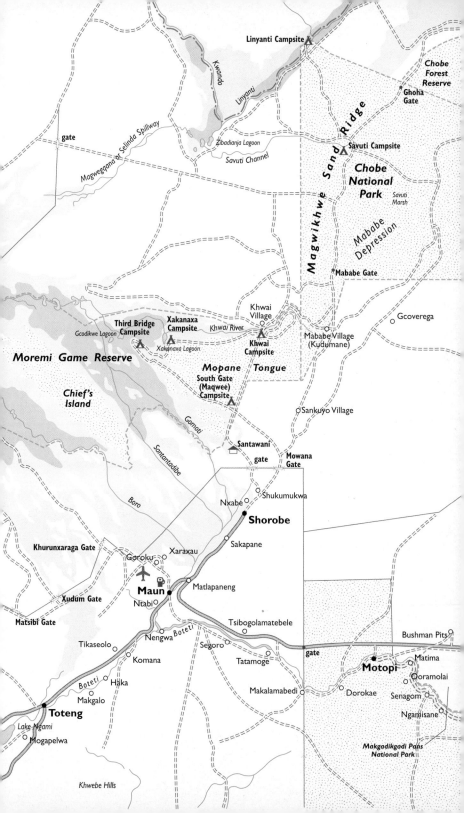

Botswana
Don't
miss...

Mokoro trip on the Delta
(CM) page 128

Birding
Carmine bee eaters *Merops nubicoides*
(RT) page 71

Wildlife
Male lion *Panthera leo*
(RM) page 469

Palm-fringed islands of the Okavango
A luxury lodge
(CM) page 273

Tsodilo Hills
left Laurens van der Post panel
right Rhino panel at the foot of the Female Hill
(CM) page 345

Aerial view of Okavango Delta
(CM) page 241

Author

AUTHOR

Chris McIntyre went to Africa in 1987, after reading physics at Queen's College, Oxford. He taught with VSO in Zimbabwe for almost three years and travelled around extensively. In 1990 he co-authored the UK's first *Guide to Namibia and Botswana*, published by Bradt, before spending three years as a shipbroker in London. After that, Chris concentrated on what he enjoys: Africa. In 1996 he wrote the first guidebook to Zambia for Bradt, and later their acclaimed Namibia guide. Whilst keeping these updated, he is now managing director of Expert Africa – a specialist tour operator which organises a variety of high-quality trips throughout Africa, including Botswana. He maintains a keen interest in development and conservation issues, is a Fellow of the Royal Geographical Society, and contributes photographs and articles to various publications, including *The Times*, *Wanderlust*, *BBC Wildlife* and *Travel Africa*. Based in west London, Chris spends two or three months each year researching in Africa, but can usually be contacted by email on chris.mcintyre@expertafrica.com.

PUBLISHER'S FOREWORD   Hilary Bradt

The first Bradt travel guide was written in 1974 by George and Hilary Bradt on a river barge floating down a tributary of the Amazon. It was followed by *Backpacker's Africa*, published in 1979. In the 1980s and '90s the focus shifted away from hiking to broader-based guides to new destinations – usually the first to be published on those places. In the 21st century Bradt continues to publish these ground-breaking guides, along with guides to established holiday destinations, incorporating in-depth information on culture and natural history alongside the nuts and bolts of where to stay and what to see.

Bradt authors support responsible travel, with advice not only on minimum impact but also on how to give something back through local charities. Thus a true synergy is achieved between the traveller and local communities.

* * *

A few years ago I 'won' a trip to Botswana in a charity auction. It was a packed itinerary: five different lodges in ten days. It goes without saying that I loved it – the best safari experience I've had in Africa – but what added to the enjoyment immeasurably was Chris's guide. We used it for previews of the lodges, finding it spot on every time, and for more information on the wildlife we could expect to see. Again spot on. This new edition will inform and delight a host of future travellers.

Second edition January 2007
First published 2003

Bradt Travel Guides Ltd, 23 High Street, Chalfont St Peter, Bucks SL9 9QE, England.
www.bradtguides.com
Published in the USA by The Globe Pequot Press Inc, 246 Goose Lane,
PO Box 480, Guilford, Connecticut 06475-0480

Text copyright © 2007 Chris McIntyre
Maps copyright © 2007 Bradt Travel Guides Ltd
Illustrations copyright © 2007 Individual photographers and artists

ISBN-10: 1 84162 166 8   ISBN-13: 978 1 84162 166 1
British Library Cataloguing in Publication Data
A catalogue record for this book is available from the British Library

Photographs Chris McIntyre (CM), Martin Harvey/Alamy (MH), Tricia Hayne (TH), Rob McDowell (RM), David MacCallum-Price (DM), Richard du Toit (RT), Ariadne Van Zandbergen (AZ)
Front cover Elephant calves in the Okavango Delta (MH)
Back cover Leopard *Panthera pardus* in camelthorn tree (CM)
Title page Lion cub *Panthera leo* (DM), Malachite kingfisher *Alcedo cristata* (CM), Fireball lily *Scadoxus multiflorus* (TH)
Illustrations Annabel Milne, Carole Vincer   **Maps** Terence Crump, Steve Munns
Typeset from the author's disc by Wakewing
Printed and bound in Italy by Legoprint SpA, Trento

Major Contributors

Tricia and Bob Hayne updated the sections on Maun, Chobe and Kasane for this edition. As former editorial director of Bradt Travel Guides, Tricia is only too familiar with the minutiae of putting together a guidebook, and enjoys seeing it from the other side of the coin. She and Bob have also helped to update Chris's guides to Namibia, Zambia and Zanzibar.

Judi Helmholz counts travel consultant, entrepreneur, safari guide, chicken farmer and 'facilitator' among her occupations. She lives beside the Zambezi with her husband, Arthur, several rottweilers and 4,000 chickens. She is active in Livingstone's Tourism Association and conservation, and contributed much of the information for the Livingstone chapter.

Octavia Kenny studied Old English literature and archaeology at Oxford and York, before becoming a museum curator, with a particular interest in oral history. Octavia researched and wrote most of the history in the first chapter, and kept her cool during a long research trip to the Kalahari. She currently lives and writes in London, and travels as much as possible.

Mike Unwin is a freelance natural-history writer and illustrator, and author of Bradt's *Southern African Wildlife: A Visitor's Guide*. Mike contributed much expert natural history information, and wrote most of the chapter on the Kalahari's great salt pans. He now lives in England, having spent seven years in southern Africa pursuing wildlife around all corners of the region. In 2000, he won the BBC Wildlife Magazine Travel-Writing competition.

Contents

Acknowledgements   VII

Introduction   IX

PART ONE   GENERAL INFORMATION   I

Chapter 1   History and Economy   3
History 3, Economy 16

Chapter 2   People and Culture   19
People 19, Language 34, Education 37, Cultural
guidelines 37, Giving something back 39

Chapter 3   The Natural Environment   43
Physical environment 43, Flora and fauna 53,
Conservation 62

Chapter 4   Planning and Preparation   67
When to go 67, Entry requirements 73, Getting there and
away 74, Organising and booking your trip 77, Money and
budgeting 88, What to take 92

Chapter 5   Health and Safety   99
Before you go 99, In Botswana 103, Safety 113

Chapter 6   Into the Wilds   117
Driving 117, Bush camping 121, Walking in the bush 125,
Boating 128, Minimum impact 130

Chapter 7   Botswana Today   133
Getting around 133, Accommodation 135, Food and
drink 135, What to buy 137, Organising and booking 137,
Communications and media 139, Other practicalities 142

PART TWO   THE GUIDE   145

Chapter 8   Maun   147
Getting there and away 147, Orientation 149, Getting
around 149, Where to stay 150, Where to eat and
drink 159, Nightlife 161, Shopping 161, Other
practicalities 162, What to see and do 164, Tourist
information, travel agents and tour operators 167, The
road north of Maun: to Moremi and Chobe 173

Chapter 9   Kasane and the Northeast   175
Kasane 175, Around Kasane 188

Chapter 10 **Chobe National Park and Forest Reserve** **191**
Background information 191, When to visit 196, Chobe
riverfront 198, Driving from Kasane to Savuti 205, Chobe
Forest Reserve 209, Liambezi area 211, Ngwezumba
pans 211, Savuti 212, Driving south from Savuti 220,
Linyanti 222

Chapter 11 **Linyanti, Selinda and Kwando Reserves** **225**
Background information 225, Linyanti concession
(NG15) 226, Selinda concession (NG16) 230, Kwando
concession (NG14) 237

Chapter 12 **The Okavango Delta – Moremi Game Reserve** **241**
Background information 241, The Mopane Tongue 248,
The private areas of Moremi (NG28) 264

Chapter 13 **Okavango Delta – Private Reserves around Moremi** **273**
Gudigwa (NG12) 276, Khwai community concessions
(NG18 and NG19) 276, Kwara Reserve (NG20) 276,
Xugana, Camp Okavango and Shinde (NG21) 280,
Vumbura and Duba Plains (NG22 and NG23) 284,
Community area (NG24) 289, Jao, Kwetsani, Jacana and
Tubu camps (NG25) 290, Abu Camp and Macatoo
(NG26) 294, Pom Pom, Kanana and Nxabega
(NG27A) 299, Delta, Oddballs, Gunn's and Eagle Island
(NG27B) 303, Xigera, Mombo and Chief's Camp
(NG28) 309, Gubanare and Xudum (NG29 and
NG30) 309, Chitabe and Sandibe (NG31) 314, Stanley's,
Baines' and budget mokoro trips (NG32) 318, Sankuyo
Tswaragano Community Trust (NG33) 322, Sankuyo
Community Trust and Starling's (NG34) 323, Mankwe
(NG43) 326

Chapter 14 **The Okavango Panhandle and Northwest Kalahari** **329**
The Panhandle 329, The delta's western fringes 338, The
northwest Kalahari 345

Chapter 15 **The Kalahari's Great Salt Pans** **365**
Background information 365, Getting organised 372, Nxai
Pan National Park 373, Makgadikgadi Pans 380,
Makgadikgadi Pans National Park 395

Chapter 16 **The Central Kalahari** **405**
Background information 405, Practical information 410,
What to see and do 416, Rakops 420

Chapter 17 **Livingstone and the Victoria Falls** **421**
History 421, Geology 423, Useful information 425,
Livingstone 425

Appendix 1 **Wildlife Guide** **469**
Appendix 2 **Language** **489**
Appendix 3 **Further Information** **491**
  Index **497**

LIST OF MAPS

African continent showing faults	47
Aha & Gcwihaba Hills, Nokaneng & Tsao	357
Botswana colour section, ii–iii	
Central Kalahari	404
Central Kalahari Game Reserve, northern	412–13
Chobe riverfront to Savuti	192–3
Chobe riverfront area	200
Gcwihaba Caverns	362
Guma Lagoon	342
Great Salt Pans	366–7
Kasane	178
Kasane & the northeast	176
Khwai (North Gate) area	247
Kwando, Selinda & Linyanti	224
Land above sea level	44
Livingstone	430–1
Livingstone & Victoria Falls	424
Livingstone & the Zambezi	422
Makgadikgadi superlake	46
Maun centre	152–3
Maun, lodges north of	157
Maun overview	146
Mohembo, Shakawe & Tsodilo Hills	335
Moremi overview	242–3
North Gate (Khwai) area	247
Ntwetwe Pan & Makgadikgadi Pans National Park	392–3
Nxai Pan & Kgama-Kgama Pan	378
Nxai Pan National Park	374
Okavango, cross section of	48
Okavango Delta colour section, iv–v	
Okavango's faults	48
Okavango, private reserves, camps & lodges	274–5
Panhandle & NW Kalahari	328
Piper's Pan	419
Savuti area	214
Sua Pan	387
Tsodilo Hills	348
Vegetation	54
Xakanaxa	254

VI

Acknowledgements

Writing this book has been a team effort; I'm indebted to many that have made researching a pleasure and this book possible. Firstly thanks to African expert and fellow author, Philip Briggs, for the original text of the *Wildlife Guide* appendix, and for allowing me to build on it. Also to Janice Booth, for her box on *Women travellers* and, with Hilary Bradt, for invaluable input on drafts of several chapters. Thanks also to Dr Felicity Nicholson and Dr Jane Wilson-Howarth for their expertise on health matters. Thanks to Wilderness Safaris for kind permission to borrow from diagrams for the illustrations in *Chapter 3*.

Thanks to my patient colleagues at Expert Africa – several of whom are authorities on travel in Botswana in their own right; also to Noel Josephides and John der Parthog for their good humour whilst I travel. Thanks to many of Expert Africa's travellers who have commented on drafts, and helped with feedback after their trips, but especially Peter & Julie Dodd, Martin Kendall, Peter & Sue Egan, and Sue Granger & Peter Dalby. Others are many, and I hope will forgive their omission.

On a personal note, my fiancée, Susie, made a great travelling companion during a particularly punishing research trip; I'm looking forward to many more trips with her in the future! Duncan, Purbs, Occy, Fritz and Simon all helped with different aspects of previous books, and all are remembered here with thanks. On a professional basis Colin Bell, Peter Sandenbergh and Dave van Smeerdijk gave valuable help, as did Julie Brenner-Clifford and Rob Clifford.

Others went far out of their way to help or guide me around Botswana. I hope that those who aren't mentioned here will forgive the accidental omissions. Some who spring to mind include: Annelies from Drumbeat; Bev & Guy from Guma; Dendy Barker; Willem & Sally Barnard; Oreeditse Bojosi; Joyce Bestelink & Simon Paul; Rowan Calder; Lloyd & Sue Camp; Sarah Collins; Russell Crossey; Dany at AHS; Stephanie Drew; Elaine Dugmore; Roger & Sophie Dugmore; Beth Engelhart; Erica from Bushways; Tim Fincham; Carol-Ann Green; Doug & Sandi Groves; Adam & Brigitte Hedges; Heidi, Britt and team at Leroo-la-Tau; Caroline Helfer; Graham Hemson; Jan & Suzi from Huab; Map Ives; Nicky Keyes; Fiona Kimmins; Lorraine Kirk; Laura at Audi Camp; Louis at TRS; Alex Lugg; Guy Symons & Edurne Martinez; Ewan Masson; Matt & Lorna from Muchenje; Maureen at Landela; Glyn Maude; Suzy Lumsden & Ian Michler; Trust Mpotshane; Mike Myers; Craig Nesbitt; Estelle Oosthuysen, for Tsodilo comments; Karl Parkinson; Mike & Angie Penman; Phil & Kay Potter; Phil & Nicky at Ker & Downey; Ryan Powell; Geoff & Nookie Randall; Richard Randall; Susan Rothbletz; Sarah & Steve at Phakwe; Robert Schaerer; Ishmael Sebosaha; Sharon at Kubu; Rosi Slogrove; Ian Tema; Vikki & Richard Threlfall; Redmond Walsh; Alwyn van der Watt; Laura and Brent at Travel Wild; and Grant Woodrow, for help with the rhinos. Also Ralph, Paula, Bianca, Julie and especially Catherine from the Uncharted team; Diane Wright; Helen Simmans, Sally Brunning, Debra

Fox, Shona Bagley from CC Africa; Randall and, especially, Eliza Deacon at EBS; Karin, Kevin Leo-Smith, Mark Tennant and the Kwando team; PJ, Barney & Gogs from OHS; and also Connie, Kuda, Brian & Jan at Linyanti Explorations.

In writing this, I'm aware that there are many above who know much more about Botswana than I. However, three experts really stand out: Alec Campbell, Mike Main and Veronica Roodt. All have written amazing, scholarly works on Botswana which have been a real inspiration, and all kindly offered their help to me. Beside their erudite works (recommended in *Appendix 3, Further Information*), this book pales – but I hope that it may introduce Botswana, and their works, to a wider audience.

Finally, Bradt's team who've worked with me on this have been supremely patient and encouraging: Hilary Bradt, James Rice, Steve Munns, Sally Brock, John King and, especially, Tricia Hayne – who contributed much more than any normal editorial director, and without whom this book would simply never have been finished. That which is good and correct owes much to their care and attention; errors and omissions are all my own.

Introduction

Botswana meant little to me at first; it was never in the news. Then, finding myself in Zimbabwe, I remembered an old friend's enthusiasm for the Okavango Delta. So, in April 1988, three of us set off from Victoria Falls and hitched a lift in an open pick-up into Chobe. We were badly prepared, but even our lack of food and close encounters with hyenas added to the magic. No fences here; everything was so wild.

From Maun we splashed out on a few days' camping trip on a mokoro. Whilst the boatman spoke little English, the Delta was magical, almost surreal – like floating on a tropical fish-tank with animals everywhere around. The Okavango's lush greenery contrasted with the harsh dryness in the rest of the subcontinent. Iridescent birds flashed past, whilst terrapins sunbathed and otters played. All added to the feeling of paradise; we left entranced.

Thus started my love affair with the country. Since then I've been lucky enough to return many times. I've been guided by some of the best, learning more about the bush and its animals and plants. I've flown over the dry Kalahari and the verdant Delta, mesmerised by the ancient patterns of watercourses, islands and game trails. And I've walked and driven around, exploring for myself on the ground, exhilarated by the sense of freedom. Yet still I feel as if I've only scratched the surface of Botswana, and I always leave wanting to return.

It's tempting here, by way of introduction, to list the highlights of Botswana's main areas, one-by-one, describing each to entice the reader. But to do this would be misleading, as Botswana has just three main attractions for me.

First is the wildlife. Whether this is your first safari or your 50th, Botswana won't disappoint. The sheer variation of the country, from the arid Kalahari to lush, well-watered forest glades, ensures tremendous variety. Botswana is serious about its big game. It has spectacular herds of elephants and buffalo, and prolific populations of predators. Experienced safari enthusiasts can bounce across the bush following a pack of wild dogs: Botswana has probably the continent's best population of these highly endangered predators. Yet often it's the country's smaller residents that will keep you entertained, from tiny painted reed frogs and barking geckos, to troops of entertaining meerkats.

Second – and the underlying reason why many come here – is the feeling in Botswana that you're within an endless pristine wilderness, almost devoid of human imprint. For city-dwellers, such space is the ultimate luxury. In Botswana, animals wander freely across vast reserves which are measured in thousands of square kilometres, not hectares. Exploring these wilder corners is invariably deeply liberating.

Third, and missed by some, is Botswana's rich history. It's often barely hinted at but, veiled and mysterious, it's all the more enticing. It reveals itself in the paintings at Tsodilo, and the magic that seems to surround those hills. You'll catch a glimpse of it as you search for Stone Age arrowheads on the Makgadikgadi Pans.

And standing on an ancient river-bed, or the wave-washed hills around Savuti, it's hard not to think back and wonder what forces shaped this country, long before you, or any Europeans, first set eyes on it.

Back in the present, the world is changing fast. Most of the earth's great wilderness areas are under threat. The 21st century is an age when even the earth's wildest corners must earn their keep, adapt or change irrevocably. Botswana's government has been a beacon of prosperity and stability amidst a troubled continent. Financed largely by income from some of the world's largest diamond mines, it has set many examples of how to run a country. Taking a long-term view, its thriving tourist industry is the envy of the continent: minimising impact by admitting only small numbers who pay handsomely to rejuvenate themselves in its pristine environments. Then it has channelled much of the revenue back to the poorer communities in the areas concerned. This first-rate approach has been a steady, growing strategy to increase responsible tourism to Botswana. It hasn't been a quick way for the country to get rich through tourism, but it has been a sustainable one.

However, Botswana's diamonds aren't forever. Current deposits are running out, and whilst new ones are discovered, many expect the industry's output is likely to plateau and decline within a few decades at most. When this happens, it will leave a gaping hole in the economy. Tourism is the obvious way to fill this, but exactly how is unclear. With only a sketchy understanding of Botswana's appeal for overseas visitors, large companies are tempted to build big new hotels in efforts to increase the number of visitors. But more tourists may not mean more revenue for Botswana; if the country's sense of wilderness is destroyed, then it'll rip the heart out of the experience that is found here today. It'll devalue it to the point where it ceases to attract the high-spending visitors that currently come here on safari. Increasing numbers could bring diminishing returns.

So my plea to the reader is two-fold. First, go now and support Botswana's small-scale camps and responsible tourism; the country needs you. Second, having committed many of Botswana's secret corners to paper here, I ask you to use this guide with respect. Botswana's wild areas need great care to preserve them. Local people are easily offended, and their cultures eroded, by a visitor's lack of sensitivity. Enjoy – but be a thoughtful visitor, for the country's sake.

NOTE ON DATUM FOR GPS CO-ORDINATES For all the GPS co-ordinates in this book, note that the datum used is WSG 84 – and you must set your receiver accordingly before copying in any of these co-ordinates.

All GPS co-ordinates in this book have been expressed as degrees, minutes and decimal fractions of a minute. This is the same format as used by the 1998 edition of the Shell map, but differs from the 2001 Contimap, which uses degrees, minutes and seconds.

Note that Google Earth satellite images for some of the lodges, camps and key GPS locations in this book can be accessed directly from links on the on-line version of this guide at www.botswana-travel-guide.com.

Part One

GENERAL INFORMATION

Location Southern Africa, between 20° and 30° east, and between 18° and 27° south

Size 581,370km²

Climate Subtropical. Summer (Nov–Mar): 19–35°C; winter (Jun–Aug): 5–23°C. Rainy season Nov–Mar

Status Republic

GDP US$10,500 per capita (2006 estimate)

Currency Pula (BWP, abbreviated to P)

Exchange rate US$1 = P6.07, £1 = P11.97, €1 = P8.08 (December 2006)

Population 1,680,863 (2001 census), 1,639,833 (2006 estimate)

Population growth per year 0.04% (2006 estimate)

Life expectancy at birth 47 years (2006 official estimate)

Infant mortality 53.7/1,000 live births (2006 estimate)

Economy Major earners: diamonds, copper, nickel

Capital Gaborone, population 186,007 (2001 census), almost 250,000 (2005 estimate)

Other main towns Francistown, Lobatse, Selebi–Phikwe, Orapa

Language English (official), Setswana (national), Shona, other local languages

Religion Christianity, traditional beliefs

Flag Broad, royal-blue horizontal stripes, divided by black central stripe bordered by narrow white stripes

National anthem *Fatshe leno la rona*, which translates to 'Blessed be this noble land'

Public holidays 1–2 January, Good Friday, Easter Monday, 1 May (Labour Day), Ascension Day, 1 July (Sir Seretse Khama Day), 3rd Mon–Tue in July (President's Day), 30 September (Independence Day), 1 November, 25–26 December

Time GMT +2

Electricity 220 volts

Weights and measures Metric

International telephone code +267

History and Economy

We can learn a lot about Botswana today by looking back into its history. Its far distant past, explaining some of the main features of its landscapes, is covered as part of *The Natural Environment*, at the start of *Chapter 3*. A potted overview of Botswana's more recent human history is given here, casting some light on its current politics and economics.

HISTORY

EARLY PEOPLES Read about the country's geological history and it's framed in terms of hundreds, or at least tens, of millions of years. Thus it's sobering to realise how relatively recent any human history is, and how much more compressed its timescales are.

Our knowledge about early human life in Botswana is derived from archaeology and from oral histories, which go back about 700 years. Written records only date from the arrival of Europeans in the 18th and 19th centuries. Most of these are personal accounts, which are interesting, but subjective. In many places the story is confused and incomplete, or even deliberately misleading (see *A note on 'tribes'* at the start of *Chapter 2*).

However, from the archaeology we know that the ancestors of the Khoisan (see pages 4–5) were once widely dispersed throughout the continent and probably had exclusive occupation of southern, central and eastern Africa from about 60,000 years ago up to the last 3,000 years. Skeletons of a Khoisan-type people, dating back 15,000 years and more, are found throughout southern and eastern Africa. It is believed to be these people who made the rock paintings of people and animals that are found all over eastern and southern Africa and even in the Sahara Desert. The earliest paintings have been found in Namibia (the 'Apollo 11' cave) and are thought to date back 26,000 years.

Rock paintings found in the Kalahari, at the Tsodilo Hills, are evidence that the living was good enough to allow the people to develop a vibrant artistic culture. Most experts believe that many of the paintings have deeper significance, probably connected with spiritual, religious or mythological beliefs. It is impossible to interpret them accurately without an in-depth knowledge of the culture and beliefs of those who created them. Unfortunately no group today claims historical responsibility. The local Zhu Bushmen claim that their god, Gaoxa, made the paintings.

The animals of Africa, such as antelope, eland, rhinos and giraffe, are the subject of many paintings. The images beautifully capture the form and the spirit of each animal. Humans also appear; one painting at the Tsodilo Hills shows a group of 15 men exhibiting the permanent erection, or semi-erection, which is a distinctive feature of San men from birth to death. Later paintings, featuring black men and sometimes war, are thought to depict the arrival of the Bantu farmers.

3

The San The San were perfectly adapted to their desert environment and had learnt to survive its harsh extremes of climate – drought and unrelenting heat and sun in the winter, and heavy rains and floods in the summer.

Predominantly hunter-gatherers, it is thought that at various times, when the climate was more favourable, the San may also have owned and grazed stock. Several times in past millennia the climate of Botswana has been much wetter, and at others much drier than it is at the moment. Periodically the huge pans that are a distinctive feature of the landscape, such as at Makgadikgadi and Nxai, became great lakes, full of water and supplied by several rivers. Probably some San groups took advantage of plentiful supplies of water to acquire stock. Now the rivers have dried up and the Okavango Delta has receded, the pans are full of water only during the rainy season and the San are herders no longer. There are also more recent records of them owning and trading copper from secret mines in the Kalahari, and bartering it for iron.

The Khoe Around 3000BC, Late Stone Age hunter-gatherer groups in Ethiopia, and elsewhere in north and west Africa, started to keep domestic animals, sow seeds, and harvest the produce: they became the world's first farmers.

By around 1000BC these new pastoral practices had spread south into the equatorial forests of what is now the Democratic Republic of Congo, to around Lake Victoria, and into the northern area of the Great Rift Valley, in northern Tanzania. However, agriculture did not spread south into the rest of central/southern Africa immediately. Only when the technology, and the tools, of iron-working became known did these practices start their relentless expansion southwards.

It's thought that during the last centuries BC many Khoe-speaking peoples in northern Botswana converted their lifestyle to pastoralism – herding cattle and sheep on the rich pastures exposed by the retreating wetlands of the Okavango Delta and Lake Makgadikgadi.

It used to be thought that the Khoe acquired their stock during the (black) Iron Age, from Bantu-speaking farmers who are thought to have migrated into their area around 1,500 years ago. However, finds of sheep bone dating back 3,000 years now suggest that the Khoe had obtained stock long before the arrival of the Bantu, probably from east Africa where they had been herded for thousands of years. The Khoe spread, migrating with their livestock through central Namibia, as far south as the Cape of Good Hope, by about 70BC.

When the first Dutch settlers saw the Khoe in about AD1600 they lived in groups with a leader, but were split into smaller clans under their own headman. The clans came together only in times of stress or war. Because water was vital for the stock animals, the Khoe dug wells that were owned exclusively by the clan and group. In times of drought, when water was scarce, fights might erupt over these waterholes. Then each clan sent men to fight to protect the group's interests.

Each clan lived in a village, which was built inside a circular thorn hedge. In the centre were thorn enclosures to pen and protect the stock, surrounded by a circle of houses. Khoe houses are of a 'bender' or dome tent construction type; that is, long flexible poles are bent to form arches and the ends stuck into the ground. They are then covered with mats. When the clan needed to move to find more water or grazing these huts were simply taken down and strapped onto the back of their animals.

Tlou and Campbell describe one such village, which is known to have existed at Toromoja on the Boteti River around AD1200. A group of Khoe known as the Bateti lived there and kept long-horned cattle, sheep and goats, but they lived mainly on fish, zebra and other animals which they caught in the pits they dug by the river. They also ate plants, particularly water-lily roots. They had San servants who hunted and collected wild food for them. Sometimes they traded skins and ivory for iron tools, copper and tobacco, with the people living at Maun in the northwest, or the Toutswe people to the southeast.

Archaeologically speaking the Khoisan peoples were examples of Late Stone Age cultures; that is, their tools and weapons were made of wood, bone and stone. The Late Stone Age refers not to a period of time, but to a method and style of tool construction. Human beings had made stone tools for millennia and the name Late Stone Age refers to stylistic refinements and to the manufacture of tools developed for specific uses.

Specifically, experts define the transition from Early to Middle Stone Age technology as indicated by a larger range of stone tools often adapted for particular uses, and signs that these people had a greater mastery of their environment. This was probably in progress around 125,000 years ago in Botswana.

They normally characterise the late Stone Age by the use of composite tools, those made of wood and/or bone and/or stone used together, and by the presence of a revolutionary invention: the bow and arrow. This first appeared in southern Africa, and throughout the world, about 15,000 years ago. Skeletons of some of these Late Stone Age hunters had a close physical resemblance to the modern Khoisan people.

The Bantu-speaking farmers

The next people to arrive in Botswana were the Bantu-speakers. This collective term refers to a number of different tribes, from a related linguistic group, who gradually migrated down into southern Africa, from north of the Equator, over the course of thousands of years. The date of their arrival in Botswana is hard to pinpoint.

The Bantu were grain farmers (agriculturalists) as opposed to pastoralists or hunter-gatherers and they brought Iron Age technology with them; that is their tools and weapons were made of iron. Physically these Iron Age farmers were much taller and heavier than the Khoisan, and they became the ancestors of the modern black Africans in southern Africa.

Crucial to the production of iron is a smelting furnace capable of reaching very high temperatures. Associated with the Iron Age is a new kind of pottery, which also had to be fired at high temperatures. Archaeologists use the finds of pottery and iron to date the arrival of the new people on the landscape of Botswana.

It is thought that the Bantu-speakers arrived in two main waves, bringing western and eastern Bantu languages. From West Africa, Late Stone Age farmers on the upper Zambezi were converted to the use of iron tools by about 300BC. From east Africa, Early Iron Age farming spread south along the east coast as far as the Zambezi by around 20BC.

By 200BC, in the Okavango–Makgadikgadi region, people were making a kind of pottery which archaeologists think was Khoe pottery influenced by western Iron Age (Bantu) styles, suggesting an initial contact between the two groups. The major Bantu influx probably occurred around the first few centuries AD, and the ancestors of the Khoisan people, with their simple Stone Age technology and hunter-gatherer existence, just could not compete. Since then the Khoisan have gradually been either assimilated into the migrant groups, or effectively pushed into the areas which could not be farmed. Thus the older Stone Age cultures persisted for much longer in the Kalahari (which is more difficult to cultivate) than in the rest of the country.

In theory, the stronger iron weapons of the Bantu should easily have made them the dominant culture. However, it took a very long time for Bantu language and culture to replace that of the Khoe – as late as the 19th century people were still speaking Khoe on the Boteti River. This supports a theory of communities living peacefully there, side by side, for a thousand years or more.

There is some evidence of inter-marriage or inter-breeding between the two groups and the Batswana today have a mixture of Bantu and Khoisan features and they are noticeably lighter in skin colour than Bantu-speakers further north. They also tend to have the almond-shaped eyes, high cheekbones and thin lips of the Khoisan.

More immigrants There are numerous problems with compiling a historical record of Bantu history in Botswana. We are dependent on oral history and archaeological records, and the two sometimes conflict with each other. The situation is very complex because of the number and mobility of the tribes involved.

The earliest dated Iron Age site in Botswana is an iron-smelting furnace in the Tswapong Hills, which is dated to around AD190. There is evidence of an early farming settlement of beehive huts made of grass matting, dating to around AD420 by the Molepolole River and a similar one has been found coexisting with Khoisan sites in the Tsodilo Hills, dating to around AD550.

By the 4th or 5th century AD, Iron Age farmers had certainly settled throughout much of southern Africa. As well as iron-working technology, they brought with them pottery, the remains of which are used by archaeologists to work out the migrations of various different groups of these Bantu settlers. These migrations continued, and the distribution of pottery styles suggests that the groups moved around within the subcontinent: this was much more complex than a simple north–south influx. Many of the tribes roamed over the whole of southern Africa, before various colonial authorities imposed artificial country borders in order to carve out territories for themselves.

This situation was complicated more recently by the prolonged and horrifically bloody tribal wars of the 19th century, known to historians as the Difaquane Wars.

TSWANA HISTORY The Tswana rose to domination from among a number of powerful dynasties that spread out from the western Transvaal, around AD1200–1400. During the period AD1500–1600 the Phofu dynasty in western Transvaal disintegrated with junior brothers forming breakaway, independent chiefdoms. Oral history traditions explain this as a response to drought. The archaeological record shows populations expanding into open country in small villages with cattle corrals, but by around AD1700 the settlements were often larger towns built of stone and situated on hills, reflecting the growth of hostile states, and the need for a strong defence.

The Difaquane Wars The whole of southern Africa was subject to increasing disruption, migration and war from about 1750 onwards, as trading and raiding for ivory, cattle and slaves spread inland from the coasts of Mozambique, the Cape Colony and Angola. The tribes often captured opponents during battle and sold them to slave raiders. Some of the battles themselves may have been slave raids against an enemy tribe.

Paramount amongst the aggressors in these wars was an ambitious Zulu leader named Shaka, who controlled a large slice of Natal by around 1810. The Ngoni people, which includes the Zulu nation, refer to the wars which Shaka initiated as the Mfecane, or 'the crushing.' However, the Tswana people, who were amongst the victims of Shaka's wars of expansion, refer to them as the Difaquane, which means 'the scattering.' Because they scattered, so they dispersed others.

A good explanation of this period is covered in John Reader's excellent *Africa: A Biography of the Continent* (see *Appendix 3, Further Information*). He summarises the root causes:

Thus they [the Zulus] were trapped in 'the trans-continental cross-fire of interrelated European plunder systems.' It was the unrelenting advance of settlers from the west, and the predacious demands of slavers in the east – exacerbated by intermittent drought – that set southern Africa in turmoil during the early eighteenth century. Not Shaka, not the Zulus, not the Mfecane.

Eventually, after the wars passed in the 1840s, the Tswana states of Ngwaketse, Kwena and the Ngwato rose to prosperity. They organised their people into wards with their own chiefs, but all paying tribute to the king. The states were in competition over trade benefits for ivory and ostrich feathers, down new roads, south to the Cape Colony. These roads also brought Boer trekkers and Christian missionaries to Botswana.

One of the Tswana kings, Sechele of the Kwena (1829–92), was baptised by David Livingstone, who passed through Botswana on his missionary travels. However it was the Ngwato, who superseded the Kwena in trading supremacy, who produced the most remarkable and famous dynasty – and upon whom the following pages will concentrate.

Ngwato dynasty In *Serowe: Village of the Rain Wind* (see *Appendix 3, Further Information*), Bessie Head describes this remarkable dynasty, beginning with the reign of Khama the Great. He was king when the capital of the Bamangwato (Ngwato) moved to Serowe in 1902. Previously the capital had been 100 miles away at Shoshong, and then at Palapye, but each time the tribe was forced to move on when water sources dried up. In 1902 two rivers, the Sepane and the Manonnye, flowed through Serowe, although both have subsequently dried up.

Khama the Great Khama was the eldest son of Segkoma I, who was the chief when David Livingstone, the missionary explorer, first moved northwards through Botswana in the 1840s. Whilst the capital had still been at Shoshong, Livingstone had converted Khama and his brothers to Christianity. Although their father had allowed the missionaries to stay with them, and was interested to talk to them, he had refused to give up the traditional ways.

Eventually this led to a war between father and son, which Khama won, becoming king of the Bamangwato. Khama was a poetic visionary who changed the customs of his people in line with his Christian beliefs, and who foresaw the need for strong protection in the colonial carve up of Africa, and campaigned strongly for the British Protectorate of Bechuanaland. (See also *Chapter 2, People and Culture*.)

Segkoma II In 1916 Khama was kicked on the knee by a horse. At this time he invited his son Segkoma II, who had been in exile for ten years governing his own branch of the Bamangwato, to come home and rule at Serowe. This he did, and subsequently ruled at Serowe for nine years, although for most of that time he remained in the shadow of King Khama. Most importantly Khama insisted that Segkoma marry a woman given to him by the Bamangwato, and the heir from this marriage was Seretse, who would later become the first president of Botswana.

Tshekedi Khama Following the death of Khama, and shortly afterwards of Segkoma II, Tshekedi Khama (Khama's son from a late second marriage) stepped in as regent until the four-year-old Seretse should come of age.

Where Khama was a visionary and politician, Tshekedi was full of pragmatic common sense and his rule, from 1926 to 1959, is marked by educational advances and self-help projects. When he first became leader there was only a primary school in Serowe. Then Tshekedi used his own money to send the young people of the village to South Africa for further education. From there they came home to teach in the village school. Later a secondary school and subsequently a college were built, using the voluntary labour of what were known as the age regiments (see page 38). Also known as the mephato, these were groups of young men of about the same age, usually formed from those who had graduated from the tribal initiation ceremony (known as bogwera) at the same time. They could be called upon to carry out services for the good of the community, ranging from routine community tasks to helping out with emergencies.

Moeng College of higher education is exciting for the principles on which it was founded, which gave equal weight to traditional knowledge and craft skills alongside academic instruction. As an experiment in social relations the houses built for the teaching staff were the equivalent of houses for white government officials. It was the only college in southern Africa at the time where houses for white and black teachers were equal and where they lived together in the same hostel.

Seretse Khama During the reign of Tshekedi, a problem arose over the future of Seretse Khama. Seretse was educated abroad, in London, Fort Hare and Oxford. In 1948 Seretse wrote to inform his uncle that he wanted to marry an Englishwoman, Ruth Williams. Tshekedi opposed the marriage on the grounds that a king or chief could not do as he pleased because he was the servant of the people, and an heir to the chieftaincy was at stake. Traditionally the chief's wife was chosen by the *morafe* or tribal group. Seretse insisted on his right to choose his own wife and married the Englishwoman.

They were still arguing when the British took matters into their own hands. In a case that created international scandal, the British government barred Seretse from the chieftaincy of the Bamangwato, and exiled him for six years. They invited him to Britain, where they forced him to stay. They also banned Tshekedi Khama from entering the Bamangwato reserve.

Secret documents have since confirmed that this British intervention was in order to satisfy the South African government, which objected to Seretse Khama's marriage to a white woman at a time when the policy of racial segregation, apartheid, was being enforced in South Africa.

Seretse, Tshekedi and their people fought against this banishment. The Bamangwato refused to pay taxes, sent delegations to the British and led protests. They refused to accept a British nominated chief and many people, including women, were flogged for this refusal.

Finally Tshekedi visited Seretse in London and the two resolved their differences. Seretse returned to Botswana with Ruth. Although a condition of his return was that he remained barred from the chieftancy, both he and Tshekedi continued to play an active role in the politics of Botswana, and were instrumental in the lead-up to independence.

Traders The earliest Europeans to come to Botswana were adventurers, explorers, hunters and missionaries. Travel in Botswana was very expensive, even then. A year's travel could cost up to £600 – equivalent to what a soldier of the period might earn during 30 years in the army. So early travellers came to trade for ivory, which made them huge profits with which to finance their expeditions. They travelled in wooden wagons, drawn by oxen or horses, and brought guns, beads, clothing and other, less valuable items, which they bartered for significant amounts of ivory.

One of the biggest problems on the journey was the lack of water. There were often stretches of 50km or more without any. Water would be carried on the wagons, but not enough for both men and beasts. Sometimes the oxen died of thirst. There are stories of the wagons being unhitched and the oxen led to the nearest water – which could be some kilometres distant – and then returning to pull the wagons further. Oxen often died from drinking bad water or from tsetse fly bite, while horses died of tick bite. A distance of 20km per day was thought to be a good rate of travel.

However, a wagon that did make it could return with about 200 elephant tusks – worth around £1,200 when sold in Cape Town. As they heard tales of huge profits, more traders began to venture into the region and gradually introduced money, which had been unknown until then. Previously barter and exchange systems functioned in the village – one goat equals one woven grass basket, and so on. Subsequently money became important in trade and people were forced to either sell something, or sell their labour, to get money. Little paid work could be found in Botswana, so large numbers of people were forced to emigrate to find work, often in the mines in South Africa.

Meanwhile the traders began to settle in Botswana at Shoshong, though the Bamangwato chiefs, Segkoma and Khama, were keen to prevent them from going further into the interior, so that they could maintain their trading supremacy.

The missions Following the traders came the missionaries, and missionary societies, who were already active in South Africa. Robert Moffat of the London Missionary Society (LMS) established a station at Kudumane, which succeeded in bringing Christianity to the Batswana and in training African evangelists to spread the word. It was to Kudumane that David Livingstone came in 1841. In 1845 he married Moffat's daughter, Mary, and they settled among the Bakwena.

Although ostensibly a missionary, Livingstone's main interest was exploration and in 1849 Livingstone and his party became the first whites to see Lake Ngami. He died in 1873 while looking for the source of the Nile, in Zambia.

Khama and his Bamangwato family at Shoshong were converted by the missionaries of a German Lutheran society, although he later joined the London Missionary Society Church. Most missionaries tried to change local Setswana customs, which they considered heathen and inferior to European Christian customs. Most of all they fought against the medicine men, who defended the old traditional customs. However, despite leaders like Khama who abolished male and female initiations, rain-making and beer drinking, some customs still flourish because people like them.

The early missionaries affected disinterest in politics, although they inevitably supported Christians against non-Christians. Their position was always precarious because they needed to retain the goodwill of the chiefs to remain in their mission posts. However, during the Protectorate, missionaries who knew they had the backing of the British government became quite cavalier, demanding the removal of chiefs who resisted Christianity.

Although the missionaries tried to destroy local cultures, they also provided education and established the first schools. They introduced useful tools such as the plough and the wagon, taught gardening and crop irrigation. The missionaries' wives taught sewing and baking and helped to nurse the sick and deliver babies.

Botswana and the British British foreign policy in southern Africa had always revolved around the Cape Colony, which was seen as vital to British interests in India and the Indian Ocean. Africa to the north of the Cape Colony had largely been ignored. The Boers were on the whole left to their farming in the Transvaal area, since they posed no threat to the Cape Colony.

However, from the 1850s to the 1870s the Batswana leaders appealed to the British for protection against the Boers, who had formed their own free state ruling the Transvaal, but were continually threatening to take over Tswana lands in Botswana.

David Livingstone's *Missionary Travels and Researches in South Africa* excited great interest in England. This account of his journeys across southern Africa in the 1840s and 50s had all the appeal that undersea or space exploration has for us now. Further, it captured the imagination of the British public, allowing them to take pride in their country's exploration of Africa, based on the exploits of an explorer who seemed to be the epitome of bravery and righteous religious zeal.

Livingstone had set out with the conviction that if Africans could see their material and physical well-being improved – probably by learning European ways, and earning a living from export crops – then they would be ripe for conversion to Christianity. He was strongly opposed to slavery, but sure that this would disappear when Africans became more self-sufficient through trade.

In fact Livingstone was almost totally unsuccessful in his own aims, failing to set up any successful trading missions, or even to convert many Africans permanently to Christianity. However, his travels opened up areas north of the Limpopo for later British missionaries, and by 1887 British mission stations were established in Zambia and southern Malawi.

When Germany annexed South West Africa (now Namibia) in 1884, the British finally began to take those threats seriously. They became afraid that the Boers might link up with the Germans and prevent British access to the 'north road', leading to the interior of Africa – now Zambia and Zimbabwe. It was really to safeguard this road that the British finally granted Botswana protection in 1885. Significantly, the German government was told about the British Protectorate of Bechuanaland before the chiefs in Botswana.

Cecil John Rhodes Initially the British government had fully intended to hand the supervision of the Protectorate over to the government of the Cape Colony, but the Cape was unwilling to take on the responsibility and the potential expense.

In 1886, the Boers discovered large gold deposits in the Witwatersrand (around Johannesburg). The influx of money from this boosted the Boer farmers, who expanded their interests to the north, making a treaty with Khama's enemy to the east, the powerful Lobengula. This in turn prompted the British to look beyond the Limpopo, and to back the territorial aspirations of a millionaire British businessman and prominent Cape Colony politician, Cecil Rhodes. By 1888 Rhodes, a partner in the De Beers consortium, had control of the lucrative diamond-mining industry in Kimberley, South Africa. He was hungry for power, and dreamt of linking the Cape to Cairo with land under British control.

Rhodes was fuelled by the belief that other areas of Africa had great mineral wealth and he wanted to colonise them and reap that wealth. In order to do so he formed the British South Africa Company (BSAC) in 1889. At that time, if companies or individuals could obtain concessions to African land from the owners, they were able to colonise it for the Crown. The British government expected that these concessions would be obtained honestly. However they were often gained fraudulently, by persuading illiterate African chiefs to sign (or put their mark on) documents which were presented to them as treaties, but which actually appropriated their lands.

The immediate reason for forming the BSAC was in order to colonise the land of the Amandabele and the Mashona (now Zimbabwe). In 1888 Rhodes' men had obtained, by trickery, a treaty known as the Rudd Concession from the King of the Amandabele, Lobengula. This granted Rhodes all mineral rights on the king's land.

Although the king rejected the treaty when he discovered its real intention, Rhodes was nevertheless granted a royal charter by the British government.

The British also promised to transfer the Bechuanaland Protectorate to the BSAC, on condition that Rhodes first obtained the agreement of the Batswana rulers. Rhodes wanted the Protectorate, because he needed the right to build a railway across Bechuanaland. He further wanted to annex the Protectorate to Rhodesia (now Zimbabwe), and from there attack the Boer state of Transvaal from the north.

Rhodes and other British businessmen had stakes in the highly profitable gold mines at Witwatersrand (Johannesburg), but the state was controlled politically by the Boers. Rhodes wanted British rule in the Transvaal, to protect his profits from the gold mines.

The three chiefs In 1895 three Batswana chiefs, Khama, Bathoen and Sebele, travelled to London to plead a case against the British government handing over the Protectorate to Rhodes, whom they did not trust. Some Batswana chiefs had already signed concessions with the BSAC, but in nearly all cases they did not realise that they had given away their land. It was, in any case, against Setswana law to sell or give away land. Rhodes attempted to stop the kings in Cape Town and prevent them from going to Britain but he was unsuccessful.

In a meeting with Joseph Chamberlain, then the British Colonial Secretary, the three chiefs criticised the BSAC and asked that:

- Bechuanaland should remain a Protectorate directly under the Queen.
- Their independence should be preserved.
- Their lands should not be sold.
- Liquor drinking should be prohibited in their areas.

Chamberlain told them that the British government could not go back on its promise to transfer the Protectorate to the BSAC. However, he also said that the company would obey the Queen, so it was the same as being governed by her. Hence the chiefs must reach an agreement with the BSAC. Then he went on holiday.

Instead the chiefs toured England, seeking the support of the British people against the company. Their campaign was organised by the London Missionary Society, and supported by temperance groups, anti-slavery and humanitarian groups and businesses that feared the effect of a costly war if the transfer went ahead. Chamberlain returned from holiday to find letters to this effect. Worried that the affair might become an election issue and lose the government votes, he agreed to the chiefs' demands, with the provisos that they must all cede the land which Rhodes required for the railway, and that taxation would be introduced to pay for the administration of the Protectorate.

The Jameson Raid A month later, in October 1895, Rhodes found a pretext for attacking the Transvaal. The raid was led by Dr S Jameson on behalf of the non-Boer whites or 'Uitlanders' in the Transvaal, who had complained of unequal treatment by the Boers. This famous raid, which came to be known as the Jameson Raid, was carried out from within the Bechuanaland Protectorate. However, it failed. The anticipated uprising of the Uitlanders never happened, so the raiders soon surrendered to the Boers.

The fact that Britain had allowed the Protectorate to be used to attack another country caused an international scandal. The British government, angered at being brought into disrepute by Rhodes, refused to transfer the Protectorate to the BSAC, and removed control of the Tswana lands that had been obtained for the raid.

It was the failure of the Jameson Raid, and Rhodes' subsequent if temporary disgrace, which protected the independent future of Botswana. Rhodes did later receive land for a railway strip and some blocks of 'Crown Land' – the Gaborone, Lobatse and Tuli blocks. These, together with the Tati Block and Ghanzi, which had been settled earlier, became the only European areas in Bechuanaland.

The Protectorate Britain continued to administer the Protectorate for 70 years, through the Anglo-Boer War (1899–1902) and two world wars. However, Britain disliked spending money on her colonies, and from the time the Union of South Africa was formed in 1910 it was always intended to transfer the Protectorate to the Union. The Batswana continued to fight against it, especially as they witnessed the poor treatment of black Africans in that country.

By 1955, the policy of the British government had changed. This was due in part to the problems with Seretse and Tshekedi Khama and the Bamangwato (see page 8), and partly because of South Africa's gradual move towards apartheid and away from the more egalitarian values of the post-war society that was emerging in the UK and the rest of the West.

In 1956 Seretse, who was supported by many groups in Britain, including Members of Parliament, spoke strongly against the British government's intervention. Tshekedi also turned against the British, accepting Ruth as the rightful wife and demanding Seretse's return to Bechuanaland. He believed that the British wanted to use the problem to break his tribe, and as an excuse to transfer the Protectorate to South Africa.

However, by then the issue of transferring the Protectorate to South Africa's control was dead in the minds of the British government. Clearly Botswana would have to be diplomatically protected from South Africa's ambitions, but the British didn't seem to have a plan for it beyond that.

MODERN HISTORY
The dangerous decade The years between 1955 and 1966 were a dangerous, formative decade in Botswana's history. For a detailed, insider's view of it read *Botswana: The Road to Independence*, by Peter Fawcus and Alan Tilbury. The authors were two of Britain's most senior administrators who were at the sharp end of steering relations between Britain and the Protectorate during this period.

Whilst the British government couldn't see into the future, supporters of Seretse Khama had organised political movements as early as 1952. Eventually a legislative council was set up in 1961, based on an interim constitution and limited national elections. Then Seretse Khama joined the legislative council, and the Protectorate's new executive council.

Meanwhile local politics was developing rapidly. The Bechuanaland People's Party (BPP) was founded in 1960, and later split into two factions, which were eventually to become the Botswana Independence Party (BIP) and the Botswana People's Party (BPP).

Both factions espoused a fairly radical agenda calling for immediate independence, the abolition of the chiefs, nationalisation of some lands and the removal of most whites from the civil service. With the material support of other nationalist movements in Ghana and Tanzania, 1960–61 saw support for the BPP grow rapidly in the townships of eastern Botswana.

From his position on the inside of government, Seretse Khama could see the danger that these parties posed to the constitution that was developing, and to the smooth running of the civil service after independence. Hence early in 1962, under a morula tree in Gaborone, he and five others (Ketumile Masire, A M Tsoebebe, Moutlakgola Nwako, Tsheko Tsheko and Goareng Mosinyi) formed the Botswana

Democratic Party (BDP) to campaign for a more ordered transition to independence. All were experienced, educated men and between them had strong links throughout the country, in both the educated elites and the poorer rural communities.

In particular, Seretse Khama and Ketumile Masire, as president and general secretary of the party, formed a strong partnership, without any signs of the feuds and splits that had beset the opposition. One was from the north, the other from the south; one a chief, the other a commoner. Gradually their conservative message began to win over the electorate. This was helped by the fear that any radical new government could provoke problems with South Africa – which still apparently had an appetite for control of Bechuanaland.

Independence Fawcus and Tilbury observe that from 1956 to 1966 'constitutional and political development far outstripped economic and social advance. The thought that independence might be at the end of the road only emerged in the early 1960s and was discounted by Lord Hailey as late as 1963.'

Fortunately since about 1956 there had been a slow build-up in Britain's financial grants to the Protectorate. By 1963 a £10 million plan was in place for development that covered the transition period around independence. This included the immediate start to constructing a new administrative capital, at Gaborone – as previously Bechuanaland had been administered from Mafikeng, over the border in South Africa.

During this time, Sir Ketumile Masire, Bechuanaland's first deputy prime minister and second president, commented that there was a high 'degree of consultation and co-operation between the local representatives of the British government and the people of Botswana' and that there was 'immense goodwill on both sides'. Perhaps this, more than anything else, explains how the transition was completed so peacefully.

On 1 March 1965 a remarkably peaceful election was held, with voters placing coloured symbols in envelopes to allow for the largely illiterate electorate. This worked without problems. The Bechuanaland Democratic Party (BDP) won 28 out of the 31 seats, and on 3 March 1965 Seretse Khama became the country's first prime minister. Within this new administration, a number of senior British public servants were kept on – including the minister of finance and the attorney general, and a senior civil servant in each of the ministries.

This clear victory for the BDP, and stable administration, gave the new government the platform from which to amend the constitution. The new Setswana name of the Republic of Botswana was chosen for the country, and on 30 September 1966, Sir Seretse Khama became the first president.

Politics since independence

1966–80: President Sir Seretse Khama Seretse Khama inherited a poor country. In 1965 the population stood at about 550,000 with a low level of literacy, and the country was gripped by a bad drought. Fortunately Britain was sympathetic to continuing to cover substantial costs of the new nation's administration costs, although with the discovery of diamonds at Orapa in 1967 by geologists from De Beers, and the subsequent mining operations which began in 1971, this assistance was only needed for six years after independence.

Botswana had long been in the Southern African Customs Union – and in 1969 it succeeded in renegotiating the terms of this, to become more financially independent. (Previously it had received a fixed percentage of total customs union income, rather than the income that was due directly from its own territory.)

During the 1970s Botswana's economy grew steadily, typically by around 12–13%, as Botswana extended its basic infrastructure for both mining development and basic social services for its population. Despite threats from, amongst others, the Marxist-leaning Botswana National Front (BNF), Sir Seretse Khama steered the country on a fairly moderate line – and the BDP were consistently re-elected in generally fair elections.

With civil war in Rhodesia throughout the 1970s, and apartheid regimes in South Africa and South West Africa (Namibia), Botswana's position was tricky. It accepted refugees from neighbouring countries, but refused to be used as a base for resistance organisations. Such neutrality was often severely tried, not least when, in February 1978, the Rhodesian army crossed the border and massacred 15 Botswana soldiers at Leshoma.

Zimbabwe gained independence in 1980, and the same year saw the foundation of the Southern African Development Coordination Conference (SADCC) with the aim of co-ordinating the region's disparate economies in the face of the huge economic muscle wielded by South Africa's apartheid regime.

Sir Seretse Khama died in July 1980 and, as envisaged by the constitution, was succeeded by his deputy, Sir Ketumile Masire. He left behind him an impressive legacy of a stable, prosperous country amidst a changing subcontinent. He had skilfully steered Botswana, with foresight and prudence, during perhaps its most vulnerable period – leaving it with the firm foundations of a democratic tradition, and well-trained executive and administrative branches of government.

The 1980s: President Sir Ketumile Masire Masire's succession was mandated by another victory for the BDP in a general election to the national assembly in 1984 – although at the same time they lost control of all the town councils except Selebi-Phikwe. This sign of discontent was widely ascribed to the high levels of unemployment.

Just as the 1970s had witnessed upheavals in Rhodesia, so the 1980s saw the intensification of pressure on the white regime in South Africa to give way to majority rule.

Botswana continued to welcome refugees, but refused to harbour bases for the ANC's war on apartheid in South Africa. During this period Botswana had a delicate balancing act to play. Like most countries it was calling for an end to apartheid, and geographically it was one of the 'front line' states in the battle against apartheid. However, Botswana's economy was so dependent on its southern neighbour that it couldn't afford to apply the sanctions which most countries were calling for.

In 1981 tensions arose with South Africa over the supply of military equipment from the USSR for the Botswana Defence Force (BDF), though by 1986 Britain and the USA were offering hardware to the BDF to deter South African incursions into Botswana.

Meanwhile on its eastern border, relations with Robert Mugabe's ZANU government were businesslike rather then terribly friendly. The early 1980s saw Mugabe's notoriously ruthless Fifth Brigade terrorising Matabeleland – the province adjacent to Botswana. Zimbabwean refugees flooded into Botswana including, in March 1983, the leader of ZAPU, Mugabe's opposition in the elections, Joshua Nkomo.

Nkomo left for London rapidly, but later allegations that the refugee camps were harbouring armed dissidents caused problems, culminating in a border skirmish in 1983 between the BDF and 'armed men wearing Zimbabwean military uniforms'. It wasn't until April 1989 that Botswana felt able to revoke the 'refugee' status for Zimbabwean nationals and, soon after, the refugees left – although Botswana continued to have many illegal migrants from Zimbabwe.

Internally, political tensions between the BDP and the BNF peaked in early 1987 with a referendum on constitutional amendments to the electoral system, which was boycotted by the BNF. However, by October 1989, the BDP demonstrated its substantial support by winning 65% of the votes in an election (the result of which was again challenged by the BNF in several constituencies). In October the new national assembly returned Masire to the president's office for a third term.

During this time there were several incursions into Botswana by South African troops – including two raids on alleged ANC offices in Gaborone in 1985 and 1986. But a few years later, tensions began to ease as South Africa's President De Klerk started to set his country on a course for majority rule. One of his first steps was independence for Namibia in 1990.

1990–98: President Sir Ketumile Masire The early 1990s saw several corruption scandals in which a number of ministers resigned – including, in March 1992, the vice president, Peter Mmusi. (Contrast these with the paucity of resignations that occur during corruption scandals in most governments and you'll realise this is a good sign, not a bad one, for the integrity of Botswana's government!)

Another general election was held on 15 October 1994, with the BNF triumphing in the urban areas, winning 13 seats (37.7% of the vote), while the BDP continued to command the support of the rural constituencies, which elected it to 40 seats (53.1% of the vote). The elections had been peaceful, with around a 70% turnout, and at last Botswana had an opposition party capable of a serious challenge to the BDP.

There was some unrest in early 1995, with several days of violence between the BDF and demonstrators (mainly students and the unemployed) during which one person was killed. However, most of this was sporadic and short-lived.

During this time relations with Botswana's neighbours were generally good. However, in 1992 a border squabble arose between Botswana and Namibia over a tiny island (called Sedudu by Botswana, and Kasikili by Namibia) in the Chobe River. See page 186 for more details of this argument. A potentially much more serious issue arose in 1996 when Namibia announced plans to construct a pipeline to take water from the Okavango River at Rundu. Given that this would impact directly on the Okavango Delta, the possibility of such a pipeline remains a source of great concern for Botswana.

Then in 1998 an influx of refugees from Namibia's Caprivi Strip arrived, including Mishake Muyongo, who had been suspended as president of the Namibia's opposition party, the Democratic Turnhalle Alliance. He and other leading Caprivians had campaigned for independence for the province. By 1999, over 2,000 refugees were living near Gaborone. Namibia's extradition demands were refused, although eventually a settlement was brokered by the UNHCR whereby the most prominent refugees were granted asylum in Denmark, and the rest returned to Namibia under an amnesty.

Internal electoral reform had long been on the agenda in Botswana, with some consensus about the need for it from all the political parties. In 1997 various amendments to the constitution were passed, including a reduction in the voting age from 21 to 18 years old, the establishment of an electoral commission which is independent of the government, and a measure to restrict the president to a maximum of two terms in office.

Masire reshuffled the cabinet slightly in September 1997, and soon announced that he planned to retire in 1998.

1998–present: President Festus Mogae On 31 March 1998 Sir Ketumile Masire retired as president. The following day the vice president, Festus G Mogae, head of the BDP, was inaugurated. His new cabinet was virtually identical to the old one; the only new minister was Lt General Seretse Ian Khama, son of Botswana's first president (the late Sir Seretse Khama). Ian Khama had been commander of the

Botswana Defence Force, and soon became vice president. Both men have remained in office following elections in 1999 and 2004.

Meanwhile, the same year, infighting in the opposition, the BNF, led to a split, with dissident members forming the Botswana Congress Party (BCP). After 11 of the BNF's 13 deputies joined this, the BCP was declared the official opposition in mid-July 1998.

The next elections are scheduled for 2009. There's every expectation that these will be on time, free and fair – like the previous elections. The main opposition, the Botswana National Front, has done little to spell out how it would change the running of the country, although its continued presence does help to hold the BDP to account, and maintain at least some democratic debate. Meanwhile the long experience of the ruling party, and the general success that they have made of the country and its economy, tend to suggest that the BDP will again retain power.

Into the future Botswana is highly regarded by the world community. It has maintained one of the world's highest growth rates since independence, using its diamond revenues to change from one of the world's poorest countries into a prosperous 'middle-income' country.

President Festus Mogae was born in 1939 and trained at Oxford as an economist. He served as executive director at the IMF for Anglophone Africa, and later in various senior government posts including governor of the Bank of Botswana, before becoming vice president in 1992. He has a thorough understanding of economics and although not one for high-profile media splashes on the world stage, he is likely to make a first-rate job of running the country. There is nothing to indicate that anyone on the domestic political scene will be able to mount an effective challenge to the BDP or President Mogae in the near future.

Looking to the next few years, Botswana will have some major challenges to face up to. Unemployment is becoming a problem: officially it is 23.8%, but unofficial estimates claim closer to 40%. HIV/AIDS infection rates are amongst the highest in the world, and it remains to be seen how the government will cope.

The relative instability of Zimbabwe, on Botswana's eastern border, is a cause for concern – although it seems unlikely that this will impact on Botswana significantly, except for a possible influx of refugees and economic migrants.

Perhaps the most interesting issue, and a litmus test of the government's foresight, will be their preparations for the gradual demise of the country's diamond industry. Diversification is essential, and tourism must surely be a crucial part of this mix, but replacing such a huge sector of the economy will be difficult.

ECONOMY

OVERVIEW In economic terms, Botswana is very much one of Africa's success stories, reflecting both the country's natural mineral wealth and a political and social stability which far outweighs that of its neighbours. In the 30-year period following independence in 1966, the economic growth rate averaged just over 9% a year, marking the economy out as the fastest growing in the world, according to the World Bank. By the turn of the century, the growth rate had stabilised at around 7% a year, and the country had foreign reserves of some US$6.3 billion. The annual rate of inflation was estimated at 8.6% in 2005.

Fundamental to this growth has been the exploitation of Botswana's diamond mines, although other growth sectors have been in telecommunications and financial services. Attempts to stimulate the manufacturing sector, however, have proved less successful, with the closure in 2000 of the Hyundai assembly plant, which exported vehicles to South Africa. Although manufacturing represents only

5% of the country's GDP, the closure represented a loss to the economy of US$144 million per year, or nearly half of its total manufacturing output at that time.

The Botswanan government is all too conscious of the country's narrow revenue base and continues to seek means to diversify this. The introduction in 2001 of value added tax (VAT), and privatisation of state-owned companies such as the Botswana Telecommunications Corporation (BTC) and Air Botswana are additional measures aimed at bringing significant income into the treasury coffers.

In recent years, this rosy picture has been heavily overshadowed by the threat of disease. Botswana has one of the highest HIV/AIDs levels in the world, currently affecting over a third of the population, and responsible for 26.7% of all deaths in 2003. The average life expectancy is officially 47 years, but is widely considered to be much lower.

ECONOMIC DEVELOPMENT Prior to independence, Botswana's economy was primarily based on farming, particularly cattle. Even in 1993, some 46% of the country's land was permanent pasture, while a further 1% was given over to arable farming. Since the 1970s, however, the extraction of mineral resources, particularly diamonds, has become big business, and today the sector accounts for a significant proportion of the country's wealth. Other areas of importance include tourism and cattle raising.

Total exports in 2000 – the latest figures that are available from the Botswanan authorities – were valued at around US$2.6 billion, with the bulk of these, some 77% in 1998, going to European Union countries. Other markets included South Africa (18%) and Zimbabwe (3%). Diamonds account for about 75% of all exports, but other goods include agricultural products, foodstuffs, brewing, metal products, paper products and textiles. Export business is the responsibility of the Botswana Export Development and Investment Agency.

In the same year, Botswana's imports were valued at around US$2.2 billion, with around three-quarters of these coming from South Africa, which is also the source of most of the country's electricity. Goods imported range from foodstuffs and textiles to machinery and petroleum products. The country's other trading partners include Europe, where 10% of the country's total imports originate, and South Korea, at 5%.

Botswana is an associate member of the European Union, whereby products manufactured in the country enter EU markets free from duties and quotas. In the United States there are no restrictions on textile products from Botswana. Within Africa, Botswana is a member of the Southern Africa Customs Union (SACU), an economic bloc comprising South Africa, Botswana, Namibia, Lesotho and Swaziland. Goods produced in Botswana enter the markets of the other four member states free of duty or any other restrictions. Botswana is also an active member of the Southern African Development Community (SADC), a body which groups together 14 countries within the region.

Diamond mining Botswana's economic success is founded on its natural resources, particularly diamonds. Today, it is the leading producer of gem-quality diamonds in the world, representing one-third of the country's GDP. Since mining began in 1971, the industry has catapulted the economy on to a course of sustained growth over most of the last three decades.

The majority of diamond mining is carried out by Debswana, a 50/50 partnership between De Beers and the Botswanan government. The company has three large, open-cast operations, responsible for almost the entire diamond yield of the country as a whole. The largest and richest of these mines is at Jwaneng, in the south of the country. Founded in 1973, but only in production since 1982, the mine is one of the largest in the world. Also founded in the same year was the mine at Letlhakane, which was in production by 1977. The third mine is at Orapa.

In addition to diamonds, the country is rich in copper and nickel, with salt, soda ash, potash, coal, iron ore and silver to be found as well. Although diamonds account for some 60% of the country's prospecting licences, the government is seeking to diversify its mineral output.

Tourism Botswana's natural environment is a significant attraction for tourists, as highlighted in this guide. The government's policy of encouraging small numbers of upmarket visitors to its pristine wilderness areas is proving successful within the overall aim of protecting the environment. In the last couple of years, however, the tourist industry has been thrown off balance by the knock-on effect from unrest in neighbouring Zimbabwe. This is largely because countries within southern Africa have elected to promote the region as a whole, rather than the individual countries, as a result of which many tourists choose to combine several countries in the area in one trip. Unfortunately, therefore, the problems in that one country have caused a drop in visitors to the region as a whole.

The number of visitors to the country continues to grow steadily. According to the Botswanan government, the country welcomed 923,132 overseas visitors in 2001, an increase of over 60% in just five years; that figure now tops one million. Within Africa, visitors from South Africa alone accounted for around half the total. Further afield, the majority of visitors originated in Europe, with considerable numbers also coming from the USA. Tourism is thus an increasingly important source of revenue for the government, and of employment within individual communities. In order to increase the benefits from tourism without adverse impact on the environment, attempts are being made to diversify into smaller 'ecotourism' projects that will benefit local communities at ground level, and to offset the negative effects of a clash between tourism projects and the needs of local people.

Workforce In 2005, the total workforce in Botswana was estimated at 288,400. Industrial relations are good, with virtually no worker unrest or strikes. In the same year, Botswana's GDP was some US$17.24 billion, representing a growth rate that year of 4.5%. At US$10,500, GDP per capita was the highest in Africa. The overall rate of literacy in the country is nearing 80%, a direct result of the financial success of the mining industry to the country's economy. Nevertheless, almost a third of the population is considered to be below the poverty line, and although the rate of unemployment is officially said to be 23.8%, unofficial figures place it at nearer 40%.

Foreign investment The combination of political stability, low rates of taxation and the lack of exchange controls, which were abolished in 1999, makes Botswana attractive to investors. Pursuit of the government's policy of privatisation is also significant in this area.

There are strict rules both for foreign ownership and for foreign investment in companies listed on Botswana's small stock exchange, which was established in 1995. Private investors hold less than a tenth of the total market capitalisation. No one foreigner may own more than 10% of the issued capital of a publicly quoted company, while foreign ownership of the free stock of a local company trading on the exchange may not exceed 55%. Repatriation of funds is regulated by law. For further information, contact the Administrator, PO Box 41015, Khama Crescent, 4th floor, Finance House, Gaborone; ☏ 30 5190/3740; f 37 4079.

2

People and Culture

PEOPLE

THE POPULATION The most recent census statistics (2001) put Botswana's population at 1,680,863, with a population growth per year of 0.47%. Unofficial figures, however, show a slight decline in the population to an estimated 1,639,833 in 2006, while others indicate a downturn in population growth to just 0.04%.

This growth rate is low by African standards, and results from about 49% of fertile women using contraceptives. This is exceptional for sub-Saharan Africa and reflects the educated people with a prosperous and generally developed economy (Botswana's GDP is around US$10,500 per capita).

UNICEF's statistics indicate that 95% of the population has access to safe water, 66% to adequate sanitation, and that well over 90% of children under one have been immunised with polio, diphtheria and the BCG triple vaccine shots. These are very good levels by the continent's standards, and are no doubt helped by the government's policy of paying the full cost of all these vaccines.

Primary school enrolment is around 98/99% for boys/girls, and secondary school enrolment is around 61/68%. Literacy is 74/80% for men/women. This pattern of the girls generally receiving more education is unusual in Africa, where sons are often favoured by their parents over daughters – but given women's pivotal role in bringing up children and running households in this traditional society, it bodes well for the future.

About 49.6% of the population is under 18, and the average life expectancy is officially about 47 years, although some rate it as low as 33. It's sobering to note that even the official estimate of life expectancy has been going down recently, largely due to the impact of the high rate of AIDS infection in the country.

However, these statistics say nothing of what Botswana's people are like. If you venture into the more rural areas, take a local bus, or try to hitchhike with the locals; you will often find that people are curious about you. Chat to them openly, as fellow travellers, and you will find most to be delightful. They will be pleased to assist you where they can, and as keen to help you learn about them and their country as they are interested in your lifestyle and what brings you to Botswana.

That said, it's not uncommon, especially in the towns, to find people surly and largely uninterested sometimes . . . just as they are in London, or New York, or many modern cities.

A NOTE ON 'TRIBES' The people of Africa are often viewed, from abroad, as belonging to a multitude of culturally and linguistically distinct tribes – which are often portrayed as being at odds with each other. Whilst there is certainly an enormous variety of different ethnic groups in Africa, most are closely related to their neighbours in terms of language, beliefs and way of life. Modern historians eschew the simplistic tag of 'tribes', noting that such groupings change with time.

Sometimes the word tribe is used to describe a group of people who all speak the same language; it may be used to mean those who follow a particular leader or to refer to all the inhabitants of a certain area at a given time. In any case, tribe is a vague word that is used differently for different purposes. The term 'clan' (blood relations) is a smaller, more precisely defined, unit – though rather too precise for our broad discussions here.

Certainly, at any given time, groups of people or clans who share similar language and cultural beliefs do band together and often, in time, develop 'tribal' identities. However, it is wrong to then extrapolate and assume that their ancestors will have had the same groupings and allegiances centuries ago.

In Africa, as elsewhere in the world, history is recorded by the winners. Here the winners, the ruling class, may be the descendants of a small group of immigrants who achieved dominance over a larger, long-established community. Over the years, the history of that ruling class (the winners) usually becomes regarded as the history of the whole community, or tribe. Two 'tribes' have thus become one, with one history – which will reflect the origins of that small group of immigrants, and not the ancestors of the majority of the current tribe.

Botswana is typical of many African countries. Currently historians and linguistics experts can identify at least 26 different languages spoken here. As you will see, there are cultural differences between the people in different parts of the country. However, in many ways these are no more pronounced than those between the states of the USA, or the different regions of the (relatively tiny) UK.

There continues to be lots of inter-marriage and mixing of these peoples and cultures – perhaps more so than there has ever been, due to the efficiency of modern transport systems. Generally, there is very little friction between these communities (whose boundaries, as we have said, are indistinct) and Botswana's various peoples live peacefully together.

THE SAN There is not another social/language group on this planet which has been studied, written about, filmed and researched more than the San, or Bushmen, of the Kalahari. Despite this, or indeed because of it, popular conceptions about them, fed by their image in the media, are often strikingly out of step with the realities. Thus they warrant a separate section devoted to them here. The aim of these next few pages is to try and explain some of the roots of the misconceptions, to look at some of the realities, and to make you think. Despite having spent a lot of time with San in the Kalahari, it is difficult to separate fact from oft-repeated, glossy fiction. If parts of this discussion seem disparate, it's a reflection of this difficulty.

Recent scientific observations on the Khoisan Our view of the San is partly informed by some basic anthropological and linguistic research, mostly applying to the Khoisan, which is worth outlining to set the scene.

Anthropology The first fossil records that we have of our human ancestors date back to at least about 60,000 years ago in east Africa. These are likely to have been the ancestors of everyone living today.

Archaeological finds from parts of the Kalahari show that human beings have lived here for at least 40,000 years. These are generally agreed to have been the ancestors of the modern Khoisan peoples living in Botswana today. (The various peoples of the Khoi and the San are known collectively as the Khoisan. All have relatively light golden brown skin, almond shaped eyes and high cheekbones. Their stature is generally small and slight, and they are now found across southern Africa.)

Historians, anthropologists and social scientists are divided, and often perplexed, about what name to use for the people known as 'Bushmen'. The confusion is compounded by the mix of different tribal tags used in historical texts, often for reasons of political correctness.

San, Bushmen, San/Bushmen, Khoisan, Khoi are all used, often apparently randomly. In Botswana you'll also hear RAD (Remote Area Dweller) or Masarwa/Basarwa used, but the former is exceedingly vague and the latter often considered insulting. Some avoid the term 'Bushmen', regarding it as debasing and sexist, often using 'San' in preference – which others claim to be a derogatory Nama word. Meanwhile 'Khoisan' is a language grouping, not a specific race or tribe, and encompasses the Khoi (or Khoe or Khoi-Khoi or Khoi-khoin), and hence also Namibia's Damara and Nama people. All have similar 'click' languages, but they live very differently from many of the people that we think of as the Bushmen.

Ideally, we would use the term by which these people use themselves, but there lies the rub. Ask villagers in the Kalahari and they will describe themselves as members of the Ju-/wasi, the !Kung, the Hai-//omn – or any one of a dozen other language groups. (See page 22 for an explanation of the !, / and // in these names.) If we used these much more precise linguistic terms (see *Language*, later in this chapter, for a few of the main ones), they would overly complicate our discussions and require an accuracy that is beyond me.

These people have no label for the broad racial category that we regard as 'the Bushmen'. They simply don't think of themselves as belonging to one race of people. Therefore, the concept of an overall grouping of people that we call 'Bushmen' must have originated from someone other than the people themselves. In truth, it is an invention of those who came to this corner of Africa later – a legacy of colonialism in its broadest sense.

Given the questionable validity of any term, I have used San throughout this book: not because I believe it to be more accurate than the alternatives, but simply because this is a term that is widely used in southern Africa, and widely understood elsewhere. It's also the term adopted by the Kalahari People's Fund, and agreed by various San communities in Namibia (see www.kalaharipeoples.org). That said, it's a vague term; just try to make it precise and you'll realise how inadequate it is. I apologise if it is, in any language, derogatory; it isn't meant to be.

Language research Linguists have grouped all the world's languages into around 20 linguistic families. Of these, four are very different from the rest. All these four are African families – and they include the Khoisan and the Niger-Congo (Bantu) languages.

This is amongst the evidence that has led linguists to believe that human language evolved in Africa, and further analysis has suggested that this was probably amongst the ancestors of the Khoisan.

The Khoisan languages are distinguished by their wide repertoire of clicking sounds. Don't mistake these for simple: they are very sophisticated. It was observed by Dunbar in 'Why gossip is good for you' (see *Appendix 3, Further Information*) that, 'From the phonetic point of view these [the Khoisan languages] are the world's most complex languages. To speak one of them fluently is to exploit human phonetic ability to the full.'

At some point the Khoisan languages diverged from a common ancestor, and today three distinct groups exist: the northern, central and southern groups. Languages gradually evolve and change as different groups of people split up and

Cultural sensitivity isn't something that a guidebook can teach you, though reading the section on cultural guidelines, at the end of this chapter, may help. Being sensitive to the results of your actions and attitudes on others is especially important in this area.

The San are often a humble people, who regard arrogance as a vice. It is normal for them to be self-deprecating amongst themselves, to make sure that everyone is valued and nobody becomes too proud. So the less you are perceived as a loud, arrogant foreigner, the better.

Very few foreigners can pick up much of the local language without living here for a long time. (Readers may already realise that spellings of the same word can vary greatly.) However, if you want to try to pronounce the words then there are four main clicks to master. In the well-documented Ju/'hoansi language, these are:

/ a dental click, a sucking sound, made by putting the tongue just behind the front teeth.

// a clucking sound, like that used in English to urge on a horse.

! a sharp popping sound, like a cork coming out of a bottle, made by pulling the tongue down quickly from the roof of the mouth.

(a soft popping sound, made by putting your tongue just behind the ridge at the back of the front teeth (this is usually the hardest).

move to new areas, isolated from their old contacts. Thus the evolution of each language is specific to each group, and reflected in the classifications described later in this chapter.

According to Mike Main in *The Visitor's Guide to Botswana* (now *The African Adventurer's Guide*, see *Appendix 3, Further Information*), the northern group are San and today they live west of the Okavango and north of Ghanzi, with representatives found as far afield as Angola. The southern group are also San, who live in the area between Kang and Bokspits in Botswana. The central group is Khoe, living in central Botswana, and extending north to the eastern Okavango and Kasane, and west into Namibia, where they are known as the Nama.

Each of these three Khoisan language groups has many dialects. These have some similarities, but they are not closely related, and some are different to the point where there is no mutual understanding. Certain dialects are so restricted that only a small family group speaks them; it was reported recently that one San language died out completely with the death of the last speaker.

This huge number of dialects, and variation in languages, reflects the relative isolation of the various speakers, most of whom now live in small family groups as the Kalahari's arid environment cannot sustain large groups of people living together in one place as hunter-gatherers.

Genetic discoveries Most genetically normal men have an X- and a Y-chromosome, whilst women have two X-chromosomes. Unlike the other 22 pairs of (non-sex) chromosomes that each human has, there is no opportunity for the Y-chromosome to 'swap' or 'share' its DNA with any other chromosome. Thus all the information in a man's Y-chromosome will usually be passed on, without change, to all of his sons.

However, very rarely a single 'letter' in the Y-chromosome will be altered as it's being passed on, thus causing a permanent change in the chromosome's genetic sequence. This will then be the start of a new lineage of slightly different Y-chromosomes, which will be inherited by all future male descendants.

In November 2000, Professor Ronald Davis and a team of Stanford researchers (see *Appendix 3, Further Information*) claimed to have traced back this lineage to a single individual man, and that a small group of east Africans (Sudanese and Ethiopians) and Khoisan are the closest present-day relatives of this original man. That is, their genetic make-up is closest to his. (It's a scientific 'proof' of the biblical Adam, if you like.)

This is still a very contentious finding, with subsequent researchers suggesting at least ten original male sources ('Adams') – and so, although interesting, the jury remains out on the precise details of all these findings. If you're interested in the latest on this, then you'll find a lot about this on the web – start searching with the keywords: 'Khoisan Y chromosome'.

Historical views of the San Despite much evidence and research, our views of the San seem to have changed relatively little since both the Bantu groups and the first Europeans arrived in southern Africa.

The settlers' view Since the first Bantu farmer migrated south through east Africa, the range of territory occupied by the foragers, whose Stone Age technology had dominated the continent, began to condense. By the time the first white settlers appeared in the Cape, the Khoisan people were already restricted to Africa's southwestern corners and the Kalahari.

All over the world, farmers occupy clearly demarcated areas of land, whereas foragers will move more and often leave less trace of their presence. In Africa, this made it easier for farmers, first black then white, to ignore any traditional land rights that belonged to foraging people.

Faced with the loss of territory for hunting and gathering, the foragers – who, by this time were already being called 'Bushmen' – made enemies of the farmers by killing cattle. They waged a guerrilla war, shooting poison arrows at parties of men who set out to massacre them. They were feared and loathed by the settlers, who, however, captured and valued their children as servants.

Some of the Khoisan retreated north from the Cape – like the ancestors of Namibia's Nama people. Others were forced to labour on the settlers' farms, or were thrown into prison for hunting animals or birds which had been their traditional prey, but which were now designated property of the crown.

This story is told by Robert J Gordon in *The Bushman Myth: The Makings of a Namibian Underclass* (see *Appendix 3, Further Information*). He shows that throughout history the hunter-gathering San have been at odds with populations of settlers who divided up and 'owned' the land in the form of farms. The European settlers proved to be their most determined enemy, embarking on a programme of legislation and massacre. Many San died in prison, with many more shot as 'vermin'.

Thus the onslaught of farmers on the hunter-gatherers accelerated between the 1800s and the mid-1900s. This helped to ensure that hunter-gathering as a lifestyle only continued to be practical in marginal areas that couldn't be economically farmed – like the Kalahari. Archaeological evidence suggests that hunter-gatherer peoples have lived for about 60,000 years at sites like the Tsodilo Hills.

Western views of the San in the 1800s Though settlers in the Cape interacted with Khoisan people, so did Europe and the US, in a very limited way. Throughout the 1800s and early 1900s a succession of Khoisan people were effectively enslaved and brought to Europe and the US for exhibition. Sometimes this was under the guise of anthropology, but usually it didn't claim to be anything more than entertainment.

One of the first was the 'Hottentot Venus' – a woman who was probably of Khoisan extraction who was exhibited around London and Paris from 1810 to 1815, as an erotic curiosity for aristocrats.

A string of others followed – for example, the six Khoisan people exhibited at the Coney Island Pleasure Resort, beside New York, and later in London in the 1880s, and billed as the 'missing link between apes and men', or the 'wild dancing bushman' known as Franz brought to England around 1913 by Paddy Hepston (see Q N Parsons' piece in *Botswana Notes & Records*, detailed in *Appendix 3, Further Information*).

Impressions of the San from the 1950s In the 1950s a researcher from Harvard, John Marshall, came to the Kalahari to study the Kung! San. He described a peaceful people living in harmony with nature, amidst a land that provided all their needs. The groups had a deep spirituality and no real hierarchy: it seemed like the picture of a modern Eden. (Especially when viewed through post-war eyes.) Marshall was a natural cameraman and made a film that follows the hunt of a giraffe by four men over a five-day period. It swiftly became a classic, both in and outside of anthropological circles.

Further research agreed, with researchers noting a great surfeit of protein in the diet of the Kung! San and low birth rates akin to modern industrial societies.

Again the San were seen as photogenic and sources of good copy and good images. Their lives were portrayed in romantic, spiritual terms in the book and film *The Lost World of the Kalahari* by Laurens van der Post (see *Appendix 3, Further Information*). This documentary really ignited the worldwide interest in the San and led to subsequent films such as *The Gods Must be Crazy*. All the images conveyed an idyllic view of the San as untainted by contact with the modern world.

The reality The reality was much less rosy than the first researchers thought. Some of their major misconceptions have been outlined particularly clearly in chapter 13 of John Reader's *Africa: A Biography of the Continent* (see *Appendix 3, Further Information*). He points out that far from an ideal diet, the nutrition of the San was often critically limited, lacking vitamins and fatty acids associated with a lack of animal fat in their diet. Far from a stable population with a low birth rate, it seems likely that there had been a decline in the birth rate in the last few generations. The likely cause for this was periods of inadequate nourishment during the year when the San lost weight from lack of food, stress and the great exertions of their lifestyle.

In fact, it seems likely that the San, whom we now see as foragers, are people who, over the last two millennia, have become relegated to an underclass by the relentless advance of the black and white farmers who did not recognise their original rights to their traditional land.

San today and the media Though scientific thought has moved on since the 1950s, much of the media has not. The San are still perceived to be hot news.

The outpost of Tsumkwe is the centre for many of the San communities in Namibia. It's a tiny crossroads with a school and a handful of buildings, in a remote corner of northeastern Namibia. Despite its isolation, in 2001 this desert outpost hosted no less than 22 film crews. Yes, really, that's an average of almost two each month – and I'm not counting a whole host of other print journalists and photographers.

Talk to virtually any of the directors and you'll realise that they arrive with very clear ideas about the images that they want to capture. They all think they're one of the first, they think they're original, and they want to return home with images which match their pre-conceived ideas about the San as 'the last primitive hunter-gatherers'.

As an example, you'll often see pictures in the media of San hunters in traditional dress walking across a hot, barren salt pan. When asked to do these shoots the San's usual comment is, 'Why, there's no point. We'd never go looking for anything there.' But the shots look spectacular and win prizes . . . so the photographers keep asking for them. From the San's perspective, they get paid for the shots, so why not pose for the camera? I'd do the same!

Thus our current image of the San is really one that *we* are constantly re-creating. It's the one that we expect. But it's doesn't necessarily conform to any reality. So on reflection, popular thinking hasn't moved on much from Marshall's first film in the 1950s.

Current life for the San Looking at the current lifestyle of the San who remain in the more remote areas of the Kalahari, it's difficult not to lapse into a romantic view of ignoring present realities. There are too many cultural aspects to cover here, so instead I've just picked out a few that you may encounter.

Nomads of the Kalahari Perhaps the first idea to dispel is that the San are nomads. They're not. San family groups have clearly-defined territories within which they forage, called a *n!ore* (in the Ju/'hoansi language). This is usually centred on a place where there is water, and contains food resources sufficient for the basic subsistence of the group.

Groups recognise rights to the *n!ore*, which is passed on from father to first-born son. Any visiting people would ask permission to remain in these. Researchers have mapped these areas, even in places like the Central Kalahari.

Hunter-gatherers Any hunter-gatherer lifestyle entails a dependence on, and extensive knowledge of, the environment and the resident fauna and flora found there. In the Kalahari, water is the greatest need and the San know which roots and tubers provide liquid to quench thirst. They create sip wells in the desert, digging a hole, filled with soft grass, then using a reed to suck water into the hole, and send it bubbling up the reed to fill an ostrich egg. Water-filled ostrich eggs are also buried at specific locations within the group's 'area'. When necessary the San will strain the liquid from the rumen of a herbivore and drink that.

Researchers have observed that any hunting is done by the men. When living a basic hunting and gathering lifestyle, with little external input, hunting provides only about 20% of their food. The remaining 80% is provided largely by the women, helped by the children, who forage and gather wild food from the bush. By age 12 a child might know about 200 plant species, and an adult more than 300.

Social system The survival of the San in the harsh environment of the Kalahari is evidence of the supreme adaptability of humans. It reflects their detailed knowledge of their environment, which provides them not only with food, but with materials for shelter and medicine in the form of plants.

Another very important factor in their survival is the social system by which the San live. Social interaction is governed by unwritten rules that bind the people in friendship and harmony, which must be maintained. One such mechanism is the obligation to distribute the meat from a large kill. Another is the obligation to lend such few things as are individually possessed, thereby incurring a debt of obligation from the borrower.

They also practise exogamy, which means they have an obligation to marry outside the group. This creates social bonds between groups. Such ties bind the society inextricably together, as does the system of gift exchange between separate groups.

Owing to the environmental constraints a group will consist of between 80 and 120 people, living and moving together. In times of shortage the groups will be much smaller, sometimes consisting of only immediate family – parents, grandparents and children. They must be able to carry everything they possess. Their huts are light constructions of grass, and they have few possessions.

Because no one owns property, no one is richer or has more status than another. A group of San has a nominal leader, who might be a senior member of the group, an expert hunter, or the person who owns the water rights. The whole group takes decisions affecting them, often after vociferous discussions.

Hunting The San in the Kalahari are practised hunters, using many different techniques to capture the game. Their main weapons are a very light bow, and an arrow made of reed, in three sections. The arrowhead is usually poisoned, using one of a number of poisons obtained from specific plants, snakes and beetles. (Though most San know how to hunt with bows and arrows, the actual practice is increasingly uncommon when it's not done to earn money from observing visitors.)

All the hunters may be involved in the capture of large game, which carries with it certain obligations. The whole group shares in the kill and each member is entitled to a certain portion of the meat.

There are different methods for hunting small game, which only the hunter's family would usually share. One method for catching spring hares involves long, flexible poles (sometimes four metres long) made of thin sticks, with a duiker's horn (or more usually now a metal hook) fastened to the end. These are rammed into the hare's hole, impaling the animal, which is then pulled or dug out.

Trance dancing Entertainment for the San, when things are good, usually involves dancing. During some dances, which may often have overtones of ritual or religion, the dancers may fall into a trance and collapse.

These trances are induced by a deliberate breathing technique, with a clear physiological explanation. Dances normally take place in the evening, around a fire. Then the women, children and old people will sit around and clap, whilst some of the younger men will dance around the circle in an energetic, rhythmic dance. Often this is all that happens, and after a while the excitement dies down and everyone goes to sleep.

However, on fairly rare occasions, the dancers will go into a trance. After several hours of constant exertion, they will shorten their breathing. This creates an oxygen deficiency, which leads to the heart pumping more strongly to compensate. Blood pressure to the brain increases; the dancer loses consciousness and collapses.

Issues for the future As commented above, foragers throughout the world are perceived to have less valid claims on lands than the farmers, who usually occupy more clearly demarcated areas of land.

Firstly, as a matter of policy, Botswana doesn't allow any of its policies to favour one ethnic group or another. This is generally held to be a very sensible policy, framed to avoid creating ethnic divisions and strife. However, having such a disadvantaged position, it's much more difficult for the San to access their rights than most other groups.

Secondly, the San are not recognised within the power structure accorded to the various chiefs of Botswana's other tribal groups. There's no San representation in the House of Chiefs (Botswana's second legislative chamber), and no traditional land rights accorded to them. This puts them at a major political disadvantage.

Thirdly, under Botswana law hunting and gathering isn't recognised as a formal

THE 'BUSHMEN' OF THE CENTRAL KALAHARI GAME RESERVE

The following text has been contributed by Survival International.

We know this land belonged to our great grandparents. But now, just because we are Bushmen, our land is being taken from us.

Bushman woman, Central Kalahari Game Reserve

Survival International is a worldwide organisation supporting tribal peoples. It stands for their right to decide their own future and helps them protect their lives, lands and human rights.

Today there are more than 150 million tribal people worldwide, including at least 70 uncontacted tribes. Almost all are persecuted relentlessly – they are flooded by dams, wiped out by disease, driven from their homes by logging and mining, and evicted by settlers. However, with the support of people outside, these threats can be averted and tribal peoples can live healthy and secure lives: there is nothing inevitable about their demise.

Survival has been supporting the Gana and Gwi 'Bushmen' of the Central Kalahari Game Reserve (who are the indigenous people of this region) for over 15 years. For all this time the Botswana government has expressed its desire to relocate the Gana and Gwi, together with their neighbours the Bakgalagadi, out of the reserve, in spite of the fact that the reserve was actually created to provide a home for the Bushmen, and the wildlife they hunt. The Bushmen's life in the reserve was gradually made impossible, especially by heavily restricting the hunting on which the Bushmen depend for their food.

In two big operations, in 1997 and 2002, the authorities trucked out virtually all those Bushmen who had not previously succumbed to a combination of inducement and pressure. The government also destroyed the Bushmen's water supplies and borehole. Some observers believe that behind the evictions lurk the prospect of huge riches from the diamond deposits known to be in the reserve (Botswana's economy largely depends on diamonds). The government has now relocated these people to bleak 'resettlement' camps where they live on government handouts and are reduced to boredom, alcoholism and despair; many are desperately struggling to return to their homes in the reserve.

Until they were evicted from their land, the Gana and Gwi lived self-sufficient lives. Of the entire 'Bushmen' population, they are virtually unique in having maintained hunting as central to their way of life. In modern-day Botswana, however, this lifestyle is widely seen as 'primitive' and an embarrassment to a 'developing' country. The president, for example, has said, 'How can you have a Stone Age creature continue to exist in the age of computers? If the Bushmen want to survive, they must change or otherwise, like the dodo, they will perish.'

Survival is the only international organisation supporting tribal peoples worldwide which does not accept funding from any national government. For more information about our campaign with the Gana and Gwi, contact: Survival International (☎ + 44 (0) 207 687 8700; www.survival-international.org).

category of land use – so in local disputes the needs of the San are frequently subjugated to those of Botswana's farmers.

The resulting disenfranchisement has led many of the San into situations of extreme poverty. Alcoholism is a problem amongst some San populations. Today the government provides schools in villages where the supply of water and drought relief food encourages the people to stay. But with no recent farming tradition, self-sufficiency is difficult. Others work on cattle farms or game farms and reserves.

The following is taken from a speech given by President Mogae on 7 November 2002, in which he sought to refute a connection between diamond exploration in the CKGR and the relocation of the Basarwa.

In view of the extended campaign of deception which has been waged by Survival International, it is necessary for me to set the record absolutely straight on a number of matters of fact which, fortunately, are easily verifiable by those, including Survival International, who care to do so. These facts are:

- Despite exploration over many years, beginning in the mid-1960s, no commercially mineable mineral deposit has been found inside the CKGR. There is neither any actual mining nor any plan for future mining inside the reserve.
- A diamond deposit was discovered at Gope, inside the CKGR, in 1980. After extensive testing, including the sinking of a trial shaft which still exists, it has been determined that the deposit cannot be economically mined. The area remains the subject of a retention licence, but all activity has ceased and there is no plan to resume.
- The activity associated with past mineral prospecting, including the sinking of a borehole at the location, attracted a small number of Basarwa to abandon a more nomadic lifestyle and adopt a settled existence in the area. The borehole has subsequently been disconnected because prospecting activity in the area has ceased. This was criticised by Survival International on the absurd notion that the government was terminating the 'traditional' water supply of the Basarwa.
- The programme of assisted relocation of Basarwa from areas of the CKGR, where it is virtually impossible to provide any kind of basic human infrastructure, began in 1997 after having been the subject of consultations since 1985. It was in no way related to any plan, real or fictitious, to commence diamond mining in the CKGR.
- The great majority of the Basarwa communities are anxious to seize the opportunity for an improvement in the quality of their lives and the lives of their children. Even some of those who are apparently resisting such opportunities have found the means to advance the lives and the future prospects of their own families, by tapping into the fruits of economic development which are already available to them outside the CKGR.

The relocation exercise, which is accepted as being in the best interests of the majority of the Basarwa and of the nation as a whole, has been carried out in the most sensitive and constructive manner possible. The government has devoted significant resources to assist the Basarwa in their new settlements. Funds have been allocated for infrastructural developments, such as schools, health posts, water reticulation and other social amenities. Apart from land for residential and commercial purposes, people have been given cattle and goats, and more than P30 million (US$5 million) has been expended on projects to improve the new settlements. In a world where governments stand accused of many terrible crimes, it does seem strange that the Botswana Government should have to defend itself against the charge of improving the lives of its citizens.

Central Kalahari Game Reserve This is one of the most contentious issues facing Botswana today – with much rhetoric from all quarters.

The Central Kalahari Game Reserve (CKGR) was proclaimed in 1961 in the last days of the British Protectorate with the intention of placating international concern over the well being of the San, by safeguarding it for the San hunter-gatherers who were living there. Although for ease of administration it was designated as a game reserve, the needs of its people was a prime motivating factor in its declaration.

In the early 1960s the population here was estimated at around 5,000 people; by the 1996 it had reduced to an estimated 1,482. The largest settlement, a small village called Xade, had a borehole which supplied water, and a few basic buildings. As early as 1986 a government white paper spelled out that the policy was for the residents of the CKGR to be relocated outside the reserve. The story since then has been one of the government using carrots and sticks to attain this aim.

Supporters of the San's right to remain have alleged that since the mid-1990s the government and its servants, including the park's game scouts, have been applying more and more pressure on the local people, forcing them to resettle to new locations outside the reserve. The best known of these is named, with Orwellian flair, New Xade. They allege that San individuals have been beaten and otherwise coerced into moving, and that even the water supply has been stopped for those who stay. In return, the government denies that they have ever used force. They say that water and other services have been withdrawn from Xade for reasons of practicality and cost, and that any relocations have been voluntary.

It seems likely that the government has, at best, been a little 'over-zealous' in its resettlement policy, and at worst it may have committed serious injustices to the people in the reserve. For me, the most pertinent question is 'Why bother?' as the official line that it's to protect the game seems implausible, given all the bad press that this generates for them throughout the world. There are two obvious theories. One recognises that the government is putting an increasing emphasis on tourism, and is concerned that the presence of the San will detract from the tourist's experience. A second suggests that the government wants to clear the way for the possibility of exploiting mineral claims in the area – diamond prospectors have long been looking for another find like Orapa beneath the Kalahari.

A case against the government has been brought by the San people. The first judge to rule on the case announced, on 13 December 2006, that the government had acted legally; two further judgements were to follow.

Hope for the future? Perhaps one of the few rays of hope is that as a consequence of the prevailing image of the San, visitors really are willing to pay to see something of their 'traditional culture'. Hence the springing up of various traditional villages and tourism projects in both Botswana and neighbouring Namibia.

These vary from really interesting, genuine insights into the people and their skills, to little more than curiosity shows put on for the benefit of visitors.

I'd probably argue that virtually all are worthwhile for the San – provided that they bring a substantial income into the community involved, and do so without actively harming the people's self-esteem. Meanwhile from experience of the best, I know they can be absolutely fascinating personal interactions for the visitor, as well as acting to reinforce the community's own self-esteem and value in their own skills, whilst bringing much-needed money into the community.

What's become very, very clear is that making such a tourist–community interaction really successful for both parties needs the permanent commitment of someone on the ground who has been working with the community for a long period – and understands both the community and the tourists. Without this, such projects invariably fail.

OTHER SOCIAL GROUPS

The Khoisan The Khoisan group includes the San people, discussed at length in the previous sections, and the Khoe, covered here.

The Khoe The San are often described as hunter-gatherers and the Khoe as pastoralists. The distinction is not quite so clear-cut, but it is generally useful. The Khoe, who live in central Botswana and Namibia, have herds of cattle, but continue to source some of their food from hunting and gathering, supplemented by milk products.

The ownership of animals is a mark of status in these groups, so laws are required to protect property and status. Because of the intrinsic value of the animals, the Khoe milk their herds but do not kill them for food; stock animals are only killed to mark special occasions.

The ownership of property (stock) has created a more rigid and complex social structure. Property creates wealth, which can be inherited after the death of the owner, and so laws of inheritance have been developed. Wealth brings with it the power to control others, thus creating leaders. It also leads to a wealth-based economy that depends on the exchange of goods and work that have an economic value. What must be freely given among the San must be bought and paid for among the Khoe.

Little is known about the religious beliefs of the Khoe, though they believe in a Supreme Being and it is thought that some beliefs are similar to the San and can be traced back to a common source.

Bantu-speaking peoples After a complex history of conflict, a number of tribes of Bantu origin can now be found in Botswana. As discussed on pages 19–20, today the word 'tribe' has colonial connotations, but unfortunately we do not have a suitable alternative. Likewise, definition by ethnic group is not considered politically correct in Botswana; all people are primarily Batswana (the people of Botswana), and only secondarily Bayei, Bakwena, European etc. Tribal names are frequently preceded by 'Ba', which means 'the people of . . .'. Sometimes you'll also see the term 'Matswana' used to mean a person from Botswana.

Tswana Although the same name applies to all the people of Botswana, the Batswana (or Tswana) are also the largest ethnic group in the country. As an aside, colonial partitioning led to three-quarters of the Tswana actually living in South Africa. The name embraces a number of different offshoots. The Tswana speak Setswana, which is the second language of Botswana, English being the official language.

The Basubiya, the Hambukushu and the Bayei Around AD1600 these three groups of river-dwelling people all lived close together in the region to the south of the Chobe River. Their closeness is reflected in the similarity of their customs. Significantly, their system of inheritance meant that wealth and status were not passed to the first son, but through to the children of the father's eldest sister. So a man inherited the chieftancy if his mother was the eldest sister of the chief.

The Basubiya According to tradition, after a fight over a lion skin the Bayei were defeated by the Basubiya. They moved away to the Linyanti River, but they still came under the rule of the Basubiya.

Meanwhile, the Hambukushu were driven from their homeland by the expansionist and tribute-seeking Chief of the Balozi, whose capital was at Katima Mulilo (now in western Zambia.) To avoid paying the tribute and escape his attentions, the Hambukushu left the Zambezi River and moved nearer to the Chobe and Linyanti rivers, into a region which was already occupied by the Bayei.

The Basubiya eventually grew very powerful and had a large state which stretched from Luchindo on the Chobe river, westwards towards the Okavango. Eventually they were defeated by the Balozi and incorporated into the Lozi empire until its collapse in 1865. According to Campbell, the Basubiya were mainly agriculturalists who also kept some cattle, sheep and goats. They cultivated the floodplains, which they prepared by hoeing in the autumn before the winter floods and planting crops such as millet, sweet reeds and melon when the floods had receded. Today they still live in the northwest and Chobe Districts of the country.

Bayei (and Banoka) In response to the Basubiya invasion, the Bayei moved away from the Chobe River, into the Okavango, and between 1750 and 1800 they firmly established themselves in the area of the delta around Lake Ngami. This shallower, southern section of the delta perfectly suited the Bayei, who lived mainly from fishing. They also kept cattle, but used them only as pack animals. In the Delta they encountered a group of Khoe, called the Banoka, (otherwise known as the River Bushmen), who had adapted their hunter-gatherer skills to the environment of the delta.

The two peoples seem to have coexisted peacefully and even swapped skills. For example the Bayei taught the Banoka to fish with nets where before they had only used baskets. The Bayei made nets from the twisted fibres of succulent plants, which they then trawled behind their boats, called mekoro. A mokoro (mekoro is the plural form) is a dugout canoe that is poled from the rear. In return the Banoka taught the Bayei how to dig pits, filled with sharp pointed sticks, in the middle of a game trail, to trap unsuspecting animals on their way to the river.

A prize catch for the Bayei was the hippo, which they sometimes hunted from their mekoro. Their method, like the old whale hunters, was to harpoon the hippo from the boat. Instantly the hippo would take flight, towing the mokoro in its wake. The hunters had to kill the hippo with their spears, before it either broke loose or killed them. This they did by attempting to reach the bank in their boats, tying the rope attached to the harpoon to a tree and waiting for the hippo to tire before approaching it with spears. Hippos are notoriously bad tempered and dangerous and are liable to attack if they are surprised in the water. Mekoro today are more likely to be transporting tourists for a spot of hippo watching, and may well be made of fibreglass instead of wood, but they are still often poled by a Bayei man.

Another favourite method of hippo hunting was to place a spear weighted with rocks suspended from a tree over a hippo trail. Hippos live in the water during the day, but come out at night to graze and they tend to keep to the same tracks.

The Hambukushu Meanwhile the Hambukushu found that settling on the Chobe did not take them far enough from the Balozi tribute seekers, so they moved again and settled in the more northerly, upper reaches of the Okavango Delta. Being agriculturalists as well as hunters and fishermen, they preferred the deeper water there. Unlike the lower regions, this area did not flood when the rains came and so was more suitable for agriculture. They cleared the bush and planted crops along the river, such as millet, sugar cane, pumpkins and root crops.

Like the Bayei, the Hambukushu used mekoro boats, but instead of poling them standing up, they sat down and used paddles to propel them through the deeper water.

Alec Campbell's *The Guide to Botswana* (see *Appendix 3, Further Information*) describes how the Hambukushu hunted for elephants:

> They took the blade of a spear which had a barb in it and fixed this into a heavy piece of wood. They dug shallow holes on paths used by elephants and then set these spear blades facing upwards. The elephant stood on this, driving the blade deep into the bottom of its foot, after which it couldn't walk. When it was weak, men came with axes and slashed the tendons in its back legs so that it fell down and could be speared.

Today the Hambukushu are most famous for their beautiful hand-woven baskets, which are internationally recognised for their craftsmanship and design. The wide variety of basket types reflects the numerous purposes for which they were traditionally used, ranging from enormous grain storage baskets, to tightly woven beer baskets for holding the local brew. Unfortunately, the baskets are now being produced commercially, which enables the makers to earn a reasonable living, but has led to over-exploitation of the natural resources from which the baskets are made. The Hambukushu are also renowned as rain-makers, another skill which they have exploited commercially by selling their services to neighbouring tribes.

The Ovaherero and the Ovambanderu The Ovaherero and their relatives the Ovambanderu are pastoralists, who keep large herds of sheep, goats, and especially cattle, which have a religious significance for them. According to their oral history tradition they seem to have moved southwest from central Africa, probably to escape the spread of the tsetse fly which spreads sleeping sickness and kills cattle and people.

The religious life of the tribe was of great importance. The tribe was divided into religious clans under a priest/chief. He owned the most cattle and he maintained a sacred herd on behalf of the tribe. On his death the priesthood and the care of the sacred herd passed to his son. The Ovaherero practised ancestor worship, and one of the priest's main religious duties was appeasing the dead relatives of the tribe.

As pastoralists the clans led their herds in search of grazing but each clan had a designated area. Within this area the women built round huts from a framework of branches covered with mud. The huts were built in a circle around corrals for the animals. As well as tending the herds, the men hunted with wooden spears, (their only iron came from trading with the Batswana). The women also collected wild food and made *omaere*, a kind of sour milk which was their staple food.

Most of the Ovaherero today live in Namibia, though some are also found in Botswana, where they fled following the German–Herero War at the beginning of the 20th century. In the 19th century the Ovaherero were living in what is now northern Namibia, but were becoming increasingly unhappy about their loss of land to the German colonists. In January 1904 their leader, Samuel Maherero, ordered a Herero uprising against the colonial forces.

Initially the Hereros had success in taking many German farms and smaller outposts, and in severing the railway line between Swakopmund and Windhoek. However, later in 1904, the German General von Trotha led a large German force including heavy artillery against the Hereros. By August 1904 the Hereros were pushed back to their stronghold of Waterberg, with its permanent water-holes.

On 11 August, the Germans attacked, and the battle raged all day. Though not decisive, the Hereros' spirit was beaten by the superior firepower and they fled east, into the Kalahari and towards Maun. Many perished; the rest settled in what is now northern Botswana.

They had lost their cattle and were forced to work as servants to another tribe, the Batawana. However they soon rebuilt their herds and also learnt agriculture from the Batawana, which they used to supplement their traditional diet of soured milk. The Ovaherero are recognisable today because the women continue to dress in the clothes they were taught to wear by Victorian Christian missionaries, including long bulky dresses and headdresses.

The Bakalanga The Bakalanga are the second largest population group after the Tswana, despite having been divided by colonial boundaries. Today over 75% of them live in Zimbabwe. Those in Botswana live mainly in the area around Francistown, although they are scattered as far afield as Maun, Palapye, Serowe, Mahalapye and Mochudi. Their origins are unclear, though some of them have probably lived in the region of the upper Shashe River for at least a thousand years. For the last 600 years they have been ruled by other peoples, but interestingly their conquerors have always ended by inter-marrying with the Bakalanga and adopting their customs and language.

The Bakalanga are primarily agriculturalists and this is reflected in their religion and culture, but cattle and goats are also kept, usually by the chief on behalf of his tribe. The chief would give cattle to people who had performed services to the tribe, or those who needed them in order to get married or to sacrifice to the ancestors. The primary importance of agriculture is shown by the traditional marital gifts of specially forged iron hoes that were given to the bride's parents to symbolise the continuity of her livelihood.

The Kagalagari This name is applied to different people of varied descent who currently live in the Kalahari Desert. There are five major groups who have settled in different areas of the Kalahari. They all have their own tribal names and customs and they speak a variety of languages – the combined form of which is a Sotho language, not a dialect of Tswana.

Of these five groups the Bakgwatheng remain in the east of the Kalahari on the fringes of the desert, which receives sufficient rainfall for their crops of sorghum, melons and beans. They also keep small herds of cattle, sheep and goats, and mine and work iron. As the iron ore was not available in the heart of the Kalahari these factors all restricted them to the desert's fringe.

The Bangologa and the Babolaongwe, on the other hand, are pastoralists with large herds of sheep and goats, and a few cattle. They obtain most of their food from hunting and gathering, so they are not reliant upon agriculture and they trade for iron, so they were able to live a nomadic existence within the desert.

Others
White Botswanans The current white population of Botswana is much lower than that of her surrounding neighbours, and many of these are not permanent residents. This reflects the unusual history of Botswana: the fact that the country was a 'Protectorate' rather than a colony.

Note that these small numbers of white Botswanans are very different from the expatriate community (see below), who are often white but simply working in the country on a temporary basis. Many white Botswanans will trace their families back to colonial immigrants who came over during British rule, but most are citizens of Botswana rather than, say, British. This is generally an affluent group of people, a number of whom own and run their own businesses.

Expatriates Totally distinct from the permanent population of citizens of Botswana who are white, there is also a significant 'expat' community in Botswana. These foreigners usually come to Botswana for two or three years to work on short-term contracts, often for multi-national companies or aid agencies. Most are highly skilled individuals who come to share their knowledge with local colleagues – often teaching skills that are in short supply in Botswana.

There is also a significant number of foreigners working in the safari industry. These are often residents of other southern African nations who come to guide or manage camps for a few years, although as work permits become increasingly difficult to obtain, the number of expats in the safari business is slowly starting to fall.

RELIGION Officially Botswana is a Christian country, although the number of practising Christians is estimated at only around 20% of the population. These mostly belong to the Catholic, Anglican, Methodist, Lutheran and Zion Christian Church (where its members are noted for the khaki dress worn when attending). Services are usually in Tswana, though the larger churches in the main towns also have English services, and the smaller, rural ones will sometimes use the local languages. Faith healing is often incorporated into services.

Other religions, such as Islam, are only represented in the larger towns; their following is small, mainly amongst expat workers.

As usual in the subcontinent, many of Botswana's religions blend Christian beliefs with aspects of traditional beliefs. In times of crisis or ill health, most people are as likely to seek out a traditional healer as they are to visit a priest or a hospital. Though more often still, they will pursue both a traditional and a more Western approach at the same time. (From a medical standpoint, the best practices of traditional healers are increasingly lauded throughout southern Africa as holistic approaches, which can complement Western medicine.)

People's traditional beliefs depend largely on ancestry, differing widely from tribe to tribe, but generally incorporating a great respect for ancestors, a belief in their continued existence in the spirit world, and a certainly that the spirits affect everyone's day-to-day lives.

LANGUAGE

According to data from *Ethnologue: Languages of the World* (*www.ethnologue.com*) there are at least 26 languages spoken in Botswana. The official languages are English and Setswana: 70% of the population speak Setswana. Many people are at least bilingual, speaking English and their mother tongue, and possibly Setswana or Afrikaans, depending on what is locally required to get work.

It's interesting to note here that all the world's languages have been grouped into around 20 linguistic families. Of these, four are very different from the rest. All these four are African families – and they include the Khoisan and Niger-Congo (the Bantu languages). The Khoisan languages are amongst the world's most complex languages; this is part of the evidence that has led linguists to believe that human language evolved in Africa, and probably amongst the ancestors of the Khoisan.

For more scientifically minded readers, here's a list of most of Botswana's main language groups, with their linguistic family roots and a few brief notes on where they're spoken. This tells you the history of that language, starting with the main group to which it belongs, and defining it more specifically. Thus English and Afrikaans are both Indo-European languages, and more specifically Germanic and West. That means they both originally derive from one ancient language, West Germanic. The classification of the Khoisan and Bantu languages gives a similar view of their history and relationships. Obviously information below is best read in conjunction with the previous section on social groups.

LANGUAGES OF THE BANTU FAMILY

Tswana *Classification: Niger-Congo, Atlantic-Congo, Volta-Congo, Benue-Congo, Bantoid, Southern, Narrow Bantu, Central, S, Sotho-Tswana (S30), Tswana.* Around 70% of the population speak Tswana (also known as Setswana). Some official business is conducted in Tswana, the media often use English and Tswana interchangeably, and it's a lingua franca between different citizens who don't speak English.

Tswapong *Classification: Niger-Congo, Atlantic-Congo, Volta-Congo, Benue-Congo, Bantoid, Southern, Narrow Bantu, Central, S, Sotho-Tswana (S30), Tswapong.* Several thousand speakers, in the Central District and Mahalapye Sub-district.

Kagalagadi *Classification: Niger-Congo, Atlantic-Congo, Volta-Congo, Benue-Congo, Bantoid, Southern, Narrow Bantu, Central, S, Sotho-Tswana (S30), Kgalagadi.* Estimated total of about 35,000 speakers in Botswana.

Birwa *Classification: Niger-Congo, Atlantic-Congo, Volta-Congo, Benue-Congo, Bantoid, Southern, Narrow Bantu, Central, S, Sotho-Tswana (S30), Sotho.* Estimated total of about 10,000 speakers in Botswana.

Kalanga *Classification: Niger-Congo, Atlantic-Congo, Volta-Congo, Benue-Congo, Bantoid, Southern, Narrow Bantu, Central, S, Shona (S10).* Estimated total of about 160,000 speakers in Botswana.

Ndbele *Classification: Niger-Congo, Atlantic-Congo, Volta-Congo, Benue-Congo, Bantoid, Southern, Narrow Bantu, Central, S, Ngui.* Estimated total of about 10,000 speakers in the Northeast District, though this is the main language over the border in Zimbabwe's Matabele Province.

Herero *Classification: Niger-Congo, Atlantic-Congo, Volta-Congo, Benue-Congo, Bantoid, Southern, Narrow Bantu, Central, R, Herero.* Estimated total of about 31,000 speakers scattered among other ethnic groups, often having their own area in towns and villages. This is one of Namibia's major ethnic groups.

Yeyi *Classification: Niger-Congo, Atlantic-Congo, Volta-Congo, Benue-Congo, Bantoid, Southern, Narrow Bantu, Central, R, Yeye.* Estimated total of about 27,000 speakers in Botswana, with probably another 20,000 ethnic Bayeyi who do not actually speak Yeyi.

Mbukushu *Classification: Niger-Congo, Atlantic-Congo, Volta-Congo, Benue-Congo, Bantoid, Southern, Narrow Bantu, Central, K, Kwangwa.* Estimated total of about 12,000 speakers in Botswana, located in the Northwest District, especially in Gomare, and in the villages to the north of there, and in the Okavango Delta.

Subiya *Classification: Niger-Congo, Atlantic-Congo, Volta-Congo, Benue-Congo, Bantoid, Southern, Narrow Bantu, Central, K, Subia (L50).* Estimated total of about 12,000 speakers in Botswana, mostly living in the Northwest and Chobe Districts.

LANGUAGES OF THE KHOISAN FAMILY

!Xoo *Classification: Khoisan, southern Africa, Southern, Hua.* There are between 3,000 and 4,000 speakers of this Khoisan language, and its related dialects, living in Botswana.

=/Hua *Classification: Khoisan, southern Africa, Southern, Hua.* Around 1,000–1,500 speakers, living mainly in the Southern Kalahari Desert and the Kweneng District.

//Gana *Classification: Khoisan, southern Africa, Central Tshu-Khwe, Northwest.* Around 1,000 speakers living around the Ghanzi District, in villages and farms, and in the Central Kalahari Game Reserve. Speakers are also found in the Central District (Boteti Sub-district) and the cattle-posts south and west of Rakops.

/Anda *Classification: Khoisan, southern Africa, Central Tshu-Khwe, Northwest.* About 1,000 speakers live in the Northwest District, mostly around the Khwai River and Mababe Village areas.

Ksoe *Classification: Khoisan, southern Africa, Central Tshu-Khwe, Northwest.* People speaking this language are also often known as the 'River Bushmen'. Speakers of this language number around 1,700–2,000, and live in and around the Northwest District, mainly in the villages: Gan, Cadikarauwe, Mohembo, Shakawe, Kaputura, /Ao-Kyao, Sikonkomboro, Ngarange, Sekanduko, Xongoa, Cauwe, Moxatce, Dungu, Seronga, Beyetca, Gudigoa, Sikokora, Geixa, /Qom-ca, Tobere, 0/Umbexa, Djaxo, Kangwara villages.

Deti *Classification: Khoisan, southern Africa, Central Tshu-Khwe, Central.* Spoken in the Central District, Boteti Sub-district, and in the villages which are strung out along the Boteti River.

Nama *Classification: Khoisan, southern Africa, Central Tshu-Khwe, Central.* In Botswana there are about 200–1,000 Nama speakers, mostly in the Kgalagadi Disrict, around Tsabong, Makopong, Omaweneno, Tshane villages, and in the Ghanzi District, in the villages along the Ghanzi-Mamuno road. It's also spoken by a much larger population in Namibia.

Ganadi *Classification: Khoisan, southern Africa, Central Tshu-Khwe, North Central.* Spoken in the Northeastern area.

Shua *Classification: Khoisan, southern Africa, Central Tshu-Khwe, North Central.* There are around 19,000 Shua speakers in Botswana, counted together with the Tshwa group. Located in Central District and Tutumi Sub-district.

//Gwi There are around 800 speakers in villages in the Kweneng District and the Ghanzi District.

Naro *Classification: Khoisan, southern Africa, Central Tshu-Khwe, Southwest.* Botswana has an estimated 8,000 speakers of Naro.

Ju/'Hoansi *Classification: Khoisan, southern Africa, Northern.* This is one of the larger Khoisan languages, with 4,000–8,000 speakers in Botswana, and many more in Namibia – around the Tsumkwe area.

=/Kx'au//'ein *Classification: Khoisan, southern Africa, Northern.* There are about 3,000 speakers in Botswana, mostly in the Ghanzi District, in the villages and working on commercial farms.

LANGUAGES OF THE EUROPEAN FAMILY
English *Classification: Indo-European, Germanic, West, English.* English is the official language in Botswana, the language of government and schools, although official work is increasingly being carried out in Setswana (Tswana).

Afrikaans *Classification: Indo-European, Germanic, West; Low Saxon-Low Franconian, Low Franconian.* There are 20,000 people in Botswana whose native tongue is Afrikaans, mainly on the commercial farms in the Ghanzi District – however many of the white community who have close links with South Africa can communicate in Afrikaans.

EDUCATION

Botswana's education system follows a nine-year course focusing on both academic and practical skills. Examinations held at the end of standard 7 – roughly aged 14 – determine whether or not a child may continue into secondary education, and thence to technical college.

Primary education in Botswana is in theory free, and is compulsory for all children. That said, parents are charged a 'development fee' each term of P20 (US$4), and also need to equip their child with a uniform, which could set them back around P350 (US$7), including shoes. This in a country where the minimum government wage is less than US$0.50 an hour. Where parents cannot meet these fees, local authorities step in. In 2006, it is likely that school fees will be implemented across the board, with figures under discussion currently P300 for primary schools, P400 for secondary, and P750 for technical colleges.

CULTURAL GUIDELINES

Comments here are intended to be a general guide, just a few examples of how to travel more sensitively. They should not be viewed as blueprints for perfect Botswana etiquette. Cultural sensitivity is really a state of mind, not a checklist of behaviour – so here we can only hope to give the sensitive traveller a few pointers in the right direction.

When we travel, we are all in danger of leaving negative impressions with local people that we meet. It is easily done – by snapping that picture quickly, whilst the subject is not looking; by dressing scantily, offending local sensitivities; by just brushing aside the feelings of local people, with the high-handed superiority of a rich Westerner. These things are easy to do, in the click of a shutter, or flash of a dollar bill.

However, you will get the most representative view of Botswana if you cause as little disturbance to the local people as possible. You will never blend in perfectly when you travel – your mere presence there, as an observer, will always change the local events slightly. However, if you try to fit in and show respect for local culture and attitudes, then you may manage to leave positive feelings behind you.

One of the easiest, and most important, ways to do this is with **greetings**. African societies are rarely as rushed as Western ones. When you first talk to someone, you should greet them leisurely. So, for example, if you enter a bus station and want some help, do not just ask outright, 'Where is the bus to . . . ?' That would be rude. Instead you will have a better reception (and a better chance of good advice) by saying:

Traveller:	'Good afternoon.'
Local:	'Good afternoon.'
Traveller:	'How are you?'
Local:	'I am fine, how are you?'
Traveller:	'I am fine, thank you. (pause) Do you know where the bus to . . .'

This goes for approaching anyone – always greet them first. For a better reception still, learn these phrases of greeting in Setswana, or even the local language (see *Appendix 2, Language*). English-speakers are often lazy about learning languages, and, whilst most people in Botswana understand English, a greeting given in an appropriate local language will be received with delight. It implies that you are making an effort to learn a little of their language and culture, which is always appreciated.

Very rarely in one of the towns you may be approached by someone who doesn't greet you. Instead s/he tries immediately to sell you something, or even hassle you in some way. These people have learned that foreigners aren't used to greetings, and so have adapted their approach accordingly. A surprisingly effective way to dodge their attentions is to reply to their questions with a formal greeting, and then politely – but firmly – refuse their offer.

Another part of the normal greeting ritual is **handshaking**. As elsewhere, you would not normally shake a shop-owner's hand, but you would shake hands with someone to whom you are introduced. Get some practice when you arrive, as there is a gentle, three-part handshake used in southern Africa which is easily learnt.

It consists of taking each other's right hand, as for a normal handshake, but just shaking once, up and down. Then whilst leaving the thumbs linked, the grip is changed by both people raising their hands, until their arms make a right-angle. Each then grasps the other person's thumb and the top of their hand firmly. Then this is swiftly relaxed, with thumbs still interlinked, and the hands are dropped back into one last normal 'shake'.

Your **clothing** is an area that can easily give offence. Most people in Botswana frown upon skimpy or revealing clothing, especially when worn by women. Shorts are fine for walking safaris, otherwise dress conservatively and avoid short shorts, especially in the more rural areas. Respectable locals will wear long trousers (men) or long skirts (women).

Photography is a tricky business. Most people in Botswana will be only too happy to be photographed – provided you ask their permission first. Sign language is fine for this question: just point at your camera, shrug your shoulders, and look quizzical. The problem is that then everyone will smile for you, producing the type of 'posed' photograph that you may not want. However, stay around and chat for five or ten minutes more, and people will get used to your presence, stop posing and you will get more natural shots of them (a camera with a quiet shutter is a help).

TRADITIONAL CULTURE AND CHANGE

Because he was a deeply committed Christian convert, Khama, the leader of the Bamangwato, began to make changes to the traditional way of life. One of the most significant changes was the abolition of the initiation ceremonies for men and women. He reformed the *bogadi* tradition, which had meant that a woman's children belonged to her husband, even those children she had after he had died. Khama also laid down laws and regulations for his people to live by, including banning the consumption of alcohol.

One elderly man described the men's initiation ceremony or *bogwera*: 'Not only was the foreskin cut and the youths put through endurance tests, but one of us had to remain behind. He was killed in a painful way, in the secrecy of the bush. When we came home, it was made out that the youth had died because he could not stand up to the tests. Everyone knew the truth but it was treated as a deep secret. That was why Khama abolished *bogwera*.'

However, it was still important to mark the passing of boyhood into manhood, so Khama preserved the tradition of 'age regiments'. All young men had their coming of age marked by a gathering with prayers and lectures. Those who came of age at the same time formed an age regiment. From Khama's time on, the age regiments began to volunteer to work on community projects such as building schools or churches and many things were accomplished.

It was also largely due to the efforts of Khama that Botswana became a British Protectorate, known as the British Bechuanaland Protectorate. This probably saved Botswana from becoming another South Africa or Rhodesia (Zimbabwe) and resulted in Botswana's peaceful independence in 1966.

Note that special care is needed with photography near government buildings, bridges, mines, and similar sites of strategic importance. You must ask permission before photographing anything here, or you risk people thinking that you are a spy. (To be fair to the country, I've never come across such problems in Botswana, though I'd still exercise the same caution as in any other country.)

If you're travelling, and seeking directions to somewhere, don't be afraid of **asking questions**. Most people will be polite and keen to help – so keen that some will answer 'yes' to questions if they think that this is what you want to hear. So try to avoid asking leading questions. For example, 'Yes' would often be the typical answer to the question, 'Does this road lead to . . . ?' And in a sense the respondent is probably correct – it will get you there. It's just that it may not be the quickest or shortest way.

To avoid misunderstandings, it is often better to ask open-ended questions like, 'Where does this road go to?' or 'How do I drive to . . . ?'

The specific examples above can only be taken so far – they are general by their very nature. But wherever you find yourself, if you are polite and considerate to the people of Botswana that you meet, then you will rarely encounter any cultural problems. Watch how they behave and, if you have any doubts about how you should act, then ask someone quietly. They will seldom tell you outright that you are being rude, but they will usually give you good advice on how to make your behaviour more acceptable.

GIVING SOMETHING BACK

Botswana is one of the richer of the developing nations, but despite this you may see scenes of poverty when you are visiting the country, especially in more rural areas. Beggars are fairly rare in the towns, but often the least able are dependent on

When the Protectorate was finally granted, Khama expressed his gratitude and laid down the following principles of government, in a document which related primarily to the Bamangwato, but was later applied to the whole country:

I am not baffled in the government of my town, or in deciding cases among my own people according to custom. I have to say that there are certain laws of my country which the Queen of England finds in operation, and which are advantageous to my people, and I wish these laws should be established and not taken away by the Government of England. I refer to our law concerning intoxicating drinks, that they should not enter the country of the Bamangwato, whether among black people or white people. I refer further to our law which declares that the lands of the Bamangwato are not saleable. I say this law is also good; let it be upheld and continue to be law among black people and white people.

The system of traditional law to which Khama referred in this document was well established. It centered upon the chief, whose position of prestige and power carried with it the obligation that the good of the tribe must be placed above personal desire. The chief held property and land on behalf of the tribe and had always to be available to his people to settle disputes and business affairs.

There was also a tribal court, known as a *kgotla*, to help him make decisions. This consisted of the headmen of the wards into which the village was divided, and of senior tribesmen. Disputes which could not be settled within the ward were brought to the *kgotla*. There was an obligation for people to be open in all their dealings with each other and to act in the best interests of the community.

charity. Whilst giving a few coins to people is one way to put a sticking plaster over your feelings of guilt, this is not a long-term solution.

There *are* ways in which you can make a positive contribution, but they require more effort than giving to someone on the street, and perhaps this is the least you can do after an enjoyable trip to Botswana?

There is an established, trustworthy and reliable network of charities, churches and NGOs (non-government organisation). If you really want to help, then contact someone and make it happen!

LOCAL CHARITIES WORKING IN BOTSWANA One good source of information on NGOs is the website of the Botswana Council of Non-Governmental Organisations (*BOCONGO;* ✆ *3911 319;* f *3912 935;* e *bocongo@bocongo.bw; www.bocongo.bw*). Their website is a good reference site, with a brief synopsis of many of the country's groups doing valuable work. It doesn't include all charities, but is a good start to your research.

HELPING POORER COMMUNITIES Botswana has a whole range of good, small charities working at grassroots level to improve the lot of the poorest members of society here, and help them to develop economically. A few which concentrate on the north of the country, include:

Bana Ba Letsatsi Trust P Bag 114, Suite 55, Maun; ✆ 7141 3774; e banabaletsatsi@yahoo.com; http://capricorn-foundation.com/html/banabaletsatsi.html. A local charity helping with Maun's streetchildren. For details, see page 150.

Chobe Enclave Conservation Trust, Kavimba; ✆ 3950 486; f 3950 746; e gben@gov.bw. A village trust that aims to support the sustainable management of the Chobe enclave's natural resources for the benefit of the local community.

COCEPWA c/o Maun General Hospital, PO Box 12, Maun; ✆ 6864 758; f 6864 758. This 'coping centre' provides support for people infected with HIV/AIDS.

Ditshwanelo (The Botswana Centre for Human Rights) P Bag 416, Gaborone; ✆ 3906 998; f 3907 778; e ditshwanelo@info.bw. Involved all over Botswana, including a base in Kasane, Ditshwanelo works with poorer communities on a range of issues including access to water and the Chobe River.

Thuso Lutheran Rehabilitation Centre P Bag 40, Thitoyamoda, Maun; ✆ 6864 076; f 6860 539; e tlrc@botsnet.bw. Rehabilitation centre for disabled people in the community, providing vocational skills' training such as gardening, knitting, sewing and computing.

HELPING THE WILDLIFE The first thing to do if you want to help protect Botswana's wilder areas is to travel there, often; the income generated by tourism is the main hope to enable these areas to survive and thrive in the long term.

The second thing to do is to support organisations such as the following that work in promoting knowledge of Botswana's wilder areas, or in campaigning for environmental and social issues:

The Botswana Society Gaborone, Botswana; ✆ 391 9673; www.botsoc.org.bw

The Kalahari Conservation Society Plot 112, Independence Av, PO Box 859, Gaborone; ✆ 397 4557; www.kcs.org.bw

In addition, helping the country's poorer communities (see above) will, ultimately, also help preserve the wildlife areas, as without sustainable economic development there's little long-term hope for the wildlife.

There are also several good small charities that are working for different small-scale, but none the less important projects:

White rhino have been successfully re-introduced to Moremi Game Reserve (see page 245 and *Appendix 3*, page 483) and there are plans in hand to re-introduce the black rhino as well. However, this requires significant financial support. For details, contact Grant Woodrow at the Environmental Division, Okavango Wilderness Safaris (*P Bag 014, Maun;* ✆ *686 0086;* f *660 632*).

Botswana's only **animal orphanage** is in Francistown, and is owned by the Uncharted Safari Company (*Francistown;* ✆ *2412 277;* e *office@unchartedafrica.co.bw; www.unchartedafrica.co.bw*).

3

The Natural Environment

PHYSICAL ENVIRONMENT

TOPOGRAPHY Botswana lies landlocked in the heart of southern Africa, straddling the Tropic of Capricorn and covering about 585,370km^2, of which about two-thirds is in the tropics. Most of Botswana is a gently undulating sandsheet with an altitude of between 900m and 1,300m. This is punctuated by occasional isolated rock outcrops, which are rarely more than 100m tall. Two major features stand out from this: the enormous salt pans and the huge inland delta of the Okavango River.

A relatively narrow corridor of land on the southeast side of Botswana is rockier and less flat than the rest, with sandstone and granite hills leading down to the Shashe, Limpopo and Marico rivers. This land is much more suitable for agriculture, and is where most of the country's population is concentrated.

GEOLOGICAL HISTORY Looking back into Botswana's geological history gives us insights to explain how the Great Salt Pans and the Okavango Delta were formed. It's a long story though, of which I can give only a brief outline here. For a deeper and much more scholarly approach, seek out John Reader's *Africa: A Biography of a Continent* and especially Mike Main's *Kalahari: Life's Variety in Dune and Delta* (see *Appendix 3, Further Information*). Both are excellent, giving much more comprehensive discussions of the latest scientific thinking than I'm able to give here – the first in terms of Africa generally, and the second with immense detail specifically about Botswana.

Setting the scene To put discussions in perspective, and give our history a sense of scale, let me start at the beginning. . . Around 4,600 million years ago the earth's crust began to form and cool. A thousand million years later, fossils from South Africa's Barberton Mountain Land give us evidence of the first recorded, simple, single-celled bacteria.

By 3,300 million years ago more complex blue-green algae had appeared, though it took a further 2,300 million years for multicellular organisms to evolve. Palaeontologists say that around 600 million years ago there was an 'evolutionary explosion', when many different species evolved, including ancestors of most of the world's existing invertebrates.

About 230 million years ago the earth saw the emergence of both dinosaurs and the first mammals. For the next 165 million years the dinosaurs dominated the earth and the largest mammals which evolved were probably no bigger than present-day rabbits. Only around 65 million years ago, when some great calamity killed off most of the dinosaurs, did the mammals begin to rise to dominance and inherit the earth.

The super-continent Meanwhile somewhere between 135 and 10 million years ago the super-continent, Gondwanaland, broke up and the continents started to move away from each other.

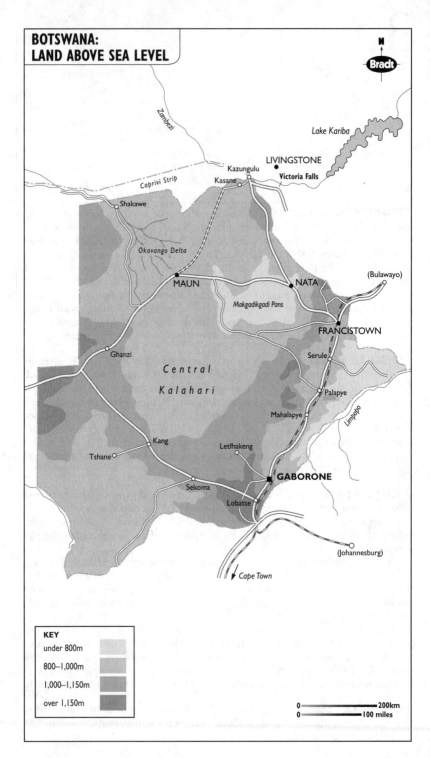

BOTSWANA:
LAND ABOVE SEA LEVEL

N

Bradt

Zambezi

Lake Kariba

LIVINGSTONE

Kazungulu

Caprivi Strip

Kasane

Victoria Falls

Shakawe

Okavango Delta

MAUN

NATA

(Bulawayo)

Makgadikgadi Pans

FRANCISTOWN

Ghanzi

Serule

Central

Kalahari

Palapye

Mahalapye

Limpopo

Kang

Letlhakeng

Tshane

Sekoma

GABORONE

Lobatse

(Johannesburg)

Cape Town

KEY

under 800m

800–1,000m

1,000–1,150m

over 1,150m

0 — 200km
0 — 100 miles

Diamond is a crystalline form of ordinary carbon formed under conditions of extreme pressure and temperature. In nature, such conditions are only found deep below the earth's surface, in the lower crust or upper mantle. Under specific circumstances, the rock matrix in which diamonds occur was subjected to such great pressure that it became fluid and punched its way up to the earth's surface in a volcanic pipe of liquid rock. This situation is similar to a conventional volcanic eruption, except that instead of basaltic magma being erupted through fissures in the crust, the volcanic material is a peculiar rock called kimberlite. This contains a wide assortment of minerals (including diamonds), often in addition to large chunks of other rocks that have been caught up in the whole process.

Such kimberlite pipes occur throughout southern Africa from the Cape to Zaire. However, only a small proportion of those discovered contain enough diamonds to be profitably worked.

Botswana mines kimberlite pipes for diamonds at Orapa and at Jwaneng. It's interesting to note that Botswana's neighbour, Namibia, has diamond deposits along its Atlantic coast. These are 'secondary diamond deposits', because they do not come directly from kimberlite pipes. Instead, Namibia's diamonds are found in areas where ancient rivers have eroded kimberlite pipes in the interior, washing diamonds down to the sea, and depositing them in sediments there.

By the time that the continents split from Gondwanaland, the basic rocks upon which southern Africa is built, the Karoo lavas, had been laid down. By about 65 million years ago – the end of the Cretaceous Period – most of the subcontinent's diamonds, gems and other mineral wealth had also been formed, and erosion was gradually wearing away at the land.

The world's earliest primate fossils are from Europe and North America, dating from around 65 million years ago, but it wasn't until about 4 million years ago that *Australopithecus* appeared in Africa – a prime candidate for being one of our earliest ancestors.

This period, as our first ancestors were evolving, is about the time when we start looking at how Botswana's landforms were created.

The Kalahari's super-lake During the Tertiary Period, which dates from about 65 million years ago, Botswana's climate was probably very arid, and as the region's rocks were gradually eroded, so the wind-blown sands accumulated and began to form what we now call the Kalahari.

Around four or five million years ago it's thought that the Okavango, Kwando and Zambezi rivers had completely different courses than they do today – probably all flowing into one channel which headed south through the Kalahari and into the Orange River and/or the Limpopo. (Different theories suggest different courses for these.)

Then, around two to four million years ago, it's thought that seismic shifts forced parts of southern and central Botswana upwards. Geologists identify the areas raised as the 'Zimbabwe–Kalahari Axis' and the 'Bakalahari Schwelle' – both of which are now watersheds in the region.

The net effect of these upward movements was to block the flow southwards of the rivers, and to form a super-lake that had its deepest parts where the Makgadikgadi Pans are today. This greater Lake Makgadikgadi existed until very recently, though its extent varied greatly over the millennia, depending on the climate and inflows. It is thought that at its greatest, it covered an area of up to

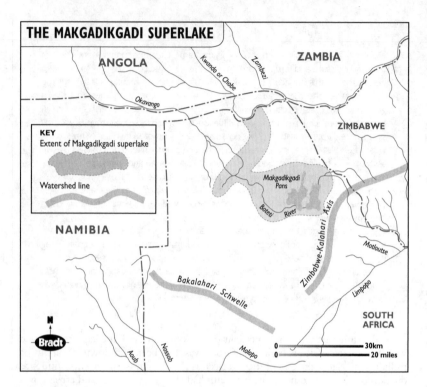

KEY

Extent of Makgadikgadi superlake

Watershed line

80,000km², and that it probably only dried up in the last 10,000 years. At its largest it probably stretched as far as Lake Ngami in the west, what is now Chobe in the north, and beyond Nata to the edge of present-day Zimbabwe in the east.

Evidence suggesting the existence of this lake is dotted around its ancient shorelines. The great Magwikwe Sand Ridge that you cross as you drive between Savuti and North Gate, probably defined one of its northwestern shorelines. Similarly, another is thought to have been the less obvious Gidikwe Sand Ridge, which lies just to the west of the western border of the present Makgadikgadi National Park.

Look at the base of several of the Kalahari's isolated hills and you'll find rounded, water-washed pebbles and rocks worn smooth over the centuries by waves. The eastern side of the Gchoha Hills, north of Savuti, are a particularly clear example of this – though all of Savuti's hills show some of this history if you look carefully.

In some areas of the Makgadikgadi you can stroll around and pick up the flint arrowheads and other tools of Stone Age encampments, which must have sat beside the shores of this lake within the last few thousand years.

From rifts to deltas At some time in the last million years (none of my sources seems to be sure exactly when), this flow into the great Lake Makgadikgadi was gradually, probably quite slowly, cut off.

Northern Botswana has a series of deep, underlying fault lines running beneath its sands. These faults are thought to be the southernmost extensions of the same system of parallel fault lines that are pulling away from each other and have formed east Africa's Great Rift Valley. These extend south, forming the rift valleys of the Luangwa and Lower Zambezi, before cutting across the Zambezi at Victoria Falls.

Here amidst the sands of the northern Kalahari they are probably at their youngest and shallowest. In Botswana and Zimbabwe these two main fault lines run parallel to each other, from northeast to southwest.

Look at a map and you'll see the Zambezi flowing roughly south through western Zambia, until it reaches a point around Victoria Falls and what's known as the Middle Zambezi Valley (around where Lake Kariba is today). Effectively the Zambezi has been diverted, flowing into the rift valley and then northeast along it. This would have starved the great lake of its largest water supply, but clearer evidence of the fault lines can be seen in the present paths of two other rivers.

Look again at the maps and you'll realise that the Kwando forms the Botswana–Namibia border, flowing southeast (roughly parallel to both the Zambezi and the Okavango). Then it clearly passes through an area where there's very little gradient, and forms a mini-delta, before abruptly changing direction to become the Linyanti River, and starts to flow northeast. (Note, in passing, the very clear parallels between the delta formations of the Okavango and Kwando/Linyanti rivers.)

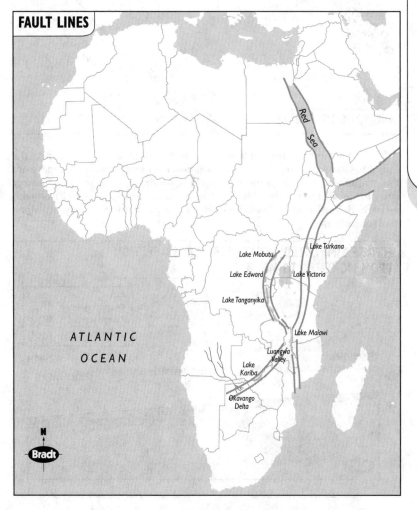

FAULT LINES

Red Sea

Lake Turkana

Lake Mobutu

Lake Edward   Lake Victoria

Lake Tanganyika

ATLANTIC

OCEAN

Lake Malawi

Luangwa Valley

Lake Kariba

Okavango Delta

N

Bradt

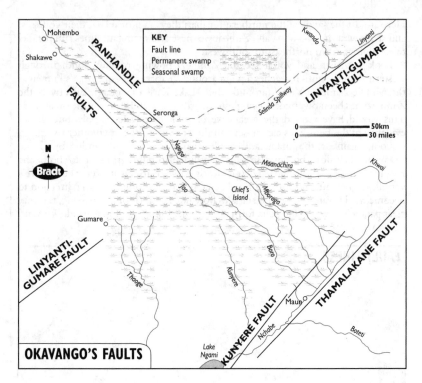

OKAVANGO'S FAULTS

This new course of the Linyanti River marks one fault line – known as the Linyanti–Gumare Fault. At Lake Liambezi, this river then seems to 'escape' from the confines of its fault to meander roughly southeast, until meeting another fault line parallel to the first. Here it is again renamed as the Chobe River, with a clearly defined course, flowing northeast and parallel to the Linyanti, along another fault line.

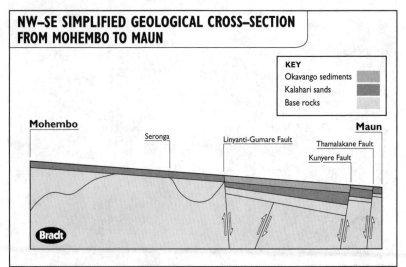

NW–SE SIMPLIFIED GEOLOGICAL CROSS–SECTION FROM MOHEMBO TO MAUN

The more northerly of these faults is the important Linyanti–Gumare Fault. The Selinda (or Magwegqana) Spillway also flows roughly along this, and further west the line cuts across the flow of the Okavango, just south of the base of the Panhandle. It effectively marks the start of the Delta proper. Parallel to this, but at the south end of the Delta, are the Kunyere and Thamalakane faults. The latter is clearly marked by the position of the Thamalakane River, which marks the most southerly extent of the Delta. Here the Thamalakane River collects the meagre outflow from the Okavango's Delta and diverts it southwest along the fault line, and ultimately into Lake Ngami and the Boteti. Maun sits in the narrow space between the Kunyere and Thamalakane faults.

Just like the parallel faults of the rift valleys further northeast, the Linyanti–Gumare Fault in the north, and the Kunyere and Thamalakane fault lines in the south are gradually pulling away from each other. Between them, the underlying base rock has dropped relative to the land outside the faults – some geologists say by as much as 300m. These have acted to 'capture' the Okavango River in a depression where the gradient is very shallow. (As an aside, just north of this, smaller faults, perpendicular to the main ones, act to restrict the Okavango's sweeping meander to the narrow confines of the Panhandle.)

Thus, in time as they gradually formed, these faults diverted the Zambezi and the Kwando rivers, and forced the Okavango to spread into its present-day delta formation.

The Great Salt Pans As its feeding rivers were diverted, the great Lake Makgadikgadi was starved of its sources. This would probably have happened over a very long period of time. We know that the climate in Botswana varied greatly, and during periods of heavier rainfalls the lake might have persisted. Geologists have identified at least five clearly different levels of the lake, each of which has its own identifying features that are still visible. And for each the size of the lake must have been totally different.

But eventually, starved of inflow in a drier climate, the lake shrank. With no known outflows, it would probably have already been very brackish. Now its remaining salts were concentrated more and more, and eventually crystallised out where the last of its waters evaporated – at its lowest point, where the pans are now. Too saline for plants to grow, this residue formed the amazingly flat surface of the Great Salts Pans that are now such a distinctive feature of the northern Kalahari.

The formation of the Okavango Delta The geological history outlined so far in this chapter explains how the Okavango has been constrained by faults, but it doesn't really help to explain how the Delta's strange and wonderful landscapes came about. That's really due to much more recent processes, of which I'll try to give you a brief summary here.

From the air Firstly, if you're flying over the Delta, note what you see. There are manmade tracks, like the straight lines of the buffalo fence, which surrounds part of the Delta. Or the close, parallel lines of bush tracks made by vehicles, sometimes curving, sometimes perfectly straight.

You'll also see more erratic, single tracks, often radiating from pans or waterholes; these are clear animal tracks. (Yes, animals have favourite paths that they like to use too.) Deeper in the Delta you'll find more and more winding drainage lines, of water channels which glint in the sun. Catch the light right and you'll realise that areas which you thought were thick, green vegetation are floodplains, which reflect the sky.

Look carefully at the 'browner' areas between these and you'll start to distinguish the dry land and the islands from the floodplains and the water. Look out for the small, round islands that often have a ring of palms around the outside of them. Note that some, at their centre, have barren patches of what looks like white salt.

Many islands will be longer. A few of these may look like a number of the small islands joined together. But many are long and narrow – we'll call them ribbon islands. Note how parallel their sides are, and how the vegetation on the edges looks that much more lush than the vegetation in the middle.

Building islands The Okavango's an amazing sight from the air – and all the more incredible if you understand a little of how its features were formed. Here are the basics of the main two methods:

Biological mechanism: round islands
The Okavango's floods are erratic and its water levels variable, sometimes giving the chance for small mounds to develop which, when flooding returns, are above the level of the flood. Often, but not always, these are termite mounds, made by the *Macrotermes michaelseni* termite.

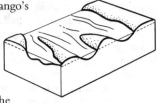

Obtruding above the water level of the subsequent flood, this allows the termites to survive, and makes a handy perch for birds. Eventually seeds take hold, and grow into shrubs and trees, fertilised by the guano from the birds that rest there. In some areas of the Delta (the Jao flats stand out in my mind) you'll see these small islands at the early stages of their formation everywhere. Often the dominant plants are wild date palms (*Phoenix reclinata*), though *Ficus* species and the usual broad-leafed trees of the Delta will follow.

Once started, the trees will transpire, sucking water up with their roots to fuel photosynthesis. This lowers the water table directly under the island, which then attracts inflows from the surrounding floodplains seeping under the island. However, the tree roots don't take up many salts, and gradually the ground water under the island becomes saturated with salts – especially silica and calcite. Eventually these crystallise out underneath the roots. As this precipitate increases, the level of the ground around the edge of the island is raised.

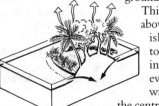

This gradually acts to enlarge the island, raising it above the surrounding floodplains. However, as the island enlarges the groundwater that moves towards the centre of the island becomes increasingly saline – and eventually toxic to plants. The wild date palms die off first in the centre, as they are the least salt-tolerant, then the broad-leaved trees, until finally the relatively salt-tolerant real fan palms (*Hyphaene petersiana*) will be the only trees in the centre. When the salt concentrations rise further they die, leaving salt-tolerant grasses like the spiky sporobolus (*Sporobolus spikatus*).

Capillary action and evaporation force the supersaturated water to the surface of the centre of the island, where salt deposits are now left and no plants can survive. This whole process is estimated to take at least 100 years, and the remaining crystalline salt deposits are known as 'trona' deposits, and are clearly visible as a white crystalline powder from the air or the ground.

Channel mechanism: linear islands The Okavango's water is at its richest in nutrients as it enters the Panhandle and the top of the Delta – as flowing over the nutrient-poor Kalahari sands of the Delta

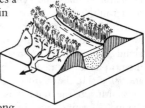

itself won't enrich it. In this Panhandle and upper Delta area, the deep waters are surrounded by the vigorous growth of papyrus (see box on papyrus on page 262 for details).

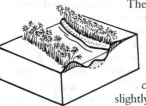

These live and die fast, forming a mat of thick vegetal matter by the side of the channel. This builds up the sides of the channel, and gradually its deeper stems are compressed and start forming peat. Meanwhile, suspended sediments are deposited on the floor of the channel. Thus the whole channel, floor and papyrus surrounds, start to rise slightly above the surrounding floodplains.

Once this happens it only takes a hippo track, or some other leakage, for the water in the channel to cut through the peat sides of the channel and the papyrus beds find a completely alternative, lower path through the floodplains. This leaves behind a dry, slightly raised line of sandy deposits, lined on either side by high beds of peat. This higher land will encourage plants to grow, forming a long, narrow island, which can be enlarged by the biological mechanisms mentioned above.

Once dry, the peat eventually burns down to a thin layer of nutrient-rich ash, which now lines this island, encouraging what biologists call 'sweet' floodplains, which support nutrient-rich grasses and other high-quality vegetation, and a rich growth of trees and bushes at the edge of these long islands.

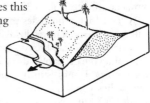

Meandering mechanism: alluvial islands Some islands in the Delta were probably built up first as sandy alluvial deposits during wetter periods in the Delta's history – as the banks beside meandering rivers. Then, when times became drier they were colonised by vegetation, and enlarged by the biological mechanisms mentioned above.

Geological mechanism: Chief's Island Chief's Island, the largest island in the Delta, is thought to have geological origins. Note that its western edge traces out a line which, if continued northwest, would coincide perfectly with the eastern faultline that constrains the Panhandle (see page 48 for a diagram showing this faultline).

Chief's Island was probably pushed up as higher land during the formative rifting/warping of the area, which fits with the observation that it is largely made up of uniform deposits of sand and clay.

CLIMATE Botswana is landlocked far from the coast and mostly in the tropics. It receives a lot of strong sunlight and most of the country is classed as either semi-arid or arid (the line being crossed from semi-arid to arid when evaporation exceeds rainfall). In many respects, most of central and northern Botswana has a sub-tropical 'desert' climate, characterised by a wide range in temperature (from day to night and from summer to winter), and by low rainfall and humidity.

Botswana's climate follows a similar pattern to that found in most of southern Africa, with rainfall when the sun is near its zenith from November to April. The precise timing and duration of this is determined by the interplay of three air-streams: the moist 'Congo' air-mass, the northeastern monsoon winds, and the southeastern trade winds. The water-bearing air is the Congo air-mass, which normally brings rain when it moves south into Botswana from Central Africa. Effectively a belt of rain works its way south across the continent, reaching its southernmost point around January or February. If you listen to any local weather forecasts, they'll probably refer to this as the Intertropical Convergence Zone, or simply the ITCZ. As the sun's intensity reduces, the Congo air-mass moves back north, leaving Botswana dry by around April. Most areas receive their heaviest rainfall in January and February. The rainfall is heavier in the north and east, and lighter in the south and, especially, the southwest.

Thus **January** and **February** are the wettest months, when many areas will have regular and often torrential downpours in the late afternoon. When there are no clouds, temperatures can peak as high as 40°C. However, it's much more usual for them to be moderated by afternoon cloud cover and to stay between about 20°C and 30°C. Humidity fluctuates during the day, typically from about 50% to 80%.

By **March** the rainfall is decreasing, though still the afternoon clouds are around. Mornings and early afternoons will often be cloudless, and a few of the nights will go below 10°C even though the average of the nightly minimums is nearer 18°C.

April and **May** are lovely months. You may catch the odd afternoon shower in April, but these are gone by May – as are most of the clouds. The maximum day temperatures are around 33°C, and while the nightly minimum average is between 10°C and 15°C, this hides the occasional chilly nights when areas of the Kalahari will record temperatures just below freezing.

June and **July** are the coolest months, with daytime average highs around 25°C concealing the occasional day when the mercury just reaches 30°C. You'll still need your shorts, T-shirt, sun-hat and sun-cream for the middle of the day, but as dusk approaches you'll quickly need warmer clothes. The average night goes down to about 6°C, but cold snaps of well below freezing (typically –5°C) are common – especially in the drier areas of the Kalahari. **August** is very similar, though not quite as cold. You'd be very unlucky for it to go below freezing, even at night, and the days will often creep over 30°C.

Typical of the pleasant climate in northern Botswana, here are the average maximum and minimum temperatures for Maun. Note that these are slightly less extreme than you might expect for somewhere in one of the Kalahari's drier environments. Similarly, expect the highs and lows of somewhere in the heart of the Delta to be more moderate than this (lower highs, and higher lows!):

	Temp °C		Temp °F		Rainfall
	max	min	max	min	mm
January	33	19	91	68	101
February	32	19	90	70	101
March	32	18	90	65	51
April	30	15	87	60	26
May	28	10	82	50	0
June	25	6	78	42	0
July	26	6	80	42	0
August	27	9	81	48	0
September	34	14	93	58	0
October	38	19	100	68	0
November	37	20	98	69	25
December	35	20	95	69	76

September and **October** are really the heart of the dry season, and the daytime heat gradually builds as these months wear on. Typical early afternoon temperatures are in the low 30s (°C), and nights will seldom fall below 10°C, though most will be nearer to 20°C. The humidity is usually very low, typically 20–40%.

November is always interesting and can be unpredictable. Often much of it will simply be a continuation of October's heat and dryness. But eventually the humidity will build and clouds start to appear in the afternoons. These will block the sun, cool the temperatures, and eventually produce some showers in the late afternoon. November mornings will generally remain fine and hot, with blue skies.

During **December** the temperatures will usually stay around 20–30°C, day and night, and rain will be an increasingly regular occurrence in the afternoon. Humidity is normally 50–60%. The hottest days may just reach 40°C, but even so the coolest nights won't go below about 10°C.

FLORA AND FAUNA

FLORA In many ways a brief description of some of the main habitats for plants is really a step through the various types of environment that you'll encounter in Botswana.

Vegetation types As with animals, each species of plant has its favourite conditions. External factors determine where each species thrives, and where it will perish. These include temperature, light, water, soil type, nutrients, and what other species of plants and animals live in the same area. Species with similar needs are often found together, in communities which are characteristic of that particular environment. Botswana has a number of different such communities, or typical 'vegetation types', within its borders – each of which is distinct from the others. The more common include:

The Natural Environment FLORA AND FAUNA

3

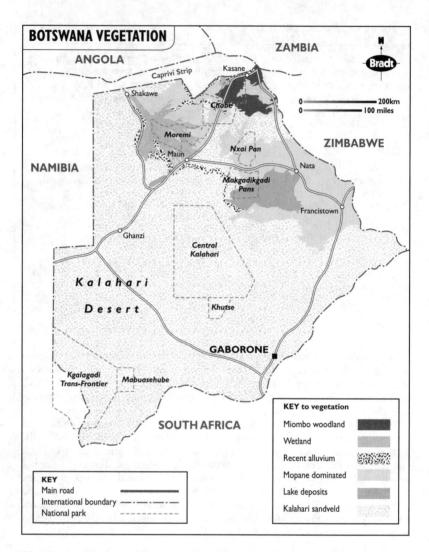

BOTSWANA VEGETATION

ANGOLA

ZAMBIA

Caprivi Strip

Kasane

Shakawe

Chobe

Moremi

ZIMBABWE

Nxai Pan

Maun

Nata

Makgadikgadi
Pans

NAMIBIA

Francistown

Ghanzi

Central
Kalahari

K a l a h a r i

D e s e r t

Khutse

GABORONE

Kgalagadi
Trans-Frontier

Mabuasehube

SOUTH AFRICA

0 ———— 200km
0 ———— 100 miles

KEY to vegetation

Miombo woodland

Wetland

Recent alluvium

Mopane dominated

Lake deposits

Kalahari sandveld

KEY

Main road

International boundary

National park

Mopane woodland The dominant tree here is the remarkably adaptable mopane (*Colophospermum mopane*), which is sometimes known as the butterfly tree because of the shape of its leaves. It is very tolerant of poorly drained or alkaline soils, and those with a high clay content. However, it doesn't thrive on the Kalahari's sands. This tolerance results in the mopane having a wide range of distribution throughout southern Africa; in Botswana it occurs mainly in the Okavango-Linyanti region, and throughout the eastern side of the country.

Mopane trees can attain a maximum height of 25m when growing on rich, alluvial soils. These are then called cathedral mopane, for their height and the graceful arch of their branches. However, shorter trees are more common in areas that are poor in nutrients, or have suffered extensive fire damage. Stunted mopane will form a low scrub, perhaps only 5m tall. All mopane trees are deciduous, and the leaves turn beautiful shades of yellow and red before falling during the late dry season. Then, with the first rains, the trees become tinged with light green young leaves. They flower around December and January, with clusters of small, yellow-green flowers.

Ground cover in mopane woodland is usually sparse; just thin grasses, herbs and the occasional bush. The trees themselves are an important source of food for game, as the leaves have a high nutritional value – rich in protein and phosphorus – which is favoured by browsers and is retained even after they have fallen from the trees. Mopane forests support large populations of rodents, including tree squirrels (*Peraxerus cepapi*), which are so typical of these areas that they are known as mopane squirrels.

Pan Though not an environment for rich vegetation, a pan is a shallow, usually seasonal, pool of water without any permanent streams leading to or from it. Mopane woodlands are full of these small pans during and shortly after the rainy season, the water being held on the surface by the clay soils. They are very important to the game that will feed here during the summer, but will dry up soon after the rains cease.

Salt pan A salt pan is, as its name implies, a pan that's salty. The huge Makgadikgadi Pans are the residues from ancient lakes. Because of the high concentrations of mineral salts found there – there are no plants there when they are dry. When they fill with water it's a slightly different story as algal blooms appear, sometimes attracting the attention of specialist filter-feeders like flamingoes.

Miombo woodland Although this would be the natural vegetation across most of neighbouring Zambia, in Botswana miombo woodland, and its associated *dambos* (see below), are uncommon. There are patches in central Chobe and the northeast of the country. It is found in areas where the soils are acid and not particularly fertile. Often they have been leached of minerals by the water run-off.

Miombo woodland consists of a mosaic of large wooded areas and smaller, more open spaces dotted with clumps of trees and shrubs. The woodland is broad-leafed and deciduous (though just how deciduous depends on the available water), and the tree canopies generally don't interlock. The dominant trees are *Brachystegia, Julbernardia* and *Isoberlinia* species – most of which are at least partially fire-resistant. There is more variation of species in miombo than in mopane woodland, but despite this it is often known simply as 'Brachystegia woodland'. The ground cover is also generally less sparse here than in mopane areas.

Dambo A *dambo* is a shallow grass depression, or small valley, that is either permanently or seasonally waterlogged. It corresponds closely to what is known as a *vlei* in other parts of the subcontinent. These open, verdant dips in the landscape often appear in the midst of miombo woodlands and support no bushes or trees. In higher valleys amongst hills, they will sometimes form the sources of streams and rivers. Because of their permanent dampness, they are rich in species of grasses, herbs and flowering plants, like orchids – and are excellent grazing (if a little exposed) for antelope. Their margins are usually thickly vegetated by grasses, herbs and smaller shrubs.

Teak forest In a few areas of the far north of Botswana, including the northern side of Chobe National Park, the Zambezi teak (*Baikaea plurijuga*), aka Rhodesian teak, forms dry semi-evergreen forests on Kalahari sand. Often these woodlands occur on fossil dune-crests. As this species is not fire-resistant, these stands are only found where fire is rare, and slash-and-burn type cultivation methods have never been used. Below the tall teak is normally a dense, deciduous thicket of vegetation, interspersed with sparse grasses and herbs in the shadier spots of the forest floor.

The teak is a lovely strong wood, with an even texture and deep red-brown colour. It is expensive, often exported, and widely used from furniture to expensive wooden floors.

Kalahari sandveld A number of trees and bushes thrive on Chobe's extensive areas of Kalahari sand, including various *Acacias*, *Terminalias* and *Combretum* species. 'Kalahari sandveld' is a general term that I'll use to describe any of these plant communities based on sand.

In appearance they range from a very open savannah with a few tall trees separated only by low undergrowth, to quite dense tickets of (often thorny) shrubs which are difficult to even walk through. If you want to be a little more technical about this, then biologists will often divide this into distinctive sub-groups, including:

Terminalia sericea sandveld occurs where you find deep, loose sand – these are unfertile areas which cover large areas of the Kalahari. The main species found here are the silver terminalia (*Terminalia sericea*), or silver cluster-leaf as it's sometimes called, and the Kalahari appleleaf (*Lonchocarpus nelsii*). These generally occur with wild seringa bushes (*Burkea africana*) and the bushwillow (*Combretum collinum*). Underneath these you'll often find the rather beautiful silky bushman grass (*Stipagrostis uniplumis*).

Acacia erioloba woodlands also occur on sand, but often where there are fossil river valleys that have an underground supply of water throughout the year. Camelthorn trees (*Acacia erioloba*) have exceedingly long taproots that reach this, sustaining large stands of these mature trees reaching an impressive 16–17m in height. They grow slowly but give good shade, so the bush cover beneath them is fairly sparse.

Acacia tortilis woodlands are not found on such deep sand; instead they prefer the fine alluvium soils, which water has deposited over time. Although it forms homogenous stands less often than the camelthorns, a number of the very distinctive, flat-topped umbrella thorns (*Acacia tortilis*) can often be seen together. Between these you'll find low grasses rather than much undergrowth. This results in a beautiful, quintessentially African, scene which fits many first-time visitors' picture of the continent as gleaned from the blockbuster film *Out of Africa*.

Moist evergreen forest

In the areas of higher rainfall and (as is more likely in Botswana) near rivers, streams, lakes and swamps, where a tree's roots will have permanent access to water, dense evergreen forests are found. Many species occur, and this lush vegetation is characterised by having three levels: a canopy of tall trees, a sub-level of smaller trees and bushes, and a variety of ground-level vegetation. In effect, the environment is so good for plants that they have adapted to exploit the light from every sunbeam.

This type of forest is prevalent in the Okavango and Linyanti areas, and beside the country's larger rivers. It's perhaps worth distinguishing here between two very different types of this forest:

Riverine forests (occasionally called riparian forests) are very common. They line many of Botswana's major rivers and are found throughout the

Okavango–Linyanti area. Typical trees and shrubs here include the jackalberry (*Diospyros mespiliformis*), African mangosteen (*Garcinia livingstonei*), sausage tree (*Kigelia africana*), large feverberry (*Croton megalobotrys*), knobthorn (*Acacia nigrescens*), marula (*Sclerocarya birrea caffra*), raintree (*Lonchocarpus capassa*) and various species of figs. Move away from the river and you'll find riparian species thinning out rapidly.

Swamp forest – or something very akin to it – occurs in tiny patches on small islands in permanently flooded areas of the Okavango. These will occasionally be flooded, and might include a mixture of fig and waterberry species, plus lots of wild date palms (*Phoenix reclinata*) and a few tall real fan palms (*Hyphaenea petersiana*).

In the centre of slightly larger small islands, where the ground is salty from Trona deposits (see page 51) you will find only spiky sporobolus grassland (*Sporobolus spicatus*) – no trees at all!

Floodplain Floodplains are the low-lying grasslands on the edges of rivers, streams, lakes and swamps that are seasonally inundated by floods. The Okavango and, to a lesser extent, the Linyanti-Chobe region has some huge areas of floodplain. These often contain no trees or bushes, just a low carpet of grass species that can tolerate being submerged for part of the year. In the midst of most of the floodplains in the Okavango, you'll find isolated small 'islands' slightly raised above the surrounding grasslands. These will often be fringed by swamp forest (see above).

Sometimes the communities of vegetation will be 'zoned' to reflect the extent and frequency of the flooding. In areas that become submerged for long periods you'll find species like wild rice (*Oryza longistaminata*) and the sedge *Cyperus articulatus*. Grasses like *Imperata cylindrica* often dominate places that generally spend less time under water.

Channels Vegetation found in permanent channels includes the giant sedge, papyrus (*Cyperus papyrus*), that dominates large areas of the Okavango, plus species like the distinctive cylindrical hippo grass (*Vossia cuspidata*), the tall maize-like phragmites reed (*Phragmites australis*), used for thatching, and the unmistakable bulrush (*Typha capensis*).

Lagoons Where the water is more still, in deep lagoons and side-channels where the surface is open but the water doesn't flow much, the bottom will often be covered with fairly stable peat deposits. This gives a stable base for many species of aquatic plants. Some are strictly submerged whilst others have floating leaves. An obvious indicator of this type of environment is the presence of waterlilies.

FAUNA
Mammals Botswana's large mammals are typical of the savannah areas of southern Africa. The large predators are here: lion, leopard, cheetah, wild dog and spotted hyena. Cheetah are found in higher densities here than in most other areas of the subcontinent, and northern Botswana has one of Africa's three strong populations of wild dogs.

Elephant and buffalo occur in large herds that roam throughout the areas where they can find water. Rhino had largely been wiped out throughout the wilds of northern Botswana, though are now being slowly reintroduced into one of the private areas of Moremi. So far only white have been brought in, but there are plans to reintroduce black rhinos too.

Antelope are well represented, with impala, springbok, tsessebe and red lechwe all numerically dominant in different areas – depending on the environment. The sheer range of Botswana's ecosystems means that if you move about there is a really wide range of totally different species to be seen.

Because the Okavango area is so well watered, its natural vegetation is very lush and capable of supporting a high density of game in the dry season. This spreads out to the surrounding areas during the earlier months of the year – accounting for the sheer volume of big game to be found in northern Botswana's parks and private reserves.

Game migrations: historical factors Like most of Africa's big game, some of Botswana's larger animals have major seasonal migrations – or at least used to have, until relatively recently. The 'big picture' was that large numbers of big herbivores put a great strain on the vegetation in any given locale, and so moving around gave the plants time to recover. Thus the basic patterns were for the game to move out into the Kalahari's drier areas during the rains, when they would have no difficulty finding small pools to drink from, and then to gradually migrate back to sources of permanent water as the dry season progressed.

The main species involved were elephant, buffalo, zebra, wildebeest and hartebeest. These migrations still occur, and do affect the game densities in many areas, although they're much reduced due to two main factors.

First, competition for land from humans and their domestic stock which has reduced the possible range of the wildlife, and caused particular problems by monopolising some of the few areas of permanent water in the Kalahari.

Second, the erection of long, game-proof, disease-control fences which have appeared across historical migration routes in the Kalahari. The first of these was in 1954, in response to the EU's insistence that to import Botswana's beef, the country must have an effective strategy for containing and dealing with outbreaks of foot and mouth disease.

The relative damage done by these two factors is still a hotly debated issue in Botswana, but the results were serious. In some years tens and possibly hundreds of thousands of animals, mostly wildebeest, died of thirst or starvation. (See pages 407–8 for further comments.) Many were in very close proximity to the fences. Some blame the fences directly; others regarded them as a scapegoat for the real cause – the scale of human encroachment on the Kalahari. Whatever the cause, Botswana no longer has migrations of this scale.

See Mike Main's *Kalahari: Life's Variety in Dune and Delta* for a rational overview of this debate; various issues of *Botswana Notes and Records* (especially 1984) for more detailed partisan arguments; and Mark and Delia Owens' book *Cry of the Kalahari* for an impassioned but one-sided view of the story of people who observed it at firsthand.

Game migrations: the current story Mention the word 'migration' and there's a tendency to picture millions of wildebeest in the Serengeti, fording rivers of waiting crocodiles and filling endless flat plains. That's not what you get in Botswana, so forget those images.

What you do find is a modest but noticeable drift of game away from the main water points of the Chobe, Linyanti and Okavango around the start of the rains – usually somewhere around November – and a gradual return as the dry season progresses. However, the precise details vary with the species of game.

Elephant and **buffalo** have broadly similar movements. As the rains come their large herds split into much smaller family groups, of which some move away from the Linyanti and Okavango systems. They spread out into the drier areas, especially the vast swathes of land dominated by mopane which lie between these areas (Wildlife Management Areas NG14/15/16/18/20; see page 64 for an explanation of WMAs). Those from the Chobe riverfront areas similarly split, heading into the Chobe Forest Reserve and the rest of Chobe National Park, while some move east of the Chobe Park into Zimbabwe's Hwange National Park, and the Matetsi area between that and the Zambezi.

From around May they start to head back, and gradually join up into larger herds, until by September and October the riverfronts of the Chobe and Kwando-Linyanti have some of the most amazing densities of buffalo and (especially) elephants that you'll find anywhere in Africa.

The migrations of **zebra** are somewhat more complex, and still the topic of research, but is seems that during the rains large herds of zebra congregate on Makgadikgadi Pans, forming an amazing spectacle (if you can find them). During the dry season these animals congregate in numbers beside the Boteti River, on the west of the game reserve.

Separate populations from the Okavango, Chobe and Linyanti areas move to more open areas of the Kalahari. Some of these groups always seem to pass through the sweet grass plains of the Savuti area around April-May, and often this coincides with their foaling season.

Wildebeest in the north of the country follow a similar pattern to the zebra, but those in the centre and south of the Kalahari are effectively now a separate population. It seems that numbers in the central area of the Kalahari have fluctuated wildly since records began; before the fences there was probably a big annual migration northeast in the dry season to Lake Xau – the nearest water point to the CKGR. Like **hartebeest** in the central Kalahari, they certainly move around with the season, but the complexities of their current migration patterns are unclear.

For more details on these and many smaller mammals, see *Appendix 1, Wildlife Guide*, page 469–88.

Animal tracks A good guide can make animal tracks come alive, helping you to make sense of what you see in the bush. Showing you, for example, that cats' tracks have three lobes at the bottom, whereas dog and hyena tracks feature only two; pointing out the cheetah's claws, usually absent from other cat tracks; or the direction in which an elephant's walking from small scuff marks around its track. The more you learn, the more you'll enjoy about the bush.

The tracks illustrated on pages 60–1 are shown in relation to each other, sizewise, and are intended as a simple introduction to the many signs of wildlife that may be seen around a waterhole, or in the sand.

Birdlife Large areas of Botswana are still covered by relatively undisturbed natural vegetation, and hunting is not a significant factor for most of Botswana's 550 recorded species of birds. Thus, with a range of natural habitats, Botswana is a superb birding destination.

There are fairly clear distinctions between the birds that you're likely to find in areas of swamp or open water, those that frequent riverine forest, and those found in the drier areas. None are endemic, though several have very restricted distributions. These include the slaty egret, which is restricted to the Okavango, Linyanti and Chobe river systems, the brown firefinch, and the Natal nightjar.

The Okavango Delta is a particularly good place for birdwatching as the habitats change from dry, to flooded, to deep-water over very short distances.

In addition to its resident bird species, Botswana receives many migrants. In September and October the Palaearctic migrants appear (ie: those that come from the northern hemisphere – normally Europe), and they remain until around April or May. This is also the peak time to see the intra-African migrants, which come from further north in Africa.

TRACKS

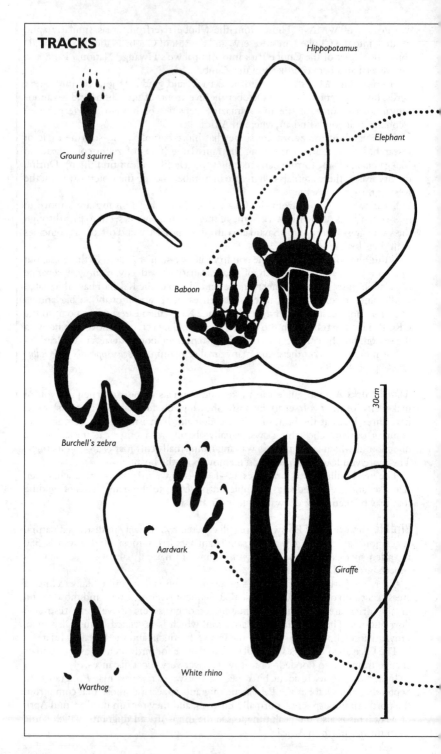

Ground squirrel

Hippopotamus

Elephant

Baboon

Burchell's zebra

Aardvark

Giraffe

30cm

Warthog

White rhino

60

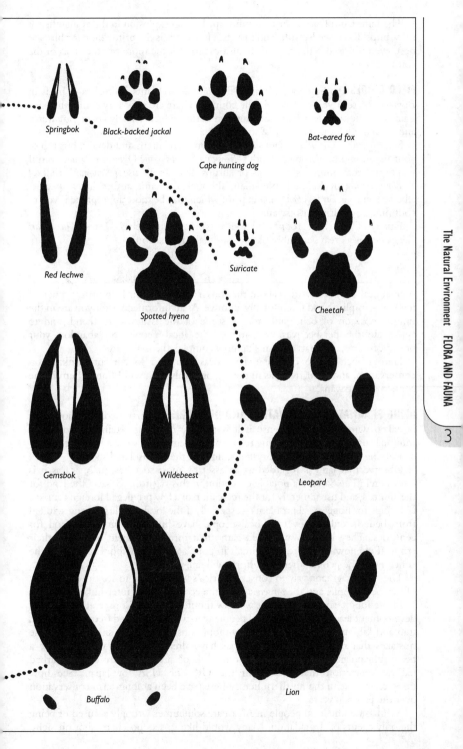

Springbok

Black-backed jackal

Cape hunting dog

Bat-eared fox

Red lechwe

Spotted hyena

Suricate

Cheetah

Gemsbok

Wildebeest

Leopard

Buffalo

Lion

The rains from December to around April see an explosion in the availability of most birds' food: seeds, fruits and insects. Hence this is the prime time for birds to nest, even if it is also the most difficult time to visit the more remote areas of the country.

FIELD GUIDES Finding good, detailed field guides to plants, animals and birds in Botswana is relatively easy within the country. There are now very comprehensive guides on the flora and fauna of southern Africa, which usually cover Botswana, and several guides dedicated just to Botswana.

See *Appendix 3, Further Information* for recommendations and details, but top of your list should be Veronica Roodt's *Trees and Shrubs of the Okavango Delta*, even if you're not that interested in trees or shrubs. I've always used *Newman's Birds of Southern Africa*, by Kenneth Newman, although the same author has a specific, albeit expensive, *Birds of Botswana* in print which may be more appropriate if you're confining your visit to Botswana.

Finally, if you have room and lots of time, then Richard Estes' *The Safari Companion* is a great general book on mammalian behaviour.

CONSERVATION

A great deal has been written about the conservation of animals in Africa; much of it is over-simplistic and intentionally emotive. As an informed visitor you are in the unique position of being able to see some of the issues at firsthand, and to appreciate the perspectives of some of the local people. So abandon your preconceptions, and start by realising how complex the issues are.

Here I shall try to outline a few ideas common to current thinking on conservation, and to many areas in the region. Only then will I frame them in the context of Botswana.

BEING PRAGMATIC: CONSERVATION AND DEVELOPMENT Firstly, conservation must be taken within its widest sense if it is to have meaning. Saving animals is of minimal use if the whole environment is degraded, so we must consider conserving whole areas and ecosystems, not just the odd isolated species.

Observe that land is regarded as an asset by most societies, in Africa as it is elsewhere. (The San are a notable exception in this regard.) To 'save' the land for the animals, and use it merely for the recreation of a few privileged foreign tourists, is a recipe for huge social problems – especially if the local people remain excluded from benefit and in poverty. Local people have hunted animals for food for centuries. They have always killed game that threatened them or ruined their crops. If we now try to protect animals in populated areas without addressing the concerns of the people, then our efforts will fail.

The only pragmatic way to conserve Africa's wild areas is to see the *development* of the local people, and the *conservation* of the ecosystems, as inter-linked goals.

In the long term, one will not work without the other. Conservation without development leads to resentful local people who will happily, and frequently, shoot, trap and kill animals. Development without conservation will simply repeat the mistakes that most developed countries have already made: it will lay waste a beautiful land and kill off its natural heritage. Look at the tiny areas of undisturbed natural vegetation that survive in the UK, the USA, or Japan. See how unsuccessful we in the northern hemisphere have been at long-term conservation over the past 500 years.

As an aside, the local people in Africa are sometimes wrongly accused of being the only agents of degradation. Many would like to see 'poachers' shot on sight, and slash-and-burn agriculture banned. But observe the importation of tropical hardwoods by the West to see the problems that our demands place on the natural environment in the developing world.

In conserving some of Africa's natural areas and assisting the development of her people, the international community has a vital role to play. It could effectively encourage African governments to practise sustainable long-term strategies, rather than grasping for the short-term fixes which politicians seem universally to prefer. But such solutions must have the backing of the people themselves, or they will fall apart when the foreign aid budgets eventually wane.

In practice, to get this backing from the local communities it is not enough for a conservation strategy to be compatible with development. Most rural Africans are more concerned about where they live, what they can eat, and how they will survive, than they are about the lives of small, obscure species of antelope that taste good when roasted.

To succeed in Africa, conservation must not only be *compatible* with development, it must actually *promote* it. Conservation efforts must also actively help the local people to improve their own standard of living. If that situation can be reached, then local communities can be mobilised behind long-term conservation initiatives.

Governments are the same. As the famous Zambian conservationist, Norman Carr, once commented, 'governments won't conserve an impala just because it is pretty.' But they will work to save it *if* they can see that it is worth more to them alive than dead.

The continent's best current strategies involve trying to find lucrative and sustainable ways to use the land. They then plough much of the revenue back into the surrounding local communities. Once the local communities see revenue from conservation being used to help them improve their lives – to build houses, clinics and schools, and to offer paid employment – then such schemes rapidly get their backing and support.

Carefully planned, sustainable tourism is one solution that is working effectively. For success, the local communities must see that the visitors pay because they want the wildlife. Thus, they reason, the existence of wildlife directly improves their income, and they will strive to conserve it.

It isn't enough for people to see that the wildlife helps the government to get richer; that won't dissuade a local hunter from shooting a duiker for dinner. However, if he is directly benefiting from visitors, who come to see the animals, then he has a vested interest in saving that duiker.

It matters little to the average rural African, or ultimately to the wildlife, whether these visitors come to shoot the wildlife with a camera or with a gun. The vital issue is whether or not the hunting is done on a *sustainable* basis (ie: only a few of the oldest animals are shot each year, so that the size of the animal population remains largely unaffected).

Photographers may claim the moral high-ground, but should remember that hunters pay far more for their privileges. Hunting operations generate large revenues from few guests, who demand minimal infrastructure and so cause little impact on the land. Photographic operations need more visitors to generate the same revenue, and so generally cause greater negative effects on the country.

HIGH REVENUE, LOW VOLUME In the late 1980s Botswana's parks, and especially the Chobe riverfront area and Moremi, were being badly over-used. Many visitors were self-contained South Africans who would arrive with all their food and kit. They bought little in Botswana except their cheap park-entry tickets, and contributed little to the nation's economy.

In an effort to reduce numbers, and stave off serious environmental (and aesthetic) problems due to too many visitors, it was decided to increase the park fees by a factor of ten. This worked miraculously – reducing the number of visitors and their impact, but retaining the same level of revenue for the parks authorities.

At the time this was revolutionary, even though now it seems obvious. Thus Botswana's policy of 'high revenue, low volume' tourism was born. Most of Botswana's wild areas are expensive to maximise revenues and keep environments pristine – and they're the envy of Africa for having a good, working system that is delivering increasing revenues as well as many local development initiatives. For the last 15 years this basic policy has been in place, and it's extended way beyond the national parks, and evolved to embrace virtually the whole of northern Botswana, going beyond the official national parks and game reserves

NATIONAL PARKS AND RESERVES The national parks, like Chobe, and the game reserves, like Moremi, work on a simple system. Nobody lives in these (the San in the CKGR being the exception). Anyone can visit, provided they pay the fees. These are scaled to be cheapest for citizens of Botswana, reasonable for residents and more costly for visitors. (See *National Parks and Wildlife Service* in *Chapter 8, Maun*, for these charges.)

Private concessions or reserves Outside of the national parks and game reserves, northern Botswana has been divided up into a series of wildlife management areas (WMAs). See the maps on pages 242–3 and 274–5 for some of these. Those in northwestern Botswana, in Ngamiland, are numbered NG1, NG2 etc, up to NG51. These areas are normally referred to in Botswana as 'concessions' although in this guide I have used this term virtually interchangeably with the phrase 'private reserve' or simply just 'reserve'.

Within each of these the government, via the local 'land board', has defined who owns the wildlife, and what can be done with it. In some hunting is forbidden, in most limited (controlled and sustainable) hunting is allowed.

Community concessions In most of these concessions, the approach taken centres around Community Based Natural Resource Management (CBNRM), a modern phrase for a strategy which tries to reconcile conflicts over resources between the people and the wildlife in it's broadest sense.

CBNRM is based on the premise that the people living next to a resource are the ones best suited to protecting that resource, as they would lose most if that resource is lost, and gain most if it's managed well. There is also an ethical consideration: for example, the people that pay the costs of living near wildlife (destruction of crops, livestock and loss of human life) benefit from its conservation. Local people need to be involved in the decision-making process and need to benefit from the areas around them, and CBNRM tries to make this possible.

Thus in most of Botswana's concessions, the local communities now make decisions about how they are run, and they reap the rewards if they are run well and successfully. See the box in *Chapter 13* entitled *The anatomy of a community partnership*, about NG22 and NG23, for an example of one such arrangement.

TOURISM Botswana lies in the heart of sub-Saharan Africa – and its tourism is the envy of the continent in many ways. It's regarded, quite rightly, as having some of the continent's best wildlife areas, which are still in generally pristine condition.

What's more, the expansion of tourism from the nucleus of the national parks to the areas around them has gradually increased the area effectively protected for wildlife since the 1980s. Areas that were devoted to hunting are now becoming solely photographic. This is enlarging the contiguous area in northern Botswana available for the wildlife, helping to ensure that the game populations increase in size, and become more viable.

A final word here goes to Peter Sandenberg, who has been running safari camps and tourism operations in this area for longer than most. He observes that 'One of the greatest changes since coming to this area in 1983 has been the remarkable increase in animal numbers and species' diversity.'

Changing economics of tourism Tourism isn't yet as important to Botswana as diamonds or beef production. However, it is increasing every year, and is providing substantial employment and also bringing foreign exchange into the country, which gives the politicians a reason to support conservation.

When the diamonds run out – within the next few decades – Botswana needs to have an alternative, and renewable, source of income . . . and tourism is one of the most obvious contenders. The difficulty for the government will be trying to increase substantially tourism's revenues whilst still keeping tourism a premium product, and hence at a low density.

How you can help more The visitor on an expensive safari is, by his or her mere presence, making a financial contribution to development and conservation in Botswana. See page 40 for ways in which you can support small local charities which directly help the people of Botswana. When on safari, one very simple thing that you can do to help is to question your safari operator, in the most penetrating of terms:

- Besides employment, how do local people benefit from this camp?
- How much of this camp's revenue goes directly back to the local people?
- What are you doing to help the people living near this reserve?
- How much control do the local people have in what goes on in the area in which these safaris are operated?

If more visitors did this, it would make a huge difference. If safari operators felt that their clients wanted them to be involved with community development, then they would rapidly get more involved.

Hunting issues Big-game hunting, where visiting hunters pay large amounts to kill trophy animals, is practised on a number of private reserves and concessions. Just like photographic tourism, this is a valuable source of revenue in the long term for people living in the country's concessions.

In practice, there is room for both types of visitors in Botswana: the photographer and the hunter. The national parks, and some of the private reserves nearest the parks (eg: NG23, NG27A and NG27B), are designated for photographic visitors; here no hunting is allowed.

Controlled sustainable hunting is allowed in many of the private reserves, although a few of these maintain a policy of no hunting (eg: the concessions run by Wilderness Safaris, like NG15 and NG26).

Most of the others have divided their concessions into areas where hunting is allowed, and places where it is not. Any photographic camps are usually built in the non-hunting areas.

Integral to this approach is that the concessions provide a buffer between the pristine national parks and the land around where sustainable hunting is allowed. This would protect the national park's animals from any incursions by poachers, whilst the park acts as a large gene pool and species reservoir for the private concessions.

Poaching Having just mentioned poaching, it's perhaps worth commenting that Botswana has very, very little poaching. There is always a little small-scale poaching of game 'for the pot' by local people . . . but large-scale commercial poaching operations are virtually unknown here.

Occasionally there's a complaint about poachers coming across the river from Namibia – putting the blame on poachers from neighbouring countries is a very usual tactic in this part of the world. However, the Kwando, Linyanti and Chobe rivers, and the rest of the country's borders, are so well patrolled by the Botswana Defence Force (BDF) that this seems unlikely.

4

Planning and Preparation

WHEN TO GO

See the section on *Climate*, pages 52–3, for a detailed description of the weather that can be expected, and note that Botswana's rainy season should occur between around December and April, with January and February usually being the wettest months.

The **dry season** (May to November) is the easiest time to travel, as then you are unlikely to meet rain and can expect clear blue skies. This is ideal if this is your first trip to Africa, or if seeing lots of big game is top of your wish-list.

Within this, you'll find June–August the coolest, when night temperatures in the Kalahari can drop below freezing. Then from September onwards the heat gradually builds up. The interior areas of the Kalahari, including central Chobe and the Great Salt Pans, get very hot towards the end of October. Occasions when it reaches over 40°C in the shade have earned this the tag of 'suicide month'.

That said, note that in the Okavango, where there are large areas of water and green vegetation, the extremes of temperature are much more pleasant and moderated: the nights in August never reaching freezing, and the days in October are never unbearable.

Everywhere November is a variable month. Some days will be hot. Some will be cooler, as gathering clouds shield the country from the sun. Sometimes these bring welcome showers; sometimes they simply build, and with them come tension and humidity.

The **wet season**, December to March, is totally different, although the days can still vary enormously from one to the next. Even within a day, skies can change from sunny to cloudy within minutes and then back again. Downpours are usually heavy and short – and usually late in the afternoon – although there are often a few days when the sky remains grey and overcast. You will need a good waterproof for the rainy season, but I've always felt that the rains were seldom long enough to stop you doing anything.

Having said this, I visited in February 2006 – when the rain didn't ever seem to end, and the skies remained grey for days, I should perhaps recant this. In fact, I take the view that Africa's weather is just becoming harder to predict, and I was unlucky!

There simply isn't one 'best time' to visit Botswana, or any of its wild areas. Here is some guidance on various issues to help you decide what the best time for your visit would be. . .

TRAVELLING Travelling around Botswana in the dry season often has its challenges, but in some places in the wet season it's a totally different game. Then the areas of pure sand are still fine to drive on, and even a bit firmer than they are when it's hot and dry.

Driving yourself In some areas where the soil has a high clay content, the bush tracks become quagmires – the track from Rakops to the Central Kalahari's scout camp near Kuke Corner is a fine example, as are most of the Makgadikgadi Pans. Some tracks, especially those in the Delta-Linyanti region, like the route between Xakanaxa and North Gate, become submerged completely. Thus travel in Botswana during the wet season requires careful research, and scrupulous attention to your emergency precautions. If you're heading for somewhere remote in the wet season, then travelling with two or more vehicles is wise.

Flying around In contrast, the weather is seldom a problem if you're flying into one of Botswana's safari camps. All are used to the vagaries of the weather and the water levels, although it may affect your activities. Similarly, if you're heading out on a budget mokoro trip or safari, it shouldn't affect your trip significantly – though your vehicle may need the occasional push!

Although there are less visitors around during this period, Botswana's flight schedules don't change much, and only a few of its camps will close. (Many will close during this period for a few weeks of planned maintenance or any building work that's needed. Those that remain open are often very quiet – so if you've often been to Africa in the dry season, then this is a fascinating time to visit – like being introduced to a different side of an old friend.)

VEGETATION During the wet season, the foliage runs wild. The Kalahari springs into life as the bush turns many shades of green. Open clay pans become small pools in the bush and it's a time of renewal, when a gentler light dapples Botswana's bush.

When the rains end, the leaves in the Kalahari gradually dry and many eventually drop. More greys and browns appear, and good shade becomes harder to find. Eventually, by late September and October, most plants look dry and parched, coloured from straw yellow to shrivelled brown.

However, note that large areas of the Okavango have their own permanent water supply – regulated more by the annual floods than the rainfall – and so don't follow this pattern so clearly. See the box on *The Okavango's annual flood*.

GAME From the point of view of most herbivores, the wet season is much more pleasant than the dry season. During the wet, most animals live in enormous salad bowls, with convenient pools of water nearby. It's a good time to have their young and eat themselves into good condition.

Visitors who have been to Africa before will often find something special about seeing all the animals when they aren't struggling with thirst and a lack of vegetation. It gives a sense of luxuriance and plenty, which isn't there in the dry season.

Before people started to have a big impact on Botswana's landscape (which, arguably, has only been in the last 150 years or so), many of the animals here used to follow regular seasonal migration patterns, often over very large distances. It was the same throughout Africa originally; many species, and especially the herding species of plains game, would move around to where the best food sources were to be found.

Despite the changes wreaked by man since then, the remnants of these migrations still happen. Understanding them will help you to work out what the best times are to visit the various parks – so first read the section on *Game migrations* in *Chapter 3* for detailed comments.

The finer details of each area are covered under sections entitled *When to go* which are spread throughout the book, but in very general terms:

THE OKAVANGO'S ANNUAL FLOOD

This very complex variable is really a minor point for most visitors – who will find the Okavango Delta enchanting whenever they visit. However, the flooding levels will have some influence on some of your activities, and may even influence your choice of where you want to visit in the Delta.

The water levels at any point in the Okavango Delta depend mainly on three variables: first, the local rainfall in your location; second, the height of the seasonal flood of the Okavango; and third, your location within the Delta – the further north you are in the Okavango, the more water you're likely to have.

The local summer rains and the arrival of the seasonal floods are generally out of sync by around two to six months, depending on exactly where you are within the Delta. This represents the time taken for the peak of the rains in the Okavango River's main catchment area – the Angolan highlands – to make it down the Okavango River and into the various different areas of the Delta.

These annual floods have for years been monitored very carefully at Mohembo, where the river enters Botswana – see the graph below. From this we know that the peak of the flood at Mohembo generally occurs between mid-March and mid-May – just after the local summer rains in the region of the Delta have come to an end. Given the tiny gradient and very slow flow rate, this surge of water from Angola can take up to six months to work its way from the Panhandle to the far extremities of the Delta's waterways.

Hence expect the highest water levels in most areas of the Delta to occur after the rains – from about May to August. After that, levels will generally fall until around February, when the local rains start to slowly raise water levels prior to the main flood.

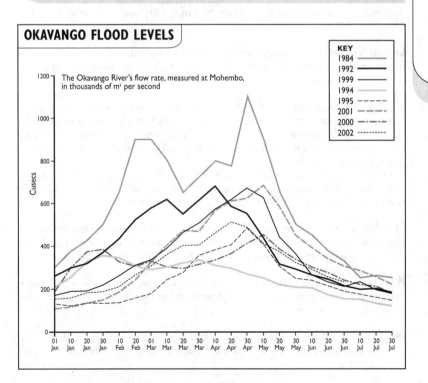

OKAVANGO FLOOD LEVELS

The Okavango River's flow rate, measured at Mohembo, in thousands of m³ per second

Planning and Preparation   WHEN TO GO

4

Chobe Areas with riverfront are at their best July–October; the Savuti Marsh area is totally different, with some good game all year. Savuti Marsh is probably at its best around March–April–May and (if the rains have arrived) November – when herds of zebra and plains game are passing through.

Kwando/Linyanti Follows the same basic pattern as Chobe's riverfronts – so it is best in the late dry season, when it's the only source of water for miles around.

Okavango/Moremi The central areas of the Delta have permanent water all year, and equally permanent populations of animals all year round. Thus many game species stay here all year, and densities of animals (excluding elephant and buffalo) don't change that much. However, in the dry season the permanent populations of game found on the edges of the Delta are swelled by an influx of animals from the parched Kalahari. Thus, the game densities on the accessible edges of the Delta often rise significantly as the dry season progresses.

Nxai Pan Can be erratic, but always used to be at its best when wet, from December to March – though often still very good into May and June. However, the artificial pumping of a waterhole a couple of kilometres north of the gate has changed this pattern. During the rest of the year, you'll find plains game staying here in numbers, often accompanied by a few lion.

Makgadikgadi Pans The pans themselves can be superb when wet, December to April; large herds of zebra and other plains grazers appear. On their western border, the Boteti River (or at least its channel, as the river seldom flows!) follows the opposite pattern, attracting game at the end of the dry season, around August to early November.

Central Kalahari Game congregates in the huge grassy valleys here, most famously in Deception Valley, when the vegetation is lush during and shortly after the rains, from about December to May.

The bottom line is probably that if game viewing is your over-riding priority, or this is one of your first trips to Africa, then you'll be better visiting during the dry season. Then the animals are much easier to spot, as no thick vegetation obscures the view, and they are forced to congregate at well-known water points, like rivers, where they can be observed.

However, more experienced African travellers are missing out if they never travel during the rains – as it's completely different and can be superb. A few specific highlights of Botswana's animal calendar would include:

Feb–Apr Most of the herbivores are in their best condition, having fed well on the lush vegetation. It's a perfect time to catch huge concentrations of springbok and oryx on the short grass plains of the Central Kalahari's fossil river valleys.

May–Jun Probably my favourite time to be in Botswana (and most of southern Africa!). It's a great time to visit Savuti Marsh, and in the Okavango the floodwater moves down the Delta.

Jul–Aug Leopard are generally easier to see, as they come out more during the twilight hours. Later in the year, they often wait until it is cool, only appearing later in the evening.

Sep–Oct Elephant and buffalo tend to amalgamate into larger, more spectacular herds. (They splinter again just before the rains.) Lion sights become more frequent, as they spend more time near the limited remaining water sources.

Nov Can be a great month as often the rains haven't arrived, leaving amazing game densities in the riverfront areas (yet visitors are thin on the ground and prices are low). However, too many cloudless days can mean high midday temperatures.

Dec–Jan Crocodiles are nesting, and so found on or near exposed sandbanks. Various baby animals start to appear in November, followed by most of the mammals that calve sometime during the rainy season.

BIRDLIFE The birdlife in Botswana is certainly best when the foliage is most dense, and the insects are thriving, ie: in the wet season. Then many resident birds are nesting and in their bright, breeding plumage. This coincides to a large extent with the 'summer' period, from around October to March, when the Palaearctic migrants from the Northern Hemisphere are seen.

To give you an idea of the richness of the avifauna here, in the Okavango-Linyanti-Chobe areas during the rainy season it isn't difficult for competent ornithologists to record 100 different species between dawn and midday. Really energetic birdwatchers can notch up as many as 200 different species in a 24-hour period in somewhere as rich as the northern Chobe riverfront area. A real enthusiast might count about 320 species (out of the 550 or so which occur) during a two-week trip here.

The highlights of Botswana's birding calendar include:

Mar–Jul Wattled cranes and other opportunists follow the floods in the Okavango, snapping up drowning insects and reptiles.

Aug–Oct 'Fishing parties' of herons, egrets and storks will arrive at pools as they dry up, to feed on the stranded fish.

Sep–Nov Nesting carmine bee-eaters colonise soft vertical riverbanks, skimmers nest on exposed sandbanks, and large breeding colonies of storks and herons gather at places like Gcodikwe Lagoon. Migrant waders appear beside the edge of most pans and lagoons.

Nov–Apr Most of the weavers are in breeding plumage.

Feb–Apr Red bishop birds, yellow-billed storks and the spectacular paradise whydahs have their breeding plumage on display. If the rains have been good then the flamingos may be nesting on Sua Pan; ostriches gather in numbers on the pans of the Central Kalahari.

Apr–Jun Juvenile birds of many species abound as this season's young are fledged and leave their nests.

PHOTOGRAPHY I find the light clearest and most spectacular during the rainy season. Then the rains have washed the dust from the air, and the bright sunlight can contrast wonderfully with dark storm clouds. The vegetation's also greener and brighter, and the animals and birds often in better condition.

However, it will rain occasionally when you're trying to take shots, and the long periods of flat, grey light through clouds can be very disappointing; you'll get few good shots then. Sometimes it can seem as if you're waiting for the gods to grant you just a few minutes of stunning light, between the clouds. A much more practical time is just after the rains, around April to June, when at least you are less likely to be interrupted by a shower. (This is one of my reasons for being a fan of May as a great time to travel!)

The dry season's light is reliably good, if not quite as inspirational as that found during the rains. You are unlikely to encounter any clouds, and will get better sightings of game to photograph. Do try to shoot in the first and last few hours of the day, when the sun is low in the sky. During the rest of the day use a filter (perhaps a polariser) to guard against the sheer strength of the light leaving you with a film full of washed-out shots.

During the hotter months around October, you're also likely to encounter more bush fires than normal, which can leave a thin pall of smoke covering a large area. (This was especially a problem last time I was up in the Linyanti area, as smoke from the many manmade fires in Namibia seemed to blanket the area.)

GENERAL AMBIENCE One of the biggest reasons for coming to the Okavango – and you may only realise this once you've visited – is not the game or the birds. It's simply the whole general ambience of being able to float over lily-covered lagoons with the sun on your back and a gentle breeze in your hair. This is certainly best when the skies are fairly clear of clouds – from April to November.

OTHER VISITORS Most tourists to Botswana visit during the dry season, from around May to November. Within that season, the period from mid-July to mid-October is definitely the busiest – although Botswana's small camps/lodges and private reserves ensure that it never feels busy, even when everywhere is full. (In fact, the country's capacity for tourism remains tiny compared with that of South Africa, Kenya or Tanzania.)

Most of those visiting outside of this season are cognoscenti, who visit early or late in the season – May to July or late-October to November – when the camps are quieter and often costs are lower.

A much smaller number of visitors come during the rains, from December to April, when camps will often be quiet for days. This often means that they will give visitors a much more personal experience, with private drives; their rates are often lower too, and they're usually far more flexible about bringing children on safari.

Much of the blame for this 'glut or famine' of visitors lies with overseas tour operators. Many who advertise trips here just don't know Botswana well enough to plan trips which work during the rainy season. It's much easier for them to make blanket generalisations, telling enquirers who don't know any better that it's 'not interesting' or that 'you won't see any game' if you visit in the wet season. None of this is true, as long as you choose your destinations carefully, but of course most people don't know this in advance.

While the rains are not the ideal time for everybody's trip, they are a fascinating time to visit and should not be dismissed without serious thought.

WALKING SAFARIS For safe and interesting walking, you need the foliage to be low so that you can see through the surrounding bush as easily as possible. This means that the dry season is certainly the best time for walking – and even then I'd counsel you to choose where you visit very, very carefully as standards of walking guides can be highly variable. (See my comments on the safety of walking safaris on pages 125–8.)

I wouldn't advise anyone looking for a serious walking trip to visit Botswana in the wet season. Walking through shoulder-high grass is nerve-racking with the best of walking guides, and only two or three operations in Botswana are really likely to have anything like that calibre of guide. The best months for walking are May to October, though away from the moderating influence of the Okavango's waters, October can be very hot for longer walks.

COSTS OF TRIPS Aside from the airfares to get here, which vary in their own way (see *Getting there and away*, later on in this chapter), some safari operators also lower their rates when business is quieter. Generally July to October is the peak season when prices are highest; January and February is the green season when prices are lowest, and the rest of the year falls somewhere in between.

ENTRY REQUIREMENTS

VISAS If you need a visa for Botswana, then you must get one before you arrive. Contact your local Botswana embassy or high commission – who are also the best source to verify that the information here is still current.

Currently visitors holding passports from the following countries **do not need a visa**:

- All EC (European Community) countries
- USA, South Africa, Scandinavian countries, Uruguay, Western Samoa and countries from the former Yugoslavia
- All Commonwealth countries (except Ghana, India, Sri Lanka, Nigeria and Mauritius – whose citizens do need visas).

Citizens from these countries will be granted a one-month entry permit on arrival. Though Botswana hasn't changed these rules often in the past, it's always wisest to check with your local embassy before you depart – or on the government's website: www.gov.bw/tourism/entry_req/entry_req.html.

The prevailing attitude amongst both Botswana's government and its people is that visitors are generally very good for the country as they spend valuable foreign currency – so if you look respectable then you will not find any difficulties in entering Botswana.

Given this logic, and the conservative nature of Botwana's local customs, the converse is also true. If you dress very untidily, looking as if you've no money when entering via an overland border, then you may be questioned as to how you will be funding your trip. Very rarely, you may even be asked for a return ticket as proof that you do intend to leave. Dressing respectably in Botswana is not only courteous, but will also make your life easier.

Visa extensions Visitors can stay for a maximum of three months in a 12-month period, and it's a serious offence to stay longer without permission. If you want longer than a month, then you must renew your permit at the nearest immigration office. If you want to stay longer than three months, then apply to the Department of Immigration, PO Box 942, Gaborone; ⚲ 374545 – preferably before entering Botswana.

If you wish to work, then work permits can be obtained from the Department of Labour, Private Bag 002, Gaborone; ⚲ 360100. Note that Botswana is now quite strict about granting work permits only for jobs for which a suitably qualified Botswana citizen is not available.

ⓔ BOTSWANA'S DIPLOMATIC MISSIONS ABROAD For an up-to-date list of Botswana's diplomatic missions, see the useful government website www.gov.bw. Currently

the relevant page to look for is www.gov.bw/tourism/embassies/embassies.html.
Current missions include:

Australia (High Commission) 5 Timbarra Cres,
O'Malley Act 2606, Canberra; ☎ 612 6290 7500;
f 6286 2566
China (Embassy) Unit 811 IBM Tower, Pacific Century
Place, #2A Gong Ti Bellu, Cha Oyan District, Beijing
100027; ☎ 6539 1616; f 6539 1199
Ethiopia (Embassy) PO Box 22202, Code 1000, Addis
Ababa; ☎ 01 715 422/23; f 01 717 215
European Union, Belgium (Embassy) 169 Av
Terveuren, B-1150 Brussels; ☎ 02 735 2070 or 735
6110; f 02 735 6318
Japan (Embassy) Shiba Amerex Bldg No 2, 4-5-10
Shiba Minato-Ku, Tokyo; ☎ 03 5440 5676; f 03
5765 7581; www.botswanaembassy.or.jp
Namibia (High Commission) 101 Klein Windhoek, PO
Box 20359, Windhoek; ☎ 061 221 941–7; f 061
236 034
South Africa (High Commission) 24 Amos St, Colbyn,
PO Box 57034, Arcadia 0007, Pretoria; ☎ 012 342
4761–4; f 012 342 1845

Sweden (Embassy) Tyrgatan 11, PO Box 26024,
10041 Stockholm; ☎ 08 723 0035; f 08 723 0087
UK (High Commission) 6 Stratford Place, London
W1C 1BA; ☎ 020 7499 0031; f 020 7409 782
United Nations, New York (Permanent Mission), 103
East 37th St, New York, NY 10016, USA; ☎ 212 889
2277, 2331, 2772, 2491; f 212 725 5061
United Nations, Switzerland (Permanent Mission) 80
Rue de Lausanne, 1202 Geneva; ☎ 022 906 1060;
f 022 906 1061
USA (Embassy) 3400 International Drive NW, Suite
7M, Washington DC 2008; ☎ 202 244 4990: f 202
244 4164
Zambia (High Commission) 5201 Pandit Nehru Rd,
PO Box 31910, Lusaka; ☎ 01 252 058; f 01 253
895
Zimbabwe (High Commission) 22 Phillips Av,
Belgravia, PO Box 563, Harare; ☎ 04 729 551/3;
f 04 721 360

BOTSWANA'S NATIONAL TOURIST BOARD OFFICES Until relatively recently, Botswana
had done little in the way of tourism promotion overseas. However, now that
tourism is becoming increasingly recognised as Botswana's best base for a
sustainable income after its diamonds run out, resources are being mobilised very
effectively to raise Botswana's profile as a destination for tourists.

Currently these efforts are concentrating on four representatives, in four
different countries:

Germany Karin Zwiers Interface International GmbH,
Petersburger Str 94, D-10247, Berlin; ☎ 030 4225
6027; f 030 4225 6286; e 100762.3614@
compuserve.com; www.interface-tourism.com
Japan Kinki Nippon Tourist Co Ltd, Club Tourism
Division, Shikjuku Hand Wind, 6-3-1 Nishi-Shinjuku,
Shinjuku-Ku, Tokyo 160-8308; www.knt.co.jp

UK Southern Skies Marketing, Old Boundary House,
London Rd, Sunningdale, Berks SL5 0DJ; ☎ 01344
298982; f 0870 706 0116; e botswanatourism@
southern-skies.co.uk; www.botswanatourism.org.uk
US Henry Kartagener, Kartagener Associates Inc, 631
Commack Rd, Suite 1A, Commack, NY 11725; ☎ 631
858 1270; f 631 858 1279; e kainyc@att.net

GETTING THERE AND AWAY

✈ **BY AIR** The vast majority of visitors to northern Botswana fly via the gateways of
Maun and Kasane, which is effectively serviced by the nearby airports at Victoria
Falls (in Zimbabwe) and Livingstone (in Zambia).

Air Botswana does not fly outside southern Africa, and there are relatively few
other airline links to Botswana. Most common for many visitors to the region is to
fly to Livingstone (three-letter airline code: LVI) via Johannesburg, and then leave
from Maun (code: MUB), again routing via Jo'burg (code: JNB). There are also
two flights a week between Cape Town (code: CPT) and Maun; these go out and
back on the same days: Fridays and Sundays – although Air Botswana does change
its timetables every year.

Botswana's capital, Gaborone (code: GBE), is relatively rarely visited if you're on your way to or from northern Botswana – although occasionally you might stop in Gaborone as you fly between Maun and Jo'burg.

However you arrange your flights, remember some basic tips. First, make sure your purchase is protected. Always book through a company that is bonded for your protection – eg: in the UK this means holding an ATOL licence (Air Travel Organiser's Licence) – or use a credit card.

Second, note that airlines seldom give the best deals direct. (The notable exception to this is some clever marketing by sophisticated airlines like the 'World Offers' periodically pushed by British Airways.) Generally you'll always do better through a discounted flight centre or a tour operator.

Third, book the main internal flights at the same time – with the same company – that you book your flights to/from Johannesburg. Often the airline taking you to Africa will have cheap deals for add-on regional flights within Africa. You should be able to get Jo'burg–Livingstone flights, or Maun–Jo'burg flights, at discounted rates provided that you book them at the same time as your return flights to Jo'burg. Further, if you book all your flights together with the same company, then you'll be sure to get connecting flights, and so have the best schedule possible.

Never be talked into getting an apparently cheap return to Jo'burg on the basis that you'll be able to then get a separate ticket to Maun; it'll cost you a lot more in the end.

From Europe Johannesburg is invariably the best gateway as it's widely served by many carriers. From Europe, British Airways, South African Airways, Lufthansa and Air France (to name but a few) have regular flights to Jo'burg. Generally these are busy routes which fill up far in advance, so you're likely to get cheaper fares by booking well ahead rather than at the last minute; this is a virtual certainty during the busiest season from July to October, and in December–January around the Christmas period.

For a return from Jo'burg to London with a decent airline, expect to pay around £550/US$1,000 for most of the year, and around £650/US$1,200 in the busiest period from mid-July to the end of August; for flights departing after 9 December, you'll be lucky to pay less than £850/US$1,500. Unless there's some major international upset, these flights become progressively more expensive as you get closer to the departure. So as with most long-haul destinations, book early for the cheapest flights.

One-way flights between Jo'burg and Maun, with Air Botswana, should cost around £122/US$220. One-way flights between Jo'burg and Livingstone (with the South Africa-based Nationwide Airlines) or Victoria Falls (with British Airways or South African Airways) should cost around £135/US$243.

Booking all your flights at once should save a lot of money as good add-on rates between Maun from Jo'burg of nearer £75/US$100 one-way are possible through good tour operators who have access to special add-on rates for Air Botswana's flights.

From North America If you are coming from the US then you will certainly need to at least pass through Johannesburg. It's often easiest to also route via London or another European capital. There isn't much of a discounted long-haul flight market in the US, so booking all your flights in the US will not always save you money.

Investigate the flight prices between the US and Botswana bought in the US. Look especially closely at fares with Delta and South African Airways direct from the US to Jo'burg – and talk to 'consolidators' who are the nearest that the US gets to having discounted ticket agents.

Then compare these to buying a US-London return in the US, and London-Botswana tickets from a good source in London. London is Europe's capital for cheap flights, and increasingly visitors from the US are discovering that flights bought from the UK, as well as trips from UK tour operators, offer better value than those in America.

From Australasia Both Quantas and British Airways fly between Jo'burg and Sydney or Perth, whilst South African Airways services routes to Asia, including Singapore.

From Windhoek or Lusaka It is possible, although rarely either easier or cheaper, to approach Botswana from one of the region's other capitals, Lusaka and Windhoek.

Travel between Windhoek and Maun ought to be easy, as both Air Botswana and Air Namibia service this route about two or three times per week. However, in practice they both use small 19-seater planes, which are often full months in advance, and they both frequently change their schedules with relatively little regard to their passengers' pre-arranged plans. If you plan to use this route as part of a fixed itinerary, you have been warned.

Travel from Lusaka to Kasane is easier and more reliable, though slower. Think of it in two stages: between Lusaka and Livingstone, and Livingstone and Kasane. Lusaka to Livingstone is a long six-hour drive (though there is an efficient and cheap coach line for the more adventurous) or a short 90-minute flight. There are a handful of good, small Zambian charter companies that will organise a charter flight on this route, or seats on a scheduled charter two or three times a week. Expect a cost of around US$175 per person.

See below for options to get between Livingstone and Kasane, but note that now it's very, very easy to arrange to be transferred across by vehicle and boat for about US$55 per person one-way.

OVERLAND Most overland border posts open from about 06.00 or 08.00, to 16.00 or 18.00, although some of the busier ones, on main routes connecting with South Africa, stay open a few hours later than this.

To/from Zimbabwe Botswana has several border posts with Zimbabwe, of which the two most important are the one on the road between Kasane and Victoria Falls, at Kazungula (open 06.00–18.00) and the one on the main road from Francistown to Plumtree (and hence Bulawayo), at Ramokgwebane (open 06.00–18.00).

The third is a much smaller post at Pandamatenga (open 08.00–16.00). This is 100km south of Kasane, and sometimes used by visitors as a neat short cut into the back of Zimbabwe's Hwange National Park.

To/from Zambia Despite their territories meeting only at a point, Botswana does have one border crossing with Zambia: a reliable ferry across the Zambezi linking Kazungula with its namesake village in Zambia. This ferry costs about US$0.50 for foot passengers, or about US$25/£17 per vehicle, and runs from 06.00 to 18.00, weather permitting.

To/from Namibia Despite the long length of its border with Namibia, Botswana has very few border posts.

The most important of these by far is the post on the Trans-Kalahari Highway, the route between the towns of Ghanzi and Gobabis. The Botswana side of this, Mamuno, is open 08.00 to 16.00, and so is the Namibian post at Buitepos on the other side.

There are two other main crossings. One is at Mohembo (north of Shakawe and at the south end of Namibia's Mahango National Park) and the other is across the Chobe River at Ngoma. Both open from 06.00 to 18.00.

There are two other possible crossings that you should know about. One is the option to cross the Kwando River by boat (only as part of an organised safari with these lodges), between the Botswana's Kwando concession, and Lianshulu Lodge in Namibia's Caprivi Strip. This obviously links two private areas, but the customs and immigration formalities are now in place to allow such a crossing.

The other is the road between Tsumkwe, in Namibia, and Nokaneng, on the west of the Delta, which is opening as an official border post. In doing so it will gradually, and probably radically, alter the options for routes in that whole area. Let's hope it has a positive effect on the Bushman communities in that region, and not the negative one that is widely feared.

To/from South Africa South Africa has always been Botswana's most important neighbour politically and economically, and for many years (even before South Africa was welcome in the international fold) it was in a 'customs union' with South Africa and Namibia. Thus it's no surprise to find a range of border posts with South Africa. In order from northeast to southwest these are:

- Pontdrift (open 08.00–16.00)
- Platjan (open 08.00–16.00)
- Zanzibar (open 08.00–16.00)
- Martin's Drift (open 08.00–18.00) to Groblersbrug
- Parr's Halt (open 08.00–16.00) to Stockpoort
- Sikwane (open 07.00–19.00) to Derdepoort
- Tlokweng, near Gaborone (open 08.00–16.00) to Kopfontein
- Ramotswa (open 07.00–19.00) to Swartkopfonteinhek
- Pioneer Gate, near Lobatse (open 07.00–19.00) to Skilpadshek
- Ramatlabama (open 07.00–20.00) to Ramatlabama
- Phitshane Molopo (open 07.30–16.30) to Makgobistad
- Bray (open 08.00–16.00)
- Makopong (open 08.00–16.00)
- Tshabong (open 08.00–16.00) to McCarthy's Rest
- Middlepits (open 08.00–16.00)
- Bokspits (open 08.00–16.00)

ORGANISING AND BOOKING YOUR TRIP

How you organise your holiday depends on what kind of a trip you're taking. Generally the more expensive the trip, the more organisation it needs.

ORGANISING A FLY-IN TRIP Most tourists who come to Botswana for a few weeks' safari fly between a series of remote safari camps; this is by far the easiest and most popular way to visit the country. Combinations of the Okavango Delta, and the Kwando-Linyanti and Chobe areas are most common, with relatively few people venturing further south or west into the Kalahari.

When to book? These trips are not cheap, but they are not difficult to arrange for a knowledgeable tour operator who knows Botswana. If you have a favourite camp or operation, or will be running to a tight schedule, then book as far ahead as you can. Eight to ten months in advance is perfect. Bear in mind that most camps are small, and thus easily filled. They organise their logistics with military precision and so finding space at specific camps at short notice, especially in the busier months, can be tricky.

Unless you're lucky, or book very early, expect one or two of your chosen camps to be full. Usually there will be good alternatives available. That said, it's fairly rare for visitors to have a really bad time in any of the upmarket camps in Botswana, as standards are generally high – so don't be put off just because your first choice isn't immediately available.

The exception to this is usually the rainy season – when camps often close for maintenance for a few weeks; those that do stay open, however, are seldom full.

How much? Safaris in Botswana are not cheap. The standards for an average fly-in safari camp are high, but so are the prices. Expect to pay around US$700–750 per person sharing per night, between June and October. This will include all meals, laundry, activities and local drinks. The very top camps will cost substantially more. Light aircraft transfers from Maun to the camps will cost around US$150 one way.

Depending on the particular camps, April, May, and November should cost less. Expect something nearer US$500-600 per person sharing per night – which again includes everything except the internal flights.

Prices in the wet season are generally lower (the exception being the camps in the Kalahari); then a rough cost of US$300-400 per person sharing per night should be quite realistic.

If you stay for a longer spell with some camps (and 'longer' can mean anything from three to seven nights), or groups of camps, then these rates will drop slightly; if you fly between camps every day or two, only spending one or two nights at each camp (not recommended) then they'll rise.

None of these trips are cheap, so you should expect a good level of service and knowledge from the operator who is arranging it for you. If you don't get it, go elsewhere.

How to book? It's best to arrange everything at the same time, using a reliable, independent tour operator. Many operators sell trips to Botswana, but few know the country and the camps. Insist on dealing directly with someone who does. If the person you're dealing with hasn't visited most of the places that you're thinking of going to, or many of the camps, then find someone who has.

Botswana's areas, camps and lodges do change, so up-to-date local knowledge is vital in putting together a trip that runs smoothly and suits you. Make sure that whoever you book with is bonded, so your money is protected if they go broke. If you're unsure, pay with a credit card. Never book a trip from someone who hasn't spent time there – you are asking for problems.

Booking directly with the Botswana companies is possible, but piecing together a jigsaw of complex transfers and flights can be tricky. All the operators in Botswana are primarily interested in selling space at their own camps and lodges – regardless of whether these are the best camps for you or not. It's wise to seek out an independent operator.

European, US and other overseas operators usually work on commission for the trips that they sell, which is deducted from the basic cost that the visitor pays. Hence you should end up paying the same whether you book through an overseas operator or with a company in Botswana.

Perhaps because of the UK's historical links, or the high number of British safari-goers, there seems to be more competition amongst UK tour operators than elsewhere. Hence they've a reputation for being generally cheaper than US operators for the same trips – and the best usually work out much cheaper than similar trips booked directly.

Botswana's larger safari groups Most of the larger groups of camps have offices outside of Botswana who hold their booking sheets and take reservations. These usually work largely with the overseas travel trade, which has special contracts with them. So, paradoxically, booking a fly-in safari through one of these offices below in southern Africa is usually more expensive than arranging it through a specialist tour operator based outside Africa.

Illustrating this clearly, Botswana's largest operator, Okavango Wilderness Safaris (which markets many camps in Botswana), comments on their website that they have deliberately not included any of their contact details on their site. They add that they believe that bookings should be done in your home country through a specialist travel agent or tour operator. There are a number of superb Africa specialist travel agencies and tour operators who love Africa – and 'talk, breathe, eat and sleep' the continent. These people have created businesses in their home countries specialising in selling quality safaris in Africa. We suggest you book your safari through one of these companies.

However, if you want a direct contact, then the booking offices of some of the larger groups are outside Botswana (most started off based in Johannesburg, South Africa, for ease of communications):

CC Africa (inc AfroVentures) Main booking office, P Bag X27, Benmore 2010, South Africa; ☎ +27 11 809 4300; f +27 11 809 4400; e bookings@ccafrica.com; www.ccafrica.com. See page 169 for details.

Desert & Delta Main booking office, Bryanston 20201, South Africa; ☎ +27 11 706 0861/2; f +27 11 706 0863; e reservations@desertanddelta.com; www.desertdelta.co.za. See page 169 for details.

Orient-Express Safaris Main booking office, Sandton 2146, South Africa; ☎ +27 11 274 1800; f +27 11 481 6065; e reservations@orient-express-safaris.co.za; www.gametrackers.orient-express.com. See page 171 for details.

Sanctuary Lodges Main booking office, Sandton 2146, Johannesburg, South Africa; ☎ +27 11 438 4650; f +27 11 787 7658; e southernafrica@sanctuarylodges.com; www.sanctuarylodges.com. See page 172 for details.

Wilderness Safaris (aka Okavango Wilderness Safaris) Main booking office, Rivonia 2128, Johannesburg, South Africa; ☎ +27 11 807 1800; f +27 11 807 2110; e enquiry@wilderness.co.za; www.wilderness-safaris.com. See page 171 for details.

Note that the above is only a list of the companies with booking offices outside Botswana; see pages 168–72 for the companies in Maun – where most of the rest of Botswana's major safari companies are located.

Which tour operator? Botswana looks on the surface like an easy country to sell, and you'll find scores of brochures that feature a trip or two there. The vast majority will include only camps from one local operator – perhaps using only Wilderness Safaris, or only Gametrackers' camps, or visiting nothing but Desert & Delta places. This is a really bad sign, as no one operator in Botswana has a monopoly of the best camps.

However, start asking detailed questions about the alternatives and you'll rapidly sort the best from the rest. Don't let anyone convince you that there are only half-a-dozen decent safari camps in Botswana; that's rubbish. If your operator doesn't know most of the camps in this book – and offer a wide choice to suit you – then find one that does. Booking a fly-in trip with one of the top overseas tour operators will usually cost you the same or less than if you contacted Botswana's camps directly – plus you should have independent advice, full financial protection, and experts to make all the arrangements for you.

Here I must, as the author, admit a personal interest in the tour-operating business. I organise and personally run the southern African operations of the UK operator Expert Africa (☎ 020 8232 9777; f 020 8758 4718; e info@expertafrica.com;

www.expertafrica.com). We are currently one of the leading tour operators to Botswana – based on my team's detailed personal knowledge of the country. We organise trips for travellers to Africa from all over the world, especially the UK and America.

Our fly-in trips start at about US$4,000/£2,250 per person for a 10-night/11-day safari, including flights from London, accommodation, meals, drinks, laundry and game activities. Call us for a free, detailed colour brochure, or you can download one directly from our website – where you'll see links to detailed satellite photographs of Botswana, with close-ups of many of the camps marked.

UK For a fair comparison, I recommend that you contact the best tour operators to Botswana, who include:

Aardvark Safaris RBL House, Ordnance Rd, Tidworth, Hants SP9 7QD; 01980 849160; e mail@ aardvarksafaris.com; www.aardvarksafaris.com. Recently founded, small upmarket operator featuring much of Africa including Madagascar, with good knowledge of Botswana.

Abercrombie & Kent St George's Hse, Ambrose St, Cheltenham, Glos GL50 3LG; 0845 0700 610; e info@abercrombiekent.co.uk; www.abercrombiekent.co.uk. Long-established, large, posh operator worldwide, with a wide choice of Africa trips. (Note that Botswana's Sanctuary Lodges are owned by A&K's owner.)

Africa Explorer 5 Strand on the Green, London W4 3PQ; 020 8987 8742; e john@africa-explorer.co.uk; www.africa-explorer.co.uk. Tiny but knowledgeable company that has unusual, large 6-wheeled self-contained vehicles for hire across northern Botswana.

African & Indian Explorations Afex House, Holwell, Burford, Oxon OX18 4JS; 01993 822443; e info@africanexplorations.com; www.africanexplorations.com. Old-school operator featuring India, sub-Saharan Africa, Madagascar & the Seychelles; don't be fooled by their very limited website.

Audley Travel New Mill, New Mill Lane, Witney, Oxfordshire, OX29 9SX; 01993 838530; e Africa@audleytravel.com; www.audleytravel.com. Specialist tailormade operator with worldwide coverage including Botswana.

Cazenove & Loyd 9 Imperial Studios, 3–11 Imperial Rd, London SW6 2AG; 020 7384 2332; e info@cazloyd.com; www.cazloyd.com. Bespoke posh operator with tailor-made trips to east/southern Africa and South America. Good local knowledge and service with a high price tag.

Cox & Kings Gordon House, 10 Greencoat Pl, London SWIP 1PH; 020 7873 5000; e cox.kings@ coxandkings.co.uk; www.coxandkings.co.uk. Long-established operator famed for its Indian trips. Also features more recent programmes to the Middle and Far East, Latin America and Africa, including fly-in trips to Botswana.

Expert Africa (formerly Sunvil Africa) 9 & 10 Upper Sq, Old Isleworth, Middx TW7 7BJ; 020 8232 9777; f 020 8758 4718; e info@expertafrica.com; www.expertafrica.com. This is a team of enthusiastic Africa experts run by Chris McIntyre – this book's author. I like to think that we have the best range of fly-in and mobile-safari trips to Botswana!

Gane & Marshall 7th floor Northway Hse, 1379 High Rd, London N20 9LP; 020 8445 6000; f 020 8445 6615. Established tailormade operators to east & southern Africa, South America and the Indian Ocean.

Hartley's Safaris The Old Chapel, Chapel Lane, Hackthorn, Lincs LN2 3PN; 01673 861600; e info@hartleys-safaris.co.uk; www.hartleys-safaris.co.uk. Old-school, established tailor-made specialists to east/southern Africa, and Indian Ocean Islands – with close historical connections to Botswana.

Nomad African Travel UK 14 Sharpe's Hill, Narrow, Bury St Edmunds, Suffolk IP29 5BY; /f 01284 810101; e nomadat@onetel.com; www.nomadafricantravel.co.uk. Small operator concentrating mainly on set-departure tours to southern Africa, including camping trips around Botswana including on the banks of the Zambezi.

Okavango Tours and Safaris Marlborough House, 298 Regents Park Rd, London N3 2TJ; 020 8343 3283; e info@okavango.com; www.okavango.com. Established specialists to east/southern Africa, and Indian Ocean. Not part of the Maun company of the same name, but linked indirectly to Delta Camp and Oddballs.

Rainbow Tours 305 Upper St, London N1 2TU; 020 7226 1004; e info@rainbowtours.co.uk; www.rainbowtours.co.uk. Established specialists to southern Africa and Madagascar with a strong ethical streak and a varied Botswana programme.

Safari Consultants Orchard House, Upper Rd, Little Cornard, Suffolk CO10 0NZ; ↘ 01787 228494; e bill@safariconsultantuk.com; www.safari-consultants.co.uk. Very old-school tailor-made specialists to east/southern Africa and Indian Ocean with a competent Botswana programme.

Safari Drive The Trainer's Office, Windy Hollow, Sheepdrove, Lambourn, Berks RG17 7XA; ↘ 01488 71140; e info@safaridrive.com; www.safaridrive.com. Specialist African operator with first-class knowledge of Botswana. They concentrate on self-drive trips using well-equipped Land Rovers.

Steppes Africa 51 Castle St, Cirencester, Glos GL7 1QD; ↘ 01285 650011; e africa@steppestravel.co.uk; www.steppestravel.co.uk. This posh tailor-made specialist features most of Asia, Central and South America, the Indian Ocean and central and southern Africa.

Tim Best Travel 68 Old Brompton Rd, London SW7 3LQ; ↘ 020 7591 0300; e info@timbesttravel.com; www.timbesttravel.net. Bespoke operator concentrating on South America, Australia, the Indian Ocean and Africa, including top-end fly-in lodges in Botswana.

Tribes Travel 12 The Business Centre, Earl Soham, Woodbridge, Suffolk IP13 7SA; ↘ 01728 685971; e bradt@tribes.co.uk; www.tribes.co.uk. An interesting selection of trips worldwide, based on fair-trade principles, include some innovative Botswana options.

Ultimate Travel Company 27 Vanston Pl, London SW6 1AZ; ↘ 020 7386 4646; e enquiry@theultimatetravelcompany.co.uk; www.ultimatetravelcompany.co.uk. Wide-ranging operator with programmes to Asia, Central and South America, the Caribbean, and Africa from the Nile to the Cape.

Wild about Africa Sunvil House, Upper Sq, Old Isleworth, Middx TW7 7BJ; ↘ 020 8758 4717; e safari@wildaboutafrica.com; www.wildaboutafrica.com. An offshoot of Expert Africa which specialises in group trips around Namibia and Botswana — has a wide range, from budget small-group departures to top private mobile safaris.

Wildlife Worldwide Chameleon House, 162 Selsdon Rd, South Croydon, Surrey CR2 6PJ; ↘ 0845 130 6982; f 0845 130 6984; e sales@wildlifeworldwide.com; www.wildlifeworldwide.com

Zambezi Safari & Travel Co Ermington Mill, Ivybridge, Devon PL21 9NT; ↘ 01548 830059; e info@zambezi.com; www.zambezi.com

Whoever you book through, make sure first that the company has in place a 'bond' to protect your money in case they go bust. The most usual form of this in the UK is the ATOL licence; if a company doesn't have one of these then question them very carefully indeed. All the companies above have good track records, and currently have ATOL bonds for your protection.

Other tour operators who feature Botswana include:

USA

Africa Adventure Company 5353 North Federal Highway, Suite 300, Fort Lauderdale, Florida 33308; ↘ +1 800 882 9453; e safari@africa-adventure.com; www.africanadventure.com

Adventure Center 1311 63rd St, Suite 200, Emeryville, California 94608; ↘ 510 654 1879; f 510 654 4200; www.adventurecenter.com

Adventure Travel Desk (ATD) 308 Commonwealth Rd, Wayland, MA 01778; ↘ 800 552 0300 or 508 653 4600; f 508 655 5672 e atd@african-safari.com; www.african-safari.com

David Anderson Safaris 4635 Via Vistosa, Santa Barbara, CA 93110; ↘ 800 733 1789 or 805 967 1712; f 805 964 8285; www.davidanderson.com

Ker & Downey 6703 Highway Bd, Katy, Texas 77494; ↘ + 1 800 423 4236; e info@kerdowney.com; www.kerdowney.com. See page 170 for details.

Australia

The Classic Safari Company Top floor, 109 Queen St, Woollahra, NSW 2025; ↘ 01 300 130 218 or 02 9327 0666; fax 02 9327 0667; e info@classicsafaricompany.au; www.classicsafaricompany.au

African Wildlife Safaris 1st Floor, 259 Coventry St, South Melbourne, Victoria 3205; ↘ 03 9696 2899; e info@africanwildlifesafaris.com.au; www.naturalfocussafaris.com

Southern Africa

Jenman African Safaris 7 Lancaster Rd, Kenilworth, Cape Town 7702, South Africa; ↘ +27 21 683 7826; e info@jenmansafaris.com; www.jenmansafaris.com. Overland trip specialists.

Nomad African Travel Zambia PO Box 60060, Livingstone, Southern Province, Zambia; \/f +260 332 2769; e nomad@microlink.zm; www.nomadafricantravel.co.uk. Small operator concentrating mainly on set-departure tours to southern Africa, including camping trips around Botswana including on the banks of the Zambezi.

Pulse Africa PO Box 2417, Parklands, Johannesburg 2121, South Africa; \ +27 11 325 2290; e info@pulseafrica.com; www.pulseafrica.com.

Tricks of the trade If you're looking for a company who knows what they're doing, then look very carefully at their brochure. Start with the text: is it factually correct? If not, that's a really bad sign. Is it free of clichés? If so that's a rare but very positive sign. A more subtle check is to look at their pictures. Notice if they have used pictures which are 'standard', which you've seen in a dozen other brochures, or if they're one-off shots that you don't see anywhere else.

Companies with the best local knowledge have staff who spend a lot of time visiting Africa. They do this because they love it, and not just because it's their work. Most will enjoy taking their own pictures, even if they're sometimes not quite as professional as they might be. Thus in their brochures the pictures will usually be originals, and the company's team will usually be able to tell you where and when most of them were taken.

Companies who don't visit so often will use pictures taken for them by people in Botswana. These same pictures are usually copied to many overseas operators and agents – who then reproduce them in their own brochures and promotional work. That's why you'll often see these same 'standard' pictures in half a dozen totally different brochures. Usually this indicates that the company producing the brochure hasn't visited the place for themselves – and so won't be able to advise you from firsthand experience.

Finally, when discussing trips, don't hesitate to ask the person helping you if they have been to this area/lodge – and if so, when. You'll always get the best advice (and the best chance of problem-free trips) from people who know the places that you're thinking of going to personally. Make sure you insist on this.

Suggested fly-in itineraries Most fly-in trips to Botswana last between ten days and three weeks, and are often limited more by travellers' available budgets than anything else. The Okavango Delta, Kwando-Linyanti and Chobe areas are the most common destinations, but Deception Valley Lodge, beside the Central Kalahari, and Jack's Camp, in Makgadikgadi, also have their own landing strips and are sometimes added on to the start or end of trips.

Less commonly, it's quite possible to plan a trip that's part mobile or self-drive, followed by a few days of relative luxury at a fly-in camp or two (usually in the Delta).

Concentrating on the fly-in element, the key to an interesting fly-in trip is variation: making sure that the different camps that you visit really are different. For me this means that they're in different environments and have different activities. So mix deep-water camps with shallow-water ones, and forested areas with open ones. That way you'll not only have the greatest variety of scenery, of which there's a lot in the Delta, but also see the widest variety of game.

I also prefer to mix camps run by different companies – one from Wilderness, one from CC Africa and one from Kwando for example. I find that this makes a more interesting trip than staying at camps which are all run by the same company (sometimes in predictably similar styles).

When flying in, the costs of visiting the camps in the parks are very similar to the costs of those in the private concessions. Because of the ability to do night drives, to drive off-road, and (sometimes) to go walking, I generally prefer to use camps in private areas. Hence I've included relatively few of the camps which are inside the parks here.

For most trips, if you work on spending around three nights at each camp that you visit, that's ideal. Four would be lovely, though often visitors haven't got that much time (or money), whereas two nights is OK for some camps, but a fraction too short for most.

Here I'll give you a few ideas for combinations of areas that I think work well together, giving a real variation to trips. These are **not** lists of my all-time favourite camps; I have deliberately chosen not to pick out just my favourites. (Simply because the type of camps that I love – the simpler, smaller ones with their emphasis on guiding and wildlife – may not be so ideal for you.)

Instead, these are trips in which I think the various areas, camps and experiences go well together – and demonstrate what I mean about varying the areas that you stay in and the companies that you use.

Livingstone, Kwando-Linyanti and Okavango Delta: 11 nights/12 days
- 2n Livingstone, a hotel or lodge
- 3n Selinda, NG16 – mostly open, permanently dry areas best for game viewing
- 3n Kwara, NG20 – for deep-water motorboat trips plus some game viewing in areas of denser vegetation
- 3n Kwetsani, NG25 – for picturesque shallow-water mokoro trips, plus some game viewing in open floodplains

Livingstone, Kwando-Linyanti, Okavango and the Pans: 15 nights/16 days
- 2n Livingstone, a hotel or lodge
- 3n Lagoon, NG15 – dry-land game viewing in mostly riverine forest
- 4n Vumbura, NG20 – for some deep-water, some shallow-water mokoro trips, and some game viewing in an open floodplain environment.
- 3n Sandibe, NG31 – for shallow-water trips and game viewing in a more forested environment
- 3n Jack's Camp – something totally different on the great salt pans

Just the Okavango Delta: 11 nights/12 days
- 3n Xakanaxa Camp, Moremi – for dry-land game viewing
- 2n Xugana, NG21 – transfer here from Xakanaxa by boat for deep-water trips
- 3n Nxabega, NG31 – for shallow-water trips and game viewing
- 3n Deception Valley Lodge – something totally different in the Kalahari

After reading this book you'll realise there are so many possibilities that you'd be wise to talk through your wishes with someone who knows the camps and can work out what's best for you.

ORGANISING A BUDGET OR BACKPACKING TRIP If you're backpacking then usually you're more restricted by money than by time. Many of the side-trips and safaris that you take will be organised at the time, on the ground – and trying to do too much in advance might be counter-productive.

So, read the book, and head off. Start by heading towards Maun or Kasane, keeping your eyes open and talking to people you meet to see what's going on. And enjoy! Much of the joy is the unpredictability of these trips; if you want everything fixed and arranged then backpacking isn't really for you!

ORGANISING A MOBILE SAFARI Mobile trips in Botswana range from cheap-and-cheerful budget safaris to absolutely top-class operations running privately guided trips for small family groups. Thus generalising amongst them is difficult.

That said, as a general rule, the more they cost, the further in advance they should be booked. The cheaper ones often survive on last-minute bookings from people who turn up; the more costly private ones can be booked-up years in advance.

Ideally, talk to someone who has been on safari with the mobile operator that you're considering before booking with them. If this isn't possible then don't hesitate to ask a lot of questions before you decide which trip is right for you. You'll be stuck with your guide and group for a week or more, so it's vital to make the right choice.

You'll find most of these companies are based in Maun, with only a few elsewhere – like Kasane. The best often have overseas tour operators who know them well, and will sell their trips at around the same price (or even cheaper) than they do directly.

ORGANISING A SELF-DRIVE TRIP Describing the roads in Botswana is like describing Dr Jekyll and Mr Hyde. The tarred main routes, and most of the roads in the towns, are beautifully smooth roads with excellent signposts. They're often delightfully free of traffic; a dream to drive on. They're eminently suitable to potter around in a normal 2WD Toyota Corolla or Citi Golf.

However, by contrast the tracks through the national parks and more remote areas can become nightmares. Inexperienced or badly prepared drivers will find themselves seriously challenged, with deep sand in the dry season, and glutinous mud when it's wet – often compounded by a complete lack of signposts or directions.

If you want to hire a self-drive vehicle for the trip, then you must treat Botswana's two personas very differently. Your biggest decision is your vehicle, as this will make or break your trip.

Hiring a 2WD If you are sticking to the towns and tar roads then hire a 2WD from one of the normal hire companies – Avis, Budget or Imperial would be the obvious three. Contacting them directly, a small saloon (Group A) for about two weeks will cost you around US$45/£25 per day, including comprehensive CDW (Collision Damage Waiver; see pages 85–6) insurance cover. This includes a free mileage allowance of 120km per day, but outside that you'll pay an extra P1.50 or so per kilometre – and if you're travelling around then you'll find the mileage will add up! See *Car hire* in the chapters on Kasane and Maun for the relevant contact details.

Hiring a 4x4 If you want to explore Botswana in your own 4x4, then the obvious solution would appear to be to hire one locally. Again, contacting them directly you'll find a twin-cab 4x4 hired for about two weeks will cost you around US$90/£50 per day, including comprehensive CDW insurance cover. Again, this includes a free mileage allowance of 120km per day, but again outside that you'll pay an extra fee per kilometre.

However, think carefully. What you need to drive into the bush in Botswana is a serious, fully equipped vehicle – and what you'd be hiring off-the-peg isn't, in my view, up to the job. You need a vehicle that you can rely on, with long-range tanks, a high-lift jack, a spade and decent tow-rope, extra fuel cans if necessary and all the other bits and pieces that make all the difference. Perhaps most vitally, you need to have confidence that if anything goes wrong, there's a system in place to help you swiftly.

South African 4x4s One South African company to consider is Britz; it has offices in Australia, New Zealand and Johannesburg (*Kempton Park 1620, Jo'burg, South Africa;* ✆ *+27 11 396 1860;* e *info@britz.co.za; www.britz.co.za*). They offer five different types of vehicles, including their 'Nomad' Land Rovers and their 'Safari 4x4' which is basically a twin-cab Toyota Hilux. The Land Rovers cost about

US$183/£102, the Toyota (US$167/£93 per day, including unlimited mileage. These come with stoves, fridges and roof tents.

As with many apparently cheaper car deals, expect there to be various additions – in this case start with US$32/£18 per day for their full CDW cover, and US$113/£63 for their '4x4 recovery kit' (tow-ropes, tyre repair, radiator repair, torch, safety triangle, spanners, and screwdrivers).

The main drawbacks are that they don't have an office in Botswana, and the drive from Maun to Jo'burg is well over 1,000km – realistically that's a two- to three-day drive in a Land Rover. This lack of back-up is also reflected in the small print of their hire agreement – which means that you would pay a heavy price for serious accidents (see below).

In addition to Britz, other specialist operators in this field include:

Bushtrackers \ +27 11 465 5700; e bushtrackers@iafrica.com; www.bushtrackers.co.za
Drive Africa \ +27 21 447 1144; e mycar@driveafrica.co.za; www.driveafrica.co.za

Kwenda Safaris \ +27 11 608 4199; e kwenda@iafrica.com; www.kwenda.co.za
Off Road Africa \ +27 21 794 0806; e info@offroadafrica.com; www.offroadafrica.com

Backed-up 4x4s Most of the companies mentioned above simply deal with hiring out vehicles; they don't get involved with helping you plan your trip or give you any advice. A step up from this, in both price and completeness, are companies that provide not only a vehicle, but also put their expertise at your disposal. They cost more, but if you're not living in southern Africa then it's probably what you need.

Safari Drive are specialist African operators (see page 81) based in the UK. They're the only overseas company that I know of who still regularly sends self-driving clients to Botswana. They can advise you on self-drive trips from personal experience.

Safari Drive use probably the region's best fleet of bush-equipped Land Rovers, and their support team has bases in Maun, Kasane, Victoria Falls and Windhoek. I've used these for all my research trips to Botswana, and they come fully equipped with everything that you'll need for comfortable bush camping, from long-range fuel tanks, roof (or ground) tents and fridges to the washing up bowls, condiments and crockery that really make a trip comfortable.

Probably more important than the kit is that they provide you with a service before you leave, planning your trip based on their detailed local knowledge. Their team in Maun makes the tricky campsite bookings with the national parks office. Most importantly, they offer first-rate back-up in Botswana – based around a well-connected team on the ground who know all the local operators, and have the contacts and know-how to help you speedily if any problems occur.

Expect these Land Rovers and the service to cost around US$261/£145 per day, including all the equipment and full insurance cover. The only added extras might be an optional satellite phone, for which they charge around £10 per day (plus call charges).

Checking the fine print The devil's in the detail, especially if you're looking at any of the cheaper options. You should check any rental agreement very carefully, so that you know your position. Preferably also discuss any questions or queries with someone within the company that is supplying you with the vehicle. A few specific pointers may help:

CDW insurance The insurance and the Collision Damage Waiver (CDW) clauses are worth studying particularly closely. These spell out the 'excess' that you will pay in the event of an accident. These CDW excesses vary widely, and often explain the difference between cheap rental deals and better, but more costly, options.

Some hire companies have very high excesses (ie: the amounts that you pay if you have a major accident). An 80% CDW is normal – which means that you will always pay 20% of the cost of any damage. However, look around and you should be able to reduce this to zero – although most hiring companies will still want a deposit, in case you damage or lose any of their vehicle's equipment.

Other fine print Though accidents are fortunately uncommon, they do happen. Then it's very important to get the situation resolved swiftly and carry on with your trip. Some of the companies have quite onerous terms – so be aware of these before you agree to take the vehicle. For example, Britz state that if you have a single-vehicle accident, then a replacement vehicle can be collected from the closest branch – which is likely to be at least two days' drive away from most of Botswana's parks.

However, you are responsible for the costs of getting there, and also for the costs of returning the damaged vehicle to the original rental station (usually Jo'burg). There's no refund if you can't reach a replacement vehicle – and if you do take a replacement, then a new rental contract and insurance conditions will apply.

Suggested self-drive itineraries
If you're driving yourself outside the national parks, and have lots of time, then you can afford to have total flexibility in your route, and plan very little. However, if you're coming for a shorter time, and want to use any of the campsites in the national parks, then you would be wise to arrange your trip carefully in advance. Note that campsite bookings in the national parks can be quite difficult to get, and are fixed when you have them. Effectively, this commits you to a specific route and schedule.

Perhaps the most obvious and instantly rewarding trip for your first self-drive trip across Botswana would be between Livingstone and Maun. This is best done in the dry season.

Livingstone, Chobe, Moremi and Maun: 11 nights/12 days This really is the fastest trip that you should consider through this area if you want to have time to enjoy the parks. Allowing more time would be better, and another 3–4 nights camping in the parks (including both Third Bridge and Xakanaxa for a few nights each) would improve it enormously.

- 2n Livingstone – hotel/lodge (or campsite)
- 2n Ihaha Campsite, Chobe
- 2n Savuti Campsite, Chobe
- 2n North Gate (Khwai) Campsite, Moremi
- 2n Xakanaxa or Third Bridge Campsite, Moremi
- 1n Maun – hotel/lodge (or campsite)

Of course it can easily be reversed. Some prefer Livingstone at the start, to relax after the flight. Others prefer to leave it until the end, with the highlight of seeing Victoria Falls (and buying curios) at the end. If you do start at Livingstone, then consider picking up your vehicle on the day that you leave for Ihaha, as this could save you a few days of vehicle hire.

I recommend that you use a hotel or lodge, rather than camp, for your first and last few days – I find that this makes my trips much easier and gives me time to get organised more easily at the start and end.

The Panhandle plus Tsodilo, Aha & Gcwihaba Hills: 14 nights/15 days To visit the hills of the northwest Kalahari, ideally consider a trip based out of Maun:

- 1n Maun – hotel/lodge (or campsite)
- 2n Drotsky's Cabins, Shakawe
- 3n Tsodilo Hills – camping (spend longer here if possible)
- 3n Nxamaseri Lodge or Guma Lagoon Camp, Panhandle
- 2n Aha Hills – camping
- 2n Gcwihaba Hills – camping
- 1n Maun – campsite or hotel/lodge

If you plan to do this trip during the rains then I'd reduce the time at Drotsky's and Nxamaseri (or Guma) and increase my time in the hills of the Kalahari. I love the Tsodilo Hills – and could spend a lot longer there than three days – but you might not feel the same!

If done in the dry season, August or after, then you might tag on a few days after Maun to visit the Boteti River area, where the game concentrations should then be good. Certainly whenever you go, I'd visit Tsodilo before Aha; it's that little bit more accessible. Do remember to fill up with fuel at Etsha 6 between your time in Tsodilo and the Aha/ Gcwihaba area.

Nxai Pan and the Central Kalahari Game Reserve: 20 nights/21 days If you're experienced in the African bush, feel a lot more adventurous, and don't mind the idea of spending hours digging yourself out of mud, then consider a trip to Nxai and the northern part of the Central Kalahari Game Reserve. This would probably be at its best between February and May, though going later in that period will make the travelling much easier.

- 1n Maun – hotel/lodge (or campsite)
- 2n South Camp, Nxai Pan
- 2n North Camp, Nxai Pan
- 3n Nata Lodge – lodge (or campsite)
- 1n Leroo-La-Tau – campsite (or lodge)
- 1n Deception Valley, CKGR – campsite at north end, CKD1-6
- 2n Sunday Pan, CKGR – campsite
- 1n Tau Pan, CKGR – campsite
- 1n Phokoje Pan, CKGR – campsite
- 2n Piper Pans, CKGR – campsite
- 2n Deception Valley, CKGR – campsite towards the south side, CKL2 or 3
- 1n Leroo-La-Tau – lodge (or campsite)
- 1n Maun – hotel/lodge (or campsite)

As with any rainy-season trip, or excursion into the Central Kalahari Game Reserve, you should be doing this with a minimum of two vehicles, and safety precautions like taking a satellite phone might be a good idea.

Making bookings If you're driving a 2WD on the tar, then you can afford to find a campsite in Maun or Kasane when you get there. If you need a room, then you only need to book one in advance during the busy season. For the rest of the year you shouldn't have a problem finding one.

Generally, finding a campsite outside the national parks is not a problem. Even at places like Tsodilo and Gcwihaba Hills, there are currently no regulations. There you can just turn up and camp.

However, campsites within the national parks **must** be booked in advance – or you simply will not be allowed to stay there. See the section on *Organising and booking* in *Chapter 8* for the finer details of this – and do it as early in your trip-planning as possible. Any lodges at which you plan to stay should also be reserved in advance.

$ MONEY AND BUDGETING

Botswana has probably Africa's strongest and most stable currency, underpinned by the huge annual earnings of its diamond industry. The unit of currency is the pula – a word that also means 'rain' in Setswana, and hence tells you something about the importance of water in this country. Theoretically each pula is divided into 100 thebe, although one thebe isn't worth that much, so most prices are rounded to the nearest ten thebe. The pula's exchange rate is free-floating on the world market, so there is no black market for the currency.

As a result, US dollars, euros and UK pounds sterling are easily changed – and most of the more international businesses in the tourism sector set their prices in US dollars. Rates of exchange in December 2006 were as follows:

£1 = P11.97
US$1 = P6.07
€1 = P8.08

There is no 'black market' in foreign currency in Botswana, as the pula floats freely on the international money markets. Thus don't expect to see any shady characters on the street hissing 'change money' as you pass; I never have. (If you do, then assume they're con-men trying to dupe visitors who don't know any better!)

INFLATION

Inflation has generally been relatively modest in Botswana. Between 1993 and 1998 the rate of inflation averaged 10.2%, but in the early 1990s it subsided to below 10% and by June 2002 the rate (based on a consumer price index) was 5.9%. However, since then it's risen and in August 2006 it stood at 10.7%. More up-to-date statistics can be found on the Bank of Botswana's website: http://bankofbotswana.bw/.

The rough trends (showing the lowest/highest interbank rates during each period) have been as follows:

		Rate of exchange of pula	
Date	to US$	to British £	to SA rand
1998 Jan–Jun	3.64/4.49	6.22/7.35	0.72/0.78
1998 Jul–Dec	4.21/4.93	7.18/8.21	0.79/0.79
1999 Jan–Jun	4.30/4.75	7.27/7.68	0.74/0.78
1999 Jul–Dec	4.50/4.73	7.26/7.70	0.74/0.78
2000 Jan–Jun	4.55/5.33	7.50/8.04	0.74/0.76
2000 Jul–Dec	5.04/5.56	7.34/8.04	0.68/0.76
2001 Jan–Jun	5.13/5.80	7.31/8.28	0.69/0.71
2001 Jul–Dec	5.61/6.31	7.96/9.20	0.47/0.71
2002 Jan–Jun	5.93/6.94	8.66/10.07	0.51/0.63
2002 Jul–Dec	5.46/6.39	8.69/9.85	0.58/0.64
2003 Jan–Jun	4.74/5.54	7.53/9.07	0.60/0.68
2003 Jul–Dec	4.20/5.04	7.27/8.12	0.64/0.69
2004 Jan–Jun	4.43/5.07	7.90/9.21	0.60/0.78
2004 Jul–Dec	4.25/4.90	8.18/8.87	0.71/0.77
2005 Jan–Jun	4.28/5.62	8.14/10.15	0.73/0.84
2005 Jul–Dec	5.24/5.71	9.55/10.15	0.80/0.90
2006 Jan–Jun	5.09/6.06	9.38/11.71	0.86/0.94

As can be seen from the table of historical exchange rates, Botswana's currency has generally gradually declined in value against the US dollar and the British pound over the last eight years. By comparison, its rate against the South African rand has been rather more variable – as the rand has had substantial exchange rate swings against the major currencies in recent years.

Given the strength of Botswana's economy, this pattern seems likely to continue in the foreseeable future: with the pula gently declining relative to the world's major currencies.

BUDGETING Like anywhere else, the cost of visiting Botswana varies with the style in which you travel, and the places where you spend your time. However, Botswana's costs are usually relatively high.

If you plan to get the most from what Botswana has to offer, you will probably need an average of US$540/£300 per day. This is high by African standards, but what you get for it is high quality, and includes everything: your activities, food, drinks, accommodation, and even the odd charter flight between camps. You'll then be staying at a handful of small safari camps, each of which is situated in a different, but often stunning, corner of a pristine wilderness. This is one of the world's top wildlife experiences – the kind of magical trip at which Botswana excels.

At the other end of the spectrum, if you travel through Botswana on local buses, camping and staying near the towns, then the country isn't too expensive. A budget of US$72–108/£40–60 per day for food, accommodation and transport would suffice. However, most backpackers who undertake such trips won't be able to afford to visit any of the camps or more remote wildlife locations – which I think means that it's scarcely worth visiting Botswana.

Between these two extremes, at around US$140–200/£80–120, you'll find some relatively basic budget-style safaris run out of Maun which will give you a real experience of the national parks and the Okavango Delta. They won't match what you'd find in the private concession areas, or further into the Delta, but they will make you glad you came to Botswana and probably harden your determination to return when you've a lot more money!

One of these mid-range options, though only one for those with substantial African experience, is to hire a fully equipped 4x4. Such a choice enables you to camp, buy food, and drive yourself around. This requires driving ability and planning, and isn't something to undertake lightly. But then four people in a decent vehicle (a slight squash, unless you're very well organised) would cost around US$140/£80 per person per day, including the vehicle, camping kit, equipment, park fees and food. Such trips are really much better for two people per vehicle, but in that case the daily costs would work out nearer US$200/£120 each.

Budgeting for safaris Botswana isn't a cheap country to visit. This is due to a combination of the high costs of the logistics needed to operate in remote areas, plus the deliberate policy of the government to maximise revenues from tourism, whilst preserving the pristine nature of the country by using high costs to limit the number of visitors. That said, different kinds of trips need very different budgeting.

For backpackers Camping at organised sites is by far your cheapest way to stay in most areas of Botswana, and always a good bet if you're relatively self-sufficient and have the equipment with you. If you do then expect to pay around US$2.70–4.50/£1.50–2.50 per person camping per night.

Restaurant meals in the towns are cheap compared with Europe or America: expect to pay US$7–10/£4–6 for a good evening meal, including a local beer or

4

two. Imported drinks are always more expensive than those from southern Africa – but as southern Africa has some first-class breweries and wineries, this really is seldom an issue. European wines and spirits, as you might expect, are ridiculously priced (and so make excellent gifts if you are visiting someone here). You will pay well over US$120/£65 for a bottle of decent French champagne!

For self-drivers If you have your own rugged 4x4 with equipment and the experience to use it and survive safely in the bush, then you will be able to camp and cook for yourself. This is then an affordable way to travel and see those remote areas of Botswana which are open to the public.

Your largest expense will be the hire of a decent and well-equipped vehicle. (Taking anything less into remote areas of wild bush is really very foolish.) See page 117 for more comments on this, but expect it to cost around US$230–290/£130–160 per day, including all your camping kit.

Your next largest expense will probably be park and camping fees in the national parks. These can be substantial: expect a total of about P175 (US$34/£19) per person per day for both park entry and camping fees. Note, however, that there are still many interesting areas outside of the national parks – including parts of Makgadikgadi, the Tsodilo Hills, Aha Hills, Gcwihaba Caves and various offbeat areas of the Kalahari.

The cost of food depends heavily on where you buy it, as well as what you buy – but most people will probably do one large shop in Maun or Kasane at the start of their trip, topping up on perishables as they progress. If you are sensible then US$12.50–18/£7–10 per day would provide the supplies for a good, varied diet without having to be at all stingy.

For mobile safaris The question 'how much are mobile safaris?' is as tricky to answer as 'how long is a piece of string?' It depends on where your trip is visiting, what the equipment, staff and guides are like, and how big the group is. In short, these trips vary greatly. To choose you must carefully prioritise what you want, what will suit you, and what you can afford to pay. Note also that prices for higher-end trips are heavily dependent upon the time of year that you travel.

On a bargain-basement trip for backpackers you will put up your tent, do the camp chores and even supply your own sleeping bag and drinks. On this you can expect to visit the parks, but not to have your time there maximised (parks are costly relative to staying outside them!). This would cost you around US$140–180/£80–100 per day per person sharing.

By contrast, a luxurious mobile safari, visiting pristine areas in the company of a small group with a top professional guide might cost up to US$350–540/£200–300 per person per day, including superb meals and all your drinks.

Between these two extremes, you ought to be able to get a trip of a decent quality for something around US$250–300/£140–170 per person per night sharing. Then expect to be camping in comfortable tents, with a small camp staff who will organise them, cook your meals and do all the chores.

As a final thought, if you value having a really comfortable bed at night, but still want the continuity of a good professional guide to stay with your group throughout the trip; if you like the idea of putting in a lot of time and energy game viewing in the parks, and don't mind a lot of time in a vehicle, then look at a mobile trip which moves between the lodges. These cost around US$480–600/£270–330 per person per day, including superb meals and all your drinks.

For fly-in safaris to lodges and camps Again, the prices for fly-in trips vary considerably – though they're never cheap, and there's relatively little difference between the few bottom-end camps, and the vast majority of middle-market camps that provide good experiences in good areas.

Expect the most basic camp which offers only mokoro activities (which are cheaper to run than vehicles or boats) to cost around US$215/£120 per person per night sharing.

Otherwise a mid-range camp in a good area will usually be around US$410–540/£230–300 per person per night sharing, all-inclusive. By going off-season, or to slightly more offbeat, marginal areas, this can be reduced. However, note that quality of accommodation is only one factor in the price: some of the smallest, simplest bushcamps are amongst the most expensive places to stay.

If money really is no object, then there are a few really top-end places that cost a lot more than this. Abu and Mombo spring to mind. For these, you'll pay double this or more. But then, some would argue, you're getting the pinnacle of what Africa has to offer.

Having said this, there are two obvious caveats. Firstly, none of the prices here include flight transfers. These probably average out at about US$110/£60 per person per transfer, though working them out precisely is a complex business.

Secondly, you will almost always be quoted a rate for a 'package' of camps and flights; that's normal and often cannot be broken into its components.

Thirdly, note that although the prices for camps given in this guide indicate what you can expect to pay (in 2006, though the figures in US$/£ don't change much from year to year) if you book directly, this really should be a maximum figure. You will usually be able to get them a little cheaper – and this is especially applicable to the more costly lodges – if you book through a good tour operator. See the section on *Organising a fly-in safari*, at the end of this chapter, and note that, like airline tickets, the better rates for lodges are usually available indirectly.

TIPPING Tipping is a very difficult and contentious topic – worth thinking about carefully. Read the section on *Local payments*, page 131, and realise that thoughtlessly tipping too much is just as bad as tipping too little.

Ask locally what's appropriate; here I can only give rough guidance. Helpers with baggage might expect four or five pula for their help, whilst sorting out a problem with a reservation would be P12–18 (US$2–3/£1–2). Restaurants will often add an automatic service charge to the bill, in which case an additional tip is not usually given. If they do not do this, then 10% would certainly be appreciated if the service was good.

At safari camps, tipping is not obligatory – despite the destructive assumption from some visitors that it is. If a guide has given you really good service then a tip of about P30 (US$5/£2–3) per day per person would be a generous reflection of this. A similar bonus for a mokoro poler might be around P20 (US$3/£2) per day per person. If the service hasn't been that good, then don't tip.

Always tip at the end of your stay – not at the end of each day/activity. Do not tip after every game drive. This leads to the guides only trying hard when they know there's a tip at the end of the morning. Such camps aren't pleasant to visit and this isn't the way to encourage top-quality guiding. It's best to wait until the end of your stay, and then give what you feel is appropriate in one lump sum.

However, before you do this find out if tips go into one box for all of the camp staff, or if the guides are treated differently. Then ensure that your tip reflects this – with perhaps as much again divided between the rest of the staff.

HOW TO TAKE YOUR MONEY If you are changing money at one of the main banks, then there is minimal difference in the rates between presenting a travellers' cheque, or presenting pounds sterling or US dollars in cash. This perhaps makes travellers' cheques preferable from a security point of view, as they are refundable if stolen. (AMEX travellers' cheques are probably the most widely recognised.)

However, outside of the banks you really need to have pula to use, especially for smaller transactions and anything bought by the roadside. In the more rural locations, nobody will accept anything else. Petrol stations accept only cash in pula; they do not usually accept credit cards.

In the towns you'll find people who, if pressed, will accept small denominations of US dollars. Because of the risk of forgeries, people are suspicious of larger denomination notes. US$100 and even US$50 bills are often rejected in shops and even banks. So always bring a mixture of US$5, US$10 and US$20 notes. US$1 notes make useful (generous) tips for porters.

South African rand are sometimes accepted, though not as widely as dollars or pounds – and they're not very popular. Most hotels, restaurants and safari camps will accept credit cards, pounds sterling, US dollars, or travellers' cheques.

BANKS If you need to change foreign currency, receive bank drafts, or do any other relatively complex financial transactions, then the banks here are perfectly capable and efficient. Their opening times vary, but expect them to start around 08.00 and finish by 14.30 during the week. Some may close a few hours earlier than this on Wednesday. On Saturday, only the bigger banks open, typically 08.00–11.00.

Cashpoint (ATM) machines can be found in most large towns, including Maun and Kasane – and they work with foreign credit cards.

WHAT TO TAKE

This is an impossible question to answer fully, as it depends on how you intend to travel and exactly where you are going. If you are flying in for a short safari holiday then you need not pack too ruthlessly – provided that you stay within your weight allowance. However, note that smaller, privately chartered planes may specify a maximum weight of 10–12kg for hold luggage, which must be packed in a soft, squashable bag. Once you see the stowage spaces in a small charter plane, you'll understand the importance of not bringing along large or solid suitcases.

If you are backpacking then weight becomes much more important, and minimising it becomes an art form. Each extra item must be questioned: is its benefit worth its weight?

If you have your own vehicle then neither weight nor bulk will be so vital, and you will have a lot more freedom to bring what you like. Here are some general guidelines:

CLOTHING For most days all you will want is light, loose-fitting cotton clothing. Pure cotton, or at least a cotton-rich mix, is cooler and more absorbent than synthetic materials, making it more comfortable in the heat.

For men shorts (not too short) are fine in the bush, but long trousers are more socially acceptable in the towns and rural villages. (You will rarely see a respectable black man in Botswana wearing shorts outside a safari camp.) For women a knee-length skirt or culottes is ideal. Botswana's dress code is generally conservative: a woman wearing revealing clothing in town implies that she is a woman of ill repute, whilst untidy clothing suggests a poor person, of low social standing.

These rules are redundant at safari camps, where dress is casual, and designed to keep you cool and protect skin from the sun. Green, khaki and dust-brown cotton is de rigueur amongst visitors at the more serious camps. Wardrobes full of shiny, new safari gear will generally earn less respect than battered old green shirts and khaki shorts.

At the less serious camps you'll see a smattering of brighter coloured clothes amongst many dull bush colours, the former usually worn by first-time visitors who are less familiar with the bush. Note that washing is done daily at virtually all camps, so few changes of clothes are necessary. A squashable hat and a robust pair of sunglasses with a high UV-absorption are essential.

Finally avoid anything which looks military. Leave all your camouflage patterns at home. Wearing camouflage is asking for trouble anywhere in Africa. You are very likely to be stopped and questioned by the genuine military, or at least the police, who will assume that you are a member of some militia – and question exactly what you are doing in Botswana. Few will believe that this is a fashion statement elsewhere in the world.

FOOTWEAR If you plan to do much walking, either on safari or with a backpack, then lightweight walking boots (with ankle support if possible) are sensible. This is mainly because the bush is not always smooth and even, and anything that minimises the chance of a twisted ankle is worthwhile. Secondly, for the nervous, it will reduce still further the minute chance of being bitten by a snake, scorpion or other creepy-crawly, whilst walking.

Because of the heat, bring the lightest pair of boots you can find – preferably go for canvas, or a breathable Gore-tex-type material. Leather boots are too hot for wearing in October, but thin single-skin leather is bearable for walking in July and August. Never bring a new pair, or boots that aren't completely worn in. Always bring several pairs of thin socks – two thin pairs of socks are more comfortable than one thick pair, and will help to prevent blisters.

For mokoro trips, or generally relaxing at camp during the day, rafting sandals are ideal. These are sandals with a strong sole and firmly fitting straps which are waterproof. At night around camp you'll need to cover your feet/ankles against mosquitoes, and so lightweight boots of some sort are ideal.

CAMPING EQUIPMENT If you are coming on an organised safari, then even the most simple bushcamp will mean tents with linen, mosquito nets and probably an en-suite shower and toilet. However, if you're planning on doing any camping, then note that equipment is easier to buy in Europe or North America, and see Camping equipment for backpackers on pages 122–4 of *Chapter 6* for ideas of what you should bring.

OTHER USEFUL ITEMS Obviously no list is comprehensive, and only travelling can teach you what you need, and what you can do without. Here are a few of my own favourites and essentials, just to jog your memory. For visitors embarking on an organised safari, camps will have most things but useful items include:

- Sunblock and lipsalve – vital for protection from the sun
- Binoculars – totally essential for game viewing
- A small pocket torch (see page 123)
- 'Leatherman' tool – never go into the bush without one
- A small water bottle, especially on flights (see Camping equipment)
- Electrical insulating tape – remarkably useful for general repairs
- Camera – long lenses are vital for good shots of animals
- Basic sewing kit – with some really strong thread for repairs
- Cheap waterproof watch (leave expensive ones, and jewellery, at home)
- Couple of paperback novels
- Large plastic 'bin-liner' (garbage) bags, for protecting luggage from dust
- Simple medical kit and insect repellent

And for those driving or backpacking, useful extras are:

- Concentrated, biodegradable washing powder
- Long-life candles – African candles are often soft, and burn quickly
- Nylon 'paracord' – bring at least 20m for emergencies and washing lines
- Hand-held GPS navigation system, for expeditions to remote areas
- Good compass and a whistle
- More comprehensive medical kit

MAPS AND NAVIGATION

Finding the right map Botswana has an excellent range of detailed 'Ordnance Survey' type maps available cheaply in Maun and Gaborone. See *Maun*, page 149, for details. However, many were made many years ago, and tracks have changed since. Thus unless you have a lot of time to interpret them, and can afford to carry around lots of maps, they're of limited use.

There are several very good maps designed specifically for visitors, but unfortunately these are very rarely available outside southern Africa. The ones that you're most likely to find in bookshops and map stores outside Africa are generally fine if you're visiting the towns and simply want to know roughly where the parks are.

Amongst these is the Macmillan *Botswana Traveller's Map*. This is certainly easy on the eye, with colour photographs, descriptions, mini street plans, and even a list of lodges and hotels, places of interest, a wildlife identification chart and a calendar of festivals.

In a similar vein is the *Globetrotter Travel Map of Botswana* (New Holland, UK). Again this has clear colouring, showing all the tarred roads and parks beautifully, and includes town plans of Francistown, Gaborone and Maun, and even distance and climate charts.

Similarly, the ITMB map of *Botswana* (aka the *International Traveller Map*) includes sections on the history, geography and people of Botswana, plus a small street plan of Gaborone and paragraphs on each of the main national parks.

However, I view all the above as useless – or worse – if you actually plan to head anywhere remote in the bush. The locations of their tracks and camps are mostly out of date, and the idea of using them to navigate anywhere off the tar is completely fanciful.

The alternatives, which stand head-and-shoulders above the rest, are the Shell maps and the InfoMap. The first of the these was the ground-breaking *Shell Tourist Guide to Botswana*, which incorporated a short but very informative 60-page booklet on the country – effectively an impressive mini guidebook – and a serious, well-researched, original map. These were produced by Veronica Roodt, an expert on the flora and fauna of the area (see *Appendix 3, Further Information* for her excellent books on the flora, and also www.veronicaroodt.co.za).

Originally this was published in 1998, and what really made the difference was that, on the reverse, were smaller, inset maps of all the main parks, complete with a number of GPS waypoints. It was this information which revolutionised independent trips around Botswana, and effectively opened the doors for more travellers into some of the country's less-known areas like the Central Kalahari. (This map is now in its second edition.)

Since then Shell have also published more detailed *Chobe* and *Moremi* maps. These have much more specific coverage of the game-viewing tracks in the park – utilising satellite images, and including bird and animal checklists. Both are worth having, in addition to the main Botswana map, if you're visiting these parks.

The InfoMap (formerly called the *ContiMap* because of its sponsorship from Continental tyres) is the second map that you ought to consider getting. It covers half of the country on each of its sides, with no insets. It's been researched primarily by Mike Main – a very knowledgeable and experienced Botswana traveller (see *Appendix 3, Further Information*) – and has an extensive range of reliable GPS points. These include some of the more offbeat roads outside the parks, and are especially good on areas like the Makgadikgadi Pans and south of Ghanzi.

So if you're going into the bush in Botswana, best to take both the Shell maps, and the ContiMap. Between them you'll have the best information available.

In the UK Because of the general lack of availability of the Shell and InfoMap in the UK, Expert Africa (see page 80 for contact details) has imported stocks of all three Shell maps and also the InfoMap to the UK. These are available to anyone with a UK postal address – even if you're not travelling with Expert Africa to Botswana. Just send them a cheque payable to Expert Africa and your address, and they will send you the maps that you want, normally by return. Currently the costs are:

- £15 for the Shell Guide to Botswana (map and booklet)
- £5 each for the Shell maps to Moremi and Chobe
- £10 for the ContiMap map of Botswana

Although see their website page www.expertafrica.com/books_and_maps.asp to check these prices, and for more details of this offer, and please add £2 per order for postage and packing.

GPS systems If you are heading into one of the more remote parks in your own vehicle, then you really should invest in a hand-held GPS: a Global Positioning System. Under an open, unobstructed sky, these can fix your latitude, longitude and elevation to within about 10m, using a network of American military satellites that constantly pass in the skies overhead. They will work anywhere on the globe.

What to buy Commercial GPS units cost from around US$160/£100 in Europe or the USA. As is usual with high-tech equipment, their prices are falling and their features are expanding as time progresses.

I have been using a variety of Garmin GPS receivers for years now. The early ones ate batteries at a great rate and often took ages to 'fix' my position; more recent models not only have endless new functions and far better displays, but also use fewer batteries, fix positions much more quickly, and usually even work when sitting on the car's dashboard.

Whatever make you buy, you don't need a top-of-the-range machine. Pre-loaded maps are still a waste of time in Africa, as none of them have the detail that you need.

What a GPS can do A GPS should enable you to store 'waypoints' and build a simple electronic picture of an area, as well as working out basic latitude, longitude and elevation. So, for example, you can store the position of your campsite and the nearest road, making it much easier to be reasonably sure of navigating back without simply re-tracing your steps.

It will also enable you to programme in points, using the co-ordinates given throughout this book and by the Shell and ContiMaps, and use these for navigation. See page x for important comment on datums. Thus you should be able to get an idea of whether or not you're going in the right direction, and how far away your destination is.

When you return home, if you have a fast internet connection then knowing the GPS co-ordinates for a place will enable you to see satellite images of the place

Ariadne Van Zandbergen

EQUIPMENT Although with some thought and an eye for composition you can take reasonable photos with a 'point-and-shoot' camera, you need an SLR camera if you are at all serious about photography. Modern SLRs tend to be very clever, with automatic programmes for almost every possible situation, but remember that these programmes are limited in the sense that the camera cannot think, but only make calculations. Every starting amateur photographer should read a photographic manual for beginners and get to grips with such basics as the relationship between aperture and shutter speed.

Always buy the best lens you can afford. The lens determines the quality of your photo more than the camera body. Fixed fast lenses are ideal, but very costly. A zoom lens makes it easier to change composition without changing lenses the whole time. If you carry only one lens, a 28–70mm (digital 17–55mm) or similar zoom should be ideal. For a second lens, a lightweight 80–200mm or 70–300mm (digital 55–200mm) or similar will be excellent for candid shots and varying your composition. Wildlife photography will be very frustrating if you don't have at least a 300mm lens. For a small loss of quality, tele-converters are a cheap and compact way to increase magnification: a 300 lens with a 1.4x converter becomes 420mm, and with a 2x it becomes 600mm. Note, however, that 1.4x and 2x tele-converters reduce the speed of your lens by 1.4 and 2 stops respectively.

For wildlife photography from a safari vehicle, a solid beanbag, which you can make yourself very cheaply, will be necessary to avoid blurred images, and is more useful than a tripod. A clamp with a tripod head screwed on to it can be attached to the vehicle as well. Modern dedicated flash units are easy to use; aside from the obvious need to flash when you photograph at night, you can improve a lot of photos in difficult 'high contrast' or very dull light with some fill-in flash. It pays to have a proper flash unit as opposed to a built-in camera flash.

DIGITAL/FILM Digital photography is now the preference of most amateur and professional photographers, with the resolution of digital cameras improving the whole time. For ordinary prints a 6 megapixel camera is fine. For better results and the possibility to enlarge images and for professional reproduction, higher resolution is available up to 16 megapixels.

Memory space is important. The number of pictures you can fit on a memory card depends on the quality you choose. Calculate in advance how many pictures you can fit

using programmes like Google Maps and Google Earth. See Expert Africa's website (*www.expertafrica.com*) for an amazing demonstration of satellite images of lodges that are possible.

What a GPS can't do A GPS isn't a compass, and when you're standing still, it can't tell you which direction is which. It can only tell you a direction if you're moving. (That said, some of the most expensive GPSs do now incorporate electronic compasses that can do just this!)

Secondly, it can give you a distance and a bearing for where you might want to go . . . but it can't tell you how to get there. You'll still need to find a track. You should NEVER just set out across the bush following a bearing; that's a recipe for disaster.

Thirdly, it can't replace a good navigator. You still need to be able to navigate and think to use a GPS effectively. If you're clueless on navigation then driving around the bush in Botswana will get you into a mess with or without a GPS.

on a card and either take enough cards to last for your trip, or take a storage drive on to which you can download the content. A laptop gives the advantage that you can see your pictures properly at the end of each day and edit and delete rejects, but a storage device is lighter and less bulky. These drives come in different capacities up to 80GB.

Bear in mind that digital camera batteries, computers and other storage devices need charging, so make sure you have all the chargers, cables and converters with you. Most hotels have charging points, but do enquire about this in advance. When camping you might have to rely on charging from the car battery; a spare battery is invaluable.

If you are shooting film, 100 to 200 ISO print film and 50 to 100 ISO slide film are ideal. Low ISO film is slow but fine grained and gives the best colour saturation, but will need more light, so support in the form of a tripod or monopod is important. You can also bring a few 'fast' 400 ISO films for low-light situations where a tripod or flash is no option.

DUST AND HEAT Dust and heat are often a problem. Keep your equipment in a sealed bag, stow films in an airtight container (eg: a small cooler bag) and avoid exposing equipment and film to the sun. Digital cameras are prone to collecting dust particles on the sensor which results in spots on the image. The dirt mostly enters the camera when changing lenses, so be careful when doing this. To some extent photos can be 'cleaned' up afterwards in Photoshop, but this is time-consuming. You can have your camera sensor professionally cleaned, or you can do this yourself with special brushes and swabs made for the purpose, but note that touching the sensor might cause damage and should only be done with the greatest care.

PROTOCOL In some countries, it is unacceptable to photograph local people without permission, and many people will refuse to pose or will ask for a donation. In such circumstances, don't try to sneak photographs as you might get yourself into trouble. Even the most willing subject will often pose stiffly when a camera is pointed at them; relax them by making a joke, and take a few shots in quick succession to improve the odds of capturing a natural pose.

Ariadne Van Zandbergen is a professional travel and wildlife photographer specialising in Africa. She runs The Africa Image Library. For photo requests, visit www.africaimagelibrary.co.za or contact her on ariadne@hixnet.co.za.

Accessories Most GPS units use quite a lot of battery power, so bring plenty of spare batteries with you. Also get hold of a cigarette lighter adapter for your GPS when you buy it. This will enable you to power it from the car whilst you're driving, and thus save batteries.

Warning Although a GPS may help you to recognise your minor errors before they are amplified into major problems, note that such a gadget is no substitute for good map work and navigation. They're great fun to use, but shouldn't be relied upon as a sole means of navigation. You MUST always have a back-up plan – and an understanding of where you are – or you will be unable to cope if your GPS fails.

PHOTOGRAPHY AND OPTICS Outside of Gaborone, optical equipment isn't widely available in Botswana – so bring everything that you will need with you. Film, though, is widely available, albeit slightly more expensive than in Europe and the USA, and with less choice. If you have a specific film that you want to use, bring a large stock with you. Remember, too, that film deteriorates rapidly in the heat, especially after exposure, so aim to keep it somewhere shady and cool, and away from heat sources like sunlight.

Pictures taken around dawn and dusk will have the richest, deepest colours, whilst those taken in the middle of the day, when the sun is high, will seem pale and washed-out by comparison. Beware of the very deep shadows and high contrast which are typical of tropical countries – film just cannot capture the range of colours and shades that our eyes can. If you want to take pictures in full daylight, and capture details in the shadows, then you will need a good camera, and to spend some time learning how to use it fully. By restricting your photography to mornings, evenings and simple shots you will get better pictures and encounter fewer problems.

The bush is very dusty, so bring plenty of lens-cleaning cloths, and a blow-brush. Take great care not to get dust into the back of any camera, as a single grain on the back-plate can be enough to make a long scratch which ruins every frame taken.

For further information, see the *Photographics tips* box on pages 96–7.

Binoculars For a safari holiday, a good pair of binoculars is essential. They will bring you far more enjoyment than a camera, as they make the difference between merely seeing an animal or bird at a distance, and being able to observe its markings, movements and moods closely. Do bring one pair per person; one between two is just not enough.

There are two styles: the small 'pocket' binoculars, perhaps 10–12cm long, which account for most popular modern sales – and have only been in production since the 1980s. These were popularised by the makers of compact and autofocus cameras, and are now often made in the Far East. Then there are the larger, heavier styles, double or triple that size, which have been manufactured for years. Many of the remaining manufacturers of these are in the CIS, Germany or Austria.

The small ones are now mass-produced at around US$160/£100, whilst the larger ones vary widely in cost and quality. If you are buying a pair, then consider getting the larger style. The smaller ones are fine for spotting animals; but are difficult to hold steady, and very tiring to use for extensive periods. You will only realise this when you are out on safari, by which time it is too late.

Around 8 x 30 is an ideal size for field observations, as most people need some form of rest, or tripod, to hold the larger 10 x 50 models steady. Get the best-quality ones you can for your money. The cheapest will be about US$60/£40, but to get a decent level of quality spend at least US$300/£200. You will be able to see the difference when you use them.

5

Health and Safety

with Dr Felicity Nicholson and Dr Jane Wilson-Howarth

There is always great danger in writing about health and safety for the uninitiated visitor. It is all too easy to become paranoid about exotic diseases that you may catch, and all too easy to start distrusting everybody you meet as a potential thief – falling into an unfounded us-and-them attitude towards the people of the country you are visiting.

As a comparison, imagine an equivalent section in a guidebook to a Western country – there would be a list of possible diseases and advice on the risk of theft and mugging. Many Western cities are very dangerous, but with time we learn how to assess the risks, accepting almost subconsciously what we can and cannot do.

It is important to strike the right balance: to avoid being excessively cautious or too relaxed about your health and your safety. With experience, you will find the balance that best fits you and the country you are visiting.

BEFORE YOU GO

TRAVEL INSURANCE Visitors to Botswana should always take out a comprehensive medical insurance policy to cover them for emergencies, including the cost of evacuation to another country within the region. Such policies come with an emergency number (often on a reverse-charge/call-collect basis). You would be wise to memorise this, or indelibly tattoo it in as many places as possible on your baggage.

Personal effects insurance is also a sensible precaution, but check the policy's fine print before you leave home. Often, in even the best policies, you will find a limit per item, or per claim – which can be well below the cost of replacement. If you need to list your valuables separately, then do so comprehensively. Check that receipts are not required for claims if you do not have them, and that the excess which you have to pay on a claim is reasonable.

Annual travel policies can be excellent value if you travel a lot, and some of the larger credit-card companies offer excellent policies. However, it can often be better to get your valuables named and insured for travel using your home contents insurance. These year-round policies will try harder to settle your claim fairly as they want your business in the long term.

IMMUNISATIONS Having a full set of immunisations takes time, normally at least six weeks, although some protection can be had by visiting your doctor as late as a few days before you travel. Ideally, see your doctor or travel clinic (see below) early on to establish an inoculation timetable.

Legal requirements No immunisations are required by law for entry into Botswana.

Recommended precautions Preparations to ensure a healthy trip to Botswana include checking on your immunisation status: it is wise to be up-to-date on

tetanus, polio and **diphtheria** – now available as an all in one vaccine (Revaxis) that lasts for ten years. Regular travellers are advised to have **hepatitis A** immunisation (eg: Havrix Monodose or Avaxim). The course comprises two injections given about a year apart (total cost about £100) and lasts for 25 years. It may be available on the NHS so check with your GP.

The newer **typhoid** vaccines (eg: Typhim Vi) last for three years and are about 85% effective. Oral capsules (Vivotif) are currently available in the US (and soon in the UK); if four capsules are taken over seven days it will last for five years. They should be encouraged unless the traveller is leaving within a few days for a trip of a week or less when the vaccine would not be effective in time.

Immunisation against **cholera** is is not usually required for trips to Botswana. However, in special circumstances, such as in the event of an outbreak, then you would be advised to take the oral vaccine, Dukoral. This is considered around 75% effective. Those six years or older require two doses over at least three weeks.

Vaccination against **rabies** is unnecessary for most visitors, but would be wise for those who travel for extended periods (four weeks or longer), are handling animals or are staying in rural areas where it may be difficult to reach medical help within 24 hours. Ideally three injections taken over a minimum of three weeks prior to travel are advised. But there is some benefit to be gained from even one injection if time is short.

Hepatitis B vaccination should be considered for longer trips (two months or more) or for those working with children or in situations where contact with blood is likely. Three injections are needed for the best protection and can be given over a three-week period if time is short (Engerix is the only vaccine currently licensed for this shortened programme.) Longer schedules give more sustained protection and are therefore preferred if time allows. A BCG vaccination against **tuberculosis** is no longer considered effective for adults, but the disease is treatable should you be unfortunate enough to contract it.

MALARIA PROPHYLAXIS

MALARIA PROPHYLAXIS Malaria is the most dangerous disease in Africa, and the greatest risk to the traveller. It occurs in most of Botswana (predominantly from November to June), and is most common in the north, so it is essential that you take all possible precautions against it.

Prophylaxis regimes aim to infuse your bloodstream with drugs that inhibit and kill the malaria parasites that are injected into you by a biting mosquito. This is why you must start to take the drugs before you arrive in a malarial area – so that they are established in your bloodstream from day one. Unfortunately, the malaria parasites continually adapt to the drugs used to combat them, so the recommended regimes must also adapt and change in order to remain effective. None is 100% effective, and all require time to kill the parasites – so, unless there is a medical indication for stopping, it is important to complete the course as directed after leaving the area (usually one to four weeks, depending on the regime).

It is vital that you seek current advice on the best anti-malarials to take. If mefloquine (Lariam) is suggested, start this two to three weeks before departure (if you have never used this before) to check that it suits you; stop it immediately if it seems to cause depression or anxiety, visual or hearing disturbances, severe headaches, fits or changes in heart rhythm. Side effects such as nightmares or dizziness are not medical reasons for stopping unless they are sufficiently debilitating or annoying. Anyone who suffers from depression or other psychiatric problems, is epileptic, has suffered fits in the past, or who has a close blood relative who is epileptic, should avoid mefloquine. Malarone (proguanil and atovaquone) is now considered as effective as mefloquine. It has the advantage of having few side effects and need only be continued for one week after returning. However, it is expensive and because of this tends to be reserved for shorter trips, even though it is licensed in the UK for three months. Malarone may not be suitable for everybody so advice should be taken from a doctor. Paediatric Malarone is also available and is prescribed on a weight basis in kilogrammes for children weighing 11–40kg.

The antibiotic doxycycline (100mg daily) should be considered when either mefloquine or Malarone are not considered suitable for whatever reason. Like Malarone, it need only be started one to two days before arrival but should be continued for four weeks after leaving the malarial area. It may also be used by travellers with epilepsy, unlike mefloquine, although the anti-epileptic therapy may make it less effective. About 1–3% of people taking doxycycline may develop an allergic skin reaction developing in sunlight. If this happens, the drug should be stopped. Women using the oral contraceptive should use an additional method of protection for the first four weeks when using doxycycline. Since there are restrictions for taking any of these drugs, it is important to seek professional advice before you go. Chloroquine and proguanil are no longer considered effective enough for Botswana, but may be used as a last resort.

Prophylaxis does not stop you catching malaria, however, although it significantly reduces your chances of fully developing the disease and will lessen its severity. Falciparum (cerebral) malaria is the most common in Africa, and usually fatal if untreated, so it is worth your while trying to avoid it.

It is unwise to travel in malarial parts of Africa, including most of Botswana, whilst pregnant or with young children: the risk of malaria in many areas is considerable and such travellers are likely to succumb rapidly. However, if travel is unavoidable during pregnancy then mefloquine can be used, especially during the second and third trimesters of pregnancy. Again seek expert advice well in advance.

Because the strains of malaria, and the drugs used to combat them, change frequently, it is important to get the latest advice before you travel. Normally it is better to obtain this from a specialist travel clinic than from your local doctor, who may not be up-to-date with the latest drugs and developments. For details of relevant clinics, see below. Travellers who may be in remote parts and are staying for long periods of time may wish to carry a treatment for malaria. Again the regime may change with time so always check with a professional before you go.

TRAVEL CLINICS AND HEALTH INFORMATION A full list of current travel clinic websites worldwide is available from the International Society of Travel Medicine on www.istm.org. For other journey preparation information, consult www.tripprep.com. Information about various medications may be found on www.emedicine.com. For information on malaria prevention, see www.preventingmalaria.info.

UK

Berkeley Travel Clinic 32 Berkeley St, London W1J 8EL (near Green Park tube station); ☎ 020 7629 6233
Cambridge Travel Clinic 48a Mill Rd, Cambridge CB1 2AS; ☎ 01223 367362; e enquiries@ cambridgetravelclinic.co.uk; www.cambridgetravelclinic.co.uk.
Open Tue–Fri 12.00–19.00, Sat 10.00–16.00.
Edinburgh Travel Clinic Regional Infectious Diseases Unit, Ward 41 OPD, Western General Hospital, Crewe Rd South, Edinburgh EH4 2UX; ☎ 0131 537 2822; www.link.med.ed.ac.uk/ridu. Travel helpline (☎ 0906

589 0380) open weekdays 09.00–12.00. Provides inoculations and antimalarial prophylaxis and advises on travel-related health risks.
Fleet Street Travel Clinic 29 Fleet St, London EC4Y 1AA; ☎ 020 7353 5678; www.fleetstreetclinic.com. Vaccinations, travel products and latest advice.
Hospital for Tropical Diseases Travel Clinic Mortimer Market Building, Capper St (off Tottenham Court Rd), London WC1E 6AU; ☎ 020 7388 9600; www.thehtd.org. Offers consultations and advice, and is able to provide all necessary drugs and vaccines

for travellers. Runs a healthline ($\searg$ 0906 133 7733) for country-specific information and health hazards. Also stocks nets, water purification equipment and personal protection measures.

Interhealth Worldwide Partnership House, 157 Waterloo Rd, London SE1 8US; $\searg$ 020 7902 9000; www.interhealth.org.uk. Competitively priced, one-stop travel health service. All profits go to their affiliated company, InterHealth, which provides health care for overseas workers on Christian projects.

MASTA (Medical Advisory Service for Travellers Abroad) Moorfield Rd, Yeadon LS19 7BN; $\searg$ 0870 606 2782; www.masta-travel-health.com. Provides travel health advice, anti-malarials and vaccinations. There are over 25 MASTA pre-travel clinics in Britain; call or check online for the nearest. Clinics also sell mosquito nets, medical kits, insect protection and travel hygiene products.

NHS travel website www.fitfortravel.scot.nhs.uk. Provides country-by-country advice on immunisation

and malaria, plus details of recent developments, and a list of relevant health organisations.

Nomad Travel Store/Clinic 3–4 Wellington Terrace, Turnpike Lane, London N8 0PX; $\searg$ 020 8889 7014; travel-health line (office hours only) $\searg$ 0906 863 3414; e sales@nomadtravel.co.uk; www.nomadtravel.co.uk. Also at 40 Bernard St, London WC1N 1LJ; $\searg$ 020 7833 4114; 52 Grosvenor Gardens, London SW1W 0AG; $\searg$ 020 7823 5823; and 43 Queens Rd, Bristol BS8 1QH; $\searg$ 0117 922 6567. For health advice, equipment such as mosquito nets and other anti-bug devices, and an excellent range of adventure travel gear.

Trailfinders Travel Clinic 194 Kensington High St, London W8 7RG; $\searg$ 020 7938 3999; www.trailfinders.com/clinic.htm

Travelpharm The Travelpharm website, www.travelpharm.com, offers up-to-date guidance on travel-related health and has a range of medications available through their online mini-pharmacy.

Irish Republic

Tropical Medical Bureau Grafton Street Medical Centre, Grafton Buildings, 34 Grafton St, Dublin 2; $\searg$ 1 671 9200; www.tmb.ie. A useful website specific

to tropical destinations. Also check website for other bureaux locations throughout Ireland.

USA

Centers for Disease Control 1600 Clifton Rd, Atlanta, GA 30333; $\searg$ 800 311 3435; travellers' health hotline $\searg$ 888 232 3299; www.cdc.gov/travel. The central source of travel information in the USA. The invaluable *Health Information for International Travel*, published annually, is available from the Division of Quarantine at this address.

Connaught Laboratories PO Box 187, Swiftwater, PA 18370; $\searg$ 800 822 2463. They will send a free list of specialist tropical-medicine physicians in your state.

IAMAT (International Association for Medical Assistance to Travelers) 1623 Military Rd, 279, Niagara Falls, NY 14304-1745; $\searg$ 716 754 4883; e info@iamat.org; www.iamat.org. A non-profit organisation that provides lists of English-speaking doctors abroad.

International Medicine Center 920 Frostwood Drive, Suite 670, Houston, TX 77024; $\searg$ 713 550 2000; www.traveldoc.com

Canada

IAMAT Suite 1, 1287 St Clair Av W, Toronto, Ontario M6E 1B8; $\searg$ 416 652 0137; www.iamat.org

TMVC Suite 314, 1030 W Georgia St, Vancouver BC V6E 2Y3; $\searg$ 1 888 288 8682; www.tmvc.com

Australia, New Zealand, Singapore

TMVC $\searg$ 1300 65 88 44; www.tmvc.com.au. 31 clinics in Australia, New Zealand and Singapore, including:
Auckland Canterbury Arcade, 170 Queen St, Auckland; $\searg$ 9 373 3531
Brisbane 6th floor, 247 Adelaide St, Brisbane, QLD 4000; $\searg$ 7 3221 9066

Melbourne 393 Little Bourke St, 2nd floor, Melbourne, VIC 3000; $\searg$ 3 9602 5788
Sydney Dymocks Bldg, 7th floor, 428 George St, Sydney, NSW 2000; $\searg$ 2 9221 7133
IAMAT PO Box 5049, Christchurch 5, New Zealand; www.iamat.org

South Africa and Namibia

SAA–Netcare Travel Clinics P Bag X34, Benmore 2010;

www.travelclinic.co.za. Clinics throughout South Africa.

Consult website for details of other clinics in South Africa and Namibia.

Switzerland
IAMAT 57 Chemin des Voirets, 1212 Grand Lancy, Geneva; www.iamat.org

MEDICAL KIT Pharmacies in the main towns in Botswana generally have very good supplies of medicines, but away from these you will find very little. If you're venturing deep into the wilds, then you should take with you anything that you expect to need. If you are on an organised trip, an overland truck, or staying at hotels, lodges or safari camps, then you will not need much, as these establishments normally have comprehensive emergency kits. In that case, just a small personal medical kit might include:

- antihistamine tablets
- antiseptic
- aspirins or paracetamol
- blister plasters (if you plan any serious walking)
- condoms and contraceptive pills
- insect repellent
- lipsalve (ideally containing a sunscreen)
- malaria prophylaxis
- Micropore tape (for closing small cuts – and invaluable for blisters)
- moisturising cream
- sticking plaster (a roll is more versatile than pre-shaped plasters)
- sunscreen

However, if you are likely to end up in very remote situations, then you should also consider taking the following – and know how to use them:

- burn dressings (burns are a common problem for campers)
- injection swabs, sterile needles and syringes
- lint, sterile bandage and safety pins
- oral rehydration sachets
- Steristrips or butterfly closures
- strong painkiller (eg: codeine phosphate – also useful for bad diarrhoea)
- tweezers (perhaps those on a Swiss army knife)
- water purification equipment (2% tincture of iodine with dropper is ideal)
- several different malaria treatment courses and a broad-spectrum antibiotic – plus a good medical manual (see *Further Information*, page 495).

If you wear glasses, bring a spare pair. Similarly those who wear contact lenses should bring spare ones, plus a pair of glasses in case the dust proves too much for the lenses. If you take regular medication (including contraceptive pills) then bring a large supply with you – much easier than hunting for your usual brand in Botswana. Equally, it's worth having a dental check-up before you go, as you could be several painful days from the nearest dentist.

IN BOTSWANA

HOSPITALS, DENTISTS AND PHARMACIES IN BOTSWANA Botswana's main **hospitals**, in Maun (☏ *6861 831;* m *713 04426*), Francistown (☏ *203666;* m *713 04425*) and Gaborone (☏ *390 1999; manned 24hrs*), are capable of serious surgery

Dr Jane Wilson-Howarth

Long-haul air travel increases the risk of deep vein thrombosis. Although recent research has suggested that many of us develop clots when immobilised, most resolve without us ever having been aware of them. In certain susceptible individuals, though, large clots form and these can break away and lodge in the lungs. This is dangerous but happens in a tiny minority of passengers.

Studies have shown that flights of over five-and-a-half-hours are significant, and that people who take lots of shorter flights over a short space of time form clots. People at highest risk are:

- Those who have had a clot before – unless they are now taking warfarin
- People over 80 years of age
- Anyone who has recently undergone a major operation or surgery for varicose veins
- Someone who has had a hip or knee replacement in the last three months
- Cancer sufferers
- Those who have ever had a stroke
- People with heart disease
- Those with a close blood relative who has had a clot

Those with a slightly increased risk:

- People over 40
- Women who are pregnant or have had a baby in the last couple of weeks
- People taking female hormones or other oestrogen therapy
- Heavy smokers
- Those who have very severe varicose veins

and a good quality of care; they will also treat you first and ask for money later. However, the public health system is over-stretched and under-funded, so unless your illness is critical, it will take time for you to be attended to and treated at the public hospitals. Bear in mind, too, that a large number of patients in the public hospitals have serious infectious diseases, so there's a risk of coming away from these with something worse than you had when you arrived.

Assuming that you have comprehensive medical insurance as part of your travel cover – and you should check that you have - it is probably better go to one of the better-funded **private clinics** which are found in each of the main towns. These cater for both affluent citizens of Botswana and expats/diplomatic staff/travellers. They will accept payment from genuine travel-health insurance schemes. The best way to find details of the nearest private clinics is to look up 'medical – private clinics/practitioners' in the yellow pages at the back of the phone book.

If you've a serious problem, then **MediRescue** (MRI; *www.medicalrescuebotswana*) organises medical evacuations from anywhere. They do insure individual travellers, and your own insurance company may pick up the MediRescue bills if their services were needed, but many lodges are also members, covering you whilst you are staying there (though you will still need your own medical insurance). They can be contacted by dialling ✆ 911 from a normal land line, or ✆ 112 on Macom; the emergency number in Gaborone is ✆ +267 3901 601. Alternatively, call an ambulance from a public hospital on ✆ 997.

- The very obese
- People who are very tall (over 6ft/1.8m) or short (under 5ft/1.5m)

A deep vein thrombosis (DVT) is a blood clot that forms in the deep leg veins. This is very different from irritating but harmless superficial phlebitis. DVT causes swelling and redness of one leg, usually with heat and pain in one calf and sometimes the thigh. A DVT is only dangerous if a clot breaks away and travels to the lungs (pulmonary embolus). Symptoms of a pulmonary embolus (PE) include chest pain that is worse on breathing in deeply, shortness of breath, and sometimes coughing up small amounts of blood. The symptoms commonly start three to ten days after a long flight. Anyone who thinks that they might have a DVT needs to see a doctor immediately who will arrange a scan. Warfarin tablets (to thin the blood) are then taken for at least six months.

PREVENTION OF DVT Several conditions make the problem more likely. Immobility is the key, and factors like reduced oxygen in cabin air and dehydration may also contribute. To reduce the risk of thrombosis on a long journey:

- Exercise before and after the flight
- Keep mobile before and during the flight; move around every couple of hours
- Drink plenty of water or juices during the flight
- Avoid taking sleeping pills and excessive tea, coffee and alcohol
- Perform exercises that mimic walking and tense the calf muscles
- Consider wearing flight socks or support stockings (see www.legshealth.com)
- Take a meal of oily fish (mackerel, trout, salmon, sardines, etc) in the 24 hours before departure to reduce blood clotability and thus DVT risk

If you think you are at increased risk of a clot, ask your doctor if it is safe to travel.

Pharmacies in the three main towns generally have a good range of medicines, though specific brands are often unavailable. So bring with you all that you will need, as well as a repeat prescription for anything that you might run out of. Outside of the larger towns you probably won't be able to find anything other than very basic medical supplies. Thus you should carry a very comprehensive medical kit if you are planning to head off into the wilds (see page 103).

STAYING HEALTHY Botswana is one of the healthiest countries in sub-Saharan Africa. It has a generally low population density, who are affluent by the region's standards, and a very dry climate, which means there are comparatively few problems likely to affect visitors. The risks are further minimised if you are staying in good hotels, lodges, camps and guest farms, where standards of hygiene are generally at least as good as you will find at home.

The major dangers in Botswana are car accidents (caused by driving too fast, or at night, on gravel roads) and sunburn. Both can be very serious, yet both are within the power of the visitor to avoid.

It's interesting to note that the most frequent medical reason for air evacuations from the Okavango Delta, and surrounds, is the unexpected side-effects of the anti-malarial drug Lariam.

The following is general advice, applicable to travelling anywhere, including Botswana:

Food and storage Throughout the world, most health problems encountered by travellers are contracted by eating contaminated food or drinking unclean water. If you are staying in safari camps or lodges, or eating in restaurants, then you are unlikely to have problems in Botswana.

However, if you are backpacking and cooking for yourself, or relying on local food, then you need to take more care. Tins, packets, and fresh green vegetables (when you can find them) are least likely to cause problems – provided that clean water has been used in preparing the meal. In Botswana's hot climate, keeping meat or animal products unrefrigerated for more than a few hours is asking for trouble.

Water and purification Tap water in Botswana's major towns and borehole water, which is used in most of the more remote locations, is perfectly safe to drink for local residents. However, even the mildest of the local microbes may cause a slightly upset stomach for an overseas visitor so you would be wise to use bottled or treated water at all times – and this includes cleaning your teeth! Two-litre bottles of mineral water are available from most supermarkets; these are perfect if you're in a car. Bottled water is also available at most safari camps – though think about the resources used to get it to you, and you might reflect that the local borehole water is likely to be just as good. (It's mineral water too!)

If you need to purify water for yourself in the bush, then first filter out any suspended solids, perhaps by passing the water through a piece of closely woven cloth or something similar. Then bring it to the boil, or sterilise it chemically. Boiling is much more effective, provided that you have the fuel available.

Tablets sold for purification are based on either chlorine or iodine (more effective), and are normally adequate. Just follow the manufacturer's instructions carefully. Iodine is the most effective, especially against the resilient amoebic cysts which cause amoebic dysentery and other prolonged forms of diarrhoea.

A cheaper alternative to tablets sold over the counter is to travel with a small bottle of medical-quality tincture of iodine (2% solution) and an eye dropper. Add four drops to one litre of water, shake well, and leave to stand for ten minutes. If the water is very cloudy (even after filtering) or very cold, then either double the iodine dose, or leave to stand for twice as long.

This tincture of iodine can also be used as a general external antiseptic, but it will stain things deep brown if spilt – so seal and pack its container exceedingly well. Applying a few drops is also an effective way to make leeches detach from your skin.

Avoiding insect bites The most dangerous biting insects in parts of Botswana are mosquitoes, because they can transmit malaria, dengue fever and a host of other diseases. Research has shown that using a mosquito net over your bed, and covering up exposed skin (by wearing long-sleeved shirts, and tucking trousers into socks) in the evening, are the most effective steps towards preventing bites. Bed-net treatment kits are available from travel clinics; these prevent mosquitoes biting through a net if you roll against it in your sleep, and also make old and holey nets protective. Mosquito coils and chemical insect repellents will help, and sleeping in a stream of moving air, such as under a fan, or in an air-conditioned room, will help to reduce your chances of being bitten.

DEET (diethyltoluamide) is the active ingredient in many repellents, so the greater the percentage of DEET, the stronger the effect. However, DEET is a strong chemical. Just 50% is regarded as an effective, non-toxic concentration. It will dissolve some plastics and synthetic materials, and may irritate sensitive skin. Because of this, many people use concentrated DEET to impregnate materials,

Heatstroke, heat exhaustion and sunburn are often problems for travellers to Botswana, despite being easy to prevent. To avoid them, you need to remember that your body is under stress and make allowances for it. First, take things gently; you are on holiday, after all. Next, keep your fluid and salt levels high: lots of water and soft drinks, but go easy on the caffeine and alcohol. Thirdly, dress to keep cool with loose-fitting, thin garments – preferably of cotton, linen or silk. Finally, beware of the sun. Hats and long-sleeved shirts are essential. If you must expose your skin to the sun, then use sunblocks and high factor sunscreens (the sun is so strong that you will still get a tan).

rather than applying it to themselves. An alternative to this is to use Bug Guards – wrist and ankle bands containing 100% DEET in capsule form. The capsules break on movement, but the chemical never touches the skin. One pack contains four bands, which when opened, last for two weeks. Mosquito nets, socks and even cravats can be impregnated and used to deter insects from biting. Eating large quantities of garlic, or cream of tartar, or taking yeast tablets, are said to deter some biting insects, although the evidence is anecdotal – and the garlic may affect your social life. However, recent research suggests that natural insect repellents containing both eucalyptus and citronella are just as effective as DEET containing repellents and these are certainly recommended in pregnancy.

Snakes, spiders and scorpions Encounters with aggressive snakes, angry spiders or vindictive scorpions are more common in horror films than in Botswana. Most snakes will flee at the mere vibrations of a human footstep whilst spiders are far more interested in flies than people. You will have to seek out scorpions if you wish to see one. If you are careful about where you place your hands and feet, especially after dark, then there should be no problems. You are less likely to get bitten or stung if you wear stout shoes and long trousers. Simple precautions include not putting on boots without shaking them empty first, and always checking the back of your backpack before putting it on.

Snakes do bite occasionally, and you ought to know the standard first-aid treatment. First, and most importantly, don't panic. Most snakes are harmless and even venomous species will only dispense venom in about half of their bites. If bitten, you are unlikely to have received venom; keeping this fact in mind may help you to stay calm.

Even in the worst of these cases, the victim has hours or days to get help, and not a matter of minutes. He/she should be kept calm, with no exertions to pump venom around the blood system, whilst being taken rapidly to the nearest medical help. The area of the bite should be washed to remove any venom from the skin, and the bitten limb should be immobilised. Paracetamol may be used as a painkiller, but never use aspirin because it may cause internal bleeding.

Most first-aid techniques do more harm than good; cutting into the wound is harmful and tourniquets are dangerous; suction and electrical inactivation devices do not work. The only effective treatment is antivenom. In case of a bite which you fear may be both serious and venomous:

- Try to keep calm. It is likely that no venom has been dispensed.
- Stop movement of the bitten limb by applying a splint.
- If you have a crepe bandage, firmly bind up as much of the bitten limb as you can. Release the bandage for a few minutes every half-hour.

- Keep the bitten limb below heart height to slow the spread of any venom.
- Evacuate the victim to a hospital that has antivenom.
- Never give aspirin. You may offer paracetamol, which is safe.
- Do not apply ice packs.
- Do not apply potassium permanganate.

If the offending snake can be captured without any risk of someone else being bitten, take it to show the doctor. But beware, since even a decapitated head is able to dispense venom in a reflex bite.

When deep in the bush, heading for the nearest large farm or camp may be quicker than going to a town: it may have a supply of antivenom, or facilities to radio for help by plane.

DISEASES AND WHEN TO SEE A DOCTOR
Travellers' diarrhoea with Dr Jane Wilson-Howarth
There are almost as many names for this as there are travellers' tales on the subject. Firstly, do resist the temptation to reach for the medical kit as soon as your stomach turns a little fluid. Most cases of travellers' diarrhoea will resolve themselves within 24–48 hours with no treatment at all. To speed up this process of acclimatisation, eat well but simply: avoid fats in favour of starches, and keep your fluid intake high. Bananas and papaya fruit are often claimed to be helpful.

If you urgently need to stop the symptoms, for a long journey for example, then Lomotil, Imodium or another of the commercial anti-diarrhoea preparations will do the trick. They stop the symptoms by paralysing the bowel, but will not cure the problem. They should only be used as a last resort and never if you have bad abdominal cramps with the diarrhoea.

If the diarrhoea persists for more than two days, or the stools contain blood, pus or slime, or it lasts for more than three or four days and/or you have a fever, you must seek medical advice. There are as many possible treatments as there are causes, and a proper diagnosis involves microscopic analysis of a stool sample, so go straight to your nearest hospital. The most important thing, especially in Botswana's climate, is to keep your fluid intake up. If it is not possible to reach medical help quickly then take 500mg of ciprofloxacin repeating the dose ten to 12 hours later if you still haven't reached help (remember that you should not drink alcohol whilst taking ciprofloxacin as it has extremely unpleasant side effects). Norfloxaxin is a good alternative but both drugs can only be obtained on a prescription in the UK. If the diarrhoea is greasy and bulky and is accompanied by sulphurous (eggy) burps the likely cause is giardia. This is best treated with tinidazole (four x 500mg in one dose repeated seven days later if symptoms persist).

The body's absorption of fluids is assisted by adding small amounts of dissolved sugars, salts and minerals to the water. Sachets of oral rehydration salts give the perfect biochemical mix necessary to replace what is pouring out of your bottom but they do not taste so nice. Any dilute mixture of sugar and salt in water will do you good so, if you like Coke or orange squash, drink that with a three-finger pinch of salt added to each glass. The ideal ratio is eight level teaspoons of sugar and one level teaspoon of salt dissolved in one litre of water. Palm syrup or honey make good substitutes for sugar, and including fresh citrus juice will not only improve the taste of these solutions, but also add valuable potassium.

Drink two large glasses after every bowel action, and more if you are thirsty. If you are not eating you need to drink three litres a day plus whatever you are sweating and the equivalent of what's going into the toilet. If you feel like eating, take a bland diet; heavy greasy foods will give you cramps.

If you are likely to be more than a few days from qualified medical help, then come equipped with a good health manual and the selection of antibiotics which it recommends. *Bugs, Bites & Bowels* by Dr Jane Wilson-Howarth (see *Further Information*, page 495) is excellent for this purpose.

Malaria You can still catch malaria even if you are taking anti-malarial drugs. Classic symptoms include headaches, chills and sweating, abdominal pains, aching joints and fever – some or all of which may come in waves. It varies tremendously, but often starts like a bad case of flu. If anything like this happens, you should first suspect malaria and seek immediate medical help. A definite diagnosis of malaria is normally possible only by examining a blood sample under the microscope. It is best to get the problem properly diagnosed if possible, so don't treat yourself if you can easily reach a hospital first.

If (and only if) medical help is unavailable, then self-treatment is fairly safe, except for people who are pregnant or under 12 years of age. There are a number of treatments available that can be obtained before you leave. Currently the most likely to be prescribed are Malarone or Co-artemether. It is always best to ask a doctor at a travel clinic for the most up-to-date advice. In Botswana you should always be able to get experienced local advice to tell you which will be the most effective.

Dengue fever This mosquito-borne disease may mimic malaria but there is no prophylactic medication available to deal with it. The mosquitoes that carry this virus bite during the daytime, so it is worth applying repellent if you see any mosquitoes around. Symptoms include strong headaches, rashes and excruciating joint and muscle pains and high fever. Dengue fever only lasts for a week or so and is not usually fatal. Complete rest and paracetamol are the usual treatment. Plenty of fluids also help. Some patients are given an intravenous drip to keep them from dehydrating. It is especially important to protect yourself if you have had dengue fever before. A second infection with a different strain can result in the potentially fatal dengue haemorrhagic fever.

Sexually transmitted diseases AIDS is spread in exactly the same way in Africa as it is at home, through body secretions, blood, and blood products. The same goes for the dangerous Hepatitis B. Both can be spread through sex.

Remember that the risks of sexually transmitted disease are high, whether you sleep with fellow travellers or locals. About 40% of HIV infections in British people are acquired abroad. Use condoms or femidoms. If you notice any genital ulcers or discharge, get treatment promptly.

Hepatitis This is a group of viral diseases that generally start with Coca-Cola-coloured urine and light-coloured stools. It progresses to fevers, weakness, jaundice (yellow skin and eyeballs) and abdominal pains caused by a severe inflammation of the liver. There are several forms, of which the two most common are typical of the rest: hepatitis A (or infectious hepatitis) and hepatitis B (or serum hepatitis).

Hepatitis A, and the newly discovered hepatitis E, are spread by the faecal-oral route, that is by ingesting food or drink contaminated by excrement. They are avoided in the same ways you normally avoid stomach problems: by careful preparation of food and by drinking only clean water. There are now excellent vaccines against hepatitis A (Havrix Monodose or Avaxim) and it is certainly worth getting one of these before you travel. See *Recommended precautions* on page 100.

In contrast, the more serious but rarer hepatitis B is spread in the same way as HIV (by blood or body secretions), and is avoided the same way as one avoids HIV.

There is a vaccine which protects against hepatitis B, but three doses are needed over a minimum of three weeks. It is usually considered necessary only for medical workers, people working closely with children or if you intend to travel for eight weeks or longer. If you are unlucky enough to contract hepatitis of any form, use your travel insurance to fly straight home – although most people recover within six months with lots of bed rest and a good low-fat, no-alcohol diet.

Rabies Rabies is contracted when broken skin comes into contact with saliva from an infected animal. The disease is almost always fatal when fully developed, but fortunately there are excellent post-exposure vaccines. It is possible, albeit expensive, to be immunised against rabies before you travel. You are advised to take this if you intend working with animals or you are travelling for four weeks or more to remote areas.

Rabies is rarely a problem for visitors, but the small risk is further minimised by avoiding small mammals. This is especially true of any animals acting strangely. Both mad dogs in town and friendly jackals in the bush should be given a very wide berth.

If you are bitten, scratched or licked over an open wound, clean and disinfect the wound thoroughly by scrubbing it with soap under running water for five minutes, and then flood it with local spirit or diluted iodine. Then seek medical advice.

At least two post-exposure rabies injections are needed even in immunised people. But for those who are unimmunised even more injections are needed together with rabies immunoglobulin (RIG). RIG is expensive (around US$900 a dose) and is also in very short supply – another good reason for taking pre-exposure vaccine.

You should always seek help immediately, ideally within 24 hours, but since the incubation period for rabies can be very long it is never too late to bother. The later stages of the disease are horrendous – spasms, personality changes and hydrophobia (fear of water). Death from rabies is probably one of the worst ways to go.

Bilharzia or schistosomiasis Though a low risk in Botswana, bilharzia is an insidious disease, contracted by coming into contact with contaminated water. It is caused by parasitic worms which live part of their lives in freshwater snails, and part of their lives in human bladders or intestines. A common indication of an infection is a localised itchy rash – where the parasites have burrowed through the skin – and later symptoms of a more advanced infection may include passing bloody urine. Bilharzia is readily treated by medication, and only serious if it remains untreated.

The only way to avoid infection completely is to stay away from any bodies of fresh water. Obviously this is restrictive, and would make your trip less enjoyable. More pragmatic advice is to avoid slow-moving or sluggish water, and ask local opinion on the bilharzia risk, as not all water is contaminated. It's generally thought that the Okavango Delta is not infected with bilharzia.

Generally bilharzia snails do not inhabit fast-flowing water, and hence rivers are free of it. However, dams and standing water, especially in populated areas, are usually heavily contaminated. If you think you have been infected, don't worry about it – just get a test done on your return at least six weeks after your last possible exposure.

Sleeping sickness or trypanosomiasis This is really a cattle disease, which is rarely caught by people. It is spread by bites from the distinctive tsetse fly – which is slightly larger than a housefly, and has pointed mouthparts designed for sucking blood. The bite is painful. These flies are easily spotted as they bite during the day,

Outbreaks of anthrax are relatively common among the animals in Botswana's national parks, but the Botswanan authorities monitor the situation very closely, putting affected areas off limits to visitors for a considerable period of time.

One of the most recent outbreaks occurred in September 2004 along the Chobe riverfront. In three months, a total of 848 animals were recorded as having died from the disease (during an outbreak, it's assumed that all unknown causes of death are related to anthrax), with some 85% of these being buffaloes, and elephants accounting for a further 9% or so. A recurrence of the outbreak in the same area led to the temporary closure of the riverfront between Ihaha and Serondela in October 2005, with all vehicles diverted away from the area.

To allay any fears, it's worth noting a few facts about anthrax. It is a bacterial disease caused by the spore-forming *Bacillius anthracis*, and is primarily contracted by herbivores such as cattle, goats, or sheep; outbreaks among carnivores are rare. Humans can contract the disease only if they come into direct contact with infected animals, their carcasses or material, including soil; it cannot be passed from one human to another. Fortunately the risk for travellers of getting anthrax is very low. Unless you're planning to eat the meat, or to get close enough to touch any animal or part of an animal, you're not at risk – though remember to avoid buying souvenirs made from animal skin, however tempting. For the most part, the disease occurs in the dry season when animals graze closer to the soil, where the spores can survive for a considerable period of time – hence the recurrence of outbreaks year on year. For this reason, proper disposal of carcasses, usually by incineration, is a crucial part of anthrax control measures.

Symptoms of anthrax vary, but usually occur within seven days. Most infections result from a cut or graze coming into contact with the bacteria. In this instance, what appears to be an insect bite grows within a couple of days into a painless ulcer about 1–3cm across, with a black centre, and surrounding lymph glands may swell. This type of infection usually responds well to antibiotics. Rarely, as a result of inhalation of spores, the apparent symptoms of a common cold progress to severe breathing problems, with a bleak outlook. A third form of the disease, which may follow the consumption of contaminated meat, leads to inflammation of the intestine, with potentially fatal consequences. While a vaccine is available, it is not normally recommended that visitors to Botswana should be inoculated.

and have distinctive wings that cross into a scissor-shape when they are resting. They are not common in Botswana, and a very low proportion of tsetse flies carry the disease, so a bite is not generally a cause for panic or worry.

Prevention is easier than cure, so avoid being bitten by covering up. Chemical insect repellents are also helpful. Although there is no scientific proof it is felt that dark colours, especially blue, are favoured by the flies (and also mosquitoes), so avoid wearing these if possible.

Tsetse bites are nasty, so expect them to swell up and turn red – that is a normal allergic reaction to any bite. The vast majority of tsetse bites will do only this. However, if the bite develops into a boil-like swelling after five or more days, and a fever starts two or three weeks later, then seek immediate medical treatment to avert permanent damage to your central nervous system. The name 'sleeping sickness' refers to a daytime drowsiness which is characteristic of the later stages of the disease.

Because this is a rare complaint, most doctors in the West are unfamiliar with it. If you think that you may have been infected, draw their attention to the possibility. Treatment is straightforward, once a correct diagnosis has been made.

NOTES FOR DISABLED TRAVELLERS

Gordon Rattray (www.able-travel.com)

For wheelchair users and people who have difficulties walking, Botswana is a relatively accessible safari destination. It is possible to book through a specialised operator and be sure that your needs are met, or to do enough preparation in advance and travel independently. Either way, with some endeavour, everybody can experience the unique highlights this country has to offer.

TRANSPORT

Air travel Most international travellers will arrive from Johannesburg, where the services and facilities for disabled people at least rival and often better those in Europe. Maun airport, on the other hand, the usual first stop in Botswana, does not yet have an aisle chair. This means that non-ambulant people must be manually carried from the aircraft. However, the staff are used to doing this, and with guidance from you the process should go without a hitch. Maun airport has a spacious, albeit not officially wheelchair-accessible toilet.

The shorter flights from Maun to Kasane and into the Okavango Delta are also quite possible; when I went, the pilot helped lift me to my seat, and there was room to stow my wheelchair with the luggage. However, these planes are small so a folding wheelchair is essential.

By car Vehicles in Botswana are often 4x4, and therefore higher than normal cars. This means that unless you use an operator with adapted vehicles, wheelchair transfers will be more difficult. Drivers and guides are normally happy to help, but are not trained in this skill, so you must thoroughly explain your needs and always stay in control of the situation.

It is possible to hire self-drive vehicles, but I know of no company providing cars that are adapted for disabled drivers.

Distances are large and roads are often bumpy, so if you are prone to skin damage you need to take extra care. Place your own pressure-relieving cushion on top of (or instead of) the original car seat and, if necessary, pad around knees and elbows.

Buses and trains There is no effective legislation in Botswana to facilitate disabled travellers' journeys by public transport. If you cannot walk at all then both of these options are going to be difficult. You will need to ask for help from fellow passengers to lift you to your seat; it will often be crowded and it is unlikely that there will be an accessible toilet.

RETURNING HOME Many tropical diseases have a long incubation period, and it is possible to develop symptoms weeks after returning home (this is why it is important to keep taking anti-malaria prophylaxis for the prescribed duration after you leave a malarial zone). If you do get ill after you return home, be certain to tell your doctor where you have been. Alert him/her to any diseases that you may have been exposed to. Several people die from malaria in the UK every year because victims do not seek medical help promptly or their doctors are not familiar with the symptoms, and so are slow to make a correct diagnosis. Milder forms of malaria may take up to a year to reveal themselves, but serious (falciparum) malaria will usually become apparent within four months.

If problems persist, get a check-up at one of the hospitals that specialise in tropical diseases. Note that to visit such a hospital in the UK, you need a letter of referral from your doctor.

For further advice or help in the UK, ask your local doctor to refer you to the Hospital for Tropical Diseases (see pages 101–2), or in the US to the Centers for Disease Control (see page 102).

ACCOMMODATION In general, it is not easy to find disabled-friendly accommodation in Botswana. Occasionally (more by accident than through design), showers and toilets are wheelchair accessible, but where this is not the case, you should be prepared to be carried again, or do your ablutions in the bedroom.

In Maun, Island Safari Lodge (see pages 157–8) has two 'paraplegic chalets' with roll-in showers, and Riley's Hotel (see page 154) has a bathroom where the bath has grab-handles. Other hotel options include Mowana Safari Lodge and Chobe Marina Lodge, in Kasane, and Livingstone's Royal Livingstone. There are several lodges and camps in the Okavango Delta that have a degree of accessibility, depending on your needs. It is worthwhile spending some time researching these options before you leave home. Local operators and accommodation owners can be contacted by email and will be happy to describe their facilities and equipment.

HEALTH Doctors will know about 'everyday' illnesses, but you must understand and be able to explain your own particular medical requirements. African hospitals are often basic so, if possible, take all necessary medication and equipment with you. It is advisable to pack this in your hand luggage during flights in case your main luggage gets lost.

Botswana can be extremely hot. If this is a problem for you, be careful to book accommodation with fans or air-conditioning; a useful cooling aid is a plant-spray bottle.

PERSONAL ASSISTANCE I contacted the Delta Medical Centre in Maun (✆ +267 686 1411, 2999; e deltamed@info.bw or pak@info.bw) which organised a qualified nurse to help me with personal care. Rates are negotiable.

SECURITY The usual security precautions apply, but it is also worthwhile remembering that, as a disabled person, you are even more vulnerable. Stay aware of who is around you and where your bags are, especially during car transfers and similar. These activities often draw a crowd, and the confusion creates easy pickings for an opportunist thief.

SPECIALISED OPERATORS Endeavour Safaris (e info@endeavour-safaris.com; www.endeavour-safaris.com) caters to many types of disability and senior travellers.

SAFETY

Botswana is not a dangerous country. If you are travelling on an all-inclusive trip and staying at lodges and hotels, then problems of personal safety are exceedingly rare. There will always be someone on hand to help you. Even if you are travelling on local transport, perhaps on a low budget, you will generally be perfectly safe if you are careful.

Outside of rougher parts of the main cities, crime against visitors, however minor, is rare. Even if you are travelling on local transport on a low budget, you are likely to experience numerous acts of random kindness, but not crime. It is certainly safer for visitors than the UK, USA or most of Europe.

To get into a difficult situation, you'll usually have to try hard. You need to make yourself an obvious target for thieves, perhaps by walking around at night, with showy valuables, in a less affluent area of the city. Provided you are sensible, you are most unlikely to ever see any crime here.

For women travellers, especially those travelling alone, it is doubly important to learn the local attitudes, and how to behave acceptably. This takes some practice, and a certain confidence. You will often be the centre of attention but, by developing conversational techniques to avert over-enthusiastic male attention, you should be perfectly safe. Making friends of the local women is one way to help avoid such problems.

THEFT Theft is not a problem in Botswana – which is surprising given the poverty levels amongst much of the population. The only real exception to this rule is theft from unattended vehicles, which is becoming less unusual in the larger towns. If you leave a vehicle with anything valuable on view, then you may return to find a window smashed and items stolen. Aside from this, theft is really very rare.

When staying at safari camps in the bush, you'll often find that there are no locks and keys on the doors and there is a tremendous amount of trust. Regardless of this, leaving cash or valuables lying around or easily accessible is both stupid and very unfair to the camp's staff. Your watch could easily be worth a year's salary to them; make sure you keep such items out of sight and out of the way of temptation.

Should you experience a theft in a camp, report it to the management immediately; but bear in mind that most such reports are solved with the realisation that the property's owner mislaid it themselves!

How to avoid it Like anywhere, thieves in the bigger cities here work in groups and choose their targets carefully. These targets will be people who look vulnerable and who have items worth stealing. To avoid being robbed, try not to look too vulnerable or too rich – and certainly not both. Observing a few basic rules, especially during your first few weeks in Botswana's cities, will drastically reduce your chances of becoming a target. After that you should have learnt your own way of assessing the risks, and avoiding thefts. Until then:

- Try not to carry anything of value around with you.
- If you must carry cash, then use a concealed money-belt for your main supply – keeping smaller change separately and to hand.
- Try not to look too foreign. Blend in to the local scene as well as you can. Act like a streetwise expat rather than a tourist, if possible. (Conspicuously carrying a local newspaper may help with this.)
- Rucksacks and large, new bags are bad. If you must carry a bag, choose an old battered one. Around town, a local plastic carrier bag is ideal.
- Move confidently and look as if you know exactly what you are doing, and where you are going. Lost foreigners make the easiest targets.
- Never walk around at night – that is asking for trouble.
- If you have a vehicle then don't leave anything in it, and avoid leaving it parked outside in a city.

Reporting thefts to the police If you are the victim of a theft then report it to the police – they ought to know. Also try to get a copy of the report, or at least a reference number on an official-looking piece of paper, as this will help you to claim on your insurance policy when you return home. Some insurance companies won't act without it. But remember that reporting anything in a police station can take a long time, and do not expect any speedy arrests for a small case of pickpocketing.

ARREST To get arrested in Botswana, a foreigner will normally have to try quite hard. There's no paranoia about foreigners, who are now generally seen as welcome tourists who bring money into the economy.

Janice Booth

When attention becomes intrusive, it can help if you are wearing a wedding ring and have photos of 'your' husband and children, even if they are someone else's. A good reason to give for not being with them is that you have to travel in connection with your job – biology, zoology, geography, or whatever. (But not journalism – that's risky.)

Pay attention to local etiquette, and to speaking, dressing and moving reasonably decorously. Look at how the local women dress, and try not to expose parts of yourself that they keep covered. Think about body language. In much of southern Africa direct eye-contact with a man will be seen as a 'come-on'; sunglasses are helpful here.

Don't be afraid to explain clearly – but pleasantly rather than as a put-down – that you aren't in the market for whatever distractions are on offer. Remember that you are probably as much of a novelty to the local people as they are to you; and the fact that you are travelling abroad alone gives them the message that you are free and adventurous. But don't imagine that a Lothario lurks under every bush: many approaches stem from genuine friendliness or curiosity, and a brush-off in such cases doesn't do much for the image of travellers in general.

Take sensible precautions against theft and attack – try to cover all the risks before you encounter them – and then relax and enjoy your trip. You'll meet far more kindness than villainy.

One simple precaution to avoid trouble is to ask for permission to photograph near bridges or military installations. This simple courtesy costs you nothing, and may avoid a problem later.

One excellent way to get arrested in Botswana is to try to smuggle drugs across its borders, or to try to buy them from 'pushers'. Drug offences carry penalties at least as stiff as those you will find at home – and the jails are a lot less pleasant. Botswana's police are not forbidden to use entrapment techniques or 'sting' operations to catch criminals. Buying, selling or using drugs in Botswana is just not worth the risk.

Failing this, arguing with any policeman or army official – and getting angry into the bargain – is a sure way to get arrested. It is essential to control your temper and stay relaxed when dealing with Botswana's officials. Not only will you gain respect, and hence help your cause, but you will also avoid being forced to cool off for a night in the cells.

If you are careless enough to be arrested, you will often be asked only a few questions. If the police are suspicious of you, then how you handle the situation will determine whether you are kept for a matter of hours or for days. Be patient, helpful, good-humoured, and as truthful as possible. Never lose your temper; it will only aggravate the situation. Avoid any hint of arrogance. If things are going badly after half a day or so, then start firmly, but politely, to insist on seeing someone in higher authority. As a last resort you do, at least in theory, have the right to contact your embassy or consulate, though the finer points of your civil liberties may be overlooked by an irate local police chief.

BRIBERY Bribery is not at all common in Botswana, and the government takes a very strict anti-corruption stance. Certainly no normal visitor should ever be asked for, or offer, a bribe. It would be just as illegal as offering someone a bribe back home. Forget it.

6

Into the Wilds

DRIVING

Driving around Botswana is exceedingly easy if you stick to the network of first-class tarred roads between the towns, but heading into the bush is a completely different proposition, which usually requires a small expedition.

Botswana's bush tracks are maintained only by the passage of vehicles, and aren't for the novice, or the unprepared. However, if you've been to Africa at least once or twice before, perhaps including a driving trip around South Africa or Namibia, then such trips can be a lot of fun provided that you realise that you're embarking on an adventure as much as a holiday.

To explore the more rural areas and remote parks on your own you'll need a fully equipped 4x4 vehicle, stocked with food and water for your trip. Depending on where you are going, some form of back-up is often wise. This might be a reliable satellite phone, a radio (and the know-how to use it), someone tracking your schedule – with frequent call-in points so they can look for you if you don't turn up on time, or the security of travelling in convoy with at least one other vehicle.

Having pointed out all the dangers, those who do this kind of trip often get addicted to the space and the freedom; it can be really rewarding and tremendous fun!

EQUIPMENT AND PREPARATIONS

Fuel Petrol and diesel are available in all of the larger towns. However, for travel into the bush you will need long-range fuel tanks, and/or a large stock of filled jerrycans. (Only use metal jerrycans for fuel; plastic containers are highly dangerous.)

It is essential to plan your fuel requirements well in advance, and to carry more than you expect to need. Remember that using the vehicle's 4x4 capability, especially in low ratio gears, will significantly increase your fuel consumption. Similarly, the cool comfort of a vehicle's air conditioning will burn your fuel reserves swiftly. At the time of research, the price in Maun for diesel was P4.21 per litre, and for petrol P4.25 per litre. The further you go away from the major centres, the more these prices will increase.

Spares Botswana's garages generally have a comprehensive stock of vehicle spares – though bush mechanics can effect the most amazing short-term repairs, with remarkably basic tools and raw materials. Spares for the more common makes are easiest to find; most basic Land Rover and Toyota 4x4 parts are available. If you are arriving in Botswana with an unusual foreign vehicle, it is best to bring as many spares as you can.

Navigation See the section on *Maps and navigation* in *Chapter 4* for detailed comments, but there are two good maps designed for visitors widely available –

and offices of the Surveyor General in Maun and Gaborone. It's wise to take a GPS, though learn how to use it before you arrive and never switch your brain off and rely on it totally.

COPING WITH BOTSWANA'S ROADS

Tar roads Botswana's tar roads are excellent, and a programme of tarring is gradually extending the network of roads. Note that the police do operate radar traps, especially near the towns. A speeding ticket will usually mean that you have to turn up at the nearest police station within 48 hours and pay a fine – which can be particularly inconvenient if you were just rushing out of the town and into the bush. Botswana's police are efficient; it'd be foolhardy not to obey such a summons.

Gravel roads There aren't many good gravel roads in Botswana – most are either good tar, or basic bush tracks. However, the few gravel sections can be very deceiving. Even when they appear smooth, flat and fast (which is not often), they still do not give vehicles much traction. You will frequently put the car into small skids, but with practice at slower speeds you will learn how to deal with them. Gravel is a less forgiving surface on which to drive than tar. The rules and techniques for driving well are the same for both, but on tar you can get away with sloppy braking and cornering which would prove fatal on gravel.

Further, in Botswana you must always be prepared for the unexpected: an animal wandering on to the road, a pot-hole, a sand-trap, or an unexpected corner. So it is verging on insane to drive over about 80km/h on any of Botswana's gravel roads. Other basic driving hints include:

- **Slowing down** If in any doubt about what lies ahead, always slow down. Road surfaces can vary enormously, so keep a constant lookout for pot-holes, ruts or patches of soft sand that could put you into an unexpected slide.
- **Passing vehicles** When passing other vehicles travelling in the opposite direction, always slow down to minimise both the damage that stone chippings will do to your windscreen, and the danger in driving through the other vehicle's dust cloud.
- **Using your gears** In normal driving, a lower gear will give you more control over the car – so keep out of high 'cruising' gears. Rather stick with third or fourth, and accept that your revs will be slightly higher than they normally are.
- **Cornering and braking** Under ideal conditions, the brakes should only be applied when the car is travelling in a straight line. Braking whilst negotiating a corner is dangerous, so it is vital to slow down before you reach corners. Equally, it is better to slow down gradually, using a combination of gears and brakes, than to use the brakes alone. You are less likely to skid.

Driving at night Outside of the main towns, **never** drive at night unless it's a matter of life and death. Both wild and domestic animals frequently spend the night by the side of busy roads, and will actually sleep on quieter ones. Tar roads are especially bad as the surface absorbs all the sun's heat by day, and then radiates it at night – making it a warm bed for passing animals. A high-speed collision with any animal, even a small one like a goat, will not only kill the animal, but will cause very severe damage to a vehicle, with potentially fatal consequences. And in the bush the danger of startling elephants is very real.

DRIVING TECHNIQUES You want a high-clearance 4x4 to get anywhere in Botswana that's away from the main arteries. However, no vehicle can make up for an inexperienced driver – so ensure that you are confident of your vehicle's capabilities before you venture into the wilds with it. You really need extensive practice, with an expert on hand to advise you, before you'll have the first idea how to handle such a vehicle in difficult terrain. Finally, driving in convoy is an essential precaution in the more remote areas, in case one vehicle gets stuck or breaks down. Some of the more relevant ideas and techniques include:

When and how to use a 4x4 Firstly, read your vehicle's manual. All makes are different, and have their quirks, and so you must read the manual before you set off. Note especially that you should **never** drive in 4x4 mode with fixed (or 'locked') differentials on tar roads. Doing this will cause permanent damage to the mechanics of your vehicle.

When you do encounter traction difficulties, stop when you can and put the vehicle into 4x4 – usually setting the second 'small' gear-stick to '4x4 high' is fine for most situations.

Now get out of the vehicle and check if the front two hubs of your vehicle have, at their centre, knobs to turn. (This is the case with many Toyotas, though some newer vehicles have 'automatic' hubs.) If so, you'll need to turn these to the 'lock' position – a fact forgotten by many novices that causes untold trouble for them, and endless smug amusement for old Africa hands.

When you're past the problem, using 2WD will lower your fuel consumption, though many will use 4x4 the whole time that they're in the bush. Remember to re-set your hubs to 'free' before you drive on tar again.

Driving in sand If you're in 4x4 and are really struggling in deep sand, then stop on the next fairly solid area that you come to. Lower your tyre pressure until there is a small bulge in the tyre walls (having first made sure that you have the means to re-inflate them when you reach solid roads again). A lower pressure will help your traction greatly, but increase the wear on your tyres. Pump them up again before you drive on a hard surface at speed, or the tyres will be badly damaged.

Where there are clear, deep-rutted tracks in the sand, don't fight the steering wheel – just relax and let your vehicle steer itself. Driving in the cool of the morning is easier than later in the day because when sand is cool it compacts better and is firmer. (When hot, the pockets of air between the sand grains expand and the sand becomes looser.)

If you do get stuck, despite these precautions, don't panic. Don't just rev the engine and spin the wheels – you'll only dig deeper. Instead stop. Relax and assess the situation. Now dig shallow ramps in front of all the wheels, reinforcing them with pieces of wood, vegetation, stones, material or anything else which will give the wheels better traction. Lighten the vehicle load (passengers out) and push. Don't let the engine revs die as you engage your lowest ratio gear. That probably means using '4x4 low' rather than '4x4 high.' Use the clutch to ensure that the wheels don't spin wildly and dig themselves further into the sand.

Sometimes rocking the vehicle backwards and forwards will build up momentum to break you free. This can be done by the driver intermittently applying the clutch and/or by getting helpers who can push and pull the vehicle at the same frequency. Once the vehicle is moving, the golden rule of sand driving is to keep up the momentum: if you pause, you will sink and stop.

Grass seeds in the Kalahari After the rains, the Kalahari's tracks are often knee-high in seeding grass. As your vehicle drives through, stems and especially seeds can build up in front of and inside the radiator, and get trapped in crevices underneath the chassis. This is a major problem in the less-visited areas of the

Kalahari. It's at its worst from March to June, after the rains, and in the areas of the Great Salt Pans, the CKGR, and the tracks around Tsodilo and the Aha Hills. The main tracks around Chobe and Moremi are used relatively frequently, and so have less dangerous.

This causes a real danger of overheating (see below) and fire. Firstly, the build-up of seeds and stems over the radiator insulates it. Thus, if you aren't watching your gauges, the engine's temperature can rocket. It will swiftly seize up and catch fire. Secondly, the grass build-up itself, if allowed to become too big, can catch fire due to its contact with the hot exhaust system underneath the vehicle.

There are several strategies to minimise these dangers; best apply them all. Firstly, before you set out, buy a few square metres of the tightly woven window-meshing gauze material used in the windows of safari tents. Fix one large panel of this on the vehicle's bull-bars, well in front of the radiator grill. Fix another much closer to it, but still outside of the engine compartment. Hopefully this will reduce vastly the number of seeds reaching your radiator.

Secondly, watch your vehicle's engine-temperature gauge like a hawk when you're travelling through areas of grassland.

Thirdly, stop every 10km or so (yes, really, that often) and check the radiator and the undercarriage for pockets of stems and seeds. Pay special attention to the hot areas of the exhaust pipe; you should not allow a build-up of flammable material there. Use a stick or piece of wire to clean these seeds and stems out before you set off again.

Overheating If the engine has overheated then the only option is to stop and turn it off. Stop, have a drink under a tree, and let it cool. Don't open the radiator cap to refill it until the radiator is no longer hot to the touch. Even then, keep the engine running and the water circulating while you refill the radiator – otherwise you run the risk of cracking the hot metal by suddenly cooling it. Flicking droplets of water on to the outside of a running engine will cool it.

When driving away, switch off any air-con (as it puts more strain on the engine). Open your windows and turn your heater and fan full on. This may not seem pleasant in the midday heat – but it'll help to cool the engine. Keep watching that engine-temperature gauge.

Driving in mud This is difficult, though the theory is the same as for sand: keep going and don't stop. That said, even the most experienced drivers get stuck. A few areas of Botswana (the road from Rakops to the CKGR's main gate is legendary in this respect) have very fine soil known as 'black-cotton' soil, which becomes impassable when wet.

Push-starting when stuck If you are unlucky enough to need to push-start your vehicle whilst it is stuck in sand or mud, there is a remedy. Raise up the drive wheels, and take off one of the tyres. You should have a hi-lift jack with you, and know how to use it.

Then wrap a length of rope around the hub and treat it like a spinning top: one person (or more) pulls the rope to make the axle spin, whilst the driver lifts the clutch, turns the ignition on, and engages a low gear to turn the engine over. This is a very difficult equivalent of a push start, but it may be your only option.

Rocky terrain There's not much of this in northern Botswana – but you will find some in the southeast. Have your tyre pressure higher than normal and move very slowly. If necessary, passengers should get out and guide you along the track to avoid scraping the undercarriage on the ground. This can be a very slow business.

Crossing rivers and other stretches of water The first thing to do is to stop and check the river. You must assess its depth, the type of riverbed and its current flow; and determine the best route to drive across it. This is best done by wading across the river (though in an area frequented by hippos and crocodiles this is not advisable). Beware of water that's too deep for your vehicle, or the very real possibility of being swept away by a fast current and a slippery riverbed.

If everything is OK then select your lowest gear ratio and drive through the water at a slow but steady rate. Your vehicle's air intake must be above the level of the water to avoid your engine filling with water. It's not worth taking risks, so remember that a flooded river may subside to safer levels by the next morning.

Driving near big game The only animals which are likely to pose a threat to vehicles are elephants – and generally only elephants which are familiar with vehicles. So, treat them with the greatest respect and don't 'push' them by trying to move ever closer. Letting them approach you is much safer, and they will feel far less threatened and more relaxed. Then, if the animals are calm, you can safely turn the engine off, sit quietly, and watch as they pass you by.

If you are unlucky, or foolish, enough to unexpectedly drive into the middle of a herd, then don't panic. Keep your movements, and those of the vehicle, slow and measured. Back off steadily. Don't be panicked, or overly intimidated, by a mock charge – this is just their way of frightening you away. For detailed comments, see the boxes on *Driving near elephants* in *Chapter 10*.

BUSH CAMPING

Many 'boy scout' type manuals have been written on survival in the bush, usually by military veterans. If you are stranded with a convenient multi-purpose knife, then these useful tomes will describe how you can build a shelter from branches, catch passing animals for food, and signal to the inevitable rescue planes which are combing the globe looking for you – whilst avoiding the attentions of hostile forces.

In Africa, bush camping is usually less about survival than comfort. You're likely to have much more than the knife: probably at least a bulging backpack, if not a loaded 4x4. Thus the challenge is not to camp and survive, it is to camp and be as comfortable as possible. With practice you'll learn how, but a few hints might be useful for the less experienced:

WHERE YOU CAN CAMP In national parks, there are strictly designated campsites that you should use, as directed by the local game scouts. These must be pre-booked or you are unlikely to be allowed entrance.

Outside of the parks, you should ask the local landowner, or village head, if they are happy for you to camp on their property. If you explain patiently and politely what you want, then you are unlikely to meet anything but hospitality in most areas of rural Botswana.

CHOOSING A SITE Only experience will teach you how to choose a good site for pitching a tent, but a few general points, applicable to any wild areas of Africa, may help you avoid problems:

- Avoid camping on what looks like a path through the bush, however indistinct. It may be a well-used game trail.
- Beware of camping in dry riverbeds: dangerous flash floods can arrive with little or no warning.

- In marshy areas camp on higher ground to avoid cold, damp mists in the morning and evening.
- Camp a reasonable distance from water: near enough to walk to it, but far enough to avoid animals which arrive to drink.
- If a lightning storm is likely, make sure that your tent is not the highest thing around.
- Finally, choose a site which is as flat as possible – you will find sleeping much easier.

CAMPFIRES Campfires can create a great atmosphere and warm you on a cold evening, but they can also be damaging to the environment and leave unsightly piles of ash and blackened stones. Deforestation is a major concern in much of the developing world, including parts of Botswana, so if you do light a fire then use wood as the locals do: sparingly. If you have a vehicle, consider buying firewood in advance from people who sell it at the roadside – or collect it in areas where there's more wood around.

If you collect it yourself, then take only dead wood, nothing living. Never just pick up a log: always roll it over first, checking carefully for snakes or scorpions.

Experienced campers build small, highly efficient fires by using a few large stones to absorb, contain and reflect the heat, and gradually feeding just a few thick logs into the centre to burn. Cooking pots can be balanced on the stones, or the point where the logs meet and burn. Others will use a small trench, lined with rocks, to similar effect. Either technique takes practice, but is worth perfecting. Whichever you do, bury the ashes, take any rubbish with you when you leave, and make the site look as if you had never been there. (See *Appendix 3, Further Information* for details of Christina Dodwell's excellent *An Explorer's Handbook: Travel, Survival and Bush Cookery*.)

Don't expect an unattended fire to frighten away wild animals – that works in Hollywood, but not in Africa. A campfire may help your feelings of insecurity, but lion and hyena will disregard it with stupefying nonchalance.

Finally, do be hospitable to any locals who appear – despite your efforts to seek permission for your camp, you may effectively be staying in their back gardens.

USING A TENT Whether to use a tent or to sleep in the open is a personal choice, dependent upon where you are. In an area where there are predators around (specifically lion and hyena) then you must use a tent – and sleep completely inside it, as a protruding leg may seem like a tasty take-away to a hungry hyena. This is especially true at organised campsites, where the local animals are so used to humans that they have lost much of their inherent fear of man.

Outside game areas, you will usually be fine sleeping in the open, or preferably under a mosquito net, with just the stars of the African sky above you. On the practical side, sleeping under a tree will reduce the morning dew that settles on your sleeping bag. If your vehicle has a large, flat roof then sleeping on this will provide you with peace of mind, and a star-filled outlook. Hiring a vehicle with a built-in roof-tent is a perfect solution for many, though it can take time to pack when wanting to rush off on an early-morning game drive.

CAMPING EQUIPMENT FOR BACKPACKERS If you are taking an organised safari, you will not need any camping equipment at all. If you're hiring a 4x4, then it's best to hire one here with all the kit. However, for those backpacking, there is very little lightweight kit available in Botswana. Most of the equipment is designed to be sturdy, long-lasting and carried around in vehicles. So buy any lightweight kit before you leave home, as it will save you a lot of time and trouble once you arrive. Here are a few comments on various essentials:

Tent During the rains a good tent is essential in order to stay dry. Even during the dry season one is useful if there are lion or hyena around. If backpacking, invest in a high-quality, lightweight tent. Mosquito-netting ventilation panels, allowing a good flow of air, are essential. (Just a corner of mesh at the top of the tent is *not* enough for comfort.) Don't go for a tent that's small; it may feel cosy at home, but will be hot and claustrophobic in the heat.

I have been using the same 'Spacepacker' tent (manufactured by Robert Saunders Ltd, Five Oaks Lane, Chigwell, Essex IG7 4QP, UK) for almost ten years. It's a dome tent with fine mesh doors on either side which allow a through draught, making all the difference when temperatures are high. The alternative to a good tent is a mosquito net, which is fine unless it is raining or you are in a big game area.

Sleeping bag A lightweight, three-season sleeping bag is ideal for Botswana most of the time, though probably not quite warm enough for the very coldest nights in the Kalahari. Down is preferable to synthetic fillings for most of the year, as it packs smaller, is lighter, and feels more luxurious to sleep in. That said, when down gets wet it loses its efficiency, so bring a good synthetic bag if you are likely to encounter much rain.

Ground mat A ground mat of some sort is essential. It keeps you warm and comfortable, and it protects the tent's ground sheet from rough or stony ground (do put it underneath the tent!). Closed-cell foam mats are widely available outside Botswana, so buy one before you arrive. The better mats cost double or treble the cheaper ones, but are stronger, thicker and warmer – well worth the investment.

Therm-a-Rests, the combination air-mattress and foam mat, are strong, durable and also worth the investment – but take a puncture repair kit with you just in case of problems.

Do watch carefully where you site your tent, and try to make camp before dark. My trusty Therm-a-Rests deflated badly one night in the Kalahari, sleeping near the Mamuno–Buitepos border. Breaking camp the next morning, I lifted the mat to find a large scorpion in its burrow immediately beneath the mat.

Sheet sleeping bag Thin, pure cotton sheet sleeping bags (eg: YHA design) are small, light and very useful. They are easily washed and so are normally used like a sheet, inside a sleeping bag, to keep it clean. They can, of course, be used on their own when your main sleeping bag is too hot.

Stove 'Trangia'-type stoves, which burn methylated spirits, are simple to use, light, and cheap to run. They come complete with a set of light aluminium pans and a very useful all-purpose handle. Often you'll be able to cook on a fire with the pans, but it's nice to have the option of making a brew in a few minutes while you set up camp. Methylated spirits are cheap and widely available, even in the rural areas, but bring a tough (purpose made) fuel container with you as the bottles in which it is sold will soon crack and spill all over your belongings.

Petrol- and kerosene-burning stoves are undoubtedly efficient on fuel and powerful – but invariably temperamental and messy. Gas stoves use pressurised canisters, which are not allowed on aircraft.

Torch (flashlight) This should be on every visitor's packing list – whether you're staying in upmarket camps or backpacking. Find one that's small and tough, and preferably water- and dust-proof. Head-mounted torches leave your hands free (useful when cooking or mending the car) but some people find them bulky and uncomfortable to wear. The strong and super-bright torches (such as Maglites) are excellent. Bring several spare bulbs with you; they are expensive in Maun.

Those with vehicles will find a strong spotlight, powered by the car's battery (perhaps through the socket for the cigarette lighter), is invaluable for impromptu lighting.

Water containers For everyday use, a small two-litre water bottle is invaluable, however you are travelling. If you're thinking of camping, you should also consider a strong, collapsible water-bag – perhaps 5–10 litres in size – which will reduce the number of trips that you need to make from your camp to the water source (ten litres of water weighs 10kg).

Drivers will want to be self-sufficient for water when venturing into the bush, and so carry several large, sturdy containers of water.

See *Chapter 4, Planning and Preparation*, pages 93–4, for a memory-jogging list of other useful items to pack.

ANIMAL DANGERS FOR CAMPERS Camping in Africa is really very safe, though you may not think so from reading this. If you have a major problem whilst camping, it will probably be because you did something stupid, or because you forgot to take a few simple precautions. Here are a few general basics, applicable to anywhere in Africa and not just Botswana.

Large animals Big game will not bother you if you are in a tent – provided that you do not attract its attention, or panic it. Elephants will gently tip-toe through your guy ropes whilst you sleep, without even nudging your tent. However, if you wake up and make a noise, startling them, they are far more likely to panic and step on your tent. Similarly, scavengers will quietly wander round, smelling your evening meal in the air, without any intention of harming you.

- Remember to use the toilet before going to bed, and avoid getting up in the night if possible.
- Scrupulously clean everything used for food that might smell good to scavengers. Put these utensils in a vehicle if possible, suspend them from a tree, or pack them away in a rucksack inside the tent.
- Do not keep any smelly foodstuffs, like meat or citrus fruit, in your tent. Their smells may attract unwanted attention.
- Do not leave anything outside that could be picked up – like bags, pots, pans, etc. Hyenas, amongst others, will take anything. (They have been known to crunch a camera's lens, and eat it.)
- If you are likely to wake in the night, then leave the tent's zips a few centimetres open at the top, enabling you to take a quiet peek outside.

Creepy crawlies As you set up camp, clear stones or logs out of your way with great caution: they make great hiding places for snakes and scorpions. Long moist grass is ideal territory for snakes, and dry, dusty, rocky places are classic sites for scorpions.

If you are sleeping in the open, it is not unknown to wake and find a snake lying next to you in the morning. Don't panic, your warmth has just attracted it to you. You will not be bitten if you gently edge away without making any sudden movements. (This is one good argument for using at least a mosquito net!)

Before you put on your shoes, shake them out. Similarly, check the back of your backpack before you slip it on. Just a curious spider, in either, could inflict a painful bite.

Walking in the African bush is a totally different sensation to driving through it. You may start off a little unready – perhaps even sleepy for an early morning walk – but swiftly your mind will wake. There are no noises except the wildlife, and you. So every noise that isn't caused by you must be an animal; or a bird; or an insect. Every smell and every rustle has a story to tell, if you can understand it.

With time, patience, and a good guide you can learn to smell the presence of elephants, and hear when a predator alarms impala. You can use ox-peckers to lead you to buffalo, or vultures to help you locate a kill. Tracks will record the passage of animals in the sand, telling what passed by, how long ago, and in which direction.

Eventually your gaze becomes alert to the slightest movement; your ears aware of every sound. This is safari at its best: a live, sharp, spine-tingling experience that's hard to beat and very addictive. Be careful: watching game from a vehicle will never be the same again for you.

WALKING TRAILS AND SAFARIS One of Africa's biggest attractions is its walking safaris – which attract people back year after year. However, because of the danger involved, the calibre and experience of guides when walking is far more important than when driving. Anyone with a little experience can drive you around fairly safely in a large metal vehicle, but when you're faced with a charging elephant you need to be standing behind a real expert to have much chance of survival.

Walking guides I am not confident that Botswana has progressed well towards the implementation of rigorous minimum standards for guides who lead walking safaris. Zimbabwe has for many years led the field, with a really tough training course leading to the exalted status of 'pro guide' – in many ways this is Africa's 'gold standard' of guiding.

Zambia has adopted an alternative, but also very safe, system requiring an armed scout and an experienced walking guide to accompany every walk. The scout controls the problem animal, the guide controls the group of people. It's rarely necessary to even fire a warning shot, and injuries are exceedingly rare.

However, Botswana, like South Africa, has minimum standards which I think are too low for walking guides. Thus, in my opinion, the term 'qualified guide' in Botswana doesn't mean that I should necessarily feel safe going walking with them. Thus it's mostly up to the individual safari operation to make sure its guides are experienced.

One or two operations (the Selinda Reserve, and the Footsteps operation near Shinde, both spring to mind) really concentrate on walking safaris. These take their walking very seriously, employ top walking guides, and put safety at the top of their agenda. I'm confident to go walking with such operations.

The rest are a mixed bag; some use good guides, others I've been out with I felt were actually dangerous. One good rule of thumb is the presence of a rifle. If your guide *doesn't* carry one, then I certainly wouldn't walk with them to anywhere where we were likely to see any dangerous game. (The converse doesn't apply though; carrying a rifle does not make an inexperienced guide safe.)

Often you'll see adverting for camps in the Okavango with comments along the lines that your guide is '. . . a man of the swamps, completely at one with his environment'. This is doubtless true, but doesn't imply that this same guide automatically has the foresight, command and communication skills to look after frightened foreigners whilst avoiding game in a dangerous situation. Knowing how to save himself is different from controlling a small group, and saving *them* from a nasty end.

Thus my advice is that if you want to do much walking in Botswana, go to one of the places that really concentrate on walking safaris. The rest of the time, stick to canoes, boats and driving. Only go walking with guides who are armed, know how to use their guns, and you have discussed the issues with and satisfied yourself that they have sufficient experience for you to be safe.

Etiquette for walking safaris If you plan to walk then avoid wearing any bright, unnatural colours, especially white. Dark, muted shades are best; greens, browns and khaki are ideal. Dark blue tends to attract tsetse flies, so best to avoid that if you can. Hats are essential, as is sun-block. Even a short walk will last for two hours, and there's no vehicle to which you can retreat if you get too hot.

Binoculars should be immediately accessible – one pair per person – ideally in dust-proof cases strapped to your belt. Cameras too, if you decide to bring any, as they are of little use buried at the bottom of a camera bag. Heavy tripods or long lenses are a nightmare to lug around, so leave them behind if you can (and accept, philosophically, that you may miss shots).

Walkers see the most when walking in silent single file. This doesn't mean that you can't stop to whisper a question to the guide; just that idle chatter will reduce your powers of observation, and make you even more visible to the animals (who will usually flee when they sense you).

With regard to safety, your guide will always brief you in detail before you set off. S/he will outline possible dangers, and what to do in the unlikely event of them materialising. Listen carefully: this is vital.

Face-to-face animal encounters Whether you are on an organised walking safari, on your own hike, or just walking from the car to your tent in the bush, it is not unlikely that you will come across some of Africa's larger animals at close quarters. Invariably, the danger is much less than you imagine, and a few basic guidelines will enable you to cope effectively with most situations.

Firstly, don't panic. Console yourself with the fact that animals are not normally interested in people. You are not their normal food, or their predator. If you do not annoy or threaten them, you will be left alone. No matter how frightened you are, you'll probably run slower than whatever is worrying you. So don't try to run; think your way out of the tight spot.

If you are walking to look for animals, then remember that this is their environment, not yours. Animals have been designed for the bush, and their senses are far better attuned to it than yours. To be on less unequal terms, remain alert and try to spot them from a distance. This gives you the option of approaching carefully, or staying well clear.

Animals, like people, are all different. So whilst we can generalise here and say how the 'average' animal will behave, the one that's glaring at you over a small bush may have had a really bad day, and be feeling much grumpier than normal.

Finally, the advice of a good guide is far more valuable than the simplistic comments noted here – though a few general comments on some potentially dangerous situations might be of use:

Buffalo This is probably the continent's most dangerous animal to hikers, but there is a difference between the old males, often encountered on their own or in small groups, and large breeding herds.

The former are easily surprised. If they hear or smell something amiss, they will charge without provocation – motivated by a fear that something is sneaking up on them. Buffalo have an excellent sense of smell, but fortunately they are short-sighted. Avoid a charge by quickly climbing the nearest tree, or by side-stepping at the last minute. If adopting the latter, more risky, technique then stand motionless until the last possible moment, as the buffalo may well miss you anyhow.

The large breeding herds can be treated in a totally different manner. If you approach them in the open, they will often flee. Sometimes though, in areas often used for walking safaris, they will stand and watch, moving aside to allow you to pass through the middle of the herd.

Neither encounter is for the faint-hearted or inexperienced, so steer clear of these dangerous animals wherever possible.

Black rhino There are no black rhino left in Botswana, though there are plans to reintroduce them to the heart of Moremi. If you are both exceptionally lucky enough to find one, and then unlucky enough to be charged by it, use the same tactics as you would for a buffalo: tree climbing or dodging at the last second. (It is amazing how even the least athletic walker will swiftly scale the nearest tree when faced with a charging rhino.)

Elephant Normally elephants are only a problem if you disturb a mother with a calf, or approach a male in *musth* (state of arousal), so keep well away from these. Lone bulls can usually be approached quite closely when feeding. If you get too close to any elephant it will scare you off with a 'mock charge': head up, perhaps shaking – ears flapping – and trumpeting. Lots of sound and fury. This is intended to be frightening, and it is. But it is just a warning and no cause for panic. You should just freeze to assess the elephant's intentions. When it's stopped making a fuss, back off slowly. Don't run. There is no easy way to avoid the charge of an angry elephant, so take a hint from this warning and move away.

When an elephant really means business, it will put its ears back, lower its head, and charge directly at you. This is known as a 'full charge' and they don't stop. It is one of the most dangerous situations in Africa. Then you probably have to run – but elephants are much faster than you, so think while you run. Aim to get behind an anthill, up a tall tree, or out of the way somehow.

See also the boxes on *Driving near elephants*, in *Chapter 10*, for more details of this behaviour with reference to vehicles.

Lion Tracking lion can be one of the most exhilarating parts of a walking safari. Sadly, they will normally flee before you even get close to them. However, it can be a problem if you come across a large pride unexpectedly. Lion are well camouflaged; it is easy to find yourself next to one before you realise it. If you had been listening, you would probably have heard a warning growl about 20m ago. Now it is too late.

The best plan is to stop, and back off slowly, but confidently. If you are in a small group, then stick together. Never run from a big cat. First, they are always faster than you are. Secondly, running will just convince them that you are frightened prey, and worth chasing. As a last resort, if they seem too inquisitive and follow as you back off, then stop. Call their bluff. Pretend that you are not afraid and make loud, deep, confident noises: shout at them, bang something. But do not run.

John Coppinger, one of Africa's most experienced guides, adds that every single compromising experience that he has had with lion on foot has been either with a female with cubs, or with a mating pair, when the males can get very aggressive. You have been warned.

Leopard are very seldom seen, and would normally flee from the most timid of lone hikers. However, if injured, or surprised, then they are very powerful, dangerous cats. Conventional wisdom is scarce, but never stare straight into the leopard's eyes, or it will regard this as a threat display. (The same is said, by some, to be true with lion.) Better to look away slightly, at a nearby bush, or even at its tail. Then back off slowly, facing the direction of the cat and showing as little terror as you can. As with lion – loud, deep, confident noises are a last line of defence. Never run from a leopard.

Hippo are fabled to account for more deaths in Africa than any other animal (ignoring the mosquito). Having been attacked and capsized by a hippo whilst in a mokoro, I finds this very easy to believe. Visitors are most likely to encounter hippo in the water, when in a boat or mokoro. (See the other section on hippo, below.)

However, as hippos spend half their time grazing on land, they will sometimes be encountered out of the water. Away from the water, out of their comforting lagoons, hippos are even more dangerous. If they see you, they will flee towards the water – so the golden rule is never to get between a hippo and its escape route to deep water. Given that a hippo will outrun you on land, standing motionless is probably your best line of defence.

Snakes are really not the great danger that people imagine. Most flee when they feel the vibrations of footsteps; only a few will stay still. The puff adder is probably responsible for more cases of snake bite than any other venomous snake in Boswana because, when approached, it will simply puff itself up and hiss as a warning, rather than slither away. This makes it essential to always watch where you place your feet when walking in the bush.

Similarly, there are a couple of arboreal (tree-dwelling) species which may be taken by surprise if you carelessly grab vegetation as you walk. So don't.

Spitting cobras are also encountered occasionally, which will aim for your eyes and spit with accuracy. If one of these rears up in front of you, then turn away and avert your eyes. If the spittle reaches your eyes, you must wash them out immediately and thoroughly with whatever liquid comes to hand: water, milk or even urine if that's the only liquid that can be quickly produced.

BOATING

Trips on motorboats and mekoro are very much an integral part of a safari trip to northern Botswana – they're both very different, and both a lot of fun. Almost no operators use the paddle-yourself Canadian-style canoes that are popular elsewhere in Africa (Linyanti Tented Camp is perhaps the exception which proves this rule).

BY MOKORO In *Lake Ngami and the River Okavango* (see *Appendix 3, Further Information*), the explorer Charles John Andersson describes a mokoro used by him on Lake Ngami in the early 1850s:

> The canoe in which I embarked (and they are all somewhat similarly constructed) was but a miserable craft. It consisted of the trunk of a tree, about 20 feet long, pointed at both ends, and hollowed out by means of fire and a small hatchet. The natives are not at all particular as to the shape of the canoe. The after part of some that have come to my notice, would form an angle of near forty-five degrees with their stem! Nevertheless, they were propelled through the water by the Bayeye (my boatmen were of that nation) with considerable speed and skill.
>
> The 'appointments' of the canoe, consist of a paddle and a pole, ten to twelve feet in length. The paddle-man sits well in the stern, and attends mostly to the steering;

whilst his comrade, posted at the head of the canoe, sends her along, by means of the pole, with great force and skill.

The natives, however, rarely venture any distance from the shore in their frail Skiffs.

Local inhabitants of the Okavango still use mekoro like this, but for visitors it's more usual to have simply a single poler standing up at the stern and propelling the craft with a long pole. It's very like the punting done at some universities in Britain; a gentle form of locomotion best suited to shallow waters.

Only certain trees are suitable for making mekoro; they must usually be old, straight and strong. Jackalberries (*Diospyros mespiliformis*), sausage trees (*Kigelia africana*) and kiats (*Pterocarpus angolensis*) are favourites, whilst occasionally African mangosteens (*Garcenia livingstonei*) and rain trees (*Lonchocarpus capassa*) are also used. The wood used to make the poles to propel them is less crucial, though these are often made from silver-leaf terminalia trees (*Terminalia sericea*).

The last few decades have seen a mushrooming demand for mekoro, which began to deplete the older specimens of these species in some areas. Fortunately, fibreglass mekoro, that look very similar, are now being made. Most safari camps use these now. This is worth encouraging, so if you are given a wooden craft, check with your camp that when it's no longer useable, they intend to replace it with a fibreglass version. The Delta can't afford to lose more of its oldest trees!

BY MOTORBOAT motorboats are used on the rivers, and in the deeper channels and lagoons of the Okavango. They can be a lot of fun although, used carelessly, their noise and (especially) their wake can do a lot of damage; so be sensitive to the dangers and don't encourage your guide to speed. You'll often see much more by going slowly anyhow.

Interesting variations on this theme include the stately, almost silent electric boat that's been introduced at Sandibe and the small, double-decker boat used at Kwara which affords views out over the top of the papyrus beds.

THE MAIN DANGERS It's tempting to become concerned about dangerous animals in Africa, but it's foolish to get paranoid. With common sense and a little knowledge, boat and mokoro trips are very safe – certainly no more dangerous than going on a game drive or walking safari. And if these worry you, maybe you shouldn't be heading out into the bush at all!

On motorboat trips, you'd have to try hard indeed to get into difficulties. Mekoro are also safe, though these craft are smaller and more vulnerable, so you should be aware of the dangers posed to you by hippos and crocodiles:

Hippo are strictly vegetarians, and will usually only attack a mokoro if they feel threatened. Your poler is usually standing up, so he has the best vantage-point for spotting potential dangers ahead. It's helpful if you're either silent, or making so much noise that every animal in the bush can hear you approaching!

During the day, hippopotami will usually congregate in deeper water. The odd ones in shallow water, where they feel less secure, will head for the deeper places as soon as they are aware of a nearby mokoro. Avoiding hippos then becomes a fairly simple case of steering around the deeper areas, and sticking to the shallows. This is where the poler's experience, knowing every waterway in the area, becomes valuable.

Really large and deep channels and waterways are seldom a problem, as the hippos can avoid you provided that you make enough noise so that they know you are around. Shallow floodplains are also fairly safe, as you'll see the hippo in advance, and avoid them.

Problems usually occur when mekoro use relatively small and narrow 'hippo trails' where hippos can submerge but can't get away. Then there's a danger of accidentally approaching too close. A mokoro inadvertently surprises a hippo, and/or cuts it off from its path of retreat to deeper water. Then the hippo feels cornered and threatened, and may even attack. Some camps now send mekoro out in small groups, with an armed guide in the lead mokoro – though others maintain that this isn't necessary.

An angry hippo could overturn a mokoro without a second thought, biting at it and/or its occupants. Once in this situation, there are no easy remedies. So avoid it in the first place.

Crocodiles may have sharp teeth and look prehistoric, but are of little danger to you . . . unless you are in the water. Then the more you struggle and the more waves you create, the more you will attract their unwelcome attentions. They sometimes become an issue when a mokoro is overturned by a hippo; you must get out of the water as soon as possible, either into another canoe or on to the bank.

When a crocodile attacks an animal, it will try to disable it, normally by getting a firm, biting grip, submerging, and performing a long, fast barrel-roll. This will disorient the prey, drown it, and probably twist off the limb that has been bitten. In this dire situation, your best line of defence is probably to stab the reptile in its eyes with anything sharp that you have. Alternatively, if you can lift up its tongue and let the water into its lungs whilst it is underwater, then a crocodile will start to drown and will release its prey.

I have had reliable reports of a man surviving an attack in the Zambezi recently when a crocodile grabbed his arm and started to spin backwards into deep water. The man wrapped his legs around the crocodile, to spin with it and avoid having his arm twisted off. As this happened, he tried to poke his thumb into its eyes, but with no effect. Finally he put his free arm into the crocodile's mouth, and opened up the beast's throat. This worked. The crocodile left him and he survived with only a damaged arm. Understandably, anecdotes about tried and tested methods of escape are rare.

MINIMUM IMPACT

When you visit, drive through, or camp in an area and have 'minimum impact' upon it, this means that that area is left in the same condition as – or better than – when you entered it. Whilst most visitors view minimum impact as being desirable, spend time to consider the ways in which we contribute to environmental degradation, and how these can be avoided. Most of these points apply to any areas of rural Africa.

DRIVING Use your vehicle responsibly. If there's a road, or a track, then don't go off it – the environment will suffer. Driving off-road can leave a multitude of tracks that detract from the 'wilderness' feeling for subsequent visitors. Equally, don't speed through towns or villages: remember the danger to local children, and the amount of dust you'll cause.

HYGIENE Use toilets if they are provided, even if they are basic long-drop loos with questionable cleanliness. If there are no toilets, then human excrement should always be buried well away from paths, or groundwater, and any tissue used should be burnt and then buried with it.

If you use rivers or lakes to wash, then soap yourself near the bank, using a pan for scooping water from the river – making sure that no soap finds its way back into the water. Use biodegradable soap. Sand makes an excellent pan-scrub, even if you have no water to spare.

RUBBISH Biodegradable rubbish can be burnt and buried with the campfire ashes. Don't leave it lying around: it will look very unsightly and spoil the place for those who come after you.

Bring along some plastic bags with which to remove the rest of your rubbish, and dump it at the next large town. Items that will not burn, like tin cans, are best cleaned and squashed for easy carrying. If there are bins, then use them, but also consider when they will next be emptied, and whether local animals will rummage through them first. For this reason, it's probably best not to use the bins at most national parks' campsites; better to carry out all your own rubbish to the nearest town.

HOST COMMUNITIES Whilst the rules for reducing impact on the environment have been understood and followed by responsible travellers for years, the effects of tourism on local people have only recently been considered. Many tourists believe it is their right, for example, to take intrusive photos of local people – and even become angry if the local people object. They refer to higher prices being charged to tourists as a rip-off, without considering the hand-to-mouth existence of those selling these products or services. They deplore child beggars, then hand out sweets or pens to local children with outstretched hands.

Our behaviour towards 'the locals' needs to be considered in terms of their culture, with the knowledge that we are the uninvited visitors. We visit to enjoy ourselves, but this should not be at the expense of local people. Read *Cultural guidelines*, pages 37–9, and aim to leave the local communities better off after your visit.

LOCAL PAYMENTS If you spend time with any of Botswana's more rural communities, perhaps camping in the bush or getting involved with one of the community-run projects, then take great care with any payments that you make.

Firstly, note that most people like to spend their earnings on what they choose. This means that trying to pay for services with beads, food, old clothes or anything else instead of money isn't appreciated. Ask yourself how you'd like to be paid, and you'll understand this point.

Secondly, find out the normal cost of what you are buying. For example, most community campsites will have a standard price for a pitch. Find out this price before you sleep there. It is then important that you pay about that amount for the pitch – not less, and not too much more.

As most people realise, if you try to pay less you'll get into trouble – as you would at home. However, many do not realise that if they generously pay a lot *more*, this can be equally damaging. Local rates of pay in rural areas can be very low, and a careless visitor can easily pay disproportionately large sums. Where this happens, local jobs can lose their value overnight. (Imagine working hard to become a game scout, only to learn that a tourist has given your friend the equivalent of your whole month's wages for just a few hours guiding. What incentive is there for you to carry on with your regular job?)

If you want to give more – for good service, a super guide, or just because you want to help – then either buy some locally made produce (at the going rate), or donate money to one of the organisations working to improve the lot of Botswana's most disadvantaged. See page 40 for ideas, but also consider asking around locally and you'll often find projects that need your support.

Many lodges and camps will assist with community projects, and be able to suggest a good use for donations. Increasingly they're becoming more involved in the welfare of the local communities near them, which is something in which you can encourage them.

7

Botswana Today

Tourists come to Botswana in relatively small numbers. Many pass through the airports and towns briefly, spending the vast majority of their time in the bush – trips for which they have already paid. They will probably find most of this chapter useless. However, if you're planning to venture into any of the towns, or are wondering how life really ticks in Botswana, then read on . . .

GETTING AROUND

BY AIR There are two ways to fly within Botswana: on scheduled airlines or using small charter flights. The national carrier, Air Botswana, operates the scheduled network. This is limited in scope, but generally very efficient and reliable.

Air Botswana links Maun directly with Kasane, Gaborone, Windhoek and Johannesburg. In addition, Kasane is linked to Victoria Falls and there is a new service to Johannesburg, which also stops in the Tuli Block area, in the east of the country.

The small charter flights operate out of the hub of Maun, with Kasane as a secondary focus, and ferry travellers around all the camps of northern Botswana like a fleet of taxis. They use six- to twelve-seater planes which criss-cross the region between a plethora of small bush runways. Flights are usually organised by the operator who arranges your camps as an integral part of your trip; there's no other way to reach most camps, and you'll never need to worry about arranging these flights for yourself.

Several people usually end up sharing these small flights, and the flight companies schedule the timings a few days beforehand. Expect them to take under about an hour, during which you may stop at one or two other airstrips before reaching your destination. See my comments under *From the air* in *Chapter 3, The Natural Environment*, pages 49–50, to help you understand a little about the patterns that you'll be able to see in the landscapes below.

BY RAIL There is a railway that links South Africa with Lobatse, Gaborone, Palapye, Francistown and Bulawayo (in Zimbabwe) – but that's the only railway in the country. It's reliable, but rarely used by travellers coming to northern Botswana.

BY BUS Botswana has a variety of local buses which link the main towns togather along the tarred roads. They're cheap, frequent and a good way to meet local people, although they can also be crowded, uncomfortable and noisy. In short, they are similar to any other local buses in Africa, and travel on them has both its joys and its frustrations.

There are two different kinds: the smaller minibuses, often VW combies, and the longer, larger 'normal' buses. Both will serve the same destinations, but the smaller ones go faster and stop less. Their larger relatives will take longer to fill up before they leave the bus station (because few buses ever leave before they are full), and then go slower and stop at more places. For the smaller, faster buses there is a premium of about 20% on top of the price.

DRIVING Driving in Botswana is on the left, based on the UK's model. The standard of driving is reasonably good. Most roads in the towns, and the major arteries connecting these, are tarred and are usually in superb condition. Speed limits are 80km/h outside towns, and 40km/h in the national parks – though you'd be hard pushed to get near this speed in most places. Variations on these limits are clearly signposted. Note that Botswana's police have radar equipment, and do actively set up radar traps, especially just outside the towns. It is compulsory to wear seatbelts, and this, too, is checked by the police.

At the time of research, the price of fuel in Maun was P4.21 per litre for diesel, and P4.25 for petrol.

Away from the main arteries, and throughout virtually all of the wild areas covered by this guide, the roads are simply tracks through the bush made by whatever vehicles have passed that way. They are almost never maintained, and usually require at least a high-clearance vehicle – although often a 4x4 is essential. During the wet season some of these tracks can be less forgiving, and become virtually impassable. Travelling on these bush tracks at any time of year is slow and time-consuming – but very much one of the joys of an adventurous trip to Botswana.

HITCHHIKING Hitchhiking is a practical way to get around the main towns – but very, very difficult as a means of getting around the national parks.

Hitching on the tarred roads has the great advantage of allowing you to talk one-to-one with a whole variety of people, from local businesspeople and expats to truck drivers and farmers. Sometimes you will be crammed in the back of a windy pick-up with a dozen people and as many animals. Occasionally you will be comfortably seated in the back of a plush Mercedes, satisfying the driver's curiosity as to why you were standing beside a road in Botswana at all. It can be a great way to get to know the country, through the eyes of its people, though it is not for the lazy or those pressed for time.

Waiting times can be long, even on the main routes, and getting a good lift can take many hours. If you are in a hurry then combining hitchhiking with taking the odd bus can be a quicker and more pragmatic way to travel.

The essentials for successful hitching in Botswana include a relatively neat, conservative set of clothes, without which you will be ignored by some of the more comfortable lifts available. A good ear for listening and a relaxed line in conversation are also assets, which spring naturally from taking an interest in the lives of the people that you meet. Finally, always carry a few litres of water and some food with you, both for standing beside the road and for lifts where you can't stop to eat.

Dangers of drunk driving Unfortunately, drinking and driving is relatively common in Botswana. It is more frequent in the afternoon/evening, and towards the end of the month when people are paid. Accepting a lift with someone who is drunk, or drinking and (simultaneously) driving, is foolish. Occasionally your driver will start drinking on the way, in which case you would be wise to start working out how to disembark politely.

An excuse for an exit, which I used on one occasion, was to claim that some close family member was killed whilst being driven by someone who had been drinking. Thus I had a real problem with the whole idea, and had even promised a surviving relative that I would never do the same . . . hence my overriding need to leave at the next reasonable town/village/stop. This gave me an opportunity to encourage the driver not to drink any more, and when that failed (which it did), it provided an excuse for me to disembark swiftly. Putting the blame on my own psychological problems avoided blaming the driver too much, which might have caused a difficult scene.

Safety of hitchhiking Not withstanding the occasional drunk driver, Botswana is generally a safe place to hitchhike for a robust male traveller, or a couple travelling together. However, although safer than in the UK, and considerably safer than in the USA, hitchhiking still cannot be recommended for single women, or even two women travelling together. This is not because of any known horror stories, but because women from outside of Botswana, and especially white women hitching, would evoke great curiosity amongst the local people, who might view their hitching as asking for trouble, whilst some would associate them with the 'promiscuous' behaviour of white women seen on imported films and TV programmes. The risk seems too high. Stick to buses.

ACCOMMODATION

Botswana's hotels, lodges and guesthouses have until recently been ungraded, but a nationwide programme of grading all accommodation was started during 2005.

HOTELS Hotels in Botswana's towns tend to be aimed at visiting businesspeople, in which case they're functional but boring, regardless of price level. That said, they're also generally clean and rarely unpleasant. Expect costs to be around (US$36–48/£20–27) per person sharing per night.

GUESTHOUSES In the last few years a few guesthouses have sprung up in Botswana's larger towns, including Maun, but these are still very limited, and often so suburban that they're only practical if you've got your own vehicle. Some also tend to be on the pricy side, and don't seem to be good value for money.

LODGES AND CAMPS Botswana's lodges and camps vary from palatial residences crafted by top designers to simple spots with a few small tents, and a table in the shade. Given that range, the vast majority have rooms which are at least as comfortable as a good hotel room.

When the words 'tented camp' are mentioned, forget your memories of cramped scout tents and think instead of canvas designer chic. En-suite flushing toilets, running hot and cold water and battery-powered lights are standard, while many have electric fans, and a few (eg: Orient-Express Safari camps) have air conditioning. Only the odd old stalwarts, like the delightfully simple walking trails camps at Selinda, still use traditional long-drop loos.

Note that expensive does not always mean luxurious. Some of the top camps are very simply constructed. As a quid pro quo, looking for basic, simple camps won't make your trip any cheaper. You're usually paying for virtually exclusive use of pristine wilderness areas, and will find little cost difference between a tiny bush-camp and the largest lodge. In fact, if anything there's increasingly a premium on space in the smaller camps. These need booking earlier as many find these friendlier than the larger ones.

FOOD AND DRINK

FOOD Talking of any one 'native cuisine' in Botswana is misleading, as what a person eats is dependent on where they live and what ethnic group they belong to.

In the Kalahari and Okavango there was relatively little agriculture until recently; there, gathering and fishing, supplemented by hunting, provided subsistence for the various groups.

In the kinder climes east of the Kalahari, where there is enough rain for crops, sorghum is probably the main crop. This is first pounded into meal before being mixed with boiling water or sour milk. It's then made into a paste *bogobe* – which is thin, perhaps with sugar like porridge, for breakfast, then eaten thicker, the consistency of mashed potatoes, for lunch and dinner. For these main meals it will normally be accompanied by some tasty relish, perhaps made of meat and tomatoes, or dried fish. Maize meal, or *papa* (often imported as it doesn't tolerate Botswana's dry climate that well), is now often used in place of this. (In Zimbabwe this same staple is known as *sadza*, in Zambia it's *nshima* and in South Africa *mealie-pap*.) You should taste this at some stage when visiting. Safari camps will often prepare it if requested, and it is always available in small restaurants in the towns.

Camps, hotels and lodges that cater for overseas visitors serve a very international fare, and the quality of food prepared in the most remote camps is usually amazingly high. When coming to Botswana on safari your biggest problem with food is likely to be the very real danger of putting on weight.

If you are driving yourself around and plan to cook, then get most of your supplies in Maun or Kasane. Both have large supermarkets which are well stocked – though Maun's Shoprite is by far the best.

DRINK
Alcohol Like most countries in the region, Botswana has two distinct beer types: clear and opaque. Most visitors and more affluent people in Botswana drink the **clear beers**, which are similar to European lagers and always served chilled. Castle and Lion are the lagers brewed here by South African Breweries' subsidiary. They are widely available and usually good. You'll also sometimes find the Zimbabwean Zambezi beer, and Windhoek Lager, from Namibia – which are similar and also excellent.

The less affluent residents will usually opt for some form of the **opaque beer** (sometimes called Chibuku, after the market-leading brand) – though as a visitor you'll have to really make an effort to seek this out. Most bars that tourists visit don't sell it. This is a commercial version of traditional beer, usually brewed from maize and/or sorghum. It's a sour, porridge-like brew; an acquired taste. Locals will sometimes buy a bucket of it, and then pass it around a circle of drinkers. It would be unusual for a visitor to drink this, so try some and amuse your companions.

Remember that this changes flavour as it ferments: you can often ask for 'fresh beer' or 'strong beer'. If you aren't sure about the bar's hygiene standards, stick to the pre-packaged brands of opaque beer like Chibuku.

Soft drinks Soft drinks are available everywhere, which is fortunate when the temperatures are high. Choices are often limited, though the ubiquitous Coca-Cola is usually there, along with southern African specialities like Grapetize. Diet drinks are available in the towns, but rarely seen in the small bottle stores which pepper the rural areas – which is no surprise for a country where the rural population are poor and need all the energy their food can give them.

Water Water in the main towns is usually purified, provided there are no shortages of chlorine, breakdowns or other mishaps. It's generally fine to drink.

Out in the bush, most of the camps and lodges use water from boreholes. These underground sources vary in quality, but are normally free from bugs and so perfectly safe to drink. Sometimes it is sweet, at other times the water is a little alkaline or salty. Ask the locals if it is suitable for an unacclimatised visitor to drink, then take their advice.

The water in the Okavango Delta is generally fine to drink. You'll be expected to do so during most budget mokoro trips, which is fine for most backpackers who are in Africa for long trips. There are relatively few people living in the communities in the Delta; contamination levels are very low. However, if you've a sensitive stomach, or are visiting for a short trip, then you'd be best to avoid it and stick to borehole water. (I'd recommend that you do not insist on bottled water as the costs/waste involved in transporting it to you are high, and borehole water is generally fine.)

WHAT TO BUY

CURIOS Botswana's best bargains are handicrafts, and you'll find a variety. Look especially for hand-woven baskets made from the fronds of the real fan palm (*Hyphaene petersiana*), and the many different handicrafts of the San, like jewellery made from ostrich eggshells.

There's usually a divide between the simpler outlets, perhaps direct from the producers, and the more stylish, well-located shops which often have the best pieces, but invariably charge the highest prices.

If you're starting or ending your trip in Livingstone, then don't miss the curio stalls near the border post to Victoria Falls. This is one of the region's best places for carvings (though expect to bargain hard here). Other places to include would be the various curio shops in Maun, for excellent baskets, and the small basket shop in Gumare. Ghanzi has a superb shop, Ghanzi Craft, for Bushman crafts – although it was closed for some time, it is likely that it will reopen.

There are plenty of shops at the more stylish end of the spectrum, especially in Maun, and many lodges have small shops selling curios. (Ask them if the staff or a local village makes these – and if they do, then buy some to support the initiative!)

SUPPLIES In the main towns, notably Maun, Kasane and Francistown, there are large supermarkets with extensive ranges of high-quality, mostly imported foods. Of these, the Shoprite store in Maun (part of a large southern African chain) is probably the best example in the area. Here you'll find most everyday foodstuffs that you'd want, and a lot more besides. If they have weaknesses compared with the supermarket back home, it's probably in the fresh food and vegetable section, where the logistics of transport can often make for a smaller selection than you might expect.

It's usually best to stock up with food at these main centres, as away from them the range will become sparser. Expect villages to have just a bottle stall, selling the most popular cool drinks (often this excludes 'diet' drinks), and a small shop selling staples like rice and (occasionally) bread, and perhaps a few tinned and packet foods. Don't expect anything refrigerated.

ORGANISING AND BOOKING

PUBLIC HOLIDAYS Botswana's public holidays are as follows:

1 January	New Year's Day
2 January	
March/April	Good Friday & Easter Monday
1 May	Labour Day
May	Ascension Day

7

1 July	Sir Seretse Khama Day
third Monday and	
Tuesday in July	President's Day
30 September	Independence Day
25 December	Christmas Day
26 December	Boxing Day

NATIONAL PARKS Until the late 1980s you could just arrive, pay your park fees, and visit any national park. Now things are different and the 'high-revenue, low-volume' policy (see page 64) has led to a constriction in the numbers of campsites available at each location: they are very limited. Sites must be pre-booked in Maun or Gaborone; once they're full, you'll be turned away.

This makes it *essential* to book as early as you can for a trip through the national parks – though they don't usually take bookings more than a year in advance. Hence booking 11–12 months before you plan to visit is usually ideal.

On the practical side, park opening hours are 06.00–18.30 from April to September, and 05.30–19.00 from October to March. No driving is permitted in the parks outside these hours, so it is imperative to allow plenty of time for your journey, and to be at the gates or campsite well before closing. Campers should leave sites before 11.00. The speed limit in all the national parks is 40km/h – though you'd be hard pressed to exceed this almost anywhere.

Where to book Bookings for the national parks may be made at one of two Parks and Reserves Reservations offices, which divide the country's parks in half. Both have extensive opening hours *(07.30–12.45 & 13.45–16.30 Mon–Sat & most public holidays; 07.30–12.00 Sun; closed Christmas Day)*. Bookings made at one of these offices may be paid in cash (pula, or possibly US dollars or UK sterling) or with a credit card, but (with just one exception) payment at the gates *must* be made in cash, in pula. At Sedudu Gate, near Kasane, it is possible to pay fees by credit card (Visa or MasterCard).

The northern parks For bookings to Chobe, Moremi, Nxai and Makgadikgadi: Parks and Reserves Reservations Office, PO Box 20364, Boseja, Maun; ✆ 6861 265; f 6861 264. On Kubu St, behind Maun's police station.

The southern parks For bookings to the Central Kalahari, Khutse and Botswana's side of the Kgalagadi Transfrontier Park: Parks and Reserves Reservations Office, Gaborone; ✆ 3180 774; f 3180 775; e dwnp@gov.bw. The Department of Wildlife and National Parks office in Gaborone's 'government enclave', at the opposite end of Queen's Rd.

Entry fees and permits Most organised trips will include park entry fees in their costs, but if you are travelling on your own then you must pay these directly. There are usually three sets of park fees: entry fees for the people, entry fees for your vehicle and camping fees. These depend on your nationality/immigration status, and where your vehicle is registered.

Usually camping fees are paid when the sites are booked in advance, through the office in Maun (or the one in Gaborone). Sites in the national parks are very, very limited and often booked out almost a year in advance – so it's only rarely possible to get any space by just turning up. Everybody books their trips in advance; it's the only way.

By far the best way here is to go into the office in Maun in person – or have someone do this for you. Then if what you ask for is full, you'll be able to look at the availability sheets and make an alternative plan. If you try to accomplish this by phone, fax or email then it can be a lot more difficult, and is often less successful. Currently the various fees are:

Park entry fees

per person per day	Bots citizen	Bots resident	Non-resident
Adult (18+)	P10	P30	P120
Child (age 8–17)	P5	P15	P60
Infant (7 & under)	free	free	free

Camping fees

per person per night	Bots citizen	Bots resident	Non-resident
Adult (18+)	P5	P20	P30
Child (age 8–17)	P2.50	P10	P15
Infant (7 & under)	free	free	free

Vehicle fees (per day)

Foreign-registered vehicle:	P50
Botswana-registered vehicle:	P10

To give you some idea of the total costs here, the following are based on a foreign-registered vehicle with two adult visitors coming to Moremi for seven days' camping. Their total costs for the parks would be:

Park entry fees	P1,680 = 2 x 7 x P120
Camping fees	P420 = 2 x 7 x P30
Vehicle entry fees	P350 = 7 x P50
Total costs	**P2,450** = US$408/£272

That's an average cost of P175 (US$29/£19) per person per day.

COMMUNICATIONS AND MEDIA

POST BotswanaPost, the government-owned postal service, is reliable, but often slow. They have post offices in all the larger towns, and a network of many agencies in some of the larger villages. You'll find a brief listing of these at www.botspost.co.bw and also details under 'Postal Services' in the Yellow Pages section at the back of the telephone directory. These include offices or agencies in Francistown, Ghanzi, Gumare, Gweta, Kasane, Maun, Nata, Nokaneng, Rakops, Sepopa and Seronga.

Currently letters are classified by size, with a 'standard' size being up to 120mm x 235mm x 20mm, and a 'large' one up to 229mm x 324mm x 20mm. Provided they weigh under 200g, postal rates are:

	Botswana	SADC	Europe	Elsewhere
in pula		*surface/air*	*surface/air*	*surface/air*
postcards/standard letters	0.55	0.90/1.95	0.90/3.90	0.90/4.70

SADC – the Southern Africa Development Community – is a regional grouping of states and includes Angola, the Democratic Republic of Congo (DRC), Lesotho, Malawi, Mauritius, Mozambique, Namibia, Seychelles, South Africa, Swaziland, Tanzania, Zambia and Zimbabwe.

There is a post restante service at all the major post offices.

TELEPHONE, FAX AND TELEX Botswana's telephone system is generally very good, and you can access some remarkably offbeat places by just dialling from overseas. There's often no need to redial repeatedly to get a line, as happens in so many countries in the region.

To dial into the country from abroad, the international access code for Botswana is 267. From inside Botswana, you dial 00 to get an international line, then the country's access code (eg: 44 for the UK, 1 for the USA), then omit the first 0 of the number you are calling.

Public phones Dotted around the main towns you'll find public phoneboxes, some of which take coins and others phonecards, available in P10 and P20 denominations from post offices, fuel stations and some shops. These incur the same call charges as a normal payphone. The cards have a number on the back, only revealed when you scratch it. With this you dial 1351 (a free call) from any phone, and follow the voice prompts to enter the card number and then the number you wish to call. The cost of this call is then deducted from the card's balance. You can use this repeatedly until your card's balance reaches zero.

Mobile phones Mobile phone coverage is excellent in Maun and Kasane, but very limited elsewhere. Local SIM cards can be purchased in both towns, cutting the cost of calls from a mobile significantly.

Fax and telex If you are trying to send a fax to, or within, Botswana then it's often wise to use a manual setting to dial the number. Then listen for a fax tone on the line yourself, and only when you finally hear one should you press the 'start' button on your machine to send the fax.

Telex machines are still used in some places, but are becoming less and less common. Where they do exist, they provide communication that you can instantly verify. You need not worry if your message has arrived, as the answer-back code will confirm that for you. You'll find a list of fax and telex numbers near the start of the telephone directory.

EMAIL AND THE INTERNET Like most places, Botswana is rapidly adopting email and you'll now find that most people are on email, and a lot of businesses have websites. That said, outside of the main towns, email is often limited to a radio-based service known as 'bushmail', which has a tiny bandwidth and so is only practical for simple text messages. (Never send attachments to any bushmail address!)

THE MEDIA With a small population, many in rural locations, the press here is equally small, and partly relies on the larger South African media companies. However, Botswana has several newspapers, radio and TV stations.

Independence issues Botswana's small media is generally fairly free and expresses its opinions, even when they disagree with government policy. Even media which are owned by the government are obliged by law to give basic coverage of opposition views as well as the official versions. That said, disagreements do occur on a fairly regular basis, and clearly the independent press here fights a continuing battle to remain independent.

In May 2001, all government offices were instructed to stop using the two independent weekly papers, the *Guardian* and the *Midweek Sun*, following their criticism of Vice President Ian Khama. Given that the government is the largest advertiser in these papers, this had significant commercial impact. Shortly after this, the papers' editors began proceedings against the government and, in late September, a High Court judge ruled that the advertising ban was unconstitutional as the authorities were deemed to be applying unfair financial pressure on the papers in order to curtail their right to freedom of expression.

Subsequently, the government has looked into bringing out a 'Mass Media Communications Bill' which would establish a 'press council', though critics have decried this as state censorship by another name – and it's not yet been passed through parliament.

Occasionally the press also comes into the firing line for sensationalism, which is claimed to be fuelling ethnic tensions, and once recently a High Court judge started proceedings against *Mmegi* for defamation.

In late April 2001, the head of news and current affairs at the official Botswana Television (BTV) station quit his job in protest about government interference in the station's editorial policy and programming. He alleged that officials had threatened him, and that the authorities had blocked the broadcast of a documentary on a South African woman who had been convicted of murder by a Botswana court and subsequently executed.

The press Botswana's most widely read newspapers are the *Botswana Guardian* and *Mmegi: The Reporter*; both are weekly. *Mmegi* has the largest circulation (about 27,000 copies) and comes out every Friday; it's a fairly weighty tome. Recently this has spawned a sister-publication, the *Mmegi Monitor*, which comes out on a Tuesday. Other papers include the *Botswana Gazette*, the *Midweek Sun* and the government's free weekday newspaper, the *Daily News*. For newspapers on the web, see page 496.

Radio Botswana has a couple of radio stations that broadcast around the main towns, but there's generally nothing but long-distance shortwave services away from these.

The state-run Radio Botswana has two stations, both mixing Setswana and English in their schedules, and often their programmes. The non-commercial Radio Botswana One (RB1) has no advertising and majors on news and current affairs, whilst the commercial station Radio Botswana Two (RB2) features mainly popular music from ballads, R&B, house, reggae, fusion and jazz to pop and disco. Within this you'll find the usual inane banter, as well as full news bulletins at 07.00, 13.00, 18.00 and 21.00 every weekday.

Alternative independent stations include Yarona FM (106.6MHz) and GabzFM (96.2MHz).

TV Botswana launched its first national television service on 31 July 2000. Based in new headquarters on the outskirts of Gaborone, this is part of the Department of Information and Broadcasting (which also runs Radio Botswana's two stations). This broadcasts for just a few hours in the evening, usually 17.00–21.00, and originally aimed to carry at least 60% local content.

Apparently in the months preceding the launch there was some doubt about it being on schedule, so a consultancy team from Britain's BBC was brought in. They observed that:

Ten days before the launch, the general manager and his colleagues laughed at the idea that the launch would take place on time. The government even cancelled plans for a lavish ceremony and speech by the president at the national stadium on launch day. So we booked the stadium and arranged a charity shield football match between the country's two best teams, which attracted a bigger television audience on July 31 than the abandoned show would have done.

This charity shield match has now become a regular fixture.

In Gaborone there is a private channel, Gaborone Television, which is owned by Gaborone Broadcasting Company (GBC) and funded by advertising. Throughout Botswana most people with televisions are connected to one of the large South African networks – like the MultiChoice satellite service. There is no cable TV.

OTHER PRACTICALITIES

ELECTRICITY The local voltage is 220V, delivered at 50Hz. Sockets usually fit plugs with three square pins, like the current design in the UK, though plugs with three large round pins, like those in South Africa, are also widely in use. Ideally bring adapters for both.

When staying in bush lodges and the more upmarket camps, you are relatively unlikely to have sockets in your room/tent. However, it's usually easy to arrange for items to be plugged in for you (eg: to charge the batteries in video cameras), as behind the scenes most camps run generators in order to power their kitchens and communications equipment.

ⒺDIPLOMATIC REPRESENTATION IN BOTSWANA There's often a list of Gaborone's diplomatic missions, including those in neighbouring countries when necessary, in the front of the telephone directory. Alternatively see the government website page: www.botswana-tourism.gov.bw/embassies/embassies.html. Many countries don't maintain a full embassy in Botswana, but have honorary consuls who can help their citizens in case of need. Their contacts can also be found at www.gov.bw. The following will be of most help to readers:

Angola (embassy) 5131 Kopanyo Hse, Nelson Mandela Rd, P Bag BR 11, Gaborone; ℡ 3900 204 or 3905 453; f 3975 089 or 3181 876

Austria (hon consul) Doreen Khama Attorney, PO Box 335, Gaborone; ℡ 3952 638; f 3953 876

Belgium (hon consul) Mr M C Tibone, PO Box 821, Gaborone; ℡ 3957 438; f 3957 476

Canada (consulate) PO Box 882, Gaborone; ℡ 3904 411

Denmark (consulate) Plot 10227, Mopororo Rd, Gaborone; ℡ 3953 505; f 3953 473; e rohlig@info.bw

Finland (hon consul) Mr S A Mphuchane, Trade World, PO Box 1904, Gaborone; ℡ 3901 500; f 3901 966

France (embassy) 761 Robinson Rd, PO Box 1424, Gaborone; ℡ 3973 863; f 3973 173

Germany (embassy) 3rd Floor Professional Hse, Segoditshane Way, Broadhurst, PO Box 315, Gaborone

Ghana (hon consul) Mrs Helfer, PO Box 906, Gaborone

India (high commission) 5375 President's Drive, P Bag 249, Gaborone; ℡ 3972 676; f 3974 636

Ireland (hon consul) Mr J M Walking, 1st Floor Standard House, P Bag 00347, Gaborone; ℡ 3903 333; f 3903 400

Israel (hon consul) Mr Richard Lyons, PO Box 160, Gaborone.

Italy (hon consul) Mr G R Grach, 4th Floor Tirelo House, PO Box 451, Gaborone; ℡ 3952 882; f 3975 045

Kenya (high commission) 5373 President's Drive, P Bag BO 297, Gaborone; ℡ 3951 408; f 3951 409

Namibia (high commission) PO Box 987, Gaborone; ℡ 3902 181; f 3902 248

Netherlands (hon consul) Mr P L Steenkamp/Mrs Vink (asst.), 2535 Nyerere Drive, PO Box 457, Gaborone; ℡ 3902 194; f 3951 200

Nigeria (high commission) PO Box 274, The Mall, Gaborone; ☏ 3913 561; f 3913 738

Norway (consulate) Plot No 3284, Bontleng Close, Extension 12, P Bag 242, Gaborone; ☏ 3908 648/9; f 3908 648

Russia (embassy) Plot 4711, Tawana Close, Gaborone; ☏ 3953 389; f 3952 930; e embrus@info.bw

South Africa (high commission) P Bag 00402, Gaborone; ☏ 3904 800/1/2/3; f 3905 502

Spain (hon consul) Mr Guido Renato Giachetti, Plot No. 5624, Real Estate Office Park, Lejara Rd, Broadhurst Industrial, Gaborone; ☏ 3912 641; f 3973 441

Sweden (embassy) 4th Floor Development Hse, The Mall, P Bag 0017, Gaborone; ☏ 3953 912; f 3953 942; e ambassaden.gaborone@foreign.ministry.se

UK (high commission) P Bag 0023, Gaborone; ☏ 3952 841; f 3956 105

USA (embassy) PO Box 90, Gaborone; ☏ 3953 982; f 3956 947

Zambia (high commission) PO Box 362, Gaborone; ☏ 3951 951; f 3953 952

Zimbabwe (high commission) Plot 8850, PO Box 1232, Gaborone

INTERNATIONAL ORGANISATIONS IN BOTSWANA
Contact details for a few of the larger international organisations who have offices in Botswana include:

European Commission Delegation Plot 68, North Ring Rd, Gaborone; ☏ 3941 155; f 3913 626; e eudelbwa@info.bw

Southern African Development Community (SADC) P Bag 0095, Gaborone; ☏ 3951 863; f 3972 848

United Nations Children's Fund PO Box 20678, Gaborone; ☏ 3952 752 or 3951 909; f 3951 233

United Nations Development Programme PO Box 54, Gaborone; ☏ 3952 121; f 3956 093

World Health Organisation Rizka House, 1st Floor, PO Box 1355, Gaborone; ☏ 3971 505/6; f 3959 483

World Conservation Plot 2403, P Bag 003000, Gaborone; f 3971 584; e iucn@iucnbot.bw

IMPORTS AND EXPORTS
There is no problem in exporting normal curios, but you will need an official export permit from the Department of National Parks to take out any game trophies. Visitors are urged to support both the letter and the spirit of the CITES bans on endangered species. In any case, without such permits you will probably have big problems when you try to import items back into your home country.

MAPS
The best maps of northern Botswana for most visitors are the Shell series, and the Contimap – see the section on *Finding the right map*, page 94, for more details.

However, if you want more detailed, Ordnance Survey-type maps, then by far the best plan is to go directly to the offices of the Department for Surveys and Mapping, in either Maun (see page 149) or Gaborone (*P Bag 37, Gaborone;* ☏ *3953 251*).

Each of these two offices has roughly the same variety of excellent maps on offer, although some are always out of print. A particular favourite is the 1:350,000 map of the Okavango Delta that covers the whole of the Okavango area in detail – although don't expect its safari camps to be up to date.

7

Part Two

THE GUIDE

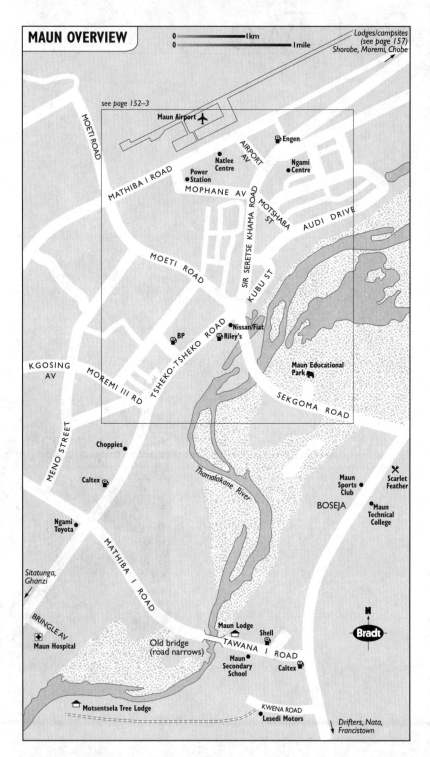

MAUN OVERVIEW

0 _____ 1km
0 _____ 1mile

see page 152–3

Lodges/campsites
(see page 157)
Shorobe, Moremi, Chobe

Maun Airport

MOETI ROAD

MATHIBA I ROAD

AIRPORT AV

Engen

Natlee Centre

Power Station

Ngami Centre

MOPHANE AV

MOTSHABA ST

SIR SERETSE KHAMA ROAD

AUDI DRIVE

MOETI ROAD

KUBU ST

TSHEKO-TSHEKO ROAD

BP

Nissan/Fiat

Riley's

KGOSING AV

MOREMI III RD

Maun Educational Park

SEKGOMA ROAD

MENO STREET

Choppies

Caltex

Thamalakane River

Maun Sports Club

Scarlet Feather

BOSEJA

Maun Technical College

Ngami Toyota

MATHIBA I ROAD

Sitatunga, Ghanzi

BRINGLE AV

Maun Hospital

Old bridge
(road narrows)

Maun Lodge

Shell

TAWANA I ROAD

Maun Secondary School

Caltex

N

Bradt

Motsentsela Tree Lodge

KWENA ROAD

Lesedi Motors

Drifters, Nata, Francistown

8

Maun

This dusty, sprawling town has been the start of expeditions into the wilds since the turn of the century, and it is now the safari capital of the country. Maun's elongated centre is dotted with modern shops and offices, while its suburbs are mainly traditionally built, thatched rondavels. Look carefully amongst these and you'll find quite a lot which incorporate old drinks cans or even bottles into their mud walls.

In the 1980s everywhere and everything here seemed geared towards the tourism bonanza. Maun had a rough-and-ready frontier feel, as contemporary cowboys rode into town from the bush in battered 4x4s. Its focal points were the camps north of town – Island Safari Lodge, Crocodile Camp, Okavango River Lodge – and the old Duck Inn opposite the airport.

Since then, Maun has changed. Government departments moved here en masse as Maun became the administrative centre for the northern and western parts of Botswana. The town's roads became sealed tar, rather than pot-holed gravel tracks, which opened the door to an influx of normal saloon cars from the rest of the country. Finally the tourism product itself changed. The pendulum swung away from last-minute budget trips bought in Maun, to upmarket safaris bought in advance from overseas. The new breed of visitors just change planes here; they seldom spend more than a few hours at Maun Airport. The town is no longer the place to book a top safari; that's usually done before you arrive.

However, for those who are driving themselves, Maun remains a centre to get organised, and perhaps a place to look at what cheaper safari options are available. It also offers an increasing number of activities to interest those who may find themselves with time on their hands between flights, or who are stopping over here before or after a safari.

GETTING THERE AND AWAY

Maun is 950m (3,100ft) above sea level, and fairly easy to reach, however you are travelling.

BY AIR Maun is well connected by scheduled Air Botswana flights. These connect with Gaborone and Johannesburg every day, and with Kasane on Mondays, Wednesdays, Fridays and Sundays.

For more detail contact Air Botswana at their stylish office near the airport (↘ 6860 391). Maun also has a number of air charter companies, where you can hire light aircraft for private flights and transfers – see pages 172–3. These can sometimes be economical if you have four or five people travelling together.

Air Namibia runs regular flights between Windhoek and Maun on Wednesdays, Fridays and Sundays, though using fairly small aircraft so these flights are frequently sold out far in advance. Note also that there are inherent risks in relying on these flights to fit in with a complex, 'fixed' trip itinerary in both countries, as the schedules for them can, and do, change relatively regularly. (There are moves to run a regular charter service on this route, but nothing's materialised yet.)

Maun Airport On the north side of town, Maun's airport is just a stone's throw from many of the local safari operators, and equally close to a number of bars, restaurants, shops and other facilities. The airport itself is fairly small and very relaxed, with none of the hassle you find at some airports. Alongside a couple of check-in desks downstairs is a bureau de change (*open daily 07.00–18.00*), though rates are not the greatest, and toilets are close by. Offices for Avis and Budget, and the tourist-information desk, are manned only intermittently, presumably when a flight is expected. Upstairs, there's a stark café where food is brought in from Riley's Hotel. At lunchtime, the 'pub meal' for around P14.50 often features traditional local fare and is said to be very good. The post-office counter in the airport has been closed, but last-minute cards can be posted just outside, next to the Bushman Crafts shop.

The airport has no left-luggage facility, though if you're passing through to visit camps in the region by light aircraft, then most safari companies will collect any spare baggage from you, and return it to you as you leave.

✈ **Air Botswana** Airport Av; ☎ 6860 391. Their main reservations office, a dramatic thatched building, is near the corner with Sir Seretse Khama Rd. It's generally easier to reconfirm flights and make further arrangements here than it is at the airport.

BY ROAD Ignoring the odd tiny bush track, there are only three significant roads linking Maun with the rest of the country:

Northeast towards Kasane Routing right through Chobe National Park, it's about 360km of bush and thick sand (accessible only by 4x4) to Kasane. For details of the track northeast of Maun, through Shorobe to Moremi and Chobe, see the separate section, *The road north of Maun: to Moremi and Chobe*, at the end of this chapter.

Southwest towards Ghanzi and Namibia It's about 286km of good tar road to Ghanzi, and thence to the Namibian border. About 2.5km beyond the Ngami Toyota garage, you'll pass the Maun Sports Complex on your left (see page 165). If you're hitchhiking then consider catching a bus or taxi, or walking this far out as it'll get you beyond most of the local traffic.

East towards Nata and Francistown Nata is about 305km due east, again along a good tar road which crosses between the Nxai Pan and Makgadikgadi national parks. If you're hitching, then at least cross to the south side of the Thamalakane River as far as the Caltex service station. If you prefer, continue for a few kilometres south until the road starts to bend west and you're beyond the outskirts and the local traffic.

Long-distance buses Maun's fairly chaotic bus station is at the southern end of Tsaro Street, alongside the local market. Here you'll find frequent departures for Francistown (*P46 one way, 7hrs*), Ghanzi (*P30, 4hrs*) and Shakawe (*up to P35, 4¹/₂–7hrs, depending on the company; quickest is the Golden Bridge Express leaving at around 08.00*), stopping at most of the larger towns on the way. To reach Kasane, hop on a bus towards Francistown and change at Nata. The first buses leave at 06.30, then run more or less hourly through the morning, but do check times beforehand, and arrive early.

ORIENTATION

Finding your way around Maun is relatively simple. Though the town stands astride the (often-dry) Thamalakane River, the main places of interest are all on the north bank. Here there are two focal points: the airport area, and the area around Riley's Garage, further south. For the purposes of distances in this guide, we have taken Riley's Garage as the centre of Maun.

MAPS Though Maun has grown a lot in recent years, there aren't any really good maps of the place apart from the town planners' survey maps, which are too detailed for most purposes, and the sketch maps in this book.

However, whilst you are in Maun, if you really want to head anywhere 'off-piste' in Botswana's bush, then there are a couple of options. The Shell maps, by Veronica Roodt, and the InfoMap have become the standard references for most travellers, and are available in most curio shops and garages in Maun. Alternatively, if you want some more traditional survey maps at a range of scales, then seek out the **Department of Surveys & Mapping**, the blue-and-white building just to the right of the stylish Air Botswana office (*Airport Av, PO Box 74, Maun;* ↘ *6860 272;* f *6860 993; open Mon–Fri 07.30–12.45, 13.45–16.30*); the entrance is round the back. Here, a very helpful team will arrange any number of maps for you from P15 (in black and white) to P40 (colour). Even if you're not exploring, the large 1:350,000 map of the Okavango Delta makes a great souvenir – though many of the camps on it are long gone. Laminated versions of many of the survey maps are available from Jacana Enterprises (see page 162); otherwise, these maps are available only in Gaborone.

GETTING AROUND

If you're around the centre, between the airport and Riley's, then walking is hot but feasible. Otherwise, you'll need some form of transport. All public-transport vehicles have blue number plates. Taxis (conspicuous for their blue number plates) can be found near the bus station (although there is talk of a new taxi rank to be built further south on Tsheko-Tsheko Road, near the new supermarket. Shared taxis hailed on the street cost P2.50 per person, and the driver will often stop and take another lift at the same time. If you're taking a taxi out to one of the camps to the north of town, expect to pay around P20.

Small combies ply frequently between the bus station at the north end of Tsaro Street, in the centre of town, and the outlying suburbs; typically, vehicles leave only when full, but they will drop you on request. Costs are just a couple of pula for the ride. The ten routes are clearly defined, with numbers painted on the front. For the visitor, the most useful routes are as follows:

Route 1 Airport, and north to Audi Camp
Route 2 Towards Maun Lodge, but not direct
Route 3 Maun Sports Complex
Route 5 Maun Lodge
Route 6 Hospital
Route 7 Maun Educational Park (and new hospital planned here)

Hitchhiking is also viable on the main arteries in and around town.

VEHICLE HIRE

🚗 **Avis** ↘ 6860 039 or 6860 258; f 6861 596;
e avismn@botsnet.bw, botswanares@avis.co.za;
www.avis.co.za. 4x4 hire from P550 per day, plus

insurance and rate per km.
🚗 **Budget** ↘ 6863 728; m 7231 1114
🚗 **Holiday Safari 4x4 Hire** ↘/f 6862 429

Tricia Hayne

To the casual observer, Botswanan society appears to retain much of its traditional, close-knit fabric based on strong family and community ties. Yet when Emily Cusack was working as a nurse in Maun in 2002, she soon noticed small numbers of children begging on the streets rather than being in school or at home. From her own resources, she set about entertaining them, collecting them up in a borrowed pick-up truck for a couple of hours' activities. Today, her organisation, Bana ba Letsatsi (the Sunshine Children) supports all children at risk, whether they are referred through official channels or come of their own accord.

It comes as a shock to learn that most of Maun's street kids are there because of tourists, but that's the harsh reality, according to Bana ba Letsatsi. Many visitors have been moved by the apparent plight of the children, taken in by their claims of hunger and destitution. While the children are indeed impoverished by Western standards, things are rarely as straightforward as they seem. Despite their claims, few of them are orphans or even destitute; the Botswanan authorities take care of children in these circumstances, feeding them and providing uniforms for their schooling. The greater demon is alcohol, with some parents in the *shabeen* from morning till night, leaving their children to fend for themselves. With no parental control, and sexual abuse a major issue, it's little wonder that they turn to the streets: begging is a lucrative occupation, for the most part serving only to keep the kids away from school and to feed their desires for sweets, junk food and glue.

Bana ba Letsatsi's aim is deceptively simple – to ease these children back into the school system so that they may eventually become productive members of society. The organisation's staff – a counsellor and two educational assistants under co-ordinator Lilian Costa – works closely with the authorities, and receives additional help from two government teachers. A day centre, initially the backbone of the organisation, provides each child aged six to 16 with breakfast and lunch, a shower, uniform, and three hours' 'no-formal' education from Monday to Friday. Younger children are taken to one of the private schools that work with the trust. Most of the youngsters walk some distance to their sanctuary, currently housed in a small compound not far from the police station on Audi Drive, although new premises are actively being sought. With the help of local companies, the children are regularly taken on outings; recently, small groups have been given their first taste of an overnight camping safari – in a country whose major attraction is its wildlife, most of these youngsters have never seen an elephant, or indeed been near the national parks.

Fortunately, funding is not an issue, with 95% of the trust's funds coming from the US. What isn't covered, however, is maintenance, so donations are welcome. And if you find yourself with room in your luggage, perhaps you could take something for the Sunshine Children – they would welcome the normal family basics, such as underwear, T-shirts or shorts; plasters and hygiene materials; footballs or volleyballs; pens and pencils. How much more rewarding than putting children on the streets in the first place.

Bana Ba Letsatsi Trust, P Bag 114, Suite 55, Maun; ✆ *7141 3774;* e *banabaletsatsi@ yahoo.com; http://capricorn-foundation.com/html/banabaletsatsi.html*

 WHERE TO STAY

Just as Maun has changed in the last decade or two, so have the places to stay. In the 1980s the few camps on the northern side of town felt like outposts in the wilderness. Places like Crocodile Camp, Island Safari Lodge and Okavango River

Lodge had the atmosphere of oases of comfort. They seemed like remote lodges and often, when the water was high enough, mokoro trips would start from the banks of the river beside the lodge, to pole adventurers into the Delta along the Thamalakane River.

Now times have changed. Better roads and more neighbours have made these camps feel less isolated and more a part of Maun. Less water in the river has put an end to mokoro trips starting in Maun. Whereas visitors (especially backpackers) used to stop for at least a night in Maun, now many simply transit briefly through the airport to fly in to a safari camp.

Hence these fine old camps have lost much of their atmosphere – though they may still be more interesting than some of the hotels and B&Bs which are the alternative. That said, the lines between camps and hotels are becoming increasingly blurred, with some of the camps heading rapidly upmarket, and the last few years have seen a handful of interesting small-scale ventures that have breathed new life into the accommodation scene, and are well worth investigation.

For ease of reference, the hotels, lodges, guesthouses and campsites below are listed alphabetically. Do note that signposts for some of the newer establishments only face south, so keep a watchful eye out for any pre-booked accommodation.

HOTELS AND LODGES While the places featured here fall neatly into the category of hotels and lodges, some of those listed under *Camping* below have excellent chalet accommodation and facilities that can make the appellation 'campsite' seem unjustified.

🏠 **Maduo Lodge** (17 rooms) Shorobe Rd, Maun; ☎ 6860 846; f 6862 161; e maduolodge@ hotmail.com. About 6km from the airport, on the way to Shorobe, this once-small guesthouse, almost opposite the Sedia Hotel, has developed into a larger place with all the atmosphere of a motel. It's friendly enough, but its basic en-suite rooms and facilities could do with some attention. *P298/343.20/376.20/442 sgl/dbl/twin/executive (with AC & fridge). B/fast P45; dinner P65 pp.*

🏠 **Maun Lodge** (30 rooms, 10 chalets, camping) Tawana 1 Rd, Plot No 459, Boseja, Maun; ☎ 6863 939; f 6863 969; e maun.lodge@info.bw; www.maunlodge.com. This small, modern, businesslike hotel does a good job, with friendly staff who try hard. It is situated on the south bank of the Thamalakane River, next to the old Tawana Road Bridge. Entering, you'll find a high lobby with a locally produced rug on the wall together with a trendy metal sculpture of pelicans.

The lodge's rooms have twin beds with ethnic-print covers, tea/coffee-making facilities, AC, TV and phone, while en suite is a bath with fixed shower. Floors are tiled and you'll find pictures on the walls, but otherwise the décor is bland. Newly built brick-and-thatch chalets around the perimeter of the site represent good value for couples or families. Similar in style to the rooms, though with a shower instead of a bath, they lack the phone but a big

plus is the parking space alongside each chalet, with this and the car park patrolled by security guards. A couple of larger chalets overlook the river. Forget the 'campsite' though – it's just a filler for an awkward corner.

A rather formal cocktail bar, restaurant (full breakfast P60, dinner P97) and conference centre are balanced by a small pool and the more relaxed open-air Boma bar, where guests may order from a range of light meals, or from the restaurant's à la carte menu, which includes both grills and vegetarian options, as well as some local dishes. Live music is played on Wednesday and Friday. *Room P538/614 sgl/dbl, suite P953, dbl chalet P437, family chalet P545, camping P50 pp. Open all year.*

🏠 **Motsentsela Tree Lodge** (7 tents, 2 chalets) Book via Travel Wild, Mathiba 1 Rd, Maun; ☎ 6860 822; f 6860 493; e travelwild@dynabyte.bw; www.botswanaholidays.com (⊕ TREELO 20°03.896'S; 23°22.881'E). After hours, lodge ☎ 6800 757. This new lodge offers something entirely different for visitors to Maun. About half an hour from Maun, it's set on a game farm that covers 3km², an excellent halfway house between the town and the bush. Most visitors are collected from the airport and stay just one night. If you're driving yourself, leave Maun on the road to Francistown, then shortly after you pass Maun Lodge, turn right at the Caltex garage, then

MAUN CENTRE

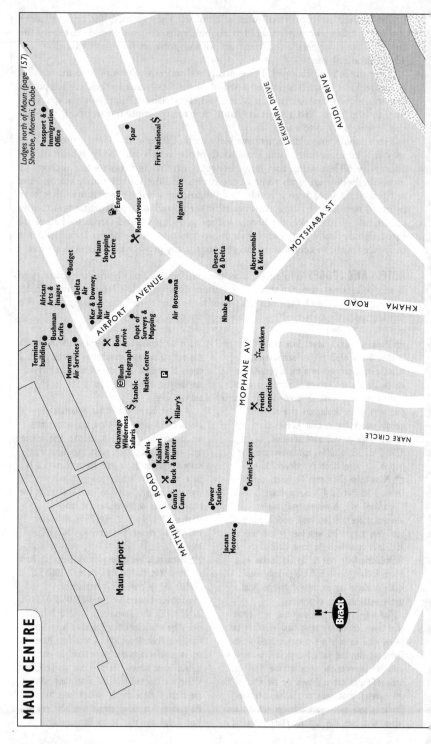

Lodges north of Maun (page 157)
Shorebe, Moremi, Chobe

Passport & Immigration Office

Spar

First National $

Engen

Rendezvous

Ngami Centre

Maun Shopping Centre

Budget

Desert & Delta

African Arts & Images

Delta Air

Ker & Downey, Northern Air

AIRPORT AVENUE

Abercrombie & Kent

MOTSHABA ST

Bushman Crafts

Air Botswana

Nhabe

LEKUKARA DRIVE

AUDI DRIVE

Terminal building

Moremi Air Services

Dept of Surveys & Mapping

Bush Telegraph

Natlee Centre

Bon Arrivé

Stanbic $

KHAMA ROAD

Okavango Wilderness Safaris

Hilary's

MOPHANE AV

Trekkers

French Connection

NARE CIRCLE

Avis

Kalahari Kanvas

Buck & Hunter

Orient-Express

MATHIBA I ROAD

Gunn's Camp

Power Station

Maun Airport

Jacana Motovac

N

Bradt

152

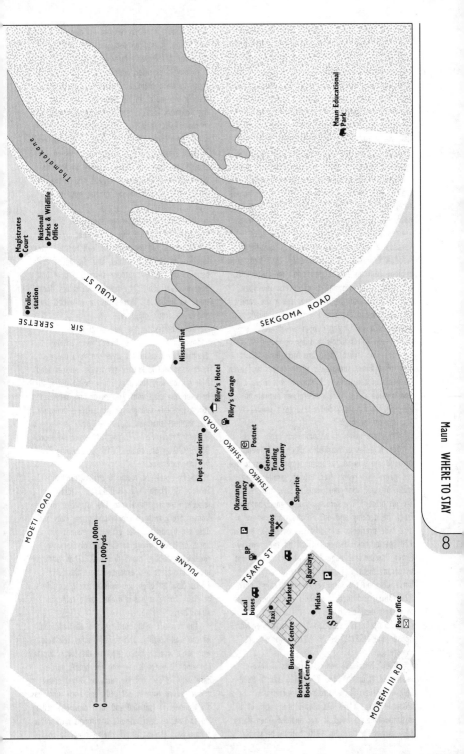

153

first right on to Kwena (signposted to Land Rover). About 50m after the tar road becomes a dirt track, bear left at the fork and continue through a village, then follow the signs more or less straight for about 8km until you reach a large sign for the lodge. Go right here, leading to the gate of Game Farm. This will be locked; be sure to get the code from Travel Wild (see page 168) *before* you set out, and note that you must have a reservation. Once inside the gate, the track leads you straight to the lodge.

The elongated central building combines a well-designed bar, lounge and dining area, all under thatch, with doors to an extensive deck set among trees and natural vegetation. Paths lead to a small pool, and beyond to well-spaced Meru-style tents, erected on stilts among the trees. From each veranda, a solid door opens on to a varnished wooden floor with sisal mats. Large twin beds with copious cushions recline under full mosquito nets, with cream curtains and chair covers. The open-plan bathroom at the back features a dbl vanity unit, a claw-foot bath and semi-private toilet, and outside is a well-screened open-air shower. 2 honeymoon suites follow a different mould — spacious and stylish, these are brick-built affairs with tiled floors, sumptuous white drapes and even an ottoman couch; their bathroom with deep bath and outside shower are modern yet entirely in keeping. Sliding patio doors lead to a small veranda at the back.

Meals are taken at a communal table, often outside. A series of marked walking trails wend through the grounds, affording opportunities to see the game that roams free: ostrich, giraffe, zebra, kudu, blesbok, springbok, impala, oryx and eland are all present. The birding, too, is good, both from the decking and out on the trails, where a bird hide overlooks a good-sized waterhole; so far, 120 species have been identified on the farm by Roger Hawker (see page 164), who can lead trips by arrangement. It is also possible to arrange horseriding on the farm (experienced riders only, P250/3hrs), and there are plans for cultural visits to villages near the lodge.
US$155 pp b/fast; US$175 pp inc dinner with house wine; US$195 pp FB. All rates inc airport transfers.
🏠 **Riley's Hotel** (51 rooms, 2 chalets) Tsheko-Tsheko Rd, Maun; ↘ 6860 204, 6860 320; f 6860 580; e resrileys @ cresta.co.bw; www.cresta-hospitality.com.. Riley's has always been more of an institution than a hotel. It was founded when Harry Riley arrived in Maun, in 1910. Initially he simply

built an extra rondavel next to his own, suitable for one visitor. It had no bed, just reed matting on the floor. A few years later he joined the 2 rondavels together, building a simple dining room between them, and soon he was running Maun's first hotel. In his book *The Lost World of the Kalahari*, Laurens van der Post described Riley's in the 1950s as a '. . . remarkable little hotel which he [Harry Riley] had founded for the odd, intrepid traveller who had been determined enough to cross the desert, as well as for the score or so of Europeans patient and courageous enough to make Maun the unique outpost of life that it is today'.

Now those first buildings form part of the manager's house, and Riley's is owned by the Cresta group. For the visitor, Riley's has a central location on the main street, and the added benefits of a lovely outdoor swimming pool and pool bar, surrounded by lawns with tables under thatched umbrellas. There's also a volleyball court, and a children's play area.

Nevertheless, by the end of 2005 the undoubted attractions of Riley's were paling against dated, corporate-style rooms, a dingy restaurant and lacklustre service. A much-needed P10 million investment in 2006 should put it firmly back on the map, with 91 new or fully refurbished rooms (possibly taking over the existing campsite), and facilities that will include a gym.
Standard room P577/750 sgl/dbl, executive room P685/930 sgl/dbl, chalet P150 pp, camping P16.50 pp. Open all year.
🏠 **Sedia Hotel** (24 rooms, 6 chalets, camping) Shorobe Rd, Maun; ╲/f 6860 177; e sedia@info.bw; www.sedia-hotel.com. The attractive, wide-fronted Sedia, with its cream and ochre walls and deep-red blinds, occupies extensive grounds 6km north of Maun Airport, to the east of the main road. Once dubbed the 'Sedi Motel', it has gradually moved upmarket and expanded since the early 1990s. Now, although not quite as costly as Riley's or Maun Lodge, it has a livelier, more colourful atmosphere.

The recently refurbished foyer is all traditional African wall-hangings and squashy sofas, complete with large wooden hippo. Most of the rooms are laid out along 2 wings facing into the hotel's gardens, each with its own outside entrance. Bright ethnic colours adorn twin or dbl beds, and each room has a telephone, TV (satellite and local channels), ceiling fan and AC; modern, en-suite bathrooms incorporate a bath with shower. Larger chalets closer to the river look rather dated, despite boasting a fridge and kitchenette (but no cooking facilities), AC, lounge with TV and a shady veranda.

At the back of the hotel, set among gardens with large lawns, is one of the area's best swimming pools, large and solar-heated. The surrounding decking is a popular venue for dining or just for drinks, while the more formal restaurant alongside comes into its own in the winter. There is also a lively bar with 2 pool tables, and a children's playground.

Beyond the lawns, a large and sprawling campsite leads down to the Thamalakane River. There is plenty of tree shade for your own tent, or a few pre-erected tents, with 2 beds, a table, chair and power point, benefit from a small, shaded veranda.

Campers have 3 or 4 well-kept showers and toilets, and they may use the hotel's pool without charge. It's possible to park next to your tent, particularly useful as the campsite isn't fenced terribly securely and security didn't seem that tight when I last stayed there, despite the presence of a night watchman. With good locks on the room's doors, this wasn't a problem for those staying in the hotel.

In front of the complex is an internet café, as well as the base for Afro Trek, who operate a good variety of budget safaris and mokoro trips (see page 168).
P475/545/590 sgl/dbl/twin room, P660/825 1/2-bedroom chalet, inc b/fast; camping P20 pp; pre-erected tents P100 pp. Open all year.

GUESTHOUSES AND B&BS In recent years a few small B&Bs have sprung up, usually run by Maun residents as a way of earning a few extra pula. They tend to be basic and functional, and as their rates are usually on a par with more upmarket lodges and hotels, have little to recommend them in terms of service and quality. Most are also way outside the centre of town, making them inaccessible unless you have your own transport. Of far greater interest are a couple of small, new initiatives offering a sense of Botswanan culture that is missing from the plethora of increasingly upmarket lodges and campsites.

 Discovery Bed & Breakfast (5 rondavels) Shorobe Rd; √f 6800 627; m 7164 9718; e discovery@info.bw. A taste of Botswanan culture comes to life in this quiet, attractive complex set around a small garden in the form of a Botswanan village. It's located about 15km north of Maun, down a 300m track to the west of the main road. Individual wood-framed rondavels, painted inside and out in traditional Setswana patterns of browns, ochres, deep reds and greens, are set on a sandy plot. Inside are twin beds with side lights and a mosquito net, with a toilet and basin behind a reed screen; communal showers are in a separate rondavel. In the reception area, which doubles as a homely dining room, Batswana crafts and baskets are on sale from P40. Evening meals combine traditional and international dishes for P100

pp. Traditional dancing on request at P150. *P225/350 sgl/dbl, B&B.*

 Marina's (8 rondavels) Shorobe Rd, Maun; √f 6801 231; f 6861 017; e marinas@dynabyte.bw. Botswanan Marina and her husband opened their innovative lodge about 8km north of Maun in 2002, with mains electricity added a couple of years later. Large, well-designed rondavels are attractively painted in cream and red, and have dbl, twin or family accommodation with fans and mosquito nets. At the back of each is a shower, toilet and basin. The circular theme continues with the outside bar, and brick paving leads to a giant dining rondavel with an ingenious upper balcony outside. For good measure, there's a good pool, with a hot tub and firepit to guard against the winter chill. *P270/390/450 sgl/dbl/family, B&B.*

CAMPS AND CAMPING Even the top hotels in Maun offer camping as well as their normal rooms, but for most campers one of the dedicated campsites is a better bet – with the definite exception of the campsite at the Sedia Hotel. Conversely, many of these camps have chalet facilities as well as camping, some of them heading seriously upmarket.

Most of these camps are north of Maun, on the road to Shorobe, with the furthest – Okavango River Lodge – 12km out of town. They're the obvious places to stay if you arrive in your own vehicle, but if you don't have transport, most will provide a pick-up/drop-off service into town at a price.

It's cheaper (P2) to catch a lift into town from the main road near any of these camps with one of the small combies that come past every few minutes. To get from town to these camps, a taxi will cost you around P20 or you can take a Route 1 combie for P2.

North of Maun

Å Alfa (14 rooms, camping) Shorobe Rd; ☏ 686 4689. The huge 'Overlanders Paradise' sign outside Alfa is a promise too far for this basic accommodation about 4km north of Maun. Chalet-style rooms are small, albeit with fridge, TV and AC. Camping is across the road.
P180/280/450 sgl/dbl/family; P90 pp budget; camping P25 pp.

Å Audi Camp (chalets, pre-erected tents, camping) Shorobe Rd, Maun; ☏ 6860 599, 6863 005; f 6865 388; e emma@okavangocamp.com; www.okavangocamp.com. The turn-off for Audi Camp is well signposted barely 300m south of Crocodile Camp's turning, about 12km from the centre of Maun on the road north to Shorobe, Moremi and Chobe. This is also the base for Audi Camp Safaris (see page 168).

The well laid-out site is on several levels, with a shady campsite under mopane trees, each pitch having its own braai and water supply; there's also a camper's kitchen. Bring your own tent, or rent one of their pre-erected tents on solid bases: either bare dome tents with camp beds and no linen, or small Meru tents (some en-suite) with beds and linen, as well as electric lights and fans. Ablutions are in an intriguingly designed circular block that has open-air showers and hot water. Firewood and ice are available, there's a limited amount of camping kit for hire, and a laundry service is also on offer.

The camp has a large thatched bar, and a restaurant area on a lower level which serves meals and snacks all day, from toasted sandwiches to steaks and vegetarian options. Near the river is a large and very popular swimming pool. The whole site is securely fenced and patrolled at night by security guards. A great little shop on site is run by Amanda Haywood, selling a range of curios as well as Sibanda hand-printed fabrics (see page 162). If you're in need of conversation, try the caged African grey parrot in the bar — though the ethics of keeping such an endangered bird caged would also provide a challenging conversation with the management.
Dome tent P120/148 per tent, sharing/sgl, Meru tent P205/240, en suite P365/410, all B&B. Camping P25 pp, power point P30 per night. Open all year.

Å Back to the Bridge Backpackers (camping) Maun; ☏ 6862 406; e thebridge@botsnet.bw;

www.dumelabotswana.com. Maun's new backpacker hang-out is tucked down a lane just north of the river bridge on the Shorobe Rd, 10km out of town. It's clearly signposted if you're heading south, but not obvious at all if you're going the other way. In that case, turn east off the road towards Shumo Island (which appears not to exist!), then left at the end of the tar, and follow the signs for about 1.5km to the camp. Owned by David, one of the original partners in Livingstone's Jungle Junction, it was opened in June 2005 on a shady site close to the old pole bridge across the river. At this point, the river flows permanently, and hippos congregate in front of the camp, while fruit bats are attracted by a large fig tree. The area used to be a vegetable garden; now, around 400 new trees have been planted around the site, which offers some lovely walks with good birding.

Alongside space for independent campers, there are a few pre-erected 'cottage' and Meru tents, each with 2 beds; the latter boast balconies over the water, and private ablution facilities. Communal reed-screened open-air ablutions are very clean. Music plays from a large, thatched central area with sand floor, where hammocks swing from the poles and tables and chairs are set out under the trees. Food is available all day, with full breakfast at P25, and pasta dishes around P25 as well; there's also a self-catering kitchen.

This is a relaxed outfit, young and friendly. Small-group trips (prices on request, depending on numbers) include mokoro trips on the edge of the Delta, some as far as the Panhandle, and desert trips into the Quebe Hills close to the Central Kalahari — considerably further afield than most of the local operators. They can also offer 4x4 vehicle hire with driver for P800 a day, plus fuel — suitable for up to 6 people.
Camping P30 pp; cottage tents P150/100 dbl/sgl; Meru tent P250.

Å Crocodile Camp (15 chalets, camping) Shorobe Rd, Maun; ☏ 6800 222; e crocamp@info.bw. Now a base for the operations of Crocodile Camp Safaris (see page 169 for alternative contact details), 'Croc Camp' as it's universally known is one of the old institutions of Maun, and was recently taken over by Tactic Tourism. Popular with the German and Dutch markets, it is well maintained, efficiently run and

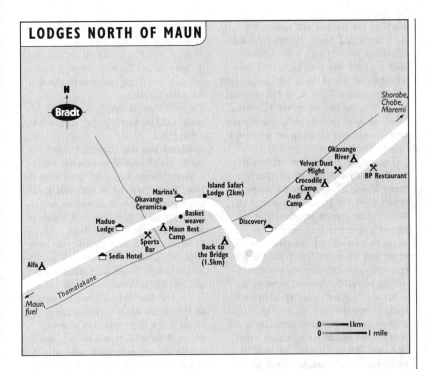

LODGES NORTH OF MAUN

Bradt

N

Shorobe, Chobe, Moremi

Okavango River

Velvet Dust Might

BP Restaurant

Crocodile Camp

Audi Camp

Island Safari Lodge (2km)

Marina's Okavango Ceramics

Basket weaver

Discovery

Maduo Lodge

Maun Rest Camp

Sports Bar

Back to the Bridge (1.5km)

Sedia Hotel

Alfa

Thamalakane

Maun, fuel

0 ——— 1km
0 ——— 1 mile

going rapidly upmarket. The entire site is wheelchair-accessible.

The camp's chalets vary in style, from the oldest design of reed and thatch, through no-frills brick-built chalets with en-suite facilities and electricity, to the largest and most upmarket of all, set at the back of the site and painted a deep red. Beautifully designed, making imaginative use of curved walls, these have large twin beds, a sofa, and French windows leading on to a veranda; cream-painted walls complement sisal rugs and deep red fabrics; extras include a hairdryer, safe, fan and mosquito nets. The aim is to have a total of 23 chalets by early 2007.

A short walk from the main camp is a separate campsite, set under a few shady *Acacia erioloba* trees, and with overland trucks benefiting from their own discrete area. The ablution block was fully refurbished at the end of 2005, with modern facilities and plenty of hot water. Plans are under consideration for the creation of individual pitches with their own water and power supplies, and the provision of pre-erected Meru tents with 2 or 3 beds.

Most of the camp's facilities overlook the Thamalakane River, which normally first flows around July, and then dries up again around December. A new, oval, thatched bar has been built here, with

plans to incorporate the dining area and conference centre by the end of 2006. Nearby is a sparkling, kidney-shaped swimming pool surrounded by a grassy area with seats, ideal for kids, and shady gardens where the tree species have been thoughtfully labelled. Set behind is the older restaurant, with breakfast at US$16, and dinner at US$27; if you want to eat here you'll need to let them know in advance.
US$105/69/53/47 pp sgl/dbl/trpl/quad; camping P25 pp. Open all year.

Island Safari Lodge (12 chalets, 4 budget rooms, camping) Shorobe Rd, Maun; ☎ 6860 300; f 6862 932; e enquire@africansecrets.net; www.africansecrets.net. Island Safari Lodge was a well-established hub when I first visited Maun in 1988. Bought back in 2003 by former owners Sean Watson and his family, it is now firmly on the up again. The lodge stands in 116ha beside the Thamalakane River about 12km north of Maun, under a forest canopy dominated by tall sycamore figs (*Ficus sycomorus*). Coming from Maun you take a well signposted left turn just before the river, then follow a really lovely stretch of track for about 2km through old riverine forest (perfectly navigable for 2WD vehicles).

Accommodation is in thatched bungalows, set among lawns and indigenous vegetation. All are fully refurbished with twin beds with mosquito nets, ceiling fans/AC, sisal flooring, TV, tea/coffee facilities, and en-suite shower — and a bench outside on which to sit and contemplate the sunset. 2 rooms are suitable for disabled visitors. Older, budget rooms are simpler, without TV and AC. By 2007, they aim to have completed the campsite, with 15 individual ablution blocks set on shady pitches, with dedicated spaces for overland trucks around the perimeter, to include a dormitory.

From the large reception area with curio shop, to the revamped long bar/restaurant (open for meals 10.00–21.00), it's evident that changes are in hand. A new pool has been built closer to the chalets, and the large old pool closer to the campsite is being refurbished, with plans to incorporate a waterfall and landscaped gardens leading down to the river. Sean is hoping to build up a reputation for activities, with possibilities including a series of walking and mountain-bike trails, canoe rental, and paintballing. Safaris are run by the affiliated Wild Attractions (see page 172), under the umbrella organisation African Secrets (not to be confused with the Kenyan company of the same name). With so many plans, it's difficult to predict which way this business will lead, but enthusiasm is definitely the watchword!
Chalet US$68/83, room US$48/63 B&B sgl/dbl; camping P20 pp. Open all year.

⚊ Maun Rest Camp (6 Meru tents, cottage, camping) Shorobe Rd, Maun; ➘ 6862 623; ➘/f 6863 472 (with answerphone); e simonjoyce@info.bw. This nice, quiet campsite on the river is also the base for a small mobile-safari operation (see page 171) run by the owners, Simon and Joyce. Find it by heading 7km north of the airport on the road to Shorobe, Chobe and Moremi.

Maun Rest Camp's campsite has 14 individual pitches, each neatly hedged with its own braai and water tap. If you don't have a tent, then brand-new Meru ones are available with twin beds, electric lights and carpets, and chairs at the front. There's also a 2-bedroom cottage with separate lounge and kitchen.

2 clean, brick-built ablution blocks (4 separate showers, loos and basins plus laundry tubs and sinks for dishes — all with copious hot water from a gas geyser) lie under large shady trees. Ask the owners to show you the birdplum tree (*Berchemia discolour*)

South of Maun

⚊ Drifters Safaris (camping) Chanoga; ➘ 7230 4472; e drifters@drifters.co.za; www.drifters.co.za. Situated

here, which is indigenous but a little uncommon, with its thick foliage and small, edible fruits.

There's no bar or restaurant at the camp, though the Sports Bar and Restaurant is barely 2 mins' walk away — so finding somewhere for a drink or dinner isn't a problem.
Camping P30 pp per night; Meru tent P220, cottage P250 per night (2 people); each additional person P50.

⚊ Okavango River Lodge (campsite, 5 chalets) Shorobe Rd; ➘/f 6863707; www.okavango-river-lodge.com. Okavango River Lodge opened in the late 1980s, and was taken over in March 2004. It stands on the opposite side of the Thamalakane River to Island Safari Lodge, about 15km north of Maun on the road to Shorobe, Chobe and Moremi.

The campsite lies beside the river, under shady acacias, with a volleyball court and small pool. There are also some simple, well-spaced chalets with twin beds, fans, nets, and en-suite shower/toilet.

The rustic little lodge has a lively and popular bar at its centre, with an ingenious system of outdoor AC that keeps drinkers cool all day. An efficient kitchen will rustle up a variety of tasty bites from the bar menu, from toasted sandwiches to T-bone steaks; there's also a wholesome set meal on offer every night (P30). Okavango River Lodge claims to have the only cricket pitch in Maun. Formerly a golf course, it is set in the open floodplain opposite camp. Whilst perhaps not very conventional, it's easy to play when the river is dry, and even more fun when it's in flood. This is a favourite with various local characters, especially on Sundays.

As well as booking activities for you, Okavango River Lodge offers its own flexible mobile camping trips to Moremi, Nxai and Makgadikgadi, the Central Kalahari, or anywhere else in Botswana. All are tailor-made. Expect a day trip to Moremi to cost around US$120 for the vehicle and driver; or US$180 pp for a 1-night/2-day trip, inc equipment, meals, drinks, park fees etc. They also organise mokoro trips of varying lengths, based 15km upriver on the Boro River in NG32, with transfers made by boat whenever possible. These range from day trips (P370 pp sharing) to longer camping trips (1-night/2-day trip P590 pp). Note that even if you pay a sgl supplement (P100) for your own mokoro, transfers need at least 2 people.
Chalet P250, camping P25 pp.

32km from Maun, this is the local base of the overland safari company, Drifters, but it's reportedly

still open to independent campers – and is well worth considering if you're heading south of the town. Coming from Maun, take the tar road towards Nata and Francistown, and just beyond the village of Chanoga turn right down a sandy track of about 1km. Here you'll find a wide riverfront location with grassy lawns, where separate thatched bar/lounge and dining areas are attractively decorated with wall hangings and baskets. There's a small pool, but the greatest attraction is the Boteti River, which when flowing attracts numerous waterbirds – including flamingos, pelicans and knob-billed ducks. Camping is on a small, tree-shaded site set to the side, with an extremely clean ablution block.
Camping P50 pp.

Å Sitatunga Camp (11 chalets, camping) Maun; ☏ 6800 380; m 7130 4292; e deltarain@ dynabyte.bw. With its location southwest of Maun, Sitatunga could feel something of an outsider, but it remains a popular choice for overlanders, and a good place for independent campers. If you're seeking peace and quiet, though, choose your days: Sundays are often busy, as this is a popular outing for Maun's residents; and Friday nights, when overland trips return from the Delta, can be very lively; the bar is open from 11.00 to late. To get there, head southwest from Maun towards Ghanzi, before turning off the main road about 12km from Riley's Garage. The lodge is about 2km from the main road down a sandy track. Route 3 combines terminate at the bridge just before the turn-off.

The large, secure campsite lies under trees, with pitches well spread out. Simple, newly built twin or dbl chalets, each with nets and power points, are set on their own, well away from the bar area. Ablutions are basic but clean, with hot water heated by wood-burning donkey-boiler. Laundry service P15–25; firewood P7 per day or load.

Beside a small pool (non-residents P10), a shaded patio makes a good chill-out area, with food available from the adjacent bar 12.00–15.30 and 17.00–21.00. There's no self-catering kitchen, but braai facilities are available. Darts, volleyball and table tennis are also on offer. A small, busy shop sells basic foodstuffs, cool drinks, wine, beer and an extensive range of ice cream. There's also a curio shop with T-shirts, hats and simple souvenirs.
Chalet P140, camping P25 pp.

✗ WHERE TO EAT AND DRINK

Maun's not really a town for fine dining, but there are a few reasonable venues, including some of the hotels and camps. There are also numerous fast-food places in town, including Nandos, Steers, Chicken King and many more. Expect a decent burger to cost upwards of P15 – and remember that you're in a country which counts beef as one of its main exports.

Of the hotels, both **Maun Lodge** and the **Sedia Hotel** have competent if uninspiring formal restaurants, with relatively high prices, but each also has an open-air venue serving restaurant meals as well as simpler bar snacks. The Boma at Maun Lodge is relaxed and quite rustic, while eating by the pool at the back of the Sedia can be fun with a good atmosphere. **Riley's** restaurant is currently very uninspiring, though refurbishment in 2006 may make a difference here. Almost all the campsites serve meals to outsiders, with **Audi Camp** highly recommended locally, while **Okavango River Lodge** is arguably the town's most frequented watering hole, particularly popular on Sundays.

In addition, there is a growing number of individual restaurants, some specialising in breakfast and lunch, and others open throughout the day. Many are within walking distance of the airport, and most are licensed, with vegetarians well catered for almost everywhere.

✗ **Bon Arrivée** Mathiba I Rd; ☏ 6800 330. Opposite the airport, this trendy and unashamedly aviation-themed bar/restaurant has a pretty eclectic menu serving everything from breakfast (P20–42) and burgers, to seafood vol-au-vent and fillet steak. It's also a popular watering hole with expats on a Friday night, and there's live jazz on Sunday afternoons. If the jokes on the menu are pretty corny, they do at least help to while away the time waiting for a delayed flight.
Open daily 07.30–22.00.

✗ **BP Restaurant & Bar** Shorobe Rd. Geared to the local market, this Botswanan restaurant is the first place you come to in Maun when driving from the

north. If you've never tried traditional Botswanan food, this is a good place to start. Clean, friendly and very good value, it serves such dishes as *papa* and beef for P8.
Open 06.30–22.30; adjoining bar open later.

✗ **Buck & Hunter** Mathiba I Rd; ☏ 6801 001. On the road parallel to the airstrip, within a short walk of the airport, this lively and popular bar was formerly the Bull & Bush (and before that, the Duck Inn). In its previous incarnation, the locals referred to it as the 'Bullet & Ambush', after its opening night when, towards the end of the evening, someone was shot. Today, it's all wood and picnic-style tables, and has taken on the mantle of serving the best pizzas in town (from P21). Otherwise, you can expect substantial bar meals at reasonable prices, such as steak and chips (P32), and a range of sandwiches and salads (around P25).
Open Mon-Thu 0.00–23.00; Fri/Sat to midnight.

✗ **French Connection** Mophane Av; ☏ 6800 625, ☏ 7175 4030. This licensed café/restaurant on the road parallel to Mathiba I Rd, is close to the airport. It is run by Marie and George, a couple of Swiss/Dutch origin who used to have a very good restaurant at Crocodile Camp. With seating outside under mopane trees, or inside for inclement weather, it's well-screened from the road, with off-road parking. The French-influenced menu ranges from homemade croissants and pâtés to fresh salads and mouth-watering baguettes. Breakfasts at P20–40 are served until 12.00, and include an innovative vegetarian breakfast at P30.50 featuring ratatouille and rösti. Packed lunches and take-aways from P25.
Open 08.00–17.00ish; dinner by arrangement.

✗ **Hilary's Coffee Shop** Mathiba I Rd; ☏ 6861 610. Hilary's has been serving since about 1995, and is one of the more interesting and reliable places to eat during the day in Maun. If you turn right out of the the airport's entrance gate, it's on the left, behind the Avis office. Well-shaded tables are outside amongst mopane trees and pot plants. Hilary and her staff make everything on the premises, from mayonnaise and salad dressing to bran muffins; the home-baked wholewheat bread is to die for, and with a little advance notice can be made to order for a camping trip, if you ask nicely . . . Expect the best home-cooked breakfasts in Maun (from P26) and tasty wholesome lunches, inc sandwiches and salads (from P17.50), daily specials (around P32), and amazing desserts and cakes.
Open Mon-Fri 08.00–16.00, Sat 08.30–12.00; evenings by arrangement only.

✗ **Power Station** Mophane Av; ☏ 6862 037. Round the corner from the Buck & Hunter, the Power Station's restaurant was closed at the end of 2005, seeking new management.

✗ **Rendezvous** Sir Seretse Khama Rd; ☏ 7287 6183. Set behind the Engen garage (the place on the main road is the take-away outlet), this rather soulless restaurant serves an unbelievable range of dishes from all corners of the globe, including pizzas, grills, Indian, Chinese and Thai food.
Open Mon–Sat 09.00–22.00.

✗ **Scarlet Feather** With its location next to a small plant nursery on the main Maun–Nata road, this new restaurant has plenty of greenery for décor. Popular at lunchtimes, it serves a range of salads and sandwiches, including plenty of interesting vegetarian dishes, while breakfast is a pick-and-mix affair from a range of options. Expect to pay around P20 for lunch. You can also order take-aways and packed lunches.
Open 07.30–15.00.

✗ **Scarlet Feather II** The modern coffee bar in the PostNet complex (see page 163) is an offshoot of the more relaxed place out at Boseja.

✗ **Sports Bar** Shorobe Rd; ☏ 6862 676. This long-standing favourite, open for dinner only, is probably the best restaurant in the area — helped by speedy service and the frequent presence of the owners. It's about 7km north of town, so you'll need transport to get here. Just head towards Chobe NP and it's on the right, just before you cross the Thamalakane River. The complex is spread over 2 levels, but the downstairs restaurant, all dark greens and reds, is separate from the bar and pool tables. The menu is fairly extensive, but it's known for great pizzas and pasta (around P40), and some excellent salads and fish. The pork knuckle — *eisvein* — comes particularly well recommended. As you'd expect, the bar area is well-stocked. Come here on a Fri night when the place rocks; there's usually a live DJ and no cover charge. It's here that Maun's younger and more affluent residents (inc lots from the safari industry) and expats dance the night away.

✗ **Velvet Dust Might** Shorobe Rd; ☏ 7141 5672, 7277 5045. North of town on the road towards Moremi, this new café and craft shop is an attractive place to combine lunch with shopping for gifts. The vivid orange and turquoise décor, mirrored by matching cushions, sets the scene; good-quality handmade jewellery, beaded lampshades, candles, batik fabrics and clothes by local artists finish the picture. Tailormade clothes to order, sometimes with in a couple of days. Serves light lunches such as baguettes and salads, and a range of desserts.
Open Mon–Fri 09.00–17.00, Sat 10.00–14.00.

NIGHTLIFE

Maun doesn't have much in the way of nightlife, except for some lively bars, the most popular being the Sports Bar and Bon Arrivée. The only nightclub, Trekkers, is on Mophane Avenue. Its reputation for safety is pretty dubious, so if you want to explore, go with a local you trust.

SHOPPING

Most shops are open Monday to Friday around 08.00–17.00, and Saturday to midday or thereabouts, unless otherwise stated, with supermarket hours considerably longer.

FOOD AND DRINK You can buy most things here that you'll find in a supermarket in Europe or North America, although the brand names may be different and the choice (especially of fresh fruit and vegetables) may not be as varied. Several of the supermarkets are near or to the south of Riley's Garage. These include Maun's oldest – and largest – **supermarket,** Shoprite (*Tsheko-Tsheko Rd,* ☎ *6860 497 or 6860 015; open daily*). There are also two branches of Spar (*behind Nandos on Tsheko-Tsheko Rd, opposite the taxi rank; nearer the airport in the Ngami Centre or 'New Mall'*), a branch of Score behind the Engen garage, and a new branch of Choppies south of Shoprite. Yet another supermarket is scheduled to open further south on the same road. For vacuum-packed meats, a good alternative would be the deli outside Riley's Garage.

Supermarkets don't sell **alcohol**, so to stock up on beer and wine you'll need to go to one of the liquor stores around town. One of the better ones is Bateman's (*almost next to Spar in Ngami Centre; open – like most off licences – Mon–Sat 10.00–19.00*).

MARKET The main local market is on Tsaro Street, virtually opposite Shoprite. Here you'll find lots of small stalls and local sellers; it's certainly worth checking out for the odd pile of fruit and vegetables. Also expect more offbeat foods, like mopane worms in season, and an assorted range of bootleg tapes and secondhand items.

SOUVENIRS, CRAFTS, BOOKS AND CURIOS There's no shortage of places that sell curios in Maun, and virtually every camp in Botswana has a small curio shop; it pays to shop around, particularly for books and crafts. It's also well worth seeking out individual workshops, or places where the work of local craftspeople is available.

African Art & Images Mathiba I Rd, ☎ 6863 584; f 6863 594; e african.art.images@dynabyte.bw. Immediately across the road from the airport, beside the Bushman Craft Shop, this is owned by the well-known wildlife film-makers, Tim and June Liversedge. In atmosphere it's reminiscent of a private art gallery, selling high-quality African art, carvings, baskets, jewellery and some beautiful photographs and prints – with correspondingly high price tags.
Botswana Book Centre Pulane Rd; ☎ 686 0853 A traditional bookshop that stocks books, magazines and newspapers including a range of titles by African writers.

Bushman Craft Shop Mathiba I Rd, ☎ 6860 025/339. Inside the gates of the airport, immediately opposite the steps to the main terminal building, this convenient shop owned by the General Trading Company (see below) sells books, postcards, crafts and curios. Barely a min's walk from the check-in desks, it's perfectly situated to dash out to whilst you're waiting for a plane.
Open daily 08.00–17.00.
Bush Telegraph See *Communications*, page 163.
The Craft Centre Mophane Av; ☎ 6863 391. In the Power Station complex, just off Mathiba I Rd, this small workshop sells local crafts inc pottery, textiles,

paper products and paintings. There's a kiln in which pottery is fired most days, having been made and glazed on the premises. Paper is also handmade here, from a mixture of recycled paper and elephant dung (yes, really), and occasional workshops and small exhibitions are staged.

General Trading Company Tsheko-Tsheko Rd; ☎ 6860 025, 6860 339. This shop, in the distinctive dark-red building almost beside Riley's Garage, has been established for years. It has a comprehensive range of books on the region, plus a good variety of carvings and crafts, some locally produced, others sourced from far away in Africa. Endless T-shirts and souvenir and safari clothing, torches, knives and all sorts of useful stuff complete the picture. Don't expect the prices to be cheap, but do expect to find some high-quality souvenirs and probably what you want.

Jazella's Natlee Centre, Airport Av; ☎ 6861 900. Jampacked full of jewellery, bags, wall hangings, books and much, much more, Jazella's is just opposite the airport.
Open Mon–Fri 08.00–18.00, weekends to 17.00.

Matlapane Baskets Shorobe Rd; ☎ 7227 1422; e thitakukushonya@yahoo.com. Award-winning master weaver Thitaku Kushonya creates her own baskets for sale from her workshop, about 8km north of Maun, opposite Marina's. Do pay her a visit – her work is excellent, and you'll learn a little of how to tell a low-quality basket from a higher-quality one that's double woven.
Open daily 06.30–18.30.

Okavango Ceramics Shorobe Rd. The company's workshop is situated next to Marina's, about 8km north of Maun, but a selection is also on sale in town, including at the Bush Telegraph (see page 163).

Sibanda's Crafts Shorobe Rd; ☎ 6800 094; m 7287 6421; e sibandas@dynabyte.bw; www.sibandas.com. Amanda Haywood sells her individually designed, hand-painted fabrics and soft furnishings both from her workshop north of Maun, just south of the Sedia Hotel, and at her shop at Audi Camp (see page 156), as well as through other outlets in town. All are of 100% cotton, printed and painted by local women. Clothes can be made to order by their own tailor.

Velvet Dust Might See *Where to eat*, page 160.

EQUIPMENT Most visitors either bring their own camping equipment, or arrive for trips which include it. Some of the tour operators who run budget trips have their own schemes for you to hire their kit for the duration of the trip. However, if you need to buy some, or you need some of your own kit repaired, then there are a few options (for vehicle spares, see pages 163–4):

Jacana Enterprises Mophane Av; ☎/f 6861 202; e jacana@botsnet.bw. An unexpected find in an office building opposite the Power Station, Jacana has a range of safari clothing and camping equipment, including good torches and knives. They also sell a range of maps (with laminated survey maps from around P85 each) and GPS equipment.

Kalahari Kanvas Mathiba I Rd, Maun; ☎ 6860 568; f 6860 035; e kalkanvas@botsnet.bw. Kalahari Kanvas, close to the airport next to Avis, started as a tiny tent-repair company in 1986, and now employs about 45 people as a major manufacturer of tents and equipment for the safari industry. They also hire out an amazing range of kit and still offer a tent-repair service. The forgetful traveller, or one without the kit, can hire just about anything here, from a knife, fork and spoon set for P0.50 per day, to a 5.9m x 10.2m

marquee/mess tent for P165 per day. A 2-person, 2.4m x 2.4m canvas bow tent costs about P37 per day; an intriguing 2-person tree-hanging tent (which 'needs no poles but a tree is very necessary') costs P25 per day; and a dbl-canvas bedroll with 75mm-thick mattress, a blanket, 2 pillows and 2 sheets costs P30 per day. Deposits are required, proportional to the items hired, and credit cards are accepted. Its best to book stuff in advance if you want it, and note that it must be returned here to the office in Maun.

PAAM Maun Shopping Centre, Sir Seretse Khama Rd; ☎ 6860 992. Despite the name (the acronym stands for Pan African Ammunition Manufacturers), this modern shop seems to specialise in the outdoors generally, with plenty of fishing gear, as well as tents, safari clothing and other equipment for sale.

OTHER PRACTICALITIES

These days Maun is, above all for most visitors, a place to restock, refuel and get organised.

BANKS AND MONEY Many places in town will accept credit cards; some will take travellers' cheques. The main **banks** (*usually open Mon–Fri 08.30–15.30, Sat 08.15–10.45*) have ATM machines that will deliver cash with most international cards (including Visa and MasterCard), which is usually the easiest, quickest and cheapest way to get pula.

Alternatively, with your passport and a little time spent in queues, you can cash travellers' cheques or obtain a manual cash advance on a credit card. The best place for these is one of the three main banks: Barclays (*opposite Shoprite;* ↘ *6860 210*), Stanbic (*opposite the airport entrance;* ↘ *686 2132*) or First National (*Ngami Centre;* ↘ *6860 919*).

There are a number of **bureaux de change** dotted around town. While they generally charge a higher commission than the banks, there's little difference in the exchange rates. Their advantage is that they offer a quicker service and longer hours. Most conspicuous are Sunny's (*Bush Telegraph opposite the airport, and PostNet complex next to Riley's;* ↘ *6862 786;* e *sunny@info.bw; open Mon–Fri 08.00–17.30, Sat/Sun 08.00–13.30*) and the First National Bank (*Ngami Centre;* ↘ *6860 919; open daily 08.00–18.00*).

COMMUNICATIONS

Post and courier The post office is on Tsheko-Tsheko Road, south of Barclays Bank. DHL has a branch here (↘ *6861 207*).

Internet Internet cafés are proliferating through the town, with the most accessible being the following:

Bush Telegraph Natlee Centre, Mathiba I Rd (opposite the airport); ↘ 6860 273. Broadband connection. P15 for 20 minutes. You can also make international calls from here at the going rate (eg: P5 per minute to the UK), plus P5 service fee. Also stocks travel essentials, and a small but tasteful range of baskets, jewellery, Okavango ceramics and Amanda Haywood's fabrics.

PostNet Riley's, Tsheko-Tsheko Rd; ↘ 686 5612. P6 for 10 min.
Open Mon–Fri 08.30–18.00, Sat to 13.00.

Business Centre Tsheko-Tsheko Rd; ↘ 686 5304.

GARAGES AND MOTOR SPARES There are several fuel stations in Maun, though at the time of writing only BP was open 24 hours. While in theory they take credit cards, don't rely on this; if the machine isn't working, you'll have to pay cash.

If you're passing through and heading off into the bush then Maun is the best place to make sure your 4x4 is in tip-top condition, with plenty of spares. Places that may be able to help include:

Exact Exhausts ↘ 6860 860; f 6862108. Specialist supplier of tyres and exhausts, located about 250m beyond the Caltex garage, near Maun Lodge on the right of the main road towards Nata and Francistown.
Lesedi Motors Kwena Rd; ↘ 686 1694. The Land Rover specialists are located just off the Francistown road, a couple of hundred metres beyond the Caltex garage.
MaxiPress Tyres On the Francistown road; ↘ 6500 588
Midas Motor Parts Tsheko-Tsheko Rd; ↘ 6860 807. Right in the centre of town, Midas is behind Barclays Bank. Open daily, inc Sun morning.
Motovac Mophane Av; ↘ 6860 872; f 6860 008. This isn't a garage, but does sell spares and accessories.
Ngami Toyota Tsheko-Tsheko Rd; ↘ 6860 252; f 6860 525. On the roundabout just north of Riley's, this is Maun's main Toyota dealer, with spares and a bodyshop. They will repair all makes, not just Toyotas.
Riley's Garage (Shell) Tsheko-Tsheko Rd; ↘ 6860 203; f 6860 556; e rg@info.bw. In the centre of town, next to the famous old hotel, this has a fuel station and workshop, and its shop carries various spares, inc tyres and batteries.
Trans-world Motors Industrial Sites Box 20092, Maun; ↘ 6862 137; f 6860 656. About 1km beyond Caltex on the road towards Francistown. Offers mechanical repairs, panel beating and spray painting.

Tyre Vision PO Box 149, Maun; ℡ 6860 107. Specialist supplier of new tyres, tubes and rims —   but mainly wholesale.

HEALTH Maun Hospital (*Bringle Av;* ℡ *6861 831;* m *7130 4426*) is located a couple of kilometres or so southwest of Riley's Garage on the Ghanzi Road. A new hospital is being planned near the educational park.

There are several pharmacies in the town, including:

Delta Medical Centre Tsheko-Tsheko Rd, opp Riley's Complex; ℡ 686 2999; e deltamed@info.bw, pak@info.bw

Okavango Pharmacy Letsego Bldg, Tsheko-Tsheko Rd, opposite Riley's Garage; ℡ 686 0043
Taurus Tsheko-Tsheko Rd; ℡ 6863 340. Close to Nandos (see page 159).

PHOTOGRAPHY Several outlets sell conventional film, including the Bush Telegraph, on Mathiba I Road; the Fuji shop, near Barclays Bank; and Maun Photolab, behind the bus station on Tsaro Road. To download digital pictures to CD, try Safari Cell (*Tsheko-Tsheko Rd;* ℡ *6864 864*) next to Barclays Bank; they also sell films and batteries.

WHAT TO SEE AND DO

Maun is really much more of a place to get organised than a destination in its own right, so few visitors are really looking for activities here. That said, if you have time to kill, here are a few suggestions. You could also visit one or two of the craftsmen listed under *Shopping* above.

ACTIVITIES The best **swimming pool** in the area is at the Sedia Hotel, open to non-residents who are using the bar and restaurant. If you're looking for something more strenuous, The Studio (*Mathiba I Rd;* ℡ *6800 578; open Mon–Sat*) behind Hilary's Coffee Shop offers day membership to the **gym** at P30. Rather more esoteric is the **cricket** pitch at Okavango River Lodge, where matches are played a couple of Sundays a month. It's also possible to organise **horseriding** for all levels (*contact Jen on* ℡ *7230 1054*); hard hats are available.

For members only, **Maun Sports Club**, opposite the technical college on the Maun–Nata road, has tennis and squash courts.

BIRDING Roger Hawker (*contact via Afro Trek,* ℡/f *6862 574;* m *7138 0632;* e *info@afrotrek.com; www.afrotrek.com*) leads birding walks of two hours or more from the Sedia Hotel. He has been a keen birdwatcher in the area for many years, some of them spent guiding and running camps in the Delta. His three-hour trip usually takes in the birds of Maun Educational Park, while his four-hour trip is long enough to reach the reedbeds and pools of the Boteti River, south of Maun. These cost about US$10 per person per hour, minimum 2 people.

CROCODILE FARM Maun's Crocodile Farm (℡ *6864 539;* e *sitatunga@info.bw; tour P10 pp*) is next door to Sitatunga Camp, on the Ghanzi road, with directions the same as for the camp (see page 159). Guided tours of the farm start on the hour between 09.00 and 16.00. You'll get to see Nile crocodiles from hatchlings to fully grown adults, and learn much about the morphology of these amazing reptiles.

MAUN EDUCATIONAL PARK Found to the east of Maun, barely 2km from the town centre, this small, fenced park (*Sekgoma Rd,* ℡ *6861 390; open daily 07.30–18.00; admission free*) is only about 3km long by 1km wide. It preserves the last of the natural habitat that used to be found in and around Maun – before goats and people wreaked havoc on its vegetation – but sadly its public areas in particular are now looking seriously neglected. Look beyond that, though, and you'll find some some fine stands of real fan palms (*Hyphaene petersiana*), various acacia thickets and some lovely riverine woodland. The park is bordered by the Thamalakane River, which attracts many aquatic bird species, whilst there are also a few open, grassy areas where you may find zebras, wildebeest and warthogs grazing. A number of other animal species, including blue wildebeest, red lechwe, kudu, impala, giraffe, chacma baboon and vervet monkey are resident, as well as a variety of smaller mammals.

In summer, a keen birdwatcher should be able to count 80 to 100 species of birds in three hours, although in winter it is more likely to be 50 to 80. Ones to look out for specially include red-necked falcon, bronze-winged courser, giant eagle-owl, lesser jacana, spotted dikkop, pied and Hartlaub's babblers, yellow-bellied eremomeia and swamp boubou. Fish eagles and crimson-breasted boubous are fairly easily seen, whilst bat hawks are sometimes spotted in the early morning or evening.

Despite its shortcomings, the park is the only place in Maun in which the public can walk freely among Botswana's native animals, so it remains a worthwhile place to visit, particularly with children. You can wander along the marked trails yourself, and cover most of the area in 2–4 hours, but serious birders would do better to contact Roger Hawker (see *Birding*, above).

MAUN SPORTS COMPLEX About 2.5km southwest of Riley's Garage on the road towards Ghanzi, this large and impressive new sports arena is used for political rallies as well as sports matches. It's worth going just to marvel at the stadium, but check in the local newspaper, *The Ngami Times*, for what's on there.

MOKORO TRIPS Several companies offer trips by mokoro, lasting from one to three days, although almost all these trips are run by the same community trust. For details see the box on page 166, and the individual tour operators on pages 168–72. It's also possible to fly in to Chief's Island for a day, with lunch, a mokoro trip and a bush walk, for US$250 pp. You'll usually need to book a day ahead with a travel agent such as Travel Wild (see page 167).

Before you shop around, it's worth explaining how these trips work. Essentially, the polers, mekoros and areas being offered by the various competing companies in Maun are all exactly the same. So by all means shop around for these trips, but be aware that what's on offer is basically the same everywhere, and will cost about the same.

The background An agreement has been made with the communities in the NG32 concession to co-ordinate mokoro trips on the Boro and Santantadibe rivers. There are a number of communities in the area, where work as polers and guides provides valuable income.

Government rules limit the numbers of visitors (and hence the impact of tourism). A maximum of 30 mekoro are allowed on each river system at any one time. These start off, and return to, one of three 'launch sites' on the Santantadibe, and one site on the Boro River.

The tour operators from Maun book slots for trips on a first-come, first-served basis; they also pay the freelance polers and guides from the community directly. It's a strict rule that there should be one professional poling guide from the villages for every party of up to eight visitors. The rest of the mekoro are usually poled by locals from the various villages who don't have this qualification.

OKAVANGO KOPANO MOKORO COMMUNITY TRUST (OKMCT)

If you're heading out on a mokoro trip from Maun, the chances are that you'll be going into the concession managed by OKMCT, a community trust that has been set up to ensure that, in line with Botswanan government policy, income generated by tourism directly benefits the community.

There are several mokoro poling stations in the concession area, all under two hours' drive from Maun. These include Boro, Ditship and Morutsha. Each mokoro takes two people, with a qualified guide poler accompanying every group of six people. Polers work on a rota basis to ensure that income derived from their work is fairly distributed throughout the community.

Essentially, OKMCT is responsible for the mokoro trails in the concession itself, but transfers to and from Maun are handled by a number of safari operators, including Afro Trek, Audi Camp, Crocodile Camp, Castro's Safaris, Delta Rain, Drifters, Okavango River lodge, Penstone Safaris and Sitatunga. Whereas transfer rates charged by tour operators will reflect their individual styles and costs, so may differ quite widely, OKMCT rates are fixed.

Guide polers and unqualified polers are paid according to an agreed scale, with the balance of fees payable made up of the concession entrance fee. The polers provide their own mekoros.

Trips here are basically mokoro trips, with short walks on the islands, and visitors usually bring all their own food and camping kit. All the polers bring is their own food – and when I last took a trip here, the poler appeared to have arranged our route to stop at friends on various islands.

Getting there and away For all of the budget mokoro trips, the operator organising it will drive you here. It takes about 90 minutes to most of the launch sites. You're not allowed to drive yourself here, and these trips must be booked through one of the participating companies in Maun. See the list of Maun operators and try one or two from those listed in the box above. There's usually no point contacting them all!

NHABE MUSEUM More of a gallery than a museum, this small venue (*Sir Seretse Khama Rd*) has constantly changing exhibits that often showcase the art of local students. A small, rather poorly displayed collection of artefacts includes musical instruments and hunting tools. '*Nhabe*', incidentally, is from the Bushman word for the sound of cattle pulling their feet out of the mud, now more usually rendered as '*ngami*'.

SCENIC FLIGHTS Short flights over the Delta in light aircraft or helicopters are offered by several companies. Rates are on a 'per-plane' basis, rather than per person, from around P1,250 per hour for a five-seater plane, plus P50 departure tax per person. Helicopter rates start from P1,825 for half an hour, for four people, but really you need at least an hour – at around P3,650. For contact details, see *Flight companies* on pages 172–3.

TRADITIONAL VILLAGE If you're seeking something of the traditional Botswanan way of life, John Davey organises half-day trips to a Bayei village outside Maun (↘ *6861 823, or book through a travel agent; US$80 pp*). We understand that this is a real opportunity to understand the life of the Bayei rather than an 'experience' set up solely with the visitor in mind.

NATIONAL PARKS AND WILDLIFE SERVICE This important office (*Kubu St, off Sir Seretse Khama Rd; open Mon–Sat 07.30–12.45 & 13.45–16.30; Sun 07.30–12.00*) in an unassuming prefabricated building is the place to book campsites for all the national parks in northern Botswana. It's much, much better to come in person, if possible, than to ring or fax. See pages 138 for more details.

TOURIST INFORMATION The Department of Tourism (*Tsheko-Tsheko Rd;* ✎ *6860 492; open Mon–Fri only*) has an office opposite Riley's, though in reality they are not set up for walk-in visitors, with just a few hotel leaflets and their own magazines available to visitors. Far better to drop in to one of Maun's travel agents if you're seeking advice on what to do in and around the area.

The local newspaper, *The Ngami Times*, is published weekly at P2.20, and is available across the city. It's useful for details of local sports and entertainment.

TRAVEL AGENTS Maun may seem to the uninitiated to be full of travel agents, but many of the companies you see are tour operators who own and run camps and safari companies (see below). However, if you look hard there is a handful of normal travel agents who (generally) know the local safari industry well, and can help you choose a trip. They are especially useful if you arrive in Maun without any arrangements and want to book a budget trip immediately. In such cases, booking through one of these agents will cost you exactly the same as booking directly with the camp or safari company.

The caveats to this are that none is well prepared for booking a range of the top-end lodges at short notice; there's very little demand for this. Secondly, some will have their own favourite camps or operators – so do ask them to be exhaustive about researching the options for you before you make a decision. Also ask them to make very clear if anyone associated with them has any links with the camps or trips that they're suggesting to you. (This shouldn't necessarily put you off booking – but you ought to know!)

Africa Pride ✎/f 6864 845; e africapride@ botsnet.bw; www.africapridebotswana.com. Based in Maun and run by owners Edurne Martinez and Carol-Ann Green, Africa Pride is a booking agent/tour operator for lodges throughout southern Africa and the Indian Ocean islands. They can arrange for Spanish, French, German and Italian interpreters to accompany trips.
The Booking Company Tsheko-Tsheko Rd; ✎ 6860 022, 6860 654; e reservations@booking.co.bw; www.thebookingcompany.net. This small and independent travel agency was started by Derek Flatt in 1990 and is now in new premises in the PostNet complex by Riley's. It is a sister-company of Safari Air, though is not directly connected to any of the lodges. Thus it can independently recommend options for you, and is another good choice for helping you to organise a last-minute mokoro trip or safari.
Okavango Tours & Safaris Power Station Bldg, Mophane Av; ✎ 6860 220; e info@

okavangotours.com; www.okavangotours.com. OTS is closely associated with Lodges of Botswana (see page 170) who own Delta Camp and Oddballs (both in NG27B). Both companies are owned by Peter Sandenbergh. That said, OTS also arrange trips to other lodges and on a variety of other safaris, if requested. It's an efficient, professional company that knows its business. Note that it's totally different from the tour operator of the same name in the UK.
Tete Travel & Tours New Mall; ✎ 6863 239; e gal@dynabyte.bw
Travel Wild Mathiba I Rd; ✎ 6860 822; e reservations@travelwild.co.bw; www.botswanaholidays.com. Opposite the airport, next to Stanbic Bank, Travel Wild is another good, independent travel agent, a friendly and helpful one-stop shop for what to do in and around Maun, and short trips into the Delta. They are also representatives for Motsentsela Tree Lodge (see page 151), on the outskirts of Maun, and the Panhandle's Shakawe Fishing Lodge (see page 334).

Maun TOURIST INFORMATION, TRAVEL AGENTS AND TOUR OPERATORS

8

SAFARI COMPANIES Looking at the length of this list, you'll realise that Maun is the safari capital of Botswana. Listed alphabetically, these range from large safari companies with many camps through to tiny operators which are little more than a guide and a vehicle. Since prices change regularly, these have not been included except where a company has no website, or to indicate particularly good value.

Note that for most of the larger operators, the contact details listed here are simply their base for logistics and operations in Maun. Many do not have booking offices here, preferring to take all reservations, and answer all queries from visitors, from dedicated reservation offices elsewhere (usually Johannesburg in South Africa).

In contrast the smaller operations may take days, or even weeks, to answer communications – sometimes because the whole team is out of the office and on safari. This kind of tiny outfit has both advantages and disadvantages, as you'll realise.

African Horseback Safaris ℆ 6863 154; e safaris@ africanhorseback.com; www.africanhorseback.com. Specialist horseriding safaris based out of Macatoo Camp on the western side of the Delta, in NG26. See pages 298 for details.

Afro Trek ℆/f 6862 574; ℆ 6886 510; e info@ afrotrek.com; www.afrotrek.com. Based at the Sedia Hotel, Afro Trek offer both 4x4 game safaris and short trips in and around Maun – including guided birding walks (see page 164).

Audi Camp Safaris ℆ 6860 599, 6863 005; e emma@okavangocamp.com; www.okavangocamp.com. Based out of Audi Camp (see page 156) north of Maun, Audi Camp Safaris run a range of budget trips in the Delta, from mobile camping trips to drive-in mokoro trips, in conjunction with local polers. Typically, trips require a minimum of 2 people and include meals, park fees, vehicle, guide and camping equipment, with travellers expected to bring their own drinks and sleeping bags, and muck in with all camp chores.

Botswana Safaris & Tours ℆ 6864 845, 6864 655; e botswanasafaris@dynabyte.bw; www.mobilesafaris.com. Run by Guy Symons (a guide trained in South Africa), Botswana Tours & Safaris has been in business since around 1989. Trips of 6–10 days using either lodge or campsite accommodation encompass all the parks and areas of interest in northern Botswana. Private mobile trips, usually concentrating on Chobe, Moremi, the Central Kalahari and the great salt pans area, are also an option. Min 6 people.

Bush Ways Safaris ℆ 6863 685; e reservations@ bushways.com; www.bushways.com. Established in 1996, Bush Ways operates small-group mobile trips with guaranteed departures, as well as tailor-made trips. Sheduled trips cover Chobe, Moremi, Nxai, Makgadikgadi and the Central Kalahari, whilst their tailor-made mobile trips go anywhere. Their custom-

built vehicles (max 12 passengers) have canvas tops and open sides (with covered sides for wet or wind). Scheduled trips, which run even if there is only one person booked, are 'semi-participation' – travellers pitch their own tents and assist with catering duties 'if they wish'. Bring your own sleeping bag and pillow (or rent these for US$25 per bag per safari). Private mobile trips can be more luxurious, though the cost is significantly greater. Bush Ways guides variously speak French, German, Spanish, English and Afrikaans; for a private safari, specify that you want a guide who speaks your language.

Butler & Lindstrom Safaris ℆ 6860 994; e sls@info.bw. This top-end company, set up in the early 1980s, offers expert-guided, tailor-made private safaris in both the national parks and a few of the region's private concession areas (where they can offer walking and night drives). Expect very comfortable camping: the large walk-in tents have en-suite showers and flush toilets; the cuisine is impressive and served in style by candlelight; the guiding is amongst the best around. Vehicles (max 5 people) are custom-built Toyota 4x4s, some open and some fitted with roof hatches.

Capricorn Safaris ℆ 6861 165; f 6862 991; e info@capricornsafaris.com; www.capricornsafaris.com. Capricorn specialises in good-value, fairly traditional mobile safaris without too many frills, and with the emphasis firmly on game viewing. Run by Adam and Brigette Hedges, who have a long pedigree from running safaris in east Africa with Dick Hedges' Safaris, Capricorn offers fixed-date trips across northern Botswana, as well as private mobile trips. Their most popular trip is a 10-night, fully serviced tented safari (no chores!), taking in 3 nights in a mobile tented camp either in Nxai Pan or the Okavango; 4 nights in Moremi, inc a boat trip and a night fly-camping on an island; and 3 nights in Chobe. Custom-built Toyota Land Cruisers (max 6 passengers) have large roof hatches for photography, a drinks fridge and a small reference library. Expect Meru-style tents, with communal hot bucket showers and long-drop toilets.

Castro Safaris ✆ 7173 1358; e castro@yahoo.com. A local operator with reportedly reliable vehicles who offers some of the cheapest day trips in Maun, at P750 pp per day, and is well recommended for budget trips. He also speaks good English. Book directly or through Travel Wild (see above).

Crocodile Camp Safaris ✆ 6860 796, 6860 265; e sales@botswana.com; www.botswana.com. From its base in the Buck & Hunter building, near the airport, CCS run Semetsi Camp (see page 308) in NG27B, on the southwest side of Chief's Island. They also manage Swamp Air. CCS have their own infrastructure and guides for mobile camping trips around Botswana, and these they build into a variety of small low/mid-budget packages. They also market mid-budget fly-in trips, often combining their own camps with other mid-range options like Okuti at Xakanaxa, or Chobe Safari Lodge. If you're in Maun and looking for something relatively inexpensive and last minute, then CCS should certainly be on your list.

CC Africa ✆ 6861 979; e ccabotswana@info.bw; www.ccafrica.com. Conservation Corporation Africa is a leading ecotourism company, committed to high quality alongside sustainable conservation development and community empowerment. Of over 35 lodges throughout east and southern Africa, they have 2 in Botswana's Okavango Delta: Nxabega and Sandibe. Guided expeditions are also on offer. Their Maun office does not handle bookings; for reservations, see page 79.

Delta Rain ✆ 6800 380, m 7130 4292; e deltarain@dynabyte.bw. In operation since the late 1990s, Delta Rain organises 1- and 2-night safaris from their base at Sitatunga Campsite (see page 159) to a private concession in the Delta. The focus of these is guided mokoro trips and game walks led by qualified guides who, like all their staff, work as part of a community-based programme. Clients must supply all camping gear, cooking equpt and food. Occasional day trips are run when there is water in the Boro River (US$100 pp), and 45min flights at US$350 per plane (max 5 people) can be organised. Advance booking essential.

Desert & Delta Safaris Tel +27 11 7060861; e reservations@desertdelta.com; www.desertdelta.com. The operators of Chobe Game Lodge, Chobe Savanna Lodge, Savute Safari Lodge,

Camp Moremi, Camp Okavango and Xugana Island Lodge also own a fleet of 8 light aircraft, enabling easy access to each lodge with regular connections to Livingstone, Victoria Falls and Maun.

Drumbeat Safaris ✆ 6863 096; e drumbeat@inet.co.bw; www.drumbeatsafaris.com. Set up in 1995 by Dutch founders Johan Knols and Annelies Zonjee, Drumbeat offers comfortable and luxury private mobile safaris throughout northern Botswana. Trips are usually guided by Johan (who speaks English, Dutch and German), whilst Annelies and her staff manage the camps. Vehicles are open 'safari outfitted' Toyota Land Cruisers (max 7 visitors); equipment and staff accompany the tour in a separate truck. Comfortable camps with Meru-style tents are usually set up on private campsites within the parks; trips inc park fees, activities, all meals, all drinks and laundry – with children welcome. Helicopter trips and luxury safari-boat cruises also available.

Eco Africa Botswana ✆ 6862 427; e rogersafaris@dynabyte.bw; www.ecoafricabotswana.com. Run by Roger and Sophie Dugmore, Eco Africa Botswana specialises in small mobile safaris and specialised photographic expeditions around all of Botswana's national parks and wilder areas. Trips are neither budget nor participatory, and are run on a leisurely basis, with camp locations moved only every 3–4 days.

Elephant Back Safaris ✆ 6861 260; e ebs@info.bw; www.abucamp.com. The booking and logistical office in Maun runs the ultra-upmarket Abu Camp, on the west of the Delta in NG26 (see pages 294–7). Don't even think about asking for any last-minute deals: they don't exist!

Game Trails Safaris ✆ 6800 369; e gametrails@botsnet.bw; www.gametrailsbotswana.com. Game Trails operates comfortable, fully serviced, mobile safaris, with walk-in tents, throughout Botswana's wilderness areas. Scheduled trips vary in length from 6 to 9 nights.

Gunn's Camp ✆ 6860 023; e sales@gunnscamp.com; www.gunnscamp.com. From its base in the Buck & Hunter building, near the airport, Gunn's Camp runs Ntswi Island in NG27B, overlooking Chief's Island in the Moremi Game Reserve. Access to the island is by light aircraft only, with mokoro excursions and game walks on offer, uninterrupted by vehicles.

Island Safari Lodge ✆ 6860 330; e enquire@africansecrets.net; www.africansecrets.net. Based out of the lodge (see pages 157–8), north of Maun, are a variety of budget mokoro trips and participation safaris that can often be booked at short notice. Island Safari have been very supportive of the

Okavango Polers' Trust and their trips based out of Mbiroba Camp (see page 332), so usually have packages which include flights there and back, and time in the Delta. You'll need to take all your food and equipment, yet stay within a modest 10kg luggage allowance. They also run trips on the Boro River in conjunction with the local polers in NG32 (see pages 321–2 for details and my comments on budget trips). These start from the lodge at around 08.00 when you're driven by 4x4 for about 2 hours to the poling station at Morutsa. After your trip you'll return downstream, and be driven back to Maun the same way. Costs range from US$78 pp (1-day trip, though this is hardly worth the effort for the minimal time that you get on the water) to US$170 pp sharing for a 1-night/2-day trip or US$240 or 2-night/3-day trip; you'll need to bring all your own food and camping kit (packed lunch supplied for day trips). A trip very like this, from Island Safari Lodge, was my first view of the Okavango and, whilst it has its limitations, I'd still regard it as remarkably good value. Island Safari's participation safaris are squarely aimed at backpackers who haven't got the transport or the kit. They'll supply an open-topped 4x4 (usually with optional canvas sunshade), which takes up to 8 passengers and a professional guide, plus dome tents, mattresses, cooking equipment, crockery, gas lamps, cooler boxes and all the rest of the paraphernalia that goes with a trip to the bush. Food is included, but soft drinks and alcohol are not. Costs for these trips vary with the destination and group size.

Ker & Downey ✆ 6860 375, 6861 226; e safari@ kerdowney.bw; www.kerdowney.com. Now based out of offices opposite the airport, Ker and Downey are two of the oldest names in the Delta. Back in 1945, Donald Ker and Syd Downey founded a hunting safari company in Kenya, to be joined in the mid-1950s by Harry Selby — who started their Botswana operations in 1962. Around 1979 they bought Khwai River Lodge, as a photographic camp, and in 1985 the photographic company Ker, Downey & Selby was split off from the hunting company, Safari South. Today it's known simply as Ker & Downey, and they run Camp Okuti, Kanana, Machaba, Shinde and its neighbouring walking trails, known as 'Footsteps across Africa'. These are all quite different camps and experiences, and the costs vary too. Reservations for Ker & Downey camps can be made through their Maun office, or their US office (see page 81).

Kgori Safaris Pharmacy House, New Mall; ✆ 686 2049; e mankwe@info.bw; www.mankwe.com. This

relative newcomer to Maun's tour operators offers a range of itineraries for 4–14 participants. They also own and run Mankwe Bush Lodge, in NG45, just south of Chobe and east of Moremi, and manage the boat station on the northwest tip of Mboma Island in Moremi (see page 258).

Kwando Safaris ✆ 6861 449; e info@kwando.co.za; www.kwando.co.za. Based in Maun, Kwando is a small, independent operator running 3 first-class camps in Botswana, as well as Songwe Village, a small camp in Zambia near Livingstone which overlooks the Zambezi's gorge, just below Victoria Falls.

Lagoon and **Lebala** are primarily dry-land camps beside the Kwando River in NG14, and Kwara has a full range of dry and wet activities, on the north side of the Delta. All are different, but all operate game drives with both a tracker and a driver — a real advantage when it comes to tracking the predators. Their focus is on enthusiastic wildlife spotting rather than excessive frills in camp, although their camps are of a high standard.

Linyanti Explorations Based in Kasane, from where they run Selinda and Zibalianja camps adjacent to the Zibadianja Lagoon on the Kwando/Linyanti system. See pages 235–6 for details.

Lodges of Botswana Power Station Bldg; ✆ 6861 154; e info@lodgesofbotswana.com; www.lodgesofbotswana.com. This Maun-based company is run by the irrepressible Peter Sandenbergh, who was one of the first to see the area's potential for backpacking tourism as well as the more usual upmarket variety. Today they own and run Delta Camp and Oddballs, in NG27B. They have particularly close links with the General Trading Company, the airline Delta Air and the Maun-based travel agent, Okavango Tours & Safaris.

Masson Safaris Plot 855, Tsanokana Ward; ✆ 6862 442; e sallie@masson-safaris.com; www.masson-safaris.com. This small family operation runs mobile photographic safaris which concentrate on game and birdlife, with a general appreciation of Botswana's more remote areas (they're especially keen on the more offbeat bits of the Kalahari: the Great Salt Pans, Tsodilo and the Central Kalahari). Ewan Masson, who has been guiding in Botswana for 20 years, leads most trips. On mobile camps expect walk-in dome tents, complete with linen, washstand, reading light and a private chemical flush loo. Game drives are taken in extended Land Rovers (max 8 guests). Both scheduled and tailor-made safaris are offered.

Maun Rest Camp Safaris ✆ 6862 623; f 6863 472 (with answerphone); e simonjoyce@info.bw. Based out of Maun Rest Camp (see page 158), owners

Simon and Joyce run fairly small, low-budget mobile safaris led by either Simon or Joyce, both of whom are qualified guides. A staff member comes along with each trip to help with the camp chores. For accommodation they use full bedrolls with linen inside stand-up-size dome tents, and are known for providing good, wholesome meals with plenty of fresh fruit and vegetables. Don't expect glossy brochures or silver service here, but do expect comfortable — not luxury — safaris at a very fair price, and a swift and efficient response to any queries. Using adapted Toyota Land Cruisers, they cover the Moremi and Chobe areas as well as the Central Kalahari, Nxai Pan, Baines' Baobabs, Makgadikgadi, Tsodilo Hills and even Drotsky's Caves. Costs include fuel, park fees, meals, drinks and VAT, as well as mokoro excursions and boat cruises if these are part of the chosen itinerary. You'd be wise to make arrangements in advance if you can, simply so they can secure bookings with the national park's campsites.

Moremi Safaris ✆ +27 11 463 3999; e info@ moremi-safaris.com; www.moremi-safaris.com. The owners of Xakanaxa Camp (see page 256) also offer lodge-based safari packages.

Naga Safaris ✆ 6800 587, 📱 7163 7250; e nagasafaris@hotmail.com. Run by local Botswanans, Naga Safaris was established in 2001. A friendly, no-frills outfit, they offer camping or lodge safaris with their own guides and cooks to the national parks, Makgadikgadi and Nxai Pans, the Central Kalahari and Victoria Falls (P550 pp per day, inc camping, food, transport and park fees). They also run day and overnight trips, both independently and with camps such as Audi Camp and Okavango River Lodge, into the Delta, Moremi or Nxai Pan for 6–8 people, costing P1,400 per vehicle, inc fuel and a guide. Camping equipment is available for hire. Transfers to/from Kasane via Nata or Chobe/Moremi cost P1,500 per vehicle.

Okavango Horse Safaris ✆ 6861 671; e ohsnx@ info.bw; www.okavangohorse.com. See pages 312–13.

Okavango Polers' Trust ✆ 6876 861; e mbiroba@ okavangodelta.co.bw; www.okavangodelta.co.bw. Based on the northern edge of the Delta, at Seronga (a village of about 3,000 people), this is a co-operative of mokoro polers who have joined together to offer budget trips in the north of the Delta. You can get to Seronga yourself, or book flights and a package through local operators in Maun. See pages 332–3 for more details and costs.

Okavango Wilderness Safaris I Mathiba I Rd; ✆ 6860 086 (for reservations or enquiries, call the Johannesburg office; see page 79). Started by safari

guides Colin Bell, Chris MacIntyre (not the author!) and Russel Friedman in Botswana in 1983, this has since grown into one of the subcontinent's leading safari organisers — with operations throughout southern Africa. They are closely linked with Sefofane, the flight company. From their office in Maun, virtually opposite the airport next to Stanbic Bank, Okavango Wilderness Safaris also market Botswana's largest selection of safari camps. These are mostly in private reserves and include: Duma Tau, King's Pool, and Savuti Camp in NG15; Vumbura Plains and Little Vumbura in NG22; Duba Plains in NG23; Kwetsani, Jacana, Jao and Tubu in NG25; Abu Camp in NG26; Jacks and San Camps in the Makgadigadi, Chitabe and Chitabe Trails in NG31; and Mombo, Little Mombo and Xigera in the Moremi Game Reserve. The style and standard of these do vary, and recently have been marketed as either 'premier' or 'classic' — with prices that vary accordingly. However, despite this, Wilderness effectively sets the baseline standard for high-quality camps in Botswana, by which other operators tend to be measured. In 2005 the company revived their mobile safaris, with luxury Discoverer trips and Classic Adventurer trips, both of which aim to recreate the atmosphere of an unhurried exploratory journey, are non-participatory and operate primarily in private concession areas. Departures are guaranteed with a minimum of 2 guests (max 8). Note that Wilderness actively advises travellers to book through their local tour operator rather than making direct bookings.

Orient-Express Safaris Airport Av; ✆ 6860 302; e gtb.mngr@info.bw; www.gametrackers.orient-express.com (for reservations, see page 79). The owners of the famous Venice-Simplon Orient Express train also have 3 upmarket lodges in Botswana: Savute Elephant Camp, Khwai River Lodge and Eagle Island Camp. Specifications in each are comparable with top hotels, very much belying their 'tent' status. Their Maun office is situated very close to the airport, between the Dept of Surveys and Mapping and the Merlin Air Service.

Penduka Safaris ✆ 6864 539; e safaris@ penduka.com.na; www.penduka.com.na. Based at Sitatunga Camp (see page 159), but no longer involved with the campsite, Penduka Safaris was started in 1963 by Izak Barnard, and has been run by his son, Willem, since the early 1990s. Penduka operates fully inclusive safaris throughout Botswana; all camp duties are taken care of by permanent staff. Excellent meals with fresh fruit and vegetables are served daily, and they provide large, spacious tents with camp beds and mattresses. Vehicles are specially adapted 4x4s with pop-top roof hatches. Trips vary in length, and some are tailor-made, but 8–12 nights would be typical.

Phakawe Safaris The Pumpkin Patch, Shorobe Rd; ↘ 6864 377; e phakawe@phakawe.demon.co.uk; www.phakawe.demon.co.uk. Run by Sabine and Steve, the successful Phakawe Safaris is based about 1km north of Maun, in the Newtown area. Its orange building with a green roof is clearly visible on the left as you drive towards Chobe. It offers some of the cheapest budget safaris around: some with scheduled departure dates, others tailor-made to suit groups of 4 or more. Costs are usually US$140 per day, inc transfers and transport (usually max 6 people per trip), parks fees, ingredients for all meals and use of simple tents, mattresses and camping kit. It doesn't include sleeping bags, drinks or any 'optional activities'. Trips are long – typically 11 days – with many options; check out their website to find out what is, and is not, included, and where their trips stay each night. Their Northern Parks trip, for example, includes 2 nights at a lodge in Maun, either side of 2 nights on a budget mokoro trip in NG32, then 6 nights through Moremi and Chobe.

Sanctuary Lodges & Camps ↘ 6862 688 (for reservations, see page 79). Abercrombie & Kent's lodges in Botswana and east Africa – including Chobe Chilwero and Chief's Camp – are now marketed under the Sanctuary Lodges brand.

Untamed African Safaris ↘ 6860 572; e untamed@dynabyte.bw; www.africa-untamed.com. The full range of mobile-safari options is available, from fully participatory budget camps to upmarket style.

Wilderness Dawning ↘ 6862 962; e wd@info.bw; www.africa-in-style.co.za/wild.htm. This reliable small mobile operator boasts that its guides all have a minimum of 10 years' guiding experience in Botswana. They offer a mix of scheduled and tailor-made safaris, taking in all the usual wildlife areas of northern Botswana. Some are aimed at mid-level budgets, with walk-in dome tents and shared toilets and hot buckets showers. Others are more luxurious, with accommodation in lodges, but the same experienced guide for the whole trip. This offers the best of both worlds in some ways – comfort of accommodation and continuity of guiding – but is on the pricey side.

Wilderness Safaris See Okavango Wilderness Safaris, page 171.

Wild Attractions ↘ 6860 300; f 6862 932; e wild-attract@info.bw; www.africansecrets.net. Affiliated to Island Safari Lodge (see pages 157–8), Wild Attractions offers a range of options from participation safaris, through mid-range to luxury safaris. Special-interest trips cater for enthusiasts in a given field, such as ornithology or entomology, while others focus on Botswanan culture.

Wild Lifestyles ↘ 6863 664; e mikepenman@botsnet.bw; www.mikepenman.com. Mike Penman isn't a guy that shrinks into the background easily, but when on good form he can be exactly the kind of large, slightly wild, old-style guide that you'd want to have between you and a charging buffalo. He's been guiding in Botswana for many years, and knows northern Botswana well. His trips range widely from the normal Maun–Chobe routes, through to more esoteric options of the Bushmen at Xai Xai and some of the private concessions. Choose from luxury mobile trips and fly-camps to specialist trips for film-makers and photographers. Accommodation is usually in fully equipped, walk-in dome tents with private bucket showers and long-drop toilets, and vehicles are Toyota HiLuxes with raised seats on the back, beneath a canvas sunshade, usually accompanied by a back-up vehicle. Mike co-presented a show (*Mad Mike & Mark*) for the Discovery Channel for some time, and often assists film companies.

FLIGHT COMPANIES With the exception of Air Botswana, all the companies mentioned here are small charter companies operating light aircraft out of Maun Airport and around the camps and lodges of northern Botswana.

I include these not because you need to ever book your own flights between the camps; you don't. That's always done for you by the camps concerned, or your tour operator back home; it's better that way.

I include a list of the main airlines and their contact details here so that, in case of emergency, you can contact them. More likely, you may want to charter a plane somewhere fairly unusual – like the Tsodilo Hills for the day, for a pleasure flight over the Delta, or even to take you to Windhoek! These details should give you some idea of who to contact to arrange this.

Note that booking inter-camp flights through the camps is invariably cheaper than chartering them directly with the airlines. For rough guidance, a nine-seater plane (ten if you include the pilot!) and an hour's flying time costs around P1,350 plus P10 pp airport departure tax. Similarly a Cessna 206 which would accommodate five passengers would cost around P700 per hour, plus P10 pp airport tax. These basic prices will usually vary very little between the various companies.

Delta Air Mathiba I Rd; ☎ 6860 044, 6861 682; e synergy@info.bw. With an office opposite the airport, Delta Air has a close association with Lodges of Botswana — and hence usually operates the transfers for Delta Camp and Oddballs. In addition, it offers all the usual charter services inc pleasure flights over the Delta.
5-seater plane P1,250 1hr plus P50 departure tax pp. Open daily 08.00–17.00.
Northern Air Mathiba I Rd; ☎ 6860 385; e nair@kerdowney.bw. Opposite the airport building, Northern Air's offices are on the corner on the right. It is part-owned by Ker & Downey, and hence is frequently used by them for inter-camp transfers. They can also arrange pleasure flights over the Delta.
Mack Air Mathiba I Rd, ☎ 6860 675; e mack.air@info.bw. Mack Air maintains a good reputation as a reliable, high-quality air charter company which doesn't have ties to any of the camps.
Merlin Air Services Mathiba I Rd; ☎ 6860 351. No guidebook to Maun would be quite complete without a mention of Merlin Services. Situated on the corner of Airport Rd, immediately outside the airport's gates, Merlin acted as a communications hub and booking centre for a few of the area's older, independent

camps — when communications meant telex and radios rather than cellphones and satellite phones.
Moremi Air ☎ 686 3632. Just next to Merlin Air Services.
Okavango Helicopters ☎ 6865 797; m 7186 6607; f 6865 798; e okavangoheli@dynabyte.bw. The name says it all! 1hr flights cover an area from Maun to just south of Moremi; ½hr gets to the veterinary fence.
P1,825 ½hr, P3,650 1hr, for 4 people. Open Mon–Fri 08.00–17.00, Sat 08.30–12.00, Sun by appointment only.
Sefofane Mathiba I Rd; ☎ 6860 778; e sefofane@info.bw. Based out of the Okavango Wilderness Safaris' block of offices, just outside the airport's gates, Sefofane is part-owned by Wilderness Safaris. Hence they organise virtually all the flying in Botswana for clients to Wilderness's camps, making them the biggest 'small' airline here. In an emergency, if they're not available on the number above, then try getting hold of them via Okavango Wilderness Safaris in Maun, or even by ringing Wilderness's Johannesburg office (see pages 79).
Wildlife Helicopters Mathiba I Rd; ☎ 6860 664; e wildheli@info.bw

THE ROAD NORTH OF MAUN: TO MOREMI AND CHOBE *Map pages 242–3*

FROM MAUN TO MOREMI GAME RESERVE Leave Maun heading northeast, passing the airport turn-off on your left. After about 10km you'll reach a large and newish roundabout with a right turn to Francistown and a left to Shorobe. Taking the left, you'll shortly pass Island Safari Lodge and Crocodile Camp.

Just under 40km after Maun you'll pass straight through the village of Shorobe. This is a good tar road, but beware of travelling too fast as you'll find domestic animals. **Shorobe** is a sizeable village about 26km north of Maun, and 53km south of Moremi Game Reserve's South Gate. It's also the northern limit of the tar road between Maun and Moremi or Kasane. Drive slowly through here as you can usually expect plenty of goats and people wandering on the road. Dotted through the village are a few small shops which sell soft drinks and very basic supplies, and there's a garish blue bar called Spyros (*open Fri–Wed 08.00–13.00, 14.00–17.00*) that could be a reasonable spot to break your journey. Otherwise, the one place that may be worth checking out is the Chorobe Craft Studio, housed in an unmissable bright-green thatched building at the northern edge of the village. On sale is a surprisingly small range of baskets and wooden sculptures, and some exuberantly painted metal washtubs, but do have a look; the money you pay is almost certainly going straight back into the local community.

Around 19km from Shorobe you'll reach the veterinary control fence, or the 'buffalo fence' as most people know it. Just 2km after the fence you'll meet a fork, signposted with a green concrete bollard. Turning left will bring you to Moremi Reserve's South Gate after about 32km. See the section on South Gate (pages 260–3) for comments on this road.

🏠 **Where to stay** There are three places beside the road that you may want to stay: one community campsite and two relatively new lodges.

Sankuyo village Sankuyo Tshwaragano Management Trust have recently developed a campsite and traditional village about 25km south of Sankuyo, south of the split between the roads to Moremi and Chobe. It lies on the main Maun–South Gate road, about 70km north of Maun, and 7km west of the Mowana Gate on the buffalo fence. This is on the eastern side of NG34 – see pages 223–6 for more on that area – but has been included here for continuity, as it's most applicable to people who are driving themselves through this area. It has community links with Santawani Lodge, about 15km south of Moremi Game Reserve's South Gate (see page 322–3).

🛖 **Kaziikini Campsite** (3 rondavels, camping) ☎ 6800 664; f 6800 665; e santawani@dynabite.bw. Now up and running again after a fire a few years ago, Kaziikini has small twin-bedded rondavels and camping on a large, tree-shaded site. At a push you could use this as a base for driving into Moremi or Chobe. There's a bar and restaurant here, but you'll need to order food at least half a day in advance. Self-drive game drives are available for P66 – you supply the vehicle, they supply the guide. *Rondavel P140, camping P45 pp.*

Lodges

🏠 **Starling's** NG34 Reserve. The Chobe road until a little north of Sankuyo, and all of the road from the veterinary fence to South Gate, are in NG34 concession. In 2006, Starling's Reserve was scheduled to be taken over as a private camp by a US tour operator. See page 326 for more details.

🏠 **Mankwe Bush Lodge** NG43 Reserve. To the east of Sankuyo is the drier NG43 concession. See pages 326–7 for more details of both the lodge and the private reserve area.

CONTINUING TO CHOBE If you're heading straight to Chobe, follow the directions above for South Gate, but just after the buffalo fence take the right turn.

This leads, after about 24km, to Sankuyo village (see above). Shortly after Sankuyo the road forks again. Take the right fork to reach Mababe village after about 30km. Leave Mababe with a left turn to head west of northwest. From there keep right as the track forks after a kilometre or so. After crossing the cut-line that marks Chobe's boundary, you'll soon be heading north towards Chobe's Mababe Gate (✪ MABGAT 19°06.182'S; 23°59.119'E), which is about 22km from Mababe Village.

Had you taken the left fork after Sankuyo, you would travel about 33km due north along the Moremi cut-line before joining the road which links the Mababe Gate with Moremi's North Gate, and crosses the Magwikhwe Sand Ridge. From this junction, a left would take you to North Gate (about 22km away), and a right would lead you across the sand ridge and, eventually (29km), back to the road mentioned above – from Mababe Village to Mababe Gate.

9

Kasane and the Northeast

KASANE

Kasane itself is just a small town standing on the southern bank of the Chobe River, in the northwest corner of Botswana, a few kilometres from its confluence with the Zambezi – where the borders of Zambia, Zimbabwe, Namibia and Botswana meet at a point.

Although Kasane is of limited interest to the visitor in itself, it is an important gateway: to the Chobe National Park, to Victoria Falls in Zimbabwe and Livingstone in Zambia, to the road across Namibia's Caprivi Strip, and to the small charter flights which ferry visitors between the various lodges in northern Botswana. So if you're just passing through the area, it's quite likely that you'll come via Kasane, if only on a transfer bus. And if you've organised your own travelling then you're likely to want to stop here, to refuel and refresh before continuing. But for many people, Kasane is a relaxing place to stay for a couple of days to take advantage of its proximity to Chobe National Park, affording opportunities of boat cruises and game drives into the park.

GETTING THERE AND AWAY
Self-drive
To/from Francistown Kasane is about 316km of good tarred road from Nata, and 506km from Francistown. It's a straight and easy drive, though not very interesting scenically; most people stop at Nata to fill up with fuel and relieve the boredom. If you are hitching or travelling by bus, then this road is easy by Botswana's standards – make an early start from Francistown and you can expect to reach Kasane by nightfall.

Note that there are often plenty of elephants on this road, so despite it being tar you should drive with caution. As with most roads in rural Africa, driving at night is asking for trouble – especially as grey elephants are well camouflaged against the grey tarmac.

To/from Zimbabwe
Kazungula There is an excellent tarred road from Zimbabwe to the Kazungula border and across into Botswana (open 06.00–18.00). This means that one of Africa's biggest centres for travellers, Victoria Falls, is a day trip away from Kasane – and, more notably, that Chobe can be visited as a day trip from the Falls.

About 2km after entering Botswana at the substantial immigration office, there's a T-junction. The right turn is for the ferry to Zambia only; left leads you immediately past a disease-control post. Here your vehicle will be driven through a puddle of insecticide and you'll be asked to stamp your shoes on an impregnated mat. You'll also be checked to make sure that you're not importing banned animal products – like fresh meat, milk, bones or skins (all part of Botswana's zealous

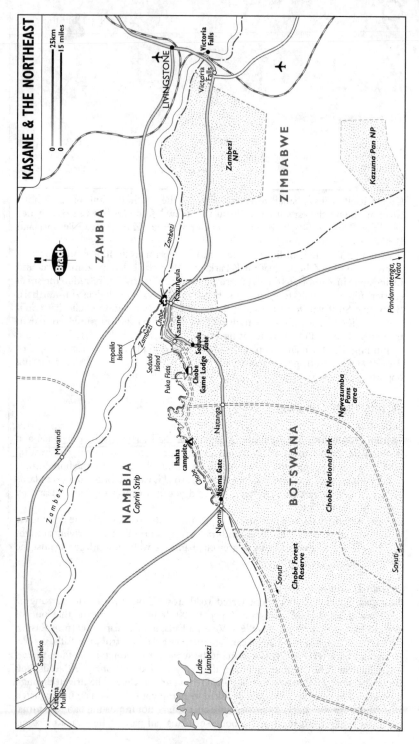

efforts to protect their national herd from diseases). Under 2km later and there's a right turn to Kasane, while straight on leads to Nata and Francistown. This is about 12km east of Kasane town.

If you're on an organised trip then it's very easy to have a road transfer arranged for you between Kasane and Victoria Falls. It'll take about two hours, and cost in the region of US$60/£35 per person, one-way.

Pandamatenga About 93km south of Kasane, and 223km from Nata, this is one of the country's few arable-farming areas. It's easily distinguished by the prominent grain silos, which tower over the surrounding sorghum and maize fields. The small border post with Zimbabwe is open 08.00–16.00. It is less than 50km from Robins Camp, deep in the heart of Zimbabwe's Hwange National Park, so it can be a convenient way to drive between Chobe and Hwange.

To/from Zambia While transfers from Livingstone airport are easily arranged and relatively inexpensive (about US$60), the Zambian government charges US$65 per person for a transit visa if visitors are not staying in Zambia overnight. If you're planning to take this route, it's well worth considering an overnight stop in Livingstone, in which case your hotel or campsite should be able to register your stay with the immigration authorities in advance, and the visa fee will usually be waived. This would also give you the opportunity to visit Victoria Falls before heading on to Kasane. The journey from Livingstone to the border takes about 50 minutes along a straight, newly tarred road of about 60km, running parallel to the Zambezi.

Kazungula About 2km from the disease-control post mentioned above is the ferry over the Zambezi to Zambia (open 06.00–18.00). This often takes quite large trucks and is a substantial size, so tends to be used either by very local traffic, or by haulage companies who wish to minimise the number of customs officials that their trucks come into contact with. Either way, it can get very busy on both sides of the river. The ferry journey costs about P45,000 (US$20) for a Land Cruiser, the precise amount depending on the vehicle's size. Foot passengers pay just P2 per person.

If you want to hitch across to Zambia, then try standing where the Zimbabwean and Zambian roads fork, hitching on both of them. The disease-control post makes a perfect hitchhiking spot to get into Kasane or to head for Nata, as vehicles have to stop here anyway.

Sesheke Heading west on the Zambian side, it's about 130km to the small town of Sesheke, the gateway to Zambia's Western Province. The tar road crosses the Zambezi at a superb new bridge, one of only six to span the width of the Zambezi anywhere along its length (the others are at Chirundu, Tete, Livingstone and Katima Mulilo, and a footbridge at Chinyingi mission). Sesheke can also be reached painlessly on good tar roads through Namibia via Ngoma.

To/from Namibia Ngoma (see pages 204–5) is the location for a bridge across the Chobe, and a border with Namibia (open 06.00–18.00). It's about 51km from the centre of Kasane by good tar road, or rather more if you take the scenic riverside road (4x4 advisable) through Chobe National Park. From Ngoma, it's a further 69km of good tar to the main town of Namibia's Caprivi Strip, Katima Mulilo.

By bus Kasane's bus station is situated behind the Shell garage in the centre of town. There are buses and regular small combies plying between Kasane and Nata,

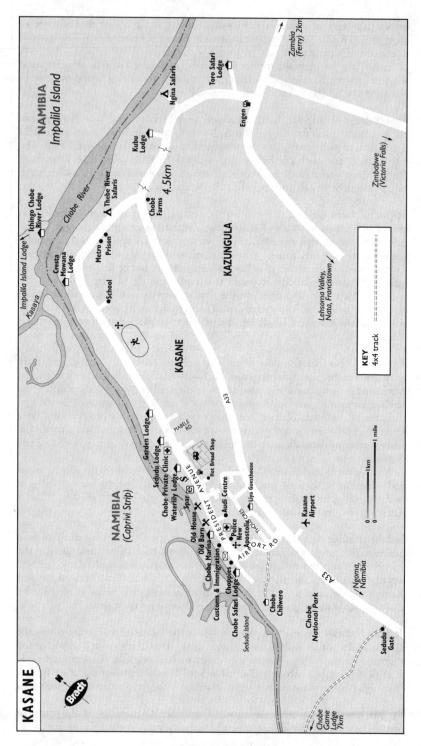

and linking on to both Francistown and Maun – but relatively little else. The most comfortable coach is the Chobe Express to Nata (*P35*), with a link from there to Francistown (*7hrs; additional P50*), or Maun (*a little longer; P70 total*). Buses leave Kasane at 06.00, 08.00 and 10.00; to get your ticket, you'll need to arrive at least half an hour early. For other journeys, get there early in the morning to be sure of getting away.

By air Kasane (airline code: BBK) is a busy gateway for the light aircraft that taxi visitors around the camps of northern Botswana, but it's otherwise fairly quiet. Most travellers coming through Kasane will also pass through Victoria Falls or Livingstone, and find it best to use the frequent flights to/from those airports to reach either Harare or Johannesburg. Do note, however, that the Zambian authorities levy a hefty US$65 per person 'visa' fee on anyone transiting the country without spending at least one night there, whereas the cost of a visa for Zimbabwe is currently US$30.

Kasane Airport Turn away from the river up a good tar road on the west side of Kasane town, just before Chobe Safari Lodge. After 1.4km you meet the main road to Ngoma at a T-junction. Turn right and after less than 1km you'll see a left turning clearly signposted to Kasane Airport.

Here there is a small, neat and very organised little airport, though being a short distance from town it's very quiet and lifeless between planes.

ORIENTATION It's fairly easy to get your bearings in Kasane. The Chobe River meanders roughly from east to west. This is the border with Namibia. On the Botswanan side, a road shadows its course near its southern bank. Kasane is a fairly linear town, spread out along that road. Most of the visitors' lodges stand on the riverbank, accessed by short side-roads.

One tar road loops around away from town and the river to reach Ngoma, the border with Namibia. This actually cuts inland through the Chobe National Park, though isn't usually of interest for game viewing. A spur from this leads north, down the sandy game-viewing roads beside the Chobe riverfront. Another tar road heads south and slightly west before bending more east and heading towards Nata and the rest of the Eastern Corridor area. The latter offers the only 2WD access to the rest of Botswana.

Maps There are few good maps of Kasane or its environs, perhaps because it's relatively easy to find your way about. For Chobe National Park, you need the excellent Shell map, by Veronica Roodt (see the section on maps on pages 94–5, and *Chapter 6*). This is usually available from African Easel bookshop, in the Audi Centre.

GETTING AROUND Most visitors to the Kasane area will either have their own transport, or they'll be visiting as part of an organised trip with an all-inclusive package – so the general lack of transport won't be a problem. If you're backpacking or want to explore alone, there are a few minibuses that ply up and down the main road from the small bus station behind the Shell garage. These are particularly useful for those staying at the eastern end of the town or in Kazungula.

Car hire For self-drive car hire just about the only choice is Avis (↘ *6250 144; f 6250 145; emergency ↘ 6251 136; www.avis.co.za*), which operates out of Mowana Safari Lodge (see page 182). Note that it'll usually be cheaper to make a reservation and pay outside Botswana (indeed, outside of Africa), rather than turn up here and take the rate at the counter.

WHERE TO STAY For such a small town, Kasane has a surprising proliferation of accommodation options for all tastes and budgets, from top-class hotels to small lodges and a range of campsites. Shared by almost all, though, is that all-important riverfront location.

When planning where to stay in this area, you should also consider the lodges that are just inside the national park (see pages 202–4), and even those on the east side of the Chobe Forest Reserve, near Ngoma (see pages 209–11). If you're just passing through Kasane, then it might make sense to choose to stay in one of the lodges outside the national park, as listed below, since they tend to be a little cheaper than those in the park, and you may also save a few days' park fees. However, if you're visiting the Kasane area specifically to see northern Chobe, and can afford to use one of the lodges in the park or near Ngoma, then you might be better there. If you're intending to camp, note that many of the campsites will not accept advance bookings from individual campers (as against overland groups), so in high season it's a good idea to arrive early.

Accommodation listed here starts with places closest to the national park, heading east along the Chobe River on President Avenue, followed by a few options that are located inland.

Along the riverfront

Chobe Chilwero Lodge (15 chalets) Sanctuary Lodges, page 172. The erstwhile delightful small bush lodge of Chobe Chilwero is now owned by A&K, the multinational luxury travel company, under their highly exclusive Sanctuary Lodges brand. Today, following complete refurbishment, it affords something of the atmosphere of a British country house in the bush.

The standards of construction and design at Chobe Chilwero are impressive. All its large timber-and-thatch bungalows have AC, imported terracotta floor tiles, sunken handmade baths, indoor and outdoor showers, and private terraces that overlook landscaped gardens with their own hammocks. The South African architect responsible for this, Jonathan Ridler, has created the atmosphere of an ethnological museum with tasteful décor including many beautiful African artefacts (while others are for sale in the classy shop). An elegant entrance hall leads through to the comfortable lounge area, a small library with an excellent selection of books and magazines, a beautifully landscaped pool (with showers, toilets and sunbeds) and a business centre for those who can't live without email. Much effort goes into the food here, with treats like breadsticks and truffles made at the lodge. The service is impeccable – but friendly – and the wine cellar extensive.

Chobe Chilwero is set high above the river, looking out over the Chobe's floodplains from behind a relatively discreet electric fence. Game drives are conducted by knowledgeable, enthusiastic guides in high-quality 4x4s, taking a maximum of 6 guests, although the lodge's location effectively limits these

to the eastern part of Chobe's riverfront. Boat cruises are also offered from 16.00 to 19.00 in small sgl-decker boats – a pleasant change from some of the larger boats on the river. Also available are fishing trips, and day trips to Victoria Falls in Zimbabwe.

Chobe Chilwero is a luxurious lodge with excellent views in an accessible spot on the edge of Chobe, and makes an ideal 2–3 day excursion from Victoria Falls or Livingstone, but is not isolated enough to offer a real wilderness experience. *From US$420 pp to US$650/845 pp sharing/sgl low/high season, inc all meals, activities, park fees, laundry, and most drinks; exc transfers. Open all year.*

Chobe Safari Lodge (71 rooms, 11 rondavels, camping) ✆ 6250 336; f 6250 437; e reservations@chobelodge.co.bw; www.chobesafarilodge.com. On a spacious site overlooking the river, on the western fringes of town, Chobe Safari Lodge is the oldest of Kasane's camps. Its wide lawns, well shaded by mature trees, attract warthogs and families of banded mongoose, as well as vervet monkeys and numerous birds. Although it is the closest lodge to the national park for boat trips, the park entrance is several kilometres by road so this proximity makes little difference if you're driving.

There's a good choice of accommodation, at varying prices, with a further 20 safari rooms planned. At the top end, both modern river rooms and the slightly larger, predominantly dark-wood safari rooms each have en-suite shower or bath and toilet, AC, TV, safe, kettle and phone, while family rooms have additional twin or bunk beds. Beds can be twin or dbl, and all have either a private balcony or small patio area overlooking lawns to the river. Simple rondavels and other rooms, inc family units, have fans rather than AC, and braai stands. For a party of 4, the family rooms are particularly good value. Meanwhile, the old established campsite by the river changes little, though it has acquired a few pre-erected tents over the years. It is still popular with overlanders, but note that independent campers may not pre-book.

Facilities include a swimming pool beside a large, tree-shaded riverfront terrace, health and beauty centre, well-stocked shop, squash court and 2 bars, with the Sedudu bar at the campsite a great place for sundowners. The restaurant runs on a set-menu system — perfectly adequate, but nothing special — with breakfast at US$15–21, braai lunch on the terrace by the pool at US$23, and dinner US$28. For lighter meals there's a snack menu with sandwiches from US$4.

Game drives (US$32/15 adults/children, exc park fees) depart at 06.00, 09.30, 13.00 and 15.30; river cruises (US$28/15) leave daily at 15.00. For something a little more intimate you can hire a small motorboat with a driver from US$33 per hr (min 2hrs) between 07.00 and 14.00, either to explore the river or to go fishing (tackle included). Other excursions take in Victoria Falls (US$60, exc visa and entry fee), or a Namibian village (US$26). *Twin river or safari room US$150 per night (family US$164), twin rondavel US$131 (family US$136). Camping US$14/11 adults/children. Packages available with Pom Pom Camp (see page 304). Airport transfer one way US$55 (Victoria Falls), US$65 (Livingstone), exc visas.*

🏠 **Chobe Marina Lodge** (66 rooms) P Bag K83, Kasane; ☏ 6252 221; f 6252 224; e reservations@chobe.botsnet.bw; www.chobemarinalodge.com. There's no mistaking the newest upmarket resort in Kasane, with its deep-red and ochre buildings that feel instantly at one with its luxuriant gardens. Built across a narrow creek, with extensive tree shade, it was opened in 2002 by the South African Three Cities Group, and is in direct competition to Mowana Safari Lodge. The spacious tiled and thatched entrance opens on to dark wooden decking, from where walkways fan out to restaurants and the bar, a curio shop, in-house tour company, private jetty, and a large pool with its own bar overlooking lawns along the river.

Rooms, inc some adapted for paraplegics, range from 2-bedroom chalets at the back, with 2 dbl beds, 2 bathrooms (1 en-suite), lounge and micro-kitchen (fridge, washing up, microwave, kettle), to rather small river-facing 'suites' with dbl bed and bath, and — best value by far — the surprisingly spacious studios, closer to the river, with just a shower. All have tiled floors, TV, AC, fan and safe, and a private balcony.

The hotel has several restaurant options, ranging from poolside tables to the 1st-floor Commissioners, where à la carte meals are served indoors or on a balcony overlooking the river (starters P30, mains P70). There's also a 100-seat conference room.

Activities, here as elsewhere, focus on the river, with well-guided river cruises — in intimate 14-seater boats or larger 2-storey affairs — and game drives. Fishing is also on offer from US$200 per ½ day. Returning by river to the rhythm and vitality of traditional dancers performing above the jetty is an occasional highlight not to be missed. *US$290/240 pp sharing, mid/low season; sgl US$440/360, inc 3 meals and 2 game activities; exc park fees.*

🏠 **Water Lily Lodge** (10 rooms) tel: 6251 775, 6252 709; f 6250 759; e janala@botsnet.bw; www.janalasafaris.com. Owned by Monica Kgaile, 'quite a character' according to one local, Water Lily Lodge is close to Barclays Bank, and was opened in 2004. From the outside it looks like a giant cream-washed rondavel, and effectively that's what it is, built around a central fountain. Nicely presented en-suite rooms overlook the river, with twin beds and mosquito nets, plus TV, desk and kettle; those downstairs have AC and doors into the garden, while upstairs, where there's a through breeze, there's just a fan, and a balcony. The restaurant's à-la-carte menu focuses on fish, steaks and chicken dishes at around P55. Outside, a small pool is set among lawns; the land between here and the river was being levelled when we visited. Activities focus on boat cruises and game drives (P100 pp, plus park fees). *P253/385 sgl/dbl inc continental b/fast.*

🏠 **Sedudu Lodge** (12 rooms) PO Box 82, Kasane; ☏ 6251 748. The simplest riverside accommodation in Kasane is in a converted house, with a few chalets built in the garden at the back. All have en-suite shower or bath, AC and tiled floors. The friendly manager, Edgar, presides over an open thatched bar to the rear. Here, meals are available on request, including local specialities such as curries and *seswa* with *papa*. Permission is currently being sought to establish a campsite between the lodge and the river. *Sgl P166, dbl/twin P277, family P554 per room.*

🏠 **Garden Lodge** (8 rooms) ✆ 6250 051; f 6250 577; m 7130 4150; e gabi@thegardenlodge.com; www.thegardenlodge.com. This small newcomer to Kasane, 5km from the national park, is relaxed, personal and well designed, a welcome addition to the more corporate style of the larger lodges. Unobtrusively tucked behind secure gates, it has a tranquil setting with attractive gardens. From the lofty central area, combining lounge and dining room, a shaded terrace overlooks the river and the lodge's private jetty. Upstairs, a rustic wooden bar is an ideal spot for chilling. En-suite twin or dbl rooms are kitted out in natural fabrics, with cane chairs and coir carpets, ceiling fans and a kettle; each looks on to the river from its own balcony, or from a terrace leading on to the lawn. A 2-storey family chalet lacks a fan or river views, but is completely detached with a private veranda. In addition to game drives (P150) and boat cruises (P120), the lodge offers small-boat fishing (from P600 per boat for 3hrs), mokoros (P50 per hr) and village walks in Namibia (P130 pp plus park fees). *US$185/260/330 sgl/dbl/trpl dinner, B&B.*

🏠 **Mowana Safari Lodge** (111 rooms) ✆ 6250 300; f 6250 301; e reservations@mowana.cresta.co.bw; www.cresta-hospitality.com; central reservations ✆ +27 11 881 1234; f +27 11 881 1222; e reservations@crestahotels.com. The Botswana flagship of the Cresta group, this luxurious hotel, conceived on a grand scale and built around a baobab tree, is well designed, airy and spacious, with imaginative use of wooden decking. Dbl and twin en-suite rooms, inc 4 suites, 16 family rooms and 2 rooms for paraplegics, are attractively finished with river views, and offer everything that you'd expect from a top international hotel, inc remote-control AC, fan, telephone, fridge and safe.

Overlooking the river are 2 restaurants and 2 bars. The main restaurant, overlooking the river, has an à la carte menu, and also does breakfast (P75–95), lunch (P105) and dinner (P125). Above it, the open-sided upstairs bar/lounge catches the breeze, with a warming wood fire for winter evenings. Outside, the less formal bar and restaurant is located above a large, modern pool with separate children's pool. Guests will also appreciate the smart curio shop, a beauty parlour that includes massages, and an internet café.

For the true business visitor there are conference facilities for up to 100 people, but most are more interested in the game drives and boat cruises that venture into Chobe National Park from the hotel's own jetty. In case that's not enough, there's also a tennis court and a 9-hole golf course, as well as evenings of traditional African culture in 'the Kgotla', or African-style meeting place. *US$310/465 pp sharing/sgl, inc 3 meals and 2 activities per day; US$199/354 pp sharing/sgl B&B. Activities US$27.50 pp, plus park fees. Open all year.*

🏠 **Thebe River Camping** (camping, 80 dorm beds, rooms) ✆/f 6250 314; e thebesafaris@botsnet.bw; www.theberiversafaris.co.za. Used mostly by overland companies and small safari groups, this family-owned site is friendly and well run, with much of the atmosphere of a popular backpackers' lodge. Located northwest of Kubu Lodge and about 5km from the centre of town, it's the base for Thebe River Safaris (see page 187) and is usually occupied by overlanders or travellers taking a trip with Thebe. Bookings are not accepted from independent campers, who take pot luck, and in high season the site may be full. Next to the campsite are a bar, a small pool, and a kitchen that will prepare meals. Transfers can be arranged from Victoria Falls and Livingstone.

A new building offering backpacker accommodation was expected to open mid-2006, with 3 dorms and en-suite rooms, and there will be a new ablution block, too. There are also plans to grass the site during this period. *P44 pp camping, approx P330 per room. Open all year.*

🏠 **Ngina Safaris** (camping) ✆ 6250 082. Included here for the sake of completeness, the campsite at Ngina is down a narrow 2km track to the west of Toro Safari Lodge. Empty when we visited, it looked somewhat forlorn, with a few dusty pitches, some pre-erected tents and a very basic ablutions block.

🏠 **Toro Safari Lodge** (26 chalets, camping) ✆ 6252 694; m 7211 1283, 7124 7383; f 6252 695; e torolodge@botsnet.bw; www.torolodge.co.bw. Opened in 2004, Toro lies to the east of Kubu Lodge, just 600m from the turn-off towards Kasane from Kazungula. The modern complex, with its ochre-painted square chalets in neat rows, seems rather soulless at first glance, but it's worth further investigation. Each of the thatched chalets is carpeted, with mains electricity, a fan and en-suite shower; those with riverfront views have DSTV and tea/coffee-making facilities, and there are plans to extend these facilities to all. Screened doors lead to a brick veranda. Behind these, individual pitches on a level, grassy site offer campers power points, a fireplace, and – a huge bonus – private ablution facilities including hot/cold showers; shade, in the form of newly planted trees, is growing rapidly. Already popular with independent travellers, the lodge is gaining interest from overland groups, lured by the standard of facilities. In the wide-fronted central area, open to the river, solid wood furniture gives an air of permanence to the popular bar and dining area, where meals are served from an immaculate kitchen, and jazz afternoons are held on Sundays. Well away from the chalets and campers, a second bar with DSTV overlooks the pool. Activities include boat cruises (from the jetty at Chobe Marina, P180 pp), game drives (P190), and fishing (P495 for 3 people/3hrs).

Riverview chalets US$70/100/115 sgl/twin/dbl, standard US$60/90/100 sgl/twin/dbl, inc continental b/fast. Camping US$10/7 adults/children; caravan US$5 extra. Discount for senior citizens. Airport transfers (Victoria Falls) P250 pp.

🏠 **Kubu Lodge** (11 chalets, 5 A-frames, camping) ℡ 6250 312; **f** 6251 092; **e** kubu@botsnet.bw; www.kubulodge.net. About 9km from the centre of Kasane and 3km from the control point at Kazungula, Kubu stands on a sloping site beside the river, clearly signposted from the main road. Botswanan-owned and run, the lodge (whose name means 'hippo' in Setswana) is friendly and personable, and immaculately kept.

The lodge's square thatched chalets are substantial wooden buildings raised off the ground with stairs up to a veranda at the front, set under shady trees in lush green lawns sloping down to the river. Each chalet is well furnished with rugs on the wooden floors, wood and metal furniture and a laundry basket; most have a dbl and a sgl bed; some have 3 sgls. Mosquito nets, screened windows and a fan keep out the resident bugs, and there's also a coffee machine. The compact bathroom has a flush toilet, shower, and basin with shaver socket.

The restaurant is a solid wooden building on 3 levels overlooking the river, with screened windows. Tables are set out under umbrellas on the veranda,

with more inside next to a small bar. A buffet lunch is P77 pp; dinner – a set menu, changed daily – costs P121. On the mezzanine area are a couple of sofas, while the top floor lies almost empty at present but would make a good place to watch birds from the small window. Nearby is a braai area and boma, and further down is a swimming pool surrounded by lawns. In the reception a large shop offers a variety of curios, a few books and postcards.

A few minutes' walk from the lodge, Kubu's campsite is popular with private campers, though its large dusty plots offer limited shade at the end of the dry season, when the trees are bare. Each of the pitches has a braai stand; some also have power points and standpipes for water. Toilets and hot showers are clean and functional, but the funky egg-shaped swimming pool could do with some attention. At the back, next to a simple open-air laundry, basic A-frame shelters have 2 beds with linen provided; the windows are gauze. Part of the campsite slopes down to the river and it's not always well lit at night, so if you eat at the restaurant make sure that you take a torch for the walk back.

Boat cruises run 10.00–13.00 or 15.00–18.30, with game drives 06.00–09.30, 10.00–13.00 and 15.00–18.00. The jetty at the lodge is used for boat cruises eastwards, up the confluence of the Chobe and Zambezi, but visitors taking game-viewing cruises west into Chobe National Park are transferred by road to Kalahari Tours in Kasane. There are also fishing trips, and the extensive grounds feature a marked nature trail, with helpful notes and a map on hand.

US$380/550/810 sgl/dbl/trpl per chalet per day, inc 2 activities, park entry fee, laundry and transfers. B&B US$175/265/225 sgl/dbl/trpl per chalet. Camping P57 pp (under 12, P38.50). Boat cruises/game drives about US$30 pp plus park fees. A-frame P88 pp. Open Mar–Jan (closed New Year).

Away from the river

🏠 **Liya Guest Lodge** (5 rooms) ℡/f 6251 450; **m** 7175 6903; **e** Liyaglo@botsnet.bw. This pleasant budget guesthouse on a suburban street above Kasane is clean and friendly. Rooms all have their own bathroom, with 2 rooms en-suite. TV in lounge. Meals are available on request (b/fast P20, lunch P26, dinner P28), or guests may use the kitchen for P30 per day. Conveniently close to the airport, and they will arrange transport.
P180/284 sgl/dbl, P195/297 en-suite sgl/dbl, P484 trpl.

🏠 **Luyi Campsite** ℡/f 6251 450; **m** 7175 6903; **e** Liyaglo@botsnet.bw. Linked to the guest lodge above is this campsite with pre-erected tents and chalets. It lies about 10km from the outskirts of Kasane. Take the main road towards Nata, then turn left at the *second* telegraph wire that crosses the road, signposted to Lisoma village. Once in the village, turn right, and ask for the campsite.
Chalets P175/260 sgl/dbl, tents P150/225 sgl/dbl.

🏠 **Elephant Valley Lodge** (⊕ CHOBEV 17°51.193'S; 25°14.585'E). Elephant Valley Lodge was built in 1999 in the Lehsoma Valley, adjacent to Chobe Forest Reserve, about 8km from Kazungula and 10km from Kasane. It's relatively easy to reach from the Kazungula–Nata road: just drive along here until you get to the *first* telegraph wire that crosses the road, then turn immediately left; the road leads to the lodge. The property is now South African-owned, but exclusively let to the American company Overseas Adventure Tours, and is not available to other visitors.

✖ **WHERE TO EAT** Between them, Kasane's hotels and lodges offer a range of restaurants, some of them very good. If you're looking for something rather less corporate, there is a handful of other possibilities:

✖ **Old Bank** Opposite Audi Centre; ✆ 6250 628. This appears to offer more than it delivers, with rather lacklustre service and a menu that appears to promise much, but seems overpriced. Light meals such as burgers P18.50; mains P35–50, with local dishes including *phane* and *papa* (mopane worms with mealie meal) at P25. Seating outside under the trees is more attractive, with picnic benches overlooking the river. *Open Mon–Thu 07.00–22.00, Fri/Sat to midnight, Sun 09.00–22.00.*

✖ **Old House** Next to Old Bank, opposite Shell garage. The unlikely combination of a sports bar with Chinese-influenced cuisine is Kasane's most popular venue for eating out in the evenings, either inside in a pub-like environment, or at picnic benches by the river. Relaxed and friendly, it's a good spot to chill out with a couple of beers as well. *Open Tue–Sun 12.00–14.30, 18.00–22.00.*

✖ **Gallery Africana & Coffee Bar** Audi Centre, ✆ 6250 944. This colourful new café, opposite Chobe Marina Lodge, doubles as a small art gallery, with a good selection of crafts and pottery from across the continent. Breakfast (P15–42), cakes and light lunches, with an interesting range of pancakes alongside staples such as burgers, salads and quiches. Drinks include fruit juices, milkshakes and a range of coffees. *Open Mon–Fri 07.30–16.30, Sat to 12.30.*

OTHER PRACTICALITIES

Banks and money Remember that you'll usually need to pay all your park fees in cash (pula) if you are entering Chobe National Park in your own vehicle (Sedudu Gate is an exception, accepting both Visa and MasterCard). Kasane is an obvious spot for changing money and has only one main bank – so the bank's 'foreign exchange' teller is usually quite busy. It's normally considerably quicker to go to one of the town's bureaux de change, where rates are only slightly lower than at the bank, and opening hours are considerably longer. In addition to the following, there's one almost next to the Shell garage, opposite Barclays.

$ **Barclays Bank** ✆ 6250 221; f 6250 269 (⊕ KASANE 17°47.97'S; 25°9.015'E). Centrally located on the river side of the road, this is a modern, architect-designed building with ATM – though I still have memories of changing money here in 1988 when it occupied a small, picturesque thatched rondavel. *Open Mon–Fri 08.30–15.30, Sat 08.15–10.45.*

$ **Cape to Cairo** Opposite Spar supermarket, with internet café. *Open Mon–Fri 08.00–19.00, Sat/Sun to 17.00.*

$ **Kasane Bureau de Change** Audi Centre; ✆ 6251 609. Efficient and friendly place offering good rates of exchange. *Open Mon–Fri 07.30–17.00, Sat to 14.00, Sun 08.00–11.30.*

Communications

Internet There are a couple of internet cafés in the town, both with broadband connections and charging P7.50 for 15 minutes; both also act as bureaux de change.

🖳 **Cape to Cairo** Opposite Spar supermarket. *Open Mon–Fri 08.00–19.00, Sat/Sun to 17.00.*

🖳 **Kasane Enterprises** Behind the shops near the bus station. Digital photos may be downloaded for around P35 for 128MB. *Open Mon–Fri 08.30, 14.00–17.00, Sat 08.00–13.00, 14.00–16.30.*

Telephone There are several coin-operated phone boxes in town, conspicuous in their bright red, blue and yellow livery. Alternatively, pop into one of the town's mobile-phone shops and buy a local SIM card – it's a lot cheaper than using your normal card.

Post and courier
DHL Kasane Enterprises, Audi Centre; ☎ 6250 234

Health
✚ **Chobe Medical Centre** Kasane Centre; ☎ 6250 888

✚ **Chobe Private Clinic** ☎ 6251 555 (24hr)
✚ **Chobe Dental Clinic** Kasane Centre; ☎ 6250 212

Shopping Kasane isn't one of the world's shopping capitals, but you'll be able to get most of what you need here.

Just east of the turn-off to Thebe River Safaris is the **Metro Cash & Carry** for large-scale shopping expeditions, with the **Village Winery** set right behind. Not far from here is **Chobe Farms**, where a wide variety of seasonal fruit and vegetables is available direct from the grower.

More accessible for most travellers are the town's two supermarkets: **Spar**, which is close to Barclays Bank, and the new **Choppies**, at the western end of town, which was scheduled to open early in 2006. For good bread, as well as pies and take-away meals, try the very popular **Hot Bread** place (*open Mon–Fri approx 08.15–16.00, Sat 08.30–11.30*) behind the Shell garage, near the bus station, where there's also a small market.

While supermarkets themselves are not licensed to sell alcoholic drinks, Spar has its own off-licence on the parade in front of the supermarket. There are other liquor stores around town, including a couple on Mabele Road opposite Sedudu Lodge, but this is the most accessible.

Gifts and souvenirs
African Easel Audi Centre; ☎/f 6250 433; www.africaneasel.com. Now just an art gallery. Open Mon–Fri and Sat am; closed 13.00–14.00. **African Window** Audi Centre. Next door to African Easel, and under the same ownership, this now stocks the range of wildlife books, local guidebooks

and more common maps previously held by the older shop, as well as crafts and cards. **Stationery Box** Audi Centre; ☎ 6251 415. Rather an empty shop that also doubles as the agent for Impalila Lodge (see pages 189–90).

Equipment
Kingfisher Trading Audi Centre. Small range of fishing equipment, and bits and pieces for camping – as

well as some secondhand books. Open 08.00–13.00, 14.00–17.00.

Vehicle repairs If you must break down, then Kasane's not a bad place to do so, as it's used as a supply base by some of the safari operators and has several garages. Certainly if you're heading across Chobe and Moremi you should make sure your vehicle's in tip-top shape before you head off. The best is probably:

Chobe Nissan ☎ 6250 673; f 6250 674. Situated near Kazungula, just past the disease-control post on the way to Nata, about 14km from the centre of town. They're agents for Dunlop tyres and

Nissan, but will service and repair most makes. They also sell spare parts, and will undertake wheel-balancing.

Other services If you need any tent repairs, then contact The Wearhouse (*☎ 6251 140 or 6250 289*) at Kazungula, just next to the Chobe Nissan garage.

The precise boundary between Namibia and Botswana in this area has been defined to follow the deepest channel of the Chobe River – a definition which works well for most river boundaries. However, the Chobe splits into many streams, whose strengths and depths seem to gradually alter over the years.

Sedudu Island (or Kasikili Island, as it's called in Namibia) is a very low, flat island which covers about 3.5km² when the waters are low, but shrinks to a much smaller size when it is flooded. It's used mainly for grazing cattle.

Both Botswana and Namibia have claimed that the island belongs to them. In the 1990s it was occupied by the Botswana Defence Force (BDF) who built several watch-towers on it – chunky structures towering over the island's grassy plains, and cunningly disguised with variegated military-pattern netting. In early 1995, both Botswana and Namibia agreed to put the issue before the International Court of Justice (ICJ) in The Hague, and in February 1996 they both agreed to abide by its eventual judgement.

Botswana argued that the northern channel was the main river channel, while Namibia maintained that southern channel was the larger one. Finally, in December 1999, the ICJ pronounced that the border should 'follow the line of the deepest soundings in the northern channel of the Chobe River around Kasikili-Sedudu Island'.

That said, the court also diplomatically ruled that 'in the two channels around Kasikili-Sedudu Island, the nationals of, and vessels flying the flags of, the Republic of Botswana and the Republic of Namibia shall enjoy equal national treatment'.

For visitors, this means that game-viewing boats from both countries are allowed on both sides of this tiny, troublesome patch of floodplain!

Local safari companies and travel agents

Because overland truck companies that are not officially registered in Botswana can't use their own vehicles in the park, there's a strong market in Kasane for day trips into Chobe.

African Odyssey ✆/f 6250 601; e odyssey@ info.bw. The safari company at Chobe Marina Lodge offers game drives, river cruises, fishing and various guided trips and walks.

Chobe Travel Shop ✆/f 6250 828; e travel@info.bw

Go Wild Safaris ✆/f 6250 468; e go.wild@info.bw. This is the in-house travel and tours agency based at Chobe Safari Lodge, offering various safaris from short game drives (P75 plus park fees for 3 hrs) to full mobile trips across the country (typically P230–320 pp per night).

Into Africa Mowana Safaris ✆ 6250 478; f 6250 469; e intoafrica@info.bw. The in-house travel and tours agency based at the Mowana Safari Lodge. Options include a 3hr breakfast cruise, half-day trips into the national park, and mokoro trails.

Janala Tours & Safaris ✆ 6251 775, 6252 709; f 6250 759; e janala@botsnet.bw; www.janalasafaris.com. This tour company also owns Water Lily Lodge (see page 181).

Linyanti Explorations ✆ 6250 505, 6250 352; e info@linyanti.com; www.linyanti.com. Based at Kazungula, near Kasane, this long-established Botswana company runs the good-value, upmarket camps in the Selinda Reserve (NG16), northwest of Chobe. See pages 235–6 for more details.

Mantis Safaris/Nkwazi Fishing P Bag K48, Kasane; ✆/f 6250 051; m 7130 4159. Small operator specialising in boat trips on the Chobe and Zambezi rivers.

Nsundano ✆ 6250 901. A small local outfit that operates from a caravan in the car park next to Barclays. Something of a jack-of-all-trades, they offer everything from airport transfers to day trips to Victoria Falls (P300 plus US$30 visa) – not to mention exchange facilities and a small range of curios.

Safari Excellence ✆/f 6250 992; e safexcel@ info.bw. Run by Stefan du Plessis and Stephanie Molloy, this small operator offers local drives and transfers, as well as longer overland safaris.

Thebe River Safaris ✆/f 6250 314; e thebesafaris@
botsnet.bw; www.theberiversafaris.co.za. As well as a
campsite (see page 182), this is the base for a
mobile-safari operation that runs tailor-made and set
trips around northern Botswana and into Zambia. It's
run by Jan, Annatjie, Jannie and Louis van Wyk, who
pitch trips as 'budget, middle or luxury' – depending
on how much effort/cash you are willing to expend.
Thebe also arranges boats, vehicles and guides for
game drives/boat trips in the park.

WHAT TO SEE AND DO The only real attraction in Kasane itself is probably **Chobe
Snake Park** (✆ 6242 391; www.chobesnakepark.org; open Mon–Sat 09.00–17.00; P20
pp unguided, P50 pp 1hr guided tour), which is in new premises close to Kubu Lodge,
about 800m from the Kazungula turn off. The park currently hosts a collection of
indigenous fauna, ranging from mambas, cobras and boomslangs to the greater
numbers of harmless snakes, with other reptiles such as lizards, geckos and
tortoises shortly to be introduced. The eventual aim is to develop the park into a
larger zoological and botanical garden, in conjunction with CARACAL: the Centre
for Conservation of African Resources: Animals, Communities and Landuse
(www.caracal.info).

If it's crocodiles that you're after, Kasane also has a **crocodile farm** open to the
public (✆ 6250 430 or 6252 534; contact Sue Slogrove).

On a quirky note, historians observe that in the early 1900s the police in the area
used a large hollow baobab tree, with a locking door, as a prison. This still stands
today, behind the present police station.

Game drives Excursions into Chobe National Park can be organised either
through your lodge, or directly with one of a handful of small local safari operators
(see pages 186–7), or you can drive yourself. Organised game drives generally head
west straight into the national park, and then cover the game drive roads and loops
around the riverfront area (see *Chapter 10* for more details of these areas). If you're
organising a trip with a local company, remember to compare the various options
available, asking how long the drive is, and how much of that time it takes to get
to the park gates and back. Typically trips last about three hours, though generally
the lodges further east will spend more of this getting to and from the park than
those further west.

Either way you're going to find yourself mostly around the eastern side of the
riverfront area, where traffic densities are relatively high.

The national park allows driving only in daylight hours, but several of the lodges
now advertise 'night drives'. Note that these are conducted outside the park, in
areas where quantities of big game are much more limited.

Boat cruises These can vary from ten-seater motorboats to double-storey boats
taking 40 or more people on a champagne breakfast. The game viewing from the
river can be surprisingly good, especially in the later afternoon during the latter
half of the dry season. Large numbers of elephants are virtually guaranteed, and
often whole herds will cross the river from one side to the other. As with game
drives, cruises can be organised through your lodge or with one of the local
operators (see pages 186–7).

Motorboat trips Many of the lodges/operators will send you out on a private little
boat with a driver and a coolbox. It's certainly my favourite way to see the Chobe
riverfront area, and probably remains one of my favourite safari experiences in
Africa. It can be magical.

The small boat gives you a lot more flexibility in what you concentrate on, and
how long you stop somewhere, as it's just a question of requesting what you want
to do from your driver/guide.

Because of the number of lodges in the area, the river can become quite full of boats at times. So if you want a quieter experience, try and arrange for a boat at the crack of dawn. Most of the cruises don't leave until 09.00, so you'll have the river almost to yourself for a few hours – apart from the occasional Namibian fisherman in a mokoro (there's no fishing allowed in the national park from Botswana).

Other options Most of the lodges and tour operators in Kasane can organise trips further afield, including mokoro trips, village walks across the river in Namibia, and excursions to Victoria Falls in Zambia or Zimbabwe.

AROUND KASANE

Although technically on Namibian soil, there are several lodges on the northern side of the Chobe River that use Kasane as a base. Many of their visitors come through Kasane, and their activities feature trips on the river beside the park.

Two of these – King's Den and Chobe Savannah Lodge – stand on land directly opposite the national park, hence I'll cover them in *Chapter 10, Chobe National Park*, page 204. Two others stand northeast of Kasane, on Impalila Island, so are discussed below. For more details of the Impalila area, and the rest of Namibia's Caprivi Strip, see one of my other guidebooks: *Namibia: The Bradt Travel Guide*.

IMPALILA ISLAND AREA Around Kazungula is the confluence of the Chobe and the Zambezi. The Zambezi flows relentlessly to the sea but, depending on their relative heights, the Chobe either contributes to that, or may even reverse its flow and draw water from the Zambezi. Trapped between the two rivers is a triangle of land, of about 700km², which is a mixture of floodplains, islands and channels that link the two rivers.

This swampy, riverine area is home to several thousand people of Namibian nationality, mostly members of Zambia's Lozi tribe. (The main local languages here are Lozi and Subia.) Most have a seasonal lifestyle, living next to the river channels, fishing and farming maize, sorghum, pumpkins and keeping cattle. They move with the water levels, transferring on to higher, drier ground as the waters rise.

The largest island in this area, Impalila Island, is at the far eastern tip of Namibia, home to around 300 people living in some 25 small villages. It gained notoriety during the 1980s as a military base for the South African Defence Forces (SADF), as it was strategically positioned within sight of Botswana, Zambia and Zimbabwe. It still boasts a 1,300m-long runway (✪ 17°46.48'S, 025°11.23'E) of compressed gravel, used today by charter airlines to bring visitors to the lodges, but the barracks are now a secondary school, serving most of the older children in the area.

The **customs and immigration post** on the island opens from 07.00 to 17.00. It's fairly laid back and informal as borders go, but remember that, if you transfer to the island from Kasane, you'll have to clear customs and immigration for both Botswana and Namibia on arrival and departure.

Flora and fauna The area's ecosystems are similar to those in the upper reaches of the Okavango Delta: deep-water channels lined by wide reedbeds and rafts of papyrus. Some of the larger islands are still forested with baobabs, water figs, knobthorne, umbrella thorn, mopane, pod mahogany, star chestnut and sickle-leafed albizia, while jackalberry and Chobe waterberry overhang the rivers, festooned with creepers and vines.

Large mammals are scarce here, and most that do occur swim over from Chobe. Elephants and buffalo sometimes swim over to Namibia, and even lions have been known to take to the river in search of the tasty-but-dim domestic cattle kept there.

Even when there are no large mammals here, the birdlife is spectacular. Large flocks of white-faced ducks congregate on islands in the rivers, African skimmers nest on exposed sandbanks, and both reed cormorants and darters are seen fishing or perching while they dry their feathers. Kingfishers are numerous, from the giant to the tiny pygmy, as are herons and egrets. However, the area's most unusual bird is the unassuming rock pratincole with its black, white and grey body, which perches on rocks within the rapids and hawks for insects in the spray.

Where to stay Visitors to the island arrive either by air at the small airstrip, or by boat from Kasane. Supplies for the lodges are normally brought in by boat from Kasane or Katima Mulilo. Because of their location, neither of the lodges can organise game drives in Chobe; they're limited to boat trips. Prices are quoted in US or Namibian dollars.

Ichingo Chobe River Lodge (7 Meru tents) \/f 6250 143 (on island); m 7131 8979; f 6250 223 (in Kasane town); e ichingo@iafrica.com; www.ichingo.com. Ichingo was the brainchild of Dawn and Ralph Oxenham, who since 1996 have run the lodge themselves. Occupying a secluded site on the south side of Impalila Island, it overlooks the quiet backwaters of some of the Chobe River's rapids, a world away from busy Kasane just across the water. It makes a super base for river trips and game viewing from boats along the Chobe River, and offers some excellent birdwatching too.

Accommodation is in rustic walk-in Meru tents, each set high above the flood levels – important in a location where the rise and fall of water is up to 2m. En-suite showers are at the back under thatch, and there's a balcony at the front, with views of the water through thick vegetation, dominated by the water-tolerant waterberry trees, *Syzygium guineese*, and the orange-fruited mangosteen, *Garcinea livinstonei*. In the evening a generator ensures a steady power supply, backed up by battery lights in each tent. Meals are taken around a large, solid wooden table in the thatched dining area/bar/lounge that fronts on to the river.

Activities are run individually, with a guide allocated to each tent for the duration of the guests' stay. Not surprisingly, the river is the main focus, with game viewing, birdwatching and fishing from motorboats, and fly-fishing in the rapids, as well as island walks through local villages to a giant baobab. Unusually for a bush lodge, the camp actively welcomes children of all ages, even when not accompanied by adults, as craft activities can usually be organised for them.
US$340 pp sharing, inc all meals, activities, airport transfer. Closed Jan.

Ichobezi (4 cabins) m 7120 2439; e info@ichobezi.co.za; www.ichobezi.co.za. For those seeking to spend longer on the river, Ichingo (see above) has introduced the 8-berth *Ichobezi*, a luxury 'safari' boat that cruises on the Zambezi and Chobe rivers, as well as into the contiguous wetlands of Namibia's Caprivi Strip. As a Namibian registered vessel, it is permitted to cruise the waters of the Chobe when the national park is closed and all Botswanan vessels must leave, so it offers a unique opportunity to watch game and experience the tranquillity of the river after dark and at sunrise.

With its crew of 5, the boat is considered an extension of the lodge, with small groups and personal attention. Each en-suite cabin has huge picture windows, so guests can sit and watch wildlife from their rooms or up on deck. This is the chance for total relaxation with a drink or in the on-board plunge pool, but for more involvement tender boats are available for fishing or birdwatching with an experienced guide.
US$340 pp sharing, inc all meals, activities, airport transfer.

Impalila Island Lodge (8 chalets) Islands in Africa, South Africa; \ +27 11 706 7207; f +27 11 463 8251; e info@islandsinafrica.com; www.islandsinafrica.com; lodge \ 6250 795. Situated on the northwest side of Impalila Island, overlooking the Zambezi's Mambova Rapids, Impalila Island Lodge has in many ways brought the island to people's attention.

Accommodation is in wooden chalets, each with twin beds or a king-size dbl. It is fairly luxurious, with much made of polished local mukwa wood, with its natural variegated yellow and brown colours. The raised-up chalets have a square design, enclosing a bathroom in one corner, giving blissfully warm showers from instant water heaters. Below the high thatch ceilings are fans for warmer days, and mosquito nets. Large adjacent dbl doors open one corner of the room on to a wide wooden veranda, overlooking the rapids. These doors have an optional mosquito-net screen for when it's hot, though are more usually glass. Being next to the river can be quite cold on winter mornings.

Activities include guided motorboat trips on the Zambezi and Chobe: the Zambezi mainly for birdwatching and fishing, while longer boat trips to Chobe offer remarkable game viewing on the edge of the national park there. Mokoro trips explore the shallower channels, and even run the gentle rapids, whilst guided and independent walks are possible on the island. Superb fishing (especially for tiger-fish, best caught on a fly-rod) is all around, and the guides are experienced enough to take beginners or experts out to try their luck.

Since the lodge was merely a project on the drawing board, the team at Impalila has worked in a very low-key but positive way to involve the local community. Currently the lodge pays into a 'community development fund' that is utilised by the community for various projects — the clinic, the school, measures to encourage preservation of wildlife and to conserve the local environment — and administered jointly with the local chief. Now there are long-term plans to start a wildlife conservancy including Impalila Island, but these could take years to realise. However, because of their excellent approach, don't miss the visits that the lodge organises to local villages, as they can be very rewarding. (Note that Impalila has a super sister-lodge, Susuwe Island Lodge, in Namibia's Caprivi Strip. It's on an island in the Kwando River, just northeast from the Kwando concession in Botswana, and is also a first-rate spot with an equally progressive approach to community involvement.)

The main part of the lodge is a large thatched bar/dining area and comfortable lounge built around a huge baobab. This is open to the breeze, though can be sheltered when cold. The wooden pool deck has reclining loungers, umbrellas, and a great view of the river. Impalila's food is excellent and candle-lit 3- or 4-course meals around the baobab make a memorable scene. It is a stylish, well-run lodge ideal for fishing, birding, or just relaxing, with the added bonus of game viewing from the river in Chobe. *N$305–455 pp sharing, inc all meals, drinks (except spirits and non-house wines), laundry and activities; 30% sgl supplement. Open all year.*

Ntwala (4 suites) Ntwala Island; contact as for Impalila (see above). The ultra-exclusive camp operated by Impalila is run on country-house lines. The style, though, combines a distinctly modern approach, white and angular, with a loose mokoro theme, and the corrugated-iron roof may come as a surprise. Each chalet has all that you would expect — and more — in the way of luxury, and comes complete with a private pool and deck with hammock, all open to the river. Guests in each suite are allocated their own boat and a personal guide, too. Facing the rapids, the central building continues the theme, with guests coming together for evening meals. *N$305–585 pp sharing, inc all meals, drinks (except spirits and non-house wines), laundry and activities; 30% sgl supplement. Open all year.*

10

Chobe National Park and Forest Reserve

Chobe National Park takes its name from the Chobe River, which forms its northern boundary, and protects about 10,700km² of the northern Kalahari. Its vegetation varies from the lush floodplains beside the Chobe River to the scorched Savuti Marsh, dense forests of cathedral mopane to endless kilometres of mixed, broadleaf woodlands. This is classic big-game country, where herds of buffalo and elephant attain legendary proportions, matched only by some exceptionally large prides of lion.

Much of the park is devoid of water in the dry season, and the vast majority of it is inaccessible, so this chapter concentrates on the four main areas of Chobe that are accessible: the Chobe riverfront, Ngwezumba Pans, Savuti, and the Linyanti. It also covers the Chobe Forest Reserve, a populated enclave almost surrounded by the park.

BACKGROUND INFORMATION

HISTORY The Chobe's original inhabitants were the Bushmen, followed by the Hambukushu, Bayei and Basubiya. The 1850s saw David Livingstone pass through the area, on his way to seeing the Victoria Falls, and a succession of big-game hunters seeking trophies and ivory. It was first protected as a game reserve in 1961, and then proclaimed a national park in 1968, which was none too late.

Despite its distant trophy-hunting past, the game density in some areas of the park remains remarkable, ensuring the park's continued popularity. Simply driving a few kilometres along the Chobe riverfront in the dry season is demonstration enough, as you'll be forced to halt frequently to allow game to wander slowly across the road, or to watch herds coming down to drink from the river.

However, perhaps more than any of Botswana's parks, Chobe has felt the impact of tourism. In the 1980s, park fees were low and the few basic campsites were full. Rubbish became a problem, solitary game viewing was almost impossible and the animals became habituated to people. While Chobe has never been busy by east African standards, its three or four basic public campsites and simple network of game-viewing roads couldn't cope with so many visitors.

Fortunately, around 1987, the government started to implement a policy of 'high cost, low density' tourism. Park fees went up and the numbers of visitors dropped. The situation has now changed. With regular increases in these park fees the flood of visitors through the park has turned into more of a moderate flow. Once again, most of the park feels like a wilderness area. Even the 'honey pot' of the northern Chobe riverfront area isn't quite as busy, though the proximity of Kasane's lodges and campsites ensure that it's never going to be that quiet either.

GEOGRAPHY The geography of Chobe National Park and adjacent Forest Reserve, and indeed most of northern Botswana, is one based on an undulating plain of

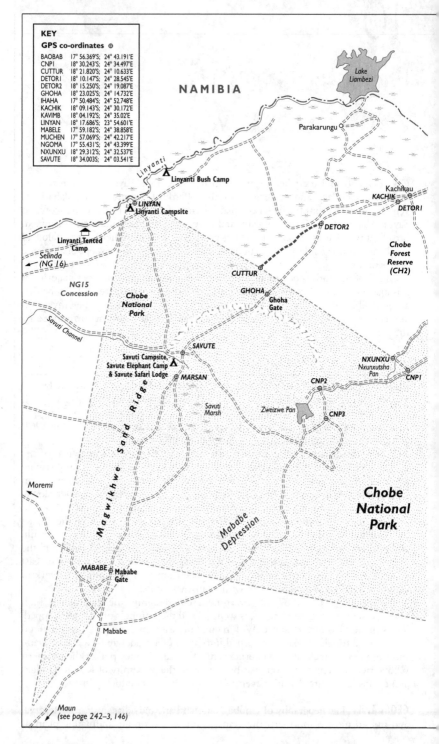

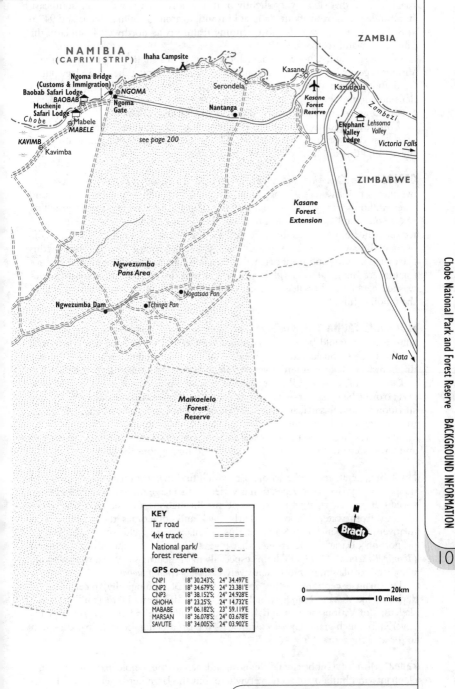

KEY

Tar road	
4x4 track	
National park/ forest reserve	

GPS co-ordinates ⊕

CNP1	18° 30.243'S;	24° 34.497'E
CNP2	18° 34.679'S;	24° 23.381'E
CNP3	18° 38.152'S;	24° 24.928'E
GHOHA	18° 23.25'S;	24° 14.732'E
MABABE	19° 06.182'S;	23° 59.119'E
MARSAN	18° 36.078'S;	24° 03.678'E
SAVUTE	18° 34.005'S;	24° 03.902'E

0 ————— 20km
0 ————— 10 miles

CHOBE RIVERFRONT TO SAVUTI

Kalahari sand that slopes very slightly from the northwest down to the southeast. Its altitude varies from about 950m at Linyanti, to around 930m at Ihaha and 942m at Savuti. In many ways its most defining feature is its northwest boundary: the Chobe–Linyanti river system.

On the ground, Chobe's geographical features are subtle rather than striking. Various vegetated sand dunes and sand ridges occur, including the large Magwikhwe Sand Ridge. Natural pans are dotted throughout the park, reaching their highest densities around the Nogatsaa and Tchinga areas, and also the Zweizwe area east of Savuti. Only occasional rounded hills break the Kalahari's flatness.

Whilst the region is bounded by great rivers, within this area there are only dry, or at least very seasonal, watercourses. The Savuti Channel is the most famous of these – and that did flow, on and off, until 1982.

GEOLOGY See *Geological history* (pages 43–52) in *Chapter 3* for a comprehensive overview of Botswana's geological past. Here it's enough to note that by around three million years ago the Kalahari's longitudinal dunes had formed, channelling rivers south and east into the Limpopo. Then, around two million years ago, a tectonic shift blocked this drainage, leaving the rivers feeding a super-lake in the heart of Botswana – Lake Makgadikgadi. Geologists think that the level of this fluctuated in time, but that it reached as far as the Savuti area. Compelling evidence for this are the great sand-ridges in the area and the presence of smooth, wave-washed pebbles and boulders – for example those found on the southern side of the Ghoha Hills.

FLORA AND FAUNA Trying to describe Chobe as a whole without any comment or sub-divisions would be very misleading. Unlike some of Africa's national parks, Chobe is best considered as a handful of totally different areas, each with a different feel, slightly different vegetation and distinct populations of animals.

Later in this chapter I'll treat separately: the wildlife highlights of the **Chobe riverfront**; the variation to be found around the **Ngwezumba Pans**; the unique situation around **Savuti**; and the isolated corner of the park that reaches northwest to the **Linyanti**. In passing, I'll also mention the circumstances of the populated Chobe Forest Reserve enclave. Meanwhile, here I'll try to give a brief overview, and cover some of the species which are found throughout the park.

Flora In general, across the whole park you'll find many similarities. Near any of the permanent rivers the vegetation is varied, with a large number of tree and bush species. It's classic riparian forest – as occurs throughout southern Africa.

Away from water, Chobe has fairly thick and sometimes thorny bush with relatively few open areas. Much of this is Kalahari sandveld, often with a high proportion of acacias and species that love deep sand, like the silver terminalia (*Terminalia sericea*). Some of Chobe, especially in the south, is covered with mopane woodland, containing almost exclusively *Colophospermum mopane*.

The main exceptions to this are a few areas of (geologically) recent alluvial deposits, like Savuti Marsh, which look totally different. Here you'll find the skeletons of various acacias and leadwoods (*Combretum imberbe*) on open plains covered in couch grass (*Cynodon dactylon*) – the latter being the principal attraction to the area for zebra.

Fauna Most of Chobe's wildlife is found across the whole park. Occasional elephants and buffalo are seen everywhere, but the large herds generally follow a highly seasonal pattern of migrations. These are principally dictated by the availability of water.

AN UNEASY ALLIANCE

Co-operative relationships between mammals and birds are unusual, but the honey badger enjoys two. Its association with the greater honeyguide is well known. This small bird uses a distinctive song to lure the honey badger to a bee's nest, whereupon it feasts on the grubs after the badger has ransacked the nest and had its fill of honey.

Less well known is the honey badger's association with the pale chanting goshawk. This relationship is of no benefit to the badger, since the goshawk – or sometimes a pair of them – simply follows the bigger predator around as it digs and forages for prey, and pounces on any rodent or reptile that slips past. The badger may have the last laugh though, since goshawk eggs and nestlings are among its 59 different prey species that have been recorded in the Kalahari.

As the dry season progresses, all the small clay pans in the bush (and particularly the mopane woodlands) dry up. Then the elephants and buffalo start to form larger herds and migrate to the permanent waters of the Chobe and Linyanti rivers. These gather in their thousands by the rivers, having come from as far away as Zimbabwe's Hwange National Park. Then, as soon as it rains and the small pans in the bush start to fill with rainwater, the animals move away again and disperse.

Many of the park's animals will follow a smaller-scale, less noticeable version of this type of seasonal migration to the water, and this is what makes the game viewing in Chobe so remarkable towards the middle and end of the dry season.

At any time of year, Chobe's big game includes blue wildebeest, Burchell's zebra, impala, kudu, tssesebe, giraffe, impala, common duiker, steenbok, warthog, baboon and vervet monkey throughout the park. Eland, sable and roan antelope also range across the park, but are relatively scarce, just as they are elsewhere in southern Africa.

Lion and spotted hyena are very common, and are generally the dominant predators, whilst leopard, cheetah and wild dog all occur, though are seen much less frequently. Both side-striped and black-backed jackal are present – though the former are found more in the north of the park, and the latter in the south. Brown hyena probably occur, though rarely, in the drier parts of the south, though they don't seem to co-exist happily with a high density of lion or spotted hyena.

Cape and bat-eared fox are found here, though again the Cape fox prefers the drier south. I once had a particularly good sighting of a whole family of bat-eared foxes in the middle of the open plains on Savuti Marsh, early in the morning on a cold September day. There are a variety of mongooses found here; the most often seen of these are probably the banded and dwarf species, both of which are social, and very entertaining to watch.

Serval, caracal, aardwolf and aardvark are found all over the park, though are only occasionally seen due to their largely nocturnal habits. Pangolin are found here too, though they're very rarely seen.

If you have the chance to take any night drives in areas adjoining the park (no night drives are allowed inside the park) then you've a good chance to spot scrub hares, spring hares, lesser bushbabies, porcupines, genets (small-spotted and large-spotted), civets, African wild cats and honey badgers.

Though white and black rhino would occur here naturally, as they should throughout northern Botswana, it's likely that by the early 1990s they had all been wiped out through poaching. There were then occasional reports of individual sightings – but a viable breeding population had been destroyed.

10

In October 2001, white rhino were finally re-introduced into the Mombo area, on Chief's Island in the Moremi Game Reserve; reintroduction of black rhinos followed shortly. The introduced animals settled in well, and have been breeding. Although numbers remain a secret, they are increasing, and are gradually spreading out – with wandering rhinos now occasionally turning up in Chobe and even Magkadikgadi.

Birdlife Over 450 species of birds have been seen in Chobe – too many to even try to list here. Thus I'll cover the birding highlights in the separate sections concerning the specific areas within the park. Note that the summer migrants generally arrive around October and leave again in March.

WHEN TO VISIT

Noting the general comments made under *Planning and Preparation*, pages 67–73, you'll generally find a wider variety of bird species here in the wet season, many of which will be in their breeding plumage.

The movement of the animals is rather more complex. Most of Chobe's larger herbivores migrate with the seasons, to find water to drink and pastures new. These movements are, to a large extent, predictable, so bear them in mind as you plan your trip to maximise your chances of good game viewing.

Like most of Africa's game migrations, the principle behind this one is simple. The animals stay close to the permanent sources of water during the driest months, then they disperse into the forests and (especially) the open grasslands at the start of the rains to take advantage of the fresh grazing and browsing.

In northern Botswana, this means that game becomes more and more prolific near the permanent watercourses – the Chobe, the Linyanti, and the edges of the Okavango – as the dry season wears on. Then as soon as the rains come, many animals head south and east into the interior's forests and plains (especially the Makgadikgadi area and Nxai Pan). This gives the vegetation beside the rivers a little time to recover, so that when the dry season returns the animals will again find some grazing near the water.

The finer details of this are more complex, and slightly different for each species. Zebra, for example, have been the focus of a research project which tracked them using radio transmitters and a micro-light aircraft, based in Savuti. This study suggested that they spend the rainy summer, from November to about February, in the Mababe depression – venturing south to Nxai Pan, and then following the Boteti River down to around Tsoe, before heading across to the Gweta area and back north to Nxai Pan.

In March and April they pass through Savuti for a few months, where they foal. This makes a particularly good foaling ground as the rich alluvial deposits from the old Savuti Channel have left the area with mineral-rich soil supporting particularly nutritious grasses. A few months later, as dryness begins to bite around July, they move again towards the Linyanti for the dry season. Finally in late October and November, they return to the Mababe area as the rains begin and the grasses start to sprout.

Similarly, Sommerlatte (see *Appendix 3, Further Information*) studied elephant movements in the park in the mid-1970s. He found that the highest wet-season concentrations were around the Ghoha Hills, the eastern side of the Mababe Depression, and the mouth the Ngwezumba River (the Nogatsaa/Tchinga pans area). Though clearly movements have changed since then, if only because the Savuti Channel has dried up.

For the visitor, this means that the game in the dry season is best in the river areas. In the wet season, and just afterwards, the interior pans are definitely worth a visit. Savuti is unusual in that, remarkably, it has good game all year, but is especially interesting around April/May and November.

GETTING ORGANISED As with most of Botswana's wilder areas, there are basically three ways to visit Chobe: on a fly-in trip, staying at the lodges and camps; on a mobile-safari trip, organised by a local safari operator; and on a self-drive trip with all your own equipment and food.

Only self-drive visitors really need to do much of their own planning, and they should take everything they'll need to live on (including supplies of water) between Maun and Kasane. Chobe is often combined with Moremi on such a trip – which, taken at a relaxed pace, typically takes about ten days. You should stock up on food, fuel and supplies before you leave.

Although it's only about 300km between Maun and Kasane across Chobe, a lot of the driving is in second gear and permanent 4x4, so prepare for fuel consumption that's perhaps two or three times your normal tar-road consumption.

There are a few small local shops in the villages of the Chobe Forest Reserve, but otherwise there's nothing available on the whole route, and certainly no fuel. The park entrance gates are open 06.00–18.30 from April to September, and 05.30–19.00 from October to March. Park rules prohibit cars on the roads between sunset and sunrise, and it would be extremely foolish to attempt to drive after dark anyway, so be careful to time your journey to give plenty of time. The speed limit in the park is 40km/h, though you'll be very unlikely ever to get near this on the deep sand racks which are the park's roads.

ORIENTATION Though the maps make Chobe look complex, it's really very simple. In the northeast corner is Kasane, and in the southwest corner the road leaves for Maun and Moremi. Most visitors drive in on one side, and exit the other – and in the middle all roads lead to Savuti. There are concessions and camps planning to open up around Chobe, which may change this, but for now work on this basis!

North of Savuti there's a 'direct' road that links it to Kasane via the Chobe Forest Reserve and the Chobe riverfront area. Then there's an indirect route that travels to Kasane via the Nogatsaa Pans area in the forested heart of the park. Most visitors choose one of these routes; see *Driving from Kasane to Savuti* on page 205–9 for a discussion of their relative merits in various seasons. In all the above I use the word 'road' loosely – to mean two adjacent tyre tracks in the sand. You need a high-clearance 4x4 for a trip to Chobe, and lots of time.

MAPS There is really only one map of Chobe that is worthwhile for normal navigation and that's the Shell Map of Chobe National Park, by Veronica Roodt. The main map itself is fairly small, but it has a good inset of the game-viewing tracks of the Chobe riverfront area, and also aerial photograph backdrops for first-rate insets of the area around Savuti and Nogatsaa. Veronica's map of Savuti is especially good for navigation!

BOOKING AND PARKS FEES If you're flying into organised camps, then your park fees will probably already be included in the price of your safari. If you're driving into Chobe then you'll need to have booked all your campsites in advance – see pages 138–9 for details of the national park's offices in Maun and Gaborone, and a scale of the fees.

You'll need to have a copy (or preferably an original) of this confirmation with you, then you'll need to pay your park fees on the gate when you arrive. Note that this is best done in pula, and that credit cards are never accepted (though for the first time US$ or £ cash became acceptable in 2001 – albeit at fixed and fairly unattractive exchange rates).

CHOBE RIVERFRONT

Perhaps the park's greatest attraction is its northern boundary, the Chobe River. In the dry season animals converge on this stretch of water from the whole of northern Botswana. Elephant and buffalo, especially, form into huge herds for which the park is famous. In November 1853 David Livingstone passed through the area and described the river:

> . . . though the river is from thirteen to fifteen feet in depth at its lowest ebb, and broad enough to allow a steamer to ply upon it, the suddenness of the bending would prevent navigation; but should the country ever become civilised, the Chobe would be a convenient natural canal.

Fortunately that kind of civilisation hasn't reached the Chobe yet – there are no canal boats to be seen – and today's traveller must make do with 4x4s or the small motorboats that weave along the river, amongst channels still ruled by hippos.

ORIENTATION The southern bank of the Chobe River is slightly raised above the river, perhaps 3–4m high. Below this is a fairly level floodplain of short green grass and reeds, through which the river follows a very meandering course, roughly west to east, with many switchbacks, loops and adjacent old lagoons.

High on the bank is the main riverfront track, which is wide but for the most part sandy. This leads from the Kasane to the Ngoma gate fairly directly. Looping off from this are game-viewing tracks. Most of those on the north side drop down to the floodplains, and then loop around by the river. Those few heading off south usually follow straight firebreaks into the dry woodlands that make up the bulk of Chobe behind the thin band of riparian forest.

You can't get lost, provided that you don't cross to the south of the main road. Head east and you'll reach Kasane, west and you'll find Ngoma.

The game densities are generally at their best between Kasane and Ihaha, although the density of vehicles is also high here. When you head west past Ihaha, towards Ngoma, you'll find an increasing number of Namibians herding cattle on the floodplain areas across the Chobe River. Game densities in the forest reserve are significantly lower than those in the park, but you do have better chances of spotting some less common species like sable and roan antelope.

For details of the roads between Kasane and Savuti, see pages 205–9.

FLORA AND FAUNA HIGHLIGHTS The Chobe River meanders through occasional low, flat islands and floating mats of papyrus and reeds. These islands, and beside the river, are always lush and green – and hence attracts high densities of game. Beside this the bleached-white riverbank rises up just a few metres, and instantly becomes dry and dusty. Standing on top of this are skeletons of dead trees, sometimes draped by a covering of woolly caper-bushes.

In several areas this bank has been eroded away, perhaps originally where small seasonal streams have joined the main river or hippo tracks out of the water have become widened by general animal use to access the floodplains. Here there are often mineral licks, and you'll see herds of animals in the dry season coming down to eat the soil as well as drink from the river.

Flora On the bank beside the river the vegetation contains many of the usual plants found in riparian forest in the subcontinent. Yet despite this it has a very distinctive appearance, different from that of any other African river – and this difference is perhaps largely due to the sheer volumes of game, and especially elephants, that visit it during the dry season.

The main tree species found in this riverine forest include Natal mahogany (*Trichilia emetica*) – which isn't found in the rest of Botswana – plus Rhodesian teak (*Baikiaea plurijuga*), large fever-berry (*Croton megalobotryus*), umbrella thorn (*Acacia tortilis*), knobthorn (*Acacia negrescens*), raintree (*Lonchocarpus capassa*), African mangosteen (*Gardenia livingstonei*), bird plum (*Berchemia discolor*), jackalberry (*Diospyros mespiliformis*) and the odd sausage tree (*Kigelia africana*).

Because of the intense pressure from elephants, you'll often see the still-standing remains of dead trees which have been ring-barked by elephants, with the termite-resistant skeletons, probably leadwoods (*Combretum imberbe*), being particularly noticeable.

These riverside forests can seem quite denuded towards the end of the dry season, which many naturally blame on heavy grazing by the game. Clearly this has an impact here, but commercial logging took place along this riverside before and during World War II and also took its toll of some of the larger trees.

Despite this, several different types of bushes thrive here. Buffalo thorn (*Ziziphus mucronata*) and knobbly combretum (*Combretum mossambicense*) are common, though Chobe's most distinctive bush must be the remarkably successful woolly caper-bush (*Capparis tomentosa*). This sometimes grows into a dense, tangled shrub, but equally often you'll find it as a creeper which forms an untidy mantle covering an old termite mound. Sometimes you'll even find it covering the crown of dead trees, or draped continuously over a series of bushes.

If you're out game viewing with a Botswana guide, then ask him or her if they know of any local medicinal uses for woolly caper-bush. The plant has very strong antiseptic qualities, and both Palgrave and Roodt (see *Appendix 3, Further Information*) report that this is one of the trees most widely used in Africa for its magico-medicinal properties.

Fauna The game densities along the Chobe riverfront vary greatly with the seasons, but towards the end of the dry season it is certainly one of Africa's most prolific areas for game. It is an ideal destination for visitors seeking big game. Elsewhere in the dry season you'll find fascination in termites or ground squirrels; but here you can find huge herds of buffalo, relaxed prides of lion, and perhaps Africa's highest concentration of elephant – huge herds which are the hallmark of the area.

One of the main attractions of the boat trips on the Chobe is that large family groups of elephants will troop down to the river to drink and bathe, affording spectacular viewing and photography. You'll find these here at any time of day, but they're especially common in the late afternoon, just before sunset.

When it's very dry you'll also find elephants swimming across the river at night to raid the relatively verdant crops and farms on the Namibian side, often coming back to Botswana during the day when the villagers feel more confident to emerge and scare them.

If you are not floating but driving, then be careful. Read my specific comments on driving near elephants, pages 208 and 210, and err on the side of caution. Most of Chobe's elephants are in family groups containing mothers with calves. They can be sensitive to any perceived threat, so keep a respectful distance from them. This can be especially difficult when you see licensed guides driving closer, but you should still keep your distance. Their experience, and general coolness in case of

10

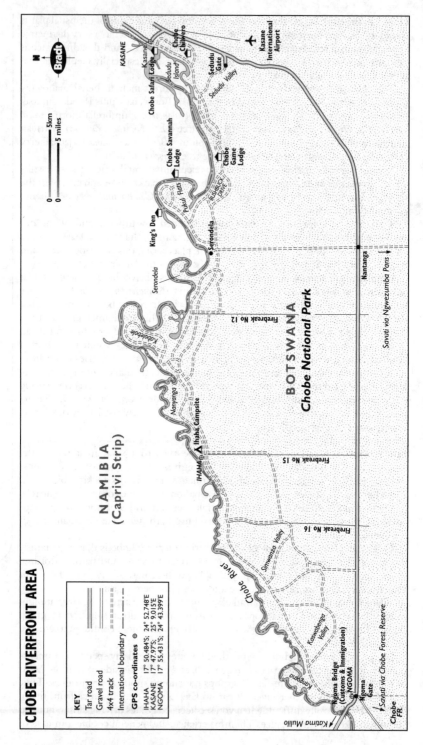

CHOBE RIVERFRONT AREA

KEY

Tar road	
Gravel road	
4x4 track	
International boundary	—·—·—

GPS co-ordinates ⊕

IHAHA	17° 50.484'S;	24° 52.748'E
KASANE	17° 47.97'S;	25° 9.015'E
NGOMA	17° 55.431'S;	24° 43.399'E

N

Bradt

0   5km
0   5 miles

NAMIBIA
(Caprivi Strip)

Kasane
KASANE ⊕
Kasane
Chobe Safari Lodge
Sedudu
Island
Sedudu Gate
Chobe
Chilwero
Kasane International
Airport

Chobe Savannah Lodge
Pukui Flats
King's Den
Chobe Game Lodge
BUSHBUCK DRIVE
Sedudu Valley

Serondela
Serondela

Kabulabola

Nunyanga

Simwanza Valley

Firebreak No 12

Firebreak No 15

Firebreak No 16

IHAHA ⊕ ▲ Ihaha Campsite

Chobe River

Kavwabenga Valley

Kasinga

Ngoma Bridge
(Customs & Immigration)
NGOMA ⊕

Ngoma
Gate

Katima Mulilo →

Chobe
FR

← Savuti via Chobe Forest Reserve

BOTSWANA
Chobe National Park

Nantanga

Savuti via Ngwezumba Pans →

elephant aggression, will allow them to do relatively safely what would be dangerous for you to attempt.

If you find your car surrounded by elephants, then try to relax. Virtually all of Chobe's elephants have seen lots of vehicles before, and so are unlikely to get too upset. Don't panic or rev your engine, just sit quiet and still until the animals have passed. Ideally switch off your engine – but this is not for the faint-hearted.

See pages 194–6 for a general comment on the game species found throughout Chobe. However, the riverfront is the best chance to see hippos, crocodiles and the odd sunbathing leguvaan (water monitor). Whilst there, also look out for the delightful Cape clawless and spotted-necked otters, which make their homes in the riverbank.

Perhaps the riverfront's most talked-about antelope is the Chobe bushbuck. This is a localised race, or perhaps a subspecies, of the bushbuck (*Tragelaphus scriptus* or, if a subspecies, then *ornata*) which has wide distribution within sub-Saharan Africa, from the edge of rainforests to the edges of the Kalahari and throughout the eastern side of southern Africa. Their colouration exhibits a lot of regional variation, and there is certainly a distinctive race which occurs only in this Chobe riverfront area – with brighter colouration and clearer markings than are found in the rest of southern Africa.

Bushbuck are small, attractive antelope which usually occur singly or in pairs. Only the males have horns, which are short and spiralled. They are well camouflaged, with a red-brown colouration, like the soil, and a covering of white spots that blend into the shadows of the riverside's thick vegetation. They will freeze if disturbed, and there are reliable reports of lions and hyena passing within 10m of a plainly visible bushbuck and not noticing it. Only if disturbed will they bolt for cover as a last resort.

Another antelope often noted here is the puku (*Kobus vardonii*) – which some sources claim is rarely seen. This is true, but only if you've never been to Zambia, where puku are probably the most common antelope. South of the Chobe they probably occur only in this Chobe riverfront area, and especially around the aptly named 'Puku Flats' peninsula of the floodplain.

The red lechwe (*Kobus leche*) is another water-loving antelope which is resident here, and easy to confuse with the puku at first glance. Look closely and you'll see that the lechwe's underparts are much lighter, their coats seem less shaggy, and the males' horns larger. Also notice that when they run, lechwe tend to hold their heads close to the ground, while puku normally run with their heads held much higher. This makes identifying them from a distance easier – and soon you'll realise that red lechwe are usually the most common antelope on Chobe's floodplains.

Waterbuck and reedbuck are also usually found in wetter areas, and so are seen around Chobe riverfront and Linyanti but not elsewhere in Chobe. Roan are also found here, but are fairly scarce, as befits an antelope that is sought-after by private game areas and is expensive to buy. Finally, the beautiful sable antelope are common nowhere, but I've seen large and relaxed herds here on several occasions. Being specialist grazers, they are more commonly found in the wooded south of the riverfront, though as sable and roan usually drink during the middle of the day, you will quite often see a small herd near the riverfront road, between Ngoma and Kasane.

Birdlife From a boat on the main river in the park you're likely to spot numerous beautiful kingfishers (pied, giant, some malachite and the occasional half-collared), with the pied seeming to be particularly numerous, perching on reeds by the river, or hovering to hold their eyes static above the river's surface. You'll also see plenty of reed cormorants and darters, various bee-eaters; hammerkops, wire-tailed swallows, a high density of fish eagles and even African skimmers (November–March only; the best place to see them is probably near Hippo Pools, beside Watercart Drive).

The fringes of the islands and floodplain are particularly good for birding, being home to many storks, herons, geese, egrets and a wide variety of plovers (blacksmiths, long-toed, crowned, wattled and, of special interest, white-crowned). Particularly unusual and worth seeking are rufous-bellied and white-backed night herons, slaty egrets, brown firefinches and wattled cranes.

For a totally different environment attracting several different species, head downstream and out of the park, to the shallow rapids dotted with rocks, which are adjacent to Impalila Island on the Chobe and Zambezi rivers. (The Chobe's are the Kasane Rapids, whilst those on the Zambezi are known as the Mambova Rapids.) In the dense waterside vegetation before the rapids look out for the shy finfoot, whilst around the rapids themselves there's a thriving population of rock pratincoles.

If you have the chance to explore the Kasai Channel (which connects the Zambezi and Chobe rivers), then do so. Technically you'll need to cross into Namibia, so this trip is probably easiest to undertake from one of the lodges on Impalila Island (see pages 189–90). Here you'll find small lagoons beside the main channel covered in water lilies, and bird species that include the uncommon lesser and purple gallinules, lesser jacanas and moorhens, pygmy geese and African rails. On the edge of these, in the adjacent reeds and papyrus beds you'll probably hear (if not see) chirping cisticolas, greater swamp warblers and swamp boubous.

Back inside the park, in the band of forest beside the river, you'll find many drier-country species, including coucals (Senegal and coppery-tailed), oxpeckers, sunbirds (you can find coppery sunbirds here), rollers (look out for the racket-tailed), hornbills, flycatchers, weavers, shrikes and francolins. Large flocks of helmeted guineafowl seem particularly visible, and are especially fond of loitering along the tracks in front of vehicles. Or so it seems!

There's a tremendously wide range of raptors here, from the ubiquitous fish eagles perching on dead trees overlooking the river, through to the huge martial eagles patrolling the drier woodlands. Other resident eagles include the uncommon western banded snake eagle, black-breasted and brown snake eagles, bateleur, tawny, long-crested, Ayres' and African hawk eagle. These are joined in the summer by migrant eagles, including Steppe and Wahlberg's eagles, and all year by many species of falcons, goshawks, harriers, kites and even the rarely seen bat-hawk.

WHERE TO STAY Many people visit the Chobe riverfront whilst staying in Kasane (see the previous chapter and pages 189–90), or possibly from a base at Ngoma (see pages 209–11). Generally the options inside the park are more expensive, but they have better locations. Within northern Chobe, there are only two choices: the basic public campsite at Ihaha or the stylish Chobe Game Lodge. There are also two lodges on the opposite side of the river which, although they are technically in Namibia, I've included here for completeness as they are primarily used to visit Chobe.

Δ Ihaha Public Campsite See page 138 for national park booking offices. About 15km west of the old site at Serondela, Ihaha (⊕ IHAHA 17°50.484'S; 24°52.748'E) is the only campsite for private visitors within northern Chobe. If you're taking the riverfront road from Kasane you can't miss this, as there are 2 sharp turns in the road and a small national park office past which you must drive. Earthwork ramparts effectively surround the site, so you have to turn away from the river road and pass through the main camp office to get there.

202

For years the only campsite in northern Chobe was at Serondela, sprawling along the riverside about 17km west of Kasane. The local animals had all lost their fear of man. Hence all the dangerous big game seemed to make a point of regularly sauntering through camp. Ignorant tourists had, over the years, fed some animals and the baboons, particularly, became a menace – aggressive, adept at stealing food if you turned your back for a second, and even able to open zips on unguarded tents.

On one occasion a lone male bounded on to the tailgate of my 4x4, snatching a packet of biscuits in its jaws from a food box, and sprinted off – all in a matter of seconds whilst I and a companion were a few steps away at the front of the vehicle. Before leaping up into the back it knew that we'd seen it and were coming back to chase it, but also knew that it was faster and so continued. It was obviously very well practised at this sort of smash-and-grab raid.

Further, Serondela was relatively close to the eastern side of the park, so it added considerably to the density of traffic in the peak dawn and dusk time for game viewing. So for several reasons the site was closed in the late 1990s and superseded by the new Ihaha site. Today, though, it is used occasionally by safari groups as a picnic site; all that remains of the campsite is the rubble of some very basic ablution blocks.

Large pitches, many with good tree shade, run parallel to the river, some with almost unlimited views across to the Namibian plains. Firm and sandy underfoot, with plenty of scrubby vegetation, this is a super place to while away hours watching the abundance of waterbirds along the river, or herds of impala or zebra grazing alongside the cattle on the other side. Two modern ablution blocks each have 2 showers, 2 flush toilets and several sinks for men and women; in theory, hot water comes courtesy of solar panels, though supply is erratic. Despite daily cleaning, the toilets in particular were in pretty poor condition when we visited, but in such a stunning location it somehow seems a trivial complaint. P30 pp.

🏠 **Chobe Game Lodge** (44 rooms, 4 suites) Desert and Delta, see page 169.

Situated about 9km from the park's Sidudu Gate, this is the largest lodge in any of Botswana's national parks. Opened in 1972, in some ways it seems like just another luxury hotel. Its design is unusual though, with tribal antiques in almost Moorish surroundings, which blend together very well. Despite its size, it has maintained a first-class reputation for personal service since I've known it; perhaps because of an experienced staff who understand how to give attention to detail.

Each of the rooms is set slightly into the bank with a barrel-vaulted ceiling and French windows on to a balcony overlooking the river, about 60m away.

Their design, together with punkah-punkah ceiling fans and AC, keep them cool through the day. Inside, the style is colonial: red-tiled floors are dotted with rugs, the furniture is solid Rhodesian teak with wicker chairs, and the comfy beds have little canopies. A minibar, safe and tea/coffee-making facilities are standard, and en-suite bathrooms have a bath with an efficient shower attachment, and electric shaver point. In the lodge's large suites, furnished equally well but with a 'lounge' as well as a bedroom, and a shower separate from the bathroom, there's a small, private swimming pool. When Elizabeth Taylor and Richard Burton chose this as a romantic place in which to be re-married, and spent their honeymoon in a suite, it was something of a PR coup!

As you'd expect, there's a large pool, a pleasant bar and upstairs a 'cigar bar' with a full-sized billiard table leading on to a terrace overlooking the river. There's also a new beauty salon with a gym, fortunately with AC, and a well-stocked curio shop. The food is good, and usually eaten outside on a covered veranda, or in the boma by the river. Breakfast and lunch are buffet-style, while dinner is even more leisurely, à la carte by candlelight.

The activities offered here are amongst the most varied of any of the region's lodges, and are very flexible: you can take as many activities as you have the time and energy for. Game drives in open-sided 4x4s typically go out 3 times a day — early or late

morning and late afternoon – for about 3hrs. It's possible to take out a small boat with a driver/guide, usually either in the late morning or the early afternoon. Short walks on the riverbank and around the forest reserve are usually best done when it's cool, and it may be possible to take a long excursion to explore the Botswana side of Kazuma Pan on foot with an armed guide. And it doesn't stop there. In the evenings, there are usually shows of wildlife videos in the conference room, which seats up to 100 (it's the only business centre in Chobe or the Okavango!), while the latest attraction is the installation of stargazing equipment on the roof.
US$630/830 pp sharing/sgl Jul–Oct; US$420 pp Nov–Mar; US$360 pp Apr–Jun, fully inclusive. Open all year.

🏠 **Chobe Savannah Lodge** (12 rooms) Desert and Delta, page 169. The smaller sister lodge of Chobe Game Lodge stands on a private concession of land on the Namibian side of the river, facing west out over the Puku Flats area. Its main centre is a dbl-storey thatch-and-timber building, which has superb views across the flat landscape of the river and its floodplains. Inside this is a lounge, library and a dining room, whilst outside is an open boma for evening fires, a plunge pool and a wooden sundeck.

The brick-and-thatch suites all have en-suite facilities with separate showers and oval baths, AC, overhead fans, minibars and tea/coffee-making facilities. It's a stylish spot, designed carefully with lots of rich dark earthy browns.

Activities here major on game viewing by motorboat, as well as sunset cruises and guided canoeing. Nature walks along the river and trips to one of the local villages are also offered.
US$630/830 pp sharing/sgl Jul–Oct; US$420 pp sharing/sgl Nov–Mar; US$360 pp sharing/sgl Apr–Jun, fully inclusive. Open all year.

🏠 **King's Den** (10 chalets, riverboat) √f 6250 814; e kingsden @ botsnet.bw. Owned by the Namib Sun Hotel group, King's Den overlooks Chobe National Park from Kasikili (Sedudu) Island. It can be reached by taking a boat west from Kasane, and is nearer to the park than any of Impalila Island's lodges. It has wooden chalets constructed on stilts on the edge of the island, all with en-suite facilities. In addition to these, there is a 13-cabin riverboat, the *Zambezi Queen*. Options for guests include game-viewing boat excursions on the Chobe River or through the Chassai Channel, as well as fishing, a visit to a traditional village, and day trips to Victoria Falls.
Prices in Namibian dollars: N$1,080/1,720 sgl/dbl, inc all meals and boat cruise.

WHAT TO SEE AND DO Game viewing and birdwatching are the main activities here; walking and night drives are not allowed in Chobe. Most visitors explore along the floodplains beside the river; this is relatively easy game viewing even without a guide.

If you're driving yourself though and have a little time to spare, don't ignore the roads away from the river on the western side of this riverfront section, particularly the Kaswabenga and Simwanza Valley roads, as well as the fire-breaks marked on Veronica Roodt's maps of Chobe. The landscape here is very different from anything else you're likely to see in Chobe. It's broken country with rocky hillsides and gullies; classic leopard country. Driving around here in October, you'll often find surprisingly good concentrations of game, despite its apparent distance from the river. This is because the game will often rest in the shade of the forest on its way to and from the river.

Ngoma border post At the westernmost point of the Chobe Riverfront is Ngoma gate (✦ NGOMA 17°55.43'S; 24°43.39'E), which marks the boundary between Chobe National Park and Chobe Forest Reserve. Turning towards the river at this point brings you to the border post at Ngoma, where on the Botswanan side is a smart, mid-1990s building perched high above the river. Namibia has a less imposing office next to the bridge on the other side of the Chobe River, about 2km further on. Both are efficient, pleasant, and generally quiet. This crossing is fine for 2WD vehicles, and opens 06.00–18.00. As with many borders, don't be alarmed if you see the odd soldier wandering around with a gun, and don't even think about taking any pictures near the bridge without permission. From the border, it's signposted 57km to Kasane, 65km to Kazungula, 115km to Savuti, and 362km to Nata.

At several checkpoints in Botswana, particularly near rivers, notices are posted warning of the problems posed by the invasive water weed, *Salvinia molesta*. Known locally as *mosthimbambo*, and more widely by its common names, giant salvinia or Kariba weed, it was first identified in the Zambezi River over 50 years ago. Since then it has become widespread throughout the southern part of the continent, migrating to the Chobe River in the 1980s.

A native of Brazil, Kariba weed is a water fern that was at one time sold for ornamental use in aquariums and garden ponds. With an exceptionally fast rate of reproduction, the plant spread rapidly from these relatively narrow confines into larger bodies of warm, relatively sluggish water. As the plant multiplies, its originally flat green leaves die back and fold together, forming an impenetrable mat that can be as much as a metre deep. The implications for waterways such as the rivers of Botswana are considerable. Not only do the matted plants create an obstruction, impacting on boat traffic and blocking irrigation pipes and water supplies, they also create an ideal breeding ground for mosquitoes and other insects. The impact on the environment is no less devastating, with indigenous plants affected by loss of light and oxygen, an effect that is compounded as decaying plants sink to the river bed and adversely affect the development of fish and other river wildlife.

Control of such a virulent plant has proved extremely difficult. While it can be sprayed, this is rarely fully effective, and the chemicals used are in themselves harmful to the environment. Rather more successful has been the introduction of a weevil imported from Australia, *Cyrtobagus salviniae*, whose adults and larvae feed on and damage the plants under the right circumstances. To date, a success rate of up to around 90% has been recorded in some areas over a period of 12 months, although success is also affected by temperature.

The problem is by no means confined to Africa. Kariba weed is on the environmental hit-list of countries across the globe, from New Zealand to the US, where both sales and ownership of the plant are now banned. In Botswana, however, the challenge is to prevent serious damage to the country's aquatic ecosystem. With this in mind, the authorities have introduced strict measures, which include controlling the boats allowed on the country's waterways, and decontamination of those that are licensed.

The conversion of the gravel road into tar from Namibia's Katima Mulilo to the Botswana border at Ngoma has taken years, but has now been completed. Thus you can now drive from Kasane into Namibia and right across the Caprivi Strip on a good tar road.

DRIVING FROM KASANE TO SAVUTI

There are two routes through Chobe National Park between Kasane (⊕ KASANE 17°47.97'S; 25°9.015'E) and Savuti. Certainly the shorter, and probably the more beautiful, is the western route, which is about 172km from Kasane to Savuti, via the Chobe Forest Reserve, and can take in the Chobe riverfront drive (above) if you have time. The alternative is the eastern route, which is about 207km long. This stays within the park and passes through the Nogatsaa Pans area.

Note that in the wet season, you're recommended to use the western route. Firstly, it's probably slightly more frequented by vehicles. Secondly, you'll find it particularly easy to get stuck in the clay soils found around the pans (both Zweizwe and Nogatsaa/Tchinga). That said, if you do brave the pans route, the birding can be particularly good at that time of year.

Don't imagine that the western route is always easy at that time. Most of this is fairly thick sand and you'll often be crossing fossil dunes with woodland on the crests and scrub or grasslands in the valleys. Veronica Roodt (see *Appendix 3, Further Information*) reports that there's a patch where water sometimes gathers just south of the Ghoha Hills. So beware of problems there after heavy rains.

EASTERN ROUTE: VIA THE PANS For the eastern route, you need to take the fast road from Kasane to Ngoma, away from the river. About 16km after the Sedudu Entrance Gate, near Kasane, you'll reach a crossroads. A right turn, north, would take you to the riverfront road in the Serondela area. Left leads you through the Nantanga Gate on to the only road through Chobe, and within 1km to the Nantanga Pans.

About 35km later there is a left turn to the complex of roads around Nogatsaa airstrip, Ngwezumba Dam and the old Nogatsaa and Tchinga campsites. Continue straight and after about 22km you'll pass another left, leading back to the same area. Shortly after this the road begins to follow the dry bed of the Ngwezumba River.

Around 22km from this (at ⊕ CNP1: 18°30.243'S; 24°34.497'E) you pass a small track on the right, which leads after almost 4km to Nxunxutsha Pan (⊕ NXUNXU: 18°29.312'S; 24°32.537'E), which is the southernmost point of the Chobe Forest Reserve.

About 60km later after the second Nogatsaa turn-off, this road takes a more southerly direction and leaves the riverbed behind (⊕ CNP2: 18°34.679'S; 24°23.381'E). About 7km later the road splits it (⊕ CNP3: 18°38.152'S; 24°24.928'E), with the right turn leading southwest through the pans. About 11km later the road turns west and finally northwest towards Savuti. This track enters Savuti by the south side of Qumxhwaa Hill (Quarry Hill) and joins the western route from Kasane just north of the channel.

At this final split in the pans route, there is an alternative left fork (which is not recommended as a route) which leads south for a few kilometres before passing Chosoroga Pan. One spur from this used to swing west around the pan and join into the roads on the south side of Savuti Marsh (from where you bear north and slightly west to reach the centre of Savuti). Another track apparently heads down directly from this pan to Mababe Village. I'm unsure of the current state of either of these tracks, so I would welcome news on either (preferably accompanied by details and GPS co-ordinates if they're navigable).

The total distance from Kasane to Savuti along the eastern route is about 207km, and it takes five or six hours to drive in the dry season. An advantage is the possibility of a midway stop at the Ngwezumba Pans, although scenically this route lacks the beauty of the Chobe River.

WESTERN ROUTE: VIA THE RIVERFRONT Taking the western route you have a choice of ways to start. If you're in a hurry, or starting late in the day, then drive the 57km to Ngoma from Kasane on the tar. Alternatively, and much more enjoyably, meander along the riverfront road (see *Chobe riverfront*, pages 198–205), which passes Serondela and Ihaha before joining up with the end of the tar road at Ngoma near the border post (see page 204). Both routes are a little over 50km, but whereas the fast route will take under an hour, the river route will take several, depending on how much you stop to watch animals or take photographs.

Either way you'll reach the scout hut at Ngoma, where you may be required to sign the register and possibly also to walk across a disinfectant mat while the wheels of your vehicle are sprayed to prevent the spread of any disease. Then you should take a left turn if you've been on the tar road (or continue more or less straight on

The final 50km or so north of the Ghoha Gate into Chobe can be very thick, heavy sand and the road has been badly churned up by trucks in the past. To avoid this, watch carefully and about 3.5km after you pass through Kachikau, there's the start of a track (⊕ DETOR1 18°10.147'S; 24°28.545'E) which bears off slightly to the right of the 'main' track (although the difference is hard to gauge) and which often makes for easier driving. Running more or less parallel to the main road, it is sometimes joined by a third track. Here and there the paths cross, most clearly at (⊕ DETOR2 18°15.25'S; 24°19.087'E), which is about 22.5km from Kachikau and 16.6km from the Ghoha Gate. At this point, you can either rejoin the main track, by turning left as indicated by the signpost towards Savuti, or continue straight on (signposted Linyanti), in which case it leads to a point on the cut-line (⊕ CUTTUR 18°21.82'S; 24°10.633'E) which is about 7.7km northwest of the gate. Thus you just need to turn left along the cut-line to return to the main track, and turn right to the gate.

For anyone heading in the opposite direction, from Savuti to Maun, you would simply turn left up the cut-line immediately after exiting the gate, and then take a right turn (⊕ CUTTUR) just after the end of a band of mopane trees.

from the riverfront road), heading roughly southwest, and signposted to Mabele (12km), Kachikau (35km), Parakarungu (70km) and Savuti (115km). This is sometimes referred to as the B334 and it appears at first to be good tar – but don't let that deceive you, for after a little over 1km it reverts to very rutted gravel. This brings you into the **Chobe Forest Reserve** (see pages 209–11).

About 11.5km past the turning you'll pass a big baobab near a few simple buildings and a large sign proclaiming **Mabele**. You'll still be able to see the Chobe floodplain off to the right, but with little game on it. Mabele has a 'hi-life' bar and a soccer pitch. Mabele General Dealer (⊕ MABELE 17°59.182'S; 24°38.858'E), on the right, is the best shop in town, though it's still very limited. The vegetation is mostly acacia species here, with lots of umbrella thorn, *Acacia tortilis*, but the scenery becomes less inspiring. Almost 22km after Ngoma you pass a police camp on the right-hand side (various prefabricated houses) which overlooks the floodplain again, then 3km or so further on you reach the sprawling town of **Kavimba**, whose landmark two baobabs stand guard on each side of the road (⊕ KAVIMB 18°4.192'S; 24°35.02'E). There's a board at the side of the road advertising a craft co-operative in the town, but little sign of any activity to back this up. And despite rumours of a community campsite, there is no evidence of this either. A little over 10km later you'll reach **Kachikau**, which is marked on some maps as 'Kachekabwe'. You can buy a limited range of drinks and foodstuffs at the shops here. There's also a forestry camp, and the smart, well-built Lizwasani Community School. In the centre of town (⊕ KACHIK 18°9.143'S; 24°30.172'E) there's a right turning signposted to Setau, a small settlement in the communal area to the north of the forest reserve, near Lake Liambezi. Ignore that turning and just afterwards you'll pass a small shop set back from the road on the left.

After Kachikau the sand starts to get deeper and the track worse (see box above for a possible detour to avoid this).

The country around here is rolling vegetated dunes, which means lots of corrugations and deep, deep sand. Plenty of leadwood trees are around, so beware of punctures (especially if you've reduced the pressures in your tyres for the sand). The long, strong leadwood spines will cause punctures in even the sturdiest of 4x4 tyres.

About 80km after Ngoma you'll meet what looks like a crossroads, although in reality you are crossing the cut-line that marks the end of the forest reserve, and the start of Chobe National Park. If you were to turn right here, then this (very

DRIVING NEAR ELEPHANTS: AVOIDING PROBLEMS

Elephants are the only animals that pose a real danger to vehicles. Everything else will get out of your way, or at least not actively go after you, but if you treat elephants wrongly there's a chance that you might have problems.

To put this in perspective, most drivers who are new to Africa will naturally (and wisely) treat elephants with enormous respect, keeping their distance – simply out of fear. Also in the more popular areas of Chobe or Moremi, where the elephants are habituated to vehicles, you'd have to really annoy an already grumpy elephant for it to give you trouble.

To give specific advice is difficult, as every elephant is different. Each is an individual, with real moods and feelings – and there's no substitute for years of experience to tell you what mood they're in. However, a few basics are worth noting.

Firstly, keep your eyes open and don't drive too fast. Surprising an elephant on the road is utterly terrifying, and dangerous for both you and the elephant. Always drive slowly in the bush.

Secondly, think of each animal as having an invisible 'comfort zone' around it (some experts talk of three concentric zones: the fright, flight, and fight zone – each with a smaller radius, and each more dangerous). If you actively approach then you breach that zone, and will upset it. So don't approach too closely: keep your distance. How close depends entirely on the elephants and the area. More relaxed elephants having a good day will allow you to get within 25m of them, bad-tempered ones that aren't used to cars may charge at 250m! You can often approach more closely in open areas than in thick bush. That said, if your vehicle is stationary and a relaxed, peaceful elephant approaches you, then you should not have problems if you simply stay still.

Thirdly, never beep your horn or flash your lights at an elephant (you shouldn't be driving yourself at night anyhow!). Either is guaranteed to annoy it. If there's an elephant in your way, just sit back, relax and wait; elephants always have right of way in Africa! The more sound and fury – like wheel spins and engine revving – the more likely that the elephant will assume that you are attacking it, and this is especially the case with a breeding herd.

Finally, look carefully at the elephant(s):

- Are there any small calves around in the herd? If so expect the older females to be easily annoyed and very protective – keep your distance.
- Are there any males in *musth* around? These are fairly easy to spot because of a heavy secretion from penis and temporal glands and a very musty smell. Generally these will be on their own, unless they are with a cow on heat. Such males will be excitable; you must spot them and give them a wide berth.
- Are there any elephants with a lot of seepage from their temporal glands, on the sides of their heads? If so, expect them to be stressed and easily irritable – beware. This is likely to have a long-term cause – perhaps lack of good water, predator pressure or something as random as toothache – but whatever the cause that animal is under stress, and so should be given an extra-wide berth.

rough and bumpy) cut-line would lead you to a spot on the Linyanti River just east of the Linyanti Campsite. If you were heading directly from Kasane to the Linyanti or Selinda concessions, you would probably use this track (the right side is better when it's wet, the left better in the dry season).

Continuing straight across the cut-line, however, and less than 1km later you'll reach the impressive Ghoha entrance gate (⊕ GHOHA 18°23.25'S; 24°14.732'E).

This is about 80km from Ngoma, and 28km from Savuti. Here you'll need to produce your camp reservations, sign in and pay any required park fees – assuming it's manned, of course.

As you enter the national park you'll see the Ghoha Hills on your left in the distance. A few kilometres later you'll pass the first of the hills, which is dotted with baobab trees. The road inside the park is generally less sandy and better than that which is outside, although it does cross the northern edge of the Magwikhwe Sand Ridge just south of the hills.

About 25km after the entrance gate you'll pass a sharp-angled right turn which leads to Savuti airstrip, and a couple of kilometres further on you'll reach the main Savuti waterhole on your right, where you'll often find game-viewing vehicles. The road eventually approaches Savuti from a northeasterly direction. Although this route is shorter (about 172km in total) and arguably more spectacular, it is generally more difficult and time-consuming to drive than the eastern route described above.

CHOBE FOREST RESERVE

Chobe Forest Reserve is an enclave largely surrounded by Chobe National Park. To the northwest of it are seasonal marshes, Lake Liambezi and, eventually, Namibia.

The reserve, and the area to the north of it – concessions known as CH/1 and CH/2 – are designated respectively for photographic safaris and community-managed hunting. The new photographic area in CH/1, beside the Linyanti River, is the location of Linyanti Bush Camp (see page 230). The flora and fauna here are essentially the same as in the Linyanti Concession; hence we have included the camp in that section.

The 'hunting' aspect of CH/2 should not deter photographic guests from visiting, as the reserve contains good populations of wildlife that are managed sustainably by the community and Hakuna Matata Safaris.

Most visitors simply pass through the southern corner of CH/2 *en route* between Kasane and Savuti. See *Western route: via the riverfront* above for more details of the drive through the area.

WHERE TO STAY You'll also find that Chobe's game-drive loops become quieter as you move east to west from the Kasane area to Ngoma. There are two lodges here in the forest reserve, so think of them as alternatives to those in the Kasane area, as well as a potentially convenient stopovers. Buffalo Ridge, the campsite near the Namibian border that was once linked to the lodge, is now closed.

Baobab Safari Lodge (8 chalets) Contact via Overseas Adventure Travel, USA; ☎ 1 800 493 6824; www.oattravel.com (◈ BAOBAB 17°56.36'S; 24°43.19'E). About 3km inside the Chobe Forest Reserve, there's a turning to the right to Baobab Safari Lodge. This is a private camp leased until the end of 2006 from Wilderness Safaris by OAT, specialists in small-group travel for the over 50s; no walk-in guests are accepted. Built on a ridge with a superb view across the plains, the rather dark stone-built central building combines dining and lounge areas. Behind and alongside sit individual stone-built chalets with pitched canvas roofs; each has twin

beds and an en-suite bathroom. As you would expect, activities focus on game drives in the national park.
Rates as part of organised group only. Open all year.
Muchenje Safari Lodge (10 chalets) ☎ 6200 013/14/15; m 7164 6017; e info@muchenje.com; www.muchenje.com (◈ MUCHEN 17°57.115'S; 24°42.361'E). Matt and Lorna Smith built Muchenje in 1996, and have owned and run it ever since. To get there follow the signs from Ngoma towards Mabele and Savuti; Muchenje is 3km along on your right.

Well-spaced wooden chalets are comfortably furnished with twin or dbl beds surrounded by a

If you get into a hair-raising situation with elephants, then you've probably not kept your distance. The key was prevention, and you failed. Now you must keep cool, with your logic ruling your fear. A few words here are inadequate – you need experience – but I'll outline some basics.

Firstly, if your vehicle is stationary and switched off, and you become unexpectedly surrounded by peaceful elephants, don't panic. Don't even start the engine, as that would startle them. Just sit there and enjoy it; there's no real cause for concern. Only when they've passed and are a distance away should you start up. When you do start: never start and move off simultaneously, which will be interpreted as the vehicle being very aggressive. Instead start up quietly, wait a little and then move.

More often a situation occurs when one from the herd will be upset with you. In that case you've approached too closely. (The key was to keep your distance – remember?) Then an annoyed elephant will usually first mock charge. This usually first involves a lot of ear flapping, head shaking and loud trumpeting – mock charges are often preceded by 'displacement activities', and the animals often show uncertainty about charging. The individual then runs towards you with ears spread out, head held high, and trumpeting loudly. This is terrifying, especially if you're not used to it. But be impressed, not surprised; elephants weigh up to 6,000kg and have had several million years to refine this into a really frightening spectacle.

However terrifying, if you stand your ground then almost all such encounters will end with the elephant stopping in its tracks. It will then move away at an angle, with its head held high and turned, its back arched, its tail raised, and the occasional head-shake. Often you'll find the 'teenagers' of the herd doing this – testing you and showing off a bit.

However, if you flee or back off rapidly during such a mock charge, the elephant will probably chase your vehicle, perhaps turning a mock charge into a full charge (see below). So, before you move, make very certain that you have a swift escape route, and that you can drive faster than the elephant can run. (In deep sand, you can forget this.)

As a fairly desperate measure, not normally needed, if the elephant is really getting too close, then increasing the revs of your engine – commensurate with the threat – will encourage the animal to stop and back down. Don't beep your horn, don't rev up and down, but do steadily press your accelerator further down as the elephant gets closer. (I've never needed to do this; it's overkill for most mock charges.)

However, if you're really unfortunate then you'll come across an upset or traumatised animal, or one that really perceives you as a threat and that makes a full charge. This is rare – expected only from injured elephants, cows protecting calves, males in *musth* and the like. Then the individual will fold its ears back, put its head down, and run full speed at your vehicle. I'm pleased that I've never faced one of these, but if you do then your only option is to drive as fast as you can. If you can't get away then I'd try revving, as above, matching its threat with your engine's noise. But I'd also start praying – this is a seriously dangerous place to be.

walk-in mosquito net. Each has a modern en-suite shower and toilet, ceiling fan, electric lights, and its own veranda overlooking Chobe's floodplain.
Discreetly tucked away is a honeymoon (or family) chalet – it sleeps up to 4 – with a second storey, a large bath tub, and an absolutely private veranda set to the side.

The wide, solid stone lodge is perched on the escarpment overlooking the floodplain, making the most of the setting. It has a dining area with a modest library, a curved central bar with plenty of seating and a large chessboard, and a small clothes/curio shop, all under a high thatched roof. Above the bar is a game-viewing platform with a great view, while outside, a small pool with loungers around it and the nearby boma share that impressive view.

Activities include game drives into the national park – using an area which tends to be more private and less busy with vehicles than those from lodges around Kasane, as less traffic reaches this far west. Bush walks (with armed guides) in the forest reserve are also offered, as is birdwatching on the river. A typical excursion for those staying 2 nights or more – which includes most guests – is a full-

day safari taking in a boat cruise along the Chobe, followed by a picnic lunch in the bush and then an afternoon game drive through the park back to the lodge. Fishing is available with advance notice only, and at extra cost, as it is arranged through a separate company.
US$225/325 pp sharing/sgl Dec–Mar; US$275/425 Apr–Jun; US$325/475 Jul–Nov, inc all meals, local drinks, activities, laundry, and transfers to/from Kasane. Open all year.

LIAMBEZI AREA

This large, shallow lake is located between the Linyanti and Chobe rivers. When full, it covers some 10,000ha, although it has been much drier, and frequently something of a dustbowl, since 1985. For most of the year, people and cattle now populate its bed.

Lake Liambezi's main source of water used to be the Linyanti River. However, even in recent years of good rain it has failed to fill the lake after filtering through the Linyanti Swamps (which themselves are very dry). Even despite good water levels in the Kwando-Linyanti system in the 2001–2 rainy season, it didn't break through as far as Liambezi.

Although over recent decades there has been a trend towards less and less water, and more villages, in the lake and the marshes around it, the early years of the 21st century have seen signs of a possible change. For the first time in many years Lake Liambezi has had a few inches of water on it, due to good rains and possibly some flow-back from the Chobe River.

NGWEZUMBA PANS

About 70km south of the Chobe River lies a large complex of clay pans surrounded by grassland plains, mopane woodlands and combretum thickets. There are well over a dozen individual pans: Noghatsau, Gxlaigxlarara, Tutlha, Tambiko, Kabunga, Cwikamba and Poha, to name but a few, and all hold water after the rains. This makes them a natural focus during the first few months of the year, when the animals tend to stay away from the permanent waters of the Linyanti and Chobe rivers.

If any of the water pumps here are working consistently then it also ensures the pans are excellent during the dry season too. However, if visiting in the heart of the dry season then check with the scouts at Savuti or Nantanga; ask if the pumps are working before you head this way.

FLORA AND FAUNA HIGHLIGHTS With water there, the pans are excellent in the dry season. Early in the dry season they're quite likely to hold water anyway – so taking the eastern route certainly makes sense around May–August. Once the natural water dries up, the pumps are vital. With water in the late dry season you can expect herds of Chobe's game interacting; it's a place to just sit and watch for hours.

Curiously, perhaps the area's most notable game doesn't need permanent water and so is found here all year. This area is perhaps the only place in Botswana where oribi antelope occur naturally. These small, elegant grazers are orange-red above, white underneath, have a dark circular scent gland under their ears and a short bush tail with a black tip. Only the males, which are very territorial, have short, straight horns. They are usually seen in pairs, or small groups, feeding in the open grasslands during the morning or late afternoon. If startled they will often emit a shrill whistle before bounding off at a rapid rate with a very jerky motion.

This is also the only area of Chobe where you've any real chance of spotting gemsbok (or oryx). This is the dominant large antelope species in the parks south of here, but it's relatively unusual to see them in Chobe. These pans, together with the complex around Zweizwe, are probably the park's best place to spot roan antelope, which never thrive in areas of dense game but seem to do well around here.

For birdwatchers the pans, and especially the larger ones like Kwikamba Pan, can be superb during the rains. Expect a whole variety of aquatic birds passing through including Egyptian and spurwinged geese, lesser moorhen, redknobbed coot, redbilled and Hottentot teal, African pochard, dabchick and even the occasional dwarf bittern. The large grassland plains here also attract grassland species such as yellow-throated sandgrouse, harlequin quail, croaking cisticola and, occasionally, Stanley's bustard.

WHERE TO STAY There used to be two campsites here, at Tchinga (alias 'Tshinga' and 'Tjinga') and Nogatsaa, but both have been strictly closed to private visitors over recent years. There are certainly HATAB camping facilities in the area, so you ought to have no problems visiting with a mobile safari run by a licensed Botswana tour operator (see pages 83–4 for an explanation).

Nogatsaa, the more northerly site, overlooks Nogatsaa Dam and used to have toilets, cold showers and a game-viewing hide. It used to be a great place for just sitting and watching the game coming to bathe and drink.

Tchinga is about 21km south of Nogatsaa, and even years ago had no facilities other than a water tank with a very temperamental mechanical pump.

SAVUTI

Unlike most game-viewing areas, Savuti isn't just about animals. Its game can be great, but that's only half the story. To understand the rest, and discover some of its spirit, you must dig into its history – from the geological past, to the first humans and then the European hunters, 'explorers' and conservationists – and learn of the reputation of some of its famous characters. Savuti seems to have more stories linked with it than all the other game areas in Botswana combined. So seek these out before you come, as only then will you really appreciate why Savuti has a legendary quality about it.

HISTORY The key to its attraction is the mysterious Savuti Channel, which is often dry (as it is now) but sometimes, inexplicably, flows. Its journey starts in the Zibadianja Lagoon, at the southern tip of the Linyanti Swamps. In past years when it flowed, it meandered a little south and then eastwards until it entered the national park about 35km away.

Continuing east, it flowed through a wide gap in the Magwikhwe Sand Ridge, around which are a number of low, rounded hills – the Gubatsaa Hills. (In former times, its flow probably formed this gap.) This is about 54km due east of the lagoon, and this is the place usually referred to as Savuti. It's also the place where the modern national park's campsite stands.

From here the channel turned abruptly south, and spilled out into the Mababe Depression, a huge flat area which was once the bed of an ancient lake (see pages 45–6 for more details), and formed the flat expanse of the Savuti Marsh, covering about 110km².

At its peak, with the channel and marsh full, it must have been like a huge drinking trough over 100km long, penetrating the heart of the dust-dry northern Kalahari. It's no surprise that it attracted huge quantities of game and, in turn, whatever people were around at the time.

San/Bushmen The early hunter-gatherers certainly had settlements here, evidenced by at least five sites in the hills around Savuti containing rock art. Archaeologists link these paintings with those in the Tsodilo Hills, and with the traditions of people of the Okavango.

A few of these sites are known to some of the guides at the lodges here, and if you are staying at one then request for your guide to take you to see them. Despite park regulations about walking, at least one of these sites now has a clear signpost to it. However, you need to think very carefully before trying this on your own – given not only the park's rules, but also the high density of lion, leopard, buffalo and elephant in the area.

The Rock Art Research Institute at the University of the Witwatersrand provides information about Bushman paintings in general on www.wits.ac.za/raru; e enquiries@rockart.wits.ac.za.

Early explorers There are many reports of this area from the early European explorers – fascinating if only to look back and see what they recorded of Savuti. In June 1851 when Livingstone passed through here the marsh was a 'dismal swamp' some 16km long, fed by both the Mababe (now called Khwai) River, which spilled over from the Okavango system, and also by the 'strongly flowing' Savuti Channel.

Chapman also crossed the channel around 1853, when he recorded it as dry. When the great white hunter, Frederick Courtney Selous, came in 1874, the channel was full and flowing into the marsh. However, when Selous came back in 1879 he noted that the channel had partially dried out, and no longer fed the marsh. Mike Main, in his excellent book on the Kalahari (see *Appendix 3, Further Information*) concludes that sometime in the 1880s the channel dried up.

Modern history It seems to have remained dry until a heavy rainy season, 1957–58, when the channel began to flow strongly once again. This continued until 1966, when it dried up once more. It then flowed from 1967 to 1981, when it seemed permanent and enhanced the area's reputation as a top game destination.

In the 1970s Lloyd Wilmot started a camp here, Lloyd's Camp, which was to put both Lloyd and Savuti on the map. Lloyd is, in fact, the son of one of the Okavango's famous crocodile hunters, Bobby Wilmot, and has many sisters, most with strong connections in the area.

A safari here was always off-beat. Lloyd built up a reputation for empathy with the game, and a total lack of fear for his own safety when dealing with it. Everyone who visited here came away with stories of remarkable animal encounters, and Savuti's reputation grew.

However, the channel's flow was gradually reducing and, in 1982, it ceased to flow completely. Gradually the water shrank into a few remaining pools, and then they dried up too. With them went the fish, hippos, crocodiles and all the other creatures that had lived there. During this time Lloyd was frequently photographed kneeling or lying in front of a thirsty elephant, excavating sand from a hole in the bottom of the channel until he reached water. This sad time was well chronicled in a video, *The Stolen River*, by Dereck and Beverly Joubert. It's also one of the main subjects of Clive Walker's book, *Savuti – the Vanishing River* (see *Appendix 3, Further Information*).

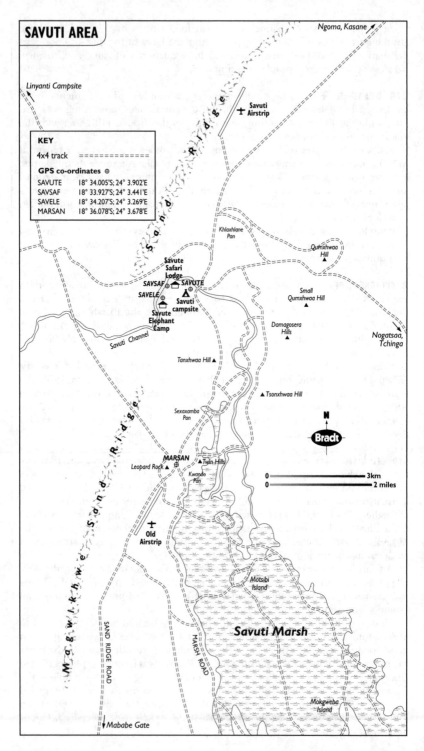

SAVUTI AREA

Ngoma, Kasane

Linyanti Campsite

Savuti Airstrip

KEY

4x4 track ===========

GPS co-ordinates ⊕

SAVUTE	18° 34.005'S; 24° 3.902'E
SAVSAF	18° 33.927'S; 24° 3.441'E
SAVELE	18° 34.207'S; 24° 3.269'E
MARSAN	18° 36.078'S; 24° 3.678'E

Khlaxhlane Pan

Qumxhwaa Hill ▲

Savute Safari Lodge

SAVSAF ⊕ ▲ SAVUTE

SAVELE ⊕

Savuti campsite

Small Qumxhwaa Hill ▲

Savute Elephant Camp

Savuti Channel

Damagosera Hills ▲

Nogatsaa, Tchinga

Tanxhwaa Hill ▲

Tsonxhwaa Hill ▲

Sexaxamba Pan

N

Bradt

MARSAN ⊕

Leopard Rock ▲

▲ Twin Hills

Kwando Pan

| 0 | | 3km |
| 0 | | 2 miles |

Old Airstrip

Motsibi Island

Savuti Marsh

M a g w i k h w e S a n d R i d g e

SAND RIDGE ROAD

MARSH ROAD

Mokgweba Island

Mababe Gate

214

Nobody really knows why it stopped, as nobody understood why it started again after almost 80 years of dryness. Explanations range from changes in the paths used by the Linyanti's hippos to tectonic shifts; see Mike Main's book, *Kalahari*, for a more detailed discussion.

However, even with the channel now dry, Savuti remains a classic area for game. Experts observe that the soil here is especially good, and the grazing particularly rich. Furthermore, there are now several permanent waterholes in the area. The oldest is pumped by the National Park, near the centre of Savuti, while two others are in front of the two lodges in the area. A further two are towards the bottom of the marsh, on opposite sides of it – and these try to attract the game, and especially the elephants, away from the centre of Savuti which has been so heavily impacted by game over the years.

ORIENTATION The Savuti Channel is a (currently dry) riverbed, which starts from the Zibadianja Lagoon, at the southern tip of the Linyanti Swamps. It flows through the Linyanti Reserve, before entering the national park about 35km away. Heading east, it first cuts through a wide gap in the Magwikhwe Sand Ridge, around which are a number of low, rounded hills – the Gubatsaa Hills. There it spreads out into the Mababe Depression, forming a large marshy area known as Savuti Marsh.

This area is now dry and known as Savuti. It's about 54km due east of the lagoon, and here within the Chobe National Park you'll find a campsite, two upmarket lodges and several waterholes.

Maps There are numerous small, winding sand roads around Savuti, relatively few landmarks and very few signs on the tracks. It's easy to become disoriented. If you want to explore the area in detail, you should have with you Veronica Roodt's excellent Chobe map (see *Appendix 3, Further Information*), and preferably also a GPS.

FLORA AND FAUNA HIGHLIGHTS

Flora Savuti's habitat is a mostly undistinguished thick thorny scrub, with camelthorn (*Acacia erioloba*) and silver terminalia (*Terminalia sericea*) making up much of it, though there are also large areas of mopane (*Colophospermum mopane*). You'll also find substantial stands of shaving-brush combretum (*Combretum mossambicense*) and Kalahari appleleaf (*Lonchocarpus nelsii*), and it's perhaps the most westerly area where you can find the lovely paper-bark albezia (*Albezia tanganyicensis*). Dotted all over the drier parts of the area are landmark baobab trees (*Adansonia digitata*); their ability to survive being ring-barked is essential to survival here.

The main contrast to these wooded areas is the Savuti Marsh. Here open plains covered with a variety of perennial grasses stand above the (geologically) recent alluvial deposits of the channel. These grasses are tolerant of the slightly higher salinity levels present, and some are particularly nutritious and a great attraction for the game when there's moisture about.

Here you'll also see the skeletons of dead trees, still standing in the flat grasslands. These were mostly camelthorns, umbrella thorns (*Acacia tortilis*) and leadwoods (*Combretum imberbe*) which are thought to have seeded and grown up between the 1880s and the 1950s, when the marsh was dry. Then when it flooded in the late 1950s they were drowned – though the hard, termite-resistant wood still stands.

On the southern side of the marsh you can see the bush gradually starting to invade the grasslands again, with the distinctive, low 'round mounds' of candle-pod acacia (*Acacia hebeclada*) leading the aggressors.

Fauna At the heart of the park, Savuti sees most of the park's species (see pages 194–6), with the exception of the Chobe bushbuck and the water-loving species. Reedbuck and waterbuck used to occur here, but even they have deserted with the demise of the channel's flow.

Now much of the interest is concentrated around the three remaining waterholes, and especially the old one pumped by the National Parks department. Here there's invariably a lot of game. Lion are frequently found lying around, and big herds will pause as they approach, or wait until their thirst overcomes their fear.

Savuti's elephants are notable for a number of old bulls which live in the area permanently, and are often individuals known to guides who have spent a lot of time in the area. These are augmented by large breeding herds which pass through. Whenever it's dry you can be sure that with such limited water resources, there's action and jostling for drinking positions at the waterhole.

In recent years, at least one of the local lion prides has grown so large that they will kill elephants to satisfy their hunger – traumatising the local elephants in the process. (The Khwai River area in Moremi has a similar phenomenon.)

Spotted hyena have always been numerous and very noticeable at Savuti. In the late 1980s and early '90s they would appear at the campsite, skulking around the bins, as soon as the sun set. After dark, and when people had gone to sleep, they'd pick up anything that they could carry, and eat anything small enough to crunch up – including, I was once assured, a glass lens from a 35mm camera! My aluminium camping cooker was stolen by a hyena once at Savuti, and still bears the scars of its strong jaw.

S M Cooper (see *Appendix 3, Further Information*) studied the clan sizes here in 1986–88, and found that there were five territorial clans in the area, and a number of transient animals passing through. The clans each averaged about 18 adult females, six males, five of unknown sex and ten cubs under two years of age – so around 39 members of each clan. They tend to prey on reliable, low-density resident game species like impala and warthog throughout the year, and augment this by feasting on the herds as they pass through the area, especially the new-born zebra foals.

Despite the presence of so many lion and hyena, leopards also do well here, perhaps helped by the presence of the rocky kopjes which make a perfect habitat for them. Daryl and Sharna Balfour have some lovely shots of leopard at Savuti in their book on Chobe (see *Appendix 3, Further Information*).

Once, when driving with one of Lloyd's guides (who shall remain nameless), we realised that there was an early-morning commotion in the air, and followed this to a young female leopard that had *just* killed an impala. The guide knew that she had a cub nearby to feed. However, our vehicle's approach had, unwittingly, frightened the leopard off its kill, and soon after we arrived so did a hyena – which proceeded to claim the prize.

Such was the maverick nature of Lloyd's Camp that this guide simply jumped out of the cab, grabbed the hind quarters of the impala, and started upon a tug-of-war with the hyena for the carcass. Spurred on by this, and the realisation that the cub would otherwise miss a meal, I joined in. Eventually we won the carcass and hauled it up on to a low branch hoping that the leopard would reclaim it.

But nature, once upset, isn't so easily put right. As we pulled back from the scene the hyena returned, stretched up on its hind legs, and plucked the impala from the branch with ease. Others swiftly joined it, devouring it within minutes. The leopard had already given up and disappeared, perhaps in disgust.

In the wet season there are still movements of buffalo, zebra and wildebeest which come on to the marsh to graze, though the huge herds of buffalo that came when the channel flowed have now stopped coming. In his guide to Botswana (see

One of Savuti's more famous residents was an elephant named Baby Huey, who had become very relaxed around people. He'd also picked up a liking for oranges, after foolish visitors fed him. Gradually he came to associate people with food. When I first visited Savuti in 1998, this was a problem.

Nobody drives around at night, but on that trip we were woken at 05.00 one morning by a vehicle driving up to our tent. The couple inside it had seen our fire burning, and come to seek sanctuary. It seems that they, and their small son, had been sleeping in the back (the pick-up section) of their 4x4 when Baby Huey had passed by. Smelling oranges, he'd used his tusk on the front cab like a can-opener on a tin, and then delved inside for a snack.

The couple were completely traumatised, and left Chobe at first light. Two days later Baby Huey was shot – and camping visitors are still banned from bringing citrus fruit into the park. And all because people were naive enough to feed the animals.

Appendix 3, Further Information) in 1968, Alec Campbell describes the scene on the marsh when the channel was flowing:

> Here the Savuti Channel carries water from the Linyanti . . . forming a marsh about a meter deep. From June to December huge herds of buffalo visit the marsh to feed in the surrounding scrub mophane and one can see as many as 6,000 daily. Out on the flats which surround it on the southern and western sides are herds of bull elephants, wildebeest, impala, giraffe, tsessebe and sometimes large numbers of zebra. Lion are also quite common.
>
> Cow elephants with their young spend much time in the taller mophane to the east of the marsh but come down to drink in the afternoon. Hippopotami and waterbuck are to be seen in the Channel especially near the mouth where it enters the marsh.

Numbers now probably don't match what was seen then, though April–May is still the prime time for the zebra and wildebeest herds to pass through, usually foaling here as they go. The precise timing of this is heavily dependent upon the local rainfall patterns.

The dry season can witness large numbers of tsessebe move on to the marsh area to graze. Occasionally, at the end of the dry season, oryx have been known to appear at the south end of the marsh, but they are very uncommon this far north. Always you'll find groups of giraffe in the acacia woodlands on the edge of the marsh and all over the area.

Finally, if you're anywhere around the hills in the area, then P C Viljoen (see *Appendix 3, Further Information*) notes that several klipspringer were spotted here on the Qumxhwaa Hill (Quarry Hill) in 1978 and 1979. This has since been confirmed by several reliable sources – including Tricia and Bob Hayne in 2005. Their existence here is remarkable, as the nearest other significant klipspringer population is probably in Zimbabwe's Hwange National Park, about 130km to the east.

Birdlife The list of bird species found in Savuti runs to over 300 species, but a couple of the more unusual include the Marico flycatcher, crimson boubou, capped wheatears, pennant-winged nightjars (only during the summer, October–January; look especially on the roads at dusk) and Bradfield's hornbill.

In addition, when you're in areas of acacia woodland then keep a look out for racket-tailed rollers and the spectacular displays of the male broad-tailed paradise whydahs in breeding plumage (February–April).

The kori bustard (*Ardeotis kori*) is one of the world's heaviest flying birds, weighing up to 17kg, and – despite a wingspan of 2.8m – it is a reluctant flyer, needing a good run-up to get airborne. On the ground, these stately birds strike conspicuous figures, and are often seen around the pans, either picking their way hesitantly across the grassland in pairs, one at least 100m from its partner, or resting in the midday shade of an acacia.

Kori bustards often associate with game herds, whose trampling hooves disturb the locusts, beetles, reptiles and other small creatures on which they feed. In turn, they sometimes provide a similar service for the carmine bee-eater (*Merops nubicoides*). This dazzling bird arrives from central Africa in October, and spreads out across the grassland in large flocks. Its usual hunting technique is to hawk for insects – particularly bees – in acrobatic sorties from a fixed perch, such as an anthill or bush, and return to the perch to dispatch and swallow the catch. In open grassland, where fixed perches are in short supply, a kori bustard provides an ideal mobile alternative.

In fact the bustard goes one better than a bush by actively stirring up food for the bee-eater, which snaps up whatever it can catch around the bigger bird's feet before settling again on its back. Bee-eaters are not known to try this trick from the backs of mammals, yet the bustard remains surprisingly tolerant of its passengers, and sometimes two or more of them will hitch a ride.

On Savuti's open areas you'll find the occasional secretary birds, Stanley's bustard, and plenty of the larger kori bustards. The Balfours' coffee-table book on Chobe (see *Appendix 3, Further Information*) has a wonderful picture of a carmine bee-eater using the back of a kori bustard as a perch from which to hawk around for insects. Kori bustards are Africa's heaviest flying birds, but heavier still is the flightless ostrich, which can sometimes be seen here. During the summer, Abdim's and white storks congregate in numbers on the marsh.

WHERE TO STAY Savuti's two luxury camps and its campsite are all close to each other. All face on to the Savuti Channel, and all are near the old bridge over the channel, just to the north of the marsh. Being a day's drive from either Kasane or Maun, most guests of the lodges fly in to Savuti's airstrip (which can take planes as large as a DC3), but visitors to the campsite usually arrive driving their own fully equipped 4x4s, complete with all their supplies.

Stay in the area for long and you'll hear of the legendary Lloyd Wilmot and his famous camp – Lloyd's Camp. This became something of an institution here, but has sadly now closed. (Lloyd still visits occasionally, but has left the safari business.) Despite this, you'll still find books and websites that haven't caught on to this. Allan's Camp and Savuti South were opened here (by Gametrackers) and subsequently closed – only to be combined and rebuilt as the Savute Elephant Camp (see below).

The current options for visitors are:

Savuti Campsite (10 pitches) See page 138 for national park booking offices. Savuti's public campsite (⊕ SAVUTE 18°34.005'S; 24°3.902'E) now has an impressive office and entrance gate, but remains a wonderful place to camp. The idea of a fence around the whole site has been abandoned, but

there's a relatively new ablution block, surrounded by an ingenious circular wall. This is designed to be elephant-proof, and also so that smaller animals like cats can easily get out over the wall, but not easily get in. The toilets, showers and laundry areas, with solar-powered hot water and electric light, are relatively clean and in good order. Many of the numbered camping pitches sit under old camelthorn trees, with pitch No 1 being particularly good. Each has its own braai stand, and a water tap ingeniously encased in concrete to prevent elephants from pulling the pipes to access the clean water (they would often make such an effort for clean water, rather than drinking from the dirty waterhole!). The size of the site, and the distance between the pitches, is such that some campers even drive to the ablution block after dark. Visibility is good, with not too much undergrowth around, though the ground can be very dusty and there may be the low whine of a water pump or a generator in the background.

Alongside the elephants for which Savuti is famed, the camp has almost nightly visits from spotted hyenas which, I once discovered, can carry away a full rucksack at high speed, despite being pursued. They will steal and eat anything, from a camera lens to a bar of soap, so leave nothing outside. Then sit back after dinner, turn off your lights, and shield your eyes from the fire. Now, when your vision has adjusted to the dark, shine around a powerful torch. With a little patience you should be able to pick out the ghostly green eyes of hyena, just beyond your firelight. (But beware of shining a torch accidentally at a passing elephant. They don't like this at all!) If you do have any hyena problems, remember that they will push their luck, but are essentially cowardly animals. Chase them and they will always run, sometimes dropping their spoils. Just be very careful of what else you might run into during the chase!

P30 pp.

🏠 **Savute Elephant Camp** (12 Meru tents) See Orient-Express Safaris, page 171. Savute Elephant Camp (✛ SAVELE 18°34.207'S; 24°3.269'E), situated close to the Safari Lodge, was the first of Gametracker's camps that I visited following their reconstruction, and I was amazed at its scale. 'Tents' is far too flimsy a word for the rooms here, each built on a large, raised platform of wooden decking about 18m x 6m. At the front, safari chairs overlook the bottom of the channel from quite a height, and behind them is a huge shaded tent of cream canvas. Inside, on the polished wooden floor, stylish soft furnishings in muted neutral colours offset twin ³/₄ size beds under a walk-in mosquito net. AC units flanking the beds augment a large ceiling fan, which, like the room's lights, can be used day and night, and there's a radiator to help take the chill off the room during winter when temperatures can drop below freezing. There's no shortage of space for the solid furnishings, including several comfy chairs, a writing-desk and a chair, not to mention an intercom system in case of emergencies. Behind the wooden headboard there's a place for suitcases, a wardrobe with a clothes rail, and, in the middle, a dressing room with twin basins, several large mirrors and acres of hardwood surround. Through polished hardwood doors you'll find separate rooms for the large shower (easily big enough for shared showers) and the flush toilet; current refurbishment plans include an additional outside shower for each chalet.

Immaculate lawns under acacia trees link the rooms with the camp's airy bar, lounge and dining room, an open-sided barn-like construction that leads on to an umbrella-shaded terrace. Set just below, a large swimming pool overlooks a pumped waterhole in the Savuti Channel, a contrast that, at the height of the dry season, may, make you feel uncomfortable as you wallow in the pool whilst stressed elephants argue over precious gulps of muddy water below you.

The lodge emphasises the quality of its food, served buffet-style on the terrace or in the dining room. It's very similar indeed to its sister camp, Khwai River Lodge (see page 250), with which it shares a professionalism marked by friendly service. Activities concentrate on 4x4 game drives during the day (night drives, and driving off-road, are not allowed in Chobe). There is also a small hide nearby, and can be arranged visits to local Bushman paintings on request.

From US$499 pp sharing low season to US$911 pp sharing high season, inc accommodation, meals, drinks, laundry & all activities. Open all year.

🏠 **Savute Safari Lodge** (12 rooms) See Desert and Delta Safaris, page 169. Savute Safari Lodge (✛ SAVSAF 18°33.927'S; 24°3.441'E) opened in March 1999 and most of its visitors reach here by plane. It's been built right next to the site of the old Lloyd's Camp, so the local wildlife is exceptionally relaxed with people – to the point that lions have occasionally been found sleeping on the paths between rooms. (There's a discreet electric fence around the lodge and, as with most wildlife camps in Botswana, guests are always escorted by the staff if walking around the camp after dark.) The lodge overlooks 3 waterholes, with a pump ensuring a permanent water supply.

Rooms, although similar in size (at least 16m x 6m) and quality to those at the Elephant Camp, are unique in Botswana. Of wooden construction, with a high thatched roof over a slightly raised, smooth wooden floor, they are light and airy, with glass sliding doors backed by mesh mosquito screens forming one entire wall (those down by the river, with a long wall of glass, are certainly the most spectacular). However, the décor is the shock: modern Scandinavian in appearance, with bright colours (mostly white with flashes of bright blue), clean lines and functional designs. If you're used to shades of green and khaki, this will surprise you. 'Ikea meets Habitat' was the description of one guest, referring to its similarity with some European furniture stores – though this is far more classy. If you're staying in several camps, or come to Africa on safari often, then the lodge's design works, and will probably seem like a refreshing change.

Each chalet has a comfortable 2-seater couch and an armchair, and thoughtful touches include chic lamps with arresting blue shades and a tea/coffee maker. The bedroom has twin or dbl beds with quality linen surrounded by a (cleverly designed) walk-in mosquito net, below a ceiling fan. On the veranda are safari chairs and roll-down blinds to cover the windows. The modern white-tiled bathroom has a sink, a glass-screened shower, a flush toilet and a large mirror. Some have large floor-to-ceiling picture windows which can be unnerving until you realise that you're not overlooked. There is no AC, though the design of the chalets helps to moderate the excesses of the climate. During the day there is electricity from a generator, backed up by battery power at night. In the central area, a huge wrought-iron candelabra hangs over tiled floors and light

wooden tables and chairs. However, meals are usually served outside, buffet style, on a covered terrace with a direct view of a waterhole in the channel (much to the delight of a local genet who often drops in for the buffet). Sharing the view is a small, shaded pool, surrounded by decking. There's a small library with various board games, and a hi-tech fireplace in the centre of the room for cold winter mornings. Above the bar, a loft area looks over the trees, ideal for an hour or so's birdwatching. A curio shop has a reasonable range of handicrafts, jewellery and clothing. Hilary Bradt and Janice Booth visited here recently, only to be woken by the yelps of wild dog which had made a kill directly under their chalet. They watched as the dogs were joined by a cohort of Savuti's numerous hyena, who then challenged the dogs for their booty – dim shapes wheeling and criss-crossing in the moonlight. Activities are limited to morning and evening game drives (private guides can be arranged for a whole day), and the occasional wander to see a Bushman painting. The young guides here when I last visited were keen on nature and enthusiastic about finding it.
US$630/830 pp sharing/sgl Jul–Oct; US$420 pp sharing/sgl Nov–Mar; US$360 pp sharing/sgl Apr–Jun, fully inclusive. Open all year.

⌂ **Savuti Camp** See *Linyanti Concession*, page 230. This is a small camp situated further up the Savuti Channel, in the private Linyanti Concession west of Savuti. It is nowhere near the marsh, nor in the area that has, historically, been known as 'Savuti'.

WHAT TO SEE AND DO Game viewing and birdwatching are the main activities here, and there's always something going on if you can find it! Start at the main waterhole, which is often the centre for action – though sadly often also quite busy with vehicles.

Driving at night is not allowed, though often the wildlife will come quite close enough if you just stay in your campsite/lodge and keep looking around you.

DRIVING SOUTH FROM SAVUTI

About 5km south of the campsite, just before the hill known as Leopard Rock, the track splits two ways. This point (✛ MARSAN 18°36.078'S; 24°3.678'E) is shown very clearly on Veronica Roodt's Chobe map. In October 1999 there was still one of Chobe's rare old signposts standing here, but since then it appears to have vanished.

The left-hand track is the **marsh road**, signposted Savuti Marsh; it's more scenic but becomes very rutted and bumpy in parts following the western side of the marsh itself. This is fine during the dry season, and you'll have great views of the marsh. It's often a particularly good area for giraffe due to the high number of acacia trees around. However, it's a bad route to choose during the rainy season, as you will almost certainly get stuck.

The right fork is the **sand-ridge road** and heads more directly towards Maun, west of the marsh. Taking this you will cut across the Magwikwe Sand Ridge about

26km south of Savuti. Don't expect this to be too obvious, as the ridge is little more than a wide, vegetated sand dune. You will climb slightly to get on to it, and drop slightly to come off – and in between the driving is more difficult than normal as your vehicle's tyres will sink deeper into the sand.

Both meet up again about 20km north of the park's Mababe Gate. The sand ridge road takes 37km to reach this, and the marsh road takes about 44km. The sign here reads: Khwai 45km, North Gate 54km and Maun 133km.

Before you reach that you'll reach the old Mababe Gate, at around (✪ OLDGAT 19°00.770'S; 23°59.360'E), which is marked on some maps as the new Mababe gate. Around here the road becomes more difficult during the rains. In contrast to Savuti's relatively lush vegetation, there is little ground cover here, and only low stunted mopane trees to protect the soil from the extremes of the elements. The road's fine earth is hard-baked when dry, and very slippery when wet.

Around 10km further on is the new Mababe Gate (✪ MABABE 19°06.182'S; 23°59.119'E), where you sign out of (or into) Chobe, and pay your park fees. Just south of this the road forks, without a signpost in sight, and you have a choice: right for Moremi, or left for Maun directly.

CONTINUING INTO MOREMI GAME RESERVE
Turn right and head west at this junction and a few kilometres later you climb slightly on to Magwikwe Sand Ridge (from about 16km to 19km after Chobe's Mababe Gate). This takes about 3km of very slow driving to plough through, and shortly after you reach the other side you enter the stunningly beautiful river valley of the Khwai River. In the dry season the contrast could not be sharper. After the unrelenting dryness of southern Chobe, the Khwai's lily-covered waterways and shady glades under huge spreading umbrella thorns (*Acacia tortilis*) are completely magical.

About 6–7km after joining the river, you'll reach the boundary between the Chobe and Moremi parks, then 22km later you'll come to the bridge over the River Khwai at North Gate (see also page 248).

Along this road (at ✪ OKAV24 19°05.500'S; 23°49.971'E), you'll find a turning north signposted to Seronga marked by one of the park's old signs, in the form of a green concrete pillar. Beware of this, especially if you're heading in the opposite direction towards Chobe, as it will lead you astray through private concessions towards Selinda (see page 230).

CONTINUING TO MAUN
Turning left, or southeast, at the fork here will lead you much more directly and quickly to Maun, effectively reaching the village of Kudumane (also known as Mababe Village) first, about 22km from the Mababe Gate. Here you'll take a right turn, passing through Sankuyo, the veterinary fence, and then Shorobe before Maun. (See pages 173–4 for this route – and if you have a GPS then set it for ✪ MAUN at 19°58.508'S; 23°25.647'E to keep you in roughly the right direction!)

If your destination is Maun, then don't imagine that travelling through the edge of Moremi (on the direct road from North Gate to South Gate) is a quick option. It'll take a good six or seven hours to reach Maun this way. You'll have some slow, heavy driving across the sand ridge, and have to pay an extra set of park fees for Moremi (even if you have just paid some for the same day in Chobe).

However, if you have pre-arranged a few nights in Moremi, then do take this road and don't miss the chance to stop off. It offers a completely different experience.

On the road to Maun, just north of Sankuyo, you'll spot a right turn to Mankwe Bush Lodge (see page 174). About 25km south of Sankuyo, the Sankuyo Tshwaragano Management Trust is reported to have recently developed a campsite and traditional village. This is signposted from the road, about 70km north of Maun.

The Linyanti River acts as a magnet for game during the dry season, just as its continuation, the Chobe, does further north. However, reaching this area does require the visitor to side-track from the established Moremi–Savuti–Ihaha route across Chobe. This means that it gets few visitors. Further, with only a few kilometres of riverfront accessible to private visitors, and some very, very thick riverside reedbeds and vegetation, it can be a disappointing area.

To the east is the CH/1 concession, which has a mixture of local villages and hunting camps within it. To the west of this is the NG15 photographic concession, the Linyanti Concession (see pages 226–30), which has several good camps, the nearest of which is Linyanti Tented Camp. Visitors driving themselves are restricted in terms of where they can go, so to see this area at its best you are probably well advised to visit one of the Linyanti's camps on a fly-in safari.

Note that despite there being a track marked on the maps from Seronga towards the Linyanti, this is not a practical one to use to get here from the west. Firstly, neither private self-drive vehicles nor mobile operators are allowed to drive through the private concessions between the Linyanti and Okavango. Secondly, as a private visitor you're not allowed to enter Chobe National Park at the Linyanti – you can only enter it from the south or the north. And thirdly, even with a GPS, navigation would be a complete nightmare, and the hunters in the centre of the concessions wouldn't be at all welcoming.

FLORA AND FAUNA HIGHLIGHTS This area has a very similar ecosystem to that of the Chobe riverfront area (pages 194–6), although the vegetation beside the water here seems to have many more large trees and to be in a more natural state. Because Chobe's Linyanti riverfront is sandwiched between two private concessions areas, it's a relatively limited size for game drives. You'll usually see large numbers of elephant at the end of the dry season, but this small stretch of the park is seldom as rewarding as the Chobe riverfront area, where the game is much more 'tame'. The presence to the east of an area where hunting is still sometimes practiced probably doesn't help relax the game – although west of Linyanti is the private Linyanti Reserve concession, which is an excellent area with a long stretch of beautiful riverfront and some very good game (see pages 226–30).

GETTING THERE AND AWAY You'd normally approach the Linyanti Campsite from Savuti. To get on to the right track, drive over the old bridge over the Savuti Channel (or what's left of it) and on to its north bank, and then turn left. Thus you pass the campsite on the other side of the channel on your left, whilst heading northwest. Ignoring various right turns, you'll approach a T-junction within a few kilometres, and take a left heading westwards. This crosses the sand ridge (though you may not notice this!) and about 5km later there are two left turnings. Ignore these. Follow the road around to the right, heading in a more northerly direction.

The first 10km of this drive is easy. It's mostly a hard, fast track that's marked clearly on Veronica Roodt's Chobe map. However, after this there's about 30km of trickier driving – very deep sand and tougher going. The scenery is gently rolling dunes, with many flatter areas of low mopane. Visiting last in October, I found large numbers of elephants on the road north. Towards the river there was also a pall of dust and wood-smoke hanging over the woods near the river, and a tremendous amount of fine, grey dust in the air. Some of this was clearly coming from fires raging across the river in Namibia.

⌂ WHERE TO STAY

⋏ Linyanti Campsite See page 138 for national park booking offices. Linyanti Campsite (⊕ LINYAN 18°17.686'S; 23°54.601'E) is about 40km from Savuti. It's a beautiful site, close to the river and very quiet, with the standard of cleanliness average for these national park sites. When last visited, it had about half a dozen green, metal rondavels with thatch over tin roofs, all in an advanced state of dilapidation. If you're camping here, then come with all your water as well as supplies — although filtering and treating river water to drink would be possible in an emergency.
P30 pp.

WHAT TO SEE AND DO With only 7km of riverfront accessible, and basically only one track to access it, the driving opportunities are limited here. However, there are plenty of reed beds next to the bank, which can be a delight for birdwatchers, and I've come across the occasional person who absolutely adores this area.

10

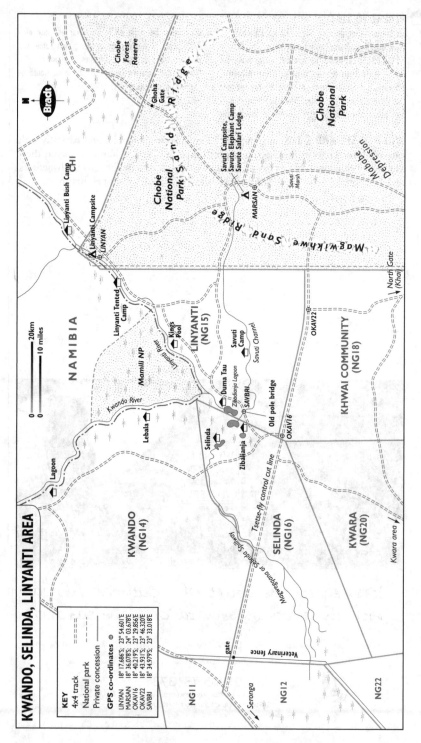

KWANDO, SELINDA, LINYANTI AREA

KEY

- ===== 4x4 track
- — — — National park
- — — — Private concession
- GPS co-ordinates ⊕

LINYAN	18° 17.686'S;	23° 54.601'E
MARSAN	18° 36.078'S;	24° 03.678'E
OKAVI6	18° 40.219'S;	23° 79.856'E
OKAV22	18° 43.931'S;	23° 44.320'E
SAVBRI	18° 34.979'S;	23° 33.018'E

N

Bradt

0   20km
0   10 miles

NAMIBIA

Chobe Forest Reserve

Ghoha Gate

Chobe National Park Sand Ridge

Chobe National Park

Mababe Depression

Linyanti Bush Camp   CHI

Linyanti Campsite

⊕ LINYAN

Savuti Campsite,
Savute Elephant Camp
Savute Safari Lodge

△ MARSAN ⊕

Savuti Marsh

Magwikhwe Sand Ridge

Linyanti Tented Camp

Mamili NP

Linyanti River

King's Pool

LINYANTI (NG15)

Savuti Channel

Savuti Camp

North Gate (Khai)

Kwando River

Duma Tau

Zibadianja Lagoon

⊕ SAVBRI

Old pole bridge

Lebala

⊕ OKAVI6

OKAV22 ⊕

KHWAI COMMUNITY (NG18)

Lagoon

KWANDO (NG14)

Selinda

Zibalianja

Magwegqana or Selinda Spillway

Tsetse-fly control cut line

SELINDA (NG16)

KWARA (NG20)

Kwara area

NG11

gate

Veterinary fence

Seronga

NG12

NG22

224

11

Linyanti, Selinda and Kwando Reserves

Almost parallel to the Okavango, the Kwando River flows south from Angola across the Caprivi Strip and into Botswana. Like the Okavango, it starts spreading out over the Kalahari's sands, forming the Linyanti Swamps. Like the Okavango, in wetter years this is a delta, complete with a myriad of waterways linking lagoons; a refuge for much wildlife. It's a wild area, much of which is on the Namibian side of the border, in the Mamili National Park, where it's difficult to access. A fault line channels the outflow from these swamps into the Linyanti River, which flows northeast into Lake Liambezi, and thence into Chobe.

Both the Kwando and the Linyanti rivers are permanent, so for the animals in Chobe and Northern Botswana they are valuable sources of water. Like the Chobe and Okavango, they have become the ultimate destination for migrations from the drier areas across northern Botswana – and also sought-after safari destinations, especially in the dry season.

In recent years this area, between the Chobe National Park and the Okavango Delta, has been split into three large concessions – Kwando in the north, Linyanti in the east, and Selinda in the middle.

In some ways these are similar, as each encompasses a large area of mopane woodlands and smaller, more prized sections of riparian forest and open floodplains on old river channels. Look at the locations of the camps and you'll realise that much of the interest lies in these floodplains and riparian forests – diverse habitats rich in species.

Away from the actual water, two fossil channels are also worthy of attention: the Savuti Channel and the Magwegqana Spillway. Both offer contrasting and interesting wildlife spectacles.

BACKGROUND INFORMATION

HISTORY The Kwando River has its headwaters in Angola, from where it flows south across Namibia's Caprivi Strip, forming one boundary between Namibia and Botswana. Progressing over the Kalahari's sands, it is thought that once – around one or two million years ago – it continued southeast, probably through the course of the present-day Savuti Channel, into the Mababe Depression to swell the vast Lake Makgadikgadi (see *Chapter 3* for more on the geological history of the region). Then, at some point in the last million years, tectonic shifts raised up a fault line running northwest which effectively 'captured' this river, and diverted it along the fault to flow into the Chobe and Zambezi Rivers, thus creating what we now call the Linyanti River.

Around the same time, a parallel fault – the Thamalakane Fault – is also thought to have halted the Okavango's course, trapping it and ultimately silting it up to form an inland delta. As the gradients in this part of the northern Kalahari are very small indeed (1:4,000 is typical of the gradient in the Okavango Delta) the routes taken by these watercourses are very susceptible to the tiniest tilts in the earth's surface. As an aside, these faults probably mark the most southerly extent of Africa's Great Rift Valley.

Like the trapped Okavango, silting gradually allowed the Kwando/Linyanti river to spread out into a small inland delta, forming what we call the Linyanti Marshes today.

There is one further geographical feature of note in this area: an ancient river course known as the Magwegqana (spelled in various ways) or the Selinda Spillway. This splits off from around the Okavango's Panhandle area, and heads northeast entering the Linyanti River system just north of the Zibadianja Lagoon. This doesn't seem to be the obvious product of any local fault lines – although it does roughly follow the line of the Linyanti–Gumare Fault. It's either some form of overflow from the Okavango Delta, or perhaps an ancient river course, or both. Either way it's highly visible from the air, and on the ground offers a rich and open environment for game.

GEOGRAPHY The geography of the various parts of this area follows on directly from its geological history, and can easily be divided into four types of environment.

Firstly, there are the Linyanti Swamps, comprised of river channels, lagoons, reedbeds and banks of papyrus. Secondly, adjacent to these is a narrow belt of riparian forest that lines these waterways – on the northern edge of the Linyanti Reserve, and the eastern edge of Kwando.

Thirdly there are two dry riverbeds, the Selinda Spillway and the Savuti Channel. Both flood periodically, but both have been dry for a number of years. There are similarities as well as differences between them, most notably the sheer width of the Spillway as it approaches the Linyanti Swamp compared with the relatively narrow Savuti Channel.

Finally, and common to all the concessions, are large areas of dry woodland dominated by large stands of mopane trees, which cover most of the three areas but are usually of least interest to the visitor on safari.

LINYANTI CONCESSION (NG15)

The Linyanti Concession covers 1,250km² of the northern Kalahari, dominated by large areas of mopane woodlands. However, its northern edge is bounded by the waters of the Linyanti River, complete with a string of lagoons and marshes. Adjacent to this is a narrow band of highly varied riparian forests which is the focus of most safari activities.

Cutting from west to east, through the centre of the concession, is the bed of the Savuti Channel. This is usually a dry sand river, where a number of waterholes attract game during the dry season.

GETTING ORGANISED

Getting there and away Getting to any of the camps in the Linyanti Concession is simple: you fly. Wilderness Safaris (who run all four camps) include light-aircraft flights in their trips into these camps, and it's very easy to fly here from Maun, Kasane, or another camp in northern Botswana.

There are two main airstrips in the concession: one on the river's floodplain near King's Pool (see page 229; ✈ KINAIR 18°26.734'S; 23°41.095'E), and another cleared from the bush between Duma Tau and Savuti Camp (see page 230; ✈ DUMAIR 18°31.948'S; 23°39.264'E).

All these camps work on the basis that the logistics are worked out well in advance. Everybody who arrives has a prior reservation (most made months earlier) and everyone arrives and leaves by light aircraft.

No self-driving visitors are allowed into these camps, even by prior arrangement. So if you just drive in, you can expect to be escorted off the property and pointed in the direction of a public road!

When to visit Note the general comments made under *Planning and Preparation*, pages 67–73, and then also the specific comments made for the Chobe riverfront, on pages 196–7 – because the Linyanti's riverfront has broadly the same kind of game movements as that area. In short: game concentrates around here when it needs the water, and spreads out when it can easily drink elsewhere.

This means that the game will be better here when it's drier, although you'll find a wider variety of bird species here in the wet season, many of which will be in their breeding plumage.

Flora and fauna Technically the Linyanti Reserve is a 'multi-purpose concession', which means that both photographic safaris and hunting are allowed. However, currently Sable Safaris and Wilderness, the companies running the reserve, have a no-hunting policy in order to concentrate on photographic tourism, and reduce the negative impacts that hunting has on the animal populations.

Flora As with the animals, in many ways the vegetation here is very similar to that of the Chobe riverfront area, though it generally seems in much better condition. It's thicker, older and more lush – though perhaps that is simply the result of much less logging by humans and slightly less pressure from the animals.

In the dry season there is usually at least 1km of open ground between the slightly raised riverbank, dotted with mature riparian forest, and the actual waters of the Linyanti. Most of this is open grassland (making a conveniently smooth runway for King's Pool), and this will flood occasionally at times of very high water in the river system.

In this area you'll find some smaller bushes, like russet bush-willows (*Combretum hereoense*) and Kalahari star-apples (*Diospyros lycoides*) – the latter also known as toothbrush bushes after a surprisingly effective use for their thinner branches. (You may also hear this called the blue bush.)

Beyond the floodplain, and up the riverbank, you'll find classic riparian forest with plenty of tall species like knobthorn (*Acacia negrescens*), raintree (*Lonchocarpus capassa*), leadwood (*Combretum imberbe*), jackalberry (*Diospyros mespiliformis*), African mangosteen (*Gardenia livingstonei*) and some marvellous spreading sycamore figs (*Ficus sycomorus*). There are some woolly caper-bushes (*Capparis tomentosa*) in the lower vegetation, but fewer of them than you'll notice beside the Chobe.

Inland, far from the river, is dominated by mopane (*Colophospermum mopane*), though there are also mixed areas, notable for their Kalahari appleleaf (*Lonchocarpus nelsii*), wild seringa (*Burkea africana*), and others in the areas of deeper sand, like old watercourses. Baobabs (*Adansonia digitata*) are dotted around infrequently.

The area around Savuti Camp is very much like this dry woodland, interlaced with sandy fossil riverbeds, whilst along the narrow Savuti Channel itself you'll find more open grassland.

Fauna All year round here you're likely to see impala, kudu, giraffe, reedbuck, steenbok, warthog, baboon and vervet monkeys throughout the area. Lion and spotted hyena are common, and generally the dominant predators, whilst leopard are often seen in the riparian forest and can be the highlight of night drives.

Cheetah occur here, but not very frequently – though the Savuti Channel is perhaps an exception to this as they are seen here periodically. Wild dog usually stay near their dens from around June to September (with July and August being the most reliable time for them), and then range widely over most of northern Botswana. A den hasn't been located here recently, though pups have occasionally been seen, so there must have been one in the region somewhere. (This is no surprise, as most dens are not found in wild areas like this.)

Blue wildebeest and Burchell's zebra are present all year, although around May they will arrive in larger numbers, remaining within reach of the water until just before the rains begin in around November–December when they head off southeast towards Savuti Marsh.

Elephants and buffalo follow a similar pattern with small groups around all year, often only bulls, but with much larger breeding herds arriving in June–July and staying until December. During this time you'll regularly find very large herds of both buffalo and elephant, hundreds strong.

Tsessebe occur, but are uncommon. In very dry years sable and roan start appearing around September–October. Eland are very rare here, and gemsbok don't occur this far north.

Waterbuck are permanent residents, especially towards the northeast of the concession. This is one of relatively few areas of Botswana where they're found. Keep a lookout around King's Pool and Linyanti Tented Camp, particularly at the interface between the mopane woodlands of the interior and the riparian forest by the river. Sitatunga are occasionally sighted from boat trips on the river.

Side-striped and black-backed jackal are around, the latter reaching the extreme northern edge of its distribution here (and so isn't common). Bat-eared fox are regularly seen; the area around King's Pool airstrip seems to be a particular favourite. Mongooses, especially banded and dwarf, are always around.

Serval, caracal, African wildcat and aardwolf occur, and Savuti Camp has a notably excellent record of sightings in the channel for these, especially serval. Aardvark are occasionally seen, and one local expert reports they used to be spotted frequently in the riverine forest near the Zibadianja Lagoon. I've no reports of pangolin here.

When you're out on night drives, you've also got a chance to see scrub hares, spring hares, lesser bushbabies, porcupines, genets (small-spotted and large-spotted), civets and honey badgers.

Birdlife In the riparian woodlands, birds of particular interest include wood owls, swamp boubous, brown firefinches, white-rumped babblers and collared sunbirds. Of particular note is the beautiful Schalow's lourie, a local race of the Knysna lourie found in this region.

There are numerous summer migrants, including carmine bee-eaters that nest here. There are several colonies in the area, including one almost opposite the Livingstone hide. Carmines tend to arrive around September and leave March–April. Some appear to have learnt to follow vehicles down the Savuti Channel, catching the crickets that jump away from the moving wheels. Others use the kori bustards, which frequent the channel as moving perches.

Other summer visitors include the thick-billed cuckoo and the narina trogon, although one expert on the area's birdlife, Mark Tennant, comments that the latter may be resident.

The raptors are well represented. Bateleur and fish eagles are probably the most numerous, but you're also likely to spot African hawk, and tawny, martial and black-breasted snake eagles. Gymnogenes are relatively common. When the first rains come in December, migrants like Wahlberg's and steppe eagles seem notably attracted to the first flush of green in the Savuti Channel – hence December to February can be a particularly good time here.

Throughout the year, western banded snake eagles are also sometimes seen, though they're not common, along with giant eagle owls, bat hawks (look out on the edge of the forest, by the river, in the evening) and the occasional Pel's fishing owl.

On the water there's a host of different species, though some of the marshes and lagoons here can be difficult to access, even from the camps. (The canoeing possible at Linyanti Tented Camp goes some way to remedying this.) Some of the more unusual residents include slaty and black egret, rufous-bellied heron, painted snipe, long-toed plover, African rail and wattled crane. African skimmers usually nest here in September, with Zibadianja Lagoon, amongst others, being a favourite spot for them.

WHERE TO STAY All four camps in the Linyanti Reserve are owned by Sable Safaris, but exclusively marketed by Wilderness Safaris (see page 171). They range from the substantial comfort of King's Pool to the much more simple bush-camp style of Linyanti Tented Camp, and are listed here from north to south. All cater exclusively for fly-in visitors and none will accept visitors who want to drive in. Also included here is Linyanti Bush Camp, in a different concession but sharing a very similar environment.

⋀ Linyanti Tented Camp (5 tents). Linyanti Tented Camp has long been one of the smallest, simplest camps run by Wilderness Safaris. Used only for their groups, it offers modest comforts in place of plush luxuries: this is an old-style safari camp, with traditional tents, far from the interior-designer chic found elsewhere.

The camp is about 10km southwest of Chobe's Linyanti Campsite (see page 223). Despite having 5 simple Meru-style tents, it will normally accept a maximum of only 8 guests at a time. All the tents have en-suite hot shower, washbasin and toilet. Together with the dining and bar area, which are also under simple canvas, they all overlook the Linyanti River. Activities here vary according to the individual group, but may include short walks and boat trips, as well as self-paddle canoeing excursions in large, Canadian-style canoes on the nearby lagoons — an activity which, despite the amount of water around, is almost unique here and not generally possible at other camps in Botswana. *Rates are quoted only as part of a group trip.*

⌂ King's Pool (10 chalets). Luxury is the keyword here — for King's Pool is one of Botswana's top 3 or 4 lodges and one of Wilderness' flagship camps. It overlooks the Linyanti River and the swamps beyond from a position (✛ KINGSP 18°26.276'S; 23°42.415'E) in the very centre of the reserve, almost 19km northeast of Duma Tau and a similar distance from Linyanti Tented Camp.

Each of the well-spaced rooms is effectively like an individual villa, on high wooden decking under a thatched roof. Extensive and stylish, they're pole framed with canvas-and-gauze wall panels, and a soundly constructed bathroom, with separate toilet.

Leather armchairs, nice fabrics in neutral colours, and a large bed under a mosquito net give a solid, conservative feel. Big folding doors lead to a deck with a small plunge pool and a *sala* — think exclusive thatched gazebo with day bed — overlooking the Linyanti River. You could justifiably just chill here and watch game on the river — and many visitors do. The central area, while not particularly cosy, is well appointed with leather chairs and extensive decking, whilst outside there's an open-air boma for meals under the stars. On the edge of camp there's a swimming pool and, separately, a hide for game viewing (though it's questionable if this offers better game viewing or birdwatching than is already possible from the balconies of the chalets). And to work off all that lazing around, there's even an open-sided thatched gym.

Activities here are mainly 4x4 game drives and night drives. These concentrate on the riverine forest areas beside the water and, when dry, the wide grassy floodplains between the river's water and the high bank. Short walks are also possible, and when the water levels are high enough (eg: around Apr–Aug) there's a dbl-decker boat for gentle river cruises.

There are 2 small game hides in the vicinity of the camp: Inkwe Hide, which is near the river on the east side of camp, and Livingstone's Hide, which is halfway between King's Pool and Duma Tau. (Almost opposite the latter, on the other side of the river, is a colony of carmine bee-eaters.) Visitors can be dropped and collected later from these, and if you book early and request it then it's theoretically possible to sleep over in one (though marketed as

11

an option, this rarely happens in practice and is not for faint-hearted visitors!).

US$660/845 pp sharing/sgl low season to US$1,235/1,420 high season; inc all meals, activities, park fees, laundry, most drinks; exc transfers. Open all year.

🏠 **Duma Tau** (10 raised tents). At the western end of the Linyanti, overlooking the Zibadianja Lagoon from its southeastern shore, Duma Tau is found just east of the source of the Savuti Channel (⊕ DUMATA 18°32.217'S; 23°33.917'E) under a canopy of mangosteen trees.

The camp has luxurious tents raised on wooden platforms, all with en-suite facilities: hot showers (one indoors and one outside) washbasins and flush toilets. There is a central dining-room, bar and lounge, and a small plunge pool for afternoon dips.

Activities centre around 4x4 game drives, and night drives which visit the riverine forest beside the Linyanti, as well as the drier areas along the upper reaches of the Savuti Channel and the mopane forest between. Short walks are sometimes possible, and a boat can be used on the lagoon and in nearby waterways when water levels are high.

Duma Tau shares the use of Livingstone's game hide with King's Pool. Visitors can be dropped and later collected here, and even sleep over if requested early enough. (I last saw the hide in passing, as a large pride of lion had brought down a buffalo within about 30m of it!)

From US$470/655 pp sharing/sgl low season to US$785/970 high season, inc all meals, activities, park fees, laundry, most drinks; exc transfers. Open all year.

🏠 **Savuti Camp** (7 raised tents). Savuti Camp (⊕ SAVUTI 18°35.834'S; 23°40.412'E) stands beside the Savuti Channel, about 42km due west of the Savuti Marsh – the area within the Chobe National Park that's commonly known as 'Savuti' (see pages 212–20). It's about 13km as the eagle flies from Zibadianja Lagoon and the rickety wooden bridge which spans the start of the Savuti Channel (⊕ SAVBRI 18°34.979'S; 23°33.018'E).

The camp has Meru-style tents raised up on individual wooden decks. All have en-suite showers, toilets and washbasins with hot and cold water. 5 have inside bathrooms; the others open to the skies with views beyond. Each has a small veranda, with everything under the cool shade of a large canvas roof. The camp has a separate dining room and bar/lounge area under a thatched roof, a star deck and a small plunge pool.

Activities concentrate on 4x4 game drives, by day and night, although walks are also possible. There are several elevated hides to visit, and the waterhole in front of the camp is the only source of water in the dry season for miles around. Hence the camp has a justified reputation for lion and elephant. What's less well known is the channel's apparently high concentration of serval, which appear with surprising regularity on the night drives here.

Note that the camp is highly seasonal, with the channel flushing a verdant green with the first rains, but subsequently becoming quite arid and harsh towards the end of the dry season in Oct–Nov. *From US$470/655 pp sharing/sgl low season to US$785/970 high season, inc all meals, activities, park fees, laundry, most drinks; exc transfers. Open all year.*

🏠 **Linyanti Bush Camp** (6 rooms) African Bush Camps; ☎ +263 9 234307; e info@ africanbushcamps.com; www.africanbushcamps.com. This stylish but fundamentally traditional camp represents something increasingly rare in Botswana: an independent, high-quality camp. Large, walk-in tents, overlooking the Linyanti Marshes, are well furnished with sisal floor rugs, twin ³/₄ beds or a king-size dbl, and good, comfortable chairs. There's an en-suite flush toilet and hot shower, plus hardwood-surround washbasins, with lighting supplied by paraffin lamps and low-voltage electric appliances. The camp has a logpile hide, similar to that at Savuti Camp, where you can effectively be surrounded by elephants protected by huge logs – which takes something of a leap of faith! Top-class guiding, provided by Zimbabwean professionals, is a huge plus.

US$660 pp sharing. Open 8 Mar–7 Jan.

SELINDA CONCESSION (NG16)

Selinda covers a long swathe of 1,350km², including a large section of the Magwegqana Spillway, the often-dry waterway that links the Okavango to the Linyanti Swamps. Most of its camps are in the far east of the concession, in a very open area where small tree-islands stand amidst large dry plains. The eastern side of the concession is largely thick mopane forest; Motswiri Camp is a seasonal camp used for hunting here.

DRIVING THROUGH THE PRIVATE CONCESSIONS

If you thought that Botswana's national parks were badly signposted, the tracks through private concessions are even worse. Basically, they've not been set up for private vehicles. A few specified transit routes, set up for use by occasional supply vehicles, are the only tracks on which you can legally drive. Venturing off these is illegal, as is camping anywhere at all here. It's effectively private land.

Many visitors here are lost – accidentally finding themselves off the main tracks in the national parks. One story, told by the team at Selinda, is of a party of apparently 'experienced' travellers in a 4x4 from South Africa who arrived in the dead of night. They'd got lost driving from North Gate to Savuti, and been slowed down by an expensive new trailer which got stuck in every patch of sand on the way. Eventually they abandoned their trailer at Selinda, swearing that they'd never return to Botswana's bush again.

So the only way to use these routes is with permission from the reserves. You'll then need your GPS, all the maps you can find, bags of common sense . . . and then you can still expect to get lost!

GETTING THERE AND AWAY The vast majority of visitors fly into the Selinda Reserve. It's certainly the easiest and quickest way, taking only about an hour from Maun or Kasane, and very easily organised by the camp or your tour operator. There's an airstrip situated halfway between the Selinda and Zibalianja camps, less than 5km from either of them.

However, it is possible to drive here, so for the sake of completeness I'll include directions. Note that these tracks are generally used much less than even the sand tracks through Chobe or Moremi, so unless you are highly self-sufficient and bush-wise you would be much, much wiser to fly. With little or zero passing traffic, you would face a major problem in the event of a breakdown, or an argument with an aggressive elephant.

Driving from Chobe's Linyanti Campsite From northern Chobe, the Selinda Reserve is easiest to approach coming from the Linyanti Campsite, driving through the south side of the Linyanti Reserve on what's known as the 'transit route'. However you intend to arrive, you must book in advance, and make sure that the Selinda team know exactly when you're arriving, and by which route you intend to approach.

Firstly, to get to the Linyanti Campsite in Chobe you must either come about 40km from Savuti (see page 222), or a similar distance along the cut-line of the Chobe Forest Reserve (see page 208), from near the Ghoha Entrance Gate. The latter is rarely used, and most people would want to stop for a few days at Savuti anyhow.

From the Linyanti Campsite in Chobe, take the only track westwards and after 4km you'll reach the edge of the Chobe National Park, with a clear signpost from 'Linyanti Investments' directing you left, away from the river, to Maun, Kwara, Kwando – and Selinda. You are now driving along the cut-line that marks the edge of the Chobe National Park. This will lead you south for about 7km, before a right turn branches off, which you should follow. This is now the transit route – sometimes signposted as 'Transit Route A' – and it continues roughly west, parallel to the river, for a further 22km. The scenery here is almost exclusively mopane woodlands.

About 10km after leaving Chobe's cut-line, you'll pass a crossroads. Then for the next 12km there are various small right turns which you must ignore – they all lead up to the Linyanti's camps (Linyanti Tented Camp and King's Pool) and most are marked clearly with 'No through road' signs.

231

This transit route is designed to allow vehicles to cross this private concession whilst causing the minimum of disturbance to the guests. Note that if you drive off the transit route, you'll be an unwelcome intruder on a private concession!

About 22km after you leave Chobe's cut-line, the road forks and you keep right, heading between north and east. (A left turn would take you to Linyanti's Savuti Camp.) About 11km later you'll reach a crossroads where you take a left on to a deep sand road. Here again there are various right turns from the road (to Duma Tau Camp) that you should ignore.

Continue for about 10km until you reach the old, rickety bridge (⊕ SAVBRI 18°34.979'S; 23°33.018'E) made of poles. This spans the start of the Savuti Channel, just south of Zibadianja Lagoon, and is the concession boundary. If it's dry then you might prefer to just drive across the channel on land to the left of the bridge, rather than across the poles themselves.

On the far side of the channel, turn right. (The alternative track, heading left, would lead along the channel to Linyanti's Savuti Camp.) You'll find a sign saying 'Selinda Concession', and the road bends to the left. It's quite striking how different the landscape is: on the left is mixed forest, and soon on the right are open plains with the odd palm island and lots of game around. To reach Selinda's HQ keep heading left, and you'll find it on the left in a forest island within a few kilometres. From there they'll direct you to your pre-arranged camp.

Driving to the Khwai River area It's about 100km to North Gate from Zibalianja Camp, taking perhaps four hours in the dry season. If you drive south through Selinda, then all the tracks will converge into one, and then cross the TFC (Tsetse Fly Control) cut-line about 9km due south of Zibalianja Camp.

This point is noted as OKAV16 (⊕ 18°40.219'S; 23°29.856'E). You'll see a wide variety of signs at this intersection, including one denoting 'military zone 1999 – no hunting beyond this point'. Another, referring to the road northwest, indicates the village of Beetsha, confirming that (believe it or not) this is the main road up to the east side of the Okavango's Panhandle area. If you were heading north from here then, rather more cheerfully, you'd read one saying 'Welcome to Selinda,' as well as others indicating Kwando and Linyanti.

From here turn left along the cut-line, heading about 10° south of east. Generally you'll find this is a good and very straight track, though there are a few patches of deep sand. As you might expect, it's all mopane woodlands here with less and less variation in the vegetation as you travel. Typical of such an environment, the area is dotted with small pans, and where the track crosses them it can become very muddy in the wet season.

After 30km of very straight road, you'll reach OKAV22 (⊕ 18°43.931'S; 23°46.320'E), where you'll take a right turn heading south and slightly east. If you had continued straight here, you would cross the Magwikwe Sand Ridge and then meet the sand-ridge road (see pages 220–1), at a T-junction west of Savuti Marsh. This track into Chobe is not used frequently; I'm unsure of its condition.

Heading south and east from OKAV22, the road isn't as straight as the cut-line, but makes its way through large areas of mostly stunted mopane. This is NG18, a concession designated for 'community utilisation of the wildlife by the Khwai Community'. See page 276 for more details on this, but note with interest that in 1999 the Khwai community had an income of US$240,000 from the sale of its hunting quotas in this wildlife area.

Passing through NG18 fairly swiftly, in the middle of a hot day in late September we spotted a few kudu, impala and steenbok, and hyena spoor on the track – so there is a fair amount of game around here.

Towards the south side of NG18 the land opens up a little and you'll pass more open areas of grassland and low bushes. A little over 35km after OKAV22 you'll reach an old airfield at OKAV23 (✣ 19°02.415'S; 23°50.194'E), which is a large, flat grassy area that seems disused now.

After this the road continues south, though the mopane changes from rather low, stunted trees to some of the most impressive continuous stands of cathedral mopane that you'll see anywhere. Only as you approach the main game area around Khwai itself do you start to find this broken down more by elephant damage, and interspersed with open areas.

Finally, about 6km south of the airstrip you'll reach a junction (✣ OKAV24 19°05.500'S; 23°49.971'E) with the main road from Moremi to Chobe. It's still marked by one of the park's old green concrete pillars that function as signs: left (northeast) 27km to Chobe and right (southwest) 14km to Moremi. Seronga, on the east of the Panhandle, is signposted back north.

Approaching this sign from Moremi can be quite confusing. The Selinda road, described above, is apparently marked as 'Chobe'. It's not unknown for careless self-drivers to make the mistake of taking this road, thinking it leads to Savuti. One party (see box page 231) who were lost for several days having done this, eventually turned up at Zibalianja Camp, desperately seeking help.

FLORA AND FAUNA

Flora The area around Selinda and Zibalianja camps is the wide mouth of the Magwegqana Spillway – which is largely composed of open floodplains dotted with small palm islands. The spillway floods only very rarely, but when it's done so in the past it has cleared, or killed off, many small trees and bushes on the plains, leaving only flat marshes and grasslands behind.

Because it hasn't flooded fully for a long time, these areas are now dry and are gradually being colonised by 'pioneer species' of invading bushes: species which can quickly take a hold and will thrive in areas which have been disturbed like this.

Chief amongst these is the wild sage (*Pechuel-loeschea leubnitziae*), which covers large areas of the spillway with its aromatic grey-green foliage. (In *Trees and Shrubs of the Okavango*, Veronica Roodt comments that 'All over Africa wild sage is used [to treat] a variety of venereal diseases.')

Another pioneer is the candle-pod acacia (*Acacia hebeclada*) which form lovely, round bushes. If you've come here after Savuti Marsh, you may have seen them on the south side of the marsh there.

Dotted amidst this are small, slightly raised 'islands' of trees. These have been here for decades, and can survive the periodic flooding – though see the comments on pages 49–52 regarding island formation if you're curious as to how such 'islands' are formed.

The trees found on these are typical in many ways of those in the riparian forests, though with the addition of lots of the real fan palms (*Hyphaene petersianna*). Some are tall trees, many are only bush-sized, but all help to make Selinda's environment a particularly attractive one. Amongst the other tree species here, African mangosteens (*Gardenia livingstonei*) seem particularly common and lush, their branches all apparently flung outwards, as if a green bomb had exploded inside.

Fauna Like the Linyanti and Kwando, there's a population of resident game, which is swelled from about June onwards by the arrival of large numbers of game which move into the reserve for its proximity to the permanent waters of Zibadianja Lagoon and the Kwando–Linyanti river system.

Permanent game includes impala, red lechwe (on the east side near the lagoon), kudu, tsessebe, giraffe, reedbuck, steenbok, warthog, baboon and vervet monkeys. Lion and spotted hyena are common, whilst leopard are seen more rarely, usually around the larger tree-islands. The very open country is certainly good for cheetah, and though I've never seen them myself, I do get regular reports of them here.

Selinda certainly is one of the best reserves for wild dog; the pack known locally as the 'Selinda pack' denned here in 2001 and 2002. Although wild dog do range over the whole of northern Botswana, if you want any chance of seeing them then you'll need a place where your guide can drive off-road, to stick with them as they hunt, and where there's lots of dry, open grassland with not too many trees, so that the driving is relatively free of obstacles.

This narrows your choice down to a few of the private reserves, but would certainly include Selinda, Mombo, Vumbura and the southern side of Kwando. I don't wish to imply here that you won't see dogs elsewhere; you will. However, if I were going out specifically to look for dogs, then I'd start in these areas.

On my last visit I followed them hunting on one occasion for over an hour. Following them at speed across the open ground, they would frequently run through the small palm islands to try and flush out any game hiding there. At the same time we'd drive around the islands, and wait for them to come out on the other side again.

Herds of wildebeest and zebra arrive around May, staying here until just around November–December. Elephants and buffalo follow a similar pattern with individuals being seen all year, and larger breeding herds arriving around June-July and staying until December. Eland, sable and roan occur here, but none of them is common.

Side-striped jackal, bat-eared fox and various mongooses are resident, as are the more nocturnal serval, caracal, African wildcat and aardwolf. Night drives will usually locate scrub hares, spring hares, lesser bushbabies, genets (small-spotted and large-spotted), civets, sometimes honey badgers or porcupines, and – rarely – aardvark.

Birdlife Virtually all of the birds typical of riparian woodlands in the neighbouring Linyanti and Kwando reserves (see pages 228–9 and 238) also occur in the tree-islands of Selinda.

In addition to this, the reserve is noted for good sightings of collared palm thrush, plus species of open grasslands like ostriches, secretary birds, kori bustards, red-crested korhaans, various sandgrouse and both common and (from November to March) harlequin quails. The family of coursers is well-represented here – with the uncommon bronze-winged and three-banded varieties occurring as well as the more widespread Temminck's and double-banded coursers.

During the summer months flocks of Abdim's and white storks can be seen, whilst raptor concentrations are always good.

WHERE TO STAY All of the camps in the Selinda Reserve are run by Linyanti Explorations (*Kasane;* ➦ *6250 505;* ➤ *6250 352;* ℮ *info@linyanti.com; www.linyanti.com*).

Linyanti Explorations started in Botswana in 1976 as the small, owner-run operation which founded Chobe Chilwero (selling it in 1999), and they solidified their reputation with the superb, simple camps of the Selinda Reserve. In the last ten years, as the ownership of Botswana's safari camps has become concentrated into fewer companies, and many of those camps have opted to prioritise luxury, Linyanti Explorations dared to be different. It stayed simple, concentrating on its wildlife and guiding – and hence has always been a firm favourite of mine!

In 2006 year it was bought by Dereck and Beverly Joubert, famous wildlife film-makers and photographers. The good news for safari-goers is that it is still being run by three of its original shareholders: Grant Nel, Andre Martens and Marianne Martens. The new owners have stopped the (controlled) hunting that took place in the west of the reserve, forged marketing agreements with Wilderness Safaris (see page 171), and spent a lot of money upgrading Selinda Camp. Meanwhile, Zibalianja and the walking trails camps retain substantially the same, fairly simple atmosphere and rates that are (at least by Botswana standards) still reasonable.

They've also refurbished and opened the Motswiri hunting camp, in the far west of the concession – which stands in a lovely spot beside the Selinda Spillway. I was lucky enough to drive from Selinda to Motswiri during the high flood of 2006. Then the Spillway flooded completely, linking the Linyanti and Okavango systems for the first time in many years. Very close to Motswiri, in the western section of Selinda, is Lechwe Island Camp, a relatively simple tented camp used on group camping trips mostly by Wilderness Safaris, while beyond lies Ketumetse Trails Camp.

Like most of Botswana's high-quality camps, bookings must be made in advance and virtually everyone flies in. Linyanti Explorations encourages travellers to book through good overseas tour operators that specialise in Africa; they include a list of suggested operators on their website.

🏠 **Selinda** (8 tents, 1 pilot/guide tent). Standing on the edge of the Selinda Spillway, Selinda Camp (⊕ SELIND 18°31.897'S; 23°31.354'E) is the reserve's main camp though it still feels small. Substantial Meru-style walk-in tents have comfortable twin or dbl beds, wooden furniture and a relaxed, comfortable feel. Each has an en-suite bathroom with stone bath at the back, partially open to the skies, with shower, washbasin and flush toilet. This is shaded by a thatched roof to keep it cool. The tents are decked out with furniture from all over Africa, including colonial-style desks and lamps made from Maasai gourds. The 24hr generator provides 220V electricity for fans, water heaters, etc.

The camp's main building is thatched and 2 storeys high, containing a bar (often self-service), a small curio shop, a comfy lounge and an upstairs dining room – where the candlelit dinners are marvellously atmospheric. Outside is a small plunge pool for when it's hot, and a boma area with central campfire for cool mornings and evenings. Note that the camp is being refurbished again in January and February 2007; the main building will become a sgl-storey horseshoe shape, with a separate lounge/reception and an extended dining room and curio shop.

The team remain enthusiastic about their activities, which concentrate on 4x4 game drives in the morning and afternoon/evening. The former can start very early in the morning (a good sign of commitment to their game spotting!), the latter

eventually becoming spotlit night drives. Short walks can also be organised, often as part of a drive. As part of its continued monitoring of the reserve, the team assists with monthly game counts that take place every full moon. Enthusiastic visitors with stamina are invited to take part. (They also undertake aerial counts 3 times a year, as part of their overall monitoring programme of the reserve, though logistics mean that these aren't open for visitors' participation.)
From US$470 to US$785 pp sharing, low to high season.

🏠 **Zibalianja** (4 tents – but usually takes 6 visitors max). Zibalianja (⊕ ZIBALI 18°35.577'S; 23°30.670'E) is probably Botswana's smallest permanent camp, built on a small tree-island amidst the plains just a few kilometres west of the Zibadianja Lagoon (the slightly different spelling for camp and lagoon is intentional).

Zibalianja has twin-bedded Meru-style tents standing on raised wooden platforms, shaded by canvas fly-sheets. Each has an en-suite bathroom, with a shower, washbasin and flushing toilet. These are of traditional design but very comfortable, with a system of 12V lighting from solar power.

There's also a small, informal dining area, though meals are often eaten outside. The camp's focal point is a supremely photogenic little bar perched on a wooden platform under its own tree just off the edge of the tree-island. This has superb views all around.

11

Activities here, and the team's enthusiasm for them, mirror those at Selinda, and the guiding when I last visited was up to its usual high standards. Zibalianja is a super little camp for those who are serious about their game viewing and birdwatching. *From US$470 to US$785 pp sharing, low to high season.*

🏠 Motswiri (3 tents)

In the face of increasing levels of luxury in much of Botswana, Motswiri is refreshingly simple. It is set under leadwood trees on the western side of the reserve, which has until recently been virtually unvisited except by hunters, but has now been taken over for photographic safaris. The camp's communal area, all chunky wood with rustic chairs and tables and tented top, is very much in keeping with the environment, as are the traditional Meru-style walk-in tents, which have twin beds, hessian floor covering, and a bathroom at the back, with open-air shower and plenty of hot water. Solar-generated power gives lighting and allows for charging of batteries too. Itineraries depend on individual guests, with no fixed times for the canoeing (a rare bonus in this part of Botswana), walks, game drives and village visits that are on offer.

From US$420 to US$690 pp sharing, low to high season

Å Lechwe Camp Although owned by Linyanti, this simple camp with dome tents is operated for scheduled 'Adventurer' trips run by Wilderness. *Rates as part of a trip only.*

🏠 Ketumetse Trails Camp (6 tents) Contact Wilderness Safaris. Another camp used by Wilderness for their scheduled trips, Ketumetse is at the other end of the spectrum. Large walk-in hexagonal-shaped tents are rather more upmarket than most, giving the camp the air of a good safari camp of the late 1990s. *Rates as part of a trip only.*

On the eastern side of Selinda, close to the Linyanti Swamps, are two walking trails camps which are normally combined into a longer trip on Selinda. A typical trip will spend about a week starting or ending at Selina and/or Zibalianja, and spend three or four days in the middle at a combination of the walking camps:

Å Walking trails camps (3 tents each) Usually referred to as simply Selinda's walking trails camps, you won't find their names, Mokoba and Tshwene, used very often. Both stand along the Selinda Spillway (the Magwegqana, towards the northeast of the reserve).

Tshwene is further west, where the spillway is still relatively narrow, standing under some lovely old leadwood (Combretum imberbe) and knobthorn (Acacia nigrescens) trees. It is one of the smallest and simplest camps that you'll find in Botswana. Mokoba is in the far northeast corner of the reserve, close to the Kwando River. Neither is more than about 6km from Selinda Camp, and typically visitors spend a few days at one of the permanent camps (Selinda or Zibalianja), then a few days walking to one of these camps, and then continue to the other camp for their last nights.

Accommodation in either of the walking camps consists of mini-Meru tents on raised platforms, which give you the option of sleeping under the stars (and under a mosquito net). These have large panels of airy (but insect-proof) mesh, and rechargeable lighting inside. Inside is enough space in which to stand, two proper single beds, a small bedside table and a couple of chairs.

A separate fly-sheet extends to create a tiny veranda, next to which you'll find a washbasin in a stand with a screen around it. Downstairs is a flushing toilet and another washbasin. Bucket showers (hot water provided on request) are separate; the showers are shared between the guests on a deck open with a superb view across the plains.

Meals are very relaxed and alfresco; the table is usually set up under the stars, and the food is good despite having only the simplest of bush kitchens.

These camps focus on walking safaris, although short night drives are also possible. Each camp takes just 4 walkers at a time (6 if all in one group) and the reserve has earned an excellent reputation as one of the very best reserves in Botswana for walking. The guides here are always armed, and accompanied by a tracker. Guiding standards are high because they are specialist walking guides.

A typical day here would be perhaps 6–8km between camps in a morning, and a shorter walk of perhaps 4–5km in the afternoon.

Rates as for Selinda and Zibalianja: from US$470 to US$785 pp sharing, low to high season.

On the northern edge of Botswana, bordering Namibia across the Kwando River, the Kwando Concession covers an enormous 2,320km² of very wild bush. It's one of Botswana's larger wildlife concessions. Beside its eastern boundary (the river) is a narrow belt of riverine forest. In the south this opens out into some large tree-islands and open floodplains. There are two photographic camps on this productive eastern side.

The vast western part of the concession includes huge tracts of thick mopane woodland. Here, far from the river, there is a seasonal hunting camp.

GETTING ORGANISED

Getting there and away Like most of Botswana's private concessions, Kwando is reached by a short flight from Maun, Kasane, or one of Botswana's other camps. Both these camps work their logistics out well in advance. Trips here are always pre-arranged, and they don't welcome drop-in visitors, nor ever really get any. There are two main airstrips in the concession: one near Lagoon, and the other near Lebala.

Thus virtually nobody would consider self-driving into these camps, even by prior arrangement. However, if you did then you'd pre-arrange your visit with the camps and take the transit route north through Selinda. It's about 14km in a straight line from Selinda to Lebala, and a further 30km by road from there to Lagoon.

WHEN TO VISIT Game viewing revolves around the reserve's riverfront on the Kwando River and its adjacent riverine forest. Thus note the comments made under *Planning and Preparation*, pages 67–73, and also the specific comments made for the Chobe riverfront area, on pages 196–7. The Kwando's riverfront has broadly similar game movements to the Chobe or Linyanti riverfronts. In short: game concentrates around here when it needs the water, and spreads away again when it can easily drink elsewhere.

This means that the game viewing improves as the land dries out. Then buffalo and elephants move into this area from the west and south and zebra and wildebeest move in from the great plains of the Chobe. Later, when it rains, so the animals will move away – although birdwatchers will find more of interest in the wet season when there's greater variety of bird species, many of which are in breeding plumage.

FLORA AND FAUNA

Flora Kwando's environment and ecosystems are similar to those of the Linyanti and Selinda reserves. The north of the reserve is most like the Linyanti Reserve, in that it's dominated by the presence of the river, which runs on its eastern border in a roughly straight line. Adjacent to this is a band of riverine forest, characteristically rich in its variety of trees. These include African mangosteen (*Garcinia livingstonei*) – which remind me of a bomb exploding, as all the stems grow out straight from the top – jackalberry (*Diospyros mespiliformis*), sausage tree (*Kigelia africana*), leadwood (*Combretum imberbe*) and knobthorn (*Acacia nigrescens*).

As you move further south in the reserve, around Lebala Camp, you're getting into the northern side of the Magwegqana Spillway, and here the riverine forest opens out, becoming a mosaic of open areas covered in low bushes and grasses. These open areas are often dominated by wild sage (*Pechuel-loeschea leubnitziae*) and interspersed with patches of forest, which become smaller and more island-like as you move further south.

These forest patches and islands contain many of the same riverine trees species, and you'll also find marula trees (*Sclerocarya birrea*), occasional baobabs (*Adansonia digitata*), and increasing numbers of real fan palms (*Hyphaene petersiana*), plus many camelthorns (*Acacia erioloba*), and the invasive candle-pod acacia (*Acacia hebeclada*).

Further south still, the land becomes even more open as you approach the reserve's southern boundary and the Selinda Reserve.

Fauna Like the Linyanti and Selinda, Kwando's resident game is augmented in about June by migrant game which arrives here from the drier areas south and west, attracted by the permanent waters of the Kwando River.

Common species found here include include impala, red lechwe, kudu, tsessebe, giraffe, steenbok, warthog, baboon and vervet monkeys. Roan, sable and common duiker also occur, but are not common. Lion, leopard and spotted hyena are common, whilst cheetah are rarely seen. Hippo and crocodiles frequent the river, along with the playful spotted-necked otters.

Herds of wildebeest and zebra are resident here from about May to December. Elephants and buffalo follow a similar pattern with individuals around all year, and larger breeding herds arriving around June–July and staying until December. These large herds are particularly common near the river during the dry season, and the elephants seem to have a penchant for aggression if approached too closely. When driving with one of the camp's guides, he would refer to them nonchalantly as 'cheeky' animals; but driving myself through the area once I found it much more nerve-racking. They reacted completely differently to the relatively passive elephants found in the busier parts of Chobe and Moremi.

Kwando is also a good reserve for seeing wild dog, especially in the south of the reserve around Lebala, helped by Kwando Safari's policy of actively 'tracking' animals across the bush, and having both a tracker and a driver/guide on each of its vehicles.

Highlights of the night drives here include Selous' mongoose, genets and aardwolf – along with more usual sightings of scrub hares, spring hares, bushbabies, genets, civets, honey badgers and porcupines.

Birdlife The birdlife here is almost identical to that of the Linyanti Reserve (see pages 228–9), with plenty of variety. I particularly remember a huge colony of carmine bee-eaters that we seemed to have discovered by accident when stopping on a drive for a 'sundowner' drink.

Sacred and hadeda ibis are particularly common in the waterways here, whilst rarer residents include slaty and black egrets, and rufous-bellied herons.

WHERE TO STAY Both the camps here are owned and run by Kwando Safaris, based in Maun. See page 170 for details.

Lagoon Camp (8 tents). Overlooking the Kwando River, Lagoon Camp (⊕ LAGOON 18°12.980'S; 24°24.790'E) is the smaller and more northerly of Kwando's 2 camps here in the riparian forest belt. It stands amidst tall, mature forest that includes some fine marula (*Sclerocarya birrea caffra*) and jackalberry (*Diospyros mespiliformis*) trees.

The large tents here are of a custom design, with 2 ¾ size beds, or a dbl, overlooking the river. The large front door can be opened into an entirely gauzed area: wonderful to wake up to! These have a solid wooden bed-head, matching the tent's wardrobe and furniture – though no fan. Outside each the veranda has 2 khaki chairs overlooking the river. All are covered by shade netting, shielded from the sun by a thatched roof. At the back of each is a private, en-suite, reed-walled enclosure with an open-air shower, a washbasin (in front of a large mirror) and a flush toilet. Hot water comes from individual gas-fired boilers.

The food at the camp is good, and served in a thatched dining room which overlooks the river. The bar's largely self-service, and an extensive curio shop has local handicrafts and some useful books. The lounge area has comfortable armchairs, a small library and various boardgames.

Game frequently wanders into camp and on my last visit here one old bull elephant came to within touching distance of the dining room as we ate brunch, in search of some tasty morsels in the tree above. It was very relaxed, apparently oblivious to the camera flashes and general fuss that it was causing.

Lagoon Camp has a plunge pool for the hotter months, but its main activities are walking and 4x4 game drives, usually one early in the morning (after coffee and biscuits), and the second in the late afternoon, which usually turns into a night drive as the light fades. With a tracker accompanying every drive, and a maximum of 6 people per vehicle, there's a willingness here to drive cross-country and actively track coveted game, such as big cats and wild dogs. The guides are enthusiastic about their big game, and sometimes positively zealous in their tracking of it.

There is also a 2-storey floating pontoon-type boat on the river, which can be used for gentle sundowner cruises. If you're keen on fishing then spinning for tiger fish and bream is also an option.

Lagoon's atmosphere is laid-back, friendly and not at all regimented — mealtimes are usually adjusted around game-viewing times, rather than vice versa. A slight minus is that the tents are quite close together (although all have canvas blinds that can be closed).
From US$415 pp low season to US$750/1,000 pp sharing/sgl high season, inc all meals, most drinks, activities, park fees. Open all year.

⌂ **Lebala Camp** (8 tents). Lebala (⊕ **LEBALA** 18°24.760'S; 23°32.540'E) is in a very different location. *Lebala* means 'open space', which is appropriate as there are lots of plains around it. It's just 14km from Selinda, and yet 26km (measured in a straight line) from Lagoon — and hence it's no surprise that its environment is close in character to that of Selinda, but quite different to the area around Lagoon.

Lebala's substantial and custom-designed tents are built on raised decking. This is mostly made of polished mukwa wood — a very colourful and durable local wood from the *Pterocarpus angolensis* tree. Each chalet encompasses a very large bedroom, with 2 ¾-size beds and a sprinkling of mukwa furniture. Outside the bedroom is a large private veranda for sitting out, with a few chairs and a table.

Canvas room-divisions separate the bedroom from the 'entrance hall' where there is a spot to put suitcases, a hat-and-coat stand, a large wardrobe and a writing desk — as well as a zipped tent door to the outside world. The large bathroom has a stand-alone claw-footed bath, with taps on the side, and also his-and-hers washbasins and a toilet. Outside is a large semicircular shower. (Hot water comes very efficiently from each room's individual gas geyser.)

Good meals are served in the separate thatched dining area, adjacent to which is a comfy lounge and bar area. This has a modest library of books, and one side open to the plains around. There's a campfire for the cooler months, and a small plunge pool for the warmer ones.

Activities here concentrate on walking and 4x4 game drives, and as with Lagoon the guides always drive with a tracker and will actively seek the game. Last time I visited, I arose late one morning, only to learn that wild dog had sprinted through camp just before sunrise.
From US$415 pp low season to US$750/1,000 pp sharing/sgl high season, inc all meals, most drinks, activities, park fees. Open all year.

12

The Okavango Delta – Moremi Game Reserve

Much of what is covered in this section – especially concerning flora and fauna, and when to visit – is applicable to the Okavango as a whole. Therefore I've covered this information here in detail, and made reference to it elsewhere where appropriate.

Remember that Moremi and its surrounding reserves are only separated by lines on a map; their ecosystems blend together seamlessly. Birds and animals move without hindrance across almost the whole of the Okavango, Linyanti and Chobe regions. Thus all the country covered in *Chapters 12–16* is really one continuous area dedicated to wildlife. The enormous size of this, together with the diversity of ecosystems that it contains, are two of the main reasons why the wildlife of northern Botswana is so spectacular.

BACKGROUND INFORMATION

HISTORY In his *Travels and Researches in South Africa* (see *Appendix 3, Further Information*) David Livingstone recounts what he was told by the local people near Lake Ngami in 1849 about the origin of a river there:

> While ascending in this way the beautifully-wooded river, we came to a large stream flowing into it. This was the Tamunak'le. I enquired whence it came. 'Oh, from a country full of rivers – so many no one can tell their number – and full of large trees.'

However, within 100 years of Europeans finding this 'country full of rivers', its environment and wildlife were under threat. In an exceedingly far-sighted move, the BaTawana people proclaimed Moremi as a game reserve in 1962, in order to combat the rapid depletion of the area's game and the problems of cattle encroachment.

Initially Moremi consisted mainly of the Mopane Tongue area; then in the 1970s the royal hunting grounds of Chief Moremi, known as Chief's Island, were added. In 1992 the reserve was augmented by the addition of a strip of land in the northwest corner of the reserve, between the Jao and Nqoga rivers. This was done to make sure that it represented all the major Okavango habitats, including the northern Delta's papyrus swamps and permanent wetlands which had not previously been covered.

As an aside, this is often cited as the first reserve in Africa that was created by native Africans. This is true, and recognises that the native inhabitants were the prime movers here, rather than the colonial authorities. However, beware of ignoring the fact that Africa's original inhabitants seemed to coexist with the wildlife all over the continent without needing any 'reserves', until Europeans started arriving.

GEOGRAPHY Moremi Game Reserve protects the central and eastern areas of the Okavango Delta. It forms a protected nucleus for the many wildlife

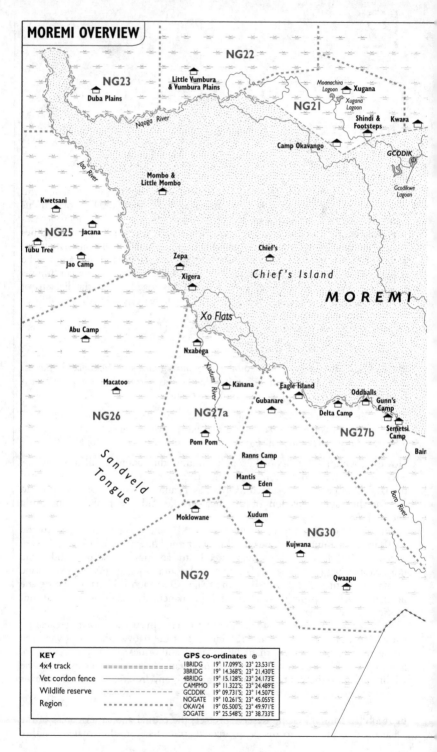

MOREMI OVERVIEW

NG22

NG23
Duba Plains

Little Yumbura & Vumbura Plains

Moanachira Lagoon
Xugana
Xugana Lagoon

NG21

Shindi & Footsteps   Kwara

Ngoga River

Camp Okavango

GCODIK

Jao River

Gcodikwe Lagoon

Mombo & Little Mombo

Kwetsani

NG25   Jacana

Tubu Tree

Jao Camp

Zepa

Chief's

Chief's Island

MOREMI

Xigera

Xo Flats

Abu Camp

Nxabega

Xudum River

Kanana

Eagle Island

Oddballs

Gunn's Camp

Macatoo

Gubanare

Delta Camp

NG27a

NG26

Semetsi Camp

NG27b

Pom Pom

Bain

Ranns Camp

Sandveld Tongue

Mantis   Eden

Boro River

Moklowane

Xudum

NG30

Kujwana

NG29

Qwaapu

KEY
4x4 track	=============
Vet cordon fence	———————
Wildlife reserve	– – – – – – –
Region	■ ■ ■ ■ ■ ■ ■

GPS co-ordinates ⊕
1BRIDG	19° 17.099'S;	23° 23.531'E
3BRIDG	19° 14.368'S;	23° 21.430'E
4BRIDG	19° 15.128'S;	23° 24.173'E
CAMPMO	19° 11.322'S;	23° 24.489'E
GCDDIK	19° 09.731'S;	23° 14.507'E
NOGATE	19° 10.261'S;	23° 45.055'E
OKAV24	19° 05.500'S;	23° 49.971'E
SOGATE	19° 25.548'S;	23° 38.733'E

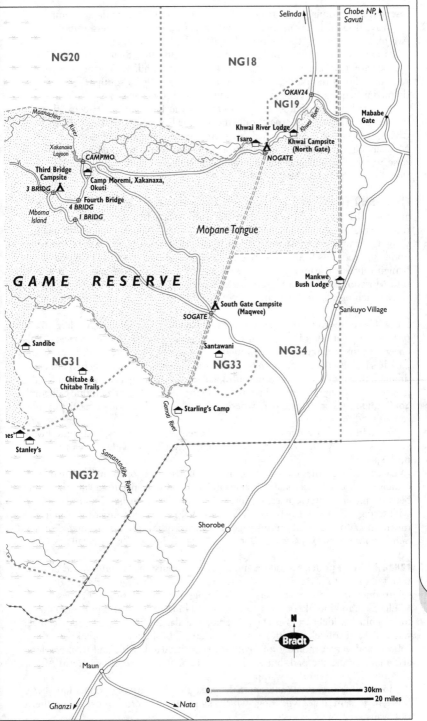

NG20

NG18

Selinda

Chobe NP, Savuti

Moanachira River

OKAV24

NG19

Mababe Gate

Khwai River

Xakanaxa Lagoon

Khwai River Lodge

Tsaro

CAMPMO

Khwai Campsite (North Gate)

Third Bridge Campsite

NOGATE

3 BRIDG

Camp Moremi, Xakanaxa, Okuti

Fourth Bridge

4 BRIDG

1 BRIDG

Mboma Island

Mopane Tongue

GAME   RESERVE

Mankwe Bush Lodge

South Gate Campsite (Maqwee)

SOGATE

Sankuyo Village

Sandibe

Santawani

NG31

NG33

NG34

Chitabe & Chitabe Trails

Gomoti River

Starling's Camp

es'

Stanley's

Santantadibe River

NG32

Shorobe

N

Bradt

Maun

Ghanzi

Nata

0   30km
0   20 miles

reserves/concessions in the region. Physically Moremi is very flat, encompassing extensive floodplains, some seasonal, others permanent, numerous waterways and two main landmasses: the Mopane Tongue and Chief's Island.

Its area is defined in some places by rivers, although their names and actual courses are anything but easy to follow on the ground. Its northern boundary roughly follows the Nqoga–Khwai river system, whilst its southern boundary is defined in sequence by the Jao, Boro and Gomoti Rivers.

It's worth noting that since the middle of the last century it seems that the western side of the Delta (specifically the Thaoge River system) has gradually been drying up. As this has happened, an increasing amount of water is entering the Moanachira–Khwai river system, on the eastern side of Chief's Island – helping to raise water levels around the Khwai River area, and increase the incidence of flooding on the roads there.

FLORA AND FAUNA The ecosystems of Moremi Reserve are amongst the richest and most diverse in Africa. Thanks to generally effective protection over the years, they have also been relatively undisturbed by man. Now with wildlife tourism thriving around the park as well as in the private concessions, we can be really optimistic about its future. The regime of conservation supported by money from benign tourism is gaining ground. As I write this, rhino have been reintroduced into Moremi: the first to be sent back into the wild areas of northern Botswana since poaching wiped them out.

Flora There are over 1,000 species of plants recognised in Moremi, yet large tracts of the reserve are dominated by just one: mopane (*Colophospermum mopane*). This covers the aptly named Mopane Tongue and parts of Chief's Island. Because the park has had effective protection for years, and the soils are relatively rich but badly drained, much of this forest is beautiful, tall 'cathedral' mopane – so called for the gracefully arching branches which resemble the high arches of a Gothic cathedral. You'll often find large areas here where there are virtually no other species of trees represented.

Beside the many waterways you'll find extensive floodplains, and some lovely stretches of classic riparian forest with its characteristically wide range of tree and bush species.

Laced through the areas of mopane you'll also find open areas dotted with camelthorn trees (*Acacia erioloba*), and sandveld communities following the sandy beds of ancient watercourses, dominated by silver terminalia (*Terminalia sericea*), wild seringa (*Burkea africana*) and Kalahari appleleaf (*Lonchocarpus nelsii*). You'll find much, much more detail on this vegetation in Veronica Roodt's essential *Trees and Shrubs of the Okavango Delta* (see *Appendix 3, Further Information* for details).

Fauna Moremi protects as dense and diverse a population of animals and birds as you'd expect to find in one of Africa's best wildlife reserves. With the reintroduction of rhino, you can see all the big five, and a lot more besides.

Elephant and buffalo occur here year-round in large numbers, and you're likely to see blue wildebeest, Burchell's zebra, impala, kudu, tsessebe, red lechwe, waterbuck, reedbuck, giraffe, common duiker, bushbuck, steenbok, warthog, baboon and vervet monkey throughout the park. Eland, sable and roan antelope also range across the park but are less common, as they are elsewhere in Africa. Sitatunga live deep in the swamps.

Lion, leopard, cheetah and spotted hyena all have thriving populations here. Moremi is central to wild dog, which range widely across most of northern Botswana.

Both side-striped and black-backed jackal occur, though the latter are more common. Brown hyena probably occur, but relatively rarely and only in the drier areas with lower densities of the other large predators. Similarly, bat-eared fox are found here, though not so commonly as in Botswana's drier areas. There is a wide variety of mongooses to be found, including the banded, dwarf, slender, large grey, water and Selous' mongoose. Meanwhile in the water, Cape, clawless and spotted-necked otters are often glimpsed though seldom seen clearly.

Serval, caracal, aardwolf and aardvark are found all over the park, though are only occasionally seen due to their largely nocturnal habits. Pangolin are also found here, and seem to be slightly less rare than in other areas of their range.

Although night drives aren't allowed within the reserve itself, some of the camps near North Gate will finish their afternoon drives outside the park, and hence do short night drives back to camp. Then you have a chance to see scrub hares, spring hares, lesser bushbabies, porcupines, genets (small-spotted and large-spotted), civets, African wildcats and honey badgers. Black-and-white striped polecats are also nocturnal, though very seldom seen.

Until 2001 rhino had been absent due to poaching, though in November of that year the first white rhino were reintroduced into the Mombo concession, in northeast Moremi. They're now free to roam, but they are effectively constrained to Chief's Island.

Birdlife Moremi boasts over 400 bird species, a great variety, which are often patchily distributed in association with particular habitats; though visiting any area, the sheer number of different species represented here will strike you as amazing.

Although there are no birds that are truly endemic to Botswana, the Okavango is a hugely important wetland for many species, amongst which are a number of rarities worth noting. Top of the Okavango's list of 'specialities' is the slaty egret. Expect to find this in shallow, reedy backwaters and pans. Besides the Okavango, this rare egret is only resident in the quieter corners of the Chobe and Linyanti rivers, and the Bangweulu Wetlands in Zambia. To identify it look for its overall slate-grey colouring, except for its lower legs and feet which are yellow, as are its eyes and some of its face, while the front of its neck is a rufous red. (The less uncommon black egret lacks the yellow on the legs and face, or the rufous neck.)

Much easier to spot are magnificent wattled cranes which can be seen in the delta fairly readily, usually in pairs or small groups wandering about wet grasslands or shallow floodplains in search of fish and small amphibians and reptiles.

For keen birdwatchers, other specials here include brown firefinch, lesser jacana, coppery-tailed coucal, Bradfield's hornbill, pink-throated longclaw and the inconspicuous chirping cisticola.

WHEN AND HOW TO VISIT See *When to go* in *Chapter 4* for more general comments on the whole of northern Botswana, and note that the best times to visit are dependent upon how you intend to visit, exactly which camps you are visiting, and why.

Flying in If you're flying into a camp in Moremi or the Delta then the season won't make much difference to the access; virtually all the camps open all year. The Okavango's camps used to close down during January and February, but now most keep open throughout the year, despite being much quieter during the green season (December to March). The exception to this has been the January to March period in 2002, when many camps closed down due to reduced bookings from America after the tragedy of 11 September 2001.

12

In terms of vehicle access to the various game-viewing areas from your camp, the rains are often less of a concern than the flood, the peak of which usually lags behind the rains by several months (depending on how far up the Delta you are). However, generally there will be the most dry land from about August to January.

Driving in If you're driving yourself into Moremi, it's important to understand that only a restricted area of the reserve will be accessible to you, and the wet season will make this access even more difficult. As the rains continue, their cumulative effect is to make many of the roads on the Mopane Tongue much more difficult to pass, while it simply submerges others.

The direct track between North Gate and Xakanaxa has been particularly problematic recently. It was waterlogged for traffic for virtually all of 2001, due to a combination of rain and floods. Thus only the experienced and well-equipped need even think about driving anywhere through Moremi between about January and April.

Most visitors who drive themselves come to Moremi in the dry season, between around May and October. Then the tracks become increasingly less difficult to navigate, although even then there are always watercourses to cross. As with all national parks, the speed limit in the park is 40km/h, with no vehicles allowed on the roads between sunset and sunrise.

Flora and fauna The flora and the birdlife are definitely more spectacular during the rains. Then the vegetation goes wild, migrant birds arrive, and many of the residents appear in their full breeding plumage. So this is a great time for birders and those interested in the plants and flowers.

The story with the animals is more complex. In most of Moremi there is water throughout the year. Higher water levels here simply means less land area available for animals that aren't amphibious. However, around the edges of the Delta, animal densities are hugely affected by the migration towards the water from the dry central areas of the country.

Thus game viewing generally gets better the later in the dry season that you go . . . although this trend is probably less pronounced in the centre of the Delta than it is at the edges.

Activities The water levels will affect the activities that you can do whilst here. In some areas mokoro trips are possible only for a few months every year, when water levels are high enough. Similarly, the game drives from a few of the camps are generally possible only when water levels are low enough.

Costs The cost of some camps in the Okavango varies with the season. This depends very much on the company owning/marketing the camps, but in general you can expect July–October to be the period of highest cost, December–March to be the time of lowest cost, and November, April, May and June to be pitched somewhere in the middle.

GETTING ORGANISED
Orientation Moremi Game Reserve covers a large tract of the centre of the Okavango Delta, and a wide corridor stretching east to link that with Chobe National Park.

At the heart of Moremi is a long, permanent island, Chief's Island, oriented from southeast to northwest. At about 60km long and around 10km wide this is the largest island in the Delta, and it's usually cut off from the mainland by waterways and floodplains. Within the eastern side of Moremi is a triangular

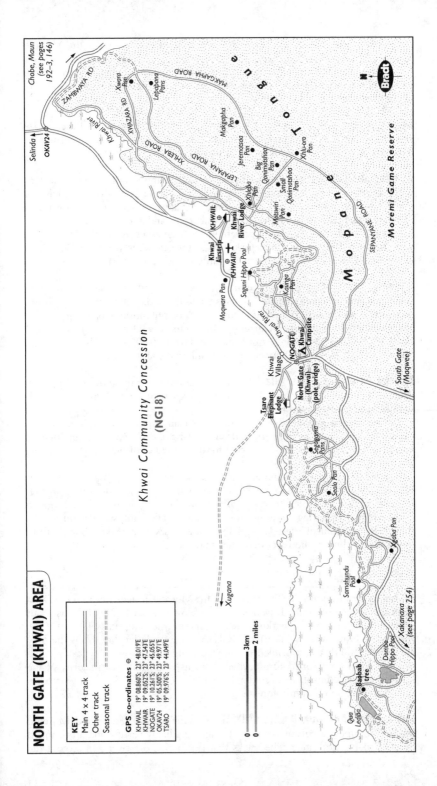

NORTH GATE (KHWAI) AREA

KEY

Main 4 × 4 track
Other track
Seasonal track

GPS co-ordinates ⊕

KHWAI	19° 08.860'S; 23° 48.019'E
KHWAIR	19° 09.052'S; 23° 47.543'E
NOGATE	19° 10.261'S; 23° 45.055'E
OKAV24	19° 05.500'S; 23° 49.971'E
TSARO	19° 09.976'S; 23° 44.049'E

Khwai Community Concession (NG18)

Chobe, Maun
(see pages
192–3, 146)

Selinda
OKAV24 ⊕

ZAMBWAYA RD

Khwai River

XWAZARA RD

XHLEBA ROAD

LEPRANA ROAD

MAKGAPHA ROAD

Xwara
Pan

Lehutana
Pans

Makgapha
Pan

Jeremotsaa
Pan

Big
Qonimotshaa

Small
Qonimotshaa
Pan

Xhu-oro
Pan

Xhleba
Pan

Matswiri
Pan

KHWAI
Khwai
River Lodge

Khwai
Airstrip ⊕
KHWAIR ✝

Moqwara Pan

Saguni Hippo Pool

Kaunga
Pan

Khwai River

Khwai
Village

NOGATE ⊕
▲ Khwai
Campsite

North Gate
(Khwai)
(pole bridge)

Tsaro
Elephant
Lodge

Sepogana
Pans

Seolo Pan

Xaba Pan

Xugana

Samahundu
Pool

Domba
Hippo Pool

Xakanaxa
(see page 254)

Baobab
tree

Qaa
Lediba

M o p a n e   T o n g u e

Moremi Game Reserve

SEPANTANE ROAD

South Gate
(Maqwee)

Bradt

N

0   3km
0   2 miles

peninsula of dry land covered (mostly) in mopane trees, known as the Mopane Tongue.

Between and around Chief's Island and the Mopane Tongue, Moremi is a mosaic of rivers, lagoons, floodplains and small islands which slowly and gradually change with the passage of time.

Maps Once again, Veronica Roodt's definitive map of Moremi Game Reserve (see *Appendix 3, Further Information*) can't be recommended too highly for visitors to Moremi, and is essential for anyone planning a self-drive trip there.

Booking and parks fees If you're flying into an organised camp, then parks fees will probably already be included in the price that you've paid. If you're driving in you'll need to have booked all your campsites in advance; see page 138 for details of the national park offices in Maun and Gaborone, and a scale of the fees.

You'll need to have a copy (or preferably an original) of this confirmation with you, then you'll need to pay your parks fees on the gate when you arrive. Note that this is best done in pula, and that credit cards are never accepted.

Opening hours The park's opening hours vary with the season, roughly corresponding to 'dusk 'til dawn'. This is when the park's gates and offices open, and you're not allowed to drive around the park before morning opening time, or after evening closing time. Currently the hours are: December, January and February: 05.30–19.30; March, April and May: 06.00–19.00; June, July and August: 06.30–18.30; September, October and November: 06.00–19.00.

Moremi Game Reserve regulations With your entry permit and booking you'll usually be given a photocopied set of the park's regulations, which are worth familiarising yourself with before you get here.

Amongst the more notable ones are strict bans on camping away from the campsites or without a valid permit; driving off-road; driving faster than 40km/h; walking away from your vehicle (except for designated campsites); and swimming anywhere.

You aren't allowed to bring any firewood into the reserve, or take any out. However you *are* allowed to collect it from within Moremi for your own use. Remember that, and collect it as you drive around during the day. If you forget to do so until you're setting up camp, you'll usually find the campsites devoid of even the smallest combustible dead twigs! (Needless to say, never take branches from living trees or bushes, however dead they may seem.)

THE MOPANE TONGUE

Within eastern Moremi, the dry triangle of the Mopane Tongue juts into the Delta from the east, between the Khwai and Mogogelo rivers. Each side of this is about 40km long, and roughly marking the corners are the campsites of South Gate (Maqwee), North Gate (Khwai) and Xakanaxa – a reminder that this is the only area of Moremi that's accessible for visitors driving themselves.

Aside from the riverine forest which lines its edges, the vast majority of the interior of this peninsula is covered in forests of mopane, including many stretches of very mature and beautiful forests.

KHWAI RIVER AND NORTH GATE (KHWAI) Near the northeastern edge of Moremi, the northernmost waterways of the Okavango gradually narrow and are spanned by a wooden pole bridge. The tracks that run beside the river and around the floodplains are often stunning in their beauty, and prolific in their wildlife. It's a spectacular area, and especially so if approached from the dusty heartlands of Chobe during the dry season.

Orientation It's easy to orient yourself here. The Okavango's waters approach from the west down the Khwai River. To the west they're flanked by floodplains, loops, meanders and lagoons, but gradually travelling east this valley narrows and concentrates the river water into a small channel.

Central to the whole area is the bridge at North Gate (now more commonly called Khwai), which spans the channel. South of this is Moremi Game Reserve, and north is the small settlement of Khwai Village, the community-controlled concessions beyond NG18 and NG19 (see page 276), and the area's airstrip. Access to the reserve is through the village of Khwai.

Although the lodges in this area are technically inside these concessions, I've included them in this chapter as their focus is essentially on this corner of Moremi.

Getting organised There are three small shops in Khwai Village, a welcome sight if you've been driving for several days and supplies are running low. Coming into the village from Savuti, the first sells just a few cans and soft drinks, but a little further on are two more shops; the second of these is a smaller shop but with a far better range, sometimes including potatoes and other fresh vegetables, and with fresh bread on Mondays. There are also baskets for sale. A signpost to the right in the village points to Lechwe Camp and Tau Camp – which I believe are sites for mobile camps in the south side of Khwai community's area, NG18. I would welcome more details of either.

Flora and fauna highlights

Flora All along the edge of the Khwai's floodplain you'll find some of the region's most beautiful, mature riverine forest. Stunning trees, tall and old abound, including a large number of camelthorn (*Acacia erioloba*) and some almost pure stands of leadwood (*Combretum imberbe*). There are also patches of acacia woodlands, usually standing on sandy patches of ground between the river valley and the mopane woodlands of the Tongue's interior.

Fauna The Khwai area seldom fails to deliver some very impressive wildlife spectacles when visited in the dry season. This is perhaps to be expected, as it marks the boundary of the Okavango's waters that flow east and north – and so is the closest drinking water for large numbers of thirsty animals in southern Chobe during the late dry season.

Of particular note are the lion prides. In 1999 one was so large that it had started taking down small elephants – a practice which visibly worried the area's large elephant herds.

I've had some particularly good leopard sightings here, seeing the cats lounging around in shady trees during the day, usually on the edge of the riverine forest. Mixed areas of broken woodlands and open areas is classic leopard territory, and because it's been protected for so long, many of the residents are very relaxed in the presence of game-viewing vehicles.

At Khwai you probably have a better chance than in most places of seeing the normally elusive roan antelope, which come down to the river to drink regularly.

Birdlife Khwai's birdlife is varied, like the habitats found here, though with only a narrow channel of water in the dry season, you'll usually have to search elsewhere for large numbers of the more aquatic species. That said, even in the dry season you will find storks (saddle-billed and marabou) and wattled cranes pacing around the open areas in search of fish, frogs and reptiles to eat.

Khwai does have a reputation, especially towards the end of the dry season, for having a very high density of raptors – with which I can concur. I've been closer to a martial eagle here than anywhere else, and had a lovely sighting of a marsh harrier hunting, and both bateleur eagles and giant eagle owls seem particularly common. So as you drive along, keep glancing into the sky and checking the tops of trees for the distinctive outline of a perched raptor.

⌂ Where to stay
The erstwhile three lodges here have now been reduced to one, Khwai River Lodge, although a second may reopen during 2006. Both lie on the north side of the river, overlooking Moremi Game Reserve, so are technically in the NG19 concession (see page 276). Both are described here for continuity. Not far away is the national park's campsite. Note that both Khwai River Lodge and the campsite must be pre-booked before you arrive; you are likely to be turned away if you simply roll up.

⌂ **Khwai River Lodge** (15 canvas rooms) See Orient-Express Safaris, page 171. I've very fond memories of the original Khwai River Lodge
(✪ KHWAIL 19°08.860'S; 23°48.019'E), with understated little bungalows amongst the leadwood trees on the edge of the river's floodplain. It was one of the Okavango's oldest lodges, and full of character. Now all that remains is the basic structure of its old office that has been preserved as a small museum and curio shop. Around this, an opulent lodge was built in the late 1990s to the same design as that used for Savute Elephant Camp (see page 219).

At its heart, set among neat grassy lawns, is a central area, slightly raised on a timber platform and topped by an enormous thatched roof. In the middle, a fireplace forms the focus of the lounge, with chess sets, a TV with wildlife videos, comfy couches and a small library. There's a bar to one side, and to the other a dining area where candles illuminate wooden tables for stylish table d'hôte dinners. In front, a telescope stands on a wide area of decking overlooking the narrow, shallow river valley. On a lower level is a firepit, for drinks outside, and a huge swimming pool built into the decking. An adjoining raised observation deck with thatched roof shelters another telescope; it's a good spot for game viewing or the occasional private dinner. A refurbished spa and gym (fortunately with AC) should appeal to the more active, while for those who can't cope with life in the slow lane, a communications area with TV, internet and photo-downloading facilities was scheduled for completion in 2006.

The lodge's large (18m x 6m) canvas rooms (far too opulent to be called tents) are built on high timber platforms facing the river valley, each a good

distance from the next. Because these are spread out in a line, the camp stretches for over 1km in length, with the furthest tents a significant walk from the centre. Each platform has a wide veranda at the front, with a hammock and wicker chairs overlooking the river. Inside, the 'tents' boast polished wooden floors, rugs and good-quality furniture with muted fabrics. Twin ³/₄-size beds, usually pushed together, have high-quality cotton bedding, bedside tables and twin electric/battery-powered lamps, all surrounded by mosquito netting. Above, 2 AC units fight a valiant if sometimes losing battle to keep the room cool. At the back of the tent are a toilet and a 2-person shower, each behind a wooden door, with outside showers a welcome addition for 2006 (2 rooms will also have private plunge pools).

Activities focus on 2 game drives per day, the first in the early morning after a light breakfast, returning late morning for a substantial brunch, and the second after dinner. Not surprisingly, service here is excellent, with more than a hint of the colonial. *From US$499 pp sharing low season to US$911 pp sharing high season, inc accommodation, meals, drinks, laundry & all activities. Open all year.*

⌂ **Tsaro Elephant Lodge** (8 rooms). Barely 2km west of North Gate, Tsaro Elephant Lodge (✪ TSARO 19°09.976'S; 23°44.049'E) was until recently another of Moremi's old, established camps. In 2001, however, the lodge was unexpectedly closed, apparently because the leaseholders were unable to reach an agreement with the local community over the terms of a new lease. When we visited in November 2005, there were rumours that a 4-year lease had been granted to a local Botswanan woman called Bonti, who had secured a government loan.

We heard that she planned to reopen in mid-2006, but so far have received no details.

⚥ North Gate (Khwai) Campsite (10 pitches) Contact the national park's booking office (see page 138). Khwai is situated on a lovely site to the south of the Khwai River, immediately on your left as you cross the pole bridge into Moremi from North Gate. It has only the most basic of facilities, with 2 simple toilet blocks, and poor maintenance has done nothing to combat the troupes of vervet monkeys and baboons that are starting to overrun the place. The monkeys in particular can be a menace, openly stealing from our vehicle as we stood close by, though it's hard not to laugh at their brazen theft. Pitches are dotted amidst tall woodlands, some along the river, where fireflies put on a mesmerising display as night falls, and the grunts of hippos form the bass notes to the general cacophony from baboons and francolins. Each site has a rather incongruous concrete table and benches – some broken – as well as an ingenious chain system combining braai facilities with a campfire

Look out for especially impressive specimens of sickle-leaved albizia (*Albizia harveyi*). Their fine leaves and flattened seedpods might look like acacias, but trees of the *Albizia* family don't have thorns. You'll also find a few huge sycamore figs (*Ficus sycomorus*), easily spotted because of their yellow-orange bark and a tendency for parts of their wide trunks to form buttresses. Old Africa hands will avoid camping directly under a fig tree, though, as their fruits are sought after by everything from baboons and bats to elephants – any of which can make for a messy tent in the morning, and a very disturbed night's sleep,

What to see and do Wherever you stay, however you travel, your activities during the day will be almost exclusively game drives, as walking and night drives are forbidden by park rules, and the Khwai is too shallow and narrow for safe boating.

Game-viewing roads and loops spread out on both sides of North Gate, to the west and east. Most stick close to the Khwai River, either exploring the river's floodplain or the adjacent band of riverine forest. You'll need Veronica Roodt's map of Moremi (see *Appendix 3, Further Information*) to get the best from these, as they're not shown on the main map of Botswana.

If you're visiting in the wet season, then consider taking one of the long drives that loop away from the river east of North Gate – like Sepanyana Road. These give you access to some of the pans in the mopane area, which might prove more productive for game at that time.

Getting there and away

By air Virtually all of the visitors to the lodges arrive at the airstrip (⊕ KHWAIR 19°09.052'S; 23°47.543'E), which is just outside Khwai River Lodge. This is a short hop from Kasane, Maun or any of the other airstrips in the region. There are no facilities at the airstrip; it's just a flattish section of low grass with a windsock next to it.

By road

Driving from North Gate (Khwai) to Savuti, Chobe Note that the reverse of this route is described in slightly greater detail in *Chapter 10*, pages 220–1. Here I've repeated the basics, as this is often a route that is taken by self-drive visitors on their first trip to Botswana, and it's one that can be confusing.

From the pole bridge at Khwai Campsite, cross to North Gate (⊕ NOGATE 19°10.261'S; 23°45.055'E), on the north side of the Khwai river, and follow the main track through Khwai Village. This bends to the right, and heads roughly northeast, passing the Khwai Airstrip (⊕ KHWAIR 19°09.052'S; 23°47.543'E) on the right. Near the airstrip, a right turn leads to Khwai River Lodge, while a few kilometres later a second right heads to Machaba.

About 8km after the airstrip, the road forks at OKAV24 (⊕ 19°05.500'S; 23°49.971'E). The branch to the north, signposted to Seronga by one of the park's old green concrete pillar signs, heads off to Selinda Reserve and the northeast side of the Delta. To reach Chobe take the right turn which initially bends east, following the stunningly beautiful Khwai River Valley.

Around 9km after this you technically cross into Chobe National Park and there's a right turn on to a cut-line road which heads due south, marking Moremi's border. This takes about 33km to join the road to Maun near the village of Sankuyo.

Ignoring that right turn, about 16km after OKAV24 the road leaves the river and splits again. Both forks join the Savuti–Maun track: head right for Maun, but left for Savuti. Shortly after you'll cross the Magwikwe Sand Ridge – a relic from the period when central Botswana was covered by the giant super-lake, Lake Makgadikgadi. (See pages 45–6 for more on the origins of this ridge.) You may not see the ridge itself, but after 3km stuck in low gears ploughing through thick sand, you'll realise that you've crossed it.

It's about 6km from the base of the sand ridge to Chobe's Mababe Gate (✪ MABABE 19°06.182'S; 23°59.119'E), and the earth on some of this road is very fine with a high clay content: hard-baked when dry; sticky and difficult when wet. At the gate, stop and sign in before continuing roughly north towards Savuti.

About 20km north of the Mababe Gate, the road splits. Both forks lead to Savuti. The right fork is the **marsh road**, which is more scenic, but can be very rutted and bumpy during the dry season, with great views of the marsh. It is certainly going to be the worse of the two during the rainy season, when you'd be wise to take the left fork, the more direct if less interesting, sand-ridge road. This stays closer to the Magwikwe Sand Ridge, climbing on to it at one point.

After about 37km on the sand-ridge road, or 44km on the marsh road, these routes converge (✪ MARSAN 18°36.078'S; 24°3.678'E) beside Leopard Hill Rock, which is about 5km south of the heart of Savuti.

Driving from North Gate (Khwai) to Xakanaxa Important note on the road between North Gate and Xakanaxa:
In recent years the main North Gate–Xakanaxa road has been largely closed because of high water levels. Before setting off along it you should always ask the warden at the camp you are leaving if it's passable. If not then you have no choice but to go via South Gate and the 'central' road through the Mopane Tongue (a total distance of about 72km).

That said, even when it's blocked by high water levels, the main problems are often in the middle of the route. Here it's possible to access some of the more northerly game-drive loops from North Gate on a drive from the east, but having seen these, you've then got to retrace your steps.

This route is really very straightforward. Start from North Gate's wooden bridge and follow the road southwest towards South Gate for less than 1km. Here you'll find a substantial right turn signposted to Xakanaxa, heading in a more westerly direction. Follow this and after about 44km it'll lead you straight there, mainly through old, established mopane woodlands.

However, the real joy of this route is the numerous side-loops which detour to the right of the road. There are endless small loops and side-roads, but if you feel lost remember that heading west and south will generally keep you going in the right direction. Heading north will go deeper into the detours and usually bring you back to the Khwai River. One particularly attractive loop, signposted 'Hippo Pool', leads to a large, shallow lake where hippos wallow in the permanent water. At one end of the pool is a tall bird hide, giving the opportunity to leave the vehicle and spend unlimited time in the heat of the day observing the waterbirds that congregate here, including Egyptian and spur-winged goose, knob-billed and white-faced duck, and woolly-necked stork. (Quite unexpectedly, a toilet has been built at the base of the hide, which suggests that this is well frequented by safari groups.)

The main problem arises when the tracks are waterlogged. When I drove this route in 1999, most of the loops were fine. A few – often those marked as 'seasonal roads' on Veronica Roodt's map of Moremi (see *Appendix 3, Further Information* – were tricky and required one to cross quite deep water in the vehicle. The scenery on the road around Qua Ledibe (*lediba* is the local word for 'lagoon'), particularly looking out west towards the Xuku floodplain, was very beautiful as we meandered between the dappled light of the forest and open lagoons.

However, west of Qua Lediba, the road became progressively more difficult, with deeper and deeper stretches of water to cross. Several times we forded water across the road, until one large pool stopped us. Forest to the left and lagoon to the right. There was no easy way around. The track was flat sand; solid not slippery. Vehicle tracks had been this way recently – a good sign.

As we considered our next move, two large trucks, run by a mobile-safari operator, approached and drove across, showing us the depth; we crossed safely. We avoided the next pool, but in a third the vehicle lurched alarmingly to the right – my passenger falling across me as I drove. The Land Rover didn't blink though and pulled us through. Nerve-racking when alone, such puddles are more fun with a party of two vehicles, as then one can pull the other out of difficulty if necessary.

Back on the main road, heading west we found a drift, where the road had been washed away. Various alternatives circled off left, finding shallower, but more slippery, places to cross. The water at the main road was deeper, but the substrate was more solid. On the whole, a safer bet.

Driving from North Gate to South Gate Again, this is a very straightforward route, on a very straight road – only without the game-drive loops of the previous route. From North Gate's wooden bridge you simply follow a substantial track for about 30km, which heads southwest, directly towards South Gate (✦ SOGATE 19°25.548'S; 23°38.733'E).

Driving from North Gate to Maun This isn't a route that people often want to take, but the quickest way is probably to follow the first part of the *Driving from North Gate (Khwai) to Savuti, Chobe* instructions, above. Then around 9km after OKAV24 (✦ 19°05.500'S; 23°49.971'E), turn right on to the cut-line which heads due south. This takes about 33km to join the road to Maun near the village of Zankuyo.

Note that crossing the Khwai River here can be tricky, and this road is especially sticky and difficult during the rainy season.

TIP OF THE TONGUE: XAKANAXA AND BEYOND
One corner of the Mopane Tongue's triangular peninsula juts towards the centre of Moremi, and at the end of the tip is Xakanaxa Lagoon. Beyond it, on three sides, is the Delta's maze of channels, floodplains, lagoons and islands. A few of the larger, closer islands, such as Goaxhlo and the large Mboma Island, are accessible via simple pole bridges. Beyond this, Moremi becomes inaccessible without a boat: that's the realm of the small, fly-in safari camps.

The patchwork of environments found here is typical of the inner reaches of the Delta. It's also phenomenally beautiful, and one of the most reliably good areas for wildlife on the subcontinent. Expect extraordinary densities of game and birdlife and, as it's been protected for years, the animals are generally very relaxed.

For the self-driving visitor, the game and scenery here is as good as it gets in Botswana – don't miss this area.

Orientation The main route from North Gate to Xakanaka roughly follows the northern edge of the Mopane Tongue. Similarly, the main road from South Gate

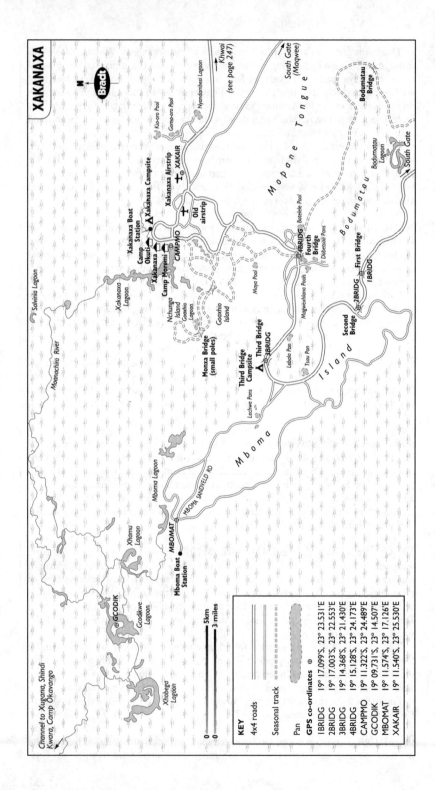

XAKANAXA

Channel to Xugana, Shindi Kwara, Camp Okavango

Moanachira River

Savhinia Lagoon

Xhobega Lagoon

Gcodikwe Lagoon

⊕ GCODIK

Xhamu Lagoon

Mboma Lagoon

Mboma Boat Station

MBOMAT ⊕

MBOMA SANDVELD RD

M b o m a   I s l a n d

Lechwe Pans

Labelo Pan

Tsau Pan

Third Bridge Campsite
⛺ Third Bridge
3BRIDG

Monxa Bridge (small poles)

Nchunga Island

Gcoaxho Island

Goaxhio Lagoon

Xakanaxa Lagoon

Xakanaxa Boat Station
Camp Station
Okuti ⌂
Xakanaxa ☗
Camp Moremi ☗
CAMPMO ⊕

⛺ Xakanaxa Campsite
Xakanaxa Airstrip
✈ XAKAIR

Old airstrip ✈

Kai-oro Pool
Gomo-oro Pool

Nyandambesi Lagoon

Khwai (see page 247)

South Gate (Maqwee)

M o p a n e   T o n g u e

Botelele Pool

⊕ 4BRIDG
Fourth Bridge
Dobetsaa Pans

Moya Pool

Magwexhana Pools

Second Bridge
⊕ 2BRIDG

First Bridge
⊕ 1BRIDG

B o d u m a t a u

Bodumataa Lagoon

Bodumatau Bridge

South Gate

Bradt

N

KEY

4x4 roads	══════
Seasonal track	══════
Pan	

GPS co-ordinates ⊕

1BRIDG	19° 17.099'S,	23° 23.531'E
2BRIDG	19° 17.003'S,	23° 22.553'E
3BRIDG	19° 14.368'S,	23° 21.430'E
4BRIDG	19° 15.128'S,	23° 24.173'E
CAMPMO	19° 11.322'S,	23° 24.489'E
GCODIK	19° 09.731'S,	23° 14.507'E
MBOMAT	19° 11.574'S,	23° 17.126'E
XAKAIR	19° 11.540'S,	23° 25.530'E

0 ___ 5km
0 ___ 3 miles

to Third Bridge roughly follows the southern edge of the Tongue. This section covers the area around and between Xakanaka and Third Bridge.

In Veronica Roodt's map of Moremi (see *Appendix 3, Further Information*) there are some detailed insets of the road layouts around this area, so make sure that you buy a copy of this before you get here. You'll also find plenty of useful references and background information on the reverse of the map.

Flora and fauna highlights Picking out the wildlife highlights for an area like this, and trying to point out what's special here, is virtually impossible. There's usually something special around every corner. It's not that you'll see different things here than you will elsewhere in Moremi, or even Botswana; it's just that you'll see them all in a very small area.

Where to stay There are three camps (catering mostly to pre-arranged fly-in visitors) and one campsite, all clustered around the Xakanaxa Lagoon, a huge open lagoon which is fed by the Moanachira River. This can be traced upstream, passing close to Camp Okavango, Shinde and Xugana, allowing these isolated water-based camps to be used as 'satellites' for sojourns of a few days into the Delta, linked by a boat journey of a few hours.

Note that because of the particularly high game densities here, and the relaxed, fearless nature of the animals, even walking around within camp can be an experience at times. Lion, hyena, leopard, buffalo, wild dogs and elephants all wander though the camps and campsites very frequently – so be careful when you are walking around, especially after dark.

Camp Moremi (11 tents) See Desert and Delta Safaris, page 169. Approaching Xakanaxa Lagoon from either of Moremi's entrance gates, Camp Moremi (✪ CAMPMO 19°11.322'S; 23°24.489'E) is the furthest left (southwest) of the adjacent camps at the tip of the Mopane Tongue.

This well-kept, established camp is set under huge old trees with lawns cropped short by the hippos that regularly graze here at night. A lot of other animals venture into camp, though elephants are kept at bay by discreet strands of electrified wire around the perimeter. A resident attraction is Pavarotti, an elderly hippo who apparently feels safer with humans around – having switched his lifestyle (to avoid other hippos) so that he's on land by day and in the water at night. But be wary – he is still a wild animal and should not be approached.

A large, square wooden construction, somewhat akin to a treehouse, comprises the camp's central area, its walls partially open to the breeze, and cooled overhead by punkah-punkah fans. Clever use of space upstairs means that there's room for a dining area, some comfy sofas and a small library stocked mostly with novels, as well as a rather modern bar. Beneath is a good curio shop (open for guests only), and nearby a boma for breakfast, brunch and high tea. A hammock swung between 2 jackalberry trees makes for lazy afternoons overlooking the river, and there's a high observation platform with a super view over Xakanaxa Lagoon. Tucked to one side is a small pool raised up on a wooden deck, with umbrella-shaded sunbeds.

Guests stay in Meru-style tents constructed on raised teak platforms, each facing the river. Each has proper doors (which must be kept locked because of kleptomaniac baboons) and is well furnished with sisal matting, bright rugs and fabrics, wooden wardrobe, luggage rack, dressing table, a table-top electric fan and director's chairs. There are also facilities for making tea and coffee. A private bathroom – with flush toilet, large, glass-screened shower, mirror and washbasin – is set next to the tent and the platform. At the end of camp, the 'honeymoon' suite (No 11: the only one with a dbl bed) is raised up quite high and has been built with flair and imagination around a marvellous old jackalberry tree (*Diospyros mespiliformis*), which has 5 separate trunks growing up right through the middle of the room.

Activities concentrate on morning and afternoon game drives, and motorboat trips around the lagoons and waterways. As Camp Okavango and Xugana (see pages 282–3) are owned by the same company, it's a good idea to combine several nights at one of these with Camp Moremi, sticking to game drives here, and transferring between them by motorboat.

US$630/830 pp sharing/sgl Jul–Oct; US$420 pp
sharing/sgl Nov–Mar; US$360 pp sharing/sgl
Apr–Jun, fully inclusive. Open all year.

🏠 **Xakanaxa** (13 tents) Moremi Safaris, Cramerview
2060, South Africa; ☎ +27 11 465 3842/3; f +27
11 465 3779; e info@moremi-safaris.com;
www.moremi-safaris.com, www.xakanaxa-camp.com.
Less than 1km northeast of Camp Moremi, Xakanaxa
has long been run by Bob and Flo Flaxman. It's a
classic old camp, solidly built among natural
vegetation, with plenty of tree shade, and one of the
few independents (ie: camps that aren't run by a
large company as part of a group) in northern
Botswana. With lighting for the most part provided
by candles and paraffin storm lanterns, there's a
strong sense of place (but there's a generator in the
day, and it's possible to charge electrical equipment).
The whole site is also wheelchair-accessible.
Xakanaka's raised, thatched dining area overlooks the
lagoon. It's memorable for a long, 18-seater table,
made from reclaimed old railway sleepers, on which
dinners are served, lit by candlelight from a
handmade wrought-iron candelabra. There's a
separate lounge/bar, and a circular area built out
over the water with a central fire, as well as a
plunge pool. Massages are available on request.

Meru-style tents stand on wooden decks, with
verandas that overlook the lagoon. Inside are solid
wooden twin beds, with a carefully chosen reference
book on each table. At the back, screened by reeds,
are a hot shower, handbasin and flush toilet. The
whole is covered by a large canvas roof with an
innovative 'irrigation' system designed to cool the air
inside.

Six tents form Pandani's, a private camp-within-
a-camp that is ideal for families or small groups: it
comes complete with its own lounge, dining room
and kitchen, pool and fire.

The camp is surrounded by a high, but discreet,
3-strand electric fence, designed purely to keep out
elephants, which can be destructive to the trees as
well as dangerous. Xakanaxa is better than most
camps in Botswana at catering for families and
children.

Activities focus on 4x4 game drives and boat
trips on to the lagoon, as well as mokoro excursions
from the boats.
US$385 pp sharing/sgl low season to US$695/990
high season, inc all meals, activities & park fees.
Open all year.

🏠 **Camp Okuti** (10 chalets) See Ker & Downey
Safaris, page 170. Sandwiched between Xakanaxa and
the campsite, Okuti has quite a tight spot in many

ways. Built in the early 1980s, it was taken over by
Ker & Downey some years ago, but didn't seem to
fit in with their more upmarket camps. With
refurbishment in hand at the end of 2005, and the
construction of a small pool, it will be interesting to
see whether or not the camp will match up with
the standards of others in the group.

For now, Okuti's small, thatched A-frame chalets,
lacking the space typical of today's safari camps, are
huddled together by the side of the lagoon, among
shady trees. Cream washed, with steeply angled
thatched roofs almost to the ground, they look
rather like something out of The Hobbit. Inside are
twin or dbl beds (a 'family unit' has 4 beds) with
sisal matting and a central fan, and at the back a
tiled shower area with toilet and washbasin. Hot
water comes from wood-fuelled 'Rhodesian' boilers,
whilst the lights run from a generator during the
day, and a battery at night.

Outside, chairs are set around a firepit by the
river near the small bar. Activities concentrate on
4x4 game drives and trips on to the lagoon by
motorboat.

Okuti was a top camp a few decades ago,
though when visited at the end of 2005, it was in
need of a refit. Until then, though, the dining area,
once canvas-topped, has a plastic-sheet roof, the
curio shop has closed, and the place generally feels
lacking in impetus. Unfortunately, because it's
effectively surrounded on all sides, there seems to be
no way that rebuilding could bring it up the
spacious standards of its neighbours.
US$395/450 pp sharing/sgl May–Jun, Nov,
US$495/635 pp Jul–Oct, US$330 pp Mar–Apr, inc
all meals, drinks, activities, laundry; transfers extra;
no children under 7. Open Mar–Nov.

▲ **Xakanaxa Campsite** (8 pitches) See page 138 for
national parks' booking offices and campsite fees. On
arrival in this area, campers are supposed to stop
and sign in at the smart warden's office which is
about 3.5km southeast of the campsite, immediately
next to Xakanaxa airstrip (✪ XAKAIR 19°11.778'S;
23°26.342'E), but in practice the office is often
unmanned. If you arrive from North Gate, you'll pass
this on your right; if you're coming from Third
Bridge or South Gate then follow the signs to North
Gate and watch for it on your left as you start to
drive east. (Don't confuse this airstrip with a disused
strip that's about 1km west of the new one.)

Lying on the east side of Camp Okuti, Xakanaxa
Campsite stretches along this tip of the Mopane
Tongue, almost adjacent to Xakanaxa Boat Station.
Its roughly marked pitches, some only just off the

dirt road (though there's no traffic to speak of), blend into one long camping area lining the river. The large ablution block was one of the cleanest we came across on our last visit, with 2 toilets, 2 showers and 2 basins for each sex. Water taps are dotted around the site, with incongruous concrete tables and benches, and braai stands of varying quality.

I've always loved these sites, and on my last visit in September the purple hanging flowers of the Kalahari appleleaf (*Lonchocarpus nelsii*) were in full force, reminding me of small jacaranda trees. However, as with Third Bridge, this is an area of particularly dense game, so always remain vigilant as you move about the campsite, making sure that you keep your eyes out for animals at all times.

⋏ Third Bridge Campsite (7 pitches) See page 138 for national parks' booking offices and campsite fees. Third Bridge (✪ 3BRIDG 19°14.368'S; 23°21.430'E) is about 8km in a straight line from Xakanaxa Campsite, although by road it's about 18km, depending on the route used. Despite their relative proximity, if you're camping in the area for 4–5 nights, then ideally try to split these between the 2 sites. Third Bridge is well located for visiting Mboma Island, and is a more open site, with plenty of tree shade. It's also rather more private, with fewer vehicles around, and is certainly my favourite site in Moremi.

Approaching from Xakanaxa you'll come to a fairly new wooden office, raised off the ground and surmounted by a radio mast. In theory, you stop here to sign in before proceeding slowly over the pole bridge; in practice, it's hardly ever manned. You'll see that the water's crystal-clear as it passes over the sandy bottom of the narrow waterway, and people used to bathe here often, but despite the apparently impenetrable stands of papyrus, there have been regular attacks by crocodiles; hence the plethora of notices warning you against swimming.

This site is sprawling, with pitches spread out across 2 almost distinct areas. It's notable for some attractive large fever-berry trees (*Croton megalobotrys*) and a particularly fine sausage tree (*Kigelia africana*). At its eastern end you'll find a small thatched ablution block, with 2 flush toilets and 2 showers for each sex. Alongside are a couple of wood-fired 'Rhodesian' boilers and a water tower – if you need hot water, you'll probably have to collect firewood, build a fire and heat it for yourself.

Specialities of this site include a troop of very cheeky baboons, who have developed stealing food into a form of sport – and they usually win. So what's good practice anywhere is absolutely vital here: lock everything away when you're not using it, or it'll be stolen. The site has a 'no rubbish' policy, and all refuse must be taken away. When we last stayed, the place was deserted, with not a baboon in sight, but visitors lunching here earlier in the day were pestered to such an extent that they returned to Xakanaxa, although not before an entire pack of cappuccino had been devoured.

What to see and do Until very recently all self-drive visitors ever did here was go on their own game drives, or perhaps take a boat trip for a few hours from one of the lodges. Recently more organised water activities have started to become available, and seem likely to become very popular in time.

Self-drive There's a lot of exploring to do in this area, which is veined with game-viewing loops and tracks. So take your time. Drive around slowly, and stop frequently. There are a number of specific areas that you might aim for, or just end up at:

Floodplain roads The network of tracks to the west of the main track between Xakanaxa and Third Bridge are probably the most rewarding in Moremi for game. Many are also very beautiful.

Goaxhlo Island and Pan Also known as Dead Tree Island, you'll recognise it by the number of skeletal trees that surround the pan of open water. Like those at Savuti, these were killed by drowning – when the channels changed and inundated the area. Most are mopane trees, and because of their resistance to termites, and semi-submerged state, they're decomposing very, very slowly indeed. This is quite an eerie sight, and photographers will find plenty to inspire them, especially if there are any animals present. Keep a particular lookout for the graceful pink spoonbills which breed here.

Dobetsaa Pans Take a left in a southerly direction, perhaps 1km after crossing Fourth Bridge on the way to Third Bridge, and you'll find a short loop leading down past a few very scenic pans. Veronica Roodt comments that this is 'one of the few places in Moremi where the African skimmer can be seen'. But even without the skimmers it's a good birdwatching spot with some very open pans.

Mboma Island West of Third Bridge is a large, long island, circled by a loop road which stretches for about 50km around it. There's a spur to this at the north end, and a short cut back to Third Bridge halfway round. It's worth spending a day here, as Mboma's environments are varied and beautiful, though different from the floodplain loops nearer to Xakanaxa. I've had great sightings of cheetah on the northern side of the island, and the south is said to be a popular haunt of buffalo herds.

Boat trips I'd strongly recommend that you take at least one trip by boat or mokoro on to the lagoons and waterways of Moremi. It's certainly worth the cost, unless you're due to be going on to a camp with water-based activities. But remember that boat fuel is costly to buy and transport, and you're in a very remote location, so these trips aren't cheap.

Two boat stations in the immediate vicinity hold the exclusive rights to take boats on to the lagoon. This exclusivity is in part to help prevent the spread of *Salvinia molesta*, or Kariba weed, an invasive plant that is posing a serious threat to Botswana's waterways. You'll need a hat, suncream and drinks, but little else except of course a camera. It is safe to leave a vehicle parked at either place.

Xakanaxa Boat Station (⊕ 19°13.98'S, 23°22.247'E). Literally adjacent to the campsite at Xakanaxa, this new enterprise (P Bag 41, Maun; e nm@info.bw; open 08.00, last departure 17.30) offers trips on to the lagoon in shallow, 8- and 12-seater aluminium boats for P240/US$55/£30 or P250/US$60/£35 per hr respectively. If you ask around at the campsite, you may well find someone to share a boat, thus cutting costs.

All the drivers are qualified guides, in as much as they can name the various birds and plants that you'll see, but their understanding of what you want may not tie up with yours. For this reason, do explain your objectives clearly before you set out, or you may find yourself being driven at breakneck speed from one side of the lagoon to the other, watching a hastily named bird rise up in fright at the approaching roar of the engine, or veering away from the occasional pod of hippo. And do ask questions – your driver may well know the answers.

There's little or no shade on the boats, so the best times to venture on to the lagoon are early morning or late afternoon, culminating in sunset over the lake. A couple of hours is really the ideal; less than that and it'll seem rushed so you'll miss out on the gentle beauty of the place. In theory there's no need to book, but the number of boats is limited so it makes sense to give them advance warning.

Mboma Boat Station Kgori Safaris, page 170. The more established of Moremi's boat stations is at the far northwest tip of Mboma Island, about an hour's drive (15km) from Third Bridge, or 3 hours (63km) from South Gate. The turn-off from the main loop road is at ⊕ MBOMAT 19°1.574'S; 23°17.126'E, with the station about 1.5km west of there. Cold drinks are available here (from P5 for water to P9 for beer) but nothing else, so be sure to bring anything else you may need, including a hat and suncream.

A 9-seater motorboat and driver can be hired for P240 per hr, or P1,250 for a full day. For a more leisurely trip, you can go out on a mokoro, with an experienced poler, for P100 per hr (for 2 people), or P430 per day. The longer trips usually leave at around 08.00, returning at about 15.00, sometimes stopping for lunch (bring your own) on one of the islands on the lagoon. Although in theory you can just turn up, it's not advisable, since if the polers are running a camping trip there may be no-one available to take out day visitors.

Overnight camping trips by motorboat can be organised in advance to 3 nearby islands: Gcodikwe 1, Gcodikwe 2 and Xhobega. These are in the area of the Gcodikwe and Xhobega lagoons, just northwest of Mboma Island; see below for a description of the Gcodikwe Lagoon with its heronries. Such trips can be fully catered, or you can bring in all your own equipment and food. You cannot, yet, stay overnight on islands as part of a mokoro trip as the water is too deep to reach any of the the the designated islands for camping. For the most part, mokoro trips explore the floodplains just off Mboma Island, on the southeastern side of the boat station.

Gcodikwe Lagoon Gcodikwe Lagoon (⊕ GCODIK 19°09.731'S; 23°14.507'E) is one of the Okavango's largest and most famous lagoons. This is a huge, oxbow lagoon that's now almost circular and has several large tree-islands in it. It is only reachable by boat. Xakanaxa is 18km away, or about 90 mins by boat. It is perhaps best visited from one of the lodges just outside of the park, the best being Kwara (6km northeast), Shinde (11km northwest) or Camp Okavango (15km west) — though you can double all these 'straight-line' distances to allow for meandering through the waterways.

These 'islands' are made up mainly of water fig trees and a little papyrus growing in shallow water.

Over the millennia these have accumulated a mass of bird guano and detritus under them to raise their levels and grow. Now they're large, but still isolated from any predators that are not aquatic. Hence they've become a vital breeding ground for the Okavango's waterbirds. Thousands of birds come to this heronry to breed, including herons, egrets, storks, ibises, cormorants and many others. Most of the nest-building activity starts around August, and breeding seems to be timed so that the chicks hatch around October and November, when water levels are low and thus the birds find fish easiest to catch. Certainly when I last visited in late February, there were only a few birds around.

Watch carefully and you'll see that the larger, more robust species like marabou and yellow-billed-storks tend to nest in the canopy of the trees, while the smaller, more vulnerable species can be found within the trees. Also keep an eye out for water snakes and leguvaans, which come here in search of chicks.

Getting there and away
By air Virtually all of the visitors to the three lodges arrive and leave via Xakanaxa airstrip, which is easily linked with any of the other airstrips in the region.

By road
Driving from Xakanaxa to North Gate It's about 44km to drive directly from Xakanaxa to North Gate; just head east from Xakanaxa airstrip (⊕ XAKAIR 19°11.778'S; 23°26.342'E). See pages 252–3 for more comments on this route, and ask advice from the camp's office before you set off as sometimes this road is blocked by high water levels. If that's the case, then you have no choice but to go the long way around, via South Gate (see the routes given below).

Driving from Xakanaxa to South Gate Many would travel from Xakanaxa to South Gate via Third Bridge, using the route described in the next section, as the scenery's more varied and, in the dry season, I'd expect the game to be better — especially around the Mboma Island area.

However, if you do need the most direct route, then a track heads southeast from near the western end of Xakanaxa's airstrip, and takes about 42km to reach South Gate. The route is generally good, even when it's wet, apart from a number of clay pans which can be sticky.

Driving from Third Bridge to South Gate (Maqwee) I always find the tracks around Mboma Island confusing, but to reach South Gate you set off west on to Mboma Island from Third Bridge. Keep bearing left when the road forks and after 3–4km you'll be travelling south. The road then bends east, south and even west until you reach another pole bridge which is known, rather unimaginatively, as Second Bridge (⊕ 2BRIDG 19°17.003'S; 23°22.553'E).

Crossing this, you'll then head southeast towards another pole bridge referred to as (surprise!) First Bridge (⊕ 1BRIDG 19°17.099'S; 23°23.531'E). From here it's an uncomplicated drive southeast to South Gate, with the vast majority of the trip through mopane woodlands. If time is on your side, there's a short, easy loop off to the south of the road, about 12km before the gate; it's clearly marked on Veronica Roodt's map of Moremi (see *Appendix 3, Further Information*). Characterised by flat, open plains, dotted with anthills and small pans, this is a great place to look out for storks, with large numbers of marabou in particular when we visited at the end of the dry season. Don't worry if you miss the connection with the main road at Xini Lagoon, which isn't at all clear on the ground when it's dry; the track links up almost seamlessly with the main road to South Gate, and the woodland landscape, just a couple of kilometres further on.

SOUTH (MAQWEE) GATE South Gate (⊕ SOGATE 19°25.548'S; 23°38.733'E), also known as Maqwee Gate, is usually treated as a transit stop by most visitors as it's in the midst of fairly unexciting mopane forest. Camp amongst the trees; there are toilets, showers and water here.

Having described it as unexciting, this may just be my failure to really get to know the area well. I've only stayed here for three individual nights, one during each of three different trips (always at the start or the end of a trip across Chobe and Moremi). However on one of those occasions, just as I was getting up, about half a dozen wild dogs gently jogged through the camp and into the forest. I don't think our roof tent has ever been packed away so rapidly – but try as we might, tracking them was a waste of time, with park rules forbidding off-road driving in Moremi!

On another trip I found a whole pack of wild dogs lounging in the road a few kilometres south of South Gate, in the NG33/34 concession area. They posed for photographs just a few metres from my vehicle for 20 minutes or so – totally unconcerned with our presence. So perhaps, especially in the earlier months of the year, South Gate warrants a closer look and more than just an overnight stop.

Orientation The geography of South Gate is very straightforward. There are no game-viewing loops as such, just five clear roads: one to Maun via the veterinary checkpoint, another to North Gate, one to Third Bridge which stays close to the southern side of the Mopane Tongue, and a fourth to Xakanaxa which cuts through the heart of the Tongue. The fifth, less frequently used, takes you to Santawani (for details of the concession, and the community-owned Santawani Lodge, see *Chapter 13*, pages 322–3).

Flora and fauna highlights
Flora Around South Gate the trees are almost all mopane (*Colophospermum mopane*), with their distinctive butterfly-shaped leaves. Tall, undamaged specimens can reach 18m in height, when they're known as 'cathedral' mopane for their gracefully arching branches. In neighbouring areas, where the nutrients are not as plentiful or the trees have been damaged by elephants, this same species grows much lower – and is known as 'stunted mopane'. In both you'll find their leaves hanging down and tending to fold together during the heat of the day, leaving little shade underneath.

This tremendously successful tree is one of the commonest species in the hot, dry areas of the subcontinent. It's notable for its tolerance of poorly drained, alkaline soils – and often occurs in areas where there's a lot of clay. Driving in mopane country during the rainy season usually involves negotiating lots of sticky, clay-filled mud-holes.

For the camper, the mopane wood is a dark-reddish colour, hard, heavy and termite-resistant. Thus even long-dead pieces won't have been completely eaten by termites. It burns exceedingly well, smelling sweetly and producing lots of heat, so think of collecting some firewood if you're passing through here on the way to

Xakanaxa or Third Bridge. (Turn each piece over, looking under it carefully for snakes and scorpions, before picking it up.)

Fauna With relatively dense forests this area can seem devoid of wildlife. But don't be mistaken; it isn't. Because the soil in mopane forest areas is often very poorly drained, it's dotted with small pans – temporary shallow ponds – during and shortly after the rains. This allows most of the big game species to leave the over-populated areas beside the watercourses and disappear into these huge areas of forests.

Elephant, zebra, impala, kudu, tsessebe, common duiker, bushbuck, steenbok, eland, roan warthog, baboon and vervet monkey can all be found here, as can lion, leopard, cheetah, spotted hyena, wild dog and many of the smaller mammals. But you will have to look much harder here for them than on the open floodplains and beside the watercourses where they congregate during the dry season.

What you are guaranteed to see here at any time of year are lots of bush squirrels (*Paraxerus cepapi*), which are so common in mopane woodlands that they're often known as 'mopane squirrels'. See *Appendix 1, Wildlife Guide*, page 488, for more details.

Birdlife The high density of small rodents in mopane woodlands, especially tree squirrels, means that it's a good place for small raptors which hunt from perches (rather than the air). These include barn owls, smaller hawks and kestrels, and even martial eagles.

Meanwhile two very common species here are the small, black-and-white Arnot's chat, which appear in pairs or small groups, often hopping about the ground or lower branches in search of small insects – memorably described by a friend on first sight as 'little flying zebras'. There's also the red-billed hornbill, which seems to be everywhere with it's heavy flap-flap-flap . . . glide. . . flap-flap-flap . . . glide . . . style of flight. Remember Rowan Atkinson's performance as the hornbill in Walt Disney's *The Lion King* and you'll never be able to watch one again without smiling.

Where to stay There's only one place to stay:

⋀ South Gate Campsite (7 pitches, 1 reserve) Contact the national park's booking office (see page 138). Immediately next to the nark gate, this campsite has the basic facilities that are a hallmark of Botswana's parks, though one of the 2 ablution blocks was newly built in May 2005. Each block has a shower and a toilet each for ladies and gents; if hot water's a necessity, there's a DIY Rhodesian boiler. Shade is provided by stands of mopane trees, with the constant buzz of cicadas for company, and each pitch has its own concrete table and benches. *P30 pp.*

Getting there and away
From South Gate (Maqwee) to Third Bridge Take the most westerly exit from the campsite and the route is very easy. After about 24km you'll pass a right turn, marked by an old green cement block. One side of this notes that Mboma and Third Bridge are off to the left. There are no indications where the right turn goes, though it actually leads around the east side of the Bodumatau Lagoon.

Keeping on the main road (to the left), you'll then pass, in order, First Bridge (⊕ 1BRIDG 19°17.099'S; 23°23.531'E) and Second Bridge (⊕ 2BRIDG 19°17.003'S; 23°22.553'E), before finally reaching the campsite at Third Bridge (⊕ 3BRIDG 19°14.368'S; 23°21.430'E).

From South Gate to Xakanaxa Usually the best route is to follow the directions to Third Bridge, above, then continue southwest to Fourth Bridge (⊕ 4BRIDG

19°15.128'S; 23°24.173'E), which at the end of 2005 was in very poor repair, although in the dry season it's possible to drive to the side. From there proceed north, keeping slightly east to Xakanaxa airstrip (✪ XAKAIR 19°11.778'S; 23°26.342'E), where you turn west. You can navigate through this labyrinth of game-viewing loops using Veronica Roodt's map, or by sticking to the main track, setting your GPS for Xakanaxa, and then keeping slightly east of the direct-line direction.

However, if it's late in the dry season and you've plenty of time, then you may want to take a detour around the Bodumatau Lagoon, which avoids Third Bridge completely. (This track is marked as 'seasonal' on most maps, and is much less reliable than the main track, especially when wet.) In that case, take the right turn at the green concrete block that is about 24km from South Gate. It's 16km to the Bodumatau Bridge from here, then a further 13km to Fourth Bridge.

One local operator refers to the first part of this road after the green concrete block as 'Elephant Alley', for its winding road through dense mopane is often frequented by elephants. Drive carefully.

From South Gate to North Gate (Khwai) A very direct, straight road leads about 30km north-northeast from South Gate to North Gate (✪ NOGATE 19°10.261'S; 23°45.055'E). There are no game-viewing loops off this road.

From South Gate to Maun Leaving the park from South Gate, after a few hundred metres there's a well-signposted fork: left for the main road directly to Maun, right to Santawani Lodge in NG33 (see pages 322–3) and the Wild Dog Research station near Chitabe (see page 323), then continuing south to Maun.

PAPYRUS

The graceful, feathery papyrus is a giant sedge which dominates large areas of the Okavango. It grows in areas of permanent swamp in thick floating mats, unmistakable for its feather-duster heads that sway in the breeze. At first it's perhaps surprising that such vigorous, lush, emerald-green vegetation thrives here with apparently few nutrients available from the clear water or the poor Kalahari sands beneath.

The secret lies in a number of remarkable adaptations. Firstly, papyri have nitrogenous bacteria between their scale-leaves which 'fix' nitrogen from the air into a form that the plants can use. Secondly they photosynthesise using a special 'carbon-4' pathway, thus making more efficient use of the sun's energy than most plants.

With these adaptations, plus water and sunshine, papyri are amongst the fastest-growing plants in the world. You'll quickly see another factor that helps them here if you cut a stem of papyrus (preferably a dying one!). Observe that although thick and strong, it's very light. So the plant is committing relatively little energy or materials to raise such a tall, strong stem.

In fact papyri store most of their energy in long, thick rhizomes which form part of the tangled floating mat. From this base, their shoots can rise up to about 2.5m high, and yet typically have a life cycle of only three months. Within this they grow swiftly to maturity, flower and die – leaving a tangle of brown, dead stems near water level. The nutrients from these old stems are withdrawn back into the rhizome, ready to power the birth of another shoot. This rapid recycling of nutrients is another of the keys to the plant's lush, vigorous growth.

LIFE IN PAPYRUS SWAMPS

Papyrus swamps are in many ways a difficult habitat. Below the waterline, little light penetrates the floating mat of dead, tangled stems and rhizomes. The constant decomposition of dead papyrus stems mean much organic debris, and water which is acidic and low in oxygen. With no light, there's no chance for algae or any other higher plantlife.

Above the waterline the stems form a dense, tangled mass. The stems themselves are fibrous, difficult to digest and very nutrient-poor. Combined with a floating base that can't support any weight, this makes life here almost impossible for most larger animals. Only the specially adapted sitatunga antelope is at home here.

For animals as small as rats and mice, the situation isn't so bad. They don't generally stay in the papyrus beds, but they are light enough to make forays there, supported by the floating mat and individual stems. Greater cane rats are the largest of these, growing up to about 80cm on a diet of papyrus shoots, reeds and other vegetation. Although they swim well, they normally live in small family groups in burrows on permanent dry land, leaving these at night to forage in the reedbeds and papyrus.

A few birds also use the papyrus for shelter and nesting, including several species of weavers, the red-shouldered widow and red bishop bird – which will tear the feathery umbels of the papyrus as material to weave their intricate nests. Many more will come into papyrus areas to hunt for fish or insects, and there will be very few trips here when you won't see at least a few malachite and pied kingfishers.

Keeping left on the main road, you should keep looking out for wildlife. I drove this way in May 1993, and about 14km from the gate the road was virtually blocked by a large pack of lazy wild dogs wandering about the road, showing little interest in our vehicle. There are several areas of sandy thornveld shortly after the gate, with some stunning, tall old camelthorn trees (*Acacia erioloba*), which are a particular favourite of the local giraffe. Within these sandier areas, the road is so wide that during the rains it can seem like a series of small lakes. Although the centres of these tend to be deeper than the edges, they are generally firm, whereas the shallower edges can be much more muddy.

To the right of this road is a non-hunting area, NG33, whilst to the left is an area managed by the community, NG34. Both are good wildlife areas, but because the land and the wildlife are managed, technically the road you are on is a 'transit route', and you are not allowed to stop and camp.

About 32km from South Gate you join the main road from Chobe National Park to Maun. Bear right for Maun or double back left for Sankuyo Village and Chobe National Park. (This road north to Chobe is referred to as 'the Mababe Road' on the signpost.) The nearest campsite is probably at Mankwe Bush Lodge (see page 178) in NG45, just north of Sankuyo Village, or the community campsite at Kaziikini (see page 174).

Shortly after that junction, about 34km from South Gate, you may need to stop to pass through the veterinary cordon fence.

After a further 17km you'll reach the sizeable village of **Shorobe** (see pages 173–4). Roadside vendors sell cold drinks, and there's a craft studio on the east side of the road, but little else to tempt the passing traveller. From here the road to Maun is tarred, passing the University of Botswana. The total journey from South Gate to the Engen garage, which is the first fuel station in Maun, is about 90km.

12

Aside from the Mopane Tongue, the only way to access any of the rest of Moremi is from one of the small private safari camps with access only by air. There are three main camps within Moremi: Mombo and Chief's Camp at the north end of Chief's Island, and Xigera right on the western edge. These are described below. However, there are a number of camps, such as those in NG19 near North Gate, which stand just outside the edge of the park, but conduct many of their activities within the park. These include the camps in NG21 (Camp Okavango, Shindi and Xugana – see pages 280–4) and the old camps along the south end of the Boro River in NG27B (Oddballs Camp, Delta Camp, Gunn's Camp, Semetsi and Eagle Island – see pages 303–9).

Because these two areas are very different I'll subdivide this concession into two sections: one covering Xigera's area, and the other concentrating on Mombo and Chief's Camp.

XIGERA If you had to place a pin on the map in the centre of the Delta, you'd probably put it near to here. The Xigera (pronounced 'keejera') area is within the boundaries of Moremi Reserve, near its western border. Technically it's within Moremi's only private concession area, NG28.

Concession history Look at an old map of the Delta and you'll realise that the western boundary of Moremi used to be further east than it is now. Then the Xigera and Mombo areas were part of the NG28 concession and outside the park. Xigera was originally built in 1986 by Hennie and Angela Rawlinson, two well-known Maun residents, at a place that Hennie called 'Paradise Island'.

Then in 1992 Moremi was expanded westwards and northwards. This was done in order to bring under its protection all the major Okavango habitats, as until then none of the northern Delta's papyrus swamps or permanent wetlands had been included. This expansion swallowed up NG28, including the Xigera and Mombo areas. Thus these camps now occupy prime sites within Moremi Game Reserve.

The lease for Xigera expired in 1998, but the Rawlinsons got it back again for another 15 years. Between December 1999 and April 2000 the camp was completely demolished, and rebuilt from scratch a short distance away. It opened in May 2000.

Getting there and away Only pre-booked guests who fly in visit this area, and all the marketing, management and reservations for Xigera are done by Wilderness Safaris (see page 171 for details).

The airstrip serving the camps is located at ✦ XIGAIR 19°23.155'S; 22°44.618'E. Note that there's no practical dry-land access to Mombo, Chief's Camp or the nearby Nxabega from here. Driving here isn't an option.

When to visit Because the focus here is more on the environment and birdlife than game per se, this area can be visited any time of the year – although the tiny Zepa bushcamp is really not designed for rainy conditions, and so closes during the rains.

What to see and do motorboat trips and mokoro excursions have always been the main activities from Xigera; from Zepa only mekoro are usually possible. That said, Xigera's team has worked hard and in 2001 they located a good area for game drives, and have come up with a way of stationing vehicles on the larger islands there. So usually, water levels permitting, it's now possible to drive there too.

Thus from about May until October, whilst the water is high, you boat to the game-drive vehicles, and then drive from there. Then it's possible to do motorboat trips as well as mokoro trips directly from the camp.

However, between about November and May, the water level is lower and it's then possible to keep the vehicles near camp and drive directly from there, though the motorboats have to be stationed in deeper water a short distance north of camp, and are reached by mokoro.

Because the camp is within Moremi Reserve, night drives, fishing and off-road driving is not allowed. Short walks are conducted, but the guides are not allowed to carry rifles.

Flora and fauna The area around Xigera is one of the Delta's few truly deep-water experiences. (Jedibe, when it was open, used to deserve this accolade. It really was surrounded by apparently endless papyrus swamps, with only the odd island. Camp Okavango, Kwara, Xugana and Shinde could also lay claim to have deep-water experiences to some extent.)

Here at Xigera you're very close to the Jao River, which feeds the Boro and is one of the Okavango's major waterways.

Flora Spending nearly all of your time on the water, you're probably going to be particularly aware of the aquatic grasses and sedges. Of these the graceful, feathery papyri (*Cyperus papyrus*) are perhaps the most striking, and certainly one of the most interesting (see box page 262).

In shallower sections you'll also find large areas of common reeds (*Phragmites australis*), and the tall miscanthus grass (*Miscanthus junceus*). There are also a few lovely stands of pure water fern (*Thelypteris interrupta*) on the edges of some of the channels and lagoons.

On the islands you'll find the normal trees of the Delta, including a good number of confetti trees (*Gynmosporia senegalensis*). The English name for these comes from the small, scented white flowers which come out around May–June, and then fall underneath the tree in large enough quantities to be scooped up.

Fauna This area isn't a bad one for big game, though that's not why I'd go to Xigera. If you're staying at Xigera then remember that the bridge across the channel, linking the camp on one island with the main vehicle track to the airstrip on the other, isn't only used by people. Many other animals find it convenient, especially at night. Spotted hyenas cross it almost religiously every night, lion regularly and leopard occasionally too. Monkeys and baboons play on it during the day. Look underneath at the fish in the clear water and you may even see the odd spotted-necked otter fishing for bream.

On the larger island elephants are often in evidence, and when I was last here the floodplain beyond my tent's veranda was dotted with lechwe. Elephant are often around, sometimes in substantial herds of 50 or so, and on game drives you've a good chance of spotting impala and tsessebe.

As you'd expect for the environment, the Xigera area has one of the highest densities of sitatunga antelope in the Delta. These lovely creatures are notoriously difficult to spot, but gliding around silently in a mokoro probably offers you the best chance possible – just keep yours eyes wide open and your mouth tightly shut!

On one occasion here recently, an eminent guide was leading a number of mekoro, trying to get as close as possible to a sitatunga. When the antelope made a break to get away, it jumped directly over one of the mekoro.

Birdlife Given the environment of large areas of permanent papyrus and swamp vegetation, plus some islands, this is a good camp for seeking the more water-dependent birds in the Delta.

Notable amongst these are the African skimmers, which usually arrive at Xigera Lagoon around September or October. About 20 pairs of these incredible birds have been noted here in recent years; if they're new to you then take a few moments to watch one of them through binoculars. You'll see it using the most amazing flying skills to place its lower mandible in the lagoon at a fixed depth, and steadily scythe through the water. Then periodically you see the bill snap shut with its catch of an unfortunate small fish. This is compulsive viewing, even if you never normally look at anything smaller than a lion; an incredible fishing technique.

Whilst floating around you can expect to see assorted kingfishers, herons, egrets and other waterbirds. Included in this list, if you're lucky, will be purple (but not lesser) gallinules, lesser jacanas, moorhens, lesser moorhens and green-backed herons. It should be a good area for bitterns (including the dwarf and little), though I've never seen one here.

Other unusual birds that enthusiastic ornithologists should look out for include chirping cisticolas, tawny-flanked prinias and palm swifts, all of which are regularly sighted here.

Where to stay
Although there are two camps here, Zepa is a tiny, almost temporary camp that is usually visited only as part of a set itinerary. For most visitors, Xigera is the only option here. Both camps are run by Wilderness Safaris (see page 171).

Xigera (10 tents). Sited on a new location (⊕ XIGERA 19°23.647'S; 23°45.535'E) on Paradise Island, Xigera Camp opened in April 2000. If you've never been to the Delta, then simply conjure up an image of a luxurious safari camp in the heart of the swamps, enveloped by a green, tropical lushness. You've probably come close to visualising Xigera.

All of Xigera's tents are raised a few metres above the island floor on wooden decks. These are widely spread out along one fringe of the island, each looking eastwards, past the easy chairs and table on the veranda and on to a small lagoon that seems to attract good game. These tents are all linked together, and to the central hub of a lounge and dining room area, by a total of about 800m of raised boardwalks.

The tented rooms themselves are part wood, part canvas. The front is made of wood, with 2 large sliding doors and huge gauze windows. It's easy to really open up for good views and airflow, the latter assisted by an efficient, free-standing, antique-style electric fan.

Inside, the dbl or twin beds are enclosed in a walk-in mosquito net, with a large trunk and easy chairs. Behind the bed is a bamboo screen and towel rack, a dressing table, twin basins, an inside

flush toilet and separate shower. Through the tent's rear door is a blissful outdoor shower.

The camp's generator charges batteries, which supply 220V electricity to the chalets constantly and even power the (very efficient) electric showers.

Overlooking a perennial channel, and the footbridge across it, is the camp's comfortable thatched dining room, bar and exceedingly cozy lounge. Close by, the camp has a small curio shop selling materials, jewellery, postcards, film, T-shirts and a few hats. There's also a small plunge pool, filled with water pumped from the Delta. This may seem superfluous in such an environment, though clearly litigious-minded visitors aren't encouraged to find 'safe' places to swim in the Delta itself!

Like Jao, Xigera feels like one of the Delta's most tropical, slow and romantic camps. It offers a great water experience, though I'd suggest that most visitors spend only 2 nights here, rather than 3 or 4 that might be the norm at a camp with more emphasis on game activities.

From US$470/655 pp sharing/sgl low season to US$785/970 high season, inc all meals, activities, park fees, laundry, most drinks; exc transfers. Open all year.

MOMBO AND CHIEF'S CAMP Mombo and Chief's share a concession within Moremi, but they are about 25km apart – which is a long way in the Okavango.

Hence, unless they want to cross paths, you'll never normally see vehicles from one camp in the other camp.

Concession history Since the mid-1980s the rights to run Mombo were owned by Jao Safaris (now defunct). They sub-leased this to many safari companies including Ker & Downey, Bonadventure (who were one of the main tour agencies when I first visited Maun in 1987) and, lastly, Wilderness Safaris. During this time, and especially the last few years, it gained a first-class reputation for game, helped by an exceedingly large and successful pack of wild dogs.

When Jao Safaris' lease expired in 1998, there was clearly going to be very stiff competition for this area. Because it was recognised as such a prime area, the Land Board (ie: the government body responsible) allowed for two sites to be put up for tender, at opposite ends of the concession. Some 29 companies entered. There was tremendous competition: the best proposal and overall management plan would win.

Eventually two bids were accepted, one from Wilderness Safaris and another from A&K (whose Botswana operations have recently become Sanctuary Lodges). Each needed to promise the government the highest possible revenue, as well as the best (that is, most sustainable and productive) management plan.

To achieve this, they both arrived at the obvious solution: each built one of the country's most upmarket camps, and attached an appropriately high price tag to it. It was the only way to make financial sense with such high concession fees.

Thus the new, much more luxurious Mombo came into being, near the old Mombo site, and Chief's Camp was built south of that, on the northwestern side of Chief's Island. The tender process had maximised the government's revenues, and pushed part of the area's tourism a step further upmarket.

Getting there and away Only pre-booked guests flying in visit this area, as there is no practical dry-land access to Chief's Island. Driving here isn't an option. Each camp has its own airstrip on Chief's Island; Mombo's airstrip is at ✪ MOMBOA 19°12.680'S; 22°47.510'E.

When to visit Because the focus here is firmly on game viewing, the dry season is the obvious time to visit. That's when the game is at its most visible and most dense. That said, from July to October the camps (especially Mombo) have substantial 'high-season supplements', which can make the costs at other times of the year seem very attractive.

If you decide to come at a less popular, and cheaper, time then remember that Chief's Island is a large, permanent island with its own large, permanent population of game. Thus you'll still see some first-rate game even if the game viewing isn't quite as good as it would have been during October.

What to see and do Game drives are the main activity here, though both camps are constricted to some extent by the park's rules. Night drives, fishing and off-road driving are not allowed – though the camps have been campaigning to have these rules softened. Short 'nature walks' are conducted, although these are restricted as the guides are not allowed to carry rifles under the park's current rules.

In addition to drives, Chief's Camp also offers mokoro trips. When the floods arrive, up to 70% of Chief's Camp's network of roads becomes covered in water, and mokoro trips can start off right at the lodge.

Flora and fauna highlights
Flora The environments found here aren't unique in the Delta, but they are old,

established, and have long been protected – and so are basically pristine and undisturbed.

Perhaps the most interesting, and certainly the most photogenic, habitats here are the shallow floodplains which surround the northern end of Chief's Island. (It's such a distinctive landscape that an image of it has remained deeply ingrained in my mind since my first visit here, in the mid-1990s.)

Looking at the whole Delta, you'll realise that this area is very close to the permanent swamps at the base of the Panhandle. Because of this, the floods here are more regular and predictable than they are lower down the Delta. This regular seasonal flooding has created a very photogenic environment of short-grass plains, amongst which are a number of tiny islands fringed by dense, feathery stands of wild date palms (*Phoenix reclinata*). For me, this is the quintessential Delta landscape – and it's sufficiently open to be excellent for game viewing.

(Away from the Okavango Delta, the only place that I've seen which is similar to this in southern Africa is the Busanga Plains of northern Kafue, in Zambia. Again, these are consistently flooded every year, and have very little disturbance.)

Go back on to the dry land of Chief's Island and you'll find a range of more familiar landscapes and floral communities. Mopane woodlands are dominant across much of the island, with some areas of impressive, tall 'cathedral' mopane (*Colophospermum mopane*), often a popular retreat for game during wetter months.

Running through this you'll find lines of Kalahari sandveld, reflecting the locations of old, long-dry watercourses. Here you will see sand-loving species like the silver cluster-leaf (*Terminalia sericea*), the Kalahari appleleaf (*Lonchocarpus nelsii*), perhaps some camelthorn (*Acacia erioloba*) and umbrella thorns (*Acacias tortilis*), and the odd leadwood tree (*Combretum imberbe*).

Where the land meets the water, there are bands of classic riverine forest including fine specimens of raintree (*Lonchocarpus capassa*), sausage tree (*Kigelia africana*), jackalberry (*Diospyros mespiliformis*), African mangosteen (*Garcinia livingstonei*), figs (mostly *Ficus sycomorus*) and some wild date palms (*Phoenix reclinata*). Throughout the area's forests you'll occasionally find huge old baobab trees (*Adansonia digitata*) – which probably have lived long enough to see the environment change around them!

Fauna The game in this area is at least as dense as anywhere else in the Okavango (or indeed the subcontinent), and because the area's a private one, the game viewing is just about the best you'll find in southern Africa. It's dense, varied, and good sightings of predators are virtually guaranteed.

See *Flora and fauna* at the start of this chapter for more extensive comments on Moremi as a whole; in this particular area impala, tsessebe, zebra and giraffe are usually the most numerous of the larger herbivores – although warthogs are remarkably common. (So numerous that they have become a major prey species for both lion and leopard.) Elephant and buffalo are resident here in good numbers, with more individual animals seen during the rains, and generally larger herds recorded as the dry season progresses.

Herds of red lechwe are common in the flooded areas when the water's high, but they rarely venture into the drier parts of the reserve. Kudu and wildebeest also occur, as do the occasional reedbuck and steenbok; sable and roan are usually never seen here.

Though the majority of the Delta's usual line-up of nocturnal animals do occur, without taking night drives most are difficult to spot. The exception seems to be honey badgers, porcupines and spring hares which are sometimes seen around the camps at night.

The area has a justified, first-class reputation for excellent sightings of all the major predators. Spotted hyena are probably the most successful large carnivore in the area, though lion are also very common – as they are in many areas of the Delta.

What's less usual is the thriving permanent cheetah population here. The sprinkling of slightly raised date palm islands and termite hills make ideal look-out posts, suiting the cheetah's hunting style perfectly. The area's open environment makes sightings of cheetah relatively frequent. I've a recent report of one sizeable pair of brothers taking sub-adult zebra and wildebeest – bigger prey than might normally be expected.

As an aside, long-standing guides comment that there were a lot more cheetahs in the Mombo area until a recent demise in the dominance of the lion and a rise in the fortunes of the hyena. This is really just a small-scale example of the constant ebb and flow of power struggles in the animal kingdom – and cheetah sightings here are still much better than in most other areas of the Delta, or indeed southern Africa!

There are good numbers of leopard around – although their appearances during the day are relatively limited. Originally Mombo, and this area, built its reputation on some of Africa's best sightings of wild dog – largely because of a very successful pack of about 40 dogs (which is a very large size for a pack) that denned here for several years in the mid-1990s. With this pack in residence, visitors were virtually guaranteed amazing sightings, and the area's dry open floodplains proved marvellous for following the animals as they hunted.

Now that pack has broken up, as is the usual process when the alpha female dies. Thus while the wild dog sightings are as good as most of the areas in the eastern Delta, they're not better as there's no sizeable pack in regular residence. That said, the fact remains that if you do see dogs here, the floodplain areas are the perfect place to be able to follow them.

Finally, a real good news story for this area, and the Delta as a whole. Black and white rhino used to occur here naturally, but by the 1980s they had been exterminated by poaching. At last, on 9 November 2001, the first white rhino were brought back into this area. Five of them were set free to roam, and have since settled down well on Chief's Island. This has been so successful that there are plans to bring in more, and in time it's likely that black rhino will also be reintroduced to the area.

Birdlife At the heart of the Delta, and with a large and diverse area of dry land and floodplains, this area of Moremi gets periodic visits from virtually all of the birds in the Delta, so singling out a few to mention here is inevitably a flawed process.

However, top of the list for a special mention are the vultures, attracted by the game densities and predator activity. Most numerous are the white-backed, hooded and lappet-faced vultures – though you'll also find a surprising number of white-headed vultures. Palm-nut vultures occur here (usually frequenting the real fan palms) though they're not common.

Also attracted by the game, both kinds of oxpecker are present here – though yellow-billed (which feed on the backs of hippos) seem more common than the red-billed variety.

As happens everywhere in the Delta, when the waters recede, isolated pools of fish are left behind. As these gradually dry up the fish become more and more concentrated, attracting the most amazing numbers of predatory birds. Pick the right day (usually one between about May and October) and the right pool, and you'll be entertained for hours by large concentrations of pelicans, saddle-billed storks, marabou storks, black egrets, grey and Goliath herons to name but a few. It's an amazing sight. In other receding pools you'll find congregations of pelicans or, in those which aren't so frantic, painted snipes can be seen if you look hard (or have a good guide!).

The short-grass floodplains here suit wattled cranes, which are often found in numbers, and on the drier plains watch for secretary birds and kori bustards. The latter occasionally have carmine bee-eaters using their backs as perches. In plains with longer grass you may be able to spot an African crake, while ostriches are very rarely seen (perhaps because there are too many large predators).

On the water look for pygmy geese and dwarf jacanas in the quieter areas, along with many species of more common waterbirds. There's often a good number of the relatively rare slaty egrets about too.

Where to stay

Both Mombo and Chief's are top-of-the-range camps in one of southern Africa's very best game areas. Both come at a high cost – though Chief's hasn't been around long enough to build up quite the same reputation that Mombo has. However, note that some safari purists contend that elements of the clientele who visit this camp are attracted more by the image of the camp rather than the reality of the game viewing, which can be to the detriment of the atmosphere at times.

Mombo (9 tents) Contact via Wilderness Safaris (see page 171). This is the flagship Wilderness Safaris camp in Botswana – one of their 4 'Premier' camps (the others are Jao, page 292; Vumbura Plains, page 288; and Kings Pool, page 229) and probably the most expensive photographic camp in Botswana.

It all stands on wooden decking raised high off the ground. The main dining area has, under a high thatched roof, a long polished wooden table for candlelit dinners. One side of this structure opens on to the decking outside, via roll-down grass blinds (used for rare bouts of inclement weather).

The adjacent lounge/bar overlooks wide floodplains and is furnished comfortably with hand-woven 'sea-grass' coffee-tables and colonial leather sofas. Next to this are the glass-fronted cases of a well-stocked small library, amidst easy chairs around a wooden Pygmy bed, imported from the Congo, which doubles for a coffee table. Behind the lounge is a large boma where traditional dinners are sometimes served, while in front on the decking is a campfire, surrounded by deck chairs, for after-dinner drinks. Near to the small plunge pool some loungers cluster in a patch of shade.

Mombo's 'tents' are very large. They're made of canvas, supported by wooden poles, and connected by raised wooden walkways. There are 5 to the east of the main area, and 4 to the west, plus Little Mombo (see below). The furthest, No 9, is the 'honeymoon tent', close to a small lounge that is used for private dinners. Each tent's large wooden door opens to reveal twin beds, or a dbl, surrounded by walk-in mosquito nets, a sofa, a

writing desk, 2 bedside tables with lamps, a free-standing electric fan and overhead fans. To one side the bathroom has a dbl indoor shower (2 shower heads and lots of space), free-standing twin sinks (the plumbing disguised by a criss-cross wooden lattice) and a rather magnificent mirror – 2m tall with a wide polished wooden frame. Underfoot is polished parquet, held together using dowels.

The zipped gauze panels at the front of each tent open on to a decked balcony, where a table, chairs and a lounger are shaded from the sun by the canvas roof. On one side is a thatched *sala*, or small gazebo, with a mattress and cushions, which makes a nice shady spot from which to watch game. That said, the area underneath the decking of the chalets themselves seems to be a popular evening spot for buffalo.

From US$1,330/1,580 pp sharing/sgl low season to US$1,510/1,760 high season, inc all meals, activities, park fees, laundry, most drinks; exc transfers. Open all year.

Little Mombo (3 tents). Continuing along the decking, past Mombo's tent No 9, you find its smaller sister camp, Little Mombo. This camp has only 3 tents and, although adjacent to the main camp, it operates as a separate entity. Its tents have the same design as those of its neighbour, and its main lounge/dining/bar area is similarly furnished, though smaller. Little Mombo has its own outdoor boma, small pool and communal *sala* – as well as individual ones for the rooms.

US$890/1,090 pp sharing/sgl Jul–Oct, US$490/620 Dec–Mar, US$695/895 Apr–Jun &

Nov, inc all meals, activities, park fees, laundry, most drinks; exc transfers. Open all year.

⌂ **Chief's Camp** (12 tents) Contact via Sanctuary Lodges (see page 172). Chief's Camp is about 25km from Mombo, just off the western side of Chief's Island. It is the pride of Sanctuary Lodges' operations in Botswana, and used extensively by A&K companies worldwide.

Chief's main area is raised on decking where its high thatch roof covers a large, open-plan area. This is dotted with expensive ethnic curios and the odd bookshelf, where there is a varied mix of interesting reading. Adjacent to this you'll find the lounge and a well-stocked bar, with wooden coffee table and weaved 'sea-grass' sofa, and a dining room with a number of tables. Here guests tend to dine with their own guide, who is generally allotted to you when you arrive (you tend to stick with the same guide and take all your drives with him/her). When last visited, Chief's food was good and imaginative, and accompanied with an impressive selection of wine.

Outside this dining/lounge area, an expanse of wooden decking acts as a veranda, where you can sit in the shade of large jackalberry (*Diospyros mespiliformis*) and marula (*Sclerocarya birrea*) trees. Slightly below this, a large (8m-long) swimming pool is surrounded by loungers and a small *sala*. Those with a passion for shopping might also seek out the efficient shop that sells T-shirts, film, books and some stylish curios.

Chief's secluded tents are slightly raised off the ground on decking. They are reached from a simple bush path, lit at night by electric hurricane lamps. Tents 1–7 are on the eastern side of the main area, the others on the west. All have private verandas overlooking the plains (which usually flood from around June to the end of August, when the water may come all the way up to the lodge).

Each tent has a wooden door and polished wood floor. Bedside the twin or dbl beds, adjustable aluminium lamps stand on the bedside tables. The décor is stylish and partly modern, partly ethnic — including masks made by the Teke people of Cameroon. But it's not at all rustic. In the tents you'll find a solid wardrobe, with roll-down canvas door, a couple of chairs and tables, a free-standing lamp and a ceiling fan, powered by 24hr electricity (110/220V).

The bathroom is adjacent to the main body of the tent, but feels different. It has proper partition walls and a brick shower cubicle with glass door, opposite which is a large glass mirror. On one side is a door leading out to a small open-air shower. The toilet is behind a wooden door, and there are twin washbasins, both with individual mirrors — completing the impression that this is the bathroom of a plush hotel rather than a safari camp.

From US$635 pp low season to US$650/845 pp sharing/sgl high season, inc all meals, activities, park fees, laundry, most drinks; exc transfers. Open all year.

13
Okavango Delta – Private Reserves around Moremi

In his book, *Lake Ngami and the River Okavango*, the Victorian-era explorer and trader Charles John Andersson wrote:

> On every side as far as the eye could see, lay stretched a sea of fresh water, in many places concealed from sight by a covering of reeds and rushes of every shade and hue; whilst numerous islands, spread over its whole surface, and adorned with rich vegetation, gave to the whole an indescribably beautiful appearance.

For modern visitors the Okavango Delta has lost none of its beauty. However, finding reliable information on the various areas from brochures can be as challenging as Andersson's expedition. This chapter aims to demystify these areas, and to identify some of the strengths and weaknesses of the areas and their camps.

It aims to cover all of the private reserves around the Okavango and the main camps within these. But before you read any of my comments, here are a few general observations on the chapter:

- I've covered the reserves in the order of their concession numbers, from NG12 to NG34.
- There are virtually no fences between these areas, so the game flows freely between them, and won't always be where I suggest it is.
- Remember that differences in environment and game can be as great within a reserve as they are between one reserve and its neighbour. Despite this some trends are evident, which I've tried to draw out.
- The marketing leaflets of the reserves usually claim that every animal/bird is found in their particular areas – particularly the 'sexy' ones like wild dogs and Pel's fishing owls! There is some truth in this, in that virtually all the animals/birds do occur in all the reserves. However, I've tried to get behind the spin with a realistic assessment of what you're most likely to see, and where you're most likely to see it. I've tried to make my comments reflect realistic probabilities, but they can't be definitive.
- I've made comments largely from my own first-hand experience, informed when in these areas by guides and experts. Occasionally, I have used reliable local sources. That said, I have not spent a year in each reserve, so my observations have been snapshots from the times that I've visited, augmented by comments from travellers sent by my travel company. They don't pretend to be comprehensive, systematic surveys, but I do believe that they're broadly representative.
- Under each reserve I've tried to cover the basics of the wildlife and the practicalities. This has necessitated some repetition, but it's a reflection of the fact that there are more similarities between the various reserves in the Delta than there are differences.

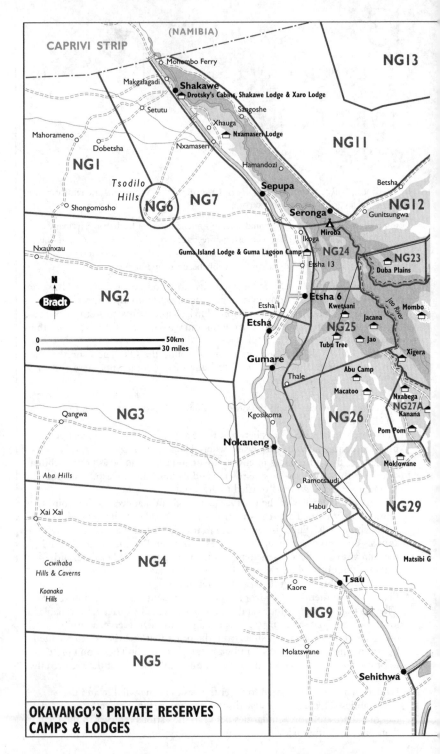

OKAVANGO'S PRIVATE RESERVES
CAMPS & LODGES

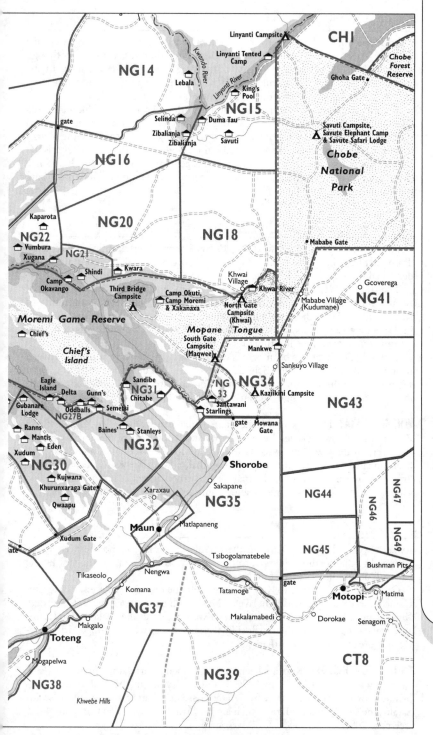

GUDIGWA (NG12)

Outside the buffalo fence, north of Vumbura and Duba Plains, the Magwegqana Spillway starts here in an environment similar to southeast Vumbura – though generally NG12's islands are bigger and its vegetation more established. In the south there is good game viewing and extensive mopane woodlands; last time I was in the area, two cheetah left Vumbura heading north to hunt in NG12.

Several villages stand on this concession's northern boundary, including Betsha (Betsaa), Eretsha (Eretsa), Kangara, Ganitsuga, Kombo and Gabamukuni. In 2003 this area received its first visitors, thanks to an exciting project to create the Delta's first upmarket, community-run 'cultural camp', Gudigwa. Sadly, soon after this the camp burned down in a bushfire, and the management and control of it have since been mired in confusion. It has not yet re-opened, but would be a very promising place to visit if it ever does.

KHWAI COMMUNITY CONCESSIONS (NG18 AND NG19)

On the southern edge of the small NG19 concession, where hunting is illegal, are Tsaro Elephant Lodge and Khwai River Lodge. For the sake of continuity, I've described these in the North Gate section, on pages 250–1 of *Chapter 12*.

The larger NG18 area, which stretches north to the Linyanti concession, east of Kwara and west of Chobe, is owned and managed by the small community of Khwai Village. Here the people have formed the Khwai Development Trust, and in 1999 they earned about P1.2 million (US$240,000) by auctioning off their hunting quota to various hunting organisations.

The only time that I've been here is when driving on the 'transit route' between Moremi and the Linyanti and Selinda reserves, which I describe briefly in *Chapter 11*, page 232. The interior of this concession appeared to be fairly monotonous mopane, but there were signs of game around.

WHERE TO STAY There two campsites here, which were to be called Xamotese and Zou, but may now be called Lechwe Camp and Tau Camp. Some details of these are given on their website (www.khwai.org) although this doesn't appear to have been updated for many years now. Failing that, contact the Khwai Development Trust (*Maun; www.khwai.org*). You may be able to contact them at e merafekhwai@ yahoo.com, e AfricanFishEagle@yahoo.com or e browner_bw@yahoo.com.

KWARA RESERVE (NG20)

Kwara covers a huge 1,750km², in the middle of the Delta's northern edge. It's bounded to the north by Selinda, to the west by Vumbura and to the east by the Khwai Community's concession, NG18.

On the south side, near to Kwara Camp itself, the reserve is adjacent to Moremi Game Reserve and the small enclave of NG21 (which includes Camp Okavango, Xugana and Shinde). This location gives Kwara access to the shallow floodplains and deep-water areas on the north side of the Delta, as well as a huge, dry game-viewing area to the north of that.

CONCESSION HISTORY Kwara's been an established safari camp for many years, since it was originally built in 1996. For several years in the mid-1990s it was privately owned and marketed by Wilderness Safaris, and was also the base for Sarah-Jane's early horse safaris, which are now run from Macatoo Camp in NG26 (see page 298).

The two main species of waterlilies in the Okavango are the day-lilies (*Nymphaea nouchali caerulea*) and the night-lilies (*Nymphaea lotus*), which are sometimes called lotus lilies. The day-lilies are more common, and the species are fairly easy to tell apart.

As you might expect, day-lilies open in mid/early morning, and close in the afternoon. Their large floating leaves have smooth edges; their flowers start off as a delicate shade of violet-purple (earning them the name of 'blue lily') with only the centre having a yellowish tinge. These last for about five days, gradually turning whiter as they age, before the stem twists and drags the pollinated seed-head under water. There it matures until the seeds are eventually released, complete with air-filled bladders to help them float and disperse better.

Night-lilies are similar but have much darker green leaves, sharply serrated at the edge. The flowers have creamy white petals, edged with yellow, and a strongly yellow centre; these flowers often lie very flat on the surface, facing directly upwards. They open in the late afternoon and close in the early morning, relying for their pollination on night-flying insects.

It was taken over by the Kwando Safaris team in 1999, to add a real Delta experience to their Lagoon and Lebala camps. They have subsequently brought Songwe Village to their portfolio, giving them a successful 'circuit' of four camps encompassing Victoria Falls, the Kwando/Linyanti region and the Okavango.

GETTING THERE AND AWAY Kwara could be reached by boat from Camp Okavango, Camp Moremi, Xugana or Shindi, but in practice virtually all visitors arrive by air to the small airstrip a short distance from camp. Like most camps in the Okavango, you can't just drop in here, and even if you could the camp wouldn't welcome you. It's essential to pre-book your visit.

FLORA AND FAUNA HIGHLIGHTS Kwara Reserve is very large, and covers a wide spectrum of environments from deep-water lagoons and thick papyrus to dry-country scrub and mopane. Thus trying to describe here any dominant species of plants or animals is at best inconclusive, and at worst completely misleading.

These are a few general notes on what you're likely to find here, plus observations of what I found most interesting on my last visit.

Flora South of the camp lie the permanent swamps; a true deep-water environment. You'll find large stands of both papyrus and phragmites reeds, often with waterberry and water fig trees dotted amongst them. Look down in some of the deeper main channels here and you'll find the water opaque, heavy with sediment.

However, in most of the lagoons and the slower channels you'll be able to see right to the Kalahari sand at the bottom, and any water creatures or plants there. Amongst the mass of weeds, ask your guide to point out the delicate web of stems belonging to one of the Okavango's many species of bladderwort (*Utricularia* species). These usually form a submerged tangle of green, hair-like stems with tiny, thin leaves. Dotted amongst these are numerous small 'bladders' which, when touched by a small invertebrate like a mosquito larva, can suck the animal in and capture it. The bladder then digests the animal, and in the process gets valuable nitrogen, which is in very short supply in the mineral-impoverished waters of the Okavango.

Much easier to locate, floating on the surface of the lagoons, you'll find the fan-shaped, serrated leaves of the water chestnut (*Trapa natans*). This is often found on the edges of the lagoons, and is interesting not so much for its white flowers, but for the horned seedpod which it forms. The barbs on this will latch on to the fur or skin of animals, as an aid to dispersing its seed. Their large size suggests that the area's numerous hippo are involved.

Move away from the water, north of camp, and you'll start entering the drier parts of the Kwara Reserve. You'll see that between the dry and wet, there's a transition zone where the bush is a mixture of ancient tree-islands surrounded by plains that were once flooded. The tree-islands here were once more distinct, and surrounded by true floodplains, but as this area has dried out, the vegetation on the plains has grown and blurred the distinction between plains and tree-islands. Similarly, the salt deposits that are often found at the heart of the tree-islands have dissipated.

Like many areas on the edges of the Delta, this is in the extremely slow process of change. This zone was once wet, and now its landscapes and vegetation are very, very gradually reverting to landforms and vegetation of the drier areas – a process that will take millennia to complete.

Here you'll find most of the Delta's usual species of trees, from African mangosteens to jackalberries and both real fan and wild date palms. Plus a few species more often seen in the drier areas of Chobe like Kalahari appleleaf (*Lonchocarpus nelsii*) and silver cluster-leaf (*Terminalia sericea*).

Fauna In the drier areas, Kwara's dominant antelopes appear to be tsessebe and impala, with very healthy populations of reedbuck, kudu and giraffe. You'll also find wildebeest, zebra, bushbuck, warthog and steenbok, plus a liberal sprinkling of elephant and the odd herd of buffalo. On the floodplains around camp, lechwe are also common, whilst deep in the papyrus there are sitatunga, though these are not often seen.

All the big cats – lion, leopard and cheetah – are around, and given the open nature of some of the environment and Kwando Safaris' policy of tracking game as actively as possible, it is a good area for wild dog. I last made a very short visit here in February 2006, which is usually a very difficult time for spotting predators. But despite the thick, green vegetation the guide and spotter managed to locate a pack of wild dogs as they killed an impala, having tracked them for several miles across the bush.

When I first visited this area in 1976, it was still in the grip of hunting, with dismal game viewing and a bleak outlook. The few game drives I went on yielded remarkably little. Antelope would flee at 500m, and we had almost no sightings of big game. Inevitably, the first people who tried to run photographic safaris here, Wilderness Safaris, couldn't make a go of the place, and it changed hands several times. Since then, the wildlife situation has changed immeasurably and for the last five or six years photographic camps have been run successfully in the area by Kwando Safaris. This is an interesting reflection of what's been happening in northern Botswana in the past ten to 15 years, in that the more interesting areas that had been used for hunting have now been supplanted by photographic camps. At the same time, the hunting safari operations have been pushed to operate in more marginal areas with environments that are of less interest to photographic visitors.

Birdlife As with the range of animals, the birdlife is inevitably varied. About 6.5km southwest of Kwara is Gcodikwe Lagoon. This is within Moremi Reserve, but Kwara is the nearest camp to it and so makes a good base for visits here. See the more comprehensive notes on pages 259 of *Chapter 12* about Gcodikwe, but note that within a boat ride you'll find one of the region's most important breeding colonies of storks, egrets, herons and spoonbills. It is at its busiest between September and November, but there are always a few birds there.

Elsewhere in Kwara you'll find a good range of the usual species found in and around the Delta. The more common residents include reed cormorants, darters, African and lesser jacanas, malachite, pied and giant kingfishers, pygmy geese, fish eagles and marsh harriers. Meanwhile the coucals are particularly well represented, with Senegal, coppery-tailed and (in summer) even black coucals all seen here. More unusual sightings include fulvous duck, swamp boubous, black and slaty egrets, black-crowned and white-backed night herons, and the occasional migrant osprey.

In the drier areas north of the permanent waterways, some of the commoner residents include blacksmith plover, red-billed francolins, double-banded sandgrouse, lilac-breasted rollers, yellow-billed hornbills, Meyer's parrots, fiery-necked nightjars, palm swifts, white-rumped babblers, red-eyed and Cape turtle doves, black-crowned Tchagras, Heuglin's robins and black-breasted snake eagles.

More unusual sightings might include western banded snake eagles, Dickinson's kestrels (often perching on palm trees), red-necked falcons, bat hawks, swallow-tailed bee-eaters, red-billed helmet shrikes, brown-throated weavers and wattled cranes.

WHEN TO VISIT As with much of the Delta, the big game here is usually more prolific during the dry season; and although many of the birds breed between December and March, Gcodikwe is generally at its most spectacular before then. That said, visiting in February still allowed me some first-class game viewing, including wild dog, as noted above. So don't write off the green season as a universally lousy time for game: it just takes a bit more tracking down then.

WHAT TO SEE AND DO Kwara is big on activities, and has a wider range available through the year than many camps in the Delta. Game drives and night drives are the norm, and the camp boasts that there are never more than six guests on a vehicle with a guide and tracker. Together with very knowledgeable guides, this makes the game-viewing experience here amongst the best in the Delta, and certainly better in the green season than most dry-land camps. Much of this is due to their willingness to actively track the game, heading off-road and into the bush at the slightest sign of something interesting.

On the water, the varied terrain means that motorboat and mekoro trips are possible all year, and the camp also has a double-decker pontoon-type boat. Climbing on top of this in the papyrus-lined channels is magical, and will give you a completely different view of the waterscape.

WHERE TO STAY Kwara Camp and the newer Little Kwara are both owned by Kwando Safaris (see page 170) and often linked with its sister camps in NG14, Lebala and Lagoon (see pages 238–9).

Kwara Camp (8 tents). Kwara (⊕ KWARAC 19°06.473'S; 23°15.867'E) stands on a small tree-island amidst floodplains. Most of its tents are raised on teak decks with good views over the surrounding plains and lagoons.

The tents measure about 3.5m x 7m x about 2m high, and are lined in a light green canvas that makes them much brighter than a normal tent. The large windows are a traditional insect-proof mesh, and they're furnished with solid teak furniture including a wardrobe, luggage rack, bedside tables, chairs and beds, all standing on a polished floor which is dotted with rugs.

The bathroom is within the tent, though in a separate part, and includes twin washbasins, a flush toilet, and an inventively designed large shower that's enclosed but surrounded by a screen that's partially open to the outside. The honeymoon suite (No 8) also has a free-standing bath as well as a shower.

Beneath a large jackalberry tree (*Diospyros mespiliformis*), Kwara's thatched bar-lounge and dining area is cosy, comfortable and slightly raised up on decking. It overlooks a shallow lagoon that often attracts good numbers of game. The camp's food is good and the bar well-stocked, as you'd expect from a high-quality camp. Nearby there's a substantial swimming pool set into the wooden decking and lined by sun loungers, and a raised look-out hide where you can spend the middle of the day reading or taking in the view. There's also a gift shop. Kwara shares a fairly informal approach with its sister camps, Lagoon and Lebala, which have all been deliberately designed slightly differently as part of a real effort by Kwando Safaris to ensure that the camps have their own individuality. While each aims to provide a very comfortable camp, the accent is firmly on the activities and the guiding rather than ever more creature comforts. *US$750/1,000 pp sharing/sgl Jun–Oct, US$525/700 pp sharing/sgl Apr–May & Nov; US$415pp rest of the year, inc all meals, activities & park fees. Open all year.*

🏠 **Little Kwara**. (4 rooms) Although Little Kwara is only 2km or so from Kwara, it is constructed very differently. Built on a tree island with rooms raised on high wooden decks, each tented room has walls and ceilings of canvas into which large mosquito-gauze windows have been set, all with roll-down flaps. Polished wooden flooring, twin 3/4 or kingsize beds, and some solid and slightly contemporary furniture set the tone, while behind a large bedhead is the dressing area. Each tent has its own en-suite bathroom complete with bath, and indoor and outdoor shower. To the front, a large sliding door of gauze leads to a private veranda set amidst the trees. Wooden walkways lead to the hub of the camp, which was completed only in late 2006.

Overlooking the lagoon, wooden decking leads to the spacious main lounge and a well-stocked bar area where guests can help themselves. Low wicker tables, trendy sofas and proper armchairs with comfy cushions all add to the sense of a tastefully designed camp. To the side is a restaurant area, and there's also a curio shop.

Activities are of the same high standard as those at Kwara, with trackers as well as guides on every vehicle. *Rates as for Kwara, above. Open all year.*

XUGANA, CAMP OKAVANGO AND SHINDE (NG21)

This concession is relatively small by Botswana's standards, but shares a long southern boundary with Moremi Reserve, and is entirely devoted to photographic safaris. To the north NG21 adjoins the Kwara and Vumbura concessions.

Within the reserve, the activities are primarily water-based, although Shinde also offers game drives and a programme of walking safaris from fly-camps.

GETTING THERE AND AWAY All the camps have their own nearby airstrips. Camp Okavango's airstrip (⊕ CAMPOA 19°07.720'S; 23°05.930'E) is a short walk behind the camp, and from the air you'll realise that this takes up most of the very small island on which the camp is situated!

Shinde's airstrip (⊕ SHINDA 19°07.070'S; 23°09.180'E) is a short drive, less than 3km, northeast of the camp. Xugana's airstrip (⊕ XUGAIR 19°02.200'S; 23°05.710'E) is slightly closer and northwest of the camp.

All guests pre-arrange their trips here, and most fly into the camps. However, because Camp Okavango and Xugana have a sister camp, Camp Moremi, on the tip of the Moremi Tongue, there are some boat transfers between these camps. It's quite common, for example, to fly into Camp Moremi for a few days of game activities, then transfer by boat to Camp Okavango for water activities, before flying out.

WHEN TO VISIT Whilst game viewing under the clouds of the green season can be quite rewarding, the attraction of sitting on a boat or a mokoro is more elusive. To appreciate the magic of boating through the Okavango, most people need at least dryness and preferably a blue sky and tropical sun.

Last time I visited Camp Moremi during the green season, the weather one morning was glorious. This prompted the enthusiastic manager to ask me why Expert Africa sends relatively few visitors to the Okavango between January and March. 'It's almost empty of visitors and often the weather's superb,' he beamed. Later that day the clouds drew in and it rained on and off for 36 hours, foiling any ideas I had about photography for the rest of my stay. Hence I'd advise that water-based camps like Xugana and Camp Okavango are best visited during the dry season.

FLORA AND FAUNA HIGHLIGHTS NG21 is adjacent, and in many ways very similar, to the southern parts of the neighbouring reserve NG20 (Kwara Reserve). Thus read my comments on the flora and fauna there (pages 277–9) for a complete picture. That said, a greater proportion of NG21 reserve is permanent swamp, as it has several large, permanent rivers flowing through it. The Moanachira passes through heading east to feed the Gcodikwe Lagoon, before flowing into the Xakanaxa Lagoon which forms the source of the Khwai River that eventually reaches to the far eastern corner of the Delta.

A less clear channel, the Mborogha, flows southeast almost to Chief's Island where it ultimately feeds into the Gomoti and Santandibe rivers, both important watercourses of the lower Delta (though in the last few decades there seems to have been a change of flow between these two major rivers, from the Mborogha to the Moanachira).

In *Okavango: Jewel of the Kalahari* (see *Appendix 3, Further Information*), Karen Ross notes that the eastern rivers, the Moanachira and Mborogha, carry far more water today than they did 100 years ago. So with all these waters concentrated into NG21 it's perhaps not surprising that it's an area where you'll find plenty of deep-water lagoons and channels.

The majority of the NG21 reserve has too much water to be one of the Delta's prime game-viewing areas, but in the dry area around Shinde you'll still find good numbers of game, including impala, lechwe, tsessebe and giraffe. Lone bull elephants are around for most of the year, whilst the breeding herds migrate here from the dry interior towards the end of the dry season.

Reedbuck, kudu, sable and buffalo are infrequently seen, while sitatunga are common in the areas of thick papyrus but rarely sighted. Zebra and wildebeest are relatively rare in this area. It's a good place to look for water-based mammals like the very common hippo and the more elusive spotted-necked otters.

The dominant predators are lion and hyena, with leopard and wild dog also found here. From around September to November 2001 a pack of dogs, known locally as the Four Rivers Pack, denned and raised pups in the area used by the Footsteps Walking Camp.

WHAT TO SEE AND DO Xugana and Camp Okavango both operate motorboat excursions to explore the lagoons, plus mokoro trips to visit the areas of shallower water nearby. Often the mokoro trips are combined with walking on the islands, though these are usually led by an unarmed poler, so read my comments on walking (pages 125–6) before you depart. Note that if you're keen to visit Gcodikwe Lagoon then Camp Okavango or Shinde are much nearer to it than Xugana.

Both water activities are primarily for birdwatching and for learning about the general environment rather than for game viewing, though it's also possible to go fishing (for bream and tiger fish normally) from the motorboats.

13

In addition to these water activities, Shinde also has permanent access to dry land and so can offer 4x4 game drives and night drives (a maximum of seven guests per vehicle) and walks accompanied by an armed ranger. However, those serious about walking would be better off spending a few nights on Shinde's Footsteps fly-camps.

🏠 **WHERE TO STAY** Of the three camps in this area, the two water-camps, Camp Okavango and Xugana, are both owned and marketed by Desert & Delta Safaris (see page 169). The third camp, Shinde, is run by Ker & Downey (see page 170).

🏠 **Xugana Island Lodge** (8 chalets). Though it's been periodically reinvented, Xugana (⊕ XUGANA 19°04.097'S; 23°06.014'E) is one of the Delta's older camps; it is said that it may have been started as a hunting camp as early as the 1960s, probably by Henry Selby (of the hunting company Ker, Downey & Selby). Subsequently, in the early 1980s, it was bought by a local businessman, David Harvey, as a private family retreat. This eventually became more commercial and in 1986 Tsaro Elephant Lodge (see page 250) became a sister camp for Xugana. Both were marketed under the banner of Hartley's Safaris. Finally both were bought by Desert & Delta Safaris in 2000.

One of the few things that hasn't changed about Xugana over the years is its location on the banks of a forested island beside a large, deep lagoon. It's a spectacular site, fitting for a camp that concentrates entirely on water-based activities. It's about 7.5km north of Camp Okavango (and yet the most direct route by boat covers about 16.8km of waterways).

The camp's lounge, bar and dining areas are set back slightly under fig and leadwood trees; all have thatched roofs and open sides which face the water. That said, the camp often makes a point of arranging their dinners alfresco, either around camp or at locations nearby.

For many years Xugana used the lagoon itself as a swimming pool, suspending a crocodile-proof wire cage in the lagoon for bathers to cool off in. Whilst environmentally admirable, some of the camp's less enlightened guests clearly found this pool's occasional murkiness off-putting, and so in 2001 a new swimming pool was built amongst the landscaped lawns at the centre of camp. These are dotted with natural vegetation, with everything protected from hungry elephants by an electric fence. (What remains of the old swimming pool is now a floating deck, used for the odd alfresco dinner on the lagoon.)

Along with the new pool, Xugana's 8 chalets were completely refurbished in 2001, basically to bring their standards up to compete with more modern camps.

Each is built of reed and thatch, raised up on wooden decking, with twin beds or a dbl under a large, walk-in mosquito net. Each has a ceiling fan under its high ceiling, which operates from the camp's generator during the day. There's a 12V lighting system in the rooms for use at night. Their bathrooms are en suite with a walk-in hot shower, flush toilet and washbasin, and outside, facing the lagoon, is a private wooden deck with a pair of canvas safari chairs.

The camp has a good small curio shop, the Xugana Gallery, with a fair selection of local books and wildlife guides, plus a few T-shirts, handicrafts and postcards.
US$630/830 pp sharing/sgl Jul–Oct, US$420 pp sharing/sgl Nov–Mar; US$360 pp sharing/sgl Apr–Jun, fully inc. Open all year.

🏠 **Camp Okavango** (12 tents, suite). On the south side of this concession, Camp Okavango (⊕ CAMPOK 19°08.118'S; 23°06.035'E) stands on the west side of Nxaragha Island amidst floodplains, lagoons and waterways. Because of its location, Camp Okavango is one of the Delta's easiest camps in the permanent swamps to arrange to visit by boat (see *Getting there and away*, above). However, it's a measure of the meandering geography of the Delta's waterways that although its sister camp, Camp Moremi, is only about 33km away as the egret flies, the most direct route by boat (coincidentally, via the Gcodikwe Lagoon) is slightly over 60km.

'Camp O', as it's usually known, was started by an American woman, Jessie Niel, in the early 1980s, and was swiftly followed by Camp Moremi in around 1985. She ran and marketed them as a pair under the banner of Desert & Delta Safaris until, around 1993 or 1994, the whole operation was taken over by a group called Chobe Holdings, associated with Chobe Game Lodge and AfroVentures — though the name was kept.

Camp Okavango is quite a large camp by Okavango standards, and its spacious thatched dining, lounge and bar area reflect this. All open out on to a large area of lawn, which is often the venue for meals outside — usually accompanied by lots of candles and flaming torches!

For seclusion during the day, there's a raised viewing hide that's been built into a sausage tree (*Kigelia africana*) and 3 knobthorn trees (*Acacia nigrescens*) near the end of the jetty. It's a good spot to relax with comfy chairs, and the view over the papyrus and reeds might interest patient birdwatchers. The plunge pool, sundeck or the sprinkling of hammocks around camp, however, are probably better venues for relaxation.

Sand paths link the tents and main areas — which is a pleasant change from the usual acres of hardwood walkways. Camp Okavango has large Meru-style tents, raised up on individual wooden platforms. These are very comfortably furnished, with twin or dbl beds, crisp linen, a teak wardrobe, luggage rack, dressing table, bedside pedestals and canvas safari chairs. You'll also find rugs on the floor and co-ordinated linens and blinds to cover the mesh windows. Each has an en-suite bathroom with a hot shower, washbasin and flush toilet.

As well as the tents, the camp also has one suite available, which they call the 'Okavango Suite'. This is the old house of the camp's former owner, Jessie Neil. It's a unique, open-plan bungalow that's clearly been built to a personal specification. At its centre is a lounge with old-style settees and, nestling in a wooden room-divider, a TV and video. On one side of this is the large bedroom, dominated by a bed shrouded in mosquito netting. On the other is a dining room built for entertaining (though if staying in the suite then even just 2 guests can arrange to have dinner served here). It's all floored, panelled and furnished in wood.

However, the suite's *pièce de résistance* is its bathroom. Down a few steps from the bedroom you'll find a black bathroom suite lit by recessed lighting in a room lined with black tiles and mirrors. Urban Gothic, circa 1970, in the heart of the Okavango. It's wonderful; don't miss it!

In addition to boat and mokoro trips, bush walks on the islands are possible, though see my comments on walking trips in Botswana (pages 125–8) before you set off. Camps like this which concentrate on water activities tend to have a slower pace than those which also offer game drives; you'll have more time to just relax. As befits this, the tents also have their own tea/coffee-making facilities and even towelling robes. The team here are also adept at varying the routine, and including the odd torch-lit barbecue on islands away from camp, and other bush surprises.

The camp's curio shop is notable for a fine collection of baskets, all made by the staff, with the proceeds going to them. There are also a few books, T-shirts and film.

US$630/830 pp sharing/sgl Jul–Oct; US$420 pp sharing/sgl Nov–Mar; US$360 pp sharing/sgl Apr–Jun, fully inc. Open all year.

⌂ **Shinde** (8 tents) Ker & Downey (page 170). Shinde stands in the heart of the NG21 Reserve, about 6km east of Camp Okavango, 12km west of Kwara and 8km southeast of Xugana. It's also been here a long time, and since the early 1980s has been under the ownership of Ker & Downey.

The central bar/dining area is built on raised, wooden decking on various levels, rising towards a canvas roof that's bowed, a little like an old ox-wagon. The camp also has a swimming pool and a well-stocked curio shop.

Shinde's tents are of several different designs, though all are in a relatively traditional safari style. 3 of these have wooden poles for frames and canvas walls, built on individual, raised wooden decks and shaded by thatched roofs. These form an 'enclave' with its own small area of decking, which can be used together for a small group of 6 who seek privacy. The rest are more traditional, walk-in, Meru-style tents protected by large shade cloths. These have mesh windows and either wooden or tiled floors dotted with rugs. Inside each you'll find a bright colour scheme dominated by lively African fabrics, wonderfully firm mattresses, bedside tables, an open armoire for clothes and a luggage rack.

2 of these tents, including the 'honeymoon suite' with its queen-size bed, have been built on raised wooden platforms. All have en-suite bathrooms with hot and cold running water, a washbasin, shower, flush toilet, a large mirror and the usual array of tiny bottles of lotions and potions that most camps supply these days. Outside each tent is a shaded porch with a couple of comfy chairs.

Recently, 3 new tents have been built for private groups overlooking an expanse of papyrus and reeds dotted with palm islands. Suitably known as The Enclave, it incorporates its own bar, boma, dining area and lounge, with a dedicated waiter and private guide.

US$515/600 pp sharing/sgl May–Jun & Nov, US$695/970 pp Jul–Oct, US$330 pp Mar–Apr, inc all meals, activities, park fees, laundry & Most drinks; exc transfers. No children under 10. Open Mar–Nov.

Shinde started to run walking trails in NG21, which they now market as 'Footsteps across the Delta'. Along with Selinda's walking trails (see page 236), this is one of the few operations in the Delta that take walking safaris really seriously.

As with any good walking safari, numbers here are small and these camps take a maximum of 6 people at a time. Accommodation is in small, twin-bedded tents. Each is lit by gaslight, with an en-suite long-drop toilet and a separate private bucket shower.

It's all very rustic, with dinner usually eaten under the stars, although standards of food are good with lots of effort made to use fresh fruit and vegetables, bake fresh bread each day despite the camp's remote locations, and (of course) to provide a well-stocked bar.

The days here revolve around walking, though occasional trips by mokoro are also possible; you can normally expect 2 walks of 3–4 hours in duration, one in the morning and one in the evening.

Children are welcome, with special activities provided, but only if the camp is booked on an exclusive basis.

US$330 pp low season to US$495/635 pp sharing/sgl high season, inc all meals, drinks, activities, laundry; transfers extra. No children under 7. Open Mar–Nov.

VUMBURA AND DUBA PLAINS (NG22 AND NG23)

Immediately north of Moremi's Mombo concession, the Vumbura and Duba Plains reserves (NG 22 and 23) share many similarities of game and landscape with Mombo. This northern area of the Delta is one of my favourites, but because of the similarity between Vumbura or Duba, if you are planning a trip to this area then it's best to include only one of them in your itinerary.

Vumbura is a varied reserve, and the areas through which you drive are often very pretty. Much of its landscape consists of wide-open plains with tiny islands – almost a cliché of the Okavango. Vumbura's game is notably diverse, so most visitors will see a wide range of antelope and have a good chance to spot the less common predators.

Duba Plains, to the west of Vumbura, is visually similar but with larger open plains. It doesn't quite have Vumbura's diversity of game, but instead is the long-standing venue for battles between large herds of buffalo and sizeable prides of lion. Thus, it will often provide a very impressive spectacle of big game.

Both can access water activities, Vumbura for the whole year, although the areas aren't quite so picturesque as, say, the Jao Flats.

CONCESSION HISTORY Until around 1997 this was a hunting area, but then Wilderness Safaris started Vumbura, Little Vumbura and Duba Plains camps.

For several years there were two small, seasonal hunting camps running in the northeast of the Vumbura concession (one of which was on the site of Kaporota). These had closed by 2001 and while the reserve is designated by the government for 'mixed wildlife utilisation', hunting is no longer practised in either area; both are now used solely for photographic safaris. (As an aside, Dereck and Beverly Joubert, the wildlife photographers, are closely involved with the Vumbura concession.)

As is increasingly the case with reserves in Botswana, both Duba and Vumbura have an element of local community involvement. Five local villages – Seronga, Eretsa, Betsaa, Gudigwa and Gunitsugwa – have some control over the concession, and derive considerable benefit from its success. Most of the staff for the camps come from these villages too, so there's a flow of revenue from these camps back to the communities by way of wages (see *The anatomy of a community partnership* on page 285, and comments on NG12 on page 276).

GETTING THERE AND AWAY All the camps here accept only pre-booked guests who fly in. Driving isn't possible without permission – and permission is never given

Though 'community-based natural resource management' is recognised as one of the main strategies for achieving sustainable development in the rural areas of Botswana, really good examples of it are few and far between. Wilderness Safaris have a strong track record with successful community projects in other countries, like Damaraland Camp in Namibia, and here in Botswana their flagship community project is the Vumbura and Duba concessions. The camps in these private reserves or concessions started in 1997 when the safari company and their partners made an agreement with the community to which the government had given management of concession areas NG22 and NG23.

The community, in this case, consists of five villages to the north of the Okavango Delta: Seronga, Eretsha, Betsha, Gudigwa and Ganitsuga. The villagers had to set up a trust, with a fully constituted board to represent all the villages and people of the area in their dealings with the government, the Land Board and the safari companies. The ten-person board is made up of two elected people from each of the five villages. Wilderness Safaris pays a six-figure US-dollar lease fee each year to the board (this is a lot of money in rural Botswana). The board decides how to use that money for the benefit of the community. Further, as part of the deal Wilderness has to employ at least 118 people from the villages (though they actually ended up giving jobs to around 150), and to deliver on a number of community projects. These projects have resulted in the setting up and supporting of a number of secondary cottage industries in the villages, like basket-weaving and vegetable gardens; in addition they have sponsored an inter-village soccer tournament; helped with transport problems; and set up village shops, mortuaries etc.

Perhaps the most difficult issue about this kind of agreement for any safari company is the short duration of the leases; the community can swap their safari company after the first year if it wishes to, then again after the second year, the fifth year and the tenth year. Given the huge investment in infrastructure and the long-term nature of the marketing, this is difficult for most safari companies to contemplate. However, Vumbura and Duba are now six years into the project, and Wilderness Safaris are slowly starting to reap the benefits of a stable, long-term relationship with the community as their partner. Equally, guests to these camps know that their safari is actively benefiting the communities in the area – and so know that they're helping the villagers and the wildlife by coming to these camps.

(though it would be only a few hours' drive from Seronga, if you knew the way!). Note that each camp has its own separate airstrip. Vumbura's (VUMAIR) is at ✷ 18°57.504'S; 22°49.063'E.

WHEN TO VISIT In common with the rest of the Okavango, you'll find the big game more diverse and prolific during the dry season, although the birdlife is generally better between December and March. Driving around the reserve can be more difficult then, as there's a lot of water around and many roads are submerged.

FLORA AND FAUNA HIGHLIGHTS Both these reserves are broadly similar in character, although Duba Plains (as you might expect) has more extensive open plains, whereas the plains at Vumbura are often partially flooded, and they're broken up by more islands, including many small palm islands.

Flora Much of these concessions consist of very beautiful, open floodplains dotted with islands, many of which are tiny. The vegetation of the larger islands is

13

dominated by many of the Okavango's usual tree species, including raintree (*Lonchocarpus capassa*), leadwood (*Combretum imberbe*), African mangosteen (*Garcenia livingstonei*), jackalberry (*Diospyros mespiliformis*), sausage tree (*Kigelia africana*) and sycamore fig (*Ficus sycomorus*).

You'll also find knobthorn trees (*Acacia nigrascens*), although relatively few of them, and some particularly large, wonderful specimens of fever-berry trees (*Croton megalobotrys*), named after the anti-malarial properties of the seeds and the bark. (These properties had been known to local African residents for centuries, but were brought to the attention of a wider audience by an article in the medical journal, *The Lancet*, in 1899. Apparently there has still not been any detailed research on these medicinal properties.)

Amongst the main bushes that you'll find here are the Kalahari star apple (*Diospyros lycioides lycioides*), which is often also called the blue bush, for its overall bluish tinge, or the 'toothbrush bush', as its roots can be peeled and used as a toothbrush. (Veronica Roodt reports that on using it 'at first my mouth burnt and I became extremely worried when my whole mouth turned yellow. The result, however, was remarkable – white teeth and fresh breath.') Another very common bush in this area is the evergreen magic gwarri bush (*Euclea divinorum*), also sometimes known as the 'toothbrush bush' for the use of its branches. Both these bushes produce dyes used to colour palm leaves used in weaving baskets in Botswana.

In the northeast of Vumbura there are some fine acacia woodlands, whilst as you travel west from Vumbura into Duba you'll find more and larger open floodplains, slightly less thick wooded islands, and more clusters of the wild date palm (*Phoenix reclinata*).

As well as the drier areas, there are many small channels near the Vumbura camps, and some open, lightly reeded lagoons. The channels are lined intermittently with a mixture of papyrus and common reeds, and periodically open out on to floodplain areas. Scenically the areas near these camps don't quite match up to the sheer beauty of the Jao Flats, as there are very few feathery real fan palms or lily-covered lagoons.

Fauna When last visited, I was very impressed by the varied line-up of antelope that I saw in the Vumbura Reserve in a few days. Unlike many of the areas further from the heart of the Delta, there wasn't just a high density of one or two species, to the virtual exclusion of the rest.

Species that you can expect to see here include tsessebe, impala, lechwe, kudu, zebra, wildebeest, giraffe, warthog and steenbok. Sable are seen fairly often, especially near the airstrip. Waterbuck are common here; Vumbura is one of the few places within northern Botswana where you'll find good numbers of them. Duiker, reedbuck and bushbuck are seen infrequently, whilst roan antelope are rare, though have been seen occasionally in the late dry season. I know of one sighting of sitatunga in Vumbura (which was one February).

Wild dogs had denned here for several years running prior to my visit, and I was lucky enough to be able to watch a beautiful pack with pups at its den, situated in the mopane woodlands on the east side of the Vumbura. However, in a thick band of mopane woodlands it wasn't possible to follow them when they moved off.

Cheetah are also resident, though, like the rest of the smaller game, they will move through the buffalo fence and out into the huge NG12, to the north. In the dry season, when many of the open floodplains are dry, it's a classic open environment that is perfect for cheetah, rather like Mombo and parts of Selinda, so it's a particularly good area in which to seek them.

Leopard are occasionally seen on night drives. Lion and spotted hyena are both relatively common. Both black-backed and side-striped jackals occur here, though the black-backed are seen much more regularly.

Moving westwards, Duba Plains is noted not only for its huge open plains, but also for having some of the best concentrations of buffalo in Botswana. Particularly large herds are found here during the dry season. These can easily number over a thousand animals, and inevitably they attract a very high concentration of lion – which in the Duba Plains area, is very much the dominant predator. The converse of this is that Duba doesn't have the same balance of species, or the diversity, that you'll usually find in Vumbura, giraffe, zebra and impala being the notable absentees, though Duba is curiously popular with warthogs!

Spotted hyena are flourishing here, despite the sizeable prides of lions, and side-striped jackals are seen fairly frequently whilst black-backed are largely absent.

Birdlife The birdlife here is as varied as you'll find in any area of the Delta with a good mix of dry and wet environments. Certainly in one afternoon of very casual bird spotting on the river from Vumbura you can expect to find a range of kingfishers (malachite, pied, and giant), jacanas, several species of egrets (including slaty), black-winged stilts, open-bill storks and reed cormorants. In addition, the open floodplains with short grass seemed to attract very good numbers of various waders plus saddle-billed storks, glossy and sacred ibises, spoonbills and – relatively unusually – pelicans.

Similarly, the birds enjoying the waterlogged plains of Duba Plains in October 2006 included wattled cranes and, an unusual treat in the Delta, flamingos.

WHAT TO SEE AND DO The Vumbura camps, and to a lesser extent Duba Plains, have year-round access to deep permanent water, and so boat trips are possible all year, with opportunities to fish if you wish. There are also mokoro excursions, 4x4 game drives and night drives (though night drives may sometimes be restricted when flood levels are very high, from May to August). Short walks are also offered by these camps, though I would generally go to a specialist walking camp if I wanted to do much walking.

WHERE TO STAY All the camps in Vumbura and Duba are marketed by Wilderness Safaris (see page 171). Vumbura, Little Vumbura and Duba Plains currently cost the same, whilst Kaparota is marketed as one of Wilderness's rustic 'Vintage Camps' and hence costs slightly less.

There is also a little-known fourth camp in this area, called Vundimtiki. This is used exclusively by one overseas tour operator from the USA. Visitors from elsewhere are unlikely to even hear about it, and I haven't visited it and so include no further comments on it here.

Little Vumbura (5 tents). Although less than 2km from its larger sister camp, Little Vumbura (⊕ LVUMBU 19°00.070'S; 22°51.710'E) feels quite separate, perhaps because it's on a small island and always approached by boat.

Little Vumbura has a small dining area and a comfy lounge/bar section. All is under canvas on decking about a metre off the ground, and attached, via a 50m jetty, to the launch area for the boats.

Over the dining room/bar stands a large waterberry tree (*Syzygium cordatum*), and the open sides of the canvas structure (which can be rolled down) are shaded by dense surrounding stands of wild date palms, a couple of fig trees (*Ficus sycomorus*) and an assortment of jackalberry trees (*Diospyros mespiliformis*). This all leaves you with the very comfortable feeling that the camp's been built from within the vegetation, and you're cocooned in a small, tropical hideaway.

The walk-in tents are comfortable, with wickerwork shelves, wardrobe and furniture. They stand on the ground and have en-suite shower cubicle, washbasin and toilet inside. A few paces away outside is a much more natural open-air shower, with a view of the surrounding floodplains.

Aside from the main area, there's also a small curio shop (with a few books, materials and local baskets for sale), a plunge pool and a wonderful open hexagonal section of decking (with a fire pit in the middle) which extends into the reeds and is used for dinner, drinks and stargazing.

Up to 2001, this little camp accepted just 8 people and was certainly one of Wilderness's hottest properties in Botswana. Now, to capitalise on this, Little Vumbura has been made slightly larger to take up to 10 people, while the main Vumbura Camp has been slimmed down in size.

From US$470/655 pp sharing/sgl low season to US$785/970 high season, inc all meals, activities, park fees, laundry, most drinks; exc transfers. Open all year.

⌂ **Vumbura Plains** (7 rooms north, 7 rooms south). This new camp falls into the 'seriously posh' bracket: a boutique lodge in the bush, split across two sites: Vumbura Plains North and Vumbura Plains South. Although these are linked by a walkway, they have separate central areas and management, so feel like two camps, softening what could otherwise be a slightly corporate effect.

Contemporary in design, each of its large, square rooms (emphatically *not* tents) of quality light wood has a big open area with voluminous white net curtains which slide on ceiling rails to act as room dividers. Mundane things like wardrobes and hanging spaces are cleverly concealed along one side. In one quarter of the room, a square sunken lounge with low seating and soft cushions is a great place for unwinding after a game drive or early in the evening. In another, a tall post with a free-standing shower looks down on a completely open concrete slab — it's quite liberating, but with its total lack of privacy, this isn't a place for the overtly modest. The shy can always choose to use the outside shower instead! Each room also boasts its own sizeable private deck with plunge pool and little *sala*, lit by soft spots. It's all quite unexpected and very different from a typical safari camp — and is already proving popular with the American market, and the moneyed glitterati.

For families, Vumbura Plains has a big plus. It's one of the few camps in Botswana to have a private family suite, with a completely separate room for children (from 8). Linking the two rooms is a private deck with three enclosed sides, which means that — unusually — children can safely be slightly independent of their parents.

The central area of each camp, linked to the rooms by wooden walkways, focuses on a wooden platform, sheltered by a roof held up on poles and set beneath indigenous trees overlooking the plains. When it's raining or blowing a gale, wooden slatted blinds protect guests from the worst of the elements, but during the dry season, this makes for dining or relaxing almost alfresco, with a cool through breeze. As everywhere else, the décor here is contemporary and quite fun: with shaggy, long-pile rugs, plenty of comfortable, soft sofas and modern objets d'art.

The stylish mode of the camp extends to meals as well: food is served to the table, and there is a choice of carefully designed dishes, rather than the usual safari camp buffet. Expect sparkling cutlery for your food, and crystal glasses to hold your choice of the wines of the day (which usually come from South Africa). A cappuccino maker is on hand throughout the day, and the bar is particularly well stocked.

As you'd expect from a Wilderness camp, the service is friendly and staff try very hard to meet the high standards set by the camp. Activities include the usual 4x4 Land Rover safaris, walking and boats/mekoro trips. There's also a small, new gym built between the camps — and shared by guests at both.

On my last visit, I found that camps like this, Mombo and King's Pool attract some of the company's more ambitious and keen guides, who certainly rank amongst the best in the company. *US$660–1,235 pp sharing, low-high season, all inc. Open all year.*

⌂ **Duba Plains** (6 tents). Of all the 'usual' fly-in camps in the Delta, Duba Plains is one of the most northern. It is north of Moremi Reserve, a 5min flight west of Vumbura.

Duba is a fairly small camp with the main dining area built on raised decking under a high thatched roof, around a large jackalberry tree. The cozy lounge/bar area is adjacent, on a slightly lower level, with armchairs and a couple of sofas around a wicker coffee table. Judicious use of sapling screens lends it a pleasant rustic feel.

The thatched guest toilet is nearby, and beyond is another area of raised decking. On one side of this is a swimming pool; opposite is an observation deck with chairs, tables and loungers. This commands a good view over the plains, and is often used for brunch. To the side of this is a quiet *sala* (a small gazebo), with a couple of wicker chairs and a bench. It's perfect for relaxing in the afternoon. About 150m from the main lounge is a small hide for birdwatchers, with a copy of *Newman's Birds of Southern Africa* for those 'hard to identify' species.

Duba's tents are linked by bush paths, and raised on decks to give good views of the plains. Outside each there's a small veranda with a table and 2 chairs, in front of the tent's wooden door. Inside, wood has been used extensively for simple, tasteful décor. The headboard at the back of dbl or twin beds extends into twin washbasins, and there's a small wardrobe and laundry basket. The tent has mosquito-proof gauze, so mosquito nets are not usually provided. Inside at the back is a flush toilet and a shower, beyond which a door opens on to raised decking where an outdoor shower has a great view of the plains.

Because of its location near the Panhandle, Duba is one the first camps in the main Delta to be flooded. From about May to the end of August the shallow-water plains around it usually have enough water for mokoro trips.
US$610/795 pp sharing/sgl low season to US$900/1,085 high season, inc all meals, activities, park fees, laundry, most drinks; exc transfers. Open all year.

COMMUNITY AREA (NG24)

Currently this is the only one of the Delta's photography-specific areas (ie: hunting is not allowed) which has no proper safari operation in it. Until about 1999 this was the location for Jedibe Camp, which had long been run by Wilderness Safaris (see page 171) and was one of their earliest camps in the Delta.

I visited Jedibe in about 1996. It was located deep within a maze of deepwater channels and papyrus, and the main activity there was exploring on motorboats. This was superb fun (although motorboats are probably the most expensive activity to run for any camp, given their thirst for fuel!) as the boats could reach some stunning areas of the most beautiful floodplains, as well as exploring the papyrus-lined channels of the main rivers. Mokoro trips, incorporating walks on the islands, were also possible but usually of secondary interest.

However, in 1999 Jedibe's lease came up for tender – which means a re-opening of negotiations between the government, the community (the Okavango Jakotsha Community Trust) and anyone who is interested in taking responsibility for the area's lease.

Since Jedibe was built, many new mixed land-and-water camps had come into existence in the Delta, and proven very successful. Furthermore their range of game drives and water activities was wider than Jedibe's options. This left Jedibe looking less commercially attractive, with a very specific, limited niche as a deepwater camp in permanent papyrus, running mainly (inherently costly) motorboats. Jedibe's northerly location, far from Maun, meant expensive transport links and running costs too.

These factors all made Jedibe less commercially attractive, at a time when the local community was expecting to get more for the concession. Eventually no agreement could be made.

If you do visit this area, then don't go for the animals. Although there are animals on the islands, this is a deep-water area and you should treat any game sightings as a bonus. Instead come for the bird and water-life. Expect lots of deep, fast-flowing channels and endless banks of papyrus, which periodically open out on to spectacular floodplains.

WHERE TO STAY There is now one, small backpacker's camp on the edge of the reserve, accessed from Etsha 6, on the Panhandle road.

13

Å **Makwena Camp** (camping only) ☏ 6874 299, 6861 206; e makwena@dynabyte.bw. This small, budget camp is about 14km from Etsha 6 on the Panhandle – usually 12km of 4x4 track from the road, followed by a 2km boat ride. It is sometimes possible to organise 4x4 transfers to/from Etsha 6.

Makwena is currently being run as a campsite for budget travellers, who will need to arrive with all food and camping equipment. From there you can transfer by boat to a fly-camp on an island, where you can hire mekoro for around P100 per day. Each mokoro seats 1–2 people.

If you want to go for longer than a day then there's a further mokoro 'sleep-out' fee, which enables you to stay out on one of the islands; note, too, that there's an entry fee into this community area of about P25 pp.

If you're interested then apparently Mr Malcolm Thomas, who works in the Co-op supermarket at Etsha 6, can get in touch with the camp from there. However, this didn't work when I last tried, as he wasn't around. It's certainly best to contact the camp at least 2–3 days in advance.

JAO, KWETSANI, JACANA AND TUBU CAMPS (NG25)

Close to the Panhandle, west of Moremi, NG25 is a particularly beautiful concession covering about 600km^2 of the upper Okavango Delta. Most of this is a fairly wet environment, with extensive floodplains, especially around the Jao Flats, though there is a substantial drier section, where the new Tubu Tree Camp is situated, to the west of the reserve. The annual flood generally reaches this reserve around April or May, instantly expanding the area of the floodplains.

GETTING THERE AND AWAY As with most camps, flying in here is the only option, and is almost always booked in advance. Driving here is totally impractical.

WHEN TO VISIT For the water activities any time is fine as long as it doesn't rain. Hence from April to November would be my choice of time to visit. However, if you're on a serious game-viewing trip then better to come towards the end of the dry season where this area's diversity of species does pick up, with dry-country species like cheetah being seen here periodically.

FLORA AND FAUNA HIGHLIGHTS The area around Jao, Kwetsani and Jacana feels very much like most people's image of the Okavango: watery and terribly picturesque. It's a lovely environment. Whilst the game diversity in the area might not quite match some of the areas further east yet, lechwe and lion are exceedingly prolific here and those alone will keep most people entertained.

The birding is also good, with enough diversity of habitat to mean that you'll find most Delta species here if you look hard enough. I've had great luck in the past here with gallinules and pink-throated longclaws.

The area around Tubu Tree Camp, on the eastern side of the concession, is much drier and totally different from the eastern part of the reserve where the three older camps are situated.

Flora The reserve's most memorable area must be the beautiful Jao Flats, a series of huge open floodplains, dotted with tiny islands that are often only a few metres across. These vast floodplains are covered in a mix of very sparse vegetation, much of which is the aptly named hippo grass (*Vossia cuspidata*), which has round, slender leaves, pointing periodically out of the water by up to a metre. Often these have a tiny flower spike on top, reminiscent of a minute papyrus head.

Much taller and denser are the stands of tall common reeds (*Miscanthus junceus*), and even areas of the attractive bulrush (*Typha capensis*). The latter have distinctive velvety seedheads and edible roots (which taste a little like chewing gum or sugar cane!). As you'd expect in such a watery area, the deeper parts have thick stands of papyrus.

There's usually plenty of open, shallow water around, and in the slow-flowing channels look out for water lettuce plants (*Ottelia ulvifolia*) underwater, with its wavy leaves, long trailing stems and delicate, trumpet-shaped flower held above the surface by a single airbladder.

The many small islands in the area are often little more than bases for the emergence of a ring of bushy wild date palms (*Phoenix reclinata*), and perhaps the odd real fan palm (*Hyphaene petersiana*), springing up through the centre of the low canopy, perhaps around a termite mound.

Also look out for the wild dagga plant (*Leonotis nepetifolia*), with its bright red flowers, like baubles from a Christmas tree. These will remain standing long after they turn brown and die. There are also thickets of the uncommon magic gwarri bush (*Euclea divinorum*), which is believed by some local people to have wood with supernatural powers. Above these you'll find rain trees (*Lonchocarpus capassa*), woodland waterberry trees (*Syzygium guineense*) and the occasional birdplum (*Berchemia discolor*).

Some of the bushes on the larger islands are more typical of drier areas, including the Kalahari appleleaf (*Lonchocarpus nelsii*), the Kalahari star apple (*Diospyros lycioides lycioides*), with its blueish tinge which sometimes gives it the name of 'blue bush'. Ask your guide and s/he may show you how its twigs can be used as a toothbrush!

Similarly these larger islands have bands of acacias, including the umbrella thorn (*Acacia tortilis*). These become more prevalent as you move further east in the reserve, where you find larger islands, with thicker belts of acacia bush and areas of mopane also. This is the area in which you'll find Tubu Tree Camp.

Fauna The majority of the reserve around the Jao Flats is a superb area for lion and lechwe, which are both exceedingly common. The lechwe occur in large herds and will frequently startle; listen to them splash as they run across the flooded grasslands. The lion are certainly the dominant predator, with a number of large prides in the area.

Other game is usually present in lower densities, but in this eastern section you can expect to spot blue wildebeest, zebra, small groups of tsessebe and elephants. Kwetsani, in particular, is noted for the increasingly relaxed bushbuck which seem to frequent its island. Sable and roan are virtually never seen here, but the large areas of papyrus are home to sitatunga, though as ever these take a lot of effort to see.

Lone male buffalo will pass through, especially from June onwards, and later in the dry season larger breeding herds move across the reserve. Elephants have a broadly similar pattern, and their herds get larger as the dry season progresses.

Cheetah aren't usually seen on the eastern side of the reserve until the waters have receded a long way, which means around October. Then they'll move west again as the waters rise in February. Leopard and hyena are seen occasionally but infrequently throughout the reserve and the year. Sightings of wild dog are very unusual (for example, there was one sighting during the whole of 1999 – but things are improving).

The western area of the reserve, accessed from Tubu, has a much drier habitat around it and you can expect giraffe, kudu and impala here in the mixed acacia woodlands.

Like most of the reserves around the Okavango, Jao Reserve had previously been used for hunting. However, questions have been raised about whether hunting in this area is ethical. It is alleged that leopard were baited and snared in numbers, and hyena shot. This would have enabled the lion prides to grow with little competition, thus satisfying the demand for lion trophies – and explain the present very high numbers of lion and relative scarcity of other predators.

Fortunately all hunting has been stopped in the Jao Reserve for several years, and the animal populations should be slowly returning to a more natural balance.

Birdlife This is a good reserve for birdwatching, particularly for some of the less common water-based species. During a few gentle boat rides on the eastern side of the reserve, I had good sightings of many of the commoner waterbirds, plus lesser jacanas, lesser moorhens, purple and green-backed herons, slaty egrets, white-faced whistling ducks, lesser moorhens, and both purple and lesser gallinules. (Both of the gallinules were seen in small lagoons close to Kwetsani.)

Meanwhile driving in the drier areas we came across a similarly good range, and noted several flocks of Meyer's parrots, Dickenson's kestrels nesting at the top of an old palm tree, wattled starlings and a tree full of open-bill storks. Then, again near Kwetsani, we found some very uncommon pink-throated longclaws (a big tick!) in a wide marshy plain where they seem to be resident.

Though not too unusual, African snipes can be found here. Listen carefully around dusk, as the sun sets and darkness falls. Then, during the breeding season, the birds fly high and zoom back to the ground. Their fanned-out tail feathers make a noise like a percussion instrument – called 'drumming'.

The western side of this reserve, around Tubu, should have a wider range of raptors than the east (Jao, Kwetsani and Jacana), simply because it's drier.

WHAT TO SEE AND DO I would visit Jao and Kwetsani primarily for their water activities – trips by boat and mokoro – which are generally on offer all year (though motorboats at Kwetsani may be restricted by water levels around October–January). That said, day and night game drives (and sometimes short walks on the islands) are also possible, and will make a bonus for your stay.

Jacana is also best regarded as a water-based camp, with motorboat and mokoro trips all year, as well as game drives when the water levels are not in high flood. Tubu is quite the opposite: a dry-land camp for game drives which can also arrange mokoro trips when the flood levels are high. A couple of nights at Jacana, and a few at Tubu, make a relatively inexpensive combination, at least by the standards of the Delta.

The comfortable game-drive vehicles in this reserve tend to use vehicles with three rows of three seats, of which a few are often left empty. When I last went walking, the guide was a capable, experienced walking guide who gave an appropriate pre-departure safety briefing and clearly knew how to use the rifle that he carried. He also escorted the mokoro trip, which I was pleased to see eschewed the easier hippo trails in favour of a more difficult, but much safer, route through a shallow floodplain. Though he's now left this reserve, I hope that the standards of safe practice which he set will remain.

🏠 **WHERE TO STAY** All four camps in the Jao Reserve are marketed and run by Wilderness Safaris (see page 171). They range from the opulence of Jao, to the relative simplicity of Jacana. All cater exclusively for fly-in visitors.

🏠 **Jao Camp** (9 rooms). Imagine what Tarzan would have built if he'd had a few million dollars and some chic Italian designers, and you're close to imagining Jao Camp (⊕ JOACAM 19°18.431'S, 22°36.071'E). Standing on the southeast side of the

Jao Reserve, Jao is one of Wilderness Safaris' flagship 'Premier' camps (the other being Mombo, which was designed by the same architect).

Arriving at Jao, you walk through a profusion of lush wild date palms before eventually finding the large, 2-storey main building. It's about 30m long and 8–10m wide, with designer-inspired scraggy thatch and hints of an Indonesian longhouse. Upstairs is the dining room, where everybody usually eats around a long elegant table (handcrafted on site, apparently, using Zimbabwean rosewood); a spacious lounge with comfy leather sofas, a chess table and stylish lamps; there's a long outside balcony where breakfast is sometimes served.

Down a magnificent flight of stairs there's a small library, a snug and a curio shop. A few paces away from this you'll find a round swimming pool and a few sun-loungers amidst the palms.

The rooms at Jao are probably the most luxurious and spacious in the Okavango region. All are on stilts, accessed by raised wooden walkways. They have one long side, facing the nearby channel, and equally scraggy thatch to match the central longhouse. Their position gives lots of privacy, though also makes the walk from the farthest rooms as much as 600m from the centre (less fit visitors can request chalets closer to the centre).

Entering at the side of the chalet, through a large, swivelling door, you find a lounge with huge coffee table, big comfy settee and a lockable safe for valuables. This is only half of the open-plan room, which also has twin (or dbl) bed(s) under a walk-in mosquito net, complete with a fan underneath. The chalets are effectively insect-proofed, though one long side of the room is made of gauzed or glass doors which can all be opened and folded back, concertina-style. This opens up the front of the chalet on to the wide balcony outside. All of the floors are held together with wooden dowels and studs rather than nails or screws and beautifully finished with 'adzed' edges to the light, wooden floorboards.

A slight partition divides the main bedroom and lounge from a dressing area with a wardrobe, an old-style claw-footed bath, and 2 conical sinks placed centrally: a stylish use of space. Another partition separates this from a toilet, then outside is an open-air shower, surrounded by circular clay walls (with a view over the channel).

Set a few metres away from each room is a *sala*, a small outside gazebo, with a mattress and cushions, under a shady thatched roof. This makes a lovely perch for relaxing in the afternoon, raised far off the ground in the heart of the date-palm forest, overlooking the channel.

In short, Jao is visually stunning and exceedingly comfortable; if you want private luxury in the Delta then it's superb. It's an obvious choice for honeymoon couples. However, it's a large camp where guests will stay in their rooms rather than mix socially, so doesn't have quite the intimate atmosphere or sociable feel that you may find at some of the smaller camps.

US$660/845 pp sharing/sgl low season to US$1,235/1,420 high season, inc all meals, activities, park fees, laundry, most drinks; exc transfers. Open all year.

⌂ **Kwetsani** (5 tents). Kwetsani (⊕ KWETSA 19°14.594'S, 22°32.200'E) faces east, towards the rising sun, from a long, narrow island about 10km northwest of Jao, its larger, more opulent neighbour. (This can take 40 mins if the roads are dry, or an hour by boat.)

The main lounge/dining room area at Kwetsani is slightly raised and stands under a high thatched roof, with one side open, overlooking an open plain. There's a dining table under part of this, a trendy metal fireplace in the centre (handy when it's cool in the morning), and an open lounge area with comfy chairs, a leather sofa and a small bookshelf. Nearby is a well-stocked bar, complete with a jackalberry, Diospyros mespiliformis, growing up through it.

The wooden decking floor extends from under the thatch on to a wide veranda, which has been built around a huge sycamore fig (*Ficus sycomorus*), a marula (*Sclerocarya birrea caffra*) and a sausage tree (*Kigelia africana*). There's usually a spotting scope standing on the deck here. Nearby is a guest washroom/toilet, which not only has a tree growing up through it, but also has half of its wall cut away to give a view. Down a sloping walkway, almost on the level of the surrounding plains, a few sun-loungers, umbrellas and chairs surround a small splash-pool (about 5m x 3m). On the other side of the lounge is a viewing platform about 3m up from the main deck – though the view from the rooms is usually as good.

The chalets are all raised off the ground, and linked by wooden walkways. 2 are south of the main area, 3 are on the north side. Each has twin beds, or a dbl, under a large mosquito net, with a fan above it. Behind the substantial wooden bed-head is a large mirror, twin washbasins and a small wardrobe with shelves. On either side of this, separate doors lead into small rooms, one containing an indoor shower, the other a toilet.

There is also a reed-walled outdoor shower on the balcony, along with several easy chairs and a table. Kwetsani is a lovely camp which, perhaps helped by its small size, had a very relaxed and positive atmosphere when I last visited.

13

US$470/655 pp sharing/sgl low season to US$785/970 high season, inc all meals, activities, park fees, laundry, most drinks; exc transfers. Open all year.

🛖 **Jacana Camp** (5 tents). Although less than 4km north of Jao, Jacana (⊕ JACANA 19°16.766'S, 22°36.619'E) is a 35min boat ride from it. Jacana was originally a basic 'trails camp'. It started life as a base for mokoro excursions for small escorted-group itineraries that run across Chobe and Moremi. However, for 2001 Wilderness changed its emphasis and was marketing it directly for individual visitors as part of the small group of 'Vintage' camps (see page 171).

It's a much smaller, simpler camp than most in the Delta, and stands on a small island in the very beautiful Jao Flats area. Like Jao, the density of date palms lends Jacana the feeling of a tropical island. The dining/bar area is a simple 2-storey structure with a canvas roof and roll-down screens around its side. Downstairs this has a neat, well stocked bar and a small lounge/reading area with easy chairs and a sofa. Upstairs is the dining area, with a polished wooden floor and a large dining table.

Behind this is a thatched hut, which they call a *hustshi*, and a few hammocks. Meals are sometimes eaten outside, in the open area behind at the centre of camp – which reminds me of eating in a traditional African *kraal*.

Each of the tents here are raised slightly on decking, and fairly small by the standards of the Delta (about 3m x 3m).

These have simple low-voltage electric lights, twin or dbl beds, and a basic wardrobe. There's a small veranda at the front with 2 canvas directors' chairs and a table. Behind each is a private toilet, shower and washbasin, which are all open to the skies. (It's lovely to have a hot shower under blue skies and palm trees, but this isn't an ideal design for use during the rains, between January and April!)

One of the camp's most entertaining features is the guest toilet, which is down a rough walkway from the main upper deck. There's an impressive cement-moulded bowl, a great view, and a pulley made in 'Heath Robinson' style to flush the toilet. In a similar vein, the camp has several painted concrete features: a hippo, a crocodile and a purple sofa that pay tribute to the builder's imagination. They may not sound fun, but they are.

From around April to September, flood levels are high and the area around the camp is flooded. Then Jacana is best visited as a base for mokoro excursions, as game drives would entail a 20min boat ride to reach the jetty, the nearest point where Jacana's vehicles can be parked.

During the rest of the year game drives are possible from the island. Though simpler than some of the Delta's camps, Jacana is a beautiful and a very good-value choice for a couple of nights, especially towards the end of the dry season. US$470/655 pp sharing/sgl low season to US$785/970 high season, inc all meals, activities, park fees, laundry, most drinks; exc transfers. Open Apr–Nov.

🛖 **Tubu Tree Camp** (5 tents). Newly opened in June 2002, Tubu is one of Wilderness Safaris' 'Vintage' camps. This means that it's one of their simpler, less expensive camps (see page 171). It has 5 small tents on decks with en-suite shower, toilet and washbasin inside, plus a separate shower outside. The separate dining and lounge areas are also raised up and tented.

Tubu is west of the other 3 camps in the concession, with access to large areas of dry mopane and acacia woodlands. From around April to September, and perhaps later, mokoro trips and fishing ought to be possible – but for the rest of the year activities are limited to game drives and walks. US$470/655 pp sharing/sgl low season to US$785/970 high season, inc all meals, activities, park fees, laundry, most drinks; exc transfers. Open all year.

ABU CAMP AND MACATOO (NG26)

At this large concession west of Moremi, the focus is more about the activities that you do here, rather than the environment. Abu Camp is the main place in the Delta for riding elephants, and Macatoo Camp is one of the Delta's two centres for horseriding. The third camp, which I won't cover here, is the relatively famous hunting camp, Selby's.

GETTING THERE AND AWAY The only option for these camps is to make advanced bookings and fly in; there's an airstrip near Abu Camp which is used by both operations. Driving here is totally impractical.

WHEN TO VISIT Because the focus of a trip here is the experience of horseriding or the interactions with elephants, it's fine as long as you avoid the rains. So visit anytime from late April or May to the middle or end of December.

FLORA AND FAUNA HIGHLIGHTS The finer details of the wildlife in this concession tend to be eclipsed by the experience of the horses that you ride, or the elephants that you're with – hence I will make only relatively sketchy comments here on the wild fauna in this area.

However, you will find here most of the Delta's usual big game, including elephant, buffalo, giraffe, blue wildebeest, kudu, tsessebe, red lechwe, impala, zebra, reedbuck, steenbok, warthog, baboons and vervet monkeys. Lion and spotted hyena are the dominant predators, with occasional appearances by leopards and wild dogs.

That said, like NG25 to the north, and NG29 and 30 to the south, I don't think that the variation and density of game is quite up to the levels of, say, central Moremi or some of the areas on the north side of the Delta. However, rest assured that you'll still see plenty of game when visiting here.

ELEPHANT-BACK SAFARIS This is the original elephant-back safari operation, run by Elephant Back Safaris (*P Bag 332, Maun;* ⚊ *6861 260;* f *6861 005;* e *ebs@info.bw; www.abucamp.com*), and has since been emulated by several camps in various parts of southern Africa. (Grey Matters, in NG26, is the Okavango's only other place which offers interactions with non-wild elephants; see page 322.) It's the Delta's most expensive place to visit and is run by Randall Jay Moore, one of its more colourful characters.

Some claim it's simply the ultimate in amazing safari experiences; others detest the whole idea of riding on trained elephants. If you can afford it, you can make up your own mind.

The elephants The camp is named after the lead elephant, Abu, which has starred in various films, including *White Hunter Black Heart* and *The Power of One*. Abu was brought over to Africa from the USA by its trainer, Randall Moore, and gradually a small herd of 12 elephants has been assembled – most of which are orphans. They range from youngsters of six months to Abu, who is 40 years old.

The experience The activities here are flexible, depending on both the guests and the elephants, but will usually include either a morning elephant ride or a whole-day excursion, travelling with the elephants to a shady spot for a long picnic lunch, and then back with them in the late afternoon. Alternatively 4x4s and, depending on water levels, mekoro or boats are always available.

Riding on an elephant involves using a large, custom-made saddle. Although comfortable, in many ways this feels more detached than walking beside them. When you're riding, the other game is largely unaware of your human presence, but the real fascination of these trips is not the other game that you see, or even the ride. It is the experience of being so close to the elephants: being able to walk beside them as they plod along and being comfortable with them at close quarters, rather than viewing them from afar.

Safety issues In common with many safari camps throughout Africa, all visitors here are required to sign an indemnity form which, basically, absolves the camp from any responsibility for your safety whilst participating in a trip. And as when visiting any camp in the bush, you accept that you're taking on certain risks to do with Africa's animals and their unpredictability that you wouldn't face sitting on the couch at home.

13

There are about a dozen trained elephants at Abu Camp at the moment. The older ones have mostly come from zoos in the USA, whilst many of the younger ones are orphans from the Kruger National Park, in South Africa. They include:

Abu – a large bull with matching tusks, born around 1960. Probably from east Africa or the Kruger Park, he was taken when small to the United States, where he was used for rides at a wildlife park in Grand Prairie, Texas. He was returned to Africa in 1988, to feature in the movie *Circles in a Forest*, and moved to Botswana in 1990. He's appeared in many films since, and Randall Moore describes him as an exceptionally calm, intelligent and gentle bull.

Cathy – the matriarch of the herd, distinguished by her shorter left tusk, is the herd's largest adult cow and was also born around 1960. She was captured in Murchison Falls National Park, Uganda, when young, and taken to a zoo outside Toronto. She returned to Africa with Abu in 1988, and came to Botswana in 1990.

Benny – a large, mature bull, Benny has a floppy right ear and no tusks. Born around 1959, he was captured in the Kruger, moved to Brookfield Zoo in Chicago and later to the Fort Worth Zoo in Texas. He returned to Africa with Cathy and Abu, though took a long time to adapt to his new surroundings and is described as 'shy and nervous'.

Mthondo mbomvo – a strong and stocky bull with a broad head and even, splayed tusks, Mthondo was born around 1975. He was originally from Zimbabwe, but translocated when young to South Africa's Pilanesburg Reserve. There he caused trouble, knocking down tents in a hunting camp and harassing visitors, and so in 1993 he was moved to this herd. Now he is regarded by the trainers as quiet and dependable.

Nandipa – one of the herd's young female elephants, distinguished by the hole in her right ear. Her tusks are even and straight, close to the trunk. She was born around 1988, orphaned in Kruger, and moved here in 1990.

The only difference here is that being in such proximity to such huge, strong animals does present a greater risk than most normal photographic safaris.

As an example of this, in early May 2000 a 27-year-old bull named Nyaka Nyaka killed one of the camp's professional guides, Andre Klocke. He had approached the elephant from behind to take its saddle off and accidentally startled the animal. The incident had equally grave consequences for Nyaka Nyaka, who was subsequently shot.

That said, no client has ever been injured by one of the elephants in 11 years of operation. Despite this sad incident, the camp prides itself on a very good safety record.

The camp

Abu Camp (5 tents). When Ker & Downey was involved with this operation, Abu Camp stood on the site that today is occupied by Nxabega (pages 302–3). The new Abu Camp also overlooks a lagoon and consists of very luxurious tents raised up on teak decking. They've been carefully designed using an interior skeleton of wooden poles with walls of canvas stretched between them. Despite being far from most people's image of a tent, they retain the zipped doors and roll-down windows of more traditional safari tents.

Inside they're all slightly different, but very stylish; they're amongst the most luxurious rooms in the Delta. Some beds are mahogany antique 'sleigh-style', whilst others are 4-posters. The floors are beautifully polished teak, dotted with matching rugs. Bathrooms are all spacious and en suite, with a stand-alone shower, flush toilet, washbasins and either a copper or a porcelain bath. Pictures, ornaments and carvings of elephants (and especially of Abu) are all over the camp. Outside each is a shaded deck with comfy canvas chairs.

Shirheni – another young female, born around 1986 and also orphaned in Kruger. She is similar to Nandipa but slightly larger in size. She moved here in 1989 and in November 2000 gave birth to a young bull, named Pula, after she was mated by a wild bull on 20 February 1999.

Pula – born to Shirheni on 27 November 2000 at 06.30, after a night of heavy rain. 'Pula' is the Setswana word for rain or success, as well as the name of Botswana's currency. At birth he was 91cm high and it took an hour before he made his first hesitant steps. He is described as very playful and confident.

Jika – has very short tusks that are close to her trunk. Another Kruger Park orphan, she was born around 1988. She also joined Elephant Back Safaris in 1990, and is described as the herd's 'dizzy blonde'!

Seba – born around 1995, and also an orphan from Kruger. Seba is said to be often surrounded by the young females in the herd, and is the star of the Walt Disney film *Whispers*, which was released in 2000.

Thando – with some distinctive 'red' hair on his head, Thando was born around 1986 and brought to Botswana as an orphan from Kruger in 1990.

Kitimetse II – her name means 'I'm Lost'. She was found at the end of 1999 after she had been injured by a crocodile and abandoned by her own wild herd. She was brought to the boma at Abu Camp, where her wounds were treated and she was slowly introduced to the rest of the herd. She seems to have been completely accepted by the other elephants, and formed close bonds with Jika, Nandipa and Shirheni. She is thought to have been born around 1996.

Mufunyani – means 'The Irritable One'. He is another orphan from Kruger who joined this herd in 1990. In February 2002, the 14-year-old bull was released back in to the wild with a satellite tracking collar, as part of a research project. So far, he is becoming accustomed to a new life as a wild elephant, but usually stays fairly close to Abu Camp.

The dining area is set on an expanse of tiered teak decking punctuated by jackalberry trees (*Diospyros mespiliformis*) and sycamore figs (*Ficus sycomorus*). This stands in front of the main lounge, which has comfy chairs and a small library. The food is good and the service attentive, as you'd expect of a camp which regularly hosts the world's glitterati as guests.

Trips take a maximum of 10 visitors, and last a fixed duration of 5 nights – always starting Wed and ending Mon (thus leaving 2 days of the week when the elephants do not have any guests to deal with).

The terms and conditions are, unusually, worth noting as they insist on a high (30%) deposit. Read them very carefully if you're thinking of booking, and be sure to book at least a year in advance. This is Botswana's most expensive camp. *From US$365 pp sharing low season to US$745 high season, inc accommodation, meals, drinks, laundry & all activities. Open Jan–Oct.*

RIDING SAFARIS For African Horseback Safaris (✆ *686 1523;* e *sjhorses@info.bw; www.africanhorseback.com*) see page 168.

These riding safaris are run by Sarah-Jane Gullick, who is English by birth and clearly has horses in her blood, having been involved in hunting, eventing and even working on a Dude ranch in Wyoming before getting hooked on Africa. She set up this operation in 1994, originally with Ker & Downey Safaris (based out of a camp called Macateer Camp).

Basic trip information Below is some basic information for these trips. Contact African Horseback Safaris if you need more precise details as they've a lot of information about their trips that they can send.

13

Riding ability required These safaris are for experienced riders aged 12 years and over. Riders over 60 need to be 'riding fit' and strong. Trips usually involve about 4–6 hours in the saddle each day. Thus riders need to feel competent about keeping up with the group, capable of riding at all paces; rising to the trot and controlling their horse at the canter. They may also be required to gallop out of trouble, so these trips do not take beginners. For safety reasons, if they think that your riding is not up to standard, you won't be allowed to ride here.

The horses The horses are a variety of thoroughbreds, Namibian Hanovarians, Arabs and Kalahari–Arab crossbreeds ranging from 14 to 16.2 hands (140–165cm) high.

Weight limits There's a weight limit of 15 stone (210lb or 95kg) per person, above which they can sometimes make special arrangements for advanced riders.

Tack and clothes Good quality English- and Western-style trail saddles are supplied, each with its own water bottle. Guests may borrow half chaps; long leather boots are impractical.

African Horseback Safaris does not supply hard hats or safety helmets; you must bring your own. They suggest that riders wear their riding clothes and boots on the plane, and bring their hat and wash bag as hand luggage, in case luggage gets delayed.

The experience See the section on Okavango Horse Safaris (pages 312–14) for more general comments about the fascinating experience of riding through the Okavango. These apply equally well to this operation. Suffice to say that once you step into the saddle, most of the Okavango's resident game will treat you and your horse as a single, composite four-legged herbivore. So antelope will relax around you, and predators will give you pause for thought!

African Horseback Safaris request visitors come for a minimum of seven nights. This will always start on arrival in camp with an introductory talk on the safari, and a safety briefing. Two guides will accompany each riding safari; they carry a first-aid kit, rifle and radio.

Such trips normally incorporate not only riding but the occasional game drive, walk and night drive. Boating, canoeing and fishing are also possible sometimes, depending on water levels. Their riding groups have a maximum of six to eight guests, and a typical seven-day trip would include a few nights spent out at a fly-camp away from the main camp. Note that these trips usually start and end on Tuesdays and Fridays, and seven- or ten-day safaris are the norm.

The riding camps These aim to be comfortable and simple, and all are staffed. As with most camps, the service is a good standard with high-quality food prepared freshly. Dinner is usually a stylish three-course affair, served by candlelight.

Macatoo Camp (4 tents). This is the main camp, used as a base. Like Okavango Horse Safaris' camps in neighbouring NG29 (see pages 312–14), this is a specialist camp, used purely for riders. Each of this small camp's large tents has twin beds, and each tent has its own en-suite shower and loo. There is a furnished mess tent, a small splash pool and a daily laundry service.

Fly-camps (set up as/where required) Longer safaris usually include a couple of nights sleeping at a mobile fly-camp, where the ablutions are a traditional bucket shower and loo.

The costs From March to May and from November to January, a stay here costs US$330 per person per night, including all meals, drinks and activities. This rises to US$445 in the high season from June to October, though if you stay seven nights or more then the cost is US$395. There's a minimum allowed stay of three or four nights, and safaris are generally timed to start and end on Tuesdays and Fridays.

Transfers to/from Maun are US$137 per person, one way. Macatoo use Abu's airstrip, which is one to two hours' drive from camp.

POM POM, KANANA AND NXABEGA (NG27A)

This large, strictly photographic concession is now effectively split between three safari companies: Ker & Downey (who run Kanana), CC Africa (who run Nxabega) and Wilderness Safaris (who took over Pom Pom).

CONCESSION HISTORY By the early 1970s there were a number of camps throughout the Delta, most of which accepted either hunting or photographic guests. One of the bigger companies involved here was Safari South, who ran many camps including Khwai River Lodge, Four Rivers Camp (near the present Kwara), Queenie, Splash, Jedibe, Machaba, Mombo, Pom Pom and Shindi.

Around 1985 Ker & Downey was split from Safari South, as a wholly owned subsidiary, to differentiate the photographic camps from those used for hunting. Ker & Downey then had four photographic camps in the Delta: Shinde, Mombo, Jedibe and Machaba.

A company called Jao Safaris owned Mombo at that time. Various contracts changed, which resulted in Ker & Downey leaving Mombo and Jedibe. (These were eventually taken up by Wilderness Safaris, in 1989.) Meanwhile, the government had designated NG27 for photographic use only, and Ker & Downey took over the running of Pom Pom, which had been another old hunting camp run by Safari South.

From 1985 Pom Pom was the only major camp here, but in 1990 they started a 'partnership' with Randall J Moore. He brought trained African elephants over from the USA to start Elephant Back Safaris (see page 295), and Ker & Downey built Abu Camp (see page 296–7), on the site that Nxabega now occupies, in the north of the reserve. In 1993 I was very excited to visit Pom Pom – and to get here I took my first flight over the Delta! It was then one of Botswana's most upmarket camps, and the rest of the clientele during my stay were from America. The combination of Pom Pom and then Abu Camp was a winning one; business was good for them. (Note that throughout this time there were also a few simple bushcamps in the area, used by various operators.) However, the following year Randall Moore tendered for, and obtained, his own concession next door: NG26. This upset the apple cart, as he then built the camp that is today known as Abu Camp – thus taking away a highly profitable chunk of business from Ker & Downey.

NG27 concession has always been subdivided. First AfroVentures (who subsequently merged with CC Africa) built Nxabega Camp on the site of the old Abu Camp, in the north. Then in 2000 Ker & Downey opened their own new camp, Kanana.

In 2001, Wilderness Safaris took over the marketing and management of Pom Pom, building a completely new small camp here, but keeping the name and location of the 'old' Pom Pom. Since then, it has again changed hands, and is now run by Chobe Safari Lodge in Kasane.

GETTING THERE AND AWAY All of these camps work only with guests flying in, usually having made their bookings months before they travel. Driving here is not possible without permission, and totally impractical.

WHEN TO VISIT Slightly less seasonal than the areas further south and west, there's still a big difference between the game densities through the seasons; they're a lot better when it's drier. As usual, the birding is as good as it gets during the wetter time of the year (December to around March).

FLORA AND FAUNA HIGHLIGHTS Travelling from south to north, the landscapes, flora and fauna change very slowly, but there are slight differences between the various parts of the reserve. Bear in mind whilst reading this that the similarities between the different areas are much greater than their contrasts.

Flora The NG27 concession is in the heart of the Delta and contains most of the environments that are to be found in the Delta. Everywhere you'll find thickets and stands of riverine forest, more open areas of invasive bushes, and occasional floodplains.

The area around Pom Pom is very open and pretty, notable for many tiny islands amidst wide open floodplains, which are often submerged between May and September. These distinct islands are often covered, or at least fringed, by real fan (*Hyphaene petersiana*) and wild date palms (*Phoenix reclinata*), and between them are large marshy floodplains. There are quite a few baobabs in the area, and the forest patches are fairly sparse.

Moving northeast to the area of Kanana, there are fewer flat, open plains and more areas colonised by expanses of wild sage. Around these are larger islands and woodland patches with plenty of the Delta's usual riverine tree species: sausage trees (*Kigelia africana*), jackalberries (*Diospyros mespiliformis*), knobthorns (*Acacia nigrescens*), the occasional marula (*Sclerocarya birrea caffra*) and the odd raintree (*Lonchocarpus capassa*). (The raintree, also sometimes called the appleleaf, gets it name from the droplets which are secreted by froghopper insects as they suck the sap from the leaves. This keeps the soil beneath the tree moist, and in exceptional cases can even form pools.)

Further northwest, around Nxabega, the forests become more in evidence with large, dense lines of broadleaf forests and patches of acacia. Mixed with these are a few open plains, fringed by real fan palms (*Hyphaene petersiana*) and stands of riverine trees. In the midst of the larger floodplains you'll see occasional islands crowned with an African mangosteen (*Garcinia livingstonei*), or perhaps a large

THE LIZARD

There's a tale of slightly fussy, older woman coming to stay on her own in a tented safari camp. Over lunch she complained about a lizard in her room, but was told this was nothing to worry about – and it'd probably vanish of its own accord soon.

That afternoon after lunch, whilst most of the camp was having a siesta, she wandered out in search of one of the staff. 'That lizard is still in my room,' she proclaimed, with agitation, to one of the managers that she found in the dining room. He then explained that this was really nothing to worry about, as lizards often came in and out of the rooms. In fact, he elaborated, 'it's very good as they're natural way of keeping the mosquito population down.' So, she could go back and sleep, relaxed in the knowledge that it wouldn't do her any harm at all.

Off she went, but 20 minutes later she was back again. She couldn't sleep, claiming that the lizard was making too much noise. Unimpressed, but determined to satisfy the guest, the manager took her back to the room – only to be completely embarrassed to find a huge monitor lizard thrashing about, trying to find a way out of the tent.

sycamore fig (*Ficus sycomorus*), growing out of an old termite mound perhaps surrounded by a few russet bush-willow bushes (*Combretum hereroense*). Some of the Nxabega's floodplains have thick coverings of hippo grass (*Vossia cuspidata*) that turn a lovely shade of orange-red around September.

Fauna The variety of game in NG27 certainly seems wider to me than that found in areas further south and west – though I feel that it's not as wide as some of the reserves on the northeast side of the Delta. Tsessebe, impala, wildebeest, lechwe, steenbok, baboon and zebra are all common and seen here very regularly. Giraffe do particularly well here, they're very relaxed amongst the many acacia thickets, and there is a good number of resident elephants.

Lion and spotted hyena are the commonest large predators, though the mixed woodland is a perfect habitat for leopard that are numerous, though only seen occasionally. Cheetah are seen here only rarely, when the reserve is at its driest (October to March); they're not at all common. Wild dog pass through periodically (as they do through most areas of northern Botswana) though not frequently. Both black-backed and side-striped jackal are common.

As with most of the Delta there's always plenty of smaller animals, too widespread to be worthy of particular comment . . . though I recall a great sighting of an entertaining troop of dwarf mongooses here once!

Birdlife The birding is good and very varied in this concession. Kanana has immediate access to the deep channel of the Xudum channel that is lined with a mixture of water figs, huge floating mats of graceful papryus and anchored sections of miscanthus grass (*Miscanthus junceus*). Amongst the birdlife, there's a notable profusion of squacco herons. However, what is really interesting in the Kanana area is the recent discovery (October 2001) of two heronries. One is small, whilst another is described as being as big as the heronry at Gcodikwe Lagoon. When found this had many birds breeding there, including yellow-billed, marabou and open-billed storks, darters, cormorants and egrets. (I haven't yet seen this, but how such a large heronry went 'unnoticed' for so long is a complete puzzle.) However fascinating, visitors must remember the problems that disturbances can cause to the birds; don't encourage your guide to approach too close to the birds.

Nxabega doesn't have the heronry, though one recent September over 500 open-billed storks and about 1,000 squacco herons were seen gathering to roost just a little west of Nxabega. It does, however, have a couple of very old pole bridges across small waterways in its reserve. These prove particularly attractive perching places for waterbirds that can then be seen while driving. (This is an advantage if, like me, you prefer a stationary base from which to use a camera and tripod, rather than a rocking boat.) There are lots of hamerkops, small herons, egrets (including a good number of slaty), black crakes and bee-eaters. Kingfishers are well represented; here I've got closer to photograph a diminutive malachite kingfisher than I ever have whilst on a boat.

Read the marketing literature for almost any camp in the Delta and you'll realise that claims for sightings of 'the elusive Pel's fishing owl' are a tedious marketing cliché. Every camp simultaneously trumpets their rarity, and yet claims you'll see one whilst staying there. That said, when I last visited Nxabega, one such owl was making predictable, regular appearances on one of the old bridges, and the guides advised that three pairs were regularly seen in different locations in the area. Meanwhile, I'm reliably informed that in 2002 a pair of Pel's fishing owls were seen in, and said to be nesting in, trees about 100m from camp.

Having said all that about the resident birds that associate with water, you'll find an equally good variety of drier-country birds in this reserve. On my last visit just amongst the eagles, I spotted tawny, bateleur, Wahlberg's and, most remarkably, a martial eagle battling with a large monitor lizard on the ground beside our vehicle, near Pom Pom. (We found both locked in combat, but at a stalemate. Eventually they disentangled themselves and the great lizard made a hasty retreat under a bush.)

Finally, on a more domestic note, the staff at Nxabega seems to have 'tamed' a pair of wild yellow-billed hornbills sufficiently for them to come along to afternoon tea on most days.

WHERE TO STAY The camps are totally different from one another, perhaps because they're run in different ways by different companies.

Kanana (8 tents) Ker & Downey (page 170). Opened in May 2000, Kanana (⊕ KANANA 19°32.577'S; 22°51.731'E) is built a few kilometres from the site of an old basic bushcamp known as Khurunxaragha Camp (which was formerly used by Wilderness for their mobile safaris, and was located near the present airfield). Kanana stands at roughly the centre of NG27, and overlooks the reedbeds of the Xudum River. This gives the camp access to a permanent, deep-water channel for boating all year.

Accommodation is in very comfortable tents that spread out on the left side of the main area. These are separated by about 20m, and so even the furthest room isn't miles from the centre of camp. They have sewn-in insect-proof groundsheets and 6 large mesh windows — even the front of the tent can be opened up into a large mesh area, giving a wonderful airy feel when it's warm.

Inside, the floor's teak, covered with sisal matting. The tents are comfortable and well furnished with a wooden wardrobe and a luggage rack, dressing table and chairs, and plenty of thoughtful touches. The raffia bedside tables have electric lights powered by solar-powered batteries — the camp's generator is usually only switched on during the day. Twin or dbl beds have good-quality cotton sheets and down pillows with blankets. A canvas divider separates sleeping space from the en-suite flush toilet, washbasin and shower (very efficient too — hot water from individual gas geysers).

Outside on the shaded veranda, to the front and side of the tents, there's a table and comfy chairs, and all the tents face the river from under a cover of riverine trees — jackalberries, knobthorns and sausage trees. These are linked by sandy paths, illuminated at night by electric lanterns, one of which passes the small, circular waist-deep plunge pool.

Kanana's main area is a U-shaped wooden building with a large tree in the centre and a long dining room, several small lounge areas (one with a small library), a bar and, down nearer the water, a 'sandpit' for fires.

Activities possible here include boat trips (including fishing for bream or catfish), mokoro excursions (often including short island walks) and game drives. Though their comfortable vehicles have been carefully thought out, with canvas pockets for binoculars and lots of space, the camp's strongest suit is its mokoro trips. It's particularly convenient that when water levels are good, these can be launched directly from the side of the lodge's main area, and into the reedbeds which surround the Xudum River.

As with most camps, Kanana works on the basis of one long safari activity after breakfast, then siesta time after lunch, and another activity after afternoon tea, before dinner. Sometimes a late-night drive is possible after dinner.
US$330 pp sharing/sgl low season to US$595/815 high season, inc all meals, drinks and activities, & laundry; exc transfers. No children under 7. Open Mar–Nov.

Nxabega (10 tents, max 18 guests) Contact CC Africa (see page 169). Built on the site of the original Abu Camp, Nxabega (⊕ NXABEG 19°29.080'S; 22°47.670'E) is the most northerly of the camps in NG27. It's about an hour's drive north of Kanana (though only around 12km as the birds fly!) and 11km south-southeast of Xigera, which is in Moremi. However, for most of the year Xigera is inaccessible by land from Nxabega because of the Boro River.

Nxabega's lounge/dining area is constructed on a grand scale from wood, stone and a high shaggy thatched roof, around a huge jackalberry tree. Inside, it is swish but understated, with clean lines and teak-panelled walls. The large dining area stands under 2 electric candelabras. Nearby in the lounge are 2 separate groups of luxurious settees. Heavy glass-topped coffee tables rest on game-skin patchworks, supporting the odd picture book, cigar boxes and a backgammon set. It's comfortably done with style and the odd striking African artefact (sadly of west rather than southern African origin!). The bar is almost hidden, but stocked exceedingly comprehensively with obscure liqueurs, imported spirits and good wines. (Unlimited house wine, beers and soft drinks are normally included in the rate, but if you want to drink their cellar of vintage wines dry, they'll charge extra!)

The rooms are of high quality, large tents raised up on platforms about a metre above the ground, overlooking the floodplain. All are well spread out, with a discreet 30–40m between them. No 1 is on the far right of the lodge (as you look over the water); Nos 6 & 7 are on either side of the main area; and No 10 (the honeymoon suite) is past the large swimming pool on the left side. Each has a shaded veranda with table and chairs outside. Inside, twin or dbl beds stand on a smooth wooden floor, draped with quality cotton sheets, down duvets and assorted pillows.

These tents are furnished well – with chairs, a dressing table, wardrobe and bedside lamps (powered by a solar-powered battery system). At the back of each tent is a small en-suite bathroom with a flush toilet, hot shower (heated by a gas geyser), and a washbasin.

Activities include day and night 4x4 game drives, mokoro excursions and boat trips (good fishing is possible on the Boro River). Nxabega's been constructed with care and generally seems to be run with a higher complement of staff than most lodges (average 2 staff per guest). This gives it an air of quality. The food is particularly good, but what I appreciated more was the flexibility that visitors have over everything, from the timings of breakfast and lunch, to the scheduling of activities. These are seldom regimented, and the staff make real efforts to organise activities to suit you. If you've ever wanted to do a late-night drive after dinner to look

for aardvarks, or a mid-day boating trip . . . Nxabega is a good choice!

US$365–745 pp sharing, low–high season, inc all meals, drinks, activities & park fees. Open all year.

⌂ **Pom Pom** (9 Meru tents) ↘ 6250 336; m 7131 1809; f 6250 437; e pompom@ chobelodge.co.bw; www.pompomcamp.com (⊕ POMPOM 19°35.072'S; 22°50.560'E). One of the original upmarket camps in the Delta, Pom Pom was taken over in 2005 by Chobe Safari Lodge in Kasane (see pages 180–1). Although it is barely 5km southwest of Kanana, a game drive between the 2 camps would take 45 mins. Pom Pom was originally opened by Ker & Downey in 1985, but rebuilt by Wilderness when they took it over in 2001.

The camp's thatched, Meru-style tents stand on the ground at the edge of an island overlooking a small, permanent lagoon. They are furnished with twin or dbl beds (there's also one family unit), a wicker chair, and a wooden dresser and wardrobe; behind a wall in each is an en-suite bathroom.

The simple bar and separate lounge have been replaced by a new central area under thatch, bringing together the restaurant, bar and a curio shop; there's also a small pool. Activities include day and night drives, mokoro trips and short walks; excursions by boat are possible only occasionally, when water levels are very high. (The main flood hits here around May, often filling the dry lagoon in a day. The area's highest water levels usually occur around Jun–Aug.) While children over 8 are welcome, families with children aged 8–12 will be taken on game drives in a private vehicle, at an additional cost of US$150 per day.

US$440/540 pp sharing/sgl Jun–Oct, US$305/405 Apr–May & Nov, inc all meals, activities, park fees, laundry, most drinks; exc transfers. Packages available with Chobe Safari Lodge. No children under 8. Open Apr–Nov.

DELTA, ODDBALLS, GUNN'S AND EAGLE ISLAND (NG27B)

Between NG30, NG32 and Moremi stands a fairly small photographic reserve, just off the southwest side of Chief's Island. This was the first area of the Okavango where tourism really took off in volume, and it's now very interesting to see it making the transition to smaller numbers of visitors, and more upmarket camps.

CONCESSION HISTORY A short history of the Delta and Oddballs camps is an interesting illustration of the transition between different types of tourism mentioned above. It started shortly after Lodges of Botswana bought Delta Camp in 1983. During their first year they not only catered to upmarket visitors, but also used the camp as a base for the mokoro trips of more budget-conscious travellers.

This mix didn't work in one camp, and so in 1984 they built a separate lower-budget camp at the other end of their island. The nickname of their first manager was 'Oddball', and so this became Oddball's Camp. Oddball's marketing was astute and well targeted, portraying a relaxed, hippie hangout where spaced-out campers could find paradise on their own island in the Delta. This became a buzzing base for budget mokoro trips in the heart of the Delta – *the* backpacker's place in the Delta, known in hostels from Nairobi to Cape Town, and beyond.

It was very successful. At first they just had showers, toilets and a (fridge-less) bar; campers brought all their own food and kit. It grew fast, eventually encompassing a shop for campers and food, as well as chilled drinks from a fully fledged bar.

When business peaked during the late 1980s and early 1990s, they had up to 120 visitors *per day* flying in, some camping for a night in the camp and others heading out on mokoro trips. Then there were no limits on how many visitors the camp could accept. The camp had a rule that every visitor had to stay at Oddball's for at least one night.

Then two things happened which changed this business. Firstly, in July 1989 the government raised its national park fees from P10 pp per week to P30 pp per day. Mokoro trips from Oddball's had always been to Moremi, and this increased their prices dramatically.

Secondly, there had long been a process of tendering for camps, whereby safari operators bid for leases to operate safari camps. In 1996 the government introduced new leases to camps in many of the Delta's reserves, insisting that safari companies not only produce large cheques for rental and royalties (per visitor), but also a 'management plan' for the reserves. These became effective in January 1997.

In drawing up these detailed management plans, the safari companies were forced to look not only at their game and environmental policies, and the sustainability of them, but also how they trained their staff, and what they were doing to help the wider community in the area. This process raised the issues of sustainability, responsible tourism and community development – and placed them in the centre of the government's decision-making process. Thus, it made them important to the safari operators.

Oddball's had started a programme of training their polers as early as 1988. Like all camps, it now insists that all of its polers have a qualification as a professional mokoro guide. The government insists that standards like these are now applied across the board for all the camps in the region.

By 1997 Oddball's alone had about 35 mokoro guides working for them. They were able to renew their leases on Oddball's and its smaller, upmarket sister camp, Delta Camp. However, the government had made a hard bargain: they had to reduce the number of visitors to a maximum combined total of 60 people at any one time. That was 40 guests at Oddball's and 20 at Delta Camp, a fraction of past numbers.

Immediately prices had to be increased in order to cover their costs from a much smaller base of visitors. In December 1999 both camps were extensively renovated; economics dictated that they had to move more upmarket, charging more, to stay in business. The camp on the Oddball's site was rebuilt in much greater style, as a fully fledged upmarket camp that could command high prices. Then the names of the two camps were switched. This newly built camp on the site of Oddball's old site is now known as Delta Camp, whilst the older camp which was once known as Delta Camp became Oddballs (without an apostrophe this time).

Thus the 1980s camp has become an upmarket camp for the next century, whilst the original budget camp has been totally rebuilt and refurbished as a new luxurious camp, to standards which are now much higher than they were.

This is a textbook example of what has happened right across Botswana. Pressure from the government, using park fees and the concessions as tools of implementation, has led to lower numbers of visitors to Botswana's wild areas, and hence to more costly safaris and more upmarket lodges. For their money visitors now get a much more exclusive experience, guided by polers who have more training and better skills than before – and are paid better as the result.

In summary: the environment benefits, the local people benefit, Botswana's finances benefit, and even the visitors get a better experience – that is, those who can still afford to visit!

GEOGRAPHY NOTE As with the whole Delta, the floods in this area are variable and unpredictable, in both duration and timing. The flood usually arrives between March and August, and remains for an average of four months. However, hydrologists note that there has been a measured decrease in the amount of water flowing down the Boro River since the late 1980s. In the 1994–95 period of water inflow, it was estimated that the lower Boro River received little over half of its long-term average. That water flow has since gradually decreased.

This could be explained by postulating that the western side of the Delta is gradually rising relative to the eastern side. Hence the Thaoge is gradually flooding less, and the Khwai is flooding more. The Boro is fairly central to the Delta, and derives its flow from the Nqoga River (the source of the Khwai River). However, it breaks from this at a very sharp, acute angle, and hence some experts suggest that it should be considered as being influenced the same way as the rivers on the western side of the Delta.

Having said all this, some say that changes in water flows could be caused simply by a hippo changing its regular path in the higher reaches of the Delta! Whatever the cause, this reduced flow isn't necessarily good or bad for the visitor; but it is a help in understanding some of the gradual changes which are happening (over decades) to the area's vegetation.

GETTING THERE AND AWAY Although years ago safari operators used to offer boat transfers up the Boro River from Maun to here, now flying in is really the only way. There are several airstrips, including Delta airstrip (⊕ DELAIR 19°31.840'S; 23°05.430'E), which is closest to both Oddballs and Delta Camp, and, about 4km southwest from there, Xaxaba airstip (⊕ XAXAIR 19°33.220'S; 23°03.510'E).

WHEN TO VISIT Though open all year, these camps rely primarily on mokoro trips and so are certainly at their best when the sun is shining and the sky blue, ie: between April and November. If you're camping out then it makes for a better trip if it's not too cold at night, thus my favourite months for visiting here would be around May–early June and September–October time.

FLORA AND FAUNA HIGHLIGHTS The Boro River and its associated floodplains dominate this reserve. A recent (1996) land survey estimated that only about 4% of the whole reserve was permanent swampland, but 75% was classed as seasonally inundated swamp and grasslands. The remaining 22% is dry land: riverine forests and grasslands on the islands. So this is a very seasonal environment, which changes annually with the floods.

Flora As noted above, there is relatively little permanent swamp here. Small patches of papyrus are found though, usually in photogenic little clumps beside the main Boro River. Look carefully and you'll also find areas of common reeds

(*Phragmites australis*), Miscanthus grass (*Miscanthus junceus*), bulrushes (*Typha capensis*) and a number of floating leafed, emergent and submerged species.

Perhaps the major feature of the area is some splendid, mature patches of riverine forests that line sections of the Boro River. Here you'll find lots of real fan palms (*Hyphaene petersiana*), often in beautiful dense stands. There's also a scattering of all the 'usual suspects' that you'd expect in riverine forest in the region, including leadwoods (*Combretum imberbe*), jackalberries (*Diospyros mespiliformis*), knobthorns (*Acacia negrescens*), sausage trees (*Kigelia africana*), large fever-berries (*Croton megalobotrys*), woodland waterberries (*Syzygium guineense*) and occasional baobab trees (*Adansonia digitata*). However, perhaps the area's most unusual flora are the huge strangler figs (*Ficus* species, probably *thonningii*, *natalensis* or *fischeri*). There are several specimens here enveloping large leadwood trees – an amazing sight.

On the larger island, and particularly on Chief's Island (in Moremi, but visited from these camps), you'll find permanently dry forest areas. These vary from mopane woodlands in areas of clay soil, to areas of acacias where there's more sand.

In the deepest areas of sand you'll find *Terminalia sericea*, the source of the best wood from which to craft traditional mokoro poles.

Adjacent to the river are large areas of very shallow floodplains. A wide variety of grasses, sedges and herbs are found in these areas with various species of *Eragrostis, Imperata, Panicum, Aristida* and *Cymbopogen* being common. Over 200 plant species have been recorded here, though the floodplains are very often dotted with a sparse covering of *Imperata cylindrica,* sometimes known as 'silver spike', with long, rigid leaf spikes growing from a rhizome, some with a small 'spikelet' at the end.

Fauna None of the camps in this reserve conducts game drives, so a visit here is usually much more about the ambience of the Delta than about spotting game. Come for the experience, let any game sightings be a bonus, and you'll have a good trip.

That said, there are good game densities in the area, and especially on the adjacent Chief's Island. Even from a mokoro you're likely to see hippopotami and crocodiles in the water. Elephants are frequently seen in the drier months, from May to October, wandering through the floodplains; from December to April they are around in smaller numbers.

When out walking on the islands there is a chance of much more game. The area's dominant antelope is the red lechwe, but you will also find tsessebe, impala, zebra, kudu, reedbuck, giraffe, warthog and buffalo. As the area becomes drier with time, blue wildebeest are being seen more often. Roan, sable and waterbuck remain absent from this area. When the flood is at its height, sitatunga are occasionally seen. With the recent re-introduction of rhino to Chief's Island, there's a very slim chance that you could bump into one of these.

The most common predators here are lion, spotted hyena and jackals. Leopard are rarely seen, but they will be relatively common as the riverine forest suits them perfectly. Wild dogs and cheetah also occur here, but are rare sightings. There was even a report from this area of a brown hyena sighting, though this is certainly a rarity here.

Birdlife Birding is an important feature of all the trips here; you'll probably spend much of your time exploring the area from a mokoro. As mentioned above, the water levels can vary hugely – in October 2002 they dropped by 15cm in just three weeks. So expect the channels and the birdlife to vary greatly through the seasons.

When water levels are lowest, around November to February, you may find skimmers on some exposed sandbanks. Meanwhile knob-billed ducks, long-toed and blacksmith's plovers, and saddle-billed storks are amongst a whole host of permanent residents. As levels rise, red-winged pratincoles gather in large flocks, and there is always a good variety of kingfishers, from giant and pied to the tiny pygmy and malachite. Woodland kingfishers – insectivorous birds which are usually seen hunting for insects in the riverine forest – appear for the summer around the end of October. They arrive with a variety of migrants, including carmine bee-eaters, aerobatics yellow-billed kites, and paradise flycatchers, the males of which have the most spectacular tails. I've a reliable report of black coucals in front of Delta Camp, but haven't seen them there myself.

Much of the Boro's channel usually sees the annual catfish run (see box on page 339), and this area is no exception. If you're lucky enough to catch this then you can spot 30 species or more in a 100m stretch of waterway. Pelicans, skimmers and a wide variety of herons, egrets, storks, stilts, snipes and cormorants all appear in quantity then, to take advantage of the abundant food.

WHAT TO SEE AND DO Though these camps differ slightly in their activities, they are essentially water-camps from which you take guided mokoro trips along the Boro River, and out on to its associated floodplains.

Most also offer walking trips on the islands – just as camps here have for decades. These generally use the bush-wise local polers as guides, whose local knowledge can be excellent (even if their communication skills in English are more variable). They will almost never be carrying any firearms for protection, so see my general comments under *Walking in the bush* in *Chapter 6*, for a further discussion of the safety issues raised by this approach.

WHERE TO STAY Of the camps in this reserve, Delta and Oddballs are run by Lodges of Botswana (see page 170); Semetsi Camp, Gunn's Camp and Gunn's Bush Camp are run from their base in Maun (see page 169); and Eagle Island Camp, Khwai River Lodge and Savuti Camp are run by Orient-Express.

Delta Camp (10 chalets). Bought by Lodges of Botswana in 1983, this camp has been run by them ever since; at the start of 2001 the new camp built on the site of the old Oddball's Camp was renamed as Delta Camp.

The camp still overlooks the Boro River, and its reed-and-thatch chalets all have open verandas looking northeast into Moremi. All have an en-suite bathroom, including a shower, toilet and washbasin.

Activities centre around mokoro trips, with walks on the islands guided by your poler. With a little advanced notice, it's possible to go on day trips with picnic lunches.

US$360/450 pp sharing/sgl Nov–Mar, May & June, US$420/490 Apr & Jul–Oct, inc meals, all drinks, activities & park fees. Maun–Delta airstrip flights US$65 each way, strict 10kg luggage allowance. Open all year.

Oddballs Palm Island Luxury Lodge (20 dome tents). Southeast of Delta Camp, but beside the same Boro River, Oddballs is still thought of as a destination in the Okavango for budget travellers, even though it's *much more* expensive than it was.

For your money, you now have your own 2.4m x 2.4m (3-person) dome tent which stands on a raised wooden deck, surmounted by a roll of reeds for shade. Outside is a view over the Delta, inside are 2 camp beds, with a mattress and pillow included, and on its veranda is a small table and 2 stools.

Unlike the backpacker's camp of old, a stay here now includes all meals and activities. It usually includes a first and last night at Oddballs itself, with the intervening nights camping out on the islands. All your camping kit and food is provided (drinks are not – you buy these separately), but you do your own cooking whilst you're on the mokoro trail. *US$180/240 pp sharing/sgl, inc meals, activities, park fees for both the camp and the mokoro trails. Maun–Oddballs airstrip flights US$65 each way, strict 10kg luggage allowance. Open all year.*

Gunn's Camp (7 tents, 1 chalet). Gunn's is situated on the Boro River, overlooking Moremi Game Reserve, and was founded and run for years by the brusque Mike Gunn. It used to be accessed as often by motorboat as by plane from Maun, and in the 1980s it ran week-long 'fitness in the

13

wilderness' courses which, amongst other things, taught you how to punt your own mokoro.

Since then it has been upgraded to a more upmarket camp. Now it has Meru tents, each with twin beds, colourful fabrics and teak furniture. All have en-suite bathrooms with flush toilets and showers at the back, and a small sitting area outside with comfy chairs. The honeymoon chalet, which is thatched and raised up on wooden decking with a large veranda, has a 4-poster bed with mosquito-net drapes. All have electric lighting run from a generator, with battery back-up.

The camp's central dining/bar area is wood and thatch, with an excellent sitting area on the 1st floor, overlooking the adjacent river and its floodplains. Nearby is the camp's small swimming pool.

Activities are organised in the morning and evening, usually involving mokoro trips and perhaps including a walk on one of the islands. If the channels are deep enough, then motorboat trips along the Boro are possible. With prior notice, it's also possible to take a mokoro and poler out for a whole-day trip, with a picnic lunch for a long stop on one of the islands.

US$325/425 pp sharing/sgl, inc meals, activities, park fees, most drinks. Maun–Gunn's Camp flight US$170 each way, strict 10kg luggage allowance. Open all year.

🏠 **Gunn's Bush Camp** This campsite near to Gunn's Camp is used as a base for mokoro excursions around the Delta. It has a restaurant, a bar, a swimming pool, and a shop where food can be bought and limited amounts of equipment are available for rental.

The options are flexible. You can bring your own camping equipment and food, or you can hire tents and kit (best booked in advance) and eat in their restaurant. That said, the equipment hire is relatively expensive: P40 per day for a 2-person tent, P10 per day for a towel! Meals cost around P25 for a full breakfast, P20 for a lunch special, and P38 for a 2-course dinner.

Activities are mokoro trips with walks on the islands. These cost about US$70 per mokoro per day, and can be as short or as long as you wish, camping on the islands as you go. Packs consisting of a day's food and equipment hire cost US$50/60 pp sharing/sgl per day; camping fees are US$10 pp per day, and park fees are US$15 pp per day. Transfers between Maun and Gunn's Bush Camp cost US$170 pp each way (10kg luggage allowance fairly keenly enforced). Thus a 4-day/3-night mokoro trip would cost around US$356 pp sharing (including

flights). Add on another US$150 each, making a total of US$506 each, if you need food and equipment – which you probably will given the strict weight limits for the flights.

From US$200/300 pp sharing/sgl low season to US$250/375 high season, inc meals, activities; exc drinks, park fees. Maun–Gunn's Bush Camp flight US$170 each way; strict 10kg luggage allowance. Open all year.

🏠 **Semetsi Camp** (8 tents). Overlooking the Boro River, and Moremi Game Reserve beyond that, Semetsi has walk-in mini-Meru tents, raised on wooden platforms. Inside are twin beds with mattresses, duvets, towels and linen. It's clean and comfortable, but fairly spartan by the standards of most camps in the Delta. Flush toilets and showers are shared, and set back from the tents.

Semetsi has a reed-walled bar and dining area, topped by a thatched roof, and a campfire outside for drinks at the end of the day. Lighting throughout the camp is by paraffin lantern, which I still think is the most beautiful way to light a camp in the bush! Laundry service is included in the costs.

Activities here normally take place mornings and evenings, generally mokoro trips including a walk on a nearby island.

From US$200/300 pp sharing/sgl low season to US$250/375 high season, inc meals, activities; exc drinks, park fees. Maun–Semetsi flight US$170 each way; strict 10kg luggage allowance. Open all year.

🏠 **Eagle Island Camp** (12 tents). One of the Delta's first photographic camps was built here at Xaxaba Island (unless you're fluent in one of the local Khoisan languages and used to the various clicks, this is usually pronounced 'Kakaaba', with 'Ka' as in 'cat.'). It was known as Xaxaba Camp and, at one point, was bought by Lloyd Wilmott (of 'Lloyd's Camp, Savuti' fame) before it was run for many years by Gametrackers (see page 171 for details). There's still a bushcamp, known as Baboon Camp, used by wildlife researchers, on the same spot today. Now the main camp nearby is this reserve's plushest: Eagle Island.

As you might expect, it's built to basically the same design and specification as its sister camps, Khwai River Lodge (pages 250) and Savute Elephant Camp (page 219). This means large, opulent canvas rooms built to high-quality standards on timber platforms, each with a wide veranda at the front and an outside lounge with a hammock and ceiling fan. They're well spread out and linked by illuminated pathways. Inside, each tent is fully furnished with polished wooden floors, rugs and luxurious furniture. The twin ¾-size beds, which are usually pushed together, have high-quality cotton bedding, bedside tables and twin lamps, not to mention the accoutrements of a top hotel such as minibars and safes. The beds are surrounded by mosquito netting and surmounted by 2 AC units (yes, really – as well as the ceiling fan!). And there's 110/220V power augmented by 24hr battery electricity. At the back, each of these tents has a separate toilet room with his and hers basins, a large shower room, and acres of polished wood. For relaxation in camp, there's a library of books and videos, and a heated pool next to the lagoon.

Activities are mainly mokoro trips and guided walks on the islands, though during high-water periods (usually Jun–Sep) motorboat trips are also practical. For most of the year there's also a large 14-seater 'sundowner cruiser' which can slowly coast along the main channels. On very rare occasions, it's been so dry here that there's not enough water for good mokoro trips, and then the camp has organised game drives. Otherwise, Eagle Island is a camp for water-based activities.

From US$499 pp sharing low season to US$911 pp sharing high season, inc accommodation, meals, drinks, laundry & all activities. Open all year.

XIGERA, MOMBO AND CHIEF'S CAMP (NG28)

Although technically in the NG28 concession, on the north and west side of Chief's Island, this concession was effectively swallowed up by Moremi Game Reserve in 1992. These three private camps and their satellites are covered in *Chapter 12, The Okavango Delta – Moremi Game Reserve*, pages 264–71.

GUBANARE AND XUDUM (NG29 AND NG30)

Together these equally large concessions cover a total of about 2,000km² on the southern edge of the Delta, sandwiched between southern Moremi and the Sandvelt Tongue. They're designated as 'multi-use' concessions, and so separate parts of each are used for hunting and for photographic trips. All pay a 'lease fee' to the local community for their use of the land.

I've only described the non-hunting camps here, which are split between two operations: a specialist horseriding operation run by Okavango Horse Safari, and a (currently inactive) photographic operation that used to be run by Landela.

GETTING THERE AND AWAY Transport here is currently only organised by Okavango Horse Safaris. Kiri airstrip (✛ KIRI 19°36.726'S, 23°02.367'E) in the northeast of NG30 is used by Gubanare, and Xudum airstrip (✛ XUDUMA – roughly 19°41'S, 22°52'E) in the centre of NG29 is used by the other camps – though the second one was out of action on my last visit. In case of emergency, it's sometimes possible to be driven into some of these camps – though it's a dusty, bumpy six hours from Maun!

These camps work on the basis that guests have prior reservations and are getting in and out by light aircraft. No self-driving visitors are allowed into these concession areas.

WHEN TO VISIT These areas on the edge of the Delta have more seasonal variation than areas further north, so the game really is significantly better later in the dry season than earlier. As with anywhere in the Delta, the wetter times of the year are better for birdwatching.

GEOGRAPHY NOTE Be aware that the western side of the Delta (from the Thaoge into Lake Ngami) has been drying up since the middle of the last century. As a result of this (or vice versa) an increasing amount of Okavango's water is finding its way into the Muanachira/Khwai system, on the eastern side of Chief's Island.

13

Thus the floodplains of the west are gradually drying out and being invaded by flora used to drier conditions, whilst the drier areas of the Khwai River, and areas like Sandibe, are gradually becoming wetter.

FLORA AND FAUNA HIGHLIGHTS Visiting one September, I concentrated my time in the area around Gubanare, which is in the far northern corner of the concession – and probably its most productive area for wildlife.

There the land was relatively dry, with only a few areas of floodplain, which is probably fairly typical of these areas towards the southwest edge of the Delta. Because of this location, the annual flood hits these areas relatively late – typically around the end of May or June. Then good water levels last until around the end of October or November.

Flora Around Gubanare there are lots of large, open plains covered in tall grass and interspersed with dry established thorny thickets. Among these are dense stands of leadwood trees (*Combretum imberbe*) and knobthorns (*Acacia nigrescens*). The latter are so numerous that their beautiful, creamy flowers combine to form a powerful perfume.

Perhaps as the result of fires in the past, there are large areas of chest-high wild sage, amidst occasional 'islands', typical of the Delta, where termite mounds are dotted among African mangosteens, raintrees, marulas, sausage trees and jackalberrys. Amongst the larger stands of trees are umbrella thorns (*Acacia tortilis*) and real fan palms (*Hyphaene petersiana*). But these islands of forest are relatively infrequent and quite poorly defined.

In the far north, the concession has a short boundary with Moremi: the Boro River, which is one of the Delta's best known channels and is lined in parts by mature riverine forest.

Overall the mixed environment contains a wide variation of tree and plant species, though it doesn't have the beauty of some of the more mature, established forests or floodplain areas.

Fauna There's a good range of species here, typical of the Delta, though game densities didn't appear to me to be very high. They are certainly highly seasonal with animals proving scarce during the rains, and then numbers improving as the land dries out in the dry season.

The dominant antelope here is probably tsessebe (in one study of the Delta these made up 70% of all lion kills), though wildebeest and impala are also fairly common, occurring frequently in small groups. Family groups of giraffe and small numbers of zebra are also seen in the drier areas, along with kudu and steenbok. Red lechwe are dominant in the wetter areas, and there's no shortage of hippos or crocodiles in the deeper waters around the Boro River.

Roan, eland and gemsbok are seen but very rarely, and generally only in the drier areas on the south side of the NG29 concession nearest to Xudum, in an area not usually visited from these camps.

Between about December and June elephants occur here in small family groups (this is typical of their behaviour in the whole region when food is plentiful). Then they tend to be most frequently found in the mopane scrub areas in the south of the concession. Later in the year, as the land dries up, they gradually coalesce into larger herds, hundreds strong, which move north and east, nearer to the heart of the Delta. Buffalo tend to occur in large herds that move through the concession in the dry season; smaller groups are seldom seen.

Of the predators, lion are by far the most common in these concessions; there is a big population here (it's probably slightly *over*-populated). Leopard are also

top **Elephant**
Loxodonta africana
(CM) page 481

centre **Hippopotamus**
Hippopotamus amphibius
(TH) page 483

right **Buffalo**
Syncerus caffer
(CM) page 483

top left	**Leopard** *Panthera pardus* (AZ) page 469	
top right	**Cheetah** *Acynonix jubatus* (CM) page 470	
above left	**Caracal** *Felis caracal* (CM) page 471	
above right	**Lioness** *Panthera leo* (CM) page 469	

above **Spotted hyena cubs**
Crocuta crocuta
(CM) page 473

centre **Wild dogs**
Lycaon pictus
(CM) page 471

right **Bat-eared fox**
Octyon megalotis
(AZ) page 472

top	**Steenbok** *Raphicerus cempestris* (CM) page 481
left	**Male kudu** *Tragelaphus strepsiceros* (CM) page 477
above	**Red lechwe** *Kobus leche* (CM) page 480
below	**Tsessebe** *Damaliscus lunatus* (CM) page 477

top   **Springbok** *Antidorcas marsupilis* (CM) page 479
right   **Giraffe** *Giraffa camelopardis* (AZ) page 484
above   **Reedbuck** *Redunca arundinum* (CM) page 480
below   **Oryx, or gemsbok** *Oryx gazella* (CM) page 476

top	**Jacana,** *Actophilornis africana,* **and waterlily** (RT)
above left	**Little bee eater** *Merops pusillius* (AZ)
above right	**Pied kingfishers** *Ceryle rudis* (CM)
below left	**Spoonbill** *Platalea leucorodia* (CM)
below right	**Red-billed hornbill** *Tockus erythrorhynchus* (CM)

above   **Lilac-breasted roller**
Coracias caudata
(CM)

right   **Saddle-billed stork**
Ephippiorhynchus senegalensis
(RT)

below left   **Pale chanting goshawk**
Accipiter gentilis spp
(CM)

below right   **Darter, or snakebird**
Anhinga anhinga
(CM)

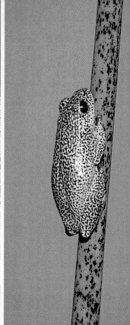

top left **Elephant shrew**
Macroscelididae spp
(RT)

top right **Reed frog**
Hyperolius argus
(CM)

centre **Banded mongoose**
Mungos mungo
(DM) page 485

above **Dragonfly**
Odonata spp
(RM)

left **Chacma baboon**
Papio cynocephalus ursinus
(CM) page 474

permanent residents, although they are shy and rarely seen, despite the night drives. I didn't see any spotted hyena on my visit, though they're almost certainly around – but perhaps restricted by the density of lion.

Cheetah are very scarce, and generally only seen in the driest of months, around October to December. Then the grass is shorter, and there's more dry land, and so less pressure from lion. At other times of the year the cheetah move away from the water, south and west out of the concession.

Recently there's been a family group of caracal which are seen fairly regularly (about once per month) near Xudum airstrip. Given how rarely these cats are seen, this represents a really good chance – so keep a sharp lookout.

Birdlife The varied habitat leads to good birdwatching, and my explorations of the Boro River area from here were excellent. Old favourites spotted included saddle-billed storks, knob-billed ducks, night herons, long-toed plovers and spurwing geese. Very large flocks of red-winged pratincoles were congregating on the exposed sandbanks, where the grass had been cropped short thanks to the grazing lechwe. May witnesses the biggest pratincole colonies here, which first appear as the Boro River begins to rise. Before that, while the sandbanks are exposed, you'll sometimes find African skimmers around.

In the area's drier grasslands black-bellied khorans are highly visible, with their eye-catching courtship displays. The wild sage areas here are often burnt and, immediately after this, wattled cranes arrive in numbers to dig up snails and other creatures that are exposed by fires.

Raptors which are frequently seen include various vultures; bateleur, fish and tawny eagles, and the occasional martial eagle. The opportunist yellow-billed kites and steppe eagles usually start arriving for the summer in late August, and whilst the smaller raptors are more scarce, black-shouldered kites are often spotted (and easily recognised because they hover in mid-flight).

THE SAFARI CAMPS There are really two totally different operations in this area, although reserves are so large that horseriders and safari campers are most unlikely to come across one another. Here I'll treat the two activities separately.

The following five safari camps have until recently been run by Landela Safaris, who used to be a substantial safari company based firmly in Zimbabwe. However, recently they have ceased operating – and the camps appear to be in some sort of legal limbo. (Their website, by contrast, is still up and running!) Sooner or later, these areas will probably have camps restarted in them, most likely on the same sites. Travellers should realise that these areas don't have the best game densities – and hence are well-suited to budget-priced safari operations. Camps in this area will be perfect for keen birdwatchers, but of limited interest to those who are more interested in game sightings.

Gubanare Camp (8 tents). In the very northern corner of NG30 (⊕ GUBANA 19°32.733'S, 22°57.832'E), Gubanare is about 11km due east of Kanana and almost exactly the same distance from its own airstrip, which is 45 mins' drive southeast of camp. It first opened in August 1999, and is just a few kilometres' drive from the Boro River, slightly upstream of the old riverside camps in NG27B.

Rann's Camp (8 chalets). Built in 1997, Rann's Camp (⊕ RANNS 19°38.032'S, 22°53.980'E) is southwest of Gubanare (NG29), about 8km southeast of Pom Pom. Note that when the flood is high, roughly between May and September, Rann's can be cut off from the airstrip – and then the only way to get here is by plane to Xudum airstrip, plus a 4x4 trip to Mantis Camp, followed by a short mokoro ride from there to the camp.

Xudum Camp (8 tents). Built around 1995, Xudum (⊕ XUDUM – 19°42.665'S, 22°52.987'E) is the oldest and the furthest south of these camps. It's situated to the south of both of its satellite walking camps, Eden and Mantis, towards the middle of the NG29 concession.

🏠 **Eden and Mantis** (4 tents each). Xudum Camp has 2 satellite walking-trails camps, Eden and Mantis, both of which were built around 1995 when Xudum was built. A third walking-trail camp — Baobab — was added at one stage but was taken down even when the others were still operational.

RIDING SAFARIS All these riding safaris are run by Okavango Horse Safaris (*P Bag 23, Maun;* ➥ *6861 671;* f *6861 672;* e *ohsnx@info.bw; www.okavangohorse.com*).

Perhaps unlike most of the other camps in this book (except African Horseback Safaris, page 168), the precise details of OHS's camps are really much less important than the arrangements made for the riding activities. Thus here I'll cover briefly the basics of these safaris, before mentioning the camps and itineraries.

Riding ability required You must be able to ride well. This isn't a place to learn to ride, or to come if you feel at all nervous on a horse. This means being able to 'post to the trot' for ten minutes at a time, being comfortable at all paces, and being able to gallop out of trouble. It is a great advantage if you are fit and a proficient rider. A separate programme can be organised for non-riding partners, on request.

The horses OHS advises that they use Pure Arab, Anglo Arab, American saddle bred, part- and full-thoroughbred, Kalahari and Kalahari cross horses. All are between 14 and 17 hands high, well schooled, responsive and have fairly even temperaments.

Weight limits The maximum weight for any rider is 95kg (15 stones or 210lb), and OHS insist that potential riders may be required to step on a pair of scales! That said, for heavier riders an alternative programme of shorter rides, game drives and walks is possible, but this must be discussed with OHS when you arrange your trip.

Tack and clothes The tack used is English style, and each saddle has a seat-saver for comfort. Australian Wintec and an assortment of leather saddles are used, including Barnsby and Kieffer. The tack is generally of a high quality and kept in good condition. Only a limited assortment of half chaps and riding gloves are kept in the camp for guests' use.

OHS produces specific 'clothes lists' for their trips, but they can do laundry in their camp. Like all operations, the air transfers dictate that you stick to a strict weight limit (excess can be left in Maun). Note that proper riding clothes, and clothes of bush colours, are important here.

Information about you To book a place on one of their trips, OHS will ask you for you age, weight, height and riding experience – as well as the more usual questions of your preference in drinks, specialised dietary requirements, allergies etc. They'll also require you to fill out an indemnity form in camp before beginning your trip, a practice which is becoming increasingly common in camps throughout southern Africa.

About the trips Having established that you can cope with the rigours of a riding safari, you have a choice between a five-day and a ten-day safari, and these are normally scheduled in advance on set dates throughout the year. This does lack flexibility, but it means you are with a group of people and get to know each other, and as a group you can cover the ground.

On all trips there's a demonstration and talk at the beginning of the safari on how to handle big game situations, as well as a familiarisation session with the tack.

After that, expect to spend between four and six hours in the saddle each day, broken by refreshment stops. Typically this means that you'll have some picnic breakfasts and lunches, and also ten-minute walks every couple of hours spent in the saddle. (This acts to rest the rider by giving him/her the chance to use different muscles, and it also helps to relieve the horse from the constant pressure of a rider's weight.)

Although the focus here is firmly on horseriding, alternative activities are often possible during afternoons which are not 'day rides'. These can include game drives, birdwatching walks, mokoro rides and night drives.

Riding in big-game country can be difficult, especially when a horse looks very much like an antelope to a hungry lion. Thus safety is a big issue; it's at the root of why this isn't a place for inexperienced riders. An extremely experienced guide, usually P J or Barney, accompanies every ride, and they do carry a .375 rifle in case of emergency.

These riding itineraries take a maximum of eight riders at once (again, for safety reasons). They will accept children, though these must be strong, competent riders (a Pony Club test pass is insisted upon). The cost for a child is the same as for an adult.

The experience Provided that you are a competent rider, seeing the Okavango from horseback can be totally magical. From the point of view of most of the rest of the Delta's animals, once you step into the saddle you become part of a four-legged herbivore (albeit a strangely shaped one). Thus generally they relax around you, so you can ride with herds of antelope without disturbing them, and see the place from a kudu's eye view. The palm islands, grassy floodplains, mopane forests and clear streams all ensure that the ground under you is always changing. Your horse will wade from island to island, where the going is normally quite good and firm along the edges – allowing the ride to move on at a trot and canter.

Having said all this, just as the herbivores perceive you as an antelope, so will the predators. Hence the emphasis on safety that a horseriding operation must have in this environment. It's not unusual to have to gallop to safety from a pride of lion – usually with the guide at the rear, gun in hand.

The riding camps These aim to be comfortable and simple, and all are staffed. Three meals a day are prepared, with saddlebag picnic breakfasts. As with most camps, they emphasise fairly healthy food with fresh vegetables and salads, and bake fresh bread each day. Dinner is often a three-course affair, usually served by candlelight at a dining table beside the campfire.

Kujwana Camp (5 tents). Kujwana is situated on the Xudum River (⊕ KUJWAN 19°44.370'S, 22°57.115'E) about 8.5km southeast of Xudum Camp. It's about 11.5km northwest of Qwaapu Fly-camp, and almost 20km southeast of Moklowana.

Accommodation here is in Meru-style tents with a shaded veranda and en-suite bathroom. This includes a long-drop toilet and a bucket shower (that's the type where the bucket is filled with hot water and raised on a pulley for you by the camp staff!). The beds are separate stretcher-type beds, with bedrolls, cotton sheets, duvets and towels provided.

Moklowane Camp (4 tents). Moklowane is the most northern of the horseriding camps

(⊕ MOKLOW 19°37.137'S, 22°49.277'E), and is situated in open floodplains only about 8km east of Rann's Camp, and barely 5km southwest of Pom Pom (in the adjoining NG29 reserve). That said, it's about 19km northwest of Kujwana, and 30km northwest of Qwaapu Fly-camp — which just goes to emphasise what a large amount of ground these horseriding safaris can cover.

Accommodation here is very similar to Kujwana, with Meru-style tents with verandas and en-suite bathrooms, complete with long-drop toilets and bucket showers.

Qwaapu and Kiri fly-camps (8 tents). Qwaapu and Kiri fly-camps are different from Kujwana and

Moklowane, firstly because they can be moved and secondly because they're a little simpler.

Qwaapu (⊕ QWAAPU 19°47.553'S, 23°02.666'E) is on the southeast side of the reserve. Kiri is often moved, depending on the water levels, but is usually somewhere on the northeast side, towards the Boro River and Kiri airstrip (⊕ KIRI 19°36.726'S, 23°02.367'E).

These camps have walk-in dome tents with separate, but private, long-drop toilets and bucket showers. There's also a central tent for dinner, though meals will often be eaten under the sky.

The costs The trips are all five- or ten-night safaris, which are usually arranged around set dates in the year. There are no trips during the rains, between December and February.

From March to May, and in November, trips cost around US$365/345 pp sharing per night for a five-/ten-night trip. This includes all accommodation, meals, drinks, guiding, riding, game drives, walks and mokoro trips. From June to October the cost is US$400 pp sharing per night, for either the shorter or the longer trip. (These prices include a fee paid to the concession of US$14 pp per night.)

Visitors who want single accommodation should add 50% to these costs, though this is usually waived if you're prepared to share a tent with another visitor. The flight between Maun and the camps costs US$90 per person, one-way (US$180 return).

CHITABE AND SANDIBE (NG31)

NG31 Reserve covers a relatively small 360km² of the eastern Okavango Delta. However, it's a superb location which looks on a map like a bite out of the southern side of Moremi Game Reserve – between Chief's Island and the Mopane Tongue. Sandibe and Chitabe share this reserve, though generally keep to their own sides of it. Sandibe have about 160km² on the northern side, and Chitabe (and the adjacent Chitabe Trails Camp) occupies the southern 200km². These two camps are relatively close, about 12km apart, and they share an airstrip.

The reserve is particularly interesting as it's experiencing a period of change. The Gomoti River, which forms the northern and eastern border of the reserve, had been dry since about 1984. It began to flow again in 1999, spilling on to the seasonal floodplains. This has dramatically increased the amount of water in this area. Previously only about 5% of Sandibe's area had water on it; now it's closer to 50% permanent water.

GETTING THERE AND AWAY All visitors to these camps pre-book their time and fly to the camps. NG31's main airstrip (⊕ CHITAA 19°27.952'S, 23°22.443'E) is about 7km north of Chitabe and 8km east of Sandibe. This is barely 60km from Maun, making it one of the closest of the Delta's airstrips for camps. However, this doesn't usually affect the price of a trip. Wilderness Safaris, for example, usually charge a set rate for a package including time at its camps and flights to/from them. This price doesn't vary with the position of the camp within the Delta.

WHEN TO VISIT As with the rest of the Okavango, the big game here is more diverse and prolific during the dry season, although the birdlife is generally better between December and March. That said, NG31 really is in the heart of the Okavango where the water is basically permanent, and so these differences aren't as great here as you'll find in some of the more outlying, western areas of the Delta.

FLORA AND FAUNA HIGHLIGHTS NG31 is a varied reserve: there are quite marked differences between the northern sides (east and west) and also between these two and Chitabe's area further south, even if the list of species which occur in both are broadly the same. There is a complex mix of environments in this reserve; what follows here is very much a simplification.

The most striking difference is that the northwest of the reserve is a wetter environment than the rest. Just north of this reserve, in Moremi, the Mboroga River flows south between the dry-land areas of Chief's Island and the Mopane Tongue. Forming a number of large lagoons, it splits into two channels. One branch, the Gomoti River, then forms part of this reserve's northern boundary, and all of its eastern side. The other branch, the Santantadibe River, is a deep, wide channel that leads to lots of lagoons and runs down this reserve's southwestern side.

Flora Sandibe overlooks the permanent Santantadibe River from within this watery side, on the reserve's northwestern corner. Around it there are plenty of open-water areas and floodplains, fringed by belts of riverine vegetation with a high proportion of real fan palms (*Hyphaene petersiana*). The islands here can be large and continuous, and on the larger of these you will find occasional baobab trees growing – an indication that they've been dry islands for a long time.

The northeastern side of the reserve, around the location of the airstrip, is a spit of dry land where the habitats seem to occur in belts. There are belts of thick mopane forest interspersed with belts of dry 'acacia thornveld', where you'll find mixed stands of camelthorn trees (*Acacia erioloba*), umbrella thorns (*Acacia tortillis*) and the very similar, but thorn-less, sickle bush (*Dichrostachys cinerea africana*); also buffalo thorn (*Ziziphus mucronata*), with its two types of thorn, which snag on any passing animal (and on clothing) and have earned it the Afrikaans name *wag-'n-bietjie*, meaning 'wait-a-bit'.

There are also bands of lower, more 'scrubby' vegetation, including classic species of deep Kalahari sand like the silver cluster-leaf (*Terminalia sericea*), and some very striking areas forested with large numbers of dead leadwood trees (*Combretum imberbe*). These trees, with their hard, termite-resistant, wood were killed by flooding when the water levels in the area changed – but will probably stand for many years, looking from the air like a river of dead trees .

Moving to the south side of the reserve, nearer to where Chitabe stands, you will find a lot of mixed forest areas with classic riverine species of trees like the large fever-berry (*Croton megalobotrys*), sausage tree (*Kigelia africana*) and jackalberry (*Diospyros mespiliformis*).

Around here there are some smaller islands surrounded by shallow floodplains covered with hippo grass (*Vossia cuspida*). The deeper channels are mostly lined by phragmites reeds (*Phragmites australis*) and miscanthus grass (*Miscanthus junceus*). These are permanent channels which don't dry up, and seem to have relatively little seasonal variation; they simply spread out on to wider floodplains when the flood finally arrives (around May or June usually).

At the southern end of the reserve is a belt of soil with a high clay content, providing the perfect substrate for large stands of mopane trees (*Colophospermum mopane*), which sometimes seem so uniform that it almost appears to be a monoculture.

Fauna This reserve has a wide range of game species, dominated by impala, tsessebe, kudu and, on the floodplains, red lechwe. Zebra are fairly numerous, blue wildebeest less so, and giraffe are very common in the bands of acacia thornveld (35 were observed together at one point on the airstrip). Reedbuck, duiker and steenbok are often seen, whilst eland and roan are found only rarely (usually towards the south of the reserve); sable seem to be totally absent.

The sightings here of buffalo and elephants seem to follow the same broad patterns. Throughout the year there are small resident herds of both around, plus odd old bulls and small bachelor groups. However, from around June to October large breeding herds pass through. Then buffalo herds can number well over 1,000, and herds of 100 elephants are not unknown.

The key to understanding this is to realise that when there has been rainfall, usually starting around November–December, the big herds move into the large swathes of mopane forest between the Okavango and the Kwando–Linyanti river system: that is, into the interior forests of Kwando (NG14), Linyanti (NG15), Selinda (NG16), Khwai Community (NG18) and Kwara (NG20). Whilst there, their water needs are sustained by the seasonal clay pans which hold water. However, when these pans start to dry up, around May or June, they move back to the areas of permanent water, including this reserve.

The reserve has plenty of lion including, when I last visited, a resident 17-strong pride. Recently they seem to have concentrated mainly on hunting buffalo, though that may have been just the natural response to having a lot of mouths to feed.

Leopard are common here, with the mixed woodlands and floodplains being an ideal habitat for them. I've had one of my best leopard sightings in Botswana near Chitabe, and hence tend to regard it as one of the country's best camps for leopard.

Cheetah stay here throughout the year, and are most frequently seen in the drier, more open eastern side of the reserve. Their populations are perhaps helped by relatively low numbers of spotted hyena.

The reserve seems to have made a name for itself for wild dog. This may partially be due to the involvement in the reserve's management of Dave Hamman, who took many of the photographs for the book *Running Wild* (see *Appendix 3, Further Information*), about the 'Mombo' pack of wild dogs in Moremi.

There certainly is a healthy population of dogs here. They seem to like the marginal floodplains, and will flush the antelopes through plains and islands to catch them. In 1999 there were three dens in the concession, though as these are usually moved from one year to the next . . . the situation is relatively unpredictable between the years. Having said this, I'd probably choose a more open and less wooded area than Chitabe if I were specifically hoping to track down some wild dogs.

Finally, on a more unusual note, this reserve seems to have had a very high incidence of pangolin sightings: they have recorded about six sightings in the last two years. (Most camps would count themselves lucky with one such sighting, as these are very rare animals.) Many of these sightings have been on full-moon night-drives, when the pangolin has been seen foraging around in the open. Aardvarks and aardwolves are also frequently seen here at night. Perhaps this, and the pangolin sightings, are really a reflection of the camps' enthusiasm for (or at least willingness to organise) serious late-night game drives, rather than a higher density of these animals in this area per se.

Birdlife A recent survey counted 386 species in this immediate area. In general, Sandibe is the better location for waterbirds. Along with many more common species, Okavango 'specials' like the Pel's fishing owl, slaty egret (thought to be the world's rarest heron), black coucal and black egret have been recorded.

Chitabe has a wider variation of dry-country birds, with its most common raptor being the bateleur eagle, though there are also good numbers of many other eagles including martial, brown snake, black snake, tawny and western banded snake eagles. Marsh harriers are found in the wetter areas, along with the inevitable fish eagles and even the uncommon migrant European marsh harriers. Look out for bat-hawks in the late evening. Less spectacular, though almost equally uncommon, brown firefinches can certainly be found here.

WHAT TO SEE AND DO The camps differ in their activities. Chitabe and Chitabe Trails are essentially dry-land camps, which concentrate on game drives and night drives, plus occasional guided walks.

Sandibe offers more of a mix of activities with game drives, boating and mokoro trips. They have recently had the huge advantage of a battery-powered boat – called *Lily* – which gives up to 12 people (more usually six or so) trips along the Santantadibe River. Its slow speed and minimal wake, combined with very quiet operation, help it to have minimal impact and thus approach the shyer game and birds more closely with less disturbance.

On mokoro trips at Sandibe, it's usual practice for an armed guide to accompany each group in a separate canoe with his/her own poler.

Unusually for the Delta, both Sandibe and Chitabe Trails welcome children. At Sandibe they're even given a 'planet manager's workbook' to keep them busy whilst teaching them about the area, and the camp staff are adept at ensuring that they don't disrupt the activities or ambience for the other guests. At Chitabe Trails there is one family room – where two halves of the room each have two beds, and share an interconnecting bathroom area.

WHERE TO STAY There are just three choices here. Chitabe and Chitabe Trails are run by Wilderness Safaris (see page 171), whilst Sandibe is run by CC Africa (see page 169). These are all very good, but very different, camps.

Chitabe Camp (8 tents). Chitabe is set on an old, established tree-island and first opened in July 1997. The whole camp is raised up on wooden decking, and walkways lead between the tents and the lounge and dining area which form the centre of the camp.

Here you'll find a large central area with a bar on one side, under thatch, and a separate dining area. Scattered around the open areas of decking are tables and chairs. One walkway leads from here down to a largish plunge pool (about 8m x 3m), and all of this is under typical tall, shard trees of riverine forests, including jackalberries (*Diospyros mespiliformis*), knobthorns (*Acacia nigrescens*) and sausage trees (*Kigelia africana*).

There are 4 tents on each side of camp, and each has a solid door which leads into a large Meru-style tent. Here you'll find twin beds, or a dbl, surrounded by mosquito netting under a fan, plus a few wicker chairs, a table and a simple wardrobe. The en-suite bathroom is part of the tent, with a shower cubicle, a washbasin and a flush toilet. There's also a (much nicer) outdoor shower, enabling you to watch the stars as you refresh. *US$470/655 pp sharing/sgl low season to US$785/970 high season, inc all meals, activities, park fees, laundry, most drinks; exc transfers. Open all year.*

Chitabe Trails (5 tents). This is a smaller version of the main Chitabe Camp, built a few hundred metres from the main camp, on the other side of the same island. It uses exactly the same style of tents and furniture as the main camp. However, here the tents are built on the ground, not on platforms, and they're linked by natural paths through the bush rather than polished wooden walkways. (One of these rooms is a new 'family unit' where 2 tents, with 2 beds each, are linked by a shared en-suite bathroom.)

Although very unprepossessing, Chitabe Trails remains one of my favourite camps in the Delta. I often prefer the Delta's smaller, more intimate camps and the experience that I had here on my last visit was magical. *US$470/655 pp sharing/sgl low season to US$785/970 high season, inc all meals, activities, park fees, laundry, most drinks; exc transfers. Open all year.*

Sandibe (8 chalets). Sandibe opened in August 1998, about a year after Chitabe, and takes its name from the Santantadibe River that it faces. It stands in a band of thick riverine vegetation, and the pathways through the camp weave between the natural bush, which has been disturbed as little as possible. There are no wooden walkways here!

The main lounge and dining area has a unique design, influenced (I'm told) by styles from Mali and even Santa Fe. The roof is 2 storeys high, supported on long tree-trunk timbers and trendily decked in shaggy thatch. Under one side of this is a small lounge, on the other are tables set for meals. Up a few steps is a small sitting area and a boardwalk with a hammock and more easy chairs. The whole structure is very open with rough wooden banisters and adobe walls.

A favourite feature of the lodge is the boma area outside, where at night they have a central fire under tall trees, surrounded by lots of magical candlelight.

As at its sister camp (Nxabega), Sandibe has a well-stocked wine cellar. Here it is kept cool in fine traditional style by an eco-friendly cool room with porous charcoal walls (ask to see this – it's how safari camps survived before refrigerators!). Though unlimited good house wine is included as part of your stay, if you want access to the vintage wines and more esoteric, imported spirits then these will cost extra.

Sandibe's relatively simple rooms are of a solid, terracotta-coloured construction with mesh windows (no glass) and big dbl doors. Inside, the twin or dbl beds have high-quality cotton sheets and linen,

covered during the day by an unusual woven leather bedspread, and a walk-in mosquito net.

In these cool rooms is a writing desk, wooden bedside tables with lamps, tall mirrors, a wall-safe for valuables and a fan high in the ceiling. There's a small toilet and wash-basin inside, plus a wonderful en-suite outdoor shower. Outside each chalet is a polished concrete veranda with chairs and a table, and a raised viewing platform for watching the wildlife.

The camp has a small circular plunge pool, perhaps 5m in diameter, surrounded by sun-loungers, and a semicircle of natural leadwood poles jutting up from the ground. There's also a curio shop, with the usual T-shirts, postcards, film, books, hats, maps, pictures, baskets and cuddly toys. Sadly they also sell imported west African and east African crafts, rather than concentrating on locally produced ones.

Like Nxabega, Sandibe has a large enough staff complement to be better than most camps at tailoring its activities to what guests want and when they want it.

From US$365 pp sharing low season to US$745 high season, inc accommodation, meals, drinks, laundry & all activities. Open all year.

STANLEY'S, BAINES' AND BUDGET MOKORO TRIPS (NG32)

This is a 'multi-purpose area', which is controlled by the local communities – and perhaps because of this operations continue to change and evolve more than they do in most of the Okavango's private areas. In the last few years, two permanent sister camps have been operating in one section of the reserve: Stanley's Camp and Baines' Camp. The Grey Matters elephant project also works in the same area. A second, quite separate, part of the reserve is used mainly for budget mokoro trips by many operators from Maun. Because these are such distinct operations, I've described them separately.

FLORA AND FAUNA HIGHLIGHTS

Flora NG32 is the concession on the other side of the buffalo fence from the relatively populated areas around Maun. It's at the southern end of the Delta, relying on the Boro and Santantadibe rivers for flooding – and last in line to receive the water. In a dry year, the floods can be very low and patchy.

This means that there are relatively few short-grass plains which are regularly flooded, but significant patches of floodplains which are only intermittently wet. These provide an idea base for a profusion of the invasive wild sage (*Pechuel-loeschea leubnitziae*), which covers large open areas with its aromatic grey-green foliage. Where they've had slightly longer to become established, you'll find the distinctive rounded outlines of candle pod acacias bushes (*Acacia hebeclada*) starting to appear in these areas – as one of the first shrubs to move in it usually indicates that an area has been dry for many years. In some of these open areas where the recent floods haven't reached you'll find a profusion of termite mounds.

Aside from this, driving around NG32 near Stanley's the vegetation seems to occur in strips, including linear expanses of riverine forest where the major tree species are leadwoods (*Combretum imberbe*), jackalberries (*Diospyros mespiliformis*), marula (*Sclerocarya birrea*) and sausage trees (*Kigelia africana*). There are relatively few areas of deep, deep sand here and not that many acacia glades, but there are some quite dense – and very attractive – concentrations of real fan palms (*Hyphaene petersiana*).

When visiting with a mokoro poler, you'll see a very different side to the area. Unless the flood has been very high, you'll probably be poling within the vicinity of the Boro or the Santantadibe. This is at the very shallowest end of the Delta, so expect large areas of miscanthus grass (*Miscantusus junceus*) and common reeds (*Phragmites australis*), plus the occasional floodplains of hippo grass (*Vossia cuspidata*).

If you do actually pole up the Boro, then you'll find the environment generally gets more interesting as you continue. After a few days, you'll leave behind some of the more boring stretches of reeds, and start finding wider floodplains around you, and more lagoons. Wherever you pole, the islands on which you stop will often be classic little palm islands fringed with palms and the riverine forest.

Fauna The game densities generally get better as you head further north in the area. Impala are probably the commonest antelope, with tsessebe a close second and red lechwe certainly dominating any areas which are flooded. Kudu, giraffe, zebra, reedbuck, warthog and occasionally wildebeest are all found here; sable, roan and waterbuck are not. Elephant and buffalo occur singly during the wetter parts of the year, and pass through in larger herds as the dry season reaches its end.

When the flood is at its height, there may be the occasional sitatunga around, but apart from a few places on the rivers, there aren't enough papyrus reedbeds to support them.

Lion are around in good numbers, and while leopard occur, they're not frequently spotted. Wild dog pass though, and sightings of them seem to increase between about October and December. However, the open wide plains where you could follow them are limited in the concession.

Cheetah are certainly around and often seen in the drier areas – on one drive here during a fairly brief visit one of the book's contributors spent a magical 25 minutes with a male cheetah as he strolled from termite mound to termite mound searching for the perfect vantage point.

Birdlife NG32 is a classic edge-of-the-Delta reserve that has a good mix of dry-country and shallow-water bird species. The most common species include red-eyed, mourning and Cape turtle doves, which all greet the morning with a variety of gentle coos. Identify the latter by their lyrical exhortations to 'work harder, work harder'.

Other birds frequently seen here include long-tailed shrikes, red-billed quelia, buffalo weavers, lilac-breasted rollers, blacksmith plovers and long-tailed and glossy starlings. Crimson-breasted shrikes provide startling flashes of red; Meyer's parrots can often be seen as a flash of colour flying at speed.

In more open areas you'll find red-billed and Swainson's francolins, flocks of helmeted guinea fowl, kori bustards and occasional ostriches. Sandgrouse are common in acacia groves, as are yellow-billed hornbills, whilst their red-billed cousins prefer the reserve's mopane woodlands.

The floodplains support a varied cast of waders and waterbirds, including the occasional wattled cranes. This is a good reserve for raptors: bateleur eagles, black-breasted and brown snake eagles are especially common, and Gabar goshawks are frequently seen.

GETTING THERE AND AWAY For those staying at Stanley's Camp, access is by air to the strip near camp; you're not allowed to drive yourself here.

WHEN TO VISIT Like most of the areas on the edge of the Delta, the game densities are better during the dry season than during the rains. So whilst from June to October is the best time to visit for game, the birdwatching is usually more interesting during the rains, from around December to March.

WHERE TO STAY

Stanley's Camp (8 safari tents) Contact Sanctuary Lodges (see page 172). Stanley's was originally built by a maverick local character, Alistair Rankin (the subject of a number of local bush myths – some involving mokoro trips, buffalo and uncomfortable nights spent in trees). It's owned and was run for several years by Sarah Collins. These origins explain why it may appear surprisingly rustic – and quite a contrast – if you arrive here from either of Sanctuary's other lodges (Chief's or Chobe Chilwero); it wasn't (re-)built or designed specifically for Sanctuary.

The open-plan dining/lounge area is simply a large canvas tent (think of a 'big top' circus), on a slightly raised wooden decking – with a large jackalberry tree (*Diospyros mespiliformis*) growing right through the centre and out the top. Under here are a couple of comfy sofas and a few leather chairs. The 'library' is slightly separate, and here you'll find a leather sofa with a couple of old wooden suitcases into which is packed a slightly eccentric collection of novels, magazines and reference books. Beside this is a chessboard, with table and chairs – a thinking option to while away hot afternoons.

Stanley's has a small curio shop with a couple of glass-fronted cabinets in which there's a selection of various souvenirs, T-shirts and a basic selection of film. It also sells baskets made by the staff, which are hanging around – all very low key and in keeping with the generally relaxed, unpretentious feel of the camp.

Most meals are social affairs, taken with everybody eating together at a long table. That said, if you're staying for a few days then you can take the opportunity to request a picnic lunch, so that you can stay out in the bush all day. After dinner in the evening, everybody usually retires for drinks and a chat to a small fire pit, outside in front of the big top.

The camp's tents, on solid red-painted concrete bases, are all to one side of the main area, connected by bush tracks. They are fairly simple, with a couple of beds, a desk with drawers and a chair, a couple of bedside tables and an old-style wooden wardrobe in one corner. Lighting is by electric 'hurricane' lamps, and there are rugs on the floor – but no fans in the rooms. Each tent has its own en-suite toilet and shower, complete with original and wood-and-canvas shower cubicles, a wooden dresser with sink and mirror (and the usual range of complimentary toiletries), and another electric lamp. Even the cracks in the floor seem to blend well with the 'bush' air of the lodge – helping to make this a very lovely, traditional old-style camp.

From US$420 pp low season to US$650/845 pp sharing/sgl high season, inc all meals, activities, park fees, laundry, and most drinks; exc transfers, a few imported drinks, laundry, elephant trips with Grey Matters (extra US$210 pp per activity).

Baines' Camp (5 rooms). Contact Sanctuary Lodges (see page 172). Named after the Victorian painter, Thomas Baines, this new camp is rather funky in design. Linked by raised wooden walkways, the 'tents' are unusual in that their solid walls are built out of recycled drink cans, wire mesh and hessian, and covered in plastic containing – why? – elephant dung! And so that guests can see how it's constructed, a section of wall in each tent is left with just cans and wire mesh. Distressed frames surround old pictures on the walls, lampshades are of ostrich eggshell, and there's an easel in each room where guests can paint. Rather more contemporary are the walls of glass, and 'star beds', which are set 4-poster style under mosquito nets, and can be rolled out on to the decking under the stars.

From US$475/619 pp sharing/sgl low season to US$865/1,125 pp high season; see Stanley's (above) for details. Open all year.

WHAT TO SEE AND DO Activities at Stanley's Camp usually revolve around 4x4 game drives and night drives, though it's normally possible to take mokoro trips for at least a few months a year – typically around June to September. The water's

LIVING WITH ELEPHANTS

Doug and Sandi Groves started this not-for-profit organisation in 1999, aiming to secure the future of their trio of elephants, and to work through various projects towards a more harmonious relationship between Botswana's elephant and human populations.

Projects undertaken include their 'Outreach programme' whereby children from Maun and nearby villages spend two days at Grey Matters (see below), interacting with the three elephants and learning about them through hands-on experience and discussions. See www.livingwithelephants.org for more details.

not consistently deep enough to run motorboat trips. Aside from these standard activities, many people here will pay the extra US$210 per activity to spend time with Doug and Sandi Groves and their elephants . . .

Grey Matters Doug Groves started out working with elephants in American zoos, including Washington Park Zoo and San Diego Wild Animal Park. Subsequently, in 1987, he came to Africa as the trainer of four elephants who were being returned from the US to South Africa for a film, *Circles in a Forest* – the first of many filming projects for him. As an aside, the main elephant involved in this was Abu, who now leads the herd at Abu Camp (NG26; see pages 296–7), the Okavango's only other operation that offers visitors time in the company of elephants which are not wild.

In 1994, Randall Moore and Ker & Downey went their separate ways – and almost simultaneously Ker & Downey invited Doug to Botswana, to set up and run an elephant-based tourism project. Now Grey Matters isn't linked to Ker & Downey, and instead works closely with Stanley's Camp – and is the base for Living With Elephants (see box above).

Elephant activities are arranged through Stanley's Camp, where all the guests stay, so guests rarely need to contact Grey Matters (\ *6863 198;* e *groves@ livingwithelephants.org*) directly.

These activities cost US$210 each, and normally consist of about four hours in the morning – a leisurely foraging walk with the camp's three elephants, which allows you to get used to observing and interacting with them at close quarters. You'll be encouraged to touch and walk with the elephants as they forage – and to view them as individuals. Riding the elephants is not part of these trips. At the end of this there's usually a picnic lunch in the bush.

The maximum number of guests at any one time is eight – if there are more people then they'll organise an afternoon walk for a second group.

Budget mokoro trips NG32 is the end destination for virtually all of the one- to four-day mokoro trips offered from Maun, which begin with a road transfer into the Delta. For full details of how to choose a trip, and what to expect, see pages 165–6.

These trips aren't really about game, although you may see some. Relax, take a bird book and a pair of binoculars, and enjoy the experience of being poled along the waterways, and seeing some of the birdlife, and water-life, close up. My first trip into the Delta was like this – and it was enchanting. Subsequently I've seen more interesting areas of the Delta, and infinitely better game, but it's still hard to beat the sheer joy that you'll get from floating around on a mokoro in such an amazing environment for the first time.

From my experience, mokoro trips are much more fun when the sun's shining and the sky is blue; grey skies and (even worse) rain do take the edge off it. Thus

There are three trained elephants with Doug and Sandi at the moment; all are orphans from culling programmes:

Jabu is short for Jabulani, which means 'happiness'; he was born in about 1986 and orphaned at the age of two by a cull in the Kruger National Park, South Africa. He is described as a proud bull who enjoys leading this small herd – playful, dependable, and the most independent and confident member of the herd. He now stands about 2.9m tall at the shoulder.

Thembi, a smaller female, is about the same age as Jabu, and was also orphaned by a cull in the Kruger. She's said to be smart and very social, and loves being the centre of attention. Originally a very insecure calf, she's gradually becoming much more confident.

Morula came to Doug in 1994 as a maladjusted 17-year-old, lacking confidence and with a troubled background. Doug comments that she started off being exceedingly submissive to him and the other elephants, but then vented frustrations on trees. He adds that she's gradually become more secure and relaxed here.

best avoid January and February if you have a choice – and ideally come between about April and November.

See my comments on walking (pages 125–8) before you go walking in search of big game with your poler – as none of these trips is likely to be led by someone that I'd describe as a professional walking guide, and none of the polers carry any guns.

SANKUYO TSWARAGANO COMMUNITY TRUST (NG33)

The small NG33 reserve is really an enclave that has been cut out of NG34. It borders Moremi, and in character is very similar to the area around South Gate and parts of NG34. However, with no major watercourse or other focal point, it's not an easy area in which to run a stand-alone operation, and the old Santawani Safari Lodge – one of the Delta's older photographic camps – finally fell into disuse. In recent years, however, the community has developed the site and re-opened the lodge.

GETTING THERE AND AWAY To reach Santawani from Moremi, leave the reserve at South Gate, take the right-hand fork after a few hundred metres, and follow this road almost due south. For the most part, it's a good, dead-straight sand road, bordering the eastern edge of Moremi Game Reserve. After about 9km, take the left-hand fork signposted to Santawani and the Wild Dog Research station. The village of Santawani, and the lodge, are a couple of kilometres or so from here, beyond the newly upgraded airstrip (✪ STWAIR 19°30.820'S, 23°37.700'E); the research station is about 1.5km from the village. To get to Maun from here, continue south on a sand track – quite deep in parts – for a further 27km to the veterinary checkpoint (*open 06.00–22.00*). From here it's another 10km, through the sprawling village of Shukumukwa, to the main road between Chobe and Maun. Turn right at the junction (✪ SANTTO S19°42.132S, 23°43.248'E) for Maun, and within 8km you'll be on the tar road. If you're coming the other way, the turning for Santawani is clearly signposted from the main road.

⌂ WHERE TO STAY

⌂ **Santawani Lodge** (6 chalets) ☎ 6800 664; f 6800 665; e santawani@dynabyte.bw, sankuyo@info.bw. The bougainvillea-covered entrance is a colourful welcome to this community-owned lodge, which was re-opened in June 2002. Square, brick-built chalets with thatched roofs sit like neat dolls' houses behind the now derelict chalets of Santawani's former owners. Set in mixed woodland, they have metal-framed windows, and a solid wooden door, with a couple of directors' chairs on a small paved patio at the front. Inside, each has twin beds with mossie nets and bedside lights, an electric fan – essential given the lack of through breeze – and en-suite shower/toilet at the rear.

The open dining room/bar and separate lounge area boast no frills, with sand floors, bare tables and basic chairs. The staff, though, are friendly and welcoming, and it's all very relaxed. (The same community runs Kaziikini Campsite to the east of Moremi; see page 174.) There's a small waterhole in front of the lodge, which claims to attract high numbers of game, including a visit by 19 lions the day before we visited.

P675 pp sharing, reduced to P575 out of season, inc all meals, 2 game drives per day. Drinks extra.

SANKUYO COMMUNITY TRUST AND STARLING'S (NG34)

NG34 covers an area of about 900km², and you drive through the eastern side of this when you leave the Moremi Reserve's South Gate and head towards Maun. It's an area with good game, and is easily accessibly (by 4x4) from Maun. Thus, and very unusually for the region, it's a private concession to which you can drive yourself.

BACKGROUND INFORMATION NG34 is run for the benefit of the local community, through the Sankuyo Tswaragano Community Trust – and it's a reserve which sees more frequent changes than most. Until about 2001 it was the location for Gomoti Camp; shortly after that closed, Starling's Camp was built here. Now that's ceased taking private bookings – and it's possible that it's become another basic, private camp for the exclusive use of the OAT groups from the USA.

Meanwhile there's long been an intermittent presence here of animal researchers, many of whom seem to have subsequently written books! Naturalist and lion researcher Peter Katz has been here for about five years. His book, *Prides*, was published in 2000, and more recently the three children staying with him and his partner have written *Lion Children*, published in 2001. They are all still in residence, at the inevitably-named 'Lion Camp', which is about 2km from Starling's Camp.

Before that, John 'Tiko' McNutt began a wild-dog research unit here in 1989. The project has broadened and developed since then, and a book that he co-authored, *Running Wild: Dispelling the Myths of the African Wild Dog*, was published in 1996.

GETTING THERE AND AWAY The old Santawani airstrip (⊕ STWAIR 19°30.820'S, 23°37.700'E), which is about 10km due south of South Gate, in NG33, should be useable. Otherwise, the only access to NG34 and this area is by 4x4 vehicle.

It takes about two hours to drive from Maun. First follow the directions for Moremi (see pages 173–4) through Shorobe, and head right up to South Gate. Within sight of the gate, about 500m from it, there's a concrete plinth just where you turn left, to drive roughly southwest down Moremi's cut-line (the straight line of cleared vegetation that separates the park from the private reserve). From there it's a straight 10.5km until the cut-line turns right. Follow this for a further 7.9km until you reach a junction (⊕ STARTU 19°31.599'S, 23°31.987'E). Here you've effectively reached the edge of the riverine forest beside the Gomoti River, and you turn to head roughly southeast and to shadow the river.

About 2.5km along here is the old site of Gomoti Camp (⊕ GOMOTI 19°32.424'S, 23°33.174'E), around which are various confusing tracks. Ignoring all of those, about 6.1km past STARTU junction you'll reach Starling's Camp

13

(⊕ STARLI 19°33.330'S, 23°34.134'E). Expect to have a number of game-viewing tracks branching off to confuse you when you're on the last section of this trip, beside the river, but follow your nose (and your GPS); it's not difficult to find.

WHEN TO VISIT Big-game animals are more prolific here during the dry season, as with the rest of the Okavango – although the birdlife is generally better between December and March. Because NG34 is on the southwest side of the Delta, the flood reaches it last. Also note that NG34 contains some of the closest dry-season watering points for the game that spreads out towards Nxai and Makgadikgadi during the rains. Around this, there is a much higher density of game in the dry season than the wet.

That said, quite a lot of the reserve is mopane woodlands, a favourite location for animals during the rains and early dry season – so expect it to have some game around all year.

FLORA AND FAUNA HIGHLIGHTS Look on a map of the reserve's vegetation and you might be struck by the amount of mopane woodlands here – which generally isn't a huge attraction for safari-goers. However, drive on the ground and you'll realise that most of the area around the Gomoti River, where Starling's Camp and its safaris are concentrated, is a much prettier combination of big open floodplains with occasional islands.

Like much of the Delta around eastern Moremi, the flood patterns here do seem to have changed recently. When Tiko McNutt first came in 1989, the Mogogelo River, near Santawani, still had water in it; since then this has dried up. The flood has been generally poor elsewhere in the area, but these indications are mixed – observe the Gomoti River, which flows seasonally, and seems to have been flooding further and better during the last few years.

With something as complex as the changes in water flows and levels in the Delta, everyone has a slightly different opinion. Perhaps one of the most pertinent comments on this was, allegedly, from local wit Willy Philips, who commented that 'the only reliable water in the Okavango is the water in the toilets'.

Flora As mentioned above, much of NG34 is quite thick, and relatively unproductive, mopane woodlands. However, the western side of the reserve, adjoining the Gomoti River and some of its floodplains, is much more interesting.

Even driving on the main road south from South Gate to Maun you'll get a flavour of this, as you pass through some superb stretches of open acacia savannah – where you'll find very good populations of giraffe, if you're not speeding through too fast. The dominant species here is camelthorn, *Acacia erioloba*, though you'll also find a few umbrella thorns (*Acacia tortilis*) and the odd old leadwood (*Combretum imberbe*) mixed amongst them. It's classic mature Kalahari sandveld – and matches many people's image of Africa. These areas run like veins through the reserve, marking out the areas of deepest sand.

Around the Gomoti River, things are different. Here you'll find plenty of lovely areas of old riverine forest, containing all the usual species including sausage trees (*Kigelia africana*), marula trees (*Sclerocarya birrea*), jackalberries (*Diospyros mespiliformis*), African mangosteens (*Gardenia livingstonei*) and sycamore figs (*Ficus sycomorus*). You'll also find knobthorns (*Acacia negrescens*), which are immediately obvious around September and October for their creamy-white flowers and almost sickly-sweet perfume. Occasionally you'll find small islands, or patches, of these standing together.

The floodplains here come in two broadly different varieties. Those plains that still regularly flood are usually covered with short grass – a photogenic environment that's easy for game viewing. The others, which have been dry for a number of years, have often been largely covered with wild sage (*Pechuel-loeschea leubnitziae*). This classic 'pioneer species' can quickly take a hold when a floodplain dries out; it thrives in areas that have recently been disturbed. Other, slower-growing species of shrubs and trees will eventually germinate and take over these areas, though not for some years yet.

Amidst all of these plains, you'll find islands, large and small. These have riverine trees and shrubs on them, including a scattering of real fan palms (*Hyphaene petersiana*) and a notably high density of knobthorn trees (*Acacia negrescens*).

Fauna I haven't spent a lot of time in this area though my first memory of it was a good one. In May 1993, I'd been driving myself through Chobe and Moremi with a friend. It had been a good trip, though we were disappointed not to have seen any wild dogs. By the time we left South Gate, in the heat of midday, we had given up trying to spot animals. We were in NG34, but didn't think of this as a wildlife reserve.

After about 14km along the main track, we slowed down to find our way blocked by a large pack of very lazy wild dogs wandering about the road, and lounging by the side of it, yet showing little interest in our vehicle. They posed for photographs, as harmless as lapdogs, for about 30 minutes until they finally wandered off – thus providing us with one of the best game sightings of our whole trip. Only now, knowing how long researchers spend following the dogs in this area, do I understand why these dogs were so totally relaxed with our vehicle.

The commonest antelope here is probably the impala, a favourite prey of wild dogs, although you'll also find good numbers of tsessebe, kudu, giraffe and warthogs. Elephant are fairly common and, like buffalo, often move through here in the dry season in large herds. Roan are seen occasionally, while a real treat is the small herds of sable which appear fairly regularly in front of camp and near the Gomoti River.

Of the predators, lion are dominant although the area certainly has a permanent presence of wild dogs also. Leopard and cheetah both occur, but aren't seen often. The landscape should suit leopard; I guess that after a few more years leopard will become less shy here, showing themselves a bit more.

Birdlife The birdlife reflects the variety that you'll find anywhere in the Delta, and obviously depends heavily on the water levels. One recent checklist for NG33 and NG34 lists 208 species, but doesn't even pretend to be exhaustive.

However, the more common birds which are most frequently seen on the Gomoti floodplain and around the camp area include the long tailed and glossy starlings, from which the lodge takes its name; plus red-eyed, Cape turtle and mourning doves; blacksmiths and crowned plovers; long-tailed and crimson-breasted shrikes; red-billed quelias; buffalo weavers; lilac-breasted rollers, and white-backed and hooded vultures. Wattled cranes and paradise whydahs are also spotted periodically.

Meanwhile in the acacia woodlands, along with the ever-present doves, you're likely to find kori bustards; large flocks of helmeted guinea fowl; red-billed and Swainson' francolins; red- and yellow-billed hornbills; Meyer's parrots; double-banded, Burchell's, Namaqua and yellow-throated sandgrouse; plus the occasional Gabar goshawk, bateleur and ostrich.

WHAT TO SEE AND DO The main activities are game drives and night drives, which are usually conducted using open-topped Toyota Land Cruisers which take a

13

maximum of seven guests. That said, when the river's dry the camp is pumping water up into a small pan in front of camp – so your veranda can also be a good venue for game sightings.

Serious walking trips are also a feature, but tour operators often advise that they will only use top professional walking guides, who are armed. ('The standard of a Zimbabwe professional guide, with experience' – which is pretty much the gold standard of guiding in southern Africa; see pages 125–6 for comments.) Thus if you are keen on walking, then I'd let them know this when you book into the camp. If they consistently live up to this promise, then Starling's will be one of the few places in the region that really offers high-quality walking trips.

Depending on the season, mokoro trips are also possible from here. Water levels for this are generally feasible from around late May to September, though obviously this varies from year to year. Similarly, the camp offers boating trips when possible. The Gomoti is rarely navigable and so they usually use one of the boat stations up at Mboma Island or Xakanaxa, in Moremi. This requires a game drive of about 90 minutes each way, but the pay-off is that you're then boating in a very interesting area at the heart of Moremi.

WHERE TO STAY Note that the number of visitors allowed to use this part of the reserve at any one time is very strictly limited – and so you cannot just turn up and hope for a space. If you find yourself travelling between South Gate and Maun and need a space for the night, then better to camp at the Kaziikini Community Campsite, on the eastern side of this concession, near Sankuyo Village (see *The road north of Maun: to Moremi and Chobe*, at the end of *Chapter 8*, page 174).

Starling's Camp (8 tents) Contact via Overseas Adventure Travel, USA; ☎ 1 800 493 6824; www.oattravel.com. Starling's Camp is now for OAT groups only and must be pre-booked through Wilderness Safaris in Maun (see page 171), and it has no campsite attached to it. At the end of 2005, we heard that Starling's had been taken over for the exclusive use of the American tour operator Overseas Adventure Travel, and thus not open to walk-in guests. I haven't been here for a few years, but if it's kept the feel of the old Starling's Camp, then you can expect walk-in Meru-style tents built on solid plinths, with en-suite flush toilets and (gas-heated) hot showers. They were clean, comfortable and functional. Lighting around the camp at night was by paraffin lamps, whilst inside the tents small lights were powered by a 12V battery system.

The camp's main social area, simple and tented, is built on a huge wooden deck with a great view over the Gomoti River and its floodplain into NG32. This stands under a huge murula tree (*Sclerocarya birrea*), around which a few smaller knobthorns (*Acacia nigrescens*) are clustered.

MANKWE (NG43)

NG43, to the east of NG33 and NG34, is really a huge (3,460km²) patch of the Kalahari, east of Moremi's South Gate and south of Chobe's Mababe Gate. It's not an area where there's easy or prolific game viewing. I include it here because it is the base for a new bush lodge, and this may prove a very convenient stop between Maun and either Moremi or Chobe. In time, as the areas under wildlife protection effectively expand, it may even become more of a game-viewing destination in its own right.

GETTING THERE AND AWAY Virtually all visitors travelling directly between Maun and Chobe will pass through a section of NG43, even if you haven't noticed it. Mankwe Bush Lodge (✪ MANKWE 19°22.030'S, 23°53.510'E) is situated in the northwest corner of the reserve, just north of Sankuyo Village, and between the roads that lead to Chobe and Moremi.

To reach it from Maun, head towards Chobe's Mababe Gate (that is, follow the directions to Sankuyo in *The road north of Maun: to Moremi and Chobe*, at the end of *Chapter 8*, pages 173–4). Shortly after Sankuto Village the track splits. The right turn goes to Chobe, the left northwest to the cut-line which runs north–south and divides Chobe from Moremi. You'll find turn-offs to 'Mankwe' signposted on both roads.

Return transfers between the lodge and Maun can also be organised by the lodge for P100 per person (for a minimum of four people).

WHAT TO SEE AND DO Mankwe really works in two different ways, with different sets of activities. Firstly, if you're just passing through on the way to Chobe, and decide to stop for a day or two, they will organise bush walks in their area led by a guide, or game drives. These can be shorter drives on NG43 itself, including afternoon/night drives with a sundowner, or whole day-drives which usually head into the Khwai River area. Night drives after dinner are also an option. These guided activities are offered for a minimum of four people – at least, you must pay for four. Bush walks (2–3 hours) are P40 per person, short (3–4 hours) game drives P60, full-day drives P100, and short (2-hour) night drives P40.

Secondly, you can use Mankwe's position close to South Gate as a base for mobile safaris into the Moremi Game Reserve, often combined with overnight trips into the Delta from Mboma Boat Station, which Mankwe Lodge runs (see page 258 for full details).

A full-day drive in Moremi or Chobe is P500 per person, and an overnight boat trip in Moremi is P880, including food and equipment – again, for a minimum of four passengers.

They're also starting to offer wilderness 4x4 trails across the NG43 concession, though these require two vehicles for safety reasons. A local guide accompanies each trip (in your 4x4), and costs P100 per day.

WHERE TO STAY

Mankwe Bush Lodge (7 Meru-style tents, camping) Contact via Kgori Safaris (page 170). Located some way from any other lodge, Mankwe (⊕ MANKWE 19°22.03'S; 23°53.51'E) opened for business in 2001. The main building is raised up on a wooden deck, with a thatched lounge, an outside boma area for sitting around the campfire, and a small splash pool. Accommodation is in fairly large Meru-style tents, set on wooden decks overlooking the surrounding plains. Inside are twin beds, simple furniture and an en-suite bathroom including a flush toilet, washbasin and a hot (gas-fired) shower.

About 1.5km from the main lodge are 6 private campsites, half under camelthorn trees and the other half under mopane trees (known as the 'camelthorn' and 'mopane' sites respectively!). Each pitch has its own small ablutions, with a flush toilet, bucket shower and washbasin. By prior arrangement, meals can be taken at the lodge. Limited firewood is available (you're asked to collect your own after the first night), but you'll need to be fully equipped, with all your own drinking water as well as food and fuel.

P1,169 pp sharing, inc all meals, activities in NG43; P624 pp sharing B&B. Camping P70 per adult per night, exc VAT. Open all year.

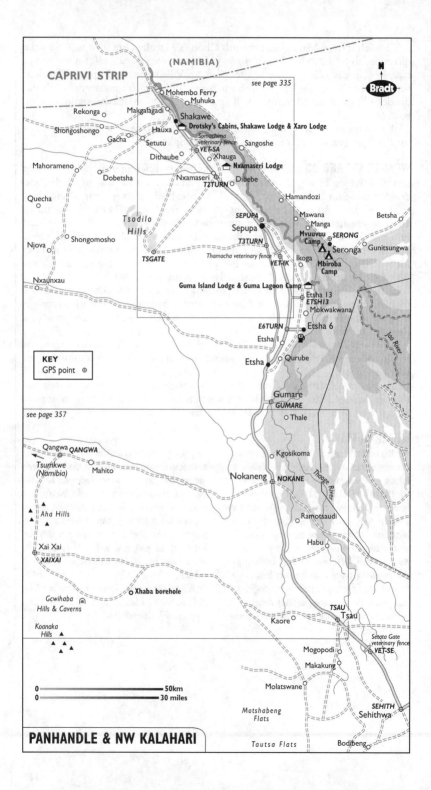

PANHANDLE & NW KALAHARI

14

The Okavango Panhandle and Northwest Kalahari

If much of the Okavango Delta is the preserve of the privileged few who can afford to fly in to exclusive safari camps, then the Panhandle presents more egalitarian options. Here you'll find the raw edge of Botswana's safari industry, camps on the edge of the Delta run by idiosyncratic owners or local communities – without marketing aids or slick glossy brochures. This is the Okavango's safari scene as it was 20 years ago!

Go west, into the Kalahari, and it's wilder still. Here there's almost nothing organised, yet the amazing Tsodilo Hills have been declared Botswana's first World Heritage Site. Adventurers will want to dig deeper here, reaching the caverns of the Gcwihaba Hills and the remote Aha range.

THE PANHANDLE

Look at a map of the Okavango Delta and you'll see that it's shaped like a frying pan, with the main river flowing down the handle, from the northwest. Thus this area gets its name.

ORIENTATION The Panhandle's western side is very easy to access with a 2WD, as the road between Sehithwa and Shakawe is tar. Once you leave the main road and the larger settlements, a high-clearance 4x4 is essential to cope with the sand in the area.

The track that follows the river on the eastern side is used much less, though it's not intrinsically difficult. Visitors very rarely travel along this as the only practical access to it is via the ferry that crosses the Okavango at Mohembo, north of Shakawe.

GEOLOGY AND GEOGRAPHY All of this area is in the Kalahari, though here it's dominated by the influence of the Okavango River. This comes south into Botswana from the Angolan Highlands, having crossed Namibia's Caprivi Strip.

GPS REFERENCES FOR PANHANDLE AND NW KALAHARI MAP			
E6TURN	19°06.706'S, 22°16.152'E	T2TURN	18°35.834'S, 21°59.986'E
ETSH13	19°00.975'S, 22°19.125'E	T3TURN	18°50.292'S, 22°10.011'E
GUMARE	19°22.242'S, 22°09.242'E	TSAU	20°10.294'S, 22°27.265'E
NOKANE	19°39.694'S, 22°11.184'E	TSGATE	18°47.275'S, 21°44.856'E
QANGWA	19°31.868'S, 21°10.281'E	VET-IK	18°50.327'S, 22°13.756'E
SEHITH	20°28.259'S, 22°42.372'E	VET-SA	18°29.256'S, 21°55.142'E
SEPUPA	18°44.150'S, 22°10.625'E	VET-SE	20°15.775'S; 22°33.926'E
SERONG	18°48.771'S, 22°24.988'E	XAIXAI	19°52.867'S, 21°04.934'E

Entering Botswana, the river's gradient is very low. However, it is constrained from spreading out by steep riverbanks on either side. Underneath the sand lies a more fundamental constraint: parallel fault lines in the earth's crust which run southeast, about 10–15km apart. Thus the river meanders gradually southeast, between them, forming a series of wide, sweeping curves and the odd ox-bow lagoon – but always remaining within the constraints of the banks.

Where the river's meanders kiss the banks at the edge of the floodplain, villages have sprung up: Shakawe, Sepupa and Seronga. The southern extent of the faultlines lies around Seronga, so south of here the river begins to spread wider to form the main body of the Delta.

FLORA AND FAUNA The Panhandle isn't a prime area for game viewing, so don't come here expecting masses of big game or you'll be disappointed. That said, you may catch glimpses of the occasional sitatunga or small herds of lechwe, and you're almost bound to see numerous hippo and crocodile.

However, there are some first-class areas for birding, and plenty of areas with deep-water channels and lagoons.

Flora Looking from the Panhandle's banks, often all you can see is a gently swaying mass of feathery papyrus heads. Here, more than anywhere else in the Delta, the environment is polarised: there's deep-water channels, and there's the papyrus beds that surround them.

Occasionally you'll find sections of phragmites reeds and, when the waters are low, open stretches of sandbanks. Sometimes the odd day-lily (*Nymphaea nouchali caerulea*) will take hold in a quiet inlet on the edge of the channel, but mainly the vegetation here is huge expanses of floating papyrus.

Birdlife The birdlife here is as varied as anywhere in the Delta, though getting to actually see the birds that inhabit the papyrus can be tricky. Some of the more sought-after sightings would be painted snipes, rufous-bellied herons, lesser jacanas, chirping cisticolas, brown-throated weavers and coppery-tailed and white-browed coucals. Greater swamp warblers and swamp boubous can often be heard calling from the papyrus, but are less easy to spot.

The Panhandle is a particularly good area for the white-backed night heron; whilst perching on the sandbanks look out for white-backed ducks (sometimes in large numbers), long-toed plovers, red-winged pratincoles and, of course, the Panhandle's most acrobatic birding attractions: African skimmers.

These distinctive, black-and-white birds fly south to the Delta between about September and December. They mainly come to breed on the sandbanks of the Panhandle which are then exposed while the water is low. Here they'll gather in small flocks, each pair excavating a shallow depression in the sand where they'll lay their eggs and raise their young.

One of the Delta's most amazing sights is to watch these birds feed. With long, graceful wings they fly fast and low, holding their elongated lower mandible just low enough to cut the water's surface. This is hollow and has sharp edges, shaped to minimise its drag in the water. When this touches a small fish near the surface, it is quickly raised against the upper mandible, trapping the fish firmly. I always marvel at their flying skill, moving their body in all directions whilst their bill traces a constant, steady path through the water.

Note that because they nest very near the waterline, on low sandbanks, their nests and young are very vulnerable to both predators and to damage from the wash caused by fast-moving motorboats. So boats operating in these areas should never be driven too fast.

Another spectacular migrant, better seen in the Panhandle than anywhere else in the Delta, is the carmine bee-eater. These come to southern Africa to breed, and stay from about October to March. They nest in large colonies, building their nests underground at the end of tunnels which they excavate into the side of sandy riverbanks. You won't forget the sight of hundreds of these bright carmine-pink birds twittering around a river bank that's holed with nests like a piece of Swiss cheese.

Above the water you'll always see fish eagles around. Marsh harriers and even the occasional migrant osprey are also sometimes seen. Beside the waters and papyrus there's the narrow band of thick riverine forest on the banks before the bush becomes that of the dry Kalahari. Here there's a wide variety of different birdlife – typical of any of the riverine areas in this region. Notable sightings here would include the tiny brown firefinch, Bradfield's hornbills, western banded snake eagles and Pel's fishing owls.

GETTING AROUND

By vehicle The main road on the west side of the Panhandle is very easy to get along in a 2WD; it's all tar and maintained to a high standard. For anywhere else in this area, you really need your own fully equipped 4x4.

By bus There are several buses per day which ply between Maun and Shakawe, stopping at the main villages on the way. The whole trip takes about seven hours and costs a total of P40. These buses will turn off to the larger centres such as Gumare and Etsha 6, but near the smaller villages they will just pick up and drop passengers on the main road. Most go from Maun to Shakawe in the morning, and back in the afternoon – but ask locally for more precise timings.

By air There are small airstrips dotted around, so if you charter a plane you can get to most places here: Shakawe, Nxamaseri, Nokaneng, Tsau and Guma Lagoon. The Tsodilo Hills have an airstrip, but you really need a vehicle whilst you're there to get the most out of it. There are no airstrips anywhere near the Gcwihaba or Aha Hills.

THE EASTERN PANHANDLE Visitors relatively rarely see this side of the Okavango's Panhandle, largely because there is little to attract visitors. However, there is a good gravel road that runs down the eastern side of the river from Mohembo to Seronga. This is how these villages get the bulk of their supplies.

Between Mohembo and Seronga you'll find a large number of small villages which survive mainly on fishing and, away from the river, a number of tiny 'cattle-post' settlements used by the people when tending their cattle in the interior of NG11 – which is fairly continuously cattle-ranching country.

The main reason for visitors to come here is for mokoro trips based out of Mbiroba Camp, run by the Polers' Trust, at Seronga. For travellers who are constrained by a relatively tight budget, this is one of the few options left to see any of the Okavango.

Getting there and away

By air Seronga has an airstrip (⊕ SERAIR 18°49.180'S, 22°25.020'E) that is now in regular use bringing visitors from Maun to the Okavango Polers' Trust, and this is now by far the easiest and most convenient way for most travellers to access this village. Check in Maun with Island Safari Lodge or Audi Camp for details of the options.

By vehicle The only practical way to access the eastern side of the Panhandle with a vehicle is to cross the Okavango River on the ferry at Mohembo, in the far north.

There appears to be another route, which every year is tried by a clueless few, following what looks like a good road on the Shell map of Botswana. This appears to go around the eastern side of the Delta and link into Seronga from the Linyanti area, via the village of Betsha.

However, the tracks on this side have very few users and no signposts. They cross a number of different private concessions and hunting areas, none of which will welcome your visit. Straying off designated transit routes will get you into trouble. Meanwhile, when the tracks meet villages they split and vanish. But perhaps the greatest danger here is of water blocking the route. It's easy to get dangerously lost in this region and to then run out of fuel, water or supplies. There's no help here, so I'd strongly advise against trying to use any of these tracks.

By bus/hitching If you're travelling without a vehicle, then both Shakawe and Sepupa are fairly easy to access on one of the local buses that run up and down the road between Shakawe and Sehithwa. There are then two ways across to the eastern side. The easiest way (and, if you're aiming for Seronga, the most convenient way) is to take the bus to Sepupa and then catch the small motorboat ferry which shuttles between Sepupa and Seronga. The alternative is to use the vehicle ferry at Mohembo, and then hitch south down the road on the eastern bank.

By boat There's a regular motorboat ferry between Seronga Boat Station (✪ SERBOA 18°49.316'S, 22°24.855'E) and Sepupa (see pages 337–8). This takes a couple of hours to reach Sepupa (it's faster in the opposite direction, downstream), via a variety of winding channels. In the highly unlikely event that you ever need to navigate yourself to Seronga by boat, the turn-off from the main channel towards the boat station is at ✪ SERTUR 18°49.776'S, 22°24.350'E.

A one-way trip on the motorboat ferry costs only about P20 per person, but you'll have to wait for the boat to fill up. Alternatively, it may be possible to arrange boat transfers here from Guma Island Lodge (see page 341) on the west side of the Panhandle, if you're staying there for a period of time. Sepupa Swamp Stop charges a minimum of P600 for a private motorboat to do the return journey between Sepupa and Seronga.

Seronga Seronga (✪ SERONG 18°48.771'S, 22°24.988'E) is a sizeable village at the base of the Panhandle. It's the regional centre for a number of small settlements to the east of it, along the northern edge of the Delta, as well as a focus for the people who still live in the northern areas of the Delta.

Where to stay There's only one option here, but it's one of the best budget options in the Delta: the base for a local co-operative of polers in the area:

Mbiroba Camp (5 chalets, rondavels, camping) Okavango Polers' Trust, Seronga; ☎ 6876 861; f 6876 939; e mbiroba@okavangodelta.co.bw; www.okavangodelta.co.bw. This is one of the region's more established community ventures, which is succeeding by offering a simple, good-value product to travellers who are not expecting 5-star luxury. Despite this, there's still a bar and a curio shop!

The camp's chalets, which were being refurbished early in 2006, are simple, 2-storey constructions with solar-powered lighting, and solar-heated water for the outdoor shower. All are of traditional Meru-style design, set on wooden decks, with up to 4 beds and an en-suite bathroom. There's also a campsite with a few simple rondavels, which share ablutions and can sleep 2 people. Limited numbers of tents and other camping equipment can be hired; expect to pay about P33 for a 2-person tent.
Chalets P250/350/450/520/590 for 1/2/3/4/6 people, rondavels P110, camping P33 pp. Mokoro P198 per day (2 people).

What to see and do Mbiroba Camp is used as a base from which to take mokoro trips into the Delta with a poler. You need to bring all your food and equipment: you'll be camping rough, without any facilities. That said, if you're prepared this is a lovely way to see the Delta. Just make sure you read *Chapter 6* before you go.

Current costs for this are P198 per mokoro (seats two) per day, plus a one-off charge of P66 for transfers, and a 'service' charge, with prices remaining remarkably stable in recent years.

THE WESTERN PANHANDLE

Mohembo border and ferry Heading north about 13km after Shakawe, you reach the area of the border with Namibia. A left turn takes you to the neat, newly built customs and immigration area for those crossing into Namibia by road (*customs post open daily 06.00–19.30*). The road straight on leads swiftly to the (free) Mohembo ferry, which usually takes a few vehicles at a time across the river, including the occasional small truck. Expect to find a lot of people waiting around here – some to cross, others to meet those who have crossed, or to buy and sell things.

Shakawe This very large fishing village stands east of the main road on the northern banks of the Panhandle of the Delta, some 281km north of Sehithwa and 13km south of the Mohembo border post on the Caprivi Strip. Driving into the village always used to feel like entering a maze of reed walls, each surrounding a small kraal, as the track split countless ways between the houses. The odd trap of deep sand was enough to stop you for an hour, and thus serve up excellent entertainment to numerous amused locals.

Today, however, Shakawe is a bustling little place. Just a stone's throw from the tar road you'll find a significant base for the army (the Botswana Defence Force), as you'd expect in one of the country's more sensitive border areas, and a major police station. If you're going to be doing anything unusual here, then stopping to ask at the police station if it is OK to proceed is always a good idea. If you've the time, take a walk along the river, just behind the police station. Sometimes there's a mokoro ferry shuttling local people to and from the eastern side of the river, full with their wares to sell or recent purchases to take back home.

Of particular importance to drivers is the Saoshoko filling station (*open daily 07.00–18.00*) close to the entrance to the village when heading north. There are also a few shops and a post office, many concentrated within the small shopping centre around the bus stop. And if you can't leave the modern world behind, then Shakawe has cellphone coverage which usually extends to Drotsky's, but not much further.

If you fancy a break before driving on, you could try a guided tour of Krokovango Crocodile Farm, 5km south of Shakawe, but there's little else to delay you here.

Getting there and away There are good daily bus services to Maun via the rest of the western Panhandle from the centre of town. Of these, the fastest is the Golden Bridge Express (P35 one way), which leaves at around 07.30 each morning, taking around 4¹/₂ hours to reach Maun. Zebra minibuses are cheaper (P28) but very cramped and take an hour longer; they also depart only when full. A third bus leaves a little later in the day. Return buses leave Maun at around the same time. Alternatively, hitchhiking is relatively easy.

On the west side of the main road, just 400m off the tarmac, you'll find a paved airstrip, with a very neat, round, thatched terminal building.

Where to stay There's nowhere practical to stay in Shakawe itself, but there are several water-based camps on the river south of town that cater mainly for fishing and birdwatching. Now that the Caprivi Strip is once more accessible to visitors, trade here has picked up so you will often need to book. Listed are the three main options, from north to south:

🏠 **Drotsky's Cabins** (6 chalets, camping) Shakawe; 📞 6875 035; f 6875 043; e drotskys@info.bw (⊕ DROTSK 18°24.868'S, 21°53.120'E). Almost 8km south of the radio mast in Shakawe you'll find a left turn off the tar road. This sandy track will lead you east, crossing the old road up the Panhandle for about 3km to reach Drotsky's Cabins. You should be able to drive across this in a normal 2WD car, though the sand can be very thick, so some driving skill is needed.

This long-established camp is run by the delightful Jan and Eileen Drotsky and their family, who have seen Shakawe change from a remote outpost to a thriving little town. It stands on a high bank, overlooking the river, which is already several kilometres wide. Below is a network of deep-water channels and large beds of papyrus. It's excellent for birdwatching or fishing, though there's little game around except for hippos and crocodiles.

Drotsky's chalets are set amongst well-watered lawns in a shaded haven under a canopy of thick riverside trees. Colourful shrubs and banana trees have been planted between them, creating the welcoming impression of a green and tropical haven.

A-frame chalets sleep either 2 or 4 people: the latter are bigger and built on 2 levels. All have low brick sidewalls supporting a tall, steeply angled thatched roof. These are insect-proofed with mesh on the window and lit by mains electricity. They all have simple furnishings, rugs on the floor, and a table-top electric fan. There's also a shady campsite with electric points. Central to the lodge is a bar (which often seems to play host to an eclectic selection of local characters) and a very large dining area, built over the river. Look out for the rather beautiful wooden top to the bar!

Drotsky's is a genuine old camp, where hospitality hasn't been learned from a manual. If you are willing to take it on its own terms, then it can be a super lodge, and offer you fascinating insights into the area, its history and its ecosystems. *P360/295 pp sgl/sharing, 4-person chalet P780, camping P75 pp, inc firewood. Breakfast P55, lunch P66, dinner P88. Boat hire from P175 per hr per boat, plus fuel, depending on size of boat; rod hire P25 per day. Transfers to or from Shakawe airport P25 pp.*

🏠 **Xaro Lodge** (8 Meru tents) Book via Drotsky's Cabins, above. Xaro (⊕ XARO 18°25.423'S,

21°56.364'E) is about 8.5km downstream from Drotsky's Cabins, its parent camp, and is usually reached from there by a 15-min boat trip. The lodge is built on an outcrop from the mainland, amidst an old, established grove of knobthorn (*Acacia nigrescens*), mangosteen (*Garcenia livingstonei*) and jackalberry (*Diospyros mespiliformis*) trees.

It was originally built in about 1984 by Hartley's Safaris, before passing through several hands until it was acquired by Jan Drotsky, whose son, Donovan, now runs the camp with his wife, Yolande.

It's hard to escape the feeling that this was once an absolutely beautiful, old-style Okavango camp. You'll still find a thatched, stone dining area with a large table in the centre and various old books on the bookshelves in the walls. Accommodation, though, is in new, Meru-style tents with en-suite facilities and sliding doors leading to a wooden deck. Look around and you'll also find a garden of succulents and cacti, banana trees and even a small baobab tree (*Adansonia digitata*) on the left of the camp as you look out on to the river.

Royal, one of the marvellous staff who has been with the family for years, recalls that the lodge has always been used for fishing and birdwatching from motorboats, never from mekoro — and that's still the situation. *P280/P350 pp sharing/sgl, inc transfer from Drotsky's. Breakfast P55, lunch P66, dinner P88. Boat hire from P175 per hr per boat, plus fuel, depending on size of boat; rod hire P25 per day. Transfers to or from Shakawe airport P55 pp.*

🏠 **Shakawe Lodge** (10 bungalows, camping) Contact via Travel Wild, Maun; 📞 6860 822; f 6860 493; e win@travelwild.co.bw (⊕ SKAKAL 18°26.059'S, 21°54.326'E). Shakawe Lodge was started in 1959, and was for decades known as Shakawe Fishing Camp. You'll find the turning to it (⊕ SHAKAT 18°26.804'S, 21°53.654'E) on the east of the main road about 5.5km north of the Somachima Veterinary Fence (⊕ VET-SA 18°29.256'S, 21°55.142'E), or 15km south of Shakawe village. The lodge stands on the bank of the Okavango River, a little less than 3km from the road. Its present owners, Barry and Elaine Price, took it over in 1975. Now the lodge offers large, thatched, brick bungalows. Each has a fan and mains power throughout, and an en-suite

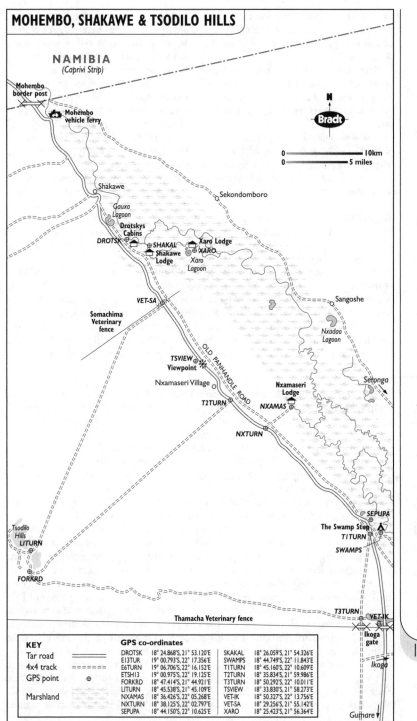

MOHEMBO, SHAKAWE & TSODILO HILLS

NAMIBIA
(Caprivi Strip)

Mohembo
border post

Mohembo
vehicle ferry

N

Bradt

0 ——————— 10km
0 ——————— 5 miles

Shakawe

Sekondomboro

Gauxa
Lagoon

Drotskys
Cabins

DROTSK

SHAKAL
Shakawe
Lodge

Xaro Lodge
XARO

Xaro
Lagoon

VET-SA

Somachima
Veterinary
fence

Sangoshe

Nxadao
Lagoon

OLD PANHANDLE ROAD

TSVIEW
Viewpoint

Nxamaseri Village

Seronga

Nxamaseri
Lodge

T2TURN

NXAMAS

NXTURN

SEPUPA

The Swamp Stop
TITURN

SWAMPS

Tsodilo
Hills
LITURN

FORKRD

Thamacha Veterinary fence

T3TURN

VET-IK

Ikoga
gate

Ikoga

KEY	GPS co-ordinates		
Tar road	DROTSK	18° 24.868'S, 21° 53.120'E	SKAKAL	18° 26.059'S, 21° 54.326'E
4x4 track	E13TUR	19° 00.793'S, 22° 17.356'E	SWAMPS	18° 44.749'S, 22° 11.843'E
GPS point	E6TURN	19° 06.706'S, 22° 16.152'E	TITURN	18° 45.160'S, 22° 10.609'E
	ETSHI3	19° 00.975'S, 22° 19.125'E	T2TURN	18° 35.834'S, 21° 59.986'E
	FORKRD	18° 47.414'S, 21° 44.921'E	T3TURN	18° 50.292'S, 22° 10.011'E
Marshland	LITURN	18° 45.538'S, 21° 45.109'E	TSVIEW	18° 33.830'S, 21° 58.273'E
	NXAMAS	18° 36.426'S, 22° 05.268'E	VET-IK	18° 50.327'S, 22° 13.756'E
	NXTURN	18° 38.125'S, 22° 02.797'E	VET-SA	18° 29.256'S, 21° 55.142'E
	SEPUPA	18° 44.150'S, 22° 10.625'E	XARO	18° 25.423'S, 21° 56.364'E

14

bathroom. All are carpeted, though very basic. There's a circular thatched boma, used as a bar/dining room, adjacent to a small lily-covered lagoon that's behind the splash pool.

Under shady trees on the riverbank, a few metres south of the main lodge, is the campsite. This is a lovely, grassy site with simple ablutions and a few metal drums that act as braai stands for cooking.

Most visitors here come to fish, though birdwatching – through the riverside forest or from boats – is also popular. Mahango Game Reserve is within reach on a day trip, though most visitors would opt to stay there as a separate destination.

Beside the bank at the lodge, look for the Okavango's only Angolan houseboat, a relic of the Angolan war from the late 1970s. Apparently it was used by 32 Battalion of the South African forces, who were stationed in the Caprivi Strip, near the site where Ngepi Campsite is now. However, it broke loose and drifted south, and has been gently rusting in Botswana ever since! Barry has some stories to tell you about this if you ask him.

Chalet P350/P550/P836.50 sgl/dbl/trpl, camping P66 pp, all inc tax. Breakfast P55, lunch P66, dinner P110. Boat hire P198 per hr, plus fuel. Visa/MasterCard accepted, or payment in any convertible currency.

Nxamaseri
Though the small village of Nxamaseri is not a stop for most visitors, I've included this section because the surrounding area is a very interesting one, offering an insight into the attractions of the Delta that is on a par with most of the reserves further east.

The Nxamaseri Channel is a side-channel of the main Okavango River. When water levels are high, there are plenty of open marshy floodplains covered with an apparently unblemished carpet of grass, and dotted with tiny palm islands. It's very like the Jao Flats, and is one of the Okavango's most beautiful corners.

Like Guma Lagoon, further south, it's fairly easily accessible due to the presence of a lodge. If you want a real Delta experience in the Panhandle, then this should be high on your list of places to visit – though getting here requires either your own vehicle or a flight.

Flora and fauna highlights
The Nxamaseri Channel is north of the point where the main Okavango River divides at the base of the Panhandle, and is a stretch of open, clear water up to about 30m wide in places. Beside the edges you'll find stands of papyrus and common reeds, whilst its quieter edges are lined by patches of waterlilies, including many night-lilies (aka lotus lilies; *Nymphaea lotus*) as well as the more common day-lilies (*Nymphaea nouchali caerulea*). Look out also for the heart-shaped floating leaves, and star-shaped white or yellow flowers of the water gentian (*Nymphoides indica*).

As with the rest of the Panhandle, this isn't a prime area for game viewing. You may catch glimpses of the odd lechwe or the shy sitatunga, and you're almost bound to see hippo and crocodile, but big game is scarce. However, the channel is a super waterway for birdwatching; home to a tremendous variety of waterbirds. Without trying too hard, my sightings included many pygmy geese, greater and lesser jacanas, lesser galinules, colonies of reed cormorants, darters, several species of bee-eater and kingfisher, green-backed herons, a relaxed black crake, numerous red-shouldered widows and even (on a cloudy morning in February) a pair of Pel's fishing owls. Beside the channel are pockets of tall riverine trees and various real fan and wild date palms, whose overhanging branches house colonies of weavers (masked, spotted-backed and brown-throated). Upstream of the lodge, on the main Okavango River, there's a colony of carmine bee-eaters at a location known locally as 'the red cliffs'. This is occupied from around early September to the end of December, but is probably at its best in late September or early October (the best time for most migrant species here). While watching for birds, keep an eye out for the elusive spotted-necked otter (*Lutra maculicollis*), which also frequents these waters.

Getting there and away Nxamaseri lies about 19km north of Sepupa, or 37km south of Shakawe. If you're approaching from the north, follow the tar road to the Somachima Veterinary Fence (⊕ VET-SA 18°29.256'S, 21°55.142'E), then after 10km you'll pass a slight rise marked by a sign as 'Tsodilo View' (⊕ TSVIEW 18°33.830'S, 21°58.273'E). From here, on a clear day, you can see the Tsodilo Hills to the southwest. Less than 3km south of this viewpoint you'll pass a sign to Nxamaseri, which leads to the village of the same name. Nxamaseri Lodge's unmarked turning (⊕ NXTURN 18°38.125'S, 22°2.797'E) is almost 9km south of this; it's just a vague track in the deep sand leading northeast to the lodge (⊕ NXAMAS 18°36.426'S, 22°5.268'E), about 5.5km from the main road. However, the lodge is surrounded by water for most of the year and self-drivers will usually be met and transferred by boat for the final few kilometres. Advanced reservations are essential; this is not a lodge to try and drop into unannounced.

Where to stay

Nxamaseri Lodge (6 chalets) Maun; ☎ 6878 015; f 6878 016; e info@nxamaseri.com; www.nxamaseri.com. This long-established camp was started as a fishing camp in about 1980. Recently bought back by the original owners, PJ and Barney Bestelink (who run Okavango Horse Safaris; see page 171), it is now run by PJ's son, Brad. It is claimed that fly-fishing in the Delta was pioneered at Nxamaseri, and certainly it remains an attraction for people who fish seriously, but to this have now been added birdwatching, visits to a local village to watch basket-making, and day trips to the Tsodilo Hills, making this a wonderful all-round lodge justifying a stay of at least 2 days.

The lodge has been built within a wonderfully thick and tropical patch of riverine vegetation. All around are knobthorn (*Acacia nigrescens*), waterberry (*Syzygium cordatum*), sycamore fig (*Ficus sycomorus*) mangosteen (*Garcinia livingstonei*), jackalberries, sausage trees (*Kigelia africana*) and some of the most wonderfully contorting python vines (*Cocculus hirsutus*) that you'll see anywhere. Sensitive refurbishment in 2006 means that the strong sense of place has been retained, but with higher standards of accommodation and food. The wide, thatched lounge/dining area is built around a couple of lofty old jackalberry trees (*Diospyros mespiliformis*), with an open frontage to the river: it's comfortable and well thought out, but not ornate. Wooden walkways lead to a dbl chalet on one side, and twin-bedded chalets to the other. All are brick with high thatched roofs and, in the front, a waist-high wall leading to a wooden deck above the river (a rainproof screen can be rolled down, but is seldom needed). With a free flow of air from outside, a walk-in mosquito net protects the beds from insects. Each en-suite chalet has a flush toilet, hot shower and washbasin, and bedside lights are powered by a generator or batteries.

The boat trips for birdwatching are first-class, and whilst there tends to be less emphasis on mokoro excursions, these are also possible (and magical) when the water levels are high and there are suitable areas of shallow water nearby. Fly-fishing and lure/spinning fishing with top-quality equipment are possible throughout the year under expert guidance at every level. The very best tiger-fishing months are Aug–Nov, while the best time for bream is Mar–Jun. During the first 3 months of the year the rain and new floodwaters are said to disturb the fish, which move out to the floodplains, so fishing in the channels can be more difficult. Nxamaseri's record tiger-fish catch is about 6.7kg, though in a normal season they'd expect to have 10–15 catches over the 6kg mark. Like most Okavango lodges, Nxamaseri operates a 'catch-and-release' system, except for the occasional bream taken for the table. They have 2 large, flat, barge-like boats which provide a very stable platform for several people fishing, and are also ideal for photography.
US$437/655 pp sharing/sgl, inc all meals and most activities, exc bar drinks and transfers. Day trips to Tsodilo Hills and full-day fishing US$50 pp. Open all year.

Sepupa Sometime spelt 'Sepopa', 223km north of Sehithwa and perhaps 58km south of Shakawe, Sepupa can be reached via a turning from the main road (⊕ SEPUPA 18°44.150'S, 22°10.625'E), which is about 1.7km away.

There you'll find a few shops including a bottle stall, a general dealer, a radio mast and a bakery advertising 'fresh palatable skilled-made bread'. Irresistible!

However, if you're not tempted then there's a turning off this linking road to the south, about halfway between the village and the main road. This is signposted to the Swamp Stop, and also leads to the motorboat ferry to Seronga.

The ferry to Seronga On the right of the Swamp Stop, a few hundred metres downstream, is the very informal mooring for the ferry. This is really just a motorboat with a shade cover. It normally leaves around 12.00–14.00, provided there are enough people, and takes 90 minutes to cross the river (diagonally downstream, via a variety of winding channels) to Seronga. A one-way trip costs P20 per person.

Where to stay There's really only one option here.

⋏ Sepupa Swamp Stop (camping plus fixed tents). The Swamp Stop itself (✪ SWAMPS 18°44.749'S, 22°11.843'E) is just a simple campsite under trees, with a few Meru tents erected on concrete bases for those who haven't brought their own tents; all share ablutions. Firewood is available.

Although it was taken over in 2005, the previous owners have marketed it well and positioned it as one of the very few remaining bases for budget safaris into the Delta, and a possible springboard for getting to Seronga, which is one of the other possible bases.

Activities include self-catering mokoro trails, with costs depending on group size and duration.

Alternatively you can take the river-taxi to Seronga, and organise trips directly with the Okavango Polers' Trust (see page 171). There are also motorboat trips, and a houseboat (with small tender boat) that takes a maximum of 12 people at a time. Both can be used for hourly or overnight trips, which can include camping on the islands. While transfers to Seronga are available, they require a minimum of 6 people, making the ferry next door a much more economical option for most people.
P25 pp camping, fixed tent P200 per night (max 2 nights). Open all year.

THE DELTA'S WESTERN FRINGES

Ordered from north to south, here's a brief listing of the main landmarks and villages on the road between Sepupa and Sehithwa. If it gets a little repetitive, then take that as a fair reflection of the road, which is long and well surfaced with tarmac. Most of this area has a low, wide verge of groundcover which is often cut – helping to ensure that big game can be seen before it is standing in front of you. But for all this visibility, the scenery is uninteresting.

Although you're travelling at times very close to the western edge of the Okavango Delta, the road passes through apparently undistinguished areas of bush. You may see the occasional animal, but with man and cattle as the dominant species in this area, only birdwatchers are likely to find much of interest on the drive.

SEPUPA TO ETSHA 13
Tsodilo turning About 0.5km south of the Sepupa junction on the main road is a smaller turning (✪ T1TURN 18°45.160'S, 22°10.609'E) on to a track which is very clearly signposted to the Tsodilo Hills. This is the most southerly approach to the hills (see page 350 for more details).

Ikoga Gate At about 211km north of Sehithwa, 12km south of the Sepupa turn-off, you will have to stop at the Ikoga Gate (✪ VET-IK 18°50.327'S, 22°13.756'E), which is a checkpoint on the Thamacha Veterinary Fence.

Ikoga turning About 206km north of Sehithwa, there's another turning east, this time to Ikoga.

The amazing phenomenon of the catfish run is unique to the Okavango Delta. It happens every year, between early August and the end of November, though its timing is difficult to predict precisely.

As the water level starts to drop in the northern part of the Panhandle, it is still rising in the southern part of the Delta. The catfish runs start in the north of the Panhandle, where the lowering water levels concentrate the Delta's smaller fish – especially the relatively small churchill (*Petrocephalus catostoma*) and bulldog (*Marcusenius macrolepidotus*) – in the channels and papyrus banks.

The main predatory species involved include the sharp-toothed catfish (*Clarias gariepinus*), a hardy, omnivorous species which grows up to 1.4m in length and 59kg in weight, and the much smaller blunt-toothed catfish (*Clarias ngaensis*). These catfish hunt in packs and a 'run' starts with the catfish swimming upstream inside the papyrus banks. Here they slap their powerful tails on the surface of the water, making a noise like a gunshot, and against the papyrus, to stun the smaller fish, their prey.

Hundreds and sometimes thousands of catfish will work their way upstream like this, making the water 'boil' with their frenzy of activity. All this noise and commotion attracts an eager audience of herons, storks, egrets, fish eagles and other fish-eating birds on the banks, while crocodiles, snakes and tiger fish lurk beyond the papyrus in the deeper channels waiting to snap up anything that escapes from the papyrus.

Although in each run the catfish swim upstream, when it's finished they pause and drift back down, subsequently re-joining other catfish and starting new runs. So as the water levels drop further down in the Delta, so the location of the runs moves south also.

These runs occur in many different sizes. There will be several per day in different areas of the Delta, each covering a distance of a few kilometres before fizzling out. A couple may be longer than this, perhaps continuing for as long as two weeks and covering a lot of distance, but these are the exception rather than the rule.

Eventually, signalled by the onset of the rising waters, the catfish will themselves move out on to the floodplains and spawn.

Etsha 13 About 32km south of the Sepupa turn-off, or 191km north of Sehithwa, is a turning (⊕ E13TUR 19°0.793'S, 22°17.356'E) which leads slightly over 3km east to Etsha 13. This small town has a few basic shops, but little more.

GUMA LAGOON On the western side of the Delta, at the very base of the Panhandle, Guma is a large, papyrus-lined lagoon. It is linked to the Thaoge River, the main eastern finger of the Okavango River system, by a short channel (40 minutes by boat from the camp or the lodge).

Guma Lagoon and the main Thoage River are excellent spots for fishing and birdwatching. This combination, with relatively easy access from Etsha 13, has encouraged two different camps to set up here.

Flora and fauna highlights Guma isn't a place for big game; it's a deep-water environment that offers good birdwatching and fishing.

The vegetation around the lagoon itself is mainly papyrus, though you'll also find large stands of phragmites reeds. You'll also find the odd waterberry (*Syzygium cordatum*) and water fig (*Ficus verruculosa*), especially in the smaller channels and backwaters.

The Okavango Panhandle and Northwest Kalahari THE DELTA'S WESTERN FRINGES

14

On the banks, the riverine vegetation is thick and lush. It includes plenty of wild date palms (*Phoenix reclinata*), river beans (*Sesbania sesban*) and potato bushes (*Phyllanthus reticulatus*), which are members of the euphorbia family and are not related to potatoes at all – but smell the air on a warm evening and you'll realise where their name comes from.

Also keep an eye out for large sour plum (*Ximenia caffra*), water pear (*Syzygium guineense*), jackalberry trees (*Diospyros mespiliformis*) and the occasional sausage tree (*Kigelia africana*) – one of which greets you as you enter Guma Lagoon Camp. Further from the water, you'll often find acacias: camelthorn (*Acacia erioloba*), knobthorn (*Acacia nigrescens*) and umbrella thorn (*Acacia tortilis*) are the main species here. There are a few baobabs (*Adansonia digitata*) in the area, but they're not common.

The more common birds include fish eagles, many species of herons, egrets, warblers, bee-eaters and kingfishers, pygmy geese and greater and lesser jacanas. Look for red-shouldered widows in the papyrus, and reed cormorants and darters sunning themselves on perches over the water.

In the riverine forest areas you can find Heuglin's robins, crested and black-collard barbets, green pigeons, various sunbirds and, in the summer, the spectacular paradise flycatchers in breeding plumage.

Getting there and away Starting at the small town of Etsha 13 (✪ ETSH13 19°00.975'S, 22°19.125'E), the route to either of the lodges at Guma Lagoon is only about 13km of very sandy 4x4 track. If you're driving a 2WD then with prior notice the lodges can arrange to collect you from Etsha 13, leaving your car somewhere safe whilst you're at Guma.

There are some small signposts on this route, but they're not always consistent and the route is far from straight. Start off by heading through the village on a track going east-southeast. Gradually this turns east, then northeast, and finally north – and the scenery gets prettier, with less domestic animals and settlements, and more small date palm islands and open floodplains.

A GPS is sensible for this route. Waypoints for one possible route, from Etsha13 to the Guma Lagoon lodges, are as follows:

ETSH13	19°00.975'S, 22°19.125'E (the village of Etsha 13);		
GUMA00	19°00.900'S, 22°19.171'E;	GUMA01	19°00.933'S, 22°19.362'E;
GUMA02	19°01.317'S, 22°20.135'E;	GUMA03	19°01.236'S, 22°20.318'E;
GUMA04	19°01.017'S, 22°20.533'E;	GUMA05	19°01.210'S, 22°21.354'E;
GUMA06	19°00.734'S, 22°22.192'E;	GUMA07	19°00.204'S, 22°22.831'E;
GUMA08	19°00.042'S, 22°22.912'E;	GUMA09	18°59.252'S, 22°22.825'E;
GUMA10	18°59.060'S, 22°22.912'E;	GUMA11	18°58.537'S, 22°22.609'E;
GUMAIL	18°58.245'S, 22°22.101'E (Guma Island Lodge);		
GUMA13	18°58.098'S, 22°22.228'E;	GUMA14	18°57.749'S, 22°22.370'E;
GUMALC	18°57.73'S, 22°22.404'E (Guma Lagoon Camp)		

There are certainly more direct routes than this, as the whole area is criss-crossed with confusing bush tracks. However, many will be seasonal and depend on the water levels, so beware of getting stuck!

Alternatively, the Island Lodge has a relatively new airstrip, or you can fly into the small airstrip at Gumare and be collected from there by the lodge. It may also be possible to fly into Seronga, and be transferred to the Island Lodge by boat from there.

What to see and do Precise activities depend on where you're staying, though boat trips are really the main draw here. On the whole, the water's deep enough to

In 1969, the war in Angola (which, in many ways, was an extension of the Cold War using African proxies) displaced a large number of mostly Hambukushu people from the Caprivi area into Botswana. There they were accepted as refugees. Initially they were received at Shakawe, but eventually the plan was to move them to a new village called Etsha, south of there.

However, whilst at Shakawe it's said that they naturally split into 13 separate groups. So when they were moved, they naturally split into 13 villages, which spread out along the western edge of the Delta, 1km apart. They were called, somewhat unimaginatively, Etsha 1, Etsha 2, Etsha 3 and so on up to the most northerly, Etsha 13.

Now the old track which links them and runs close to the Delta has been largely superseded by the new tar highway, which takes a more direct route on the east of the old road. However, you'll still find tracks linking the two, one of which is close to Etsha 13, and another close to Etsha 6.

limit the scope of mekoro for most of the year, and so motorboats are the vehicle of choice. If you're not a devout angler or birdwatcher, then just take a few rods and a pair of binoculars out and do a little of both – it's very relaxing.

Where to stay There are only two choices at this lagoon. These are each quite different and don't generally work closely together.

Guma Island Lodge also Nguma Island Lodge, Nguma Luxury Lodge (8 tents, camping) P Bag 13, Maun; \f 6874 022; e gumacamp@info.bw; www.gumalodge.com. Built on the northwestern edge of the lagoon, this lodge was opened in June 2000 by its owners, Geoff and Nookie Randall, who have lived in the area for years. (Geoff played an important part in starting the building of fibreglass mekoro in the area – and thus is partially responsible for saving an enormous number of the Delta's old trees!)

Tents are all raised up on high wooden decking. Inside you'll find comfortable twin beds made with colourful fabrics, chairs, a small table and a wooden wardrobe behind. At the back of each tent is an en-suite shower, toilet and washbasin. The power at the lodge, and the lighting in the tents, comes from the lodge's own generator and a system of back-up batteries for the lights at night.

The main lounge and dining area is a large log cabin, again raised up on decking, which houses a comfortable lounge, a dining room and a well-stocked bar. There's a better collection of local baskets and craftwork here than in most curio shops, and some are for sale in the lodge's own small shop.

The tents and main area are all widely spread out and linked by fairly high wooden walkways. This keeps everything above water if levels rise to a high

flood. Normally the ground beneath is dry, with cool lawns dotted with date palms. There are plans to install a swimming pool here.

There's also a campsite, slightly separate from the lodge, but under the same cool canopy of trees as the main lodge. Toilets and showers are simple, with wooden-clad showers and toilets, and there are also braai stands and facilities for washing up, though if you arrange it in advance, you can have your meals in the main lodge. Campers here are often serious about their fishing!

In recent years Guma has become a favourite stop for overland group trips and activities major on mokoro trips (P130 per mokoro per day). That said, various boat trips, booze cruises and fishing excursions are also possible.
P920 pp sharing, inc all meals & activities; camping P20 pp per night.. Open all year.

Guma Lagoon Camp (6 tents, camping) Postnet Maun, Suite 35, P Bag 114, Maun; \f 6874 626; e guma.property@info.bw. Barely 1km southeast of the lodge is the very different Guma Lagoon Camp, popular with anglers.

The camp focuses mainly on self-drive, self-catering visitors, although meals can sometimes be arranged if you book far enough in advance. There are campsites with toilets and hot showers, and also comfortable Meru-style tents, with clean linen and

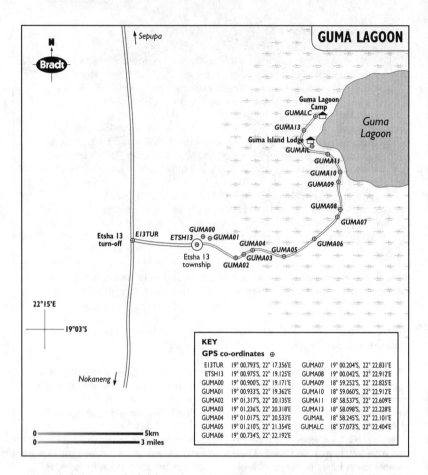

↑ *Sepupa*

N

Guma Lagoon
Camp
GUMALC

Guma
Lagoon

GUMA13

Guma Island Lodge
GUMAIL

GUMA11
GUMA10
GUMA09

GUMA08

GUMA07

GUMA06

Etsha 13
turn-off

E13TUR

GUMA00
ETSH13 ⊕ ⊕ GUMA01

Etsha 13
township

GUMA04
GUMA05

GUMA02 GUMA03

22°15'E

19°03'S

Nokaneng ↓

KEY			
GPS co-ordinates ⊕			
E13TUR	19° 00.793'S, 22° 17.356'E	GUMA07	19° 00.204'S, 22° 22.831'E
ETSH13	19° 00.975'S, 22° 19.125'E	GUMA08	19° 00.042'S, 22° 22.912'E
GUMA00	19° 00.900'S, 22° 19.171'E	GUMA09	18° 59.252'S, 22° 22.825'E
GUMA01	19° 00.933'S, 22° 19.362'E	GUMA10	18° 59.060'S, 22° 22.912'E
GUMA02	19° 01.317'S, 22° 20.135'E	GUMA11	18° 58.537'S, 22° 22.609'E
GUMA03	19° 01.236'S, 22° 20.318'E	GUMA13	18° 58.098'S, 22° 22.228'E
GUMA04	19° 01.017'S, 22° 20.533'E	GUMAIL	18° 58.245'S, 22° 22.101'E
GUMA05	19° 01.210'S, 22° 21.354'E	GUMALC	18° 57.073'S, 22° 22.404'E
GUMA06	19° 00.734'S, 22° 22.192'E		

0 ▬▬▬▬ 5km
0 ▬▬▬▬ 3 miles

open en-suite bathrooms, set in shaded areas overlooking the lagoon and furnished with beds and linen. Each of these tents has its own toilet, shower and washbasin built beside the tent. The camp has a fully equipped kitchen, with pots, pans, cutlery, cooking equipment and fridge/freezing facilities. This is next to a shaded dining/bar area with a deck extending over the lagoon.

P585–800 pp per night; camping P66 pp. Open all year.

ETSHA 6 TO TOTENG

Etsha 6 About 45km south of the Sepupa turn-off (178km north of Sehithwa) there's a signposted turning (⊕ E6TURN 19°6.706'S, 22°16.152'E). This leads, in slightly less than 3km, due east to the village of Etsha 6.

When I last drove along the main road here, there was a concentration of pot-holes in the road between the turnings for Etsha 6 and Etsha 13, so drive carefully. (That said, I only noted these because the overall standard of the tar road up the eastern side of the Delta is excellent, and pot-holes are rare on most of it.)

The town itself has the most reliable fuel in the area, from a Shell station in the centre. Thus most people passing through and travelling any distance should stop here. It's also a place where buses turn off the road to stop. Etsha 6 has a bakery and take-away, behind the bus stop, that sells good fresh bread (and some less impressive pies, chips and other fast food).

Across the road from the fuel station is a Co-op which stocks cutlery, crockery, non-perishables like tinned food, and basic staples like rice and maize in quantity. There's very little fresh produce, but they do usually have chilled soft drinks and bottled water.

There is one camp to the east of here that can be accessed from Etsha 6: Makwena Camp, in NG24 Reserve. See page 290 for brief comments.

Gumare About 146km north of Sehithwa, 37km from Nokaneng, and 77km south of Sepupa, there's a turn-off east to Gumare (◈ GUMARE 19°22.242'S, 22°09.242'E). This is one of the main towns of the Panhandle area. Signboards (only some of which are current!) crowd beside the turn-off, virtually all pointing the 700m or so west to town.

There you'll find a hospital, a school, a small community of overseas aid workers and a thriving small-business centre. Again, there's also a highly visible radio mast in town (with good cellphone coverage even for my UK phone!).

It's worth seeking out the small curio shop in town that has good local baskets at very reasonable prices, and there's a good little supermarket and also a fuel station (where, sadly, supplies can be erratic). Being about halfway between Sehithwa and Shakawe, buses travelling along this route usually detour to Gumare, and will often stop here briefly.

About 4km north of the turn-off is another turning, west from the main road, signposted to Gumare's small airstrip.

Nokaneng About 109km north of Sehithwa, 114km south of Sepupa, there's another radio mast (◈ NOKANE – 19°39.694'S, 22°11.184'E) amidst a group of houses, some of traditional design and others modern, complete with satellite dishes. Just south of the village there's a small turning to the northeast signposted to Nokaneng airstrip.

There's also a track heading east from here that leads to the Namibian border, near Tsumkwe, which opened recently, but check it before you go. Near the border, it's also possible to turn south and access the Aha Hills area, and Gcwihaba Hills and Caverns. See pages 355–63 for more on these areas.

Habu turn-off About 79km north of Sehithwa you'll find another radio mast and a signpost eastwards to the village of Habu, which is about 18km away. There you'll also find a little settlement with a few small shops.

Tsau About 43km north of Sehithwa, or 180km south of Sepupa, you'll come across a turning to the village of Tsau (also often referred to as 'Tsao'). The settlement itself is just to the east of the main road, and its prominent radio mast is quite a landmark (◈ TSAU 20°10.294'S, 22°27.265'E). Here you'll find lots of small huts, though relatively little tree or vegetation cover, and a few small, general shops.

Setata Veterinary Fence Gate At about 27.5km north of Sehithwa you'll have to stop and pass through the Setata Gate (◈ VET-SE 20°15.775'S; 22°33.926'E) in the veterinary fence.

Sehithwa Sehithwa (◈ SEHITH 20°28.259'S; 22°42.372'E) is about 29km from Toteng, and a more substantial settlement. When I last passed through here there were a lot of roadworks, apparently for a new tar road that was being built to link to the main road to Ghanzi due south of town. Locals commented that there is some cellphone coverage for about 10km north of town, though I didn't pick this up at all.

Toteng Though a significant dot on the map, Toteng (✪ TOTENG 20°21.407'S; 22°57.204'E) is little more than a road junction. It's about 64km from Maun on the good, tar road (A35) to Sehithwa, and is marked by the left turn on to the A3 road to Ghanzi, about 222km away. Today you'll find a bottle store and a general dealer at this junction, and a sprinkling of small cattle-farming homesteads in the local area.

Despite its apparent insignificance, Toteng has historical importance as a centre for the Batawana; in his *The Guide to Botswana*, Alec Campbell (see *Appendix 3, Further Information*) comments that 'When they arrived in Ngamiland in 1795 they settled at Kgwebe and later moved to Toteng.' This was also one of the areas that received an influx of Herero people after their defeat at the battle of Waterberg.

LAKE NGAMI The existence of a great lake within the Kalahari was known to Europeans from early reports of Bekwena and Batawana people, though it wasn't reached by them until the mid 19th century. Livingstone arrived on 1 August 1849, with Cotton, Oswell and Murray, narrowly beating Charles Andersson, who set out specifically to reach it from present-day Namibia.

In his book, *Lake Ngami and the River Okavango* (see *Appendix 3, Further Information*), Andersson was hugely disappointed with what he first took to be Lake Ngami. He wrote:

> At last a blue line of great extent appeared in the distance, and I made sure it was the long-sought object; but I was still doomed in my disappointment. It turned out to be merely a large hollow in the rainy season filled with water, but now dry and covered with saline encrustations.

However, he hadn't reached the lake at this stage, and after getting beyond some pans and reed beds, and over a series of sand ridges, he finally glimpsed the water, and described the moment:

> There, indeed, at no very great distance, lay spread before me an immense sheet of water bounded only by the horizon – the object of my ambition for years, and for which I have abandoned home and friends, and risked my life.

Visiting the lake is certainly easier than it was for those first explorers, though it's by no means well signposted, and at times it can still be very disappointing. Note that although very large when full, a high rate of evaporation and a very shallow profile means that the area covered by water can vary enormously.

Getting there and away The lake's bed is surrounded by a triangle of good roads, so approaching it is a matter of turning off one of these and following your nose (or, perhaps better, your compass or GPS). If you're feeling cautious then start by checking out the road which leaves Sehithwa heading south-southeast. This was a rough gravel track across the dry bed of the lake when I last travelled on it, but it may be tar now. If there's any water in the lake then it's likely to be on the eastern side of this road.

If so, then the road between Sehithwa and Toteng passes close to the northern shore. To maximise your chances of getting close to the water even when it's receded a little, strike off this about a third or half of the way from Sehithwa to Toteng, and try to find tracks heading south and slightly east. You should reach the shore within about 5km of the road.

When to visit The pithy answer to this question is: 'whenever it's full of water!'. And there lies the rub; it's only worth going if there's water in the lake, and few people will have been there and be able to tell you. Your best chance of getting up-to-date information is probably from operators in Maun, and especially the pilots, because if the lake's empty it's better to save yourself a trip. If it's just a wide expanse of clay, then you won't find it that exciting.

The state of this mystical lake varies greatly, depending upon whether the Delta's flood, which has historically been Lake Ngami's main source of water, has been high enough to overflow into the Nhabe River which feeds the lake. The lake was an empty dustbowl for the late 1980s and 1990s, but then filled to a shallow depth during 2000 and 2001. So ask around to find out what's happening.

If and when it really floods, Lake Ngami comes alive with birdlife. From October, the ducks, geese, waders and other northern migrants arrive, lining the muddy shores until the weather cools towards the end of April. The flamingos, both greater and lesser, don't choose their times so carefully – being found here in their thousands whenever the conditions are right for the algae on which they feed. They appear from the shore as a pink haze settled on the water's surface.

Where to stay There's nowhere official to stay here, but the land is open enough to camp rough – provided that you ask permission from the nearest local villagers. On my last visit the villagers suggested that I go a few kilometres away from the lake to avoid the mosquitoes. This was a very wise move. You'll need to be self-sufficient, of course; and don't count on finding any drinkable water here.

What to see and do This is purely a birding destination, though because visitors here are really very rare there are no tracks or pathways (for 4x4s or walkers) designed for birdwatchers. All the tracks have been made to serve the villagers and their many, many cattle. All this makes getting around time-consuming and at times difficult – but if there's water here then it might be worth it.

THE NORTHWEST KALAHARI

This area is Botswana at its most enigmatic. Here you'll find huge tracts of the Kalahari, punctuated only by isolated Bushman settlements. It's an area where you need to have a good 4x4 (or two), and you must be totally self-sufficient – travelling with all your own food, water, fuel and equipment.

It's not somewhere which will attract visitors for its game viewing or birdwatching, though you will find both game and birds. In fact, it's not an area that attracts many visitors at all. But old Africa hands are drawn here for its isolated ranges of hills. One displays a breathtaking cultural heritage of paintings, another hides a labyrinthine cave system, and a third – well . . . the Aha Hills are just there. On the map. In the middle of the Kalahari. Waiting to be visited.

For more information on the science and explorations of this area, interested readers are directed to numerous articles in *Botswana Notes and Records*, some of which are noted in *Appendix 3, Further Information*.

TSODILO HILLS Rising to 400m above the monotony of the Kalahari's thick bush, archaeologists say that the hills have been sporadically inhabited for about 30,000 years – making this one of the world's oldest historical sites. For only about the last millennium has this included Bantu people: previously, for thousands of years, the San lived here, hunting, using springs in the hills for water, and painting animals (over 2,000 of them) on the rocks.

For both San and Bantu, the Tsodilo Hills were a mystical place, a 'home of very old and very great spirits' who demanded respect from visitors. As told in *The Lost World of the Kalahari* (essential reading before any visit here; see *Appendix 3, Further Information*), these spirits created much trouble for some of the first Europeans to visit – and were still doing so as recently as the 1950s. Long ago it must have been, in van der Post's words, 'a great fortress of living bushman culture, a Louvre of the desert filled with treasure'.

The Tsodilo Hills remain a remarkable place, an important national monument which, in December 2001, was declared a UNESCO World Heritage Site. Whilst this should help to safeguard the hills for future generations, I can't visit without wondering what it was like when the San were here. What we regard now as the high art of an ancient people is remarkable, but it's very sad that our understanding of it is now devoid of the meaning and spirituality with which it was once imbued.

It's really worth spending several days here to search out the paintings in the Tsodilo Hills. It's a long drive across deep Kalahari sand to get here, and once you're here then even just exploring the marked trails can easily take three or four days, though a longer stay would be better.

However, after several visits over the years, I am left remembering the captivating feeling of spirituality in the hills far more than simply the images of the paintings, however remarkable. I've known this to disturb some visitors profoundly; they were uneasy to the point of wanting to flee the hills, and couldn't wait to get away, whilst others find the hills entrancing and completely magical.

So if you come here, then do so with respect and take some time to stay here – don't just come to tick it off your itinerary and leave.

A word of warning In *The Lost World of the Kalahari*, you can read Laurens van der Post's story of his first visit to the hills: of how his party ignored the advice of their guide, and disturbed the spirits of the hills by hunting warthog and steenbok on their way. Once at the hills, his companion's camera magazines inexplicably kept jamming, his tape recorders stopped working, and bees repeatedly attacked his group – and the problems only ceased when they made a written apology to the spirits.

So perhaps the spirits here are one more reason why you ought to treat the Tsodilo Hills with the very greatest of respect when you visit them.

Folklore and archaeology The Tsodilo Hills hold a special spiritual significance for the people of the region, and are of immense archaeological value to the wider world for what can be learned about some of our earliest ancestors.

Folklore The San believe the hills contain the spirits of the dead, and that their powerful gods live in caves within the Female Hill, from where they rule the world. They believe that these gods will cause misfortune to anyone who hunts or causes death near the hills.

They have many beliefs, all specific to places within the hills. For example, there's a cave on the western side of the Female Hill which contains a permanent source of water and, the San believe, a giant serpent with spiralling horns, like a kudu. If a San guide takes you around the hills, then ask them about legends and stories associated with the places that you visit on the hills.

Meanwhile the Hambukushu people, who also live in the area, believe that God lowered man to earth at the site of the hills, and he landed on the Female Hill. For proof they point to footprints engraved into the rock, high up on the hill. However, modern sceptics claim these are simply natural marks in the rock, or suggest that they might even be the footprints of dinosaurs!

Archaeology Archaeologists think that people (*Homo sapiens* as opposed to *Homo erectus*) have occupied the area for at least 60,000 years. Estimating the age of rock paintings is very difficult, and is usually done by linking a style of painting with nearby artefacts which can be scientifically dated with precision (eg: by carbon-14 dating techniques).

However, the Tsodilo Hills have been the subject of more archaeological research than most of southern Africa's sites – so we do have an idea about the people who lived here. So far, most of the evidence unearthed here dates from the Middle Stone Age period. There have been several major excavations, including ones at the Depression Shelter, the Rhino Cave and White Paintings. (See *Appendix 3, Further Information* for articles in *Botswana Notes and Records* with more details. There's also a more personal view of a visit to one of these excavations in Mike Main's *Kalahari: Life's Variety in Dune and Delta*.

Excavations at White Paintings, a site at the base of the Male Hill, indicate habitation going back at least 40,000–50,000 years. For this the archaeological team excavated as deep as 7m below ground level, finding a variety of stone blades and scrapers. It's estimated that over 55% of the raw materials for these tools don't occur in the hills, and must have been brought in from outside. This at least indicates a movement of people, and perhaps early bartering or trading networks.

Excavations at the Depression Shelter certainly indicate that people were using coloured pigments here, probably for painting, more than 19,000 years ago. However, despite what you'll often read, nobody really knows exactly how the artists made their paints. Many things have been suggested, but animal fats and derivatives of plants seem the likely binding agents, probably mixed with pigments obtained largely from ash, various minerals and plant dyes. Iron oxide, in the form of ochre, seems a particularly likely mineral to have been used.

Meanwhile much more recently, about AD800–1000, specularite was being mined here intensively. This mineral was historically used for cosmetic purposes by groups within southern Africa, further emphasising the likelihood of a long-standing trade network that included the people of the Tsodilo.

The paintings The paintings at the Tsodilo Hills chart thousands of years of human habitation, and include some of the world's most important and impressive rock art.Its special nature is augmented by the realisation that these hills are 250km from the nearest other known rock art. They are totally removed from all of southern Africa's other rock paintings. Even within the hills, some of the paintings are located on high, inaccessible cliffs, with commanding views over the landscape. This was surely a deliberate part of the paintings for the people who created them.

Campbell and Coulson, in their excellent book *African Rock Art* (see *Appendix 3, Further Information*), assert that the Tsodilo Hills 'contain some 4,000 red finger paintings composed of about 50% animals, 37% geometrics, and 13% highly stylised human figures'.

The paintings here belong to several different styles and if you take the time to look closely at them will often amaze you with their detail. Although most of the animals painted are wild, Campbell and Coulson noted that there is a much higher incidence of paintings of domestic stock than at any other similar sites in southern Africa.

The human figures include many schematic men painted with erect penises. It's thought that these could be associated with the trance dance – a traditional dance of the San in which rhythmic breathing often produces an altered state of consciousness.

Geology The Tsodilo Hills are formed from what's technically known as micaceous quartzite schists. These metamorphic rocks started out as shales, probably deposited as mud on the surface of an ancient sea. Great heat and pressure in the earth changed them, and you can see the small crystals of minerals formed during this process if you look carefully.

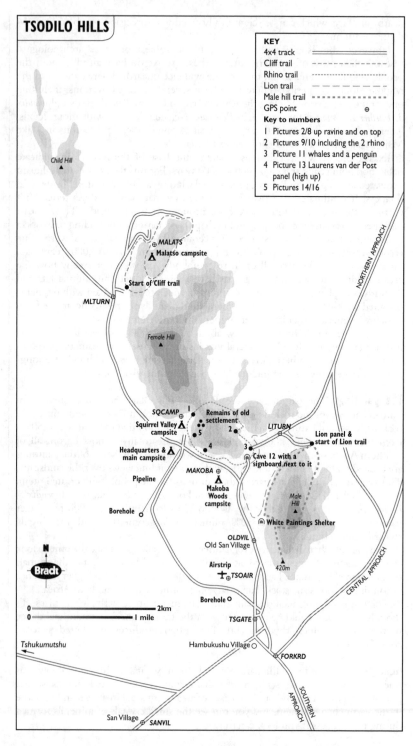

TSODILO HILLS

KEY

4x4 track	————
Cliff trail	– – – –
Rhino trail	··········
Lion trail	— — —
Male hill trail	▪▪▪▪▪▪
GPS point	⊕

Key to numbers

1 Pictures 2/8 up ravine and on top
2 Pictures 9/10 including the 2 rhino
3 Picture 11 whales and a penguin
4 Picture 13 Laurens van der Post
   panel (high up)
5 Pictures 14/16

Child Hill ▲

NORTHERN APPROACH

⊕ MALATS
▲ Malatso campsite

● Start of Cliff trail

MLTURN

Female Hill ▲

SQCAMP ⊕   1
            Remains of old
            settlement
▲ Squirrel Valley   2
  campsite   5   LITURN ⊕
                               Lion panel &
            4   3   start of Lion trail

Headquarters & ▲
main campsite   Cave 12 with a
                       signboard next to it

Pipeline   MAKOBA ⊕
                  ▲
                  Makoba
                  Woods   Male
                  campsite   Hill
Borehole ○   ▲

                  OLDVIL   ⦿ White Paintings Shelter
                  Old San Village

N

Bradt   Airstrip
                       ✚ ⊕ TSOAIR   ▲
                                         420m
| 0 | | 2km |
| 0 | | 1 mile |

                  Borehole ○   CENTRAL APPROACH

                  TSGATE ⊕

Tshukumutshu ←   Hambukushu Village ○   ⊕ FORKRD

                                    SOUTHERN
                                    APPROACH

San Village ⊕ SANVIL

GPS REFERENCES FOR TSODILO HILLS MAP

FORKRD	18°47.414'S, 21°44.921'E	OLDVIL	18°46.386'S, 21°44.782'E
LITURN	18°45.538'S, 21°45.109'E	SANVIL	18°48.147'S, 21°43.903'E
MAKOBA	18°45.688'S, 21°44.586'E	SQCAMP	18°45.385'S, 21°44.248'E
MALATS	18°43.608'S, 21°43.910'E	TSGATE	18°47.275'S, 21°44.856'E
MLTURN	18°44.243'S, 21°43.575'E	TSOAIR	18°46.870'S, 21°44.645'E

Tsodilo's schists have particularly high mica and quartz contents, and a coarse-grained surface. Conveniently, this texture means that rocks give a good grip to rubber-soled shoes, so they're relatively easy to clamber around. In many places there are piles of boulders, and you'll often need to hop between these if you want to explore the hills.

There are a few permanent springs of water in the hills, but these are very difficult to find without a local guide. They were certainly important to the early inhabitants of the area though, as they would have been the only water sources for miles around.

Flora and fauna Unlike most destinations for visitors in Botswana, a visit to the Tsodilo Hills really isn't about looking for animals, birds or plants. The focus is much more cultural and historical. That said, don't forget that you are in a very sparsely populated area of the northern Kalahari and there is wildlife around.

On the roads that approach the hills I've been very aware of fresh elephant dung, and fleeting glimpses of occasional fleeing small buck. There are certainly kudu, steenbok and duiker here permanently, as well as leopard and probably spotted hyena.

In his 1934 book *The Mammals of South West Africa* (see *Appendix 3, Further Information*), G C Shortridge records that klipspringer were found here at the hills, although I've not come across any reports of them more recently, so it seems unlikely that there is any population of them left now.

Everywhere around the hills you'll find quite a wide variety of birdlife, including the ubiquitous grey hornbills – easily heard as well as seen with their descending call of 'phe, phephee, pheephee, pheeoo, phew, pheeoo-pheeoo' (with thanks to Kenneth Newman – see *Appendix 3, Further Information* – for expressing this song so well on paper!)

Look out also for the Tsodilo gecko (*Pachydactylus tsodiloensis*) a small, nocturnal gecko with yellow and brown stripes which is endemic to these hills.

Looking at the vegetation, keep your eyes open for stands of mongongo trees (*Ricinodendron rautanenii*), which occur on the hills and sometimes in pure stands on the Kalahari's sand. These can reach 15–20m in height, and are characterised by smooth, often peeling bark on grey to light-brown stems and compound leaflets a little like the chestnut trees of Europe. After sprays of yellow flowers around October–November, they produce egg-shaped grey-green fruits from February onwards. These can be up to 3.5cm x 2.5cm in size, covered with smooth hairs. Inside these are mongongo nuts, which can be cracked open to reveal an edible kernel – one of the most important, and celebrated, foods for the San across the Kalahari. Palgrave (see *Appendix 3, Further Information*) comments that this is a protected tree in South Africa, and that its light, strong wood is sometimes used as a substitute for imported balsa wood.

Although large animals aren't prolific in this area, there is big game in the bush around the hills, including elephants, so drive carefully when you are in the area.

Getting there and away Until recently, there have been just two routes into the Tsodilo Hills from the main Shakawe–Sehithwa road. Both are difficult, sandy, 4x4-only routes that take about 2½–3 bone-shaking hours (mostly in low-range gear) to complete. Both boast an unusual type of corrugation which make the whole vehicle bounce up and down. Drive faster than about 10km/h and you find your head's hitting the ceiling. It's painful, but ensures that getting to the hills is always a long and tedious drive.

Now, however, with the development of some facilities at the hills, a third route has been opened. It's relatively smooth gravel, cutting access time to the hills down to about half an hour and, in so doing, completely changing the nature of a visit here.

The three possible driving routes, from north to south, are as follows.

Northern approach The turning from the main road is immediately next to the south side of the Somachima Veterinary Fence (⊕ VET-SA 18°29.256'S, 21°55.142'E). This is about 17.4km south of Shakawe. This route follows the fence for a little while, before forking off left. It takes about 36km to reach the hills.

This used to be the best of the routes to the hills. To find it take the track between the Male and Female Hills, head for ⊕ LITURN 18°45.538'S, 21°45.109'E, and then ignore the right turning to the start of the Lion Trail.

In February 2001 I tried this route in reverse, from the hills to the road. However, then it was very overgrown as it left the hills. It didn't appear to have been used for some time, and wasn't easily navigable. So unless this has improved, this northern track will probably swiftly become impassable and vanish back into the bush.

If you do decide to try either this route or the southern approach, then be very aware of the danger of fire from grass seeds and stems blocking up your vehicle's radiator and collecting near its hot exhaust system. You must take steps to prevent this (see pages 119–20 of *Chapter 6*).

Central approach This is the new, fast route to the hills, transformed into a reasonable gravel road around 2004; it now takes about half an hour to reach the hills from the main road. The turn for this starts on the main road at (⊕ T2TURN 18°35.834'S, 21°59.986'E). This is 4.8km southeast of the 'Tsodilo View' signpost on the road (⊕ TSVIEW 18°33.830'S, 21°58.273'E), and almost 15km south of the Somachima Veterinary Fence (⊕ VET-SA 18°29.256'S, 21°55.142'E).

From there the track heads southwest until it passes around the southern side of Male Hill and meets the southern approach at ⊕ FORKRD 18°47.414'S, 21°44.921'E, about 34km from the tarred road. You then bear right to reach the main gate (⊕ TSGATE 18°47.275'S, 21°44.856'E).

Southern approach This begins about 10km south of Sepupa, but first you must get yourself on to the untarred track that is marked on the Shell map as joining Etsha with Sepupa. To do this it'll be easiest to head to Sepupa and then, about 500m south of the turning to the village itself, take the turn-off (⊕ T1TURN 18°45.160'S, 22°10.609'E) that leads south-southwest from the main road. This is, in fact, part of the old road up the Panhandle.

About 9.5km later there's a clearly signposted turning (⊕ T3TURN 18°50.292'S, 22°10.011'E) on to a track that leads west to the hills. Follow this and after a further 22km this passes through a small cattle post. Finally you'll approach the hills from the south side, with Male Hill the first to come into view. Within sight of the hills you pass a fork in the road (⊕ FORKRD 18°47.414'S, 21°44.921'E), and soon reach the main thatched 'gate' turning (⊕ TSGATE 18°47.275'S, 21°44.856'E) about 55.5km after leaving the road at T3TURN.

If you're leaving the hills by this route then simply find the main gate (TSGATE) and then head out south of Male Hill and follow the track slightly south of east from there (a bearing averaging about 95°). Keep straight (right) where the road forks (FORKRD), and head fairly directly for T3TURN.

Hitchhiking I wouldn't try to walk or hitchhike here. With more animals around than vehicles, it would be unpleasant at best.

By air There's a good bush airstrip at the hills, so it's quite possible (albeit at significant cost) to charter a plane to get you here from Maun or elsewhere in the region. However, once on the ground you'll usually want a 4x4 to get around the base of the hills, and to the start of the various walking trails.

You may be able to persuade one of the Panhandle's lodges to send a 4x4 with a driver for your use – or if you're staying at Nxamaseri, there are regular trips here. However, the drive is so tough on their vehicles that they are reluctant to do this if you're not also spending time staying at their lodges. So however you look at this, it won't be a cheap option.

Approaching from the air you'll appreciate the hills' uniqueness within the desert, though you'll miss the excitement as they're first sighted over the treetops – and the sheer sense of achievement of having completed the long drive here.

Orientation The Tsodilo Hills rise up from the bush-covered undulations of the western Kalahari, about 45km west of the village of Sepupa. They consist of four hills, roughly in a line, with names from San folklore.

The most southerly is known as the Male Hill. This is the highest hill, rising 410m above the surrounding bush, and the San believed that the most sacred place is near the top of this. Their tradition is that the first spirit knelt on this hill to pray after creating the world, and they believe that you can still see the impression of his knees in the rock there.

Close to the Male, on its northern side, is the Female Hill, which covers almost three times the area of the Male, but only reaches about 300m in height. This seems to have most of the main rock art sites on it.

About 2km north of the Female is Child Hill, which is smaller still at only about 40m high. Then beyond this, about 2.2km northwest of the Child, is a smaller kopjie that is said by the San to be the first wife of the Male Hill, who was then left when he met the Female Hill.

Most visitors spend their time on Female Hill, and may visit the Male. Few visit the Child or the kopjie beyond, to which there are no vehicle tracks.

There are several manmade landmarks that might help you to orientate yourself when in the area of the hills:

The gate As you'll see when you arrive, there's a large and sturdy gate (⊕ TSGATE 18°47.275'S, 21°44.856'E), complete with a small office and an impressive thatched top, which makes a clear landmark. This was originally intended as a gate in a cattle fence, but when I last visited there was no fence and the gate stood on its own in splendid isolation.

Hambukushu village Just south of the gate is a small settlement with some corrals for animals. This is one possible place where you may be able to find a guide to take you around the hills.

San village The San village at the hills has, rather sadly, been moved from its old location (⊕ OLDVIL 18°46.386'S, 21°44.782'E) between the hills to a new location

(⊕ SANVIL 18°48.147'S, 21°43.903'E) about 3.8km south-southwest of there, well away from the hills. It has been alleged that this was done with the intention of 'tidying up' the area for visitors. If so, it's deeply misguided, as most visitors will want to drive out here to try and hire San guides to the hills anyway.

Tshukumutshu track On the way from the main gate to the San Village a track heads off right, on a northwest bearing of about 305°. I've followed this for 7–8km, and it remains a good track, and believe that it heads for a place called Tshukumutshu. I'd welcome more information on it if readers have gone further.

What to see and do
Apart from soaking up the atmosphere, exploring the hills and their rock art is the main reason to come here. For both you'd be wise to take a local guide with you if possible – which also helps to give the small local community some income in an area where there must be very few other opportunities for paid work.

Hiring a guide On my last visit, I drove to the San village and, with sign gestures and improvisation, tried to ask for a guide. The man of the family that I was speaking to eventually sent me off with two of the children, a boy called Xashee, aged 10, and a girl called Tsetsana, aged 16.

At first I thought that I'd been fobbed off with the children, who were silent in the presence of their family. However, as soon as we got into our car to drive back to the hills, it transpired that Tsetsana was on holiday from school, and spoke excellent English. Her brother spoke much less to us, but seemed to know more of the sites with rock art.

They bounded up the hills with bare feet, faster than we could in walking boots. They knew their way about very well and although we only followed on the 'standard' trails, we would have missed many of the paintings without their help. If you do hire a guide, expect to pay around P20–40.

The trails There are four trails that I know of on the hills: the Rhino Trail, the Cliff Trail, the Lion Trail and the Male Hill Trail. That said, one source refers to there being six trails, and several sources refer to the 'Divuyu Trail,' which I don't think exists! The best source for information will be the office at the hills, which was closed when I last visited. I'd welcome detailed descriptions of the routes, preferably with GPS positions of all the paintings, from any readers who have time to explore these trails and write to me about them.

The Rhino Trail is marked with sturdy numbered posts, indexed for a series of annotated route plans that are, apparently, being produced. I believe that Alec Campbell, a world-renowned authority on both African rock art and Botswana, has written them, and that the national museum is meant to be producing them. However, these have been 'in production' for so long that some doubt if they will ever be seen. If you can get hold of one, I'd expect them to be the best guide to the hills.

The best sites for rock art are on Female Hill, and especially towards its north end. The hills are a place to explore for yourself, preferably with a local guide. Here are a few notes from my own observations. I'm aware they may contain errors as well as omissions, but I hope that they'll spur readers to explore – and perhaps send me any corrections or additional comments.

Rhino Trail This is the only one of the trails that the author has walked, and it starts from close to the Squirrel Valley Campsite (⊕ SQCAMP 18°45.385'S, 21°44.248'E). Each of the pictures is marked with sequentially numbered posts, though in the lush vegetation of February there were some of these that neither us, nor our young guides, could locate. The GPS references here should be a help to make sure you're in roughly the right place, but you'll probably still have to search a bit to find the paintings. It's certainly best to take a local guide with you anyhow.

This trail starts with **Picture #1** (⊕ PICT1 18°45.336'S, 21°44.195'E), which is high, about 10–15m above the ground, facing a baobab on the right-hand side of a broad ravine near the campsite.

Picture #2 (⊕ PICT2 18°45.331'S, 21°44.225'E) is deeper into the ravine and higher up, at an altitude of 1,063m. There's quite a lot of steep rock-hopping to climb up this ravine at the beginning of the trail. It won't be suitable for anyone who is uncomfortable clambering around rocky slopes.

A spot that I've located nearby, and called **Picture #2A** (⊕ PICT2A 18°45.291'S, 21°44.239'E), is less than 100m north-northwest of #2, and higher up again. Here there's a beautiful picture of a rhino that's perhaps 100cm across, with gemsbok below.

By the time you reach **Picture #5**, which includes an impressive giraffe, you're at the centre of the Female Hill, and **Picture #7** is found on rocks beside a flat track here.

Picture #8 (⊕ PICT8 18°45.150'S, 21°44.576'E) is at an altitude of 1,102m (you can see the Male Hill from here); it's a picture, found under an overhang, of several men, known as 'the dancing penises'.

Pictures #9 (⊕ PICT9 18°45.437'S, 21°44.723'E) and #10 are almost adjacent to each other, on vertical walls of rock slightly off the trail. **Picture #10** has a plaque next to it reading 'Rhino Trail', and its main figures consist of two rather beautifully painted rhino. These are the most famous of Tsodilo's paintings, as they now form the logo of The Botswana Society (see page 41).

Shortly, this trail joins the main track which leads west between the Female and Male hills. Detour to the right of this, and **Picture #11** (⊕: PICT11 18°45.635'S, 21°44.862'E) is on Female Hill. It appears to be of several whales and a penguin. Arguably this is one of the pieces of evidence that indicates that the Bushmen travelled far more widely than is commonly believed, adding weight to Robert Gordon's contentions in his *Bushman Myth: The making of a Namibian Underclass* (see *Further Information*, page 494), that our view of the Bushman is often misguided.

This trail then leads around to what I'll refer to as **Cave #12** (⊕ CAVE12 18°45.673'S, 21°44.842'E), a large cave at the base of the Female Hill, facing the Male Hill. This has little in the way of paintings, but it does have a 'Museums of Botswana' board outside it urging visitors to treat the hills with respect.

Continue from here by following the main vehicle track that leads north along the west side of Female Hill. The plaque for **Picture #13** (⊕ PICT13 18°45.627'S, 21°44.436'E) stands next to a notice proclaiming 'Rhino Trail', and marks where you should turn right from the vehicle track on to a footpath which runs closer to the hill than the larger track.

When at #13, look up and slightly back at the hills and there, high up, you'll see what is now known as the 'van der Post panel'. In his inimitable style, Laurens described first seeing this:

Over the scorched leaves of the tops of the bush conforming to a contour nearby, and about a hundred feet up, was a ledge of honey-coloured stone grafted into the blue iron rock. Above the ledge rose a smooth surface of the same warm, soft stone curved like a sea shell as if rising into the blue to form a perfect dome. I had no doubt that I was looking at the wall and part of the ceiling of what had once been a great cave . . .

But what held my attention still with the shock of discovery was the painting that looked down at us from the centre of what was left of the wall and dome of the cave. Heavy as were the shadows, and seeing it only darkly against the sharp morning light, it was yet so distinct and filled with fire of its own colour that every detail stood out with a burning clarity. In the focus of the painting, scarlet against the gold of the stone, was an enormous eland bull standing sideways, his massive body charged with masculine power and his noble head looking as if he had only that moment been disturbed in his grazing. He was painted, as only a Bushman, who had a deep identification with an eland, could have painted him.

Take this footpath which follows the west side of Female Hill, heading roughly north. Very close to the path, **Picture #14** depicts rhino, warthog and several antelope. Next, less than 400m from the Squirrel Valley Campsite, **Picture #15** (✪ PICT15 18°45.556'S, 21°44.361'E) includes lots of very clearly painted giraffe, rhino, gemsbok and other antelope on a wonderfully colourful outcrop of rock.

Finally, just before arriving back at the Squirrel Valley Campsite, **Picture #16** has a curious circular design – almost geometrical – on the right. It is reminiscent of a shield, the shell of a tortoise or even a wheel.

Cliff Trail This is at the north end of Female Hill, and to find the start try heading north on the track to Malatso Campsite, and then turn right at ✪ MLTURN 18°44.243'S, 21°43.575'E. You'll reach the steep base of the cliffs, about 50m away, where there's a turning circle for vehicles.

The trail appears to circle clockwise around the northern part of Female Hill, before taking a short cut back to near its start over a col. I'd welcome a detailed description of this route and its paintings from anyone who has completed it (with GPS locations if possible).

Lion Trail This trail stays at ground level, and doesn't include any climbing. It overlaps with some of the Rhino Trail's paintings at the base of the south end of Female Hill, as well as visiting sites on the north side of Male Hill. To find its start point, take the vehicle track which heads east between Male and Female Hills, and then turn right at ✪ LITURN 18°45.538'S, 21°45.109'E, to find a turning-circle for vehicles at the base of the Male Hill.

Male Hill Trail This starts from the same place as the Lion Trail, though eventually goes up and over the top of Male Hill, including some strenuous scrambles.

Where to stay There's a relatively large, new parks office on the west side of the Female Hill which, if it's operating, should be your first point of call when you arrive at the hills. Here you'll have to sign in and pay a small entry charge, and then they will direct you to a campsite. This will either be one of the camp pitches next to the office, which is in excellent condition with pristine facilities, or one of a couple of other sites dotted around. These are wilder, as they have nothing but a fireplace, and they can be a little indistinct.

When I last visited there were no staff on duty, nor any other visitors at the hills. We stayed for three days and saw nobody apart from the local villagers.

The official campsites are listed below.

Ⱥ Makoba Woods Campsite (✪ MAKOBA 18°45.688'S, 21°44.586'E). Just beside the southern tip of Female Hill, you'll pass this as you head north to the Main Camp and office from the entrance gate.

Ⱥ Squirrel Valley Camp (✪ SQCAMP 18°45.385'S, 21°44.248'E). Nothing more than a turning circle for vehicles really, under trees at the base of Female Hill where the Rhino Trail starts. This is also known as the Baobab Campsite.

Ⱥ Malatso Campsite (✪ MALATS 18°43.608'S, 21°43.910'E). Near the far northern end of Female Hill, close to the Cliff Trail. There's an enclave here between some of the low rock outcrops from the northern end of Female Hill. (For comparison with other altitudes mentioned above, this camp at the base of the hill stands at 1,011m.) This is a lovely, remote spot – though the track to reach it was overgrown in places, and a little tricky to reach in the fast-fading light of dusk.

AHA AND GCWIHABA Over 150km southwest of the Tsodilo Hills lies an even more remote area, populated by scattered San villages and dotted with a number of hills. This is one of the most remote areas of the Kalahari, and it attracts the most experienced bush travellers simply 'because it's there'. This is expedition territory, best reserved for those who are well equipped and bush-wise.

Most go to visit the Aha Hills, which straddle the border with Namibia, and the nearby Gcwihaba Hills, which contain the well-known Gcwihaba (or Drotsky's) Caverns. These are easily located, not commercialised and fascinating to visit.

In reality, though the Gcwihaba Caverns are the only cave system here that's practical for most visitors to see, there are a number of others in the area which have been unearthed by local scientists in the last few decades. The locations of these are usually kept secret to avoid visitors damaging them or having a serious accident (which would be all too easy).

Geology and geography Turning east from Tsau, you'll soon start notice the road's gentle decline. It's entering the Gcwihaba Valley, a fossil river valley which may have been an ancient extension of the Okavango Delta. Within this, a group of six low hills protrude above the sand and rise to a maximum of 30m above the surrounding valley. (Compare this to the Male Hill at the Tsodilo, which reaches 410m.) About 40–50km northwest of these, the Aha Hills share a very similar geology and appearance.

All of these low hills are made almost exclusively of dolomite marble which, early in its formation, is thought to have been steeply folded, causing many of its strata to stand vertically. It's estimated to be about 800–1,000 million years old.

This rock has been weathered into a very jagged, sharp surface and many loose blocks which aren't always easy underfoot. Underneath, numerous faults and fractures split it. When weathered it appears a grey colour, but if you break it you'll find a pearly-white colour inside. There are occasional bands of muscovite in the marble, and beds of more recent limestone and calcrete.

About 15–20km southwest of the Gcwihaba are the Koanaka Hills. These are similar in geological origin, but essentially inaccessible to visitors. There has been some recent exploration of these (see *Discovery and Exploration of Two New Caves in the Northwest District*, in *Appendix 3, Further Information*). One of them – called the 'blue cave' – is Botswana's largest cave complex found to date.

Formation of the caves Like many cave systems in the world, the Gcwihaba Caverns have been formed by the action of acidic groundwater flowing down through the faults in the rock. This gradually dissolves the alkaline limestone over the centuries. Some of this limestone has been redeposited as stalagmites and stalactites.

That said, this simple and quite standard explanation for the cave formation doesn't entirely explain why the cave system is more or less horizontal throughout. (It has northeast and southeast entrances, and appears to have had two levels at different times.) Because of this, Cooke and Baillieul note (see *Appendix 3, Further Information*) that from the size of the caves and passages, it seems likely that very large volumes of groundwater must have moved within the rock here – perhaps an underground course of the old Gcwihaba River. This would explain the sheer size of some of the caves here.

For that to have been the case, the area's water table must have been much higher for at least one period historically, and probably two. After these levels had

14

subsided, and the caves emptied of water, then stalagmites and stalactites would have been formed gradually by a trickle-through of more moderate volumes of water (eg: rainfall) through fault-lines.

History Though people have occupied the area for at least 12,500 years, it doesn't seem as if the caves were used extensively. Excavations in Gcwihaba Caverns (in 1969 by Yellen *et al*; see *Appendix 3, Further Information*) did find evidence of charcoal, ostrich eggshell and bone fragments, thought to be the remnants of human occupation, but the finds were limited and there is no rock art here at all.

These caves were first brought to the attention of the outside world in June 1932 when the local !Kung people showed the cave to a farmer from Ghanzi, Martinus Drotsky. Hence for many years this was known as Drotsky's Cave. (As an aside, Martinus was the grandfather of Jan Drotsky, who currently runs Drotsky's Cabins, near Shakawe.)

The local !Kung refer to these hills as '/twihaba' – hence the hills, and main cave and this cave system, are now usually referred to as the Gcwihaba Hills and Caverns respectively (although you'll see this spelt in a variety of ways in various publications).

The hills and caverns were declared a national monument in 1934 and the Director of the Bechwanaland Geological Survey visited the caverns with Drotsky in 1943. The first cave survey was undertaken in 1970 by a school group from Falcon College in Zimbabwe (then Rhodesia). Various scientific explorations and surveys have been done since then, including an expedition in October 1991 by the British School's Exploring Society (including Heather Tyrrell, one of the contributors to this book).

Nowhere else in this area has had as much time or attention given to it as the Gcwihaba Caverns, though the two sinkholes in the Aha Hills have been surveyed on at least two occasions, most recently by the BSES in 1991.

The people The people of the area are mostly Ju/'hoansi Bushmen, together with a few Herero (Mbanderu). Because of the lung disease that swept through this area of the country and the subsequent eradication of cattle here in the late 1990s, work patterns have changed. Thus many people are employed by branches of the government, working to clear roads and similar public works.

A particularly detailed and interesting article on the community in the Xai Xai area, with details from a study there, can be found at www.kalaharipeoples.org/documents/Ju-pap.htm.

Flora and fauna Though visits to this part of the Kalahari are usually for caves and culture, there is some wildlife around. As with most places in the Kalahari, this area is at its most beautiful and the flora and fauna is at its most vibrant during and shortly after the summer rains (January to about April).

GPS REFERENCES FOR AHA AND GCWIHABA HILLS MAP			
DOBEVI	19°34.830'S, 21°04.428'E	QANGWA	19°31.868'S, 21°10.281'E
GCWIHA	20°01.250'S, 21°21.230'E	TSAU	20°10.294'S, 22°27.265'E
GTURN1	20°07.047'S, 22°22.291'E	WAXHUN	19°43.532'S, 21°03.489'E
GTURN2	19°39.577'S, 22°11.010'E	WAXHUS	19°46.643'S, 21°02.518'E
GTURN3	19°54.286'S, 21°09.418'E	XAIXAI	19°52.867'S, 21°04.934'E
GTURN4	19°57.556'S, 21°44.541'E			

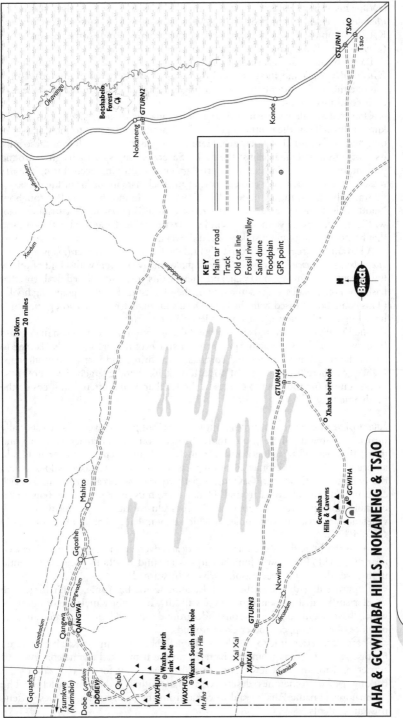

14

AHA & GCWIHABA HILLS, NOKANENG & TSAO

KEY

	Main tar road
	Track
	Old cut line
	Fossil river valley
	Sand dune
	Floodplain
⊕	GPS point

Okavango

Botshabelo
Forest

GTURN2

Nokaneng

Xaudum

Cahabadum

Cwihabadum

Konde

TSAO
GTURN1
Tsao

30km
20 miles

Mahito

Gqoshe

Gxangwadum

Qangwa
QANGWA

Gqwidum

Ggwashadum

Gquasha

Tsumkwe (Namibia)

Dobe
DOBE

Qubi

Waxha North sink hole
WAXHUN

|WAXHUS|
Waxha South sink hole
Aha Hills
Mt Aha

Xai Xai
XAIXAI

Nxanidum

GTURN3

Ncwima

Gkcadum

Xhaba borehole

GTURN4

Gcwihaba
Hills & Caverns
GCWIHA

N

Bradt

Flora This classic Kalahari environment is dominated by the silver terminalia (*Terminalia sericea*), identified by the silvery sheen on its blue-grey leaves. and the Kalahari appleleaf (*Lonchocarpus nelsii*). You'll also find some bushwillows (*Combretum callinum*) and wild seringa bushes (*Burkea africana*).

Raisin bushes (*Gwewia flava*) are here accompanied by sandpaper raisin bushes (*Grewia flavescens*) and the false sandpaper raisin bushes (*Grewia retinervis*). Rub a leaf of either of the latter between your fingers and you'll soon realise how they got their common names.

One tree worth noting here is the Namaqua fig (*Ficus cordata*). This is well known throughout the central highlands of Namibia and down to the Cape – but otherwise unrecorded in Botswana. Here you'll find it growing all over these hills, its roots often flattened against the rocks. Several strong specimens grow around the entrances to the Gcwihaba Caverns, green and thriving even during the dry season, perhaps due to the cooler, moister microclimate in the air of the caves.

Similarly, the mopane aloe (*Aloe littoralis*) is found here and throughout Namibia, but nowhere else in northern or central Botswana. It's a striking plant with a single, vertical stem, succulent leaves with serrated edges and a flower head that branches into pointed spikes of red flowers.

All around the region you'll certainly find the Devil's claw creeper (*Harpogophytum procumbens procumbens*). Recognise it by its pinky-mauve flowers with a hint of yellow in the centre in January to March, and after that its small but wicked oval fruit that has hooks on all sides – like some tiny medieval jousting ball with grappling hooks. (This could be confused with the large Devil's thorn, *Dicerocaryum eriocarpum*, which has a brighter pink flower but a much less elaborate fruit.)

The Devil's claw is found all over the Kalahari, but has recently been in demand from overseas for its medicinal properties. Extracts of this are variously claimed to aid in the treatment of intestinal complaints, arthritis, and many other ailments. Hence anywhere near a centre of population is likely to be largely devoid of these plants, but in the more remote areas of the Kalahari you'll often find it beside the sandy track.

Fauna Big game is present throughout this area, but it's relatively scarce especially near to settlements where you're more likely to come into contact with dogs and domestic stock. That said, gemsbok, springbok, eland, steenbok, duiker and kudu all occur in the area. Veronica Roodt reports seeing six very relaxed wild dog near the entrance to Gcwihaba Caverns, and there are also occasional lion, leopard, cheetah and spotted hyena around. Hence there must be a reasonable population of their antelope prey – even if these seem elusive due to the relatively thick vegetation, and lack of waterholes at which they might gather and be more easily spotted.

Given the huge distances that elephant can cover, and the spoor that I've seen near the Tsodilo Hills, I wouldn't be surprised to find lone bulls wandering around in this area during the wet season. Drivers, be warned.

If approaching this area then, whilst looking for big game, don't forget the smaller stuff. Small seasonal pans here will fill with a noisy mélange of bullfrogs which have spent the dry season underground, attracted by the water and the number of grasshoppers and crickets around.

There's no better time to see plenty of small reptiles, from the Kalahari serrated tortoise, with its bold, geometric patterns, to the flapnecked chameleon. Around sunset, and for the first few hours after that, listen out for the *click-click* of the barking gecko, sometimes described as like rattling a box of matches. The onomatopoeic name 'Aha' is said to come from the sound made by these often-unseen residents.

Inside the Gcwihaba Caverns is a different story. Some of the earlier scientists to visit the cave noted that leopard inhabit it, and found fresh spoor here. Meanwhile, its name derives from the !Kung word for 'hyena's hole'. Whilst I don't know of any more recent visitors who have come across large predators in here, you can't help but notice the bats! These can be noisy and smelly, but are otherwise harmless.

The most common species here is probably the insectivorous Commerson's leaf-nosed bat, *Hipposideros commersoni*. These are the largest insectivorous bats in southern Africa which, although they only grow to a weight of about 120g, can have a wingspan as large as 60cm. These have short, pale fawn-coloured hair all over, and black feet. Males have distinctive tufts of white fur on their shoulders. These are the bats that leave the caves in large numbers at dusk.

Also found here in numbers are the tiny Dent's horseshoe bat, *Rhinolophus denti*, which weigh a mere 6g and measure about 7cm long, with a wingspan of 20cm, when fully grown. Horseshoe bats like this are identified because of complex 'nose-leaf' structures on their face between their mouths and their foreheads (used to locate their insect prey using the animal equivalent of radar).

A third common bat here is the Egyptian (also called 'common') slit-faced bat (*Nycteris thebaica*), which is easily identified by its long, rounded ears and the 'split' running down the centre of its face. They fly efficiently but relatively slowly, eat insects, and grow to about 10cm long with a wingspan of about 24cm.

Given the presence of these bats, it's quite likely that these support a small ecosystem of invertebrates in the caves. In similar caves in Namibia, several hundred kilometres to the west of here, scientists have recently also discovered small but highly poisonous spiders. So tread carefully. . .

Birdlife As with anywhere in the Kalahari, the birds here can either survive without drinking water, or will routinely fly long distances to find it every day. Guineafowl and red-billed francolin are very common, though coqui and crested francolin do also occur here. Sandgrouse are common, particularly the namaqua and double-banded species, though you'll also find Burchell's and, occasionally, the yellow-throated varieties. Doves are here too, with cape turtle, laughing and namaqua species always around.

The area's LBJs ('Little Brown Jobbies', as keen birdwatchers refer to the plethora of smaller, brown birds whose similarities tax their identification skills) include chestnut-backed finchlarks, sabota larks and penduline tits.

Larger and more visible birds, which are easier to spot and identify, include double-banded coursers, black-bellied and red-crested khorans. Both of these khorans show interesting displays during the mating season. You may also come across of the world's heaviest flying bird here, the kori bustard, and ostriches are not unknown, though they are very uncommon.

Of the raptors, by far the commonest is the pale chanting goshawk, which is usually seen perching atop a bush, small tree or post, surveying the area. When disturbed it'll usually swoop off, flying low, to a similar perch not far away. The very similar, but slightly larger, dark chanting goshawk may also be found here, on the edge of its range. (These are distinguishable in flight, from above, as the pale variety has a white rump, whereas the dark chanting goshawk has a darker colouring and a darker, barred rump.)

Getting there and away I'm not aware of any landing strips in this area, so to get here you need at least one fully equipped 4x4, with all your food and water. There is water usually available at Xai Xai village, and a small, very basic shop at Qangwa, but it's better to bring with you everything that you might need.

As with any tracks in the Kalahari, and especially those that are rarely used, a major danger is fire caused by grass seeds and stems blocking up your vehicle's radiator, or collecting near its exhaust system. If you're driving here, especially during the first few months of the year, you must take steps to prevent this (see *Chapter 6*, pages 119–20).

There are two roads which head west from the main Shakawe–Sehithwa road, and then loop around and join up with each other around the Aha Hills. Both are very long, very sandy and hard going, though navigation is not difficult.

The northern route About 300m north of the centre of Nokaneng there's a track heading west (✪ GTURN2 19°39.577'S, 22°11.010'E). This is the longer and the sandier of the two routes, but there's relatively little mud this way so if rains have been heavy it may be the easiest route.

From Nokaneng, it twists and turns quite a lot but after a little over 120km you'll reach the tiny village of Qangwa (✪ QANGWA 19°31.868'S, 21°10.281'E), sometimes spelt 'Xangwa', or even 'Gcangwa'.

From there one track heads west towards Namibia, ultimately to Tsumkwe (✪ TSUMKW 19°35.507'S, 20°30.184'E). You take the one which leads southwest for over 10km to another small village, Dobe (✪ DOBEVI 19°34.830'S, 21°4.428'E). From there the track heads due south, and actually picks its way through the Aha Hills. It passes west of the small group of hills which contain Waxhu North Cave (✪ WAXHUN 19°43.532'S, 21°3.489'E), and east of the main range of hills, within which is found the Waxhu South Cave (✪ WAXHUS 19°46.643'S, 21°2.518'E). Finally it reaches the village of Xai Xai (✪ XAIXAI 19°52.867'S, 21°04.934'E) after about 37km.

In some literature you'll find this designated as Nxainxai, CaeCae or, more recently, /Xai/Xai. However you want to spell it, this is one of the largest villages in the area, with a population of about 300–400 Ju/'hoansi San people, and perhaps 50 Herero (Mbanderu) people. Here there is a borehole, a small school, a basic health post and small administrative centre.

From here the route turns east, becoming the route described below which ultimately ends on the main road near Tsau. About 10km east of Xai Xai you pass a clear right turn (✪ GTURN3 19°54.286'S, 21°9.418'E) which takes almost 30km to reach the Gcwihaba Hills and Cave (✪ GCWIHA 20°01.250'S, 21°21.230'E).

The southern route Although it can be confusing to locate the start of this route in the east, once you're on it, this is the best route out to the hills and caves unless there has been very heavy rain in the area.

Around Tsau (✪ TSAU 20°10.294'S, 22°27.265'E) there are a number of tracks heading roughly west to northwest. Some of these will fizzle out at smallholdings, bush homesteads and villages, whilst some join into one road which heads out towards the hills. The turning on to one of the easiest tracks (✪ GTURN1 20°07.047'S, 22°22.291'E) is found about 10.5km north of the centre of Tsau, whilst another cuts off the main road about 1.5km from Tsau.

During the dry season, the first few hours from Tsau are generally fairly easy driving, as the hard, compacted track gently descends into the fossil river valley. However, during the rains a number of wide, shallow pans hold water here, turning it into a series of connected mud-holes and a challenging route even for experienced drivers (hence in the rains you might consider taking the longer northern route instead). After that, the country becomes rolling duneland with thick sand, which is slow going but not as treacherous as the mud.

About 90km from Tsau there's a left turning (✪ GTURN4 19°57.556'S, 21°44.541'E). This passes the Xhaba borehole, a satellite cattle post of Xai Xai village, after about 26km, and then reaches the hills another 26km later. It's the quickest way to the hills. If you miss this turn-off then continue on to the main turning (⊕ GTURN3 19°54.286'S, 21°9.418'E) used by the Northern route, above, and take a left there. This is over 150km from Tsau.

Where to stay Most people camp near the main entrance to the caves, though there are sufficiently few visitors that you're unlikely to see anyone else here. Note that there is no water here (the nearest is at Xai Xai), nor any other facilities, so it's vital that you bring everything that you need with you, and take away all of your rubbish (or at least everything that cannot be burned and reduced to ash).

When using the toilet, take a spade, a box of matches and your tissue paper. Bury your waste deeply and always burn your toilet paper.

To get the best out of such an experience, you're probably wisest to come here with an experienced mobile-safari operator who – and this is vital – knows the village and villagers well. They'll also know what's possible, and enable you to get the most out of your trip, whilst the community benefits in just the same way. Operations who may be able to help include Uncharted Africa Safaris (*Francistown;* \ *2412 277;* e *reservations@unchartedafrica.com; www.unchartedafrica.com*) and Phakawe Safaris (page 172). This will be more costly than trying to do something yourself, but probably much more satisfactory.

Gcwihaba Hills and Caverns
The low, rounded hills here are not the attraction, but beneath them is a labyrinth of passages and caves, some with enchanting rock formations of stalagmites, stalactites and spectacular 'flowstones' which seem like waterfalls of rock.

Some of these chambers reach up to 10m in height, whilst other passages are so narrow that you'll need to clamber and squeeze through. All were formed by the dissolving and depositing action of acidic water on the limestone of the rocks around, though now the caves are totally dry.

What to see and do To explore the caves you'll need several good torches, plus extra batteries and bulbs (a fail-safe emergency backup is essential, as there's no one here to help you), and perhaps a lighter or matches. If you bring a huge ball of string (you'll need about 1km for it to be much use!) then remember to collect it up again and take it away with you.

There are lots of dead ends, closed-off passages and caverns to penetrate. If your curiosity flags, then remind yourself of the legend of Hendrik Matthys van Zyl, the wealthy founder of Ghanzi, who is said to have stashed a portion of his fortune here in the late 1800s.

Orientation There are two main entrances to the caves, about 250m apart. There is a route between them, but it's not straightforward or obvious, so getting through may tax your map-reading skills. (You won't be able to rely on your beloved GPS either, as they're useless under the rock ceilings of the caves!)

Most of the caves are on one level, though there is a section, slightly nearer to the south entrance than the north, where several of the corridors split into two different levels, one raised several metres above the other.

Start exploring the caves from the main (north) entrance. Here, on one of the large boulders towards the right of the main entrance hall, you'll find the inscription 'Discovered 1 June 1932, M Drotsky.'

You'll also realise that a string marks a route through the caves. Given how easy it is to get lost in here, this can be very comforting. It starts at the lower entrance, and proceeds down an increasingly steep and narrow passageway. There's a short

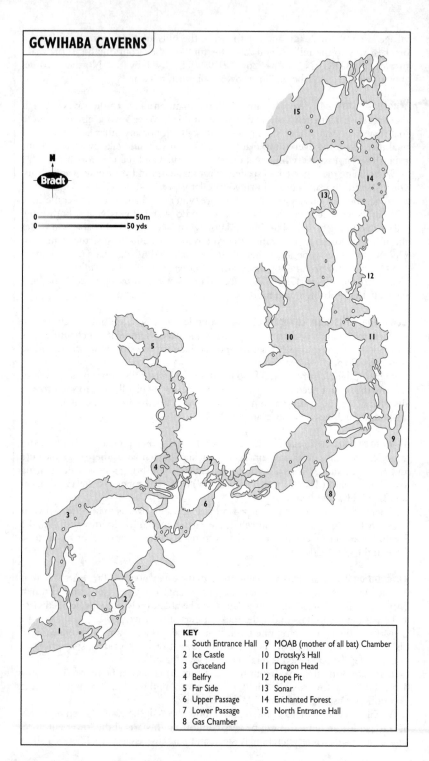

GCWIHABA CAVERNS

N
Bradt

0 ——————— 50m
0 ——————— 50 yds

15

14

13

12

5

11

10

9

4

8

6

3

7

2

1

KEY

1	South Entrance Hall	9	MOAB (mother of all bat) Chamber
2	Ice Castle	10	Drotsky's Hall
3	Graceland	11	Dragon Head
4	Belfry	12	Rope Pit
5	Far Side	13	Sonar
6	Upper Passage	14	Enchanted Forest
7	Lower Passage	15	North Entrance Hall
8	Gas Chamber		

vertical climb down into what's been christened the 'rope pit', before you emerge up the other side on to a shelf. Then it's a bit of a squeeze before you find yourself in a large chamber.

From here the route basically climbs, though there are lots of side-passages to distract you, and part way through is where there are two different levels to the passages. You'll also come across the chambers with bats in them, deep within the cave complex, before finally emerging from the southern entrance (where there's a ledge that is now used as a roost by a resident barn owl).

Aha Hills About 40–50km northwest of the Gcwihabe Hills, and visible from them, is a range of low, rounded hills: the Aha Hills. These straddle the Botswana–Namibia border, and are among the most remote and little-visited destinations in Botswana.

Like the Gcwihabe Hills, this range is made of dolomite marble that has been split by weathering into numerous faults and fractures. This presents a very jagged surface, with many loose blocks underfoot, and isn't easy to walk on.

The range covers about 245km², most of which is in Botswana, and very little of which has been properly mapped or documented. That said, it's interesting to note that on the Namibian side the range is much easier to reach than the hills in Botswana, being only about 20km from the good, gravel road which links Tsumkwe to Gam.

What to see and do In some ways the hills are attractive simply because they're so remote, and because you can camp wherever you like – though it's important, as always, that if you find yourself near a village then you ask permission to stay from the head villager.

Clambering around isn't as much fun here as in the Tsodilo Hills, simply because the rock surface is totally different. Instead of large boulders with an even surface and an easy grip, the Aha Hills are made of endless jagged little blocks. So if you do come here, stout walking shoes with strong soles make clambering around a lot easier.

Two sites on the Botswana side have attracted some interest, and both are sinkholes – large holes in the ground. The local people apparently know both simply as 'Waxhu', which means 'house of god'. Both can only be visited using specialist climbing/caving equipment, so don't be tempted to try and climb down. There are no mountain-rescue teams in Botswana!

Waxhu Cave (north; ✪ WAXHUN 19°43.532'S, 21°03.498'E) was first described in 1974 and is about 70m deep.

Waxhu Cave (south; ✪ WAXHUS 19°46.632'S, 21°02.518'E) is also known by some of its recent visitors as 'Independence Cave', because they first visited it on the fifth anniversary of Botswana's independence. This cave is about 50m deep.

Botswana Notes and Records (see *Appendix 3, Further Information*) records many more details on these sinkholes, including rough maps of them and information about the various expeditions which have explored them recently.

15

The Kalahari's Great Salt Pans

The great salt pans lie in the heart of the northern Kalahari, forming an area of empty horizons into which the blinding white expanse of the pans disappears in shimmering heat-haze. In winter, dust devils whirl across the open plains; in summer many become undulating seas of grasses beneath the turbulence of the stormy skies. It is a harsh, spare landscape, not to everybody's taste, but it offers an isolation as complete as anywhere in southern Africa, and a wealth of hidden treasures for those prepared to make the effort – including Stone Age ruins and prehistoric beaches.

The wildlife is rich, but highly seasonal and nomadic. At times you'll find great concentrations of plains game, with all their attendant predators, and, in good years, spectacular breeding colonies of flamingos crowd the shallow waters of Sua Pan. At other times the stage seems empty. But even then, there is always a cast of smaller Kalahari residents behind the scenes – from coursers and korhaans to mongooses and mole-rats.

BACKGROUND INFORMATION

ORIENTATION The tarred Nata–Maun road bisects this barren region. To the south of this lie the vast, dry depressions of Sua and Ntwetwe, with their scattered 'islands' of granite and fossilised dunes, fringed by grassland and acacia savannah. To its north is the Nxai Pan complex, including Nxai and Kgama-Kgama pans, now grassed over, and Kudiakam Pan, overlooked by the famous Baines' Baobabs.

Much of the region is unfenced ranching country, where wildlife has largely been supplanted by cattle. However, the fauna and flora are protected in a number of reserves. Makgadikgadi Pans National Park extends south of the Nata–Maun road, between the western shore of Ntwetwe Pan and the Boteti River. Nxai Pans National Park adjoins this to the north of the Nata–Maun road, and includes the Nxai Pans complex and Baines' Baobabs. The much smaller Nata Sanctuary, established to protect the seasonal breeding waterbirds of the Nata River Delta, is situated in the northeast corner of Sua Pan. Each of these areas has its own distinct attractions and seasonal peculiarities.

GEOGRAPHY The Magkadikgadi Pans consist of an immense expanse of largely flat and featureless terrain in the north of the Kalahari. The pans themselves are located roughly between the diamond town of Orapa in the south, the village of Nata in the northeast and the Boteti rivercourse in the west. This falls away northwards towards the Mababe Depression and the Chobe–Zambezi river catchment system.

At its centre lie two huge adjacent salt pans – Sua (to the east) and Ntwetwe (to the west) – which cover an estimated combined area of roughly 12,000km². Around them are a number of smaller pans, including Nxai Pan to the north and Lake Xau to the south.

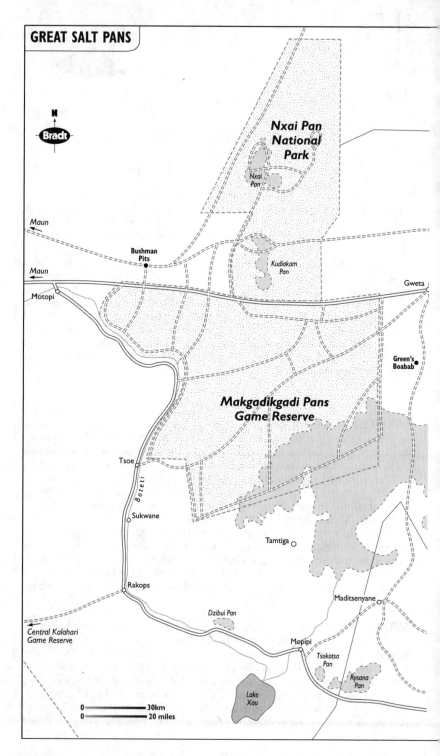

GREAT SALT PANS

N

Bradt

Maun

Maun

Bushman
Pits

Motopi

Gweta

Nxai Pan
National
Park

Nxai
Pan

Kudiakam
Pan

Green's
Boabab

Makgadikgadi Pans
Game Reserve

Tsoe

Boteti

Sukwane

Tamtiga

Rakops

Maditsenyane

Central Kalahari
Game Reserve

Dzibui Pan

Mopipi

Tsokotsa
Pan

Rysana
Pan

Lake
Xau

0   30km
0   20 miles

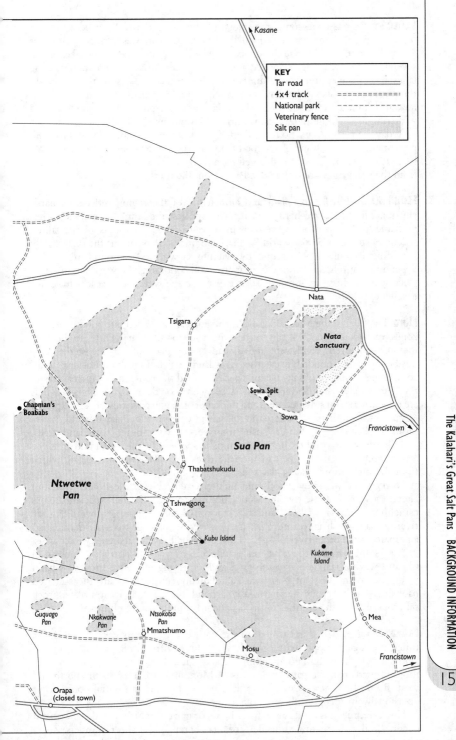

KEY
Tar road
4x4 track
National park
Veterinary fence
Salt pan

Kasane

Nata

Tsigara

Nata Sanctuary

Sowa Spit

Chapman's Boababs

Sowa

Francistown

Sua Pan

Thabatshukudu

Ntwetwe Pan

Tshwagong

Kubu Island

Kukome Island

Guquago Pan

Nkokwane Pan

Ntsokotsa Pan

Mmatshumo

Mea

Mosu

Francistown

Orapa (closed town)

GEOLOGY To grasp the complex geology of this area, you really need a broader understanding of the way in which the whole Kalahari was formed (see pages 45–9). In brief, the pans are the desiccated vestiges of the huge super-lake which, several million years ago, covered most of central Botswana and moulded the landscape of the entire region. Subsequent climate change, seismic upheavals and the diversion of rivers (the details of which divide geologists) starved this lake of its water supply, shrinking it to today's flat, caustic depressions of grey clay, and withering its surrounding wetlands into arid savannah.

Today the pans receive no more than 400–500mm of rain annually, and have no permanent standing water. After good rains, however, they briefly become shallow lakes again, fed by the seasonal Boteti river from the west – bringing the overspill from the Okavango – and the Nata River from the northeast.

FLORA AND FAUNA The plant and animal life of the region reflects its harsh climate. The plants are hardy and resilient species; the animals comprise either nomadic species that follow the rains in large seasonal movements, or specialised sedentary species adapted to arid Kalahari conditions. Populations fluctuate wildly according to rainfall. Consequently wildlife viewing is a hit-and-miss affair, depending entirely on the time of year and local conditions. However, in the right place at the right time, it can be spectacular, and the wide, open spaces make for excellent visibility.

Flora The flora of the Makgadikgadi Pans region can be graded into a loose series of zones, each determined by the soil in which it grows. At the centre lie the pans themselves: barren, windswept and devoid of any plant life. These sterile, salty dustbowls are surrounded by extensive grasslands which flourish on Kalahari sands, comprising a mixture of salt-tolerant species around the pans, coarse 'finger' grasses across the sandy plains, and nutritious 'sweet grasses' on the margins. The grasslands are punctuated with scattered trees and thickets, consisting primarily of acacia species.

Further from the pans, where the soil has a richer sand and clay mix, this acacia savannah becomes a denser bush, interspersed with other woodland trees, including various combretum and terminalia species. To the north and east, the acacias are replaced by a belt of mopane trees (*Colophospermum mopane*), which flourish on the more heavily clay soils.

To the west, the alluvial soils and hidden water-table of the Boteti riverfront support a strip of dense riverine woodland. Here typical Kalahari species, such as camelthorn (*Acacia erioloba*) and blackthorn (*Acacia mellifera*), grow alongside riverine giants such as sycamore figs (*Ficus sycomorus*), sausage trees (*Kigelia africana*) and many of the other riverine species that are usually associated with wetter areas.

Across the region, towering real fan palms (*Hyphaene petersiana*) cluster in elegant, waving stands above the grasslands, forming extensive groves of palm woodland to the west of Ntwetwe Pan. Equally conspicuous are the scattered baobabs, which sprout incongruously around the pans and on isolated rock outcrops, each with centuries of history recorded in its swollen limbs.

Fauna Fossil evidence unearthed on the pans shows that in wetter, prehistoric times, the region supported the whole spectrum of African big game – including abundant elephant, buffalo and rhino. Today, the selection of large mammals is more limited than the game-rich areas of Moremi and Chobe to the north and west. Rhino have disappeared altogether, while elephant and buffalo only occur occasionally, in small numbers on the fringes.

However, the grasslands draw huge herds of grazers, which can, despite recent declines, still rival anything outside Tanzania's Serengeti for sheer numbers. Zebra and wildebeest gather in tens of thousands, supported by smaller numbers of gemsbok, eland and red hartebeest. Movements are unpredictable, but in general the highest concentrations occur in the western Boteti region during the late dry season (August–November) and further north in the Nxai Pan area during the rainy season (December–April).

Hardy springbok are impervious to drought and remain scattered across the grasslands throughout the year. In the Nxai Pans area, the mopane woodland shelters browsers, including impala (which supplant springbok where the bush thickens), kudu, sable and tsessebe. Here, giraffe are common and a few breeding elephant frequent the fringes of the northern pans.

Another pocket of diversity occurs along the Boteti River, where the thicker bush provides cover for grey duiker, bushbuck and waterbuck. Giraffe and elephant also visit this area, while the permanent pools even support a few hippos and crocodiles – emigrants from the Okavango.

A variety of predators prowls the region. Lions generally follow the game, particularly the zebra herds in the Boteti area and the winter springbok in Nxai, but seldom occur on the pans themselves. Cheetah are most often seen around Nxai Pan, while leopard frequent the denser bush of the Boteti waterfront. Spotted hyena keep to the woodland fringes, while the brown hyena – a Kalahari specialist – is found around the pans themselves.

Wild dogs are highly nomadic and though unusual, can turn up anywhere. Here they are most often seen in the vicinity of Nxai Pan. Smaller predators include bat-eared fox, black-backed jackal, aardwolf, honey badger, African wildcat, small-spotted genet and striped polecat. Yellow mongooses are common on the grasslands, while the slender mongoose prefers acacia thickets.

Without much in the way of fruiting trees, the Makgadikgadi is not a good region for primates – except along the Boteti, where both vervet monkeys and baboons do find food and cover. However, throughout the region the lesser bushbaby, which feeds mostly on insects and acacia gum, thrives in the acacia savannah.

Other mammals of the grasslands include the ubiquitous aardvark and porcupine, and the bizarre spring hare is particularly abundant. Most smaller mammals are nocturnal, allowing them to avoid the high daytime temperatures, when a larger surface area to body ratio quickly causes overheating. On this principle a variety of rodents make their home in burrows and emerge at night, including the desert pygmy mouse, hairy-footed gerbil, and Damara mole rat (see box on page 411).

The black-tailed tree rat avoids the burning sun by hiding in tree holes, and protects the entrance to its lair with a scruffy 'nest' of twigs. At night this species can be seen scampering through the branches of a camelthorn, using its prehensile tail for added agility.

One exception to the nocturnal rule is the ground squirrel, an animal of the deep Kalahari that occurs in the sandy south of the region. This highly sociable rodent can forage in the full glare of the sun by using its tail as a parasol to cast protective shade.

Birdlife The Great Salt Pans region offers several distinct habitats for birds. The open grasslands support typical ground-nesting, arid country species such as coursers, korhaans, sandgrouse, chats, larks and pipits. Both the world's largest bird – the ostrich – and the world's largest flying bird, the kori bustard, strike conspicuous figures in this featureless terrain, while greater kestrels, pale-chanting goshawks, marsh owls and the statuesque secretary bird are among the more common resident predators.

Any isolated stands of trees are beacons for birds: red-necked falcons breed in fan palms, while baobabs provide roosts for owls and breeding sites for hornbills and rollers. Elsewhere, typical arid woodland residents dominate the thicker scrub, including red-billed francolin, grey lourie, fork-tailed drongo, pied babbler, glossy starling, white-browed sparrow weaver and a wide variety of shrikes, barbets, flycatchers, robins, sunbirds, warblers, waxbills and whydahs.

Eagles, including martial and bateleur, roam the skies. Smaller predators such as gabar goshawk and pearl-spotted owl hunt the thorn scrub, and vultures follow the herds across the region, hoping for casualties.

In summer the resident bird population is swelled by a huge influx of migrants drawn to the seasonal bonanza of seeds and insects. Some are non-breeding visitors that come from as far afield as Europe and central Africa. White storks (from Europe) and Abdim's storks (from east Africa) arrive wheeling on thermals to stalk the savannah; carmine and European bee-eaters hawk their insect prey just above the grass; shrikes, including red-backed and lesser grey, claim prominent territories on thorn bushes from where they ambush hapless lizards and grasshoppers.

Other more local breeding visitors include seed-eaters such as wattled starlings, doves, finchlarks, canaries – and the prolific red-billed quelea, whose flocks reach swarm proportions. Migrant raptors are lured by the brief abundance of prey, with many different species – including western red-footed falcons, steppe buzzards, yellow-billed kites and tawny eagles – congregating at mass termite emergences (see page 371).

After good rains, when Ntwetwe and Sua Pans turn briefly into glassy lakes, waterbirds arrive in their thousands. The shallow, saline conditions are ideal for both greater and lesser flamingos, which construct their clay nests under the blazing Kalahari sun and filter-feed on algae and brine shrimps. Meanwhile pelicans, darters, cormorants and ducks flock to the brackish waters of the Nata River delta, in the northeast of Sua Pan. Here, waders such as stilts, sandpipers and avocets forage along the shoreline, while jacanas, pied kingfishers, weavers and bishops frequent the reed beds.

Smaller fauna Further down the evolutionary scale, a variety of reptiles and amphibians thrive in Makgadikgadi's arid expanses, though most pass unseen by the visitor. Acacias, with their deeply fissured bark and abundance of insect prey, provide havens for skinks and geckos above the open grassland. At ground level, the ground agama ambushes termites from a hollow at the foot of a shady bush, while the legless Kalahari burrowing skink swims just below the surface of the sand in search of beetle larvae, and is often found drowned when pans fill up overnight. In sandier areas, barking geckos emerge from their burrows on summer evenings and fill the Kalahari night with their bizarre territorial clicking calls.

Perhaps the highlight of Makgadikgadi's smaller animals is one that few have either heard of or seen: the Makgadikgadi spiny agama (*Agama makarikarica*). This is a small species of the agama family – a lizard – that's endemic to Makgadikgadi. It feeds on termites and beetles, and lives in tunnels at the base of bushes.

The acacia woodland is home to a broad cross-section of typical bushveld reptiles, including monitor lizards (both water and rock), flapneck chameleons and leopard tortoises. Snakes encountered at ground level include black mamba, snouted cobra, African egg-eater, mole snake and the ubiquitous puff adder, while arboreal species such as boomslang and spotted bush snake hunt chameleons and birds' eggs among the thorny tangle.

To survive this harsh habitat, many frogs aestivate below ground during the dry season. Giant bullfrogs emerge from their mud cocoons after seasonal rains to take

The towers of mud built by termites, known as termitaria, are often the only points of elevation for miles across the Makgadikgadi grasslands. Not all termites build mounds – harvester termites (*Hodotermitidae*), which are common on Kalahari sands, leave little evidence of their underground tunnels above the surface – but those that do, the *Macrotermitidae* species, are responsible for one of the true wonders of nature.

Communicating entirely through pheromones, millions of blind worker termites can raise several tons of soil – particle by particle – into an enormous structure over 3m high. Below the mound lies the nest, where separate chambers house brood galleries, food stores, fungus combs (where termites cultivate a fungus that can break down plant cellulose) and the queen's royal cell. The queen produces up to 30,000 eggs a day, which means – since she lives for many years – that the millions of inhabitants of the colony are all brothers and sisters.

The whole structure is prevented from overheating by a miraculous air-conditioning system. Warm air rises from the nest chambers, up a central chimney, into thin-walled ventilation flues near the surface (you can feel the warmth by placing your hand just inside one of the upper vents). Here it is cooled and replenished with oxygen, before circulating back down through separate passages into cavities below the nest chambers. Finally, before returning to the nest, it passes through specially constructed cooling veins, kept damp by the termites. In this way, termites maintain the 100% humidity and constant temperature of 29–31°C required for successful production of eggs and young. (These conditions are exploited by monitor lizards, who seal their eggs inside termitaria for safe incubation.)

After the rains, when conditions are right, the queen produces a reproductive caste of winged males and females – known as imagoes – who leave the colonies in huge swarms to mate, disperse and establish new nests. Mass termite 'emergences' are one of the bonanzas of the bush, offering a seasonal feast to everything from frogs and spiders to kites, falcons and tawny eagles.

over temporary pans in a frenzy of breeding. These frogs are so aggressive that they have even been observed snapping at lions. The much smaller rain-frogs of the Breviceps genus, like the bushveld rain frog, *Breviceps adspersus*, have toughened feet, evolved for digging their burrows. They also appear with the rains, and gather at the surface during termite emergences, cramming in as many of the hapless insects as time will allow.

The Kalahari teems with invertebrate life. Good years bring swarms of locusts and mass migrations of butterflies to the grasslands, while countless termites demolish and carry away the dead vegetable matter that carpets the ground. Termites are fundamental to the ecology of the region. Not only do they recycle and enrich the soil, but they are also a vital prey species for everything from eagles and aardvarks to skinks and spiders.

There are 14 genera of termites, each of which has a different mode of foraging: harvester termites (Hototermitidae) nest in underground burrows, while Odontoterme termites construct the enormous raised mounds that can be seen for miles across the grasslands – each one a miracle of air conditioning.

Among a multitude of other insects are the wingless tenebrionid beetles, which scuttle rapidly across open ground on long legs and squirt a noxious fluid at attackers. More visible are the chunkier dung beetles, which swarm on strong wings to fresh animal dung, then roll it away and bury it as 'brood balls' in which their eggs are laid and their larvae mature.

On hot summer days, thickets throb with the stridulating calls of cicadas, the adults having only two weeks of life in which to mate and deposit their eggs, after up to 17 years underground larval development.

Termites and other insects feed a host of invertebrate predators. Sand divers (Ammoxennidae) are small, fast-moving spiders that paralyse termites with their venom and bury themselves if disturbed. Golden orbweb spiders (Nephiladae) string their super-strong webs between thorn bushes to ensnare flying insects.

Contrary to popular belief, sun-spiders, or solifuges (Solifugae), are not venomous, but pursue insects at high speed across the ground and despatch them audibly with powerful mandibles. You'll often see these large arachnids running across the ground at night near campfires. Though frightening at first, they're totally harmless and don't bite people!

Not so harmless are the resident scorpions, which detect the vibrations of prey through their body hairs. As a rough rule of thumb for the nervous, species with larger pincers and slimmer tails have less powerful venom than those with smaller pincers and larger tails.

Red velvet mites are parasites on larger invertebrates and often gather in sandy areas in the early morning after rain showers, looking like tiny scarlet cushions. Another tiny parasite, the voracious tampan tick, lurks in the sand beneath camelthorn trees and, chemically alerted by an exhalation of its victim's CO_2, emerges to drain the blood from any unsuspecting mammal that fancies a nap in the shade.

GETTING ORGANISED

Once you leave one of the few main roads in this area, you generally need to be in a self-sufficient 4x4 vehicle. Bringing along all your food and water with you is always a good idea, as whilst you will find water in some places, there is very little in the way of shops!

If you're venturing off across Makgadikgadi, then you really should take at least two vehicles and have a GPS and a compass; an environment of flat salt without any landmarks at all can be very disorienting, especially during a windstorm. In such a situation, breaking through the pan's crust and getting stuck can create a life-threatening situation.

MAPS The 'usual suspects' both cover this area well – the *Shell tourist map of Botswana* and the InfoMap. Both have a variety of useful GPS points. Although I find the Shell map a little easier to use, with its more detailed maps on the reverse side, the InfoMap is much newer. Take both if you can.

If you plan on exploring a lot of the pans, then you should also get hold of a copy of the excellent *African Adventurer's Guide to Botswana*, by Mike Main (see *Appendix 3, Further Information*). This has a number of carefully described routes through the area, as well as much interesting general information. However, do be aware that tracks can change, so always be vigilant.

BOOKING AND PARK FEES If you want to stay in either of the national parks then you must book ahead for a campsite. See *Chapter 7*, pages 138–9, for details of the park fees for these national parks.

Similarly Nata Sanctuary, Jack's Camp and Makgadikgadi Camp are certainly best booked in advance – though most of Sua and Ntwetwe Pans are not controlled, and so you can sleep anywhere.

Nxai Pan National Park lies to the north of the Nata–Maun road at the northern fringe of the ancient Lake Makgadikgadi basin. It is contiguous with Makgadikgadi Pans National Park, to the south of this same road. Nxai is probably the easiest area of the pans to drive yourself into, and from December to around July will also have the best game. Add in the spectacular sight of Baines' Baobabs to make a super destination for a three- to four-day self-drive trip.

Note that Nxai is usually pronounced to rhyme with 'high', unless you're familiar with the clicks of the Khoisan languages, in which case the correct pronunciation of the 'x' is actually a palatal click (ie: press tongue against the roof of your mouth, and then move down).

BACKGROUND INFORMATION

Geography The park covers an area of 2,658km², comprising Nxai Pan itself, Kgama-Kgama Pan complex to the northeast, and the Kudiakam Pan complex (including Baines' Baobabs) to the south. The baobabs were added to the original park in 1992.

The pans themselves are ancient salt lakes, ringed to the south and west with thick fossil dunes of wind-blown Kalahari sand. Today they are completely grassed over, but scattered across their surfaces are smaller pans or waterholes that fill up during the rainy season. Some of these are artificially maintained by the park authorities to provide surface water throughout the year, but the watercourses that once fed the area from the northeast have long since dried up.

The park's general topography is flat and featureless, with the famous baobabs being the most striking landmarks, and one of the higher points of elevation. To the north and east the soils become increasingly clayey, supporting the encroachment of mopane woodland and integrating with the dense mopane woodlands of the Chobe–Zambezi river catchment system.

Flora and fauna highlights

Flora The open grassland that covers the pans consists of many palatable 'sweet' grasses (eg: *Themeda* species), which sustain the large herd of grazers that invade the area in summer. These grasslands are studded with 'islands' of acacias, consisting mostly of candle-pod acacia (*Acacia hebeclada*). This is easily recognised from around October to March, as its seedpods stand upright, like candles. Other very common species here are the umbrella thorn (*Acacia tortilis*) and bastard umbrella thorn (*Acacia leuderitzii*).

During the rains, the pans sprout a profusion of wildflowers, including the spectacular brunsvigia lily (*Brunsvigia radulosa*), which brings a splash of red to the summer landscape.

Around and between the pans the vegetation differs according to soil type. Acacias are the dominant trees on sandy soils, with stands of silver clusterleaf (*Terminalia sericea*), and – particularly in disturbed areas – dense thickets of sickle bush (*Dichrostachys cineria*). Mopane (*Colophospermum mopane*) dominates the richer clayey soils to the north and east, carpeting the dusty ground with its golden butterfly leaves and bursting into a flush of green with the rains. Elsewhere, mixed sand and clay support various combretum species, with their wind-borne winged pods, while a richer selection of shrubs thrive on the lime-rich calcrete ridges, including the trumpet thorn (*Catophractes alexandrii*), Western rhigozum (*Rhigozum brevispinosum*) and purple-pod terminalia (*Terminalia prunoides*). Visit South Camp to see some fine examples of these.

Of all the area's trees, the best known must be the great baobabs (*Adansonia digitata*) – in particular the famous Baines' Baobabs that overlook Kudiakam Pan,

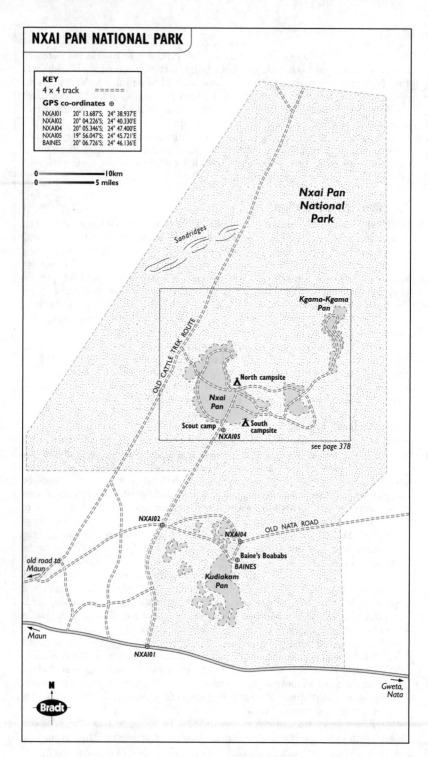

NXAI PAN NATIONAL PARK

which were painted by the renowned Victorian explorer and artist Thomas Baines on May 22 1862, and have changed little in 140 years since. They are not the only baobabs around, but they're certainly the most celebrated.

Fauna From December to April, Nxai Pan is a breeding ground for large herbivores. Game viewing can be spectacular at the start of this season, when thousands of animals are dropping their young and predators are drawn to the easy pickings. After good rains the lush green grasslands teem with huge concentrations of Burchell's zebra, blue wildebeest and springbok (here at the northeastern limit of their range), while healthy numbers of other grazers include gemsbok, eland and red hartebeest.

Large giraffe herds, sometimes over 40 strong, move across the pans between the acacia 'islands', which they prune into characteristic hourglass shapes. The mopane woodland, mainly to the north of Nxai Pan, shelters browsers such as impala and kudu, which often venture out on to the pans for the permanent waterholes and rich mineral salts. The impala is a versatile species, being able to adapt its diet to graze or browse, according to what is on offer, and Nxai Pan is one of the few areas where impala and springbok occur side by side – their habitats elsewhere generally being mutually exclusive.

In summer, small herds of breeding elephant can sometimes be seen around Kgama-Kgama Pan in the northeast of the park, while lone bulls disperse across the area at other times – generally on the fringes of the mopane. Other visitors from the north include the occasional tsessebe, at about the southern limit of their appearance in the Kalahari. In winter the great herds disperse from the pans, leaving few grazers except the hardy springbok, and a few timid steenbok that find shelter in the thickets.

Predators are well represented on Nxai Pan. Lion can be heard throughout the year: in summer they follow the zebra and wildebeest herds; during the dry season they remain to hunt springbok around the few permanent waterholes. The springbok herds also draw cheetah: Nxai Pan offers perfect open terrain for this coursing predator, and has a good reputation for sightings. Meanwhile wandering packs of wild dog occasionally turn up in pursuit of the same quarry.

Spotted hyena can sometimes be heard at night, especially when there are large concentrations of game around, while the more elusive brown hyena hunts and scavenges for smaller prey items around the pans. Black-backed jackal and honey badger are both versatile smaller predators that occur throughout the area, the latter sometimes foraging in association with the pale-chanting goshawk.

Aardwolf and bat-eared fox snap up harvester termites on the open grasslands: the former is strictly nocturnal and seldom seen; the latter may still be about at sunrise, foraging in loose family groups with ears cocked to the ground for termite rustlings.

African wildcat and small-spotted genet hunt the acacia bush after dark for small rodents and roosting birds, while by day yellow mongoose comb open sandy areas for scorpions, slender mongoose hunt the acacia scrub, alone or in pairs, and banded mongoose rummage through the woodland in large, sociable colonies.

Other smaller mammals found here include lesser bushbaby, aardvark and porcupine, with spring hare on the grassland and scrub hare in the woodland. By day, tree squirrels are common and noisy inhabitants of the mopane.

Birdlife Nxai Pan's rich avifauna comprises a mixture of grassland, acacia scrub and mopane woodland birds, with a total of 217 species recorded in Hugh Chittenden's *Top Birding Spots of Southern Africa* (see *Appendix 3, Further Information*). Each habitat has its own typical residents.

Cuckoos are not the only cheats of the bird world. Whydahs (*Viduidae*) are also brood parasites that lay their eggs in other birds' nests. Like cuckoos, each species of whydah exploits a specific host, and all of them choose waxbills (*Estrildidae*). However, unlike cuckoos, whydahs do not evict the eggs or nestlings of their host, so young whydahs grow up alongside their step-siblings, not instead of them.

To enhance the deception, a whydah's eggs – and there are usually two of them – perfectly mimic the colour of its host's clutch, and, once hatched, the whydah nestlings have exactly the right arrangements of gape spots inside their bills to dupe their step-parents into feeding them. A male whydah can even mimic the song of its host to distract it from the nest while the female goes about her devious business undisturbed. Breeding male whydahs are lively, conspicuous birds, who flaunt extravagant tail plumes in dancing display flights – though outside the breeding season they are indistinguishable from the drab females.

Three species of whydah occur in the pans region, of which the most typical is the shaft-tailed whydah (*Vidua regia*), easily recognised by the long thin tail-plumes of a breeding male, each tipped with a pennant. This species frequents sandy clearings in acacia thickets, often in association with its host, the violet-eared waxbill, and apparently without any animosity between them. The other two species are the pin-tailed whydah (*Vidua macroura*), which parasitises the common waxbill and prefers well-watered areas, and the paradise whydah (*Vidua paradisaea*), which parasitises the melba finch and is a common bird of acacia savannah.

Grassland birds include ant-eating chat, white-browed sparrow weaver, capped wheatear and pale-chanting goshawk. White-browed robin, pied babbler and chinspot batis are found in the acacia scrub. Red-billed hornbill, red-billed francolin and barred owl prefer the mopane.

The distinction between adjacent habitats is reflected in the parallel distributions of similar species. For example, double-banded coursers and white-quilled korhaans – both Kalahari specialists – occur only on the open grasslands, while bronze-winged coursers and red-crested korhaans, their close relatives, stick to the surrounding woodlands.

Resident raptors, such as bateleur, martial eagle, tawny eagle and brown snake eagle, are joined in summer by an influx of migrants, including steppe buzzard, western red-footed kestrel and yellow-billed kite. Raptor watching can be superb at this time, with more unusual species such as lesser-spotted eagle and hobby sometimes joining the throng at termite emergences.

Kori bustards, secretary birds and (in summer) white storks hunt the grasslands, and after good rains wattled cranes sometimes appear on the flashes. In spring the air resounds to the breeding displays of larks, including sabota, rufous-naped, red-capped, fawn-coloured, dusky and clapper. During summer the game herds are a focus of bird activity, with carmine and blue-cheeked bee-eaters hawking insects around the feet of springbok and zebra, red-billed and yellow-billed oxpeckers hitching rides on giraffes, and white-backed and lappet-faced vultures dropping from the sky on to carcasses.

Away from the pans, the campsites are a good place to search out the smaller passerines: violet-eared, black-cheeked and blue waxbills occur in the sandy acacia scrub together with melba and scaly-feathered finches, while shaft-tailed and paradise whydahs – brood parasites on waxbills (see box above) – dash about in extravagant breeding finery. Baobabs are always worth checking, since they often provide roosting or nesting sites for rollers, hornbills and various owls.

GETTING THERE AND AWAY To visit Nxai Pan National Park you really need a vehicle, either your own or one driven by one of the mobile-safari operators from Maun. Either way, you should come with all your fuel, water and food – there are no shops or petrol pumps here.

The route here is very easy to find, and starts with a northerly turn-off from the main Maun–Nata road (⊕ NXAI01 20°13.687'S, 24°38.937'E). This is about 134km from Maun and 158km from Nata, and is very well signposted so you're unlikely to miss it.

There's one track north here, and after 18km of fairly thick, corrugated and unpleasant sand driving, you'll reach a right turn (⊕ NXAI02 20°04.226'S, 24°40.330'E). This leads to Kudiakam Pan and Baines' Baobabs (see pages 379–80 for directions).

Continue straight, bearing north-northeast for a further 18km and you'll reach the entrance gate (⊕ NXAI05 – 19°56.047'S, 24°45.721'E), which is at the south end of the main pan.

WHEN TO VISIT The game at Nxai is fairly erratic – it can be excellent, though sometimes it will disappoint. If there has been good rains, then between December and April you have a very good chance of witnessing large herds of springbok, gemsbok, giraffe and migrating zebra, plus a scattering of other species. However, note that this is also the time when the pans are at their most treacherous, and the driving is at its most muddy.

I last visited in late May, after a year of good rains, and we had excellent general game, with very large numbers of springbok, although in three days we didn't see a single large carnivore. Reliable reports suggest that this continues until around August, when game densities start to decrease. Then as the dry season progresses and the waterholes dry up, the game becomes sparser and less dependable. Nxai can be a hot and unrewarding park at the height of October's heat.

WHERE TO STAY There are just two campsites here, both a short distance off the main Nxai Pan. Both usually have standpipes for water and, if you're lucky, you'll find working flush toilets and showers.

🏕 **South Camp** (⊕ NXAISO 19°56.159'S, 24°46.598'E) is the closest to the entrance and probably the busier site – but also the nicer one. It's situated in a grove of purple-pod terminalia trees (*Terminalia prunioides*) which cast a good shade, making it relatively cool.

🏕 **North Camp** (⊕ NXAINO 19°52.707'S, 24°47.358'E) stands in a less inspiring grove of stunted mopane trees, which don't offer nearly the same shade as the terminalias. However, if South Camp is busier then you may find more solitude here.

There's also an old, disused campsite on a short (0.8km) loop road on the eastern side of Nxai Pan, at ⊕ NXAIOL 19°55.571'S, 24°49.282'E.

WHAT TO SEE AND DO Nxai's a great park for watching the herds of plains game, and is certainly somewhere that you need to be patient. Don't rush around in search of predators; instead take your time and you'll see much more. The waterholes are very open and exposed here, so park a good distance away and you won't disturb the animals drinking.

Finally, note that the night sky here is often phenomenally clear – as it is across the centre of the Kalahari. So if you can bring a star chart as well as your route maps, you'll enjoy it all the more. First on your list should be to identify the Southern Cross, and use it to find due south.

When gazing up, try using your binoculars and you'll be amazed how many more stars you can see.

Nxai and Kgama-Kgama pans This is the main pan of the complex. It's covered with grasses and dotted with clumps of acacias – and has always provided me with the best game viewing in this park.

Getting around In the dry season you'll find most of the roads in the area of the pan are good and hard, a pleasant contrast to the thick sand that you ploughed through to reach here.

When the rains come you'll have to be much more careful as many roads on the pan itself turn very muddy. Then the sand road in will be the easiest section, and the park itself will provide the problems. Make sure your self-sufficient vehicle includes a spade, and always carry some wood with you, both for campfires and for sticking under the wheels when you get stuck.

From Nxai Pan to Kgama-Kgama Pan Visiting most recently in May, the road which leads off east towards Kgama-Kgama Pan had clearly been used very little during the previous rains, and was very overgrown.

To reach this, head east from the scout post for about 10km, passing South

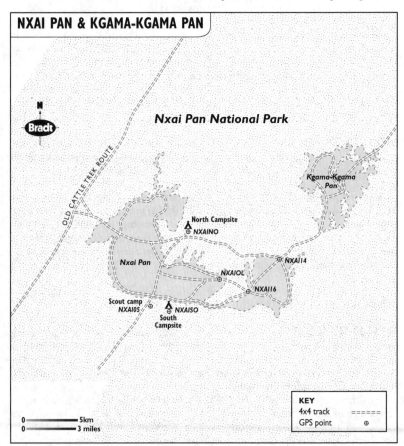

NXAI PAN & KGAMA-KGAMA PAN

N
Bradt

Nxai Pan National Park

OLD CATTLE TREK ROUTE

Kgama-Kgama Pan

North Campsite
NXAINO

Nxai Pan

NXAI14

NXAIOL

NXAI16

Scout camp
NXAIO5
NXAISO
South Campsite

KEY
4x4 track   ======
GPS point   ⊕

0 ▬▬▬ 5km
0 ▬▬▬ 3 miles

Camp on your right. This should bring you to a junction of the tracks (✪ NXAI16 19°55.803'S, 24°50.986'E). From here one track (clearly marked on most maps) leads off to loop around to the southeast and then turn north. This is in a very poor state, totally overgrown, and is fast becoming impassable.

However, another track leads off heading north of east, before turning northeast, and after almost 5km reaches another junction (✪ NXAI14 19°53.902'S, 24°52.744'E). The road northeast to Kgama-Kgama Pan was not in good shape, though later in the dry season it should be fine.

The alternative, which leads roughly west, across the north end of the small pan to the east of Nxai, heads through an interesting area of mostly mopane woodland, mixed with some denser groves of terminalias, and even in May, some of the pans here retained water. This eventually leads west to North Camp (✪ NXAINO 19°52.707'S, 24°47.358'E).

Kudiakam Pan and Baines' Baobabs
Sandwiched between Nxai Pan and the main road, Kudiakam is the largest of an interesting complex of pans lying in sparse bush east of the track to Nxai. The game here doesn't usually match Nxai's, but the main attraction is an extraordinary beautiful group of trees known as Baines' Baobabs, which stand at a spectacular site on the eastern edge of the pan. They were immortalised in a painting by Thomas Baines who came here in May 1862 with James Chapman and wrote:

> A lone circuit brought me, with empty pouch, to the clump of baobabs we had seen yesterday from the wagon; five full-sized trees, and two or three younger ones were standing, so that when in leaf their foliage must form one magnificent shade. One gigantic trunk had fallen and lay prostrate but still, losing none of its vitality, bent forth branches and young leaves like the rest . . . The general colour or the immense stems was grey and rough: but where the old bark had peeled and curled off, the new (of that peculiar metallic coppery-looking red and yellow which Dr Livingstone was wont so strenuously to object to in my pictures) shone through over large portions, giving them, according to light or shade, a red or yellow, grey or a deep purple tone.

The baobabs themselves have changed very little since Baines painted them: the one lying prostrate is still thriving, having lost none of its vitality.

Having thought of the baobabs with reference to a fairly recent Victorian painter, it's perhaps worth reminding ourselves that Baines was far from the first person here. Lawrence Robbins (see *Appendix 3, Further Information*) and others have conducted archaeological surveys of this area and discovered extensive remains dating from the Middle Stone Age period, 'especially on the eastern side within a 4km radius of the Baines baobab grove' according to Robbins. Many stone tools were found, plus ostrich eggshell remains, a zebra's tooth and the fossilised bone of a hippopotamus.

This site has been dated to about 105,000–128,000 years old, around which time this was probably a beach location on the edge of the great super-lake. This Middle Stone Age period has a special resonance, as this is the period during which we think the first *Homo sapiens* appeared.

Getting there and away The easiest way is to follow the directions to Nxai by turning off the main Maun–Nata road at ✪ NXAI01 20°13.687'S, 24°38.937'E, which is well signposted to Nxai. After heading north for 18km, you'll find a track off to the east at ✪ NXAI02 20°04.226'S, 24°40.330'E.

When I last drove this way the rusting shell of a burnt-out VW combi was a short way along this track. Either grass seeds had clogged the radiator to overheating, or the sheer effort of the deep sand here had simply been too much for it. This track splits very soon, after about 0.9km, and both roads lead to the baobabs.

Dry-season route The right fork heads almost directly for Baines' Baobabs (✪ BAINES 20°06.726'S, 24°46.136'E). It is the more direct route, but it crosses the surface of the pans, so do not try this unless you know what you're doing and are sure they will be dry. (It should be fine after about August, though don't take this as a guarantee!)

Wet-season route Taking the left fork is more reliable if you're travelling earlier in the year, as it bends around slightly to the north, taking about 14.4km to reach a crossroads at ✪ NXAI04 20°05.346'S, 24°47.400'E. Here you meet the old road between Maun and Nata; this is about 3.6km from the trees themselves. There's a network of small tracks around here, so head straight and then look for tracks off to the right, or turn right and find a track to your left – you can't miss them (✪ BAINES 20°06.726'S, 24°46.136'E).

Where to stay In the last few years, there has been an increasing number of visitors to Baines' Baobabs, and in the last decade this pan and its trees have been included in the national park to protect them. Campers were becoming a problem, and their fires a real danger to the trees, so camping is no longer allowed here.

MAKGADIKGADI PANS

The Sua and Ntwetwe pans that comprise Makgadikgadi cover 12,000km² to the south of the Nata–Maun road. The western side is protected within a national park, while the east is either wilderness or cattle ranching land.

These are amongst the largest salt pans in the world and have few landmarks. So you're left to use the flat, distant horizon as your only line of reference – and even that dissolves into a haze of shimmering mirages in the heat of the afternoon sun. During the rains this desolate area comes to life, with huge migrating herds of zebra, wildebeest, and occasionally (if the pans fill with water) pelicans and millions of flamingos. A couple of odd outcrops of isolated rock in and around the pans add to their sense of mystery, as well as providing excellent vantage points from which to view the endless expanse of silver, grey and blue.

Makgadikgadi Pans National Park lies on the west of the pans, incorporating the western end of Ntwetwe Pan and a larger adjacent area of grassland and acacia woodland. The flora and fauna there are sufficiently different, especially around the Boteti River, to warrant a separate section, towards the end of this chapter, entitled *Makgadikgadi Pans National Park* (pages 395–403).

BACKGROUND INFORMATION This section concentrates on the main salt pans, Sua and Ntwetwe, and the areas of grassland immediately around them which encompass many scattered smaller pans.

Geography and geology As discussed on page 368, Sua and Ntwetwe lie at the centre of the great prehistoric lake basin that circumscribes the whole region. On top of this is an ancient mantle of windblown Kalahari sands – deposited during the Tertiary period, as the subcontinent was levelled by erosion. Exposed rock is a rarity on the surface of this scrubbed and scoured landscape. However, beneath the sand lie ancient Karoo deposits 300 million years old, comprising basalt larva, sandstone and shales and containing such valuable minerals as gold, silver, copper and nickel.

During the Cretaceous period, 80 million years ago, rifts and buckles in the Earth's crust allowed 'pipes' of molten material – known as kimberlite – to punch their way up from below. Diamonds formed under conditions of massive heat and pressure in these kimberlite pipes. Today they are mined at Orapa, just south of Ntwetwe Pan.

A few isolated outcrops of igneous rock extrude from the surface of the pans, notably Kubu Island and Kukome Island on Sua Pan. Apart from these, and some fossilised barchan (crescent-shaped) dunes to the west, the pans themselves are flat and featureless expanses of dry, sterile salt. However, after good summer rains they are transformed into shimmering lakes, giving a glimpse of what the great super-lake must once have been like. The rainwater that pours down on them is augmented in really wet years by seasonal flows from the east: the Nata, Tutume, Semowane and Mosetse rivers. Also, again only in exceptional years, an overspill from the Okavango makes its way to the west side of Ntwetwe, via the Boteti River.

Flora and fauna highlights The saline conditions of the pans themselves have a strong local influence on their surrounding vegetation. Broadly speaking this becomes richer and more diverse the further you travel from the pan edges, creating a loose concentric series of 'succession' zones, each of which supports a distinctive fauna. These zones effectively chart the gradual demise of the ancient super-lake.

Flora There is no plant life on the surface of the pans, since nothing can tolerate the excessively high concentration of mineral salts, and wind erosion scours the exposed dusty surface, quickly denuding it of any vegetation that tries to take hold. The immediate fringes are carpeted with more-or-less uninterrupted grassland, consisting primarily of *Digitarias* species, which can survive despite the irregular herd movements. Between the pans can also be found patches of prickly salt grass (*Odyssea paucinervis*), a yellowish, spiky species that tolerates high salinity (salt crystals can sometimes be seen on the leaves).

Summer rains bring lush growth to the grasses, which flower in a wind-rippled sea of green. Then you'll also see a scattering of short-lived wild flowers bloom among the grasses, including crimson lilies, acanthus and wild hibiscus (*Hibiscus calyphyllus*). In areas of thicker sand ridges, the runners of the tsama melon (*Citrullus lanatus*) sprawls across the sand, its swollen fruit providing life-sustaining moisture for a myriad of animals, from gerbils to gemsbok. In winter, cropped and shrivelled, the grasses are reduced to a sparse golden mantle over the dusty plains, scattering their seeds to the wind.

Here and there, small hollows in the rolling grassland trap windblown detritus, creating pockets of richer soil that support scattered trees and shrubs. The commonest trees are various acacia species, such as the umbrella thorn (*Acacica tortillis*) which, with their fine leaves for minimising water loss and wicked thorns to deter browsers, are ideally suited to survive this arid environment. The hardy camelthorn (*Acacia erioloba*) thrives in areas of deeper sand, often in an almost lifeless state of disintegration, by tapping deep reserves of ground water with its long roots.

The shepherd's tree (*Boscia albitrunca*) with its distinct white trunk and dense, invaluable shade, is another versatile pioneer of sandy Kalahari soils. The grasslands are studded with stands of fan palms (*Hyphaenea petersiana*), with their hard, cricket-ball sized fruit known as vegetable ivory. Thick groves of this elegant tree occur beyond the northwest shores of Ntwetwe Pan and along the Maun–Nata road.

There are at least eight species of the pumpkin family in Botswana, of which the tsama melon (*Citrullus lanatus*), is the most distinctive and frequently seen. It is found throughout the region, and is particularly common after a good rainy season. Then, even after most of the rest of the vegetation is brown and shrivelled, you'll find tempting round melons beside the sandiest of roads – often apparently on their own.

During the dry season these become important sources of moisture for many animals, especially the gemsbok, and are also used by the local people. To get drinking water from one of these, you first cut off the top, like a boiled egg. The centre can then be cut out and eaten. Then take a stick and mash the rest of the pulp whilst it's in the melon, and this can be eaten. Take care not to eat the pips. These are best roasted and pounded, when they make an edible meal that can be cooked with water. Sometimes you'll come across a bitter fruit, which you should not eat as it may cause poisoning.

Another fairly common species is the gemsbok melon (*Citrullus naudianus*), which has similar sprawling tendrils and an oval fruit, covered in blunt fleshy spines. Unlike the tsama melon, this is a perennial plant with a long underground tuber. Inside the fruit is a jelly-like, translucent green which can be eaten raw (again, discarding the pips usually), though it doesn't taste very good. It's slightly more palatable when roasted beside the fire overnight – but I wouldn't recommend that you throw away your muesli or yoghurt before tasting it!

In the far northeast of Sua Pan, the seasonal Nata River spreads out into a small delta formation which is quite different from the rest of the region. Here there's a band of tall dry riverine forest along the banks of the Nata, and a thickening of the ground cover lining the braided channels. Phragmites reeds thrive in the brackish conditions here, and when this delta is in flood the area can seem quite lush.

Further from the pans, the grassland gives way to a denser bush. To the east, a mixed sand and clay soil supports a greater variety of woodland trees, including tamboti (*Spirostachys africana*), marula (*Scleroclarya birrea*) and monkey thorn (*Acacia galpinii*), while a belt of mopane woodland (*Colophospermum mopane*) also grows in the more heavily clayey soil around Nata and along the eastern boundary of Sua Pan.

The mighty baobabs (*Adansonia digitata*) are perhaps the region's best known and most easily identified trees. These grotesque, drought-resistant giants occur scattered around the pans and on isolated rock outcrops such as Kubu Island, where they have stood as landmarks for millennia. The swollen trunks of many are engraved with the signatures of generations of thirsty travellers. Among the baobabs on Kubu some other more unusual species take advantage of this rocky, island niche, including the African star-chestnut (*Sterculia africana*) and common corkwood (*Commiphora pyracanthoides*).

Fauna Large mammals are scarce around the pans. This is partly because of the hostile nature of the terrain, partly because this is cattle ranching country, where wild animals have been marginalised by the activities of people, and partly because of the destructive effect that veterinary control fences have had on animal migration patterns.

There is no doubt that cattle fences to the south (see page 58) have had a significant impact on the populations of herbivores, and especially the blue wildebeest. Now blue wildebeest are seldom seen around Sua Pan and certainly not in the vast herds that built up during the 1950s, when populations are estimated to have peaked at about 250,000.

Today a permanent scattering of springbok inhabit the surrounding grasslands. These hardy and versatile antelope manage without water for long periods, and withstand the harshest daytime temperatures by orientating their white rumps towards the sun to deflect the worst of its ultraviolet rays.

Other large mammals are thin on the ground, being more abundant towards the west of Ntwetwe and the adjacent grazing grounds of Makgadikgadi Pans National Park (see pages 396–8). However, a scrutiny of the pan surface can reveal the tracks of a surprising range of visitors, including rare (perhaps lost?) wandering elephants or giraffe. Zebra and gemsbok are sometimes seen trekking wearily through the heat haze as they cross the pans between grazing areas, while red hartebeest are frequent visitors to the grasslands, where they can subsist on poorer grasses than many species.

The encrusted tracks of lion or cheetah sometimes appear on the pan surface, particularly towards the west, but the comparative lack of large herbivores means that larger predators are scarce, and a wandering lion is apt to be shot by cattle ranchers. More common are the smaller nocturnal carnivores that can survive the harsh conditions and thrive on smaller pickings.

Brown hyena inhabit the area, and a habituated clan of these elusive predators may be observed at close quarters from Jack's Camp, on the western shores of Ntwetwe, where they have been studied by zoologists. Their catholic diet includes tsama melons and ostrich eggs, as well as spring hares, young springbok, smaller mammals and carrion.

Black-backed jackal, bat-eared fox and African wildcat are widespread, while yellow mongoose is common in sandy areas, where it is an accomplished killer of scorpions. At night, a legion of smaller mammals moves out across the grasslands. Spring hares thrive on damaged grassland and are common around villages, where up to 60 may occur per hectare. Their eyes shine brightly in torchlight, and casting a beam around your campsite will usually reveal at least one foraging nearby.

Aardvarks are found (though seldom seen) in open areas with plenty of termites, scrub hares hide up in acacia thickets, and porcupines occur anywhere. Acacias provide shelter for lesser bushbabies, which feed on their gum during winter when insects are less abundant. This diminutive, nocturnal primate performs astonishing leaps from tree to tree and seldom comes to the ground, progressing on its hind legs in huge hops when it does. Common rodents include typical Kalahari species such as ground squirrel, Damara mole rat, hairy-footed gerbil and black-tailed tree rat.

SPRING HARES

The spring hare is actually a true rodent, and not a hare at all. Weighing about 3kg, this bizarre animal looks like a cross between a rabbit and a kangaroo, with its long ears and thick black-tipped tail. It progresses in ambling hops on long hind legs, with forelegs clasped in front and tail balanced behind.

Spring hares live in burrows by day, in which they doze off upright, having plugged the hole with dirt. By night they graze on grass and crops, and dig for roots, corms and tubers. This animal is a prized delicacy for many nocturnal predators, including owls, honey badgers and caracals. It also figures prominently on the local human menu. It has been estimated that over 2.5 million spring hares are hunted annually in Botswana – hooked out of their holes during the day – providing the protein equivalent of 20,000 cows.

Birdlife The Makgadikgadi Pans are perhaps best known for their birdlife; specifically the great concentration of waterbirds in the Nata River delta after good rains (December–April). In good years, tens of thousands of flamingos, both lesser and greater, arrive to breed, visible from the air as a pink shimmer across the surface of the lake. They are sustained by a rich soup of algae – and brine shrimps, whose eggs lay dormant in the baked clay of the pan surface throughout the dry season.

This gathering represents the largest breeding flamingo population in southern Africa, and can peak at over 100,000 birds. However it is a very unpredictable phenomenon. Even after good rains the flamingos have a life-and-death race against time to breed before the waters dry up, and they may not return again for years. In 1976, over 5,000 young flamingos, still unable to fly, were observed from the air trekking en masse across the barren pans in search of new water when their breeding shallows evaporated. What became of them is not recorded.

The flamingos can best be seen in the Nata Bird Sanctuary (see pages 388–9). Here, when the flood is full, you will also find pelicans (both white and pink-backed), herons and egrets, cormorants and darters, waders (including avocet, blackwinged stilt, blacksmith plover, wood sandpiper and ruff), black-necked grebe, red-knobbed coot, and ducks (including red-billed teal and white-faced duck). Other species more typical of the Okavango floodplains also occur at this time, including fish eagles, saddle-billed storks and, occasionally, wattled cranes. The reedbeds themselves provide a breeding habitat for weavers, bishops and reed warblers.

The open grasslands surrounding the pans are home to many typical Kalahari ground-nesting birds, including ostriches, which are sometimes seen far out on the pans themselves, kori bustards and secretary birds. Some smaller species, including capped wheatear and ant-eating chat, take this a stage further by nesting, like rodents, in underground burrows. All four of southern Africa's sandgrouse (Namaqua, Burchell's, double-banded and yellow-throated) occur around the pans. These delicately plumaged birds are most often seen in the evening, flying rapidly towards a waterhole with rippling calls. Males will waddle in to immerse their absorbent belly feathers and carry water back many kilometres to their young on the nest.

More conspicuous by day is the boldly marked male white-quilled korhaan, who calls with a noisy 'karak karak karak' as he takes off and circles slowly in territorial display, before fluttering to the ground with yellow legs dangling. Like all korhaans, the brooding female relies on her cryptic camouflage to remain hidden. Another common species, the double-banded courser, is superbly adapted to withstand the harsh conditions of the pans. It does not need any drinking water, and can survive extreme overheating while protecting its single egg from the fierce Makgadikgadi sun.

In this largely featureless habitat, any point of elevation can prove a good spot for birds. The baobabs on Kubu island provide roosting and nesting sites for barn owls and rollers (both lilac-breasted and purple). Many tall stands of date palms harbour breeding palm swifts, and the occasional pair of red-necked falcons. Isolated thorn trees support the massive untidy nests of secretary birds or vultures (both white-backed and lappet-faced).

The acacia woodland holds a wide selection of birds typical of this habitat across the region (see *Nxai Pan*, pages 375–6). Red-billed francolin, white-browed robin and violet-eared waxbill forage low down in the thickets, while lilac-breasted roller and long-tailed shrike perch more conspicuously in the taller acacias. Bateleurs and martial eagles patrol the skies, and a host of bulbuls, babblers, hornbills, barbets, sunbirds, flycatchers and others occupy the niches in between.

The area around Nata Lodge is particularly rich in woodland species. In summer, migrant raptors such as steppe buzzard, western red-footed kestrel and yellow-billed kite join resident predators such as greater kestrel, pale chanting goshawk and marsh owl, and after good rains, Montagu's and pallid harriers may be seen quartering the grasslands in drifting, elegant flight.

Other common summer migrants include white stork, red-backed and lesser grey shrikes and European and carmine bee-eaters, while seed eaters such as red-billed quelea and black-eared finchlark arrive to breed in large numbers, taking advantage of the seasonally abundant grass seeds.

GETTING AROUND With a large number of tracks in the area, I have not even tried to describe them all in detail here. However, if you're driving around by yourself, rather than with a local guide who knows the area well, then navigation issues should preoccupy you! Outside the national park, visiting the pans is all about exploring for yourself. If you want set routes to follow, perhaps it's not for you.

If you're ready for a small expedition, then take note of the highlights and landmarks mentioned here, with GPS co-ordinates, and use the maps (mentioned on page 372) to keep some realistic idea of where you are. That said, because of the size of the pans and their very remote situation, you must follow some basic safety rules:

- Take at least one reliable GPS with you – and many more batteries than you think you'll need.
- Carry much more fuel than you expect to use.
- Carry enough water and food for your whole time in the pans area, plus a few days' safety margin.
- Travel with a minimum of two fully equipped 4x4s, and preferably also a satellite phone.
- Arrange a rendezvous for when you leave the pans, and someone to raise the alarm if you don't arrive. Leave a rough route plan with them.

It's difficult for me to emphasise enough just how dangerous the pans can be. There are periodic deaths of people who visit the area without the proper back-up and preparation, and then get into difficulties. It's different from many areas in Botswana because:

- The sun is merciless on the pan's surface; there's absolutely no shade.
- If you break through the crust of the pans to the wet silt beneath, then getting out is very difficult, even with a second vehicle. Remember: there will be no wood around, no branches to put under the wheels.
- There are so many different tracks on the pans (each diverging vehicle makes a new one), that often there simply isn't a 'right' track which most vehicles take. Thus, it may be weeks or months before someone takes the same route that you do, and passes you.

NATA Nata itself is a very small place at the junction of the tar road to Maun, Kasane and Francistown. For many years it was little more than a filling stop for most people, where the vital garage relied on hand-cranked petrol pumps, and the well-stocked Sua Pan Bottle Store was always busy.

Little has changed over time, although the place feels a lot more modern than it used to – and the nearby Nata Sanctuary has made this pan a bigger attraction than it was. It is still usually sensible to refuel when you pass through Nata.

Where to stay
Most visitors who are deliberately visiting this area stop at Nata Lodge.

Nata Lodge (20 chalets, 10 Meru tents, camping) ℡ 6211 210/260; f 6211 265; e natalodge@ inet.co.bw; www.natalodge.com. Nata Lodge lies about 10km south of Nata, and is well signposted just off the main Francistown road. It stands in a patch of sparse woodland with real fan palms and marula trees. It has recently been taken over by Chobe Safari Lodge (see pages 180–1).

There are twin beds in both thatched chalets and Meru-style tents, the latter tucked into the bush and raised up on a low platform; there are also family chalets. All have en-suite bathrooms with a shower, toilet and washbasin. Nearby is a very large, dusty camping area with good clean ablution facilities. On Saturdays there's a braai dinner (US$24); otherwise evening meals are à la carte, while other meals are buffet style, with light lunches available from a snack menu. The pool is right in front of the main lounge/dining area, with a curio shop close by. Mike Unwin reports that on his last visit he saw a family of bushbabies leaping from tree to tree, across the swimming pool.

On an ad hoc basis, the lodge organises early-morning and sunset trips into the Nata Sanctuary and on to the pans, costing US$26 pp for a 3hr trip (min 4 people). For something a bit different, quad bikes may be taken out with a qualified guide. *Chalet US$109, family chalet US$124, tents US$94; camping U$10/7 adult/child per night. Open all year.*

SUA PAN
Sua Pan is the eastern of the two twin pans, and extends roughly southwards from the town of Nata in its northeast corner. On its southern shore is the village of Mosu; to its north lies the Maun–Nata road; to its west it is divided from Ntwetwe Pan by a thin strip of grassland. Sua (sometimes spelt 'Sowa') is the Tswana word for salt, and this mineral residue from the vanished super-lake dominates the geology and ecology of the pan.

Once salt was laboriously collected from the pan surface by the San and carried away on donkeys. Today it is mined by the Sua Pan Soda Ash Company, a joint South African–Botswanan government enterprise, which supplies sodium carbonate on an industrial scale for use in the manufacture of paper, glass and steel. Their mine is situated along the Sua Spit, a tongue of grassland that extends halfway across the pan from its eastern shore.

The Nata River feeds Sua Pan from the northeast (bringing the rains from Zimbabwe) and, in good years, it floods from December to April with shallow, warm water. Where the fresh water of the river meets the saline pan, a brackish delta of silted reedbeds has formed. In summer, this corner of the pan attracts great concentrations of breeding waterbirds, notably flamingos (see *Fauna* below). This delta – an area of 230km² – is now protected within the Nata Sanctuary. The flamingos can usually be viewed from the bird hide on the eastern shore.

Evidence of the former lake exists in the form of fossil pebble beaches along the shores of Kubu Island and other granite outcrops around the pan, and fossil diatoms and molluscs on the pan surfaces. These reveal that there was a prolonged wet period about 14,000–17,000 years ago and, more recently, a flood only 1,500 years ago. Near the village of Mosu in the south, an escarpment rises some 40m above the edge of the pan, showing the erosive force of the great lake that once

GPS REFERENCES FOR SUA PAN MAP

KUBU-I	20°53.737'S, 25°49.421'E	TSHWAG	20°48.094'S, 25°45.608'E
KUKOME	20°55.001'S, 26°12.203'E	TSIVET	20°58.620'S, 25°37.178'E
KWADIB	20°54.907'S, 26°16.571'E	TURNM1	21°19.468'S, 25°33.742'E
MMATSH	21°08.590'S, 25°39.214'E	TURNM2	20°55.990'S, 25°40.015'E
THABAT	20°42.606'S, 25°47.476'E		

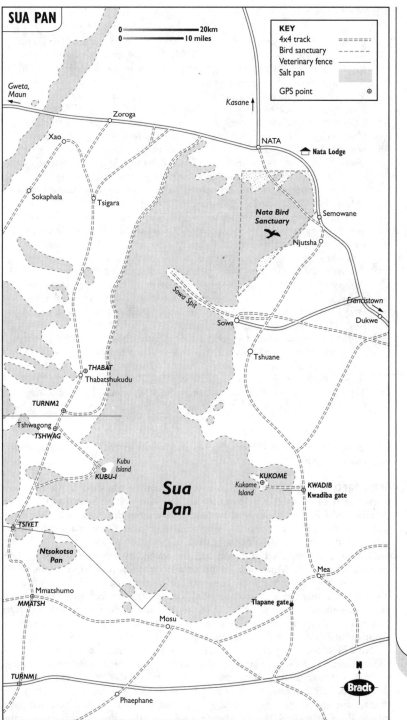

SUA PAN

0 _____ 20km
0 _____ 10 miles

KEY

4x4 track	=======
Bird sanctuary	- - - - -
Veterinary fence	————
Salt pan	▨
GPS point	⊕

Gweta,
Maun

Kasane ↑

Zoroga

NATA

⌂ **Nata Lodge**

Xao

Sokaphala

Tsigara

*Nata Bird
Sanctuary*

Semowane

Njutsha

Francistown

Sowa Spit

Sowa

Dukwe

Tshuane

THABAT
Thabatshukudu

TURNM2

Tshwagong
TSHWAG

*Kubu
Island*
KUBU-I

KUKOME

*Sua
Pan*

*Kukome
Island*

KWADIB
Kwadiba gate

TSIVET

*Ntsokotsa
Pan*

Mea

Mmatshumo
MMATSH

Tlapane gate

Mosu

TURNM1

Phaephane

N

Bradt

15

FLAMINGOS

Of the world's half-dozen or so species of flamingo, two are found within southern Africa: the greater (*Phoenicopterus ruber*) and the lesser (*Phoenicopterus minor*). Both species have wide distributions, from southern Africa north into east Africa and the Red Sea, and are highly nomadic in their habits.

Flamingos are usually found wading in large areas of shallow saline water where they filter feed by holding their specially adapted beaks upside down in the water. The lesser flamingo will walk or swim whilst swinging its head from side to side, mainly taking blue-green algae from the surface of the water. The larger greater flamingo will hold its head submerged while filtering out small organisms (detritus and algae), even stirring the mud with its feet to help the process. Both species are very gregarious and flocks can have millions of birds, though a few hundred is more common.

Only occasionally do flamingos breed in southern Africa, choosing the Makgadikgadi Pans, Namibia's Etosha Pan or even Lake Ngami. When the conditions are right (usually March to June, following the rains) both species build low mud cones in the water and lay one (or rarely two) eggs in a small hollow on the top. These are then incubated by both parents for about a month, until they hatch. After a further week the young birds flock together and start to forage with their parents. Some ten weeks later the young can fly and fend for themselves.

During this time the young are very susceptible to the shallow water in the pans drying out. In 1969, a rescue operation was mounted in Namibia when the main Etosha Pan dried out, necessitating the moving of thousands of chicks to nearby Fisher's Pan, which was still covered in water.

The best way to tell the two species apart is by their beaks: that of the greater flamingo is almost white with a black tip, while the lesser flamingo has a uniformly dark beak. If you are further away then the body of the greater will appear white, while that of the lesser looks smaller and more pink. The best place to see them in Botswana is certainly Sua Pan – although even there they will only appear if the rains have filled some of the pan.

washed against these cliffs. Here there is also one of several subterranean springs that emerge around the fringes of the pans.

Nata Sanctuary A conservation area was originally established in the northeast corner of Sua Pan with the help of the Kalahari Conservation Society in the 1980s, to protect the important seasonal wetland areas around the Nata Delta. However, although the villagers at Nata were consulted about the plans, the wider community in the area didn't benefit from it.

This area encompassed cattle-grazing land owned by four communities: Nata, Sepako, Maposa and Mmaxotae. In the early 1990s it was realised that without the support of these communities, conservation in the area couldn't be effective. Eventually, as part of a ground-breaking community project, the communities moved about 3,000 head of cattle out of the area, and fencing began. In 1993 Nata Sanctuary was opened to the public, and in the same year it won the prestigious Tourism for Tomorrow award for the southern hemisphere.

Now Nata Sanctuary conserves an ecologically sensitive and important natural environment, and also effectively returns money to the communities for doing so.

Nata Sanctuary makes a very easy place to visit for a day or two, either based at Nata Lodge or camping in the sanctuary itself. Aside from this, the pan is a remarkable area to explore, with the occasional spot like Kubu Island that has a magic all of its own. That said, there's a lot more than just Nata Sanctuary and

Kubu here – but it does need time to explore it. Read my warning under *Getting around*, on page 385; then get a copy of Mike Main's book (see *Appendix 3, Further Information*), a few good maps, and enjoy it!

There's not much traffic around, and the pans are huge and desolate, so it's best to travel in a two-vehicle party and tell someone reliable where you plan to go, and when you'll be back. This is especially important during the first part of the year when the pan is wet and there's a significant risk of getting a vehicle badly stuck in the mud.

Flora and fauna See above for notes on the general flora and fauna of the pan, but note that a number of mammals have been enclosed (or re-introduced) within the fenced boundaries of this reserve, including gemsbok, springbok, hartebeest, kudu, eland, zebra, reedbuck, jackal, fox, monkey, steenbok, squirrel and spring hare.

Getting there and away The entrance to Nata Sanctuary (*open daily 07.00–19.00, all year*) is about 17km south of Nata, next to the main road to Francistown. There's a small reception here where you must pay sanctuary entry fees of P20 per person per day, plus P10 per vehicle.

Where to stay If you're not staying at the nearby Nata Lodge then there are some simple bush campsites in the sanctuary, complete with basic long-drop toilets and cold showers. Camping here costs P25 pp per night, payable at the sanctuary reception.

Kubu Island In the southwest of Sua Pan lies an isolated granite outcrop some 10m high and 1km long, known as Kubu Island. It forms the shape of a crescent, and its slopes are terraced with fossil beaches of wave-rounded pebbles, providing startling evidence of the prehistoric lake's former water levels. Crowned with an array of ancient, gnarled baobabs and surrounded on three sides by a vast grey emptiness, Kubu has a unique atmospheric beauty.

At night, with the wind moaning through the baobabs, it is easy to imagine the waves of a great inland sea lapping at its pebble beaches. Many of the island's rocks are white, covered in ancient, fossilised guano from the waterbirds that used to perch here when it was surrounded by the lake. The moonlight reflecting off the pan's white surface gives the place an almost supernatural atmosphere, which is heightened by the mystery of Kubu's former inhabitants. The shoreline is littered with Stone Age tools and arrowheads, while concentric dry stone walls on the islands survive from a much more recent village, perhaps around AD1400–1600, and outside this are a number of stone cairns.

Archaeologists have linked these walls and cairns with the dynasty of Great Zimbabwe, and think that they were probably at the most southwestern tip of that state. In *The Riddle of the Stone Walls* (see *Appendix 3, Further Information*) Alec Campbell suggests that they could have been remote 'circumcision camps' to which the boys of the tribe were taken for circumcision and ceremonies leading to adulthood. It is suggested that perhaps ceremonies took place within the walls, and every class that 'graduated' then built a separate cairn.

Campbell also noted that the people of the nearest village, Tshwagong, hold Kubu and the nearby Thithaba Islands as sacred, and men over 16 years of age visit the islands to make contact with God, singing a particular song for rain and leaving offerings on the ground.

Note that Kubu is a national monument, and there are plans to station a warden here to ensure that visitors don't damage anything.

Getting there and away From the north there are endless possible routes to Kubu Island (⊕ KUBU-I 20°53.737'S, 25°49.421'E), and you can expect it to take about

3–4 hours from the main Maun–Nata road. Easiest is probably to take one of the many tracks that leave the main road between about 30km and 15km west of Nata. Follow your nose (or, more practically, your GPS) towards Thabatshukudu Village (⊕ THABAT 20°42.606'S, 25°47.476'E), which is about 70–75km south, depending on the track that you take.

From there it's about 10km southwest to the Tswagong Veterinary Gate, through which any north–south traffic between Sua and Ntwetwe pans passes – so tracks will lead you there. This is about 3km north of the small village of Tshwagong (⊕ TSHWAG 20°48.094'S, 25°45.608'E), from where it's about 14km in a straight line southeast to Kubu Island. (There are several tracks here, so just head southeast and follow your GPS.)

Note that the track that leaves Gweta in a south then southeasterly direction, ending at the Tswagong Veterinary Gate, passes over several long stretches of Ntwetwe Pan, and so is dangerously muddy during the earlier months of the year.

From the south, it's best to start by heading for the village of Mmatshumo (⊕ MMATSH 21°08.590'S, 25°39.214'E). You'll find a number of tracks from the Orapa–Francistown road which will lead you here; the shortest leaves the main road around ⊕ TURNM1 21°19.468'S, 25°33.742'E. From there it's about 23km to Mmatshumo. Heading north from there, there's a good view of the pan to your right after about 5km, before the track bends west and back north to cross the small Tsitane Pan, crossing the veterinary fence at ⊕ TSIVET 20°58.620'S, 25°37.178'E. Then a straight track heading north-northeast brings you to Tshwagong (⊕ TSHWAG 20°48.094'S, 25°45.608'E) after about 20km.

Note that during the dry season you can take a short cut about 7km north of the vet fence, at around ⊕ TURNM2 20°55.990'S, 25°40.015'E, which heads east-northeast across the pan to Kubu; but don't try this when the pans are wet!

Sua's landmarks
Note that you should never attempt to drive across the pan from the east side to the west, or vice versa, even during the dry season.

Sowa Pan Mine (Soda-ash factory) This modern industrial complex seems strangely out of place here, especially as it is easily reached, 40km along a tarred road. The turn-off is about 48km south of Nata on the road to Francistown.

South Islands About 7km south of Kubu, far out on the pan, are two other small islands. They too have Baobab trees and the larger one, on the east, has a series of rock cairns along its spine.

Kukome Island On the eastern shore of Sua Pan, roughly opposite Kubu, Kukome (also spelt 'Kukonje') Island (⊕ KUKOME 20°55.001'S, 26°12.203'E) has similar fossil beaches and ancient remains. To reach here, first head for the Kwadiba Veterinary Gate (⊕ KWADIB 20°54.907'S, 26°16.571'E) on the east side of Sua Pan, from where a track leads west for about 7km to Kukome Island. (Beware: the GPS point given for the Kwadiba Gate on older editions of the Shell map doesn't seem correct to me.)

Mmatshumo Village Mmatshumo (⊕ MMATSH 21°08.590'S, 25°39.214'E) is a small village on the south side of the pans, between Sua and Ntwetwe pans, as well as an important waypoint when you're navigating yourself around.

Thabatshukudu Village Thabatshukudu (⊕ THABAT 20°42.606'S, 25°47.476'E) is another village – notable for the landmark of its colourfully painted general dealer's store – and another useful waypoint when navigating yourself around.

NTWETWE PAN Ntwetwe Pan is the western twin of Sua, and is of a similar size and general topography, though aligned more east–west. It lies due south of the Nata–Maun road, between Gweta in the north and Orapa and Mopipi in the south. One finger extends to the north of the road, while to the southwest the pan breaks up into several smaller pans, including Lake Xau, just south of Mopipi. The old north–south trading route between Gweta and Mopipi crosses the centre of the pan, and the two famous isolated baobabs (Green's Baobab and Chapman's Baobab) that marked this route for early European explorers – including Livingstone, who left his initials here – still serve as landmarks for today's travellers.

Ntwetwe lacks the famous granite outcrops of Sua; its main points of elevation are fossilised barchan dunes that once crept across the surface of the lake during a dry period and were left stranded when waters rose again. Gabasadi Island is the largest of these. The profiles of the dune islands show steps and lines of vegetation which, like Sua Pan's pebble beaches, are evidence of former higher lake levels.

Stone Age sites are scattered among the smaller pans that form the western shore of Ntwetwe. At Gutsha Pan, near Chapman's Baobab, there is a perennial spring. Here the San once dug pit traps lined with poisoned stakes to trap the plentiful game that came to drink. The remains of these traps, and the calcrete blinds behind which the hunters hid, are still visible today.

What to see and do Like Sua Pan, Ntwetwe is an area for experienced Africa hands to explore in their own vehicles – though bear in mind my comments on safety under *Getting around* on page 385.

Alternatively, and much safer, there are three camps situated on the northwest side of the pan. All are expensive, even by Botswana's standards. But if you can afford their high prices, then fly in from Maun for three or four days and explore the pans and surrounding area with expert guides: on foot, by 4x4 or on quad bikes.

Where to stay Though Jack's Camp (and its sister camp, San Camp) and Makgadikgadi Camp are the only camps on the pans themselves, you could also visit this area on an excursion with Planet Baobab (see pages 401–2) near Gweta. This is a cheaper option, aimed at backpackers and people driving on the Nata–Maun road.

Makgadikgadi Camp is marketed by, and easiest to book through, Okavango Tours and Safaris in Maun (see page 167). Jack's Camp, its smaller satellite, San Camp, the new Camp Kalahari and Planet Baobab can be contacted through Uncharted Africa Safari Co (*Francistown;* ☎ *2412 277;* f *2413 458;* e *reservations@ unchartedafrica.com; www.unchartedafrica.com*).

Note that Jack's and San camps are usually reached by light aircraft from Maun; a private airstrip (⊕ SANAIR 20°29.504'S, 25°11.054'E) is ten minutes' drive from camp.

Jack's Camp (10 tents). Jack's Camp was the original camp on the pans. When all the other safari operators in Botswana focused on game and the Delta, Jack's dared to offer something totally different – and succeeded in style.

A bushcamp was originally started in this area in the 1960s, by the late Jack Bousfield. After his tragic death in an aircraft accident, his son, Ralph Bousfield, built a camp for visitors here which first opened in 1993. It's set in sparse forest of real fan palms, in grasslands on the edge of Ntwetwe Pan,

overlooking Makgadikgadi Pans National Park.

Jack's is furnished in a 'traditional east African 40s safari style'. This means it's very comfortable, with first-class attention to detail, but it's not a super-luxurious lodge by any means. Jack's green tents are classic Meru-style, built on decks and set in a palm grove. Inside, 7 of the tents have twin beds with individual canopies, while the other 3 have 4-poster dbl beds, all with down pillows and duvets, high-quality linens and even Persian rugs. Each tent has an en-suite bathroom with indoor and

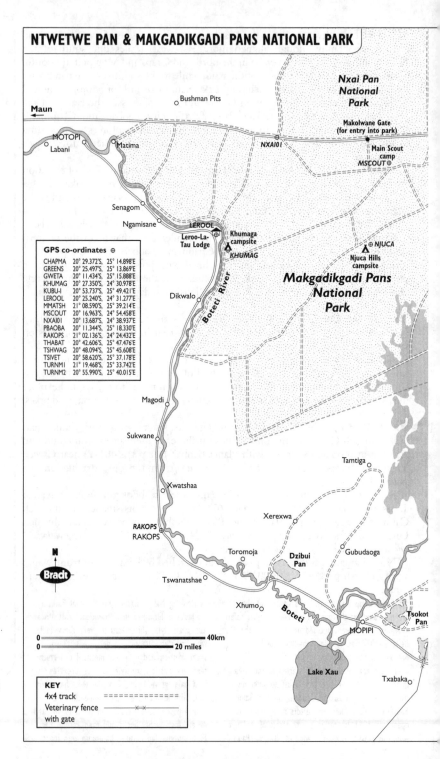

NTWETWE PAN & MAKGADIKGADI PANS NATIONAL PARK

Nxai Pan National Park

Maun →

Bushman Pits

Makolwane Gate (for entry into park)

MOTOPI
Labani
Matima

NXAI01

Main Scout camp
MSCOUT ⊕

Senagom

Ngamisane

LEROOL
Leroo-La-Tau Lodge

Khumaga campsite

⊕ *NJUCA*
Njuca Hills campsite

KHUMAG

GPS co-ordinates ⊕

CHAPMA	20° 29.372'S,	25° 14.898'E
GREENS	20° 25.497'S,	25° 13.869'E
GWETA	20° 11.434'S,	25° 15.888'E
KHUMAG	20° 27.350'S,	24° 30.978'E
KUBU-I	20° 53.737'S,	25° 49.421'E
LEROOL	20° 25.240'S,	24° 31.277'E
MMATSH	21° 08.590'S,	25° 39.214'E
MSCOUT	20° 16.963'S,	24° 54.458'E
NXAI01	20° 13.687'S,	24° 38.937'E
PBAOBA	20° 11.344'S,	25° 18.330'E
RAKOPS	21° 02.136'S,	24° 24.432'E
THABAT	20° 42.606'S,	25° 47.476'E
TSHWAG	20° 48.094'S,	25° 45.608'E
TSIVET	20° 58.620'S,	25° 37.178'E
TURNM1	21° 19.468'S,	25° 33.742'E
TURNM2	20° 55.990'S,	25° 40.015'E

Makgadikgadi Pans National Park

Dikwalo

Boteti River

Magodi

Sukwane

Tamtiga

Xwatshaa

Xerexwa

N
Bradt

RAKOPS
RAKOPS

Toromoja

Dzibui Pan

Gubudaoga

Tswanatshae

Xhumo

Boteti

Tsokot Pan

MOPIPI

0 ————————— 40km
0 ————————— 20 miles

Lake Xau

Txabaka

KEY

4x4 track ============

Veterinary fence ─×─×─
with gate

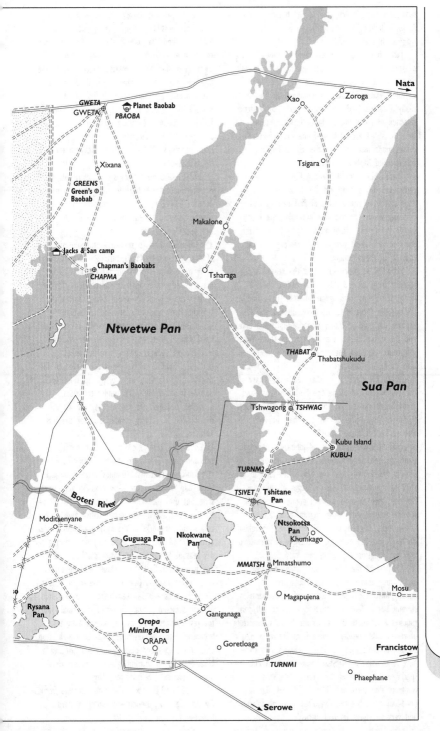

outdoor shower, flushing toilets and hot/cold water. At night, lighting is by paraffin lamp – much more magical than electricity!

Jack's has a central 'mess tent' – really a series of grand canvas pavilions. The interior is lined with amber printed cotton, whilst the green of the outside blends with the surrounding bush. This is really a canvas field museum, sheltering an eclectic selection of items (mostly local) including stone tools, fossils of extinct mega-fauna (like giant zebra), prints, maps, historical etchings, and a fair size collection of Bushman beadwork.

There's also a drinks tent, a library tent, a centralised dining tent and a separate tea tent, its floor scattered with a mass of Persian rugs and cushions, where tea and delicious cakes are usually served before the afternoon activities. Close to the tea tent is a small plunge pool where guests can cool off in the afternoon.

Activities at Jack's vary with the season. When it's dry, from around May to December, there's likely to be very little game around. That's fine, as it's not the focus of a trip here. Instead you'll explore the pans in 4x4s, on individual quad bikes and on foot, often with a San tracker. These trips will concentrate on the area's smaller wildlife, and also its history and archaeology – often including a visit to the baobabs in the area, and a part of the pan where old Stone Age flint axe-heads and arrow-heads can be just picked up off the surface. (Quite rightly, my guide insisted that they were also to be left there by us!)

When it's wet, from around January to April, the pans can become quagmires. It's often impossible to use the quad bikes, and the 4x4 drives tend to stick to the grasslands on the edges of the pans. However, then there is a much greater density of wildlife around, with many migrant birds and, if you're lucky, large herds of plains game. Throughout the year you can have the fascinating experience of walking alongside a gang of meerkats.

Amongst all the camps that I know in Africa, Jack's Camp stands out for its unique style of guiding. Anyone can find you a herd of elephants in Moremi, but to find fascination in a barren salt pan requires a lot more skill. Jack's usually uses a mixture of very capable resident guides from Botswana, plus a handful of zoology and biology graduates who come here to combine a few years' guiding with a PhD specialising on some of the local wildlife. Wits comment that these are often British, Oxbridge and good-looking – but this can often mean an informed and very intelligent level of discussion.

As the camp is outside the national park, night drives are possible – when there's often more wildlife around than during the day. Recently, thanks to the lion research that's been done from here, sightings of lion have increased hugely. Also in the last few years they've had a zoologist, Glyn Maud, based here, researching brown hyenas. He has habituated one clan to vehicles, which has enabled Jack's to virtually guarantee sightings of these very shy creatures to interested visitors. Though they occur widely, you'd be very, very lucky to see brown hyena elsewhere!

US$750/1,000 pp sharing/sgl, inc all meals, drinks, activities, laundry & park fees. Flights to/from Maun US$140 pp each way; road transfers from Gweta US$150 pp each way. MasterCard and Visa acepted. Open all year.

🏠 **Camp Kalahari** (6 rooms) At the opposite end of the spectrum to Jack's, this new camp under the same ownership is primarily for the group-trip market, but is also open to independent travellers. Visitors can expect 3m x 3m dome tents with stretcher beds and rolls of bedding, outside washbasins and warm water brought to your tent. Each pair of tents has a large shower enclosure with bucket showers, and a separate toilet enclosure. Good 3-course meals are served in the traditional mess tent, with its roll-up sides, while outside is a campfire area under the stars. Activities, however, are run as they are at Jack's, making this a winning combination for the less well heeled.

US$385 pp sharing, inc meals, activities and transfers from Gweta; exc drinks. Open all year.

🏠 **San Camp** (6 tents). 10 mins' drive from Jack's Camp, San is run by the same team in very similar style, but uses pale khaki rather than green Meru-style tents. Again, it's rustic but stylish and comfortable. It works in the same way with similar activities and approach, but is only open during the dry season. 2 tent have 4-poster dbl beds and the rest have twins. Each has en-suite flushing toilets with bucket showers (water is delivered on request).

Both Jack's and San Camp are first-rate camps offering something totally different to virtually all of the rest of Botswana's camps, though both are expensive. Either makes a great 3- or 4-night stop, best at the very end of a fly-in trip to Botswana. *US$550/750 pp sharing/sgl, inc all meals, drinks, activities, laundry & park fees. Flights to/from Maun US$140 pp each way; road transfers from Gweta US$150 pp each way. No credit cards. Open end of Apr–end of Oct.*

🏠 **Makgadikgadi Camp** (5 tents). Started in 1997, Makgadikgadi Camp stands amongst real fan palms and acacias near the edge of Ntwetwe Pan, south of Gweta. It is run by Reiner Sumerauer, the owner of Gweta Restcamp (see page 401), and marketed by Okavango Tours and Safaris in Maun (see page 167).

The tents have twin beds and en-suite shower, toilet and washbasins. The camp has a main dining area under a thatched roof, with a plunge pool nearby. Activities include short walks and trips across the pans with 4x4s and quad bikes, and bushcamps are possible.

From US$352pp sharing low season to US$418 high season, inc all meals, drinks, laundry quad biking and 4x4 game viewing. US$165 sgl supplement. Open Mar–Nov, depending on rains.

Ntwetwe's landmarks Ntwetwe Pan doesn't have anything quite so spectacular as Kubu Island, though it does have a few marvellous old baobabs and an island of its own.

Chapman's Baobab This famous landmark (⊕ CHAPMA 20°29.372'S, 25°14.898'E) was noted by Chapman when he passed with Thomas Baines in 1861. It's a big tree and visible from some distance away. Note that there are endless tracks to the west of here, many made by nearby private safari camps, and so navigation can be especially difficult, rendering a GPS essential.

Green's Baobab Less well known than Chapman's, this tree (⊕ GREENS 20°25.497'S, 25°13.869'E) is close to the only permanent spring in the area, Gutsha Pan, and still bears the inscription 'Green's Expedition 1858–1859' carved into its bark.

Gabasadi Island In the middle of Ntwetwe, to the west of the usual north–south route across the pans, Gabasadi Island is a low mound protruding from the surface of the pan. It's actually a fossilised, crescent-shaped barchan dune, which you'll realise if you climb it.

MAKGADIKGADI PANS NATIONAL PARK

Makgadikgadi Pans National Park covers about 3,900km² in a roughly square-shaped block to the west of the pans. It extends from the western edge of Ntwetwe Pan – one corner of which is incorporated within the park, fragmented into a myriad of smaller pans – westwards to the Boteti River, which marks the park's western boundary. To the north it meets the southern boundary of Nxai Pan National Park, from which it is separated only by the main Maun–Nata road.

GEOGRAPHY AND GEOLOGY About one-fifth of the reserve consists of salt pan. The rest is rolling grasslands on Kalahari sands, rising here and there into fossilised dunes and low hills of thicker sand which mark prehistoric limits of the great Makgadikgadi super-lake. The great breadth of the sandy Boteti watercourse, and the riverine woodland that lines its steep banks, are evidence of a major river that once carved a channel across central Botswana, carrying the waters of the Okavango into the Makgadikgadi basin.

Today the Boteti only flows at all after good rains, when its thin trickle is dwarfed by the channel that contains it. It hasn't properly flooded for at least ten years. As the dry season advances, this stream dwindles into a chain of rapidly shrinking pools, a few of which retain permanent water throughout the year.

FLORA AND FAUNA HIGHLIGHTS Makgadikgadi Pans National Park really contains a spectrum of environments, flora and fauna. Its east side, especially the southeast, is dominated by salt pans and grasslands – very much the same as the rest of Sua and Ntwetwe further east. Its western border, the Boteti River, is lined by thick riverine forest; here the wildlife has more in common with that found beside the Chobe or the Linyanti, or in the Okavango Delta. Between these two very different environments lies the body of the park.

Flora The vegetation on the east side of the park is very similar pattern to that of the Makgadikgadi Pans (see pages 381–2). Its diversity increases westwards as the saline influence of the pan is left behind; from the bare surface of the pan itself, through rolling grassland and the vegetated dunes of Njuca Hills, into thicker acacia scrub, and eventually to the dense riverine woodland along the banks of the Boteti River. Along the eastern border there are areas of palm-tree woodland, where groves of vegetable ivory palms (*Hyphaene petersiana*) grow among the tracts of tall grassland.

On raised ground between the salt pans, yellowish patches of prickly salt grass (*Odyssea paucinervis*) flourish, contrasting with clumps of the dark succulent *Chenopodiacea* species. Along the pan edges you may also find a cactus-like succulent, *Hoodia lugardii*, which periodically produces striking maroon flowers. The open grasslands are studded with islands of trees and denser vegetation, with such species as the trumpet thorn (*Catophractas alexandri*) and western rhigozum (*Rhigozum brevispinosum*) flowering among the acacia scrub.

Beside the deep sand of the Boteti River, camelthorns (*Acacia erioloba*), blackthorns (*Acacia mellifera*) and silver clusterleaf (*Termilalia sericea*) dominate the riverine forest, interspersed with a few other riverine giants such as sycamore figs (*Ficus sycomorus*) and sausage trees (*Kigelia africana*). Meanwhile for most of the year the 'riverbed' itself consists of a sandy channel carpeted in grasses and punctuated by occasional muddy pools of water.

Fauna In the wet season, Makgadikgadi Pans National Park boasts good concentrations of grazers that rival those of Nxai Pan to the north, and an aerial view shows the area to be latticed with a dense network of game trails. From about June onwards, herds of Burchell's zebra and blue wildebeest start a westward movement towards the lush grazing of the Boteti region, accompanied by smaller numbers of gemsbok, eland and red hartebeest. (The latter tend to come slightly later, in years when the rains have been exceptionally good.) These herds gradually congregate along the waterfront until, by November, this area becomes jam-packed with game.

In the ecozone between grassland and woodland, browsers such as kudu, bushbuck and grey duiker find a permanent home, while troops of baboons and vervet monkeys forage beneath the trees, and small numbers of giraffe and elephant often occur. This area supports a small waterbuck population, resident pairs of bushbuck (locals say the same subspecies/race as the Chobe bushbuck) and there are even a few hippo who have taken up unlikely residence in the permanent pools.

In peak season, from September to November, the area around the Boteti can offer truly outstanding wildlife watching, and the air is filled with the hiccuping calls of the milling zebra herds. However, with the arrival of the rains in December–January, the herds disperse. Some head north towards Nxai Pan, others gather in the grazing grounds of the southeast, where their migration route beyond the park to the Central Kalahari is blocked by a veterinary cordon fence. At this time, zebra and gemsbok may often be seen out on the pans in search of the mineral salts that are lacking on the Kalahari grasslands.

A healthy population of large predators, protected in the park from persecution by ranchers, includes lion, cheetah, leopard, spotted and brown hyena. Lion can be

The brown hyena (*Hyaena brunnea*) is one of the three hyena species in southern Africa, the other two being a successful scavenger and hunter, the spotted hyena, and the insectivorous aardwolf. Brown hyena are classed as 'near threatened', with a total population of under 10,000 – of which the Makgadikgadi National Park has about 50 adults.

The brown hyena has evolved to life in desert systems throughout southern Africa, where it occurs at low densities. This shy, nocturnal animal is a solitary forager that can survive independently of permanent surface water. Brown hyenas will eat virtually anything, apart from grass or herbage – and here their diet ranges from melons and scorpions to ostrich eggs or old carcasses.

As part of his PhD from Pretoria University, Glyn Maude has been running a project researching these animals for three years, based near Jack's Camp. He has habituated a clan to the presence of his vehicle, and observed that individuals will often cover over 65km in a night when foraging in the Makgadikgadi. Here lion kills are an important source of food. Over the wet season, these are often zebra and wildebeest, whilst over the dry season, when food is more scarce, they can frequently be cattle and other livestock.

Brown hyenas are not truly solitary animals; they live in clans of between two and ten members. In the Makgadikgadi, Glyn has measured clans' territories as covering 300–750km². However, clan members are rarely seen together as they forage alone, only interacting with other clan members either by a chance meeting while foraging, or at a communal den site. Some brown hyenas are not part of a clan but are nomadic, the males in particular. Clan members will often be tolerant of an intruder of the opposite sex, but will chase away same-sex intruders.

Brown hyenas are usually almost silent: their vocalisations are minimal. Long-distance communication is by a unique double scent mark deposited on grass stalks. These marks can be made as often as every 150m of foraging, and as well as communicating with other clan members, the scent mark is also a marker for the clan's territory. Defecations are also used as territorial markers and can be found in concentrations in 'latrine sites' which are often located along territorial boundaries. The presence of brown hyenas is more often indicated by their spoor or scent marks, as sightings of the animal in the wild are very uncommon.

common during peak migration, with prides knocking down more zebra than they can consume and (be warned) sometimes wandering inquisitively through the campsites. Cheetah are less common, but may turn up anywhere where there are springbok, while leopard are permanent residents of the denser bush along the Boteti. Spotted hyena, like lion, follow the dry season herds, while brown hyenas find life more productive (and less competitive) along the park's eastern side.

In the east of the park the two campsites at Njuca Hills offer a panoramic base from which to explore the wildlife of the pans and grasslands. Herds of springbok, well adapted to survive the arid and exposed conditions, are common around the pans, while steenbok – usually found in pairs – are also widespread. Nocturnal predators of the pan fringes include brown hyena, aardwolf, bat-eared fox and striped polecat, while black-backed jackal, African wildcat, honey badger and small spotted genet can occur anywhere in the park. Other small mammals include porcupine, aardvark, spring hare and scrub hare as well as a host of smaller rodents and insectivores (see the general section on pans fauna, pages 370–2).

In sandy areas, ground squirrels (here at the northern limit of their Kalahari range) forage by day in small colonies, holding up their tails as parasols against the fierce sun and dashing for their burrows at any hint of danger. These sociable rodents associate amicably with yellow mongooses, who share their burrow systems and help keep a lookout for predators.

Reptiles Perhaps the most bizarre report from this park is of some of the Boteti's larger crocodiles which, when the river drops drastically during the dry season, retreat into holes in the riverbank that they have dug for themselves. One such lair that I saw was a good 4–5m above the level of water even in May, and would have been completely high and dry by October.

Birdlife The birdlife of Makgadikgadi Pans National Park is largely the same as that elsewhere in the greater Makgadikgadi region (see pages 384–5), with a grading of species according to habitat, and a large summer influx of migrants.

The denser woodland along the Boteti also harbours more cover-loving species such as Myer's parrot, woodland kingfisher, Burchell's coucal and Heuglin's robin. Many raptors cruise the skies over the park, with gabar goshawks hunting the thickets, secretary birds stalking the savannah, and vultures following the game herds in search of carcasses. In summer, storks, bee-eaters, kites, shrikes and other migrants move in and fan out across the grasslands.

WHERE TO STAY Meno A Kwena is the newest of the lodges in this area. The more established Leroo-La-Tau and Xwaraga, both under the auspices of African Secrets, are on the western bank of the Boteti, opposite the park. Khumaga and Njuca Hills campsites are run by the national parks, and should be booked in advance in Maun (see page 138).

Meno A Kwena Tented Camp (7 tents) P Bag 053, Maun; tel: 6860 981; email: kksafari@dynabyte.bw; www.kalaharikavango.com. On the edge of quite a high bank overlooking the Boteti River, with a 30m drop to a waterhole in the riverbed, Meno A Kwena has a highly unusual

THE LIONS OF MAKGADIKGADI

Makgadikgadi is an erratic and uncertain place for lions. With the first rains, huge herds of zebra and wildebeest move out on to the plains to graze on the succulent grasses and drop their young. In the dry months this pulse of life ebbs back to the Boteti River, 50km to the west, leaving the plains largely deserted by large ungulates. The lions have had to adapt to these huge fluctuations and the unpredictability.

For some the solution is simply tracking the herds back to the Boteti for the dry months, where they must dodge the human residents on the west side of the river. Others stay behind amidst the parched grasses, swirling dust devils and spring hares. This is not the place for huge ungainly prides; rather lionesses pair up and wander over large areas, often in excess of 1,000km², in order to find sufficient food. Males typically spread their time between two or more of these small, efficient prides. They can maintain territories of almost double that, walking up to 50km a night to patrol their vast swathes of baked wasteland.

Water is unavailable for up to seven months a year for these lions, so they must gain all their moisture from their prey. Immediately after killing large prey such as gemsbok they snick open the belly and stomach, slurping up the juices before they soak away into the sand. However, large prey is hard to find during the dry season, so they will hunt aardvarks and porcupines, and they increasingly look outside the eastern and western boundaries of the park for sustenance from herds of dopey, slow-moving livestock.

Ostriches are particularly common in the eastern grasslands, and can often be seen from the main Nata–Maun road. These huge birds breed before the rains, with several females laying in a single scrape that may hold over 30 eggs. Incubation tends to rotate between the male at night (when his dark plumage is no longer vulnerable to overheating), and the female by day (when her drab plumage provides more effective camouflage). Youngsters from several broods gather together in large crèches, presided over by one adult pair, and can sometimes be seen gathering in the shadow of an adult for shade.

location for a Botswanan camp. It's also unusual in that it's independently owned and run by David Dugmore, who aims to offer a fairly simple safari experience. Not for David the normal mould of two activities per day with a rest between. While activities and drives are on offer as required, guests make their own decisions and many spend time watching wildlife at the waterhole rather than from a vehicle, or just chilling in camp after an activity.

The camp benefits from regular visits by lion. Each of its rooms is built effectively inside its own kraal – a fence of natural tree trunks with a doorway of half a dozen tree trunks that you simply push aside. Tents are traditional Meru-style, small and fairly traditional, with a couple of stretcher beds and proper mattresses, a bedside table and lamp; there's also a water flask, paraffin lantern, glasses. Outside are two safari chairs, a canvas washbasin on a stand and a small table. Within the kraal, a bucket shower has magnificent views over the river, while a traditional rondavel with bamboo reed walls houses a separate flush toilet.

Sand paths through the bush link the rooms to the main central tent. Fronted by a sandy courtyard area, this is of traditional green canvas, complete with guy ropes, and feels rather like a big top. The space is split between a fairly large bar, a dining area with huge dining table, and a lounge complete with a bright red, old-style fridge. In a separate small canvas shelter, a wrought-iron sofa and chairs are set overlooking a waterhole, while adjacent to that is a simple rock pool that does service as a plunge pool. The relaxed atmosphere is accentuated by a collection of bright sarong-like fabrics, wrought-iron furniture and a good and eclectic little bookshelf; it's the sort of place where someone might pick up a guitar and start strumming.

Perhaps more than most camps, Meno A Kwena attracts a wide range of visitors, including independent travellers, safari goers and a number of NGO workers.

US$275–400 pp sharing, low-high season, inc meals, drinks and activities.

⌂ **Leroo-La-Tau Lodge** (7 tents) ⚟ 6860 300; f 6862 932; e enquire@africansecrets.net; www.africansecrets.net (⊕ LEROOL 20°25.240'S, 24°31.277'E). Owned by Sean Watson of Island Safari Lodge in Maun, Leroo-La-Tau is situated at the eastern end of a bend in the Boteti River. Although it is now inside the perimeter fence of the park, and surrounded by it on 3 sides, it remains technically outside the park – quite a plus since, now that domestic animals can no longer graze the land, numbers of animals such as warthog and impala are on the increase.

Accommodation is in large Meru-style tents on raised wooden platforms. Most are built into the tree line, overlooking the Boteti's channel, whilst a few are set back in the bush. Each has a large veranda with chairs and table outside, and 2 dbl beds inside – complete with high-quality down duvets and quilts. They are comfortably furnished with a chair, dressing table and bedside tables, with a torch, and various toiletries and insect repellents provided. At the back, still under a shading canvas roof, is a toilet, shower and washbasin area, enclosed within an inner tent of mosquito netting. The hot water is very quick, though the water is mineral water, and so smells slightly of sulphur due to the natural chemicals in the area's groundwater.

The main lodge has one side largely made of glass, overlooking a large lawn (with small swimming pool) which leads down to the banks of the Boteti River. At one end of this is a bar, and above that a comfy sitting area with a video recorder (and a library of wildlife videos), and a lookout window. In the centre is a large and rather beautiful wooden dining table, and at the end another sitting area with a curio shop (which also sells some good books).

Activities centre on game drives and night drives from the lodge. Generally they operate in a

15

relatively narrow neck of land enclosed by a loop of the Boteti. This juts into the park, and is about 10km x 4–5km, though does have lots of riverfront – which is where the game is usually concentrated. This has the advantage of not being liable for park fees. In addition to these, they also run 'cultural trips' to the local villages.

The lodge can also be used as a base for day or overnight trips into Nxai Pan Game Reserve or overnight to the Central Kalahari Game Reserve. Expect to sleep on comfy bed-rolls in dome tents, eat around the campfire and generally get involved. Though safari activities on the west bank of the Boteti are included in the rate, if you want to take a day trip into the park itself these cost extra. (If you're going to do this, then I'd do it properly; spend 2 days there and make an overnight trip of it!)

Leroo-La-Tau is a good-quality lodge in an area that can provide remarkable game spectacles. It's relatively inexpensive for Botswana, largely because it's not well known and, without an airstrip, it's rarely included in fly-in safari circuits of the country. Regular transfers from Island Safari Lodge in Maun take an hour or so to cover the 120km journey.

US$170/320 pp sharing Nov–May & Jun–Oct, inc all meals, drinks, local activities, park fees, laundry; camping US$9 pp. Game drive US$11/14 pp. Open all year.

Å Xwaraga Campsite (5 pitches, 2 chalets). This lovely bush site is a few mins' walk from Leroo-La-Tau Lodge and under the same ownership. Its pitches lie beneath camelthorn (*Acacia erioloba*) trees, each of which used to have an adjacent water standpipe . . . until the local elephants got wind of them. There are also 2 simple thatched chalets, each of which has mosquito gauze on the windows, 4 beds and an en-suite shower and toilet at the back. Each comes supplied with cooking equipment and linen; ideal for self-catering guests. There's also a bar, a pool and a viewing platform. Game drives can be organised via the lodge.

Å Khumaga Campsite (✛ KHUMAG 20°27.350'S, 24°30.978'E). Khumaga, sometimes written 'Xhumaga,' stands within the park near the east bank of the Boteti River, about 4km south of Leroo-La-Tau. This site usually has water available, and sometimes working cold showers and flush toilets. One of the park's 2 scout camps is here.

Å Njuca Hills Campsite (✛ NJUCA 20°25.807'S, 24°52.395'E). Njuca Hills Campsite is located in the heart of the park about 38km east of Khumaga, and it's totally different. It's slightly elevated (no more than about 20m) on one of a series of low, fossilised dunes and here you'll find no water and even less firewood. The campsite is very basic, with just a long-drop toilet surrounded by what looks like a screen sprayed with concrete. Expect the main wildlife here to be barking geckos and perhaps the odd curious yellow mongoose.

Just to emphasise the safety issues raised about travelling in any of the pans, recent visitors Richard and Vikki Threlfall wrote to me: 'We broke down at Njuca Hills Campsite, and were not found until the third morning after discovering the problem! And then it was only pure chance.' Note that this happened at one of only 2 official campsites in the park, and realise that it would have taken a full-scale air search to find them if they'd been off the main routes. Do take heed of the safety issues detailed in *Getting around*, page 385, before you travel anywhere in the pans area.

WHAT TO SEE AND DO Like the bulk of Sua or the rest of Ntwetwe Pan, the Makgadikgadi Pans National Park is really an area for experienced old Africa hands to explore in their own vehicles – though bear in mind my comments on safety under *Getting around* on page 385. That said, in the late dry season you won't be quite so isolated if you stick to the road in the park which runs beside the Boteti and Khumaga Campsite which will then have quite a few visitors.

Alternatively, and much safer, stay at Jack's (or San) Camp for the pans in the eastern side of the park, and at Leroo-La-Tau for the contrasting Boteti Riverfront – exploring each of these areas with their expert local guides.

GETTING AROUND If you're driving yourself here then come armed with copies of both the Shell and InfoMap maps of Botswana (see pages 94–5 for details), with their wealth of GPS co-ordinates. Then take to heart my caveats in *Getting around*, page 385, and you're ready to explore.

First you'll need to head for one of the scout camps to sign in and pay your park fees. The main game scout camp (✛ MSCOUT 20°16.963'S, 24°54.458'E) is near the Makolwane Gate, on the Nata–Maun road. The right turn to this is about 23km east of the main turning to Nxai Pans, and about 42km east of Gweta. The scout camp is less than 10km from the road. The alternative is the scout camp at Khumaga (✪ KHUMAG 20°27.350'S, 24°30.978'E), on the western side near the Boteti.

Note that if you enter the park from the east then you should follow the cut-line north to the main road, and turn left to reach the main scout camp as swiftly as possible; meandering through the park without having paid park fees first is against the rules.

Driving around, you'll realise that the more southerly roads, crossing the pans, are particularly hard to locate; arguably they are simply non-existent, washed away with each year's rains. Equally, those around the centre of the eastern side of the park are so numerous that they're totally confusing, complicated by a whole network of tracks used by the camps in the area.

NEARBY TOWNS The small towns around here tend to be used by visitors driving themselves as simply places to refuel and replenish basic supplies; those flying into the area's camps will probably never see any of them.

Gweta Gweta (✪ GWETA 20°11.434'S, 25°15.888'E) is a small, old village about 2km south of the road between Nata and Maun, about 205km from Maun and 100km from Nata. Now it feels quite run-down, but it remains conveniently situated for exploring Makgadikgadi and Nxai Pans. There's a restcamp here, a couple of basic food stores (including the Maono Restaurant) and even a vehicle workshop for minor repairs. There is often, but *not* always, fuel available here.

Gweta is very clearly signposted south of the main road, in an area of mostly stunted mopane woodlands with the odd small clay pan. Turning off you'll first find a post office on your left, then the fuel station on your right (signposted with little pump signs) and finally the restcamp. Planet Baobab is about 5km east of town, but worth seeking out. If you're arriving by bus, ask them to stop on the road beside the turn-off to Planet Baobab.

Getting there and away If you're not driving yourself then there are very regular bus services between Maun and Francistown. They usually turn into town and stop in the centre, near the Maono Restaurant. Maun is then about three hours away and costs P20; Francistown is about four hours away, costing P25.

Where to stay The choices here are starkly different: the old and rather run-down Gweta Restcamp or the funky, rustic-trendy Planet Baobab. Either can be used as a base to explore Ntwetwe Pan or the Makgadikgadi National Park, although most visitors to these would probably camp instead. Both are really best as stopovers, with Planet Baobab doubling as a base for backpackers to take quad-bike excursions on to the pans.

🏠 **Gweta Restcamp** (28 rooms, camping)
📞 612220; e gweta@info.bw. This old restcamp has been here for years and hasn't, apparently, changed that much. It's still signposted as the 'motel' in the centre of Gweta, and has small and unimpressive rondavels, all with en-suite facilities, and an area where you can pitch a tent with toilets and showers. In the centre of the restcamp is a cool and generally pleasant thatched bar which serves

snacks as well as drinks. This should make a good stop for lunch, though on my last visit it was marred by very loud music and the staff's complete lack of any interest or attention – despite the absence of any other guests.
P95 pp sharing, P154 sgl for the room only.
🏠 **Planet Baobab** (13 huts, camping) Contact Uncharted Africa (page 391). Planet Baobab (✪ PBAOBA 20°11.344'S, 25°18.330'E) is Uncharted

Africa's venture, offering a Makgadikgadi Pans experience to a clientele who can't afford the prices of Jack's Camp, combined with somewhere interesting to stop for people driving past. Set amongst baobabs about 4km east of Gweta, it is just south of the main Nata–Maun road. If you stay here, there are 3 choices of accommodation:

The 8 traditional mud huts are actually brick clad in mud, with a thatched roof on top. Everything inside is rounded as if it's made of mud. In the 5 twin huts there are 2 beds, one built into each side of the room, each with a mosquito net, and a stylish en-suite washbasin, toilet and shower. The 3 family huts have a dbl bed and 2 built-in sgl beds. These have been very well designed, with glass in the windows and trendy mirrors on the walls.

The 5 Bushman huts are very basic, rounded shelters built using a frame of thin mopane saplings and a covering of grasses. There's a door made of sticks and grass, and inside are 2 rustic beds with a cowhide rug on a dung floor, a bedside table, an electric lantern and a mosquito net. Residents share the same ablutions as the campers. Whilst similar to camping in the dry season, I'd be a little apprehensive sleeping in one during the rains — although I am assured that they're waterproof.

The campsite has 4 showers and toilets (separated for men and women) built into a large and stylish thatched rondavel — complete with lights set into the walls and clothes-hooks made from branches. Each site has a thatched shelter and washing-up facilities to hand.

The camp's focus is a funky dining and bar area, dominated by a large, curved bar and lit by 2 chandeliers made from local beer bottles. This has tables and alcoves and a fine collection of images and interesting things on its walls. A full breakfast here is US$12, lunch is US$15 and a 3-course dinner US$25.

Fly-camping trips to the pans are covered separately (see below). However, a variety of optional activities can be organised out of a base at Planet Baobab, including the following:

Village Tour which lasts about 2 hours and includes a visit to the local primary school, Gweta's *kgotla* (traditional court), and a stop at the traditional healer. A local guide from the area will lead you, and there's always a chance to stop and sample some of the local sorghum beer (it's an acquired taste!).

Bushwalk and fireside chat which is a short guided walk for about 2 hours through the surrounding bush, concentrating on the environment, the traditional uses of plants and animals, the history of the area and perhaps some local stories.

Traditional meal at the cattlepost can be arranged with a local family: typically sorghum, mealie meal, *seswaa* (beef stew), wild spinach, mopane worms in season, wild beans and perhaps creamy baobab fruit milkshake.

US$105 per hut for family bakalanga mud hut, US$100 twin mud hut, US$30 bushman hut; camping US$10 pp (US$5 per child under 12).

🏠 **Kalahari Surf Club** This is the fly-camp of Planet Baobab. It's reached by vehicle from Planet Baobab and is the base for their quad-bike trips around the pans area. 'Accommodation' consists of a bed-roll under the stars, but with minimal dangerous game around, this is all you need and is a great way to sleep. From here you can explore the northern edge of Ntwetwe with local guides, looking at wildlife, huge baobabs, the spring at Sweet Water Pan and the stone tools which litter it, and learning a lot about the area's geology, archaeology and history. *Typical 3-day/2-night itinerary inc 1 night in a mud hut at Planet Baobab and 1 on the pans costs around US$505 pp sharing, inc accommodation, meals and activities; for a 4-day/3-night itinerary, with 1 night on the pans, expect to pay around US$625 pp sharing.*

Rakops Useful as a (hand-pumped) refuelling stop and reachable now entirely on tarmac from Maun, Rakops (✦ RAKOPS 21°02.136'S, 24°24.432'E) is notable for a tall radio mast in the centre of town, and as the last outpost passed on many trips into the Central Kalahari Game Reserve. It's also got cellphone coverage.

North of here a new tar road shadows the western side of the Boteti River, to Motopi and thence Maun. East of here, the road passes through Mopopi, around Orapa, and thence splits with one fork heading for Francistown, and the other for Palapye. All of these routes are now tarred and very good quality.

Motopi A few kilometres south of the main Maun–Nata road, this large village seemed full of road-builders and detours when I was last there. Coming from the south, the main road seemed to go through Motopi and west, although it was

Graham Hemson worked as a guide at Jack's Camp, and is studying for a PhD on lion ecology and conservation in the Makgadikgadi area as part of Oxford University's Wildlife Conservation Research Unit. In 1999 he estimated that there were about 39 lions in the Makgadikgadi area, where he investigated their impact on people, and vice versa.

Every year lions kill hundreds of domestic animals in and around the Makgadikgadi Pans National Park, which brings them into conflict with the herders and owners. In retaliation people have, in the past, laid out traps and poison, and hunted lions outside the park with ruthless efficiency. Between November 1999 and May 2000, at least 12 lions were killed here.

However, contrary to common belief, Graham's research indicated that livestock predation does not happen mainly inside the kraal, but rather out in the grazing areas and sometimes inside the park. Although lions will tackle livestock at the villages, often they can simply pick off the many untended stragglers. An interesting ecological response to the predictability of the livestock as prey is that lions that eat livestock have substantially smaller home ranges than those which are dependent on migratory prey, or scarce desert species.

Typically, this livestock predation is only a problem when wild prey is scarce. Lions are forced to change their preferences abruptly as zebra and wildebeest migrate out of their territories.

After surveying the local inhabitants, Graham found that many of the people in charge of the livestock were elderly women; often their husbands were living in town, running more lucrative family businesses. These women were physically unable to keep track of their cattle – hence a large number of stray animals make a veritable manmade buffet for lions.

Following Graham's conclusions, Botswana's Wildlife Dept has lobbied its Veterinary Department to consider re-routing a proposed disease control fence around the Makgadikgadi, to help prevent the wildlife from straying into cattle country. Meanwhile strategies have been developed to help the local people minimise their losses, and to discourage them from killing more lions before the fence is built.

possible to take a short cut along a sand track, due north through the riverbed, until about 8km later you reach the main Maun–Nata road. That said, there's probably a smooth, well-signposted alternative by now!

Orapa This is the heart of Botswana's diamond-mining operations, producing around 12.2 million carats at the turn of the millennium – that's around 12% of the world's gem-quality diamonds. This makes it by far the most important town in the country to Botswana's economy, and hence security there is very tight. You're not allowed in, or out, without permission from the diamond company Debswana, which isn't given easily. Hence it's effectively off-limits to visitors and there's a road that detours around the south side of the mine.

Whilst passing this, consider that there's also a major diamond mine at Letlhakane, about 30km from Orapa, on the Serowe road, and that there's active prospecting continuing throughout the region for more diamond pipes.

15

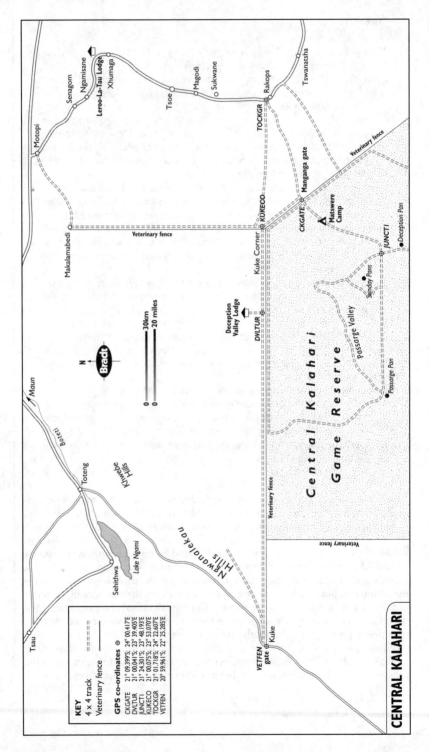

KEY

4 x 4 track
Veterinary fence

GPS co-ordinates ⊕

CKGATE	21° 09.399'S; 24° 00.417'E
DVLTUR	21° 00.041'S; 23° 39.405'E
JUNCT1	21° 24.301'S; 23° 48.193'E
KUKECO	21° 00.075'S; 23° 53.070'E
TOCKGR	21° 01.718'S; 24° 22.607'E
VETFEN	20° 59.961'S; 22° 25.285'E

CENTRAL KALAHARI

16

The Central Kalahari

Covering about 52,800km², and without a tar road anywhere near it, the Central Kalahari Game Reserve (or the CKGR, as it's usually known) is one of the world's largest game reserves. It dominates the centre of Botswana – the wider region that I refer to in this chapter as simply the 'central Kalahari'. This is Africa at its most remote and esoteric: a vast sandsheet punctuated by a few huge open plains, occasional salt pans and the fossil remains of ancient riverbeds.

The CKGR isn't for everybody. The game is often sparse and can seem limited, with no elephants or buffalo; the distances are huge, along bush tracks of variable quality; and the facilities are non-existent. So unless you have a fully equipped vehicle (preferably two) and lots of bush experience, it's probably not the place for you.

The converse is that if you've already experienced enough of Africa to love the feeling of space and the sheer freedom of real wilderness areas, then this reserve is completely magical; it's the ultimate wilderness destination.

Due to limitations of space, this is only a short introduction to the area. It's intended to give you a feel for the central Kalahari and the CKGR (the area of it which most visitors will see) and tell you how to get there and what it's like. I've assumed that most visitors will only be visiting the northern section of the park – Piper's Pan and north – as that's generally regarded as the most interesting area. It's also the obvious part of the reserve to link into a trip with the more popular northern regions of Chobe and the Okavango.

BACKGROUND INFORMATION

HISTORY The Central Kalahari Game Reserve was declared a game park in 1961, on the very eve of independence. At that time, there was increasing international publicity about the San. With the prevalent view of their 'idyllic' hunter–gatherer lifestyle came a growing concern that this was threatened, and that they might become 'extinct'. The British Protectorate of Bechuanaland was the focus for this, so the authorities decided to protect the heart of the Kalahari for the San.

At the time, there was no way to set aside one particular area for an ethnic group. Neither the British authorities nor the Tswana, who were being groomed for government, wanted any discrimination amongst its citizens based on race. This would have set a dangerous precedent, with echoes of the tribal 'bantustans' created by the apartheid regime in South Africa.

Back in the 1960s, legislation to proclaim a separate area for a separate ethnic group didn't exist. Nor was any wanted by a new country anxious to avoid ethnic divisions. Hence the heart of the central Kalahari was protected from further development or agricultural encroachment as a 'game park' – even though it was intended as a place of sanctuary for the San. Thus the Central Kalahari Game Reserve was proclaimed.

(Still to this day the Botswana government has a strict policy of not discriminating – positively or negatively – between any of the ethnic groups in the country. 'We're all Tswana' is their wise approach, designed to minimise any ethnic tensions. However, there lies the nub of a problem. If a group like the San are allowed to live and hunt in a 'game reserve', why shouldn't any other Tswana citizen? Many who are concerned for the San argue that they need positive discrimination, whilst others maintain that such moves would be racist.)

In keeping with its origins, the CKGR remained largely closed for around 30 years; visitors needed special approval and permits, which were not lightly granted. During this time its most famous visitors were probably Mark and Delia Owens, a couple of young and idealistic animal researchers from America who lived on a tree-island in Deception Valley for about seven years (1974–80), and subsequently wrote a best-selling book, *Cry of the Kalahari* (see *Appendix 3, Further Information*), based on their experiences.

Then in the late 1980s and early 1990s the park started to open up more, first allowing in organised groups with tour operators and, only in recent years, individual travellers in their own vehicles. However, numbers remain strictly limited by the number of campsites available, so it still feels very much a wilderness destination.

PEOPLE When the CKGR was declared as a reserve, a population of around 5,000 San people lived within its boundaries. In the last decade or so a borehole had been installed at the small village of Xade, where some of the park's game scouts were based. Research in 1996 estimated that the population in the reserve had fallen below 1,500, a significant proportion of whom had moved to live in the vicinity of Xade, near this fairly reliable source of water.

The government's stated policy is now to encourage relocation of the people to New Xade, a new village which has been created outside the reserve. They maintain that this will make it easier to supply the people with basic health and education services. However, this policy has attracted criticism from international human rights groups such as Survival International, who allege that the San are being coerced to move outside the reserve.

See *Chapter 2, People and culture*, pages 20–9, for more about the San and about this issue. Note that this remains a very contentious and political topic.

GEOGRAPHY AND LANDSCAPE Despite its huge area, the central Kalahari has relatively little scenic variation. The vast majority of it is covered by an enormous, undulating sandsheet. Within the CKGR itself, the north of the park contains the most varied scenery; here you'll find a network of vegetated salt pans and a few fossilised riverbeds.

FLORA AND FAUNA If you're expecting to find stark differences between contrasting environments within this Kalahari reserve, you'll be disappointed. There are subtle changes between its different landscapes, but there isn't the variation here that you'll find around Chobe or the Okavango. Because of this, the animal species found here vary little from area to area – and this is one reason why the central Kalahari is an area for old Africa hands, and not first-time safari-goers.

Flora People on their first trip through the Kalahari are often struck by just how green and vegetated it is, often in contrast to their mental image of a desert. In fact most of the Kalahari is covered in a thin, mixed bush with a fairly low canopy height, dotted with occasional larger trees. Beneath this is a rather sparse ground-covering of smaller bushes, grasses and herbs.

To be a little more precise, the central Kalahari's vegetation is dominated by *Terminalia sericea* sandveld (see page 56) standing on deep sand. The most common species within this are the silver terminalia itself (*Terminalia sericea*), the Kalahari appleleaf (*Lonchocarpus nelsii*) and Kalahari sand acacias (*Acacia luederitzii*), which occasionally form thickets. These vary from bushes to substantial trees, growing to a maximum height of around 10m. (Their flattened canopies are easily confused with the umbrella thorn (*Acacia tortilis*), earning them the alternative name of bastard, or false, umbrella thorn.)

Other common trees include the distinctive purple-pod terminalia (*Terminalia prunioides*), which seem to grow best in areas where there is more clay in the soil; shepherd's trees (*Boscia albitrunca*), with their characteristic whitish bark; and feverberry trees (*Croton megalobotrys*). Bladethorns (*Acacia fleckii*) and their close cousins the bluethorns (*Acacia erubescens*), are common bushes with fine, feathery foliage but keen, curved barbs. Inevitably you'll spot plenty of old, gnarled camelthorn trees (*Acacia erioloba*).

Beneath these you'll commonly find a variety of low bushes and shrubs including wild seringa bushes (*Burkea africana*) and bushwillows (*Combretum collinum*). Meanwhile on the ground one of the more common grasses is the lovely silky bushman grass (*Stipagrostis uniplumis*).

Look carefully, perhaps helped by a good guide, and you'll find plenty to interest you here including, during the wetter months of the year, many flowers and herbs. The beautifully curving purple flowers of the cat's tail (*Hermbstaedtia odorata*) form spectacular patches in damper areas. More entertaining are the bright red fruits of the balsam pear (*Momordica balsamina*) which, when ripe, fall to the ground and pop themselves open automatically if disturbed. In *Common Wild Flowers of the Okavango Delta*, Veronica Roodt (see *Appendix 3, Further Information*) reports that the young leaves of this plant are used as a vegetable, and while a few will use the fruits in cooking, many communities treat them as poisonous or use them in medicines.

Fauna Game viewing anywhere in the central Kalahari area can be a stark contrast to the amazing densities of game that can often be seen in the Okavango–Linyanti–Chobe region. To get the best out of the CKGR, you'll require lots of time and patience, often just watching and waiting. The big game is here, but on average it occurs in very low densities – as you'd expect in such a harsh, arid environment. The only way to get around this is, as mentioned below, to visit when it congregates on the open pans in the north.

Springbok are probably the most numerous of the **large herbivores** in the park today. That said, the game populations in the central Kalahari seem to have been fluctuating fairly wildly, at least for the last century, and perhaps longer. In his *A Comment on Kalahari Wildlife and the Khukhe Fence* (see *Appendix 3, Further Information*), Alec Campbell suggests that over this period human activities and interference have altered the balance of the wildlife populations in the Kalahari substantially, and led indirectly to population explosions and crashes.

Currently springbok disperse in small herds across the park during the dry season, but congregate in very large numbers on the short grass plains found on pans and fossil riverbeds during and shortly after the rains. (Note that this is exactly the opposite of the usual situation for many mammals, including elephants and buffalo, which gather in larger herds as the dry season progresses, only to disperse during the rains.)

These successful antelope are both browsers and grazers, which can derive all the moisture that they need from their food, provided that the plants they eat contain at least 10% water. They'll often rest by day and eat at night, thus maximising the moisture content of their fodder by including dew on it.

16

Springbok populations are very elastic: they are able to reproduce very rapidly when conditions are favourable, allowing them to rapidly repopulate after a bad drought. With good conditions females can produce two calves in 13 months, while even six-month old ewes will conceive, giving birth to their first lamb when they are barely a year old. To maximise the survival of their offspring, the females gather together in maternal herds and synchronise their births, thus presenting predators with a short-term surplus of easily caught young lambs.

The central Kalahari's population of blue wildebeest has, at times within the last century, swelled to enormous proportions. In his work *A Comment on Kalahari Wildlife and the Khukhe Fence*, Campbell (see *Appendix 3*, page 492) describes them as peaking in the 1960s when 'herds of 50 and 100 had so accumulated in the Matsheng and Okwa area that they stretched unbroken for many kilometres and numbered hundreds of thousands'. Thane Riney, an ecologist there at the time, was familiar with the vast herds of the Serengeti yet still referred to these as 'the largest herds of plains game left in Africa today'. Wildebeest populations were then estimated at up to 250,000 animals, but within a few years lack of water, grazing and the existence of veterinary cordon fences had conspired to wipe them out from much of the central Kalahari. Today you'll find small groups of wildebeest in the CKGR, but I've never seen them in large numbers.

Probably the area's most common large antelope are gemsbok (also known as oryx), which can be seen in congregations of hundreds on the short grass plains during the rains, but usually occur in smaller groupings during the rest of the year. These magnificent antelope are supremely adapted for desert living. They can survive fluctuations of their body temperature up to 45°C (when 42°C would kill most mammals) because of a series of blood vessels, known as the carotid rete, located immediately below their brain. These effectively cool the blood before it reaches the animal's brain – the organ most adversely affected by temperature variations.

Red hartebeest can also be found here in good numbers, as can eland and – an amazing sight – giraffe. Kudu occur, but generally in quite small numbers: either small bachelor groups or family groups consisting of an old male, several females and a number of youngsters. Common duiker are occasionally seen, too, but if you catch a glimpse of a small antelope bounding away from you, it's much more likely to be a steenbok.

The main **predators** here are lion, cheetah, leopard and spotted hyena, which generally occur in a low density, matching their prey species. The lion prides range over large territories and are bonded by loose associations; members spend most of their time apart from each other, living alone or in pairs, and meeting relatively infrequently. Individual lions will often hunt a variety of smaller prey, like bat-eared foxes and porcupines, as well as the larger antelope more commonly thought of as lion fodder.

Similarly the central Kalahari's leopard have a very catholic diet, ranging from mice and spring hares to ground squirrels and wild cats, plus steenbok, springbok and calves of the larger antelope.

The park's cheetah seem to be more nomadic than the lion or leopard. In other parks, where game densities are higher, cheetah often lose their kills to these larger cats. Thus the CKGR's relatively low density of predators makes it a good place for cheetah. Hence this is one of sub-Saharan Africa's better parks for spotting them – at least at times when the springbok concentrate on the pans and river beds.

Amongst the **scavengers and insectivores** found here are the brown hyena (the original object of study for Mark and Delia Owens; see *Appendix 3, Further Information*), black-backed jackal, caracal, Cape fox, bat-eared fox, aardwolf, genet and wild cat. However, as there is no facility for night drives in the reserve, only black-backed jackals are commonly seen as they aren't strictly nocturnal.

Meanwhile the diurnal yellow mongoose is sometimes seen scampering around in search of insects, and families of meerkats (or suricats) are amongst the most entertaining and endearing of all the park's residents.

Birdlife The birdlife here is very varied, with Africa's largest bird, the ostrich, doing particularly well. I've never seen more free-roaming ostrich during May, when Deception Valley seemed to be dotted by large flocks of them.

Weighing 14–19kg, kori bustard are the world's heaviest flying birds and are also common, stepping around the plains in search of insects and small reptile and mammals.

Closely related to the kori are the smaller korhaans; the white-winged black korhaan (or white-quilled korhaan) is one of the area's most obvious birds. The conspicuous black-and-white males have a harsh, raucous call and can be seen flying up and then falling back to the ground in endless display flights. Related red-crested korhaans are a little less obvious, and less common, though equally spectacular when displaying.

Doves are well represented with Cape turtle, laughing doves and, especially, Namaqua doves all being very common. All the species of sandgrouse found in southern Africa – double-banded, Burchell's, yellow-throated and Namaqua – live here. Watch in the mornings as flocks of Namaqua sandgrouse fly to waterholes. They drink and also wade into the water, where each male has specially adapted feathers on his breast, which act like a sponge to soak up water. He then flies up to 80km back to his nest, where the chicks drink from the feathers.

The central Kalahari's most common raptor is the pale-chanting goshawk: a light grey bird, with pink legs and black ends to its wings and tail. It's usually seen hunting from a conspicuous perch, perhaps a fence post beside a track or the top of a small thorn bush, or occasionally hopping about the ground foraging. If disturbed it'll usually fly off low, swooping to land on a similar perch – even if that's another fence post from which it'll shortly be disturbed again.

Black-shouldered kites and rock kestrels, both of which often hunt by hovering in flight, are common here. Bateleurs, black-breasted and brown snake eagles, martial and tawny eagles, and lanner falcons are also around, with the latter making something of a speciality of hunting birds as they come to drink at waterholes.

WHEN TO VISIT The Kalahari is really unlike any other game area in sub-Saharan Africa in that its game is probably at its most spectacular during and shortly after the rains – from around January to April. Then the animals gather where the best rain has been and the sweetest grazing is, which usually means on the pans. These can be a magnificent sight, with very large herds of springbok and gemsbok, accompanied by good numbers of giraffe and ostrich plus groups of blue wildebeest, hartebeest and eland. Inevitably these attract increased predator activity from lion, cheetah and the odd leopard.

Having said that, this is also the time when the weather, and in particular the driving conditions, can be at their least hospitable. If there has been much rain then the road from Rakops to the scout post and beyond become a series of mudholes lined by black-cotton soil, which is rock-hard when dry, but feels like treacle when wet. Meanwhile areas of pans in the park become large, shallow lakes where both navigation and traction present a challenge to any vehicle. Any group coming at this time must be fully prepared for heavy rain, and should expect to have to dig out their vehicle from the mud a number of times.

As a compromise for those who are not fond of endless mud, a favourite time to visit is just after the rains, around March–May, depending on when the rains stop.

Then most of the surface water has disappeared, and the black-cotton soil isn't nearly as treacherous as it would have been a few months earlier. The game concentrations will still be good, albeit perhaps not *quite* so spectacular, but your overall experience will probably be much more enjoyable. That is, unless you really enjoy digging your vehicle out of knee-deep mud . . .

PRACTICAL INFORMATION

GETTING THERE AND AWAY To reach the entrance gate follow the directions below, and note that the small Matswere Scout Camp, where you sign in and pay fees, is a further 8km into the park. From there it's a further 30km to the nearest campsites, those at the north end of Deception Valley.

Driving yourself Driving yourself into the central Kalahari is only a viable option for experienced and bush-wise adventurers with their own fully equipped 4x4s. Even they need at least two 4x4 vehicles and some fail-safe plan for back-up assistance in the event of an emergency. Then there are three usual routes to the park's northern entry gate.

From the Maun–Ghanzi road About 119km from Ghanzi and 167km from Maun, on the tarred Maun–Ghanzi road, you'll have to stop and pass through the Kuke Veterinary Fence (✪ VETFEN 20°59.961'S, 22°25.285'E). Immediately north of this, you'll find a good, wide gravel road that heads off on a bearing fractionally south of east. After a few kilometres, this thoroughfare bends round to the left, and there's a small turning into the bush on the right. Take this, and you'll find a simple sand track with two clear ruts for your wheels (welcome to the Kalahari!). The veterinary fence will be literally inches from your right side.

Expect only the occasional 4x4 to pass you; this isn't a busy track. Beneath your wheels you'll sometimes find patches of hard ground with bands of calcrete rocks. Then there are mud-holes, where thick clay is a sticky hazard during the rains (when this route is perfectly possible, but time-consuming). However, most of the track is good, fairly hard sand on which a reasonably experienced bush driver should be able to average 50km/h.

After about 175km, the taller bush thins out a little, leaving more open grassy areas. At times now you'll find yourself travelling parallel to several fences, and sometimes with one on each side of you. Beware of startling antelope here; they'll run in front of the vehicle with no escape, and become exhausted easily if you drive too fast.

Around 245km after the tar you'll reach a left turning (✪ DVLTUR 21°00.041'S, 23°39.405'E) which is clearly signposted to Deception Valley Lodge (see pages 415–16 for details). The lodge is about 5.3km north from here as the eagle flies, but a little further using the winding track which leads there, via the lodge's own airstrip (✪ DVLAIR 20°58.897'S, 23°39.515'E).

Almost 24km after passing this, you'll reach Kuke Corner (✪ KUKECO 21°00.075'S, 23°53.070'E). Here a gate marks the junction of several veterinary fences. To the left a straight cut-line heads due north, towards the Maun–Nata road. To the right, a well-used track follows the line of the fence, roughly south-southeast (bearing about 143°). This can be quite rutted and tedious driving, but after about 21.5km leads to the main entrance gate to the CKGR (✪ CKGATE 21°09.399'S, 24°00.417'E).

From Rakops Between Rakops and the CKGR's entrance gate there is one main track, fringed by a few detours and side-tracks. Starting at Rakops, head north out

Just below the surface of the Kalahari lies a labyrinth of tunnels excavated by the Damara mole-rat (*Cryptomis damarensis*), the only member of this endemic African family to occur in the Kalahari. Mole-rats are rodents, and unlike true moles, which are insectivores, they feed entirely on plant matter – specifically underground storage organs such as bulbs, corms, tubers and desert cucumbers.

They have plump, cylindrical bodies, short, sturdy limbs and formidable projecting incisors for chiselling out the tunnels in which they live their entire lives. Earth excavated by the teeth is shuffled backwards by the forefeet, and when enough has accumulated the mole-rat reverses up a side tunnel, pushing it to the surface to form a 'molehill'. Digging is easiest when the soil is wet, so the rains prompt a flurry of activity: in one month, one colony of 16 Damara mole-rats was recorded digging 1km of tunnels and shifting 2.5 tonnes of soil to the surface. Not bad for an animal that weighs no more than 300g.

This Herculean effort uncovers enough food to last the colony through the dry season until the next rains. Meanwhile soil is shifted around and burrows modified to create a complex of chambers, passageways and latrines.

Damara mole-rats are the most sociable of their family. This is a necessary adaptation to the harsh Kalahari environment, where numbers bring more success to a team of blind foragers in search of an erratic, scattered food supply. Their complex societies are more like those of a social insect than a mammal. A colony averages around 15–25 members, occasionally up to 40, but only one pair – the dominant male and female – are reproductive. All others help forage, dig and rear the young, but suppress their fertility, being effectively like sterile worker-termites.

The dominant female breeds all year, producing a litter of between one and five pups after an 80-day gestation in a nest chamber 2m below ground. Hierarchies are reinforced aggressively, and each year about 10% of a colony's members leave to breed and found new colonies. Mole-rats communicate underground with snorts and squeals, and drum with their hind feet on tunnel walls to relay seismic messages to mates or rivals.

Though the casual visitor is unlikely ever to see a mole-rat, a range of canny predators, notably the mole snake (*Pseudaspis cana*), have learned to watch as a pile of fresh soil accumulates and will snatch the digger just as it approaches the surface.

of town towards Motopi, and then turn left off the main road where you see a number of tracks, about 2–3km from the radio mast, around ✪ TOCKGR 21°01.718'S, 24°22.607'E.

You probably won't find one obvious track until you're a few kilometres from the tar, but if you average a bearing of about 250° then you'll be going in roughly the right direction, and will reach the entrance gate (✪ CKGATE 21°09.399'S, 24°00.417'E) after around 41km. Heading even roughly in this direction, you can't go wrong, as sooner or later you'll hit the veterinary fence that doubles as the park's boundary.

When it's wet during the earliest months of the year, this is one of the muddiest, and hence trickiest, sections of track in the region. I've heard tales of this section alone taking several days to pass, with frequent stops to dig out – so don't tackle it lightly. Later in the year, the track hardens to a roller-coaster ride where you bounce in and out of a succession of dry mud-holes; even then it's fairly slow going.

South along the cut-line This cut-line follows a veterinary fence. I haven't driven this route, but I believe it's probably the quickest route between Maun and the

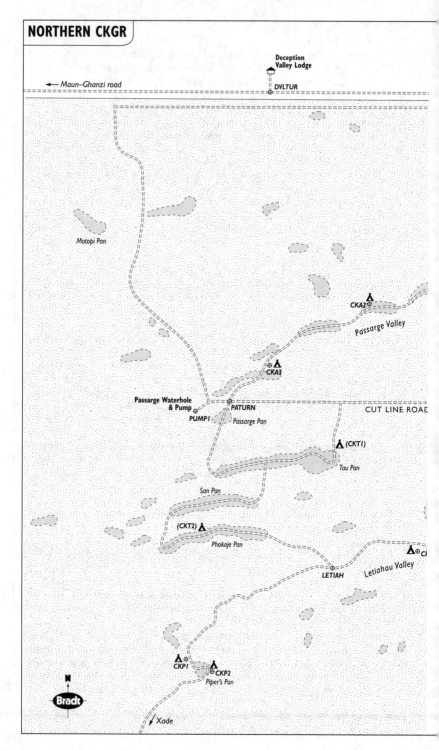

NORTHERN CKGR

Maun–Ghanzi road →

Deception Valley Lodge

DVLTUR

Motopi Pan

Passarge Valley

CKA2

CKA3

Passarge Waterhole & Pump

PUMP1

PATURN

Passarge Pan

CUT LINE ROAD

(CKT1)

Tau Pan

San Pan

(CKT2)

Phokoje Pan

Ci

Letiahau Valley

LETIAH

CKP1

CKP2

Piper's Pan

N

Bradt

Xade

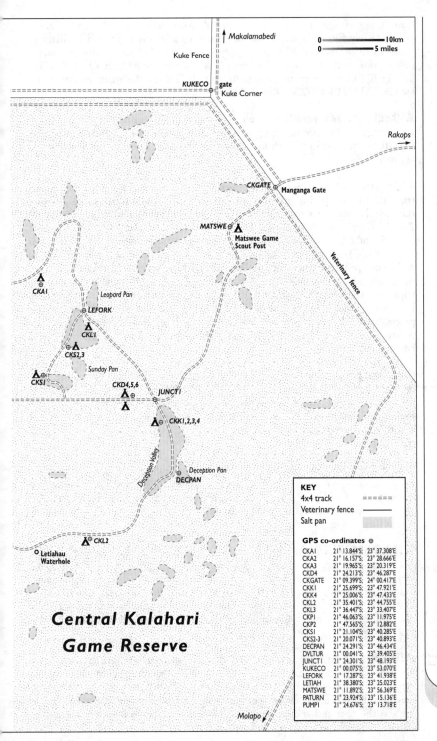

Makalamabedi

Kuke Fence

KUKECO gate
Kuke Corner

Rakops

| 0 | 10km |
| 0 | 5 miles |

CKGATE Manganga Gate

Veterinary fence

MATSWE
Matswee Game
Scout Post

CKA1

Leopard Pan

LEFORK

CKL1

CKS2,3

Sunday Pan

CKS1

CKD4,5,6

JUNCT1

CKK1,2,3,4

Deception Valley

Deception Pan
DECPAN

CKL2

o Letiahau
Waterhole

Central Kalahari
Game Reserve

Molapo

KEY

4x4 track	=====
Veterinary fence	——
Salt pan	

GPS co-ordinates ⊕

CKA1	21° 13.844'S;	23° 37.308'E
CKA2	21° 16.157'S;	23° 28.666'E
CKA3	21° 19.965'S;	23° 20.319'E
CKD4	21° 24.213'S;	23° 46.287'E
CKGATE	21° 09.399'S;	24° 00.417'E
CKK1	21° 25.699'S;	23° 47.921'E
CKK4	21° 25.006'S;	23° 47.433'E
CKL2	21° 35.401'S;	23° 44.755'E
CKL3	21° 36.447'S;	23° 33.407'E
CKP1	21° 46.063'S;	23° 11.975'E
CKP2	21° 47.565'S;	23° 12.882'E
CKS1	21° 21.104'S;	23° 40.285'E
CKS2-3	21° 20.071'S;	23° 40.893'E
DECPAN	21° 24.291'S;	23° 46.434'E
DVLTUR	21° 00.041'S;	23° 39.405'E
JUNCT1	21° 24.301'S;	23° 48.193'E
KUKECO	21° 00.075'S;	23° 53.070'E
LEFORK	21° 17.287'S;	23° 41.938'E
LETIAH	21° 38.380'S;	23° 25.023'E
MATSWE	21° 11.892'S;	23° 56.369'E
PATURN	21° 23.924'S;	23° 15.136'E
PUMP1	21° 24.676'S;	23° 13.718'E

16

CKGR, at least until the tarring of the whole road down from Motopi to Rakops is completely finished. You'll find the north end of this at the small village of Makalamabedi, west of Motopi. Simply follow this due south (driving on the eastern side of the veterinary fence) to Kuke Corner (⊕ KUKECO 21°00.075'S, 23°53.070'E), and from then continue for 21.5km to the main entrance gate (⊕ CKGATE 21°09.399'S, 24°00.417'E).

Without your own vehicle If, like most visitors to Botswana, you don't have the knowledge, experience or equipment for this kind of a trip, then to visit the CKGR you'll need to take a mobile safari to the area. There are several ways to approach this.

Join a group A few of Botswana's larger safari companies have scheduled group trips, leaving on specific pre-planned dates, which include time camping within the CKGR; see the main listings in *Chapter 4, Planning and Preparation* (pages 79–82), *Chapter 8, Maun, Tourist information, travel agents and tour operators* (pages 167–72) and *Chapter 9, Kasane and the Northeast, Local safari companies and travel agents* (pages 186–7). Check out what they have running and read between the lines to make sure you understand exactly how much of their time is within the CKGR: often, quite long trips will spend far too short a time in the park. Many of these trips will also feature Deception Valley Lodge, or even a private campsite on Deception Valley's reserve. Some of the better ones include a one-way flight, probably best done on your way out of the park at the end of your trip. Expect a return charter on a six-seater plane (up to five passengers) to Deception Valley to cost around US$300.

Organise a private mobile trip If you have a fairly generous budget, then the same operators (and many of the smaller ones) will be delighted to organise a private trip for you, for which you'll be able to specify the departure date and the timings. Expect the costs to be high though – in the region of US$200–350 per person per night. (Larger groups and longer expeditions are generally less expensive than smaller groups and shorter trips.)

Book a short trip from a lodge If you just want a few days in the park, then it's worth checking with Leroo-La-Tau, and perhaps also Deception Valley Lodge (see *Where to stay* for details). They will sometimes organise short, simple, guided camping expeditions into the park. Typically these come with a few nights either side at their lodge.

GETTING ORGANISED A visit to the CKGR requires a lot of organisation before you even start to drive there. You must book a place to stay and make arrangements to bring all your water, food, equipment and supplies. Brackish water is sometimes available at the Matswere Scout Post, near the entrance, but it isn't to drink or to be relied upon. Note that all the land outside the park falls into private farms and concessions, and so camping 'outside the gate' is not a practical option.

WHERE TO STAY You have two choices in this area: stay either within the park, using the park's demarcated campsites, or at one of the two lodges. However, these lodges are so far from the park – each is a few hours' drive from the entrance – that they're really only useful either as destinations in their own right, or as comfortable stops at the start and end of trips into the park. Neither is close enough to the CKGR to be used as a base for day trips.

Campsites inside the park The only places to stay inside the park are campsites. All of these are totally undeveloped; they're just cleared patches of ground with no water, toilets or showers. You must bring all the water you need, all your food and a spade to dig your own toilets. (Don't forget matches to burn any tissue paper before burying it!)

As for the rest of Botswana's parks, it's essential that you book and pay for these campsites in advance, or you will not be allowed in through the gate. See pages 138–9 for how to do this, and details of the costs. Each of the CKGR's campsites has a unique code: CKK1, CKK2, CKL1, CKP1 etc. I've made notes on some of these under *What to see and do*, identifying most with comments and GPS locations.

Lodges outside the park There is only one lodge really close to the park: Deception Valley Lodge. This must be booked in advance, as if full there are no nearby alternative options. Note that it is at least two hours' drive from the scout gate camp, and over three hours from the area within the CKGR known as Deception Valley. Leroo-La-Tau Lodge and its adjacent campsite, Xwarga, (see pages 399–400) stand beside the western border of Makgadikgadi Pans National Park, so are at least three hours' drive from the park's entrance gate.

🏠 **Deception Valley Lodge** (6 chalets) Pretoria 0001, South Africa; ☎ +27 11 663 6948/9; f +27 11 663 6947; e res@deceptionvalley.co.za; www.deceptionvalley.co.za. The quality of construction and furnishing used at Deception Valley Lodge ranks it as one of Botswana's top lodges. However, it is also in one of the country's more remote locations, and its relative lack of big game suits old Africa hands more than first-time visitors. Because of these factors, its prices aren't (yet) as high as you might expect.

Each chalet contains a separate large lounge and bedroom, and a smaller bathroom between them. Everything is under thatch. The focus of the lounge is a large, glass coffee-table and a very comfortable sofa. Its walls are dotted with framed Bushman artefacts, whilst lovely rugs are spread across the floors. A constant 220V electricity powers a ceiling fan in each room, a well-stocked fridge/minibar in the lounge and any number of lamps and lights, including some particularly beautiful ones which use ostrich eggshells as shades.

The bedroom has heavy teak furniture, copious wardrobe space and a couple of adjacent twin beds (or a king-size double) with mosquito nets. Sublimely comfortable mattresses are covered with notably high-quality cotton sheets and Botswana's best down quilts – which you'll need as the Kalahari's temperatures plummet at night. Everything is monogrammed with the lodge's own brown hyena logo. The 'blanket box' doubles as a lockable safety-deposit box.

Between these 2 main rooms is the equally stylish bathroom, with a flush toilet and a washbasin. A free-standing, old-style, claw-foot iron bath and an outside shower both derive hot water from an efficient gas geyser.

All around the chalet large sliding doors (with brass fittings) can be opened by day, and closed at night for warmth. These lead outside on to a shaded area of polished wooden decking, furnished with leather chairs and a table. Each of the bungalows is widely separated from the next, and linked by natural walkways lit by cute, gecko-shaped lights.

The lodge's main reception, lounge and dining areas are furnished in similar style, with equally careful attention to detail, and there's a small curio shop which sells a fairly unremarkable range of T-shirts as well as quilted warm jackets – handy if you misjudged just how cold it can get here.

Activities centre around drives and walks on the lodge's own area, which shares its southern boundary with the CKGR. (Note that drives don't normally visit the game reserve, which is too far for a comfortable day trip.) The landscape, flora and fauna here are exactly the same as in the main reserve, although being much smaller and fenced the lodge doesn't get the large wet-season congregations which are a major attraction of the CKGR.

That said, the lodge's private area encompasses a number of natural pans surrounded by larger trees, and there's a bird-hide beside one. Despite the relative lack of big game, there's plenty to look at, although this is an environment in which you would probably miss many of the smaller attractions without a good guide. The walks are often led by the lodge's San guides, and sometimes incorporate demonstrations of their traditional skills staged in a small village re-created for the purpose.

US$355/461.50 pp sharing/sgl low season to US$630/819 high season, inc all meals, drinks, laundry and game drives. Open all year.

🏠 **Leroo-La-Tau Lodge** (7 tents) Leroo-La-Tau (✦ LEROOL 20°25.240'S, 24°31.277'E), situated at the eastern end of a bend in the Boteti River, has very

comfortable chalets and a choice of activities. See pages 399–400 for full details.

🛖 **Xwaraga campsite** See page 400. This bush campsite is a few mins' walk from Leroo-La-Tau Lodge.

GETTING AROUND Just over 8km southwest of the entrance into the CKGR you'll find the small Matswere Scout Post (✦ MATSWE 21°11.892'S, 23°56.369'E). Here you can sign in and, if you ask the scouts politely, it's sometimes possible to fill up with brackish water – which is fine for showers, but not suitable for drinking. (You should have arrived with all your own water, but if you didn't, then make the most of this. There are no other waterpoints north of Xade.)

Driving conditions In the dry season, the general quality of the tracks in the park is surprising. Many of them, particularly those which follow the valleys, are really very good. You might have expected to be constantly ploughing through deep sand, but it's not like that. Of course there are patches of deep and tricky sand, and also stretches of black-cotton soil (rock hard when dry; virtually impassable if very wet), but many of the road surfaces are easy and hard when it's dry.

WHAT TO SEE AND DO

Being in a pristine area which is as remote as the CKGR is, for most visitors, an end in itself. Just being able to camp, move around and watch the wildlife at leisure in such a beautiful wilderness, with the certainty that you'll see very few other vehicles, is the real attraction here. So don't rush around looking for 'sights', as there really aren't any. Just take time to enjoy where you are!

That said, detailed here are some of the areas that you may visit, including a few notes on some of the various campsites, with their names (and booking codes). Your permit for camping in the CKGR will specify the precise campsites booked for you on each night – and these can't be changed when you're here.

If you're entering and leaving via the Matswere Scout Post then a lovely week's circuit can be made by starting around Sunday and Leopard pans, then heading north and west along Passarge Valley, south via the western link to Piper's Pan, and then returning northeast through Letiahau and Deception valleys. This is the order in which I've described these areas.

SUNDAY AND LEOPARD PANS Sunday and Leopard, just north of Deception Valley, are two fairly large pans. Either of their campsites makes a good first stop if you enter the park via Matswere and plan on heading around Passarge Valley.

The more southerly Sunday Pan has three campsites. The first (CKS1) is slightly left of the track when you're driving north, at ✦ CKS1 21°21.104'S; 23°40.285'E. Further on, the turn-off to the second and third sites (CKS2 and CKS3) is to the right, at ✦ CKS2-3 21°20.071'S; 23°40.893'E. All are pleasant, in the edge of the bush close to the main open area of the pan.

Leopard Pan is about 5km further north, and has one campsite (CKL1).

PASSARGE VALLEY This is a long valley with many pans and several campsites. Approaching from the east, it's easily reached from Leopard Pan by finding the junction of tracks to the north of the pan (✦ LEFORK 21°17.287'S; 23°41.938'E), and heading north from there.

On one morning's game-viewing, driving slowly north into the end of Deception Valley, we spotted something unfamiliar moving in the distance. Training our binoculars, we could see a woman waving. We signalled that we'd seen her and continued, eventually taking a right track to head in her direction.

Approaching with some trepidation, we found a distressed Tswana woman on her own. She'd been standing on the roof of the 4x4 all morning, trying to attract attention. In fact she was one of the park's staff who, together with a few colleagues, had been driving from the Matswere Scout Post to Xade (I never learnt why they were on a side-track off the main route!).

It seems that late the previous day the fuel filter in their old Land Rover had sprung a bad leak, marooning them there. They'd slept overnight but, with little water or food, her colleagues had set off to walk the 50km or so back to Matswere, and perhaps find visitors on the way who could help.

I spent a petrol-soaked hour under the vehicle, attempting a bush repair with no success, before offering her a lift back to the park's office. However, it transpired that this was the scout camp's only vehicle, so they wouldn't be able to do much. Hours later a better-equipped, modern Land Rover approached; it carried a bush-wise South African couple who travelled with what seemed like a garage full of spares and tools. The park workers had managed to flag this vehicle down and enlist the couple's help.

They were lucky. The park's remaining staff would have been virtually powerless to help, even if they'd known about the breakdown. Fortunately these visitors had the right tools and spare parts, so a repair was soon made. All set off again to Xade in their clapped-out Land Rover with few supplies. I hope they got there.

The morals of this story are simple:

- Don't expect any help from the park's staff: they probably won't have the vehicles or resources.
- Don't come to the CKGR without some basic spares, a simple tool kit and another vehicle to help you out.
- A satellite phone isn't totally necessary, but is a wise back-up, so bring one if possible.
- Ample food and water are absolutely essential: bring more than you expect to need.

Initially the landscape is quite a thick mixture of small trees and bushes: typical Kalahari sandveld. Then after about 13km you'll find an old green sign saying: 'Passarge Valley. Help keep this valley pristine by staying on the track'. Gradually – now heading southwest – you descend into a valley with a more open landscape and more grassland. About 9.5km further there's a turning south to Manong Campsite (✪ CKA1 21°13.844'S; 23°37.308'E), a lovely campsite set very much on its own.

Continuing in the valley for another 18km you'll then find a track to the north signposted to Kgokong Campsite (✪ CKA2 21°16.157'S; 23°28.666'E). Here the valley is really stunning: open grassland dotted with a few small tree-islands. The campsite is in the thickets just off to the side, slightly above the floor of the valley.

Further southwest, the third of Passarge's campsites is Kukama Campsite (✪ CKA3 21°19.965'S; 23°20.319'E), in a small group of trees beside a fairly scrubby pan. This is about 12km northeast of the junction with the park's main east–west cut-line track, at ✪ PATURN 21°23.924'S; 23°15.136'E.

PASSARGE PAN AND THE TRACK TO MOTOPI A little beyond the southwest end of Passarge Valley track, Passarge Pan is on the south side of the track which leads to a water pump (⊕ PUMP1 21°24.676'S; 23°13.718'E). North of here a track leads through some lovely country dotted with small pans to Motopi Pan, and ultimately to the double fence which is the northern boundary of the reserve. Note that there is no open gate here, and no way in or out of the reserve by this road. However, when you reach the fence you can take a right and follow a decent track that runs east beside the fence, and then southeast from Kuke Corner (still confined within the park's boundary fence) to the main entrance.

THE WESTERN LINK On the northeast side of Passarge Pan, the track south towards Phukwi, Tau, San and Phokoje pans starts at ⊕ PATURN 21°23.924'S; 23°15.136'E. This track is the start of the 'western link', which eventually heads south towards Piper's Pan.

You'll see from the map that this track seems to zig-zag, always heading either north–south or east–west; this is because the inter-dune valleys (with their string of pans) run east–west. These valleys usually make the best game-viewing areas. They are linked by tracks running north–south, across the top of the dunes.

Note that on this track, the first few kilometres south of the main cut-line track (⊕ PATURN) is very boggy; I'd expect this to be exceedingly challenging during the rains.

For an alternative route south, you can enter the western link via Tau Pan. To do this, first turn east along the cut-line towards the north end of Deception Valley. About 18km from ⊕ PATURN, there's a track which heads almost due south to Phukwi Pan. There is a campsite (CKT1) on this route, at Tau Pan.

The only other campsite on this side is CKT2 (⊕ CKT2 21°35.278'S; 23°16.332'E), which is roughly half-way along the track which follows Phokoje Pan. Heading east along this, the track splits off southeast from Phokoje Pan about 18km before its junction (⊕ LETIAH 21°38.380'S; 23°25.023'E) with the main track from the Letiahau Valley to Piper's Pan.

PIPER'S PAN Piper's Pan is as far south as most people visit in the northern section of the park, and as far as I'll describe in this chapter. If you are wondering if it's worth the effort to get here, the answer is a resounding 'yes'. And that's despite a badly corrugated section of road just north of this area.

Piper's Pan is only a few kilometres across, but it's a stunning stretch of perfectly flat grass. In the rains it's green, and often covered with springbok and gemsbok. By as early as May, it has usually turned a beautiful gold, like a field of ripe barley.

There are two campsites here. CKP1 (⊕ CKP1 21°46.063'S; 23°11.975'E), slightly further north, is in a grove of rather lovely trees on the west side of the track, but close to the edge of the pan.

The second site, CKP2 (⊕ CKP2 21°47.565'S; 23°12.882'E) is further south, up higher on a low fossilised dune. This is just beyond a prominent green water tank (⊕ WATANK 21°47.045'S; 23°12.755'E) which stands at the top of a fossilised dune, beside the track which leads, around 72km later, to Xade.

Around the outside edge of the pan itself there's a 7km circular track that is well worth exploring, although probably impassable during the rains. The eastern side of this (around ⊕ PIPERE 21°46.336'S; 23°15.039'E) is particularly treacherous black-cotton soil, while it often seems to disappear on the southern side. It's a lovely circuit, but very slow driving even when dry, as the hardened earth is very uneven.

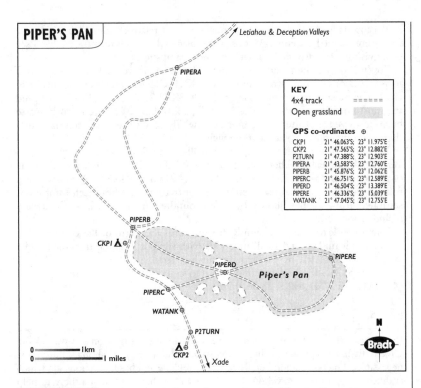

Letiahau & Deception Valleys

KEY

4x4 track ══════

Open grassland

GPS co-ordinates ⊕

CKP1	21° 46.063'S; 23° 11.975'E
CKP2	21° 47.565'S; 23° 12.882'E
P2TURN	21° 47.388'S; 23° 12.903'E
PIPERA	21° 43.583'S; 23° 12.760'E
PIPERB	21° 45.876'S; 23° 12.062'E
PIPERC	21° 46.751'S; 23° 12.589'E
PIPERD	21° 46.504'S; 23° 13.389'E
PIPERE	21° 46.336'S; 23° 15.039'E
WATANK	21° 47.045'S; 23° 12.755'E

PIPERA

PIPERB

CKP1

PIPERD

PIPERE

Piper's Pan

PIPERC

WATANK

P2TURN

CKP2

Xade

0 ━━━━━ 1km
0 ━━━━━ 1 miles

N

Bradt

LETIAHAU VALLEY Approaching from the south and Piper's Pan, the road to Matswere leads first through Letiahau and then Deception Valley. About 12km northeast of the junction (⊕ LETIAH 21°38.380'S; 23°25.023'E), which is the turning north for the western link, the track enters the picturesque Letiahau Valley. A further 4km on there's a small turning south from the road which, after about 100m, leads to a group of trees in a bushy plain where the Letiahau Campsite (⊕ CKL3 21°36.447'S; 23°33.407'E) is situated. Around 6km further east, a tiny loop takes a closer look at the permanent Letiahau waterhole.

About 20km east of the first campsite is a second one called Lekhubu (⊕ CKL2 21°35.401'S; 23°44.755'E), off on the south side of the road. Continuing east from this, the track backs around to take a more northerly line as it approaches Deception Valley.

DECEPTION PAN This open pan (⊕ DECPAN 21°24.291'S; 23°46.434'E) at the southern end of the valley is found by taking a short detour, about 1.5km from the main track. It fills with water during the rains, but for the rest of the year it's flat, cracked mud, tinged a vivid red colour by a small red water plant which flourishes when it's full.

DECEPTION VALLEY This is a long, broad inter-dune valley running roughly north–south; it's thought to be the bed of a fossil river. During and after good rains this is carpeted in luscious green grass that attracts dense concentrations of game. It's the park's most famous location, and where Mark and Delia Owens (see *Appendix 3, Further Information*) lived. If you are visiting the northern section of the park for five to six days, then my advice is for you to save this as a highlight for your last couple of days.

The Central Kalahari WHAT TO SEE AND DO

16

Because it is the park's most famous area, and relatively close (35km) to the Matswere Scout Post entrance, this is the place where you're most likely to see other visitors. It's also the area with the most campsites.

Towards the northern end of Deception Valley, on the west side, a track splits off to pass beside the four Kori campsites (CKK1–CKK4), which are about 500m apart. The most southerly one is located at ⊕ CKK1 21°25.699'S; 23°47.921'E, and the most northerly at ⊕ CKK4 21°25.006'S; 23°47.433'E. They're in fairly sparse bush on the edge of the main pan, and generally very close to any animal action there – though bushes obstruct their views.

Deception Valley's other campsites are all set north of the pan, higher up in fairly thick woodlands. There are six of these (CKD1–CKD6), three on either side of the cut-line road. CKD4 (⊕ CKD4 21°24.213'S; 23°46.287'E) consists of a roughly circular area that has been cleared of trees and bushes. Each campsite is separated from its neighbours by a few hundred metres, making them very secluded and private.

When you leave the park, simply drive towards the north of Deception Valley. There you'll find several small junctions with signposts, as the tracks along the valley are intersected by the straight cut-line road. Head east to ⊕ JUNCT1 21°24.301'S; 23°48.193'E, and continue on to sign out at the Matswere Scout Post (⊕ MATSWE 21°11.892'S, 23°56.369'E).

RAKOPS

Rakops is a small town that makes a very useful staging post on the way to the CKGR. It has telephones, cellphone coverage and a range of shops selling most necessities. The fuel station here is generally reliable and has marvellous old hand-cranked fuel pumps (marvellous, that is, provided there's someone there to help you physically pump the fuel!).

FCO TRAVEL ADVICE
know before you go
fco.gov.uk/travel

Bradt Travel Guides is a partner to the 'know before you go' campaign, masterminded by the UK Foreign and Commonwealth Office to promote the importance of finding out about a destination before you travel. By combining the up-to-date advice of the FCO with the in-depth knowledge of Bradt authors, you'll ensure that your trip will be as trouble-free as possible.

www.fco.gov.uk/travel

17

Livingstone and the Victoria Falls

Livingstone is probably better oriented towards visitors than any other corner of Zambia. In spite of this, visitors travelling north from Zimbabwe are attracted simply by the Victoria Falls. Until recently the town of Livingstone often remained unseen. In the past, some have even viewed it with suspicion, being bigger and less well known than the small Zimbabwean town which shares the name of the waterfall. As a result of Zimbabwe's political instability, however, much of this has changed in recent years. Zimbabwe is now considerably more expensive than Zambia, and the requirement for high-priced visas has not helped. Add to this concerns over safety, and fuel and food shortages, and it's not hard to see why Livingstone, and the lodges on the Zambian side of the river, are going from strength to strength.

The Zimbabwean and Zambian sides offer different views, and it is worth seeing both sides to appreciate the whole waterfall. Yet while this chapter aims to give details of both, it incorporates far more information on Livingstone, reflecting the situation on the ground. Livingstone has developed and become popular in its own right; it's now the destination of first choice for most people visiting the Victoria Falls. Historians might note that most adventure activities like rafting, bungee jumping and microlighting originally started on the Zambian side of the falls, before being taken over by more commercial Zimbabwean companies.

HISTORY

We can be sure that the falls were well known to the native peoples of southern Africa well before any European 'discovered' them. After the San/Bushmen hunter-gatherers, the Tokaleya people inhabited the area, and it was probably they who christened the falls *Shongwe*. Later, the Ndebele knew the falls as the *aManza Thunqayo*, and after that the Makololo referred to them as *Mosi-oa-Tunya*.

However, their first written description comes to us from Dr David Livingstone, who approached them in November 1855 from the west – from Linyanti, along the Chobe and Zambezi rivers. Livingstone already knew of their existence from the locals, and wrote:

I resolved on the following day to visit the falls of Victoria, called by the natives Mosioatunya, or more anciently Shongwe. Of these we had often heard since we came into the country: indeed one of the questions asked by Sebituane [the chief of the Makololo tribe] travelling was, 'Have you the smoke that sounds in your country?' They did not go near enough to examine them, but, viewing them with awe at a distance, said, in reference to the vapour and noise, 'Mosi oa tunya' (smoke does sound there). It was previously called Shongwe, the meaning of which I could not ascertain. The word for a 'pot' resembles this, and it may mean a seething cauldron; but I am not certain of it.

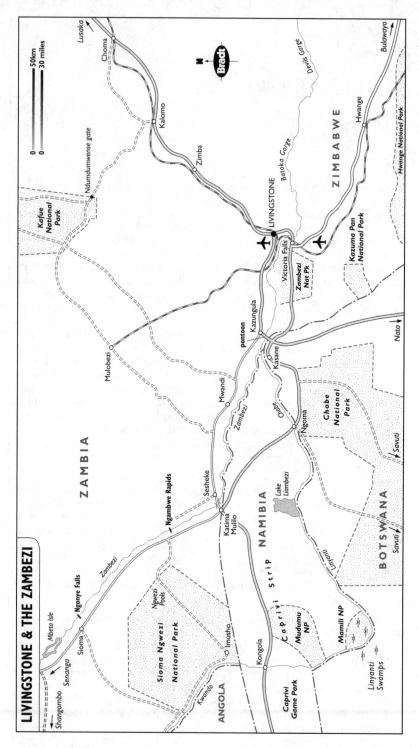

LIVINGSTONE & THE ZAMBEZI

0   50km
0   30 miles

Bradt

ZAMBIA

ZIMBABWE

NAMIBIA

Caprivi Strip

ANGOLA

BOTSWANA

Lusaka

Choma

Kalomo

Zimba

Ndumdumwense gate

Kafue National Park

Mulobezi

LIVINGSTONE

Victoria Falls

Zambezi Nat Pk

Batoka Gorge

Devils Gorge

Hwange

Hwange National Park

Kazuma Pan National Park

Kazungula

pontoon

Kasane

Mwandi

Chobe

Chobe National Park

Ngoma

Savuti

Nata

Zambezi

Sesheke

Ngambwe Rapids

Katima Mulilo

Lake Liambezi

Linyanti

Savuti

Linyanti Swamps

Mamili NP

Mudumu NP

Kongola

Kwando

Imusho

Ngwezi Pools

Sioma Ngwezi National Park

Caprivi Game Park

Sioma

Ngonye Falls

Mbeta Isle

Zambezi

Senanga

Shangombo

422

Livingstone continues to describe the river above the falls, its islands and their lush vegetation, before making his most famous comment about sightseeing angels, now abused and misquoted by those who write tourist brochures to the area:

Some trees resemble the great spreading oak, others assume the character of our own elms and chestnuts; but no one can imagine the beauty of the view from anything witnessed in England. It had never been seen before by European eyes; but scenes so lovely must have been gazed upon by angels in their flight. The only want felt is that of mountains in the background. The falls are bounded on three sides by ridges 300 or 400 feet in height, which are covered in forest, with the red soil appearing amongst the trees. When about half a mile from the falls, I left the canoe by which we had come down this far, and embarked in a lighter one, with men well acquainted with the rapids, who, by passing down the centre of the stream in the eddies and still places caused by many jutting rocks, brought me to an island situated in the middle of the river, on the edge of the lip over which the water rolls.

From the autobiographical Journeys in South Africa

Those who bemoan the area's emphasis on tourism should note that there must have been sightseeing boat trips ever since David Livingstone came this way.

Being the most eastern point reachable by boat from the Chobe or Upper Zambezi rivers, the area of the falls was a natural place for European settlement. Soon more traders, hunters and missionaries came into the area, and by the late 1800s a small European settlement had formed around a ferry crossing called the Old Drift, about 10km upstream from the falls. However, this was built on low-lying marshy ground near the river, buzzing with mosquitoes, so malaria took many lives.

By 1905 the spectacular Victoria Falls bridge had been completed, linking the copper deposits of the Copperbelt and the coal deposits at Wankie (now Hwange) with a railway line. This, and malaria, encouraged the settlers to transfer to a site on higher ground, next to the railway line at a place called Constitution Hill. It became the centre of present-day Livingstone, and many of its original buildings are still standing. A small cemetery, the poignant remains of Old Drift, can still be seen on the northern bank of the Zambezi within the Mosi-oa-Tunya National Park.

In 1911 Livingstone became the capital of Northern Rhodesia (now Zambia), which it remained until 1935, when the administration was transferred to Lusaka.

GEOLOGY

The falls are, geologically speaking, probably a very recent formation. About a million years ago, the Zambezi's course is thought to have been down a wide valley over a plateau dating from the karoo period, until it met the Middle Zambezi rift – where the Matetsi River mouth is now.

Here it fell about 250m over an escarpment. However, that fast-falling water would have eroded the lip of the waterfall and gouged out a deeper channel within the basalt rock of the escarpment plateau – and so the original falls steadily retreated upstream. These channels tended to follow some existing fissure – a crack or weakness, formed when the lava first cooled at the end of the karoo period. At around the Batoka Gorge these fissures naturally run east–west in the rock, parallel to the course of the valley.

By around the Middle Pleistocene period, between 35,000 and 40,000 years ago, this process had formed the Batoka Gorge, carving it out to within about 90km of the present falls.

17

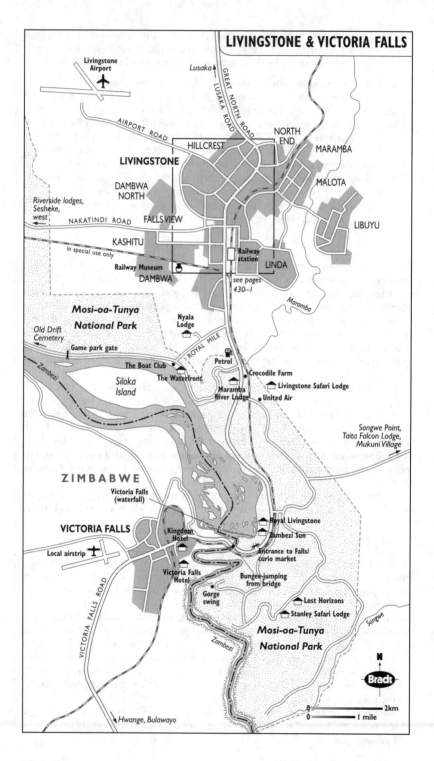

LIVINGSTONE & VICTORIA FALLS

Livingstone Airport

Lusaka

GREAT NORTH ROAD

LUSAKA ROAD

AIRPORT ROAD

HILLCREST

NORTH END

MARAMBA

LIVINGSTONE

DAMBWA NORTH

MALOTA

Riverside lodges, Sesheke, west

NAKATINDI ROAD

FALLS VIEW

LIBUYU

KASHITU

in special use only

Railway station

Railway Museum

DAMBWA

LINDA

see pages 430–1

Maramba

Mosi-oa-Tunya National Park

Nyala Lodge

Old Drift Cemetery

Game park gate

ROYAL MILE

Petrol

Zambezi

The Boat Club

The Waterfront

Crocodile Farm

Livingstone Safari Lodge

Siloka Island

Maramba River Lodge

United Air

Songwe Point, Taita Falcon Lodge, Mukuni Village

ZIMBABWE

Victoria Falls (waterfall)

VICTORIA FALLS

Royal Livingstone

Kingdom Hotel

Zambezi Sun

Local airstrip

Entrance to Falls/ curio market

Victoria Falls Hotel

Bungee-jumping from bridge

Gorge swing

Lost Horizons

Stanley Safari Lodge

Songwe

VICTORIA FALLS ROAD

Mosi-oa-Tunya National Park

Zambezi

N

Bradt

0   2km
0   1 mile

Hwange, Bulawayo

However, as water eroded away the lip of the falls, its valley gradually turned north, until it was almost at right angles to the basalt fault lines which run east–west. Then the water began to erode the fissures and turn them into walls of rock stretching across the valley, perpendicular to it, over which gushed broad curtains of water.

Once such a wall had formed, the water would wear down the rock until it found a fault line behind the wall, along which the water would erode and cause the rock subsequently to collapse. Thus the new fault line would become the wall of the new falls, behind the old one. This process resulted in the eight gorges that now form the river's slalom course after it has passed over the present falls. Each gorge was once a great waterfall.

Today, on the eastern side of the Devil's Cataract, you can see this pattern starting again. The water is eroding away the rock of another fault line, behind the line of the present falls, which geologists expect will form a new waterfall a few thousand years from now.

USEFUL INFORMATION

TOURIST INFORMATION Both Livingstone and Victoria Falls have tourist information offices where you can expect pleasant, friendly staff working with limited resources. Livingstone's is the Zambia National Tourist Board or ZNTB (↘ *321404/87;* e *zntblive@zamnet.zm; www.zambiatourism.com; open Mon–Fri 08.00–13.00 & 14.00–17.00, Sat 08.00–12.00*), at the tourist centre next to the Livingstone Museum, where Mosi-oa-Tunya Road bends into the centre of town. You can pick up brochures and get referrals, but agents and tour operators are usually better geared to assist you with actual bookings.

The Victoria Falls office is a small bungalow opposite Wimpy on Park Way.

For details of local tour operators, see page 467.

IMPORTANT NOTE ON VISAS In recent years both Zambia and Zimbabwe have changed their rules on visas, requiring more payments for crossing the borders. Zimbabwe's visas proved the major problem, seeming excessive to the operators in the falls area, who relied for their livelihood on a free flow of people across the border. (Visitors may stay on one side, but would want to take part in activities on both sides.)

Fortunately, for those visiting Zambia, a deal has been reached whereby you can enter Zambia without having to pay for an entry visa provided you are staying overnight, your holiday/arrangements have been pre-booked outside the country via a Zambian tour operator and your operator gives your passport details at least 24 hours in advance to the immigration authorities at point of entry. This is strictly enforced at all points of entry.

Essentially, operators or hotels need to put your name on a list down at the border post, and if successful you pass through free. Some tour operators actually cover the cost of your Zambia entry visa while others do not: thus it's always best to enquire at the time of booking. So remember to book your Zambian accommodation or activity in advance by a few days, and you generally won't need to pay.

LIVINGSTONE

ORIENTATION Livingstone town itself is fairly compact and surrounded by several small township suburbs, sprawling out from its centre. It has an estimated population of 140,000. Much bigger than Victoria Falls, the town has two main business areas, concentrated along its main street, the all-important Mosi-oa-

Tunya Road. Sections of this are lined with classic colonial buildings with corrugated-iron roofs and wide wooden verandas, some beautifully restored and others in a state of disrepair. The larger and busier central business district begins atop a small hill just past the museum, while in the lower part of town is a smaller but growing retail area known as '217'. Navigation is easy, even without a map, though signposts are often missing or may point to establishments no longer in existence.

Drive north out of the city, and the main street leading to the capital becomes Lusaka Road. Head south for about 10km and you reach the Zambezi River and Victoria Falls themselves, and the border post to cross into Zimbabwe via Victoria Falls Bridge. Many visitors choose to stay here at the border post, most at one of Sun International's two hotels which are close to the falls.

Travel west from town on Nakatindi/Kazungula Road and you soon find yourself parallel to the Zambezi, following its north bank upstream towards Kazungula and the ferry to Botswana. Signposts to the left point to small, exclusive lodges, perched at picturesque spots on the river's bank.

GETTING THERE AND AWAY

By air Livingstone's international airport (✆ 321153, 323322, m 097 790733; f 324235; e nacliv@zamnet.zm) is just 5km northwest of the town centre on Airport Road. It is currently going through a further phase of upgrading and redevelopment, which will transform its current facilities and service. As it stands, it has pleasant waiting rooms, airline offices, a bank and Bushtracks desk, as well as a bar and snack bar, plus sundries (sweets, postcards, stamps etc) and curio shops for last-minute purchases. Be warned, though, that once you've passed through to the departure side of passport control, the only bar has no catering facilities (aside from chocolate and crisps) and there is nowhere to purchase books or newspapers. There is, though, a small private lounge, for which entry – open to all – costs US$15, to include unlimited drinks (with rather basic snacks). There is a departure tax of US$20 per person for flights leaving Zambia, and about US$5 on domestic routes, payable in the main terminal building *before* going through security and proceeding to check-in. Airport personnel are friendly and helpful.

The airport is served by a number of scheduled airlines and charter companies (Livingstone–Johannesburg fares US$130–160, slightly more expensive in the opposite direction).

✈ **Nationwide Airlines** ✆ 322251, Sun's Activity Centre ✆ 323360; f 324575; e nationwide@ zamnet.zm or reslvi@nationwideair.co.za; www.flynationwide.co.za. This South Africa-based carrier has daily flights from Johannesburg at competitive prices, sometimes several flights a day. Nationwide was the first major carrier to come into Livingstone and remains the only carrier to fly every day of the week.

✈ **British Airways/Comair** ✆ 322827; f 322873; e bamnvfa@mweb.co.zw. Flights 5 times weekly on Johannesburg–Livingstone route, Mon,Wed, Thu, Fri and Sun. Flights typically depart Johannesburg mid-morning and return early afternoon. Fares US$134–154 one way, double for return, with those booked in the other direction rather more expensive.

✈ **South African Airways** ✆ 323033/2/1; f 323034; e saalivingstone@zamnet.zm. New on the scene. Flies Mon, Thu, Sat. Costs about US$150 for direct flights between Livingstone and Johannesburg.

✈ **Zambian Airways** ✆ 322967 or Lusaka 01 257655; f 323080; e livingstone@ zambianairways.com or reservations@ zambianairways.com; www.zambianairways.com. Daily scheduled flights to Lusaka, departing midday with connections around Zambia. Flies to Johannesburg via Lusaka. The return ticket is open-ended and you get 30kg of luggage allowance free, with only US$0.50 per extra kg. Flights to Lusaka cost about US$180 one way; Livingstone–Lusaka–Johannesburg US$280 one way.

Of the charter companies that fly into Livingstone, the following have offices here:

✈ **Proflight** Lusaka ☎ 01 271032/5; f 01 271139; m 097 335563; e proflight@iconnect.zm; www.proflight-zambia.com (shares offices with Livingstone Air Safaris). Professionally run, service-oriented airline that offers both scheduled and charter flights throughout Zambia including meet and greet service for all flights. No scheduled flights LVI–LUN yet. Seat-rate charter between LVI and Lower Zam is US$390 pp each way, min 4 persons. Flights scheduled to connect to international flights whenever possible. Any IATA agent should be able to book flights on Proflight via BSP system. Have largest fleet of aircraft in the country: 18-seater executive twin-engine Jetstream 32, 8-seat executive twin engine Piper Chieftain (leather seats and spacious interiors), 5-seat twin engine Beechcraft Baron (fast and comfortable, perfect for small groups on longer trips), 4-seat sgl engine Cessna 206 (short

flights) and 2 x 9-seat twin engine Britten Norman Islanders (ideal for bush camp strips and small cargo).

✈ **Livingstone Air Safaris** ☎/f 323224/321248; e livingstnair@zamnet.zm. Offers flights from Livingstone to numerous camps throughout Botswana, Zambia, Namibia and Zimbabwe in 3-seat C182 and 5-seat C210 aircraft. There is a strict luggage restriction of 12kg max pp (in soft bags only).

✈ **Star of Africa Air Charters** ☎ 322285, m (263) 11 211 088; e starofafrica@zamnet.zm. Based in Lusaka, they operate charters throughout Zambia and also seat rates on selected routes.

Airport transfers can be pre-booked through all tour operators or with Bushtracks the local favourite if your lodge doesn't offer this service. Rates: from US$15 pp into town, around US$30 to Victoria Falls, or from US$30 to Kazungula ferry/Botswana border.

By bus The main terminus for local buses is on the corner of Senanga Road and Akapelwa Street, just behind Mosi-oa-Tunya Road, opposite Barclays Bank, and beside the town market. Some also leave from around the post office, where a range of buses gathers in the early morning, and most head towards Lusaka. If you want to go west to Sesheke or Kazangula you'll need to get a minibus from the Mingongo Bus Station down the Nakatindi Road. Expect the first buses to leave around 06.30, and the last around 11.00, depending upon demand (and note that music played may be at ear-splitting levels). Tickets are bought on the bus, and cost around US$10/Kw40,000 for a one-way fare to Lusaka on a large bus. If you're backpacking, you can expect the attentions of bus touts. Since buses leave only when they're full, and fares are only slightly cheaper than those on the 'luxury' buses (see below), it's not usually worth the extra time and hassle unless you want a truly local experience. There are a number of private coaches running scheduled services to Lusaka, for which you'll need to book a ticket several hours in advance, and preferably the day before, at the point of departure. Each coach operates from a different place, so be sure to get to the right stop. The trip takes around five to six hours, depending on the company, and fares are US$12/Kw45,000 one way.

🚌 **CR Carriers** The largest of the local coach services, operating from the corner of Mosi-oa-Tunya Rd and Akapelwa St, opposite Barclays Bank, has 5–6 buses a day to Lusaka, with some onward services to Chipata, Ndola and Kitwe. The first departs from Livingstone at 06.00, and the last at 14.00. There are also onward services to Chipata

(5–6hrs), Ndola (4–5 hs) and Kitwe (5–6hrs).
🚌 **RPS** 2 buses a day leave for Lusaka from their depot next to the Hungry Lion (see page 444). Onward services connect to Mongu (6–7hrs) and Mansa (11–12hrs).
🚌 **Euro Coaches** Leave from outside the post office. There is 1 coach a day to Lusaka.

In addition to these, Intercape Mainliner runs a return service from Windhoek in Namibia to Victoria Falls, stopping at Kasane in Botswana, right on the Zambian border. This is a popular option for those travelling to or from Namibia, as you can avoid paying the visa fee for Zimbabwe by travelling via Botswana. The journey from Kasane to Livingstone takes an hour or so, and costs about Kw12,000 by minibus or Kw100,000 by taxi. Tickets must be booked in advance, either online at www.intercape.co.za, or at the Intercape Mainliner offices in Windhoek or Victoria Falls.

By train The railway station (*reservations:* ✏ *321001 ext 336*) is well signposted about 1km south of the town centre on the way to the falls, on the eastern side of Mosi-oa-Tunya Road.

While buses are faster and cheaper than trains, there is nevertheless a viable rail service from Livingstone. Most useful of these is the *Zambezi Express* train, which runs overnight between Livingstone and Lusaka three times a week, though timetables are generally unreliable. Bookings can only be made on the day of departure at the railway station, and can only be confirmed by payment – thus you must go in person.

Driving west If you have a vehicle and intend to head west, into Namibia's Caprivi Strip, Botswana, or western Zambia, then Nakatindi Road continues past the lodges by the river and, after about 60km, to Kazungula – where Namibia, Botswana, Zimbabwe and Zambia all meet at a notional point. Here you can continue northwest within Zambia to Sesheke, or take the ferry across the Zambezi into Botswana, near Kasane.

GETTING AROUND

By taxi Livingstone town is small enough to walk around, as is the falls area. However if you are travelling between the two, or going to the airport, or in a hurry, then use one of the plentiful – if battered – light-blue taxis that congregate near Shoprite at the main taxi stand or on Mosi-oa-Tunya Road near the main bureaux de change. All taxis are supposed to carry a fare chart, though you may be lucky to see one. A taxi between town and either the falls or the airport will cost around US$8–10/Kw30,000–40,000 per person depending upon the number of passengers. From the airport to town is about US$8/Kw32,000, from the airport to the falls/border is about US$10–12/Kw40,000–50,000 or more, and out to the riverside lodges will cost from around US$15/Kw60,000. Taxi drivers are not allowed into the game park. Competition amongst taxi drivers can be fierce, so be sure to negotiate for the best deal and agree on the price in advance. The city council has recently, and controversially, approved minibus licences in the hope of reducing the taxi population and providing more affordable transport for local people.

Tour operators While you can negotiate to hire a taxi for the day to take you around town, to the falls and into the game park, you'll have a more informative trip with the licensed and more knowledgeable tour operators.

For companies, see page 467.

By bus A minibus to the falls from the market in the centre of Livingstone will cost around US$1.50/Kw6,000 one way. Expect to be crammed like sardines! A much better choice is the **Bus that Thunders**, which cruises back and forth from the town centre to the falls all day long with key stops along the way. Departing from the Livingstone Museum, this 19-seater tourist bus offers convenient hop-on, hop-off transport along the following route: museum–Ngolide Lodge–Falls Park Shopping Centre–Crismar–Waterfront–Crocodile Park–Maramba River Lodge–Sun International Hotels–Victoria Falls (Zambian side).

By car Most lodges and hotels in and around Livingstone have secure parking, as do many restaurants. If you're parking on the street in town, you're likely to come across any number of volunteers to look after your car or to wash it for you. There's nothing organised about this; but if you're prepared to trust someone then – in spite of considerable protestations to the contrary – a tip of about US$0.30–0.50/Kw1,000–2,000 should be about right, depending on the length of time you're away. There are several 24-hour petrol stations on the main Mosi-oa-Tunya Road; the only ones with unleaded fuel are the newly built Engen at the entrance to Falls Park Shopping Centre, and Vuma complex just past Tunya Lodge to the south of town.

Car hire If you don't have a vehicle and wish to explore the area at your own pace, you can hire a car with or without a driver. Alternatively, you can hire a 4x4 with full kit if you wish to do self-drive safaris.

- 🚗 **AJ Car Hire & Tours** Liso House (rm 306), Mosi-oa-Tunya Rd; \/f 322090. Vehicles for self-drive or chauffeured hire include 5-seater Toyota saloons (US$40/day plus US$0.50/km), an 8-seater Toyota Hiace minivan (US$55/day plus US$0.50/km) and a 26-seater Mitsubishi bus (US$100/day plus US$1/km). Prices are subject to taxes and possible extra charges. Transfers, tours and activity bookings are also available.
- 🚗 **Batoka Sky Transport** Maramba Aerodrome, off Sichango Rd; \ 320058; f 324071; e info@ batokasky.co.zm. 14-seater luxury Mercedes Benz minibus and Toyota Land Cruiser safari vehicles at US$150/day or US$0.75/km (whichever is highest).
- 🚗 **Foley Hire Ltd** \/f 320888; e foleys@ zamnet.zm. From day-rental Land Rovers to fully kitted-out, expedition-ready, multi-day hires, take your pick. The choice ranges from basic 110 Defenders to fully equipped 110 and 130 Defenders, with the Discovery on order. A basic 110 Defender, without extras, costs around US$100 per day, inclusive of insurance and with unlimited mileage. An equipped vehicle is nearer US$200 per day. One-way

drop-offs are sometimes possible, at a cost.
- 🚗 **Monomotapa** Falls Trading (turn off Mosi-oa-Tunya Rd on to Nakatindi Rd and it's one block up on the left-hand corner); \ 320771 or 097 806459; f 320678; e solankis@zamnet.zm. A wide range of vehicles for hire from 4-seater Lexus to 60-seater Mitsubishi coach at competitive rates.
- 🚗 **Voyagers Zambia Ltd** \/f 323454; e carrental@voyagers.com.zm; www.voyagerszambia.com. Reservations through main office at Sun International's Falls Activity Centre, though there's a small office at the airport. Vehicles from self-drive Toyota Corollas to chauffeur-driven Toyota Hilux 4x4s, with rates at US$35–70 per day, excluding 17.5% VAT, mileage and countless insurances available (up to US$25/day extra). Also hires motorcycles, trucks with dropside bodies and luxury buses. All-inclusive rates (minimum 3 days with up to 150km/day) US$65–120, excluding VAT. Chauffeur-driven vehicles from Sun Activity Centre to Livingstone town or Victoria Falls town cost US$10/vehicle plus US$5 pp for 2 hours, then US$5/hr up to 4 hours.

By bicycle or moped Bikes can be hired individually, or with a guide, from Cliff Sitwal (the 'Zambezi Cowboy') at the shop next to Mo-Money on Mosi-oa-Tunya Road. Prices for a half day are around US$10–20 per person for a tour with a guide, depending on distance, with a range of options that include riverside rides, market and village tours and birdwatching. Bikes or mopeds may also be hired from Voyagers (see *Car hire*, above) or The Waterfront. Bikes are US$7 per half day, US$12 full day; mopeds US$20 half day, US$30 full day (credit card and motorbike licence required). You should check that your travel insurance covers you for two-wheeled transport; some don't.

🏠 **WHERE TO STAY** In the past five years, Livingstone has experienced a boom in tourism and now offers a great variety of places to stay for all types of travellers and budgets. Whereas, previously, accommodation was limited to a handful of luxury lodges, a few backpackers and guesthouses and several hotels of widely varying standards, now you will find excellent choices in all price ranges, with many providing the service, standards and amenities that international visitors have come

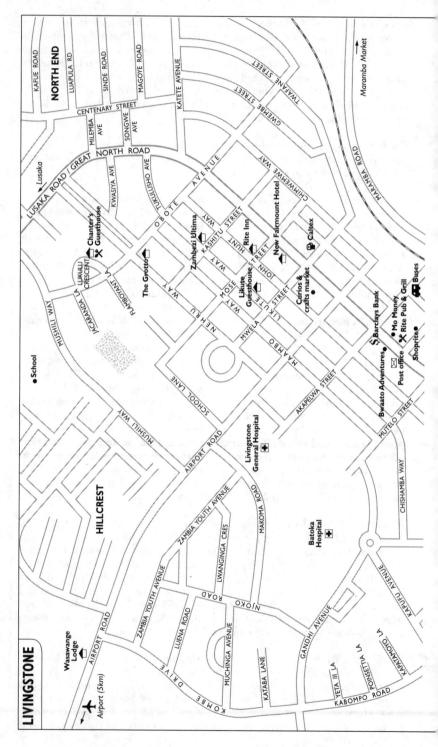

LIVINGSTONE

NORTH END

Kafue Road
Luapula Rd
Sinde Road
Magoye Road

Centenary Street
Milemba Ave
Songwe Ave
Katete Avenue
Kwasiya Ave

Lusaka Road / Great North Road
Lusaka

Twafane Street
Gwembe Street

Maramba Market

Obote Avenue
Kashitu Way
Hunt Street
Rite Inn
Chimwemwe Way
New Fairmount Hotel
Caltex

Chanter's Guesthouse
Jacaranda La Lukulu Crescent
Flamboyant La

The Grotto
Zambezi Ultima
Likute Guesthouse
John Street
Curios & crafts market

Mose Way
Nehru Way
Mwela Way
Mushili Way

School

Barclays Bank
Mo Money
Rite Pub & Grill
Buses
Shoprite
Post office
Bwaato Adventures
Mutelo Street

HILLCREST

Airport Road
Mushili Way
School Lane
Maambo Way
Likute Street
Akapelwa Street

Livingstone General Hospital

Zambia Youth Avenue
Lwanginga Cres
Makoma Road
Nioko Road
Chishamba Way

Batoka Hospital

Zambia Youth Avenue
Luena Road
Muchinga Avenue
Kombe Drive
Kataba Lane
Gandhi Avenue

Wasawange Lodge
Airport Road
Airport (5km)

Yeta III La
Poinsettia La
Kaptamoyo La
Kapatu III Avenue
Kabompo Road

430

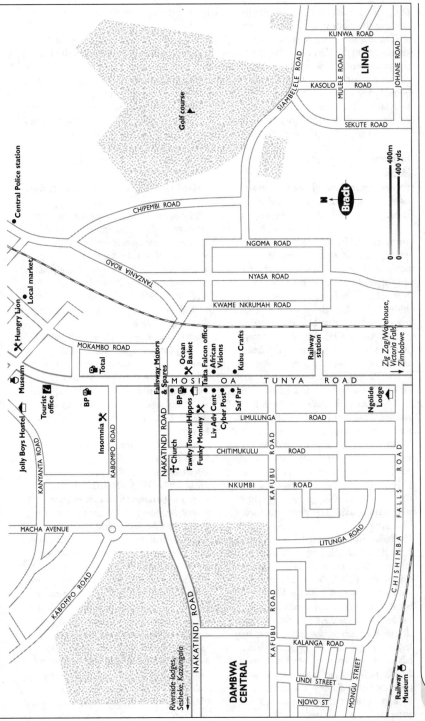

to expect, If the choice is overwhelming, knowing the options in advance will make finding the right place much easier.

The Zambian side of the falls is spread out and has numerous bush lodges in lovely situations on the Zambezi River, a short distance from town yet close enough to enjoy the attractions and activities of the falls. Further upstream, near the Botswana border, the lodges and camps of the Kazungula area are ideal for those seeking a more remote getaway with river-based diversions. Zimbabwe has very few equivalents.

At the cheaper end of the market, staying in a guesthouse, where you may meet African travellers, adds a multi-cultural dimension to your visit, while backpacker accommodation tends to cater strictly to the international budget traveller.

In town
Hotels

⌂ **New Fairmount Hotel** (73 twin rooms, family rooms, 3 suites) Mosi-oa-Tunya Rd; ℡ 320723/8, 321136, 320075; f 321490; email: nfhc@zamnet.zm. In the centre of town, between Mose and Mwela streets, this is a large, old hotel of Moorish design in sparkling white plaster that was once the town's focal point. The hotel has been refurbished and its newly upgraded rooms are clean with en-suite facilities, AC, mini fridge, satellite TV and even a DVD/video player. These are set around white-painted concrete courtyards at the back, where there's a good swimming pool and plenty of shady sitting places. The hotel has a restaurant serving Zambian and international dishes, plus a casino and disco, both popular local nightspots at weekends. It also has one of Livingstone's only squash courts. A desk for Bwaato Adventures occupies a corner of the cavernous entrance lobby, while a small arcade with beauty salon and shops hides in a courtyard behind. In front is ample covered parking under the watchful eye of 24hr security. A convenient location combined with many amenities makes the hotel good value. *US$47/61 sgl/dbl, US$94 family room (sleeps 3), US$150 Elephant suite (up to 4), US$115 Hippo suite (sleeps 2); US$320 Presidential suite (up to 4), all inc b/fast.*

⌂ **Ngolide Lodge** (16 rooms) 110 Mosi-oa-Tunya Rd; ℡ 321091/2; f 321113; e ngolide@zamnet.zm. On the south side of town, as the main road leaves Livingstone for the falls, this lodge has a large thatched roof and small gardens in front with a secure car park It's more of a hotel than a lodge, well built and compact, but a bit austere. Its rooms all lead off a central quadrangle. Each has a high thatched ceiling, polished floors, stone bathrooms, twin or dbl beds with mossie nets and AC. Rooms are comfortable, and each has its own tea/coffee maker and satellite TV. There is a licensed bar and the Indian restaurant, tucked in at the back, is among the best in Livingstone.

US$41/56 sgl/dbl, US$67 dbl suite, US$84 trpl/twin, inc full b/fast.

⌂ **Protea Hotel Livingstone** (80 rooms) no tel/fax yet; e mauro@zamnet.zm (general manager for enquiries) or info@proteahotels.com; www.proteahotels.com. On Mosi-oa-Tunya Road adjacent to the Falls Park Shopping Centre (about 0.5km past railway line crossing on left side as you head towards the falls). This new hotel, part of the South African Protea Hotels group, is scheduled to open in April 2007. It promises good 3-star accommodation of modern African design with a swimming pool, indoor and outdoor dining, conference rooms and secure car park. 40 rooms will contain 2 queen beds for a maximum of 2 adults and 2 children, while the remaining half will be king rooms for 2 adults. All rooms will have luxury bathrooms, A/C, room safes, electronic door locks, tea and coffee-making facilities and telephone. *Around US$120 per room B&B. Book online via website or email..*

⌂ **Wasawange Lodge** (18 rondavels, 2 rooms) Airport Rd; ℡ 324066, 324141/2; f 324067; e waslodge@zamnet.zm; www.tourvicfalls.com. Situated 2km from the town centre and the same distance from the airport, Wasawange Lodge is a comfortable small hotel with a few ethnic touches. Its spacious rooms are individual rondavels with en-suite facilities, AC, a fridge/minibar, in-room coffee/tea, mosquito repellers and satellite TV. Clean and well-serviced, they have high wooden ceilings, large mirrors and rugs to cover nice stone floors. The place is popular with business visitors for its in-house conference rooms and has a good restaurant, bar, swimming pool, sauna and jacuzzi. Because of its popularity and small size, you will often need to book in advance to get a room. Transfers and all activities can be arranged. *US$80 sgl, US$100 dbl, US$105 trpl or executive suite, B&B.*

Guesthouses Even the most unobservant visitor in Livingstone can't help but notice the multitude of signs pointing to guesthouses all over town, but standards vary immensely. Many are new to tourism and others cater to the local market rather than to overseas visitors. One thing is for certain, the Western image of a guesthouse – a charming bed and breakfast inn – is not to be found here . . . yet. Rather, a 'guesthouse' can be anything from a small, rustic hostel (or worse) to a converted house or quasi-mini-hotel. Although few can be described as charming or quaint, they are functional and offer yet another alternative in the budget and mid-range category. Some are old, converted homes with smallish rooms, limited facilities and lower prices; others are newly constructed with restaurant, bar, pool, air conditionaing and other mod-cons, priced accordingly. Interior decorating leans towards the basic and functional (a few have ethnic touches), or tends to be overblown, with an abundance of velvet, chrome and multi-patterned fabrics. Inevitably new places crop up all the time in Livingstone's ever-expanding tourist industry so it's worth looking around to see which place catches your eye and which location suits you best. Always make sure you ask to see the room and facilities before booking in, as there's no shortage of choice – it's a buyer's market.

🏠 **Chanter's Guesthouse** (3 rooms) Lukulu Crescent; ☎ 323412 ; www.chanters-livingstone.com. Run by former Lusaka hotelier Richard Chanter, Chanter's is both a restaurant and a small guesthouse, one of the first in Livingstone. It stands in a leafy residential area on the northern side of Livingstone, perhaps 2km from the centre. To reach it, follow Mosi-oa-Tunya Rd towards Lusaka, and turn left on to Obote Av just before the road bends to the left. Lukulu Crescent is the 4th right turn; it is not named on some maps, but is well signposted. Rooms are basic and functional, with wooden parquet floors, twin beds, satellite TV (all showing the same station) and a bath with shower attachment in the tiled, en-suite bathroom. 2 rooms have ceiling fans and one is AC. The public rooms are more stylish, with tables and chairs extending on to a patio and garden at the back that includes a swimming pool. Good food is served all day, with a nice variety on offer.
US$22 sgl, US$25 dbl per night, inc basic continental b/fast; à la carte options for b/fast are available, but cost extra.

🏠 **Guestmate Inn** (5 rooms) 394 Obote Rd; ☎ 323939; m 097 777 520. The sign at the entrance says, 'Come as a guest, leave as a mate!' Rooms in this rather basic guesthouse have twin or dbl beds and en-suite bathrooms. Neither AC nor mossie nets are provided, but you do get satellite TV and a continental b/fast. There are plans to construct some chalets and a swimming pool at the back.
US$17 pp in sgl room, US$20 2 people in sgl room, US$25 dbl bed.

🏠 **Likute Guesthouse** (14 rooms) 62 Likute Way, behind Fairmount Hotel; ☎ 323661. This clean and welcoming guesthouse offers self-contained rooms with fans, mossie nets, satellite TV, alarm clocks and a nice lounge in a small walled complex. The staff are friendly and the location is convenient.
US$20–25 per room, depending on room; inc b/fast; other meals available upon request.

🏠 **Namel's Guest Lodge** (7 rooms) Lusaka Rd; ☎ 324274; e namelslodge@zamnet.zm. From the centre of town, head towards Lusaka up the main road to the top of the hill. Just past the water tower, you will see several guesthouses in a row, including Namel's on the left, clearly signposted on the wall. Recently built, this clean guest lodge offers en-suite rooms, each equipped with safe deposit boxes, coffee/tea-making facilities, fridge, satellite TV and AC. There's a good swimming pool in the grounds, and 24hr security is provided in the ample parking area. Namel's caters to Lusaka business travellers, but is also a good choice for couples and families with their own transport. Rooms at the back are the best and quietest. Lunch and dinner are not offered, but self-catering facilities are available for a nominal charge.
US$35/50 sgl/dbl, US$60 family, US$55 twin, inc full English b/fast.

🏠 **Rite Inn** (9 rooms) 301 Mose St; ☎ 323264; f 324201; e riteinv@zamnet.zm. Set in a small, secure courtyard within walking distance of town, Rite Inn has clean and attractive twin-bedded rooms decorated in an African motif. Each has a well-tiled bathroom, AC, mini-fridge, coffee/tea service, digital safe and satellite TV. The reception area and rooms are adjacent to a sparkling swimming pool, surrounded by a large concrete patio, though without poolside furniture. The street-side carport is patrolled around the clock, although you can park inside the courtyard upon request. There are no meals or kitchen facilities, but the rooms here are among the nicest we've seen. *US$45 inc continental b/fast.*

🏠 **Southern Comfort Lodge** (8 rooms) 75 Lusaka Rd; ☎ 323103, 097 895088; e cliffbanda2003@yahoo.co.uk. Situated along 'Guesthouse Row' on the main road to Lusaka, by Namel's and Wane guesthouses. The main building is large and spacious with decorative tiles leading to well-sized rooms with fans, fridges and satellite TV. Each is en suite with a creatively tiled bathroom. There is a large, rather flamboyant lounge, and a kitchen and dining area. Parking is inside a walled gate. *US$20/22 sgl/dbl, inc b/fast.*

🏠 **Wane Guest Lodge** (7 rooms, house) Lusaka Rd; ☎ 324058, 097 881536, 096 755742; f 324058; e wangull@zamnet.zm. The lodge is located on 'Guesthouse Row' at the top of the hill coming into town, about a 10-min walk from the town centre. Look for the sign on the main road and the name on the entrance gate. The self-contained bedrooms and separate, fully furnished, self-catering family house are clean and well-appointed. Each is air conditioned, with a bath, colour satellite TV, telephone, mini-fridge and tea/coffee. There is a full restaurant and bar, serving international and Zambian dishes, as well as 24hr room service, around-the-clock security and courtesy bus service. Meals in the restaurant are US$5. *US$40–50 sgl, US$60–70 dbl, depending on room, inc full English b/fast. Family suite US$96 per night.*

🏠 **Zambezi Ultima Guesthouse** (14 rooms) 36 Likute Way; ☎ 323534. Situated on a large plot in the residential section of town, this guesthouse has 3 twin rooms, 9 dbls and 2 suites, all apparently painted with the same colour as Livingstone's blue taxis. Even so, the newer en-suite rooms in the garden area are nice enough and the hotel has a pool, dining room, common DSTV (Digital Satellie TV), and kitchen facilities. All rooms have baths and fans, 9 have AC, but none has mossie nets and there are no telephones. *US$35–65, depending upon sgl/dbl and room; inc full English b/fast.*

🏠 **Zig Zag** (12 rooms) Industrial Rd; ☎ 322814; m 095 780180; e zigzag@zamnet.zm; www.zigzagzambia.com. Near the railway crossing just off Mosi-oa-Tunya Rd, look for the signpost indicating the turn to Zig Zag, which is on the edge of town. Originally a coffee house, restaurant and craft market (see page 448), Zig Zag now includes accommodation in its spacious garden complex in the form of a block of en-suite twin/dbl and family rooms. These are nicely furnished with tiled bathrooms and ethnic décor. Zig Zag's private 1-acre compound has much to offer the visitor: an enticing pool surrounded by gardens and shady green trees, a children's play area, souvenir shopping, satellite TV lounge and a lovely spot to dine in its on-site restaurant, serving excellent cappuccinos, extensive b/fasts and freshly prepared meals 08.00–20.00 daily. There is also a gift shop selling local crafts, toiletries, clothes and jewellery. *Dbl/twin en suite with AC US$30/35 pp sharing/sgl, family room (sleeps 4: 1 dbl bed, 1 bunk bed) US$70 inc full English b/fast.*

Backpackers For the budget-minded, nothing beats Livingstone's popular backpackers' hostels. Generally clean, convenient and cheap, they are ideal for independent travellers – but can be crowded at times. As a one-stop shop, they offer shared and private rooms, camping, booking agency, restaurant, bar, kitchen, laundry, pool and even a built-in social life.

🏠 **Fawlty Towers Lodge & International Backpackers** (42 dorm beds, 13 rooms, camping) 216 Mosi-oa-Tunya Rd; ☎/f 323432; e ahorizon@zamnet.zm; www.adventure-africa.com. Just south of the turn-off to Nakatindi/Kazungula Rd, you can't miss this popular international backpackers' place. Look for the colourful wrought-iron burglar bars shaped like rising suns. Enter through the large gates covered by straw mats, and you come to the reception and lounge with satellite TV and free internet facilities. Upstairs in the main building are 4 dorms sleeping 6, 1 sleeping 4, 1 trpl and 1 dbl, all sharing toilets and showers. There's also a reading lounge, self-catering kitchen and dining room serving a full English b/fast for about US$4. Behind the main building, you'll find a spacious private garden area shaded by mango trees and coloured with bougainvillea where you can relax in the hammock or go for a dip in the inviting swimming pool surrounded by lawns. Campers on the lawns share toilets and showers, all clean with hot and cold running water. Also in the garden area are 8 dbl en-suite rooms, 3 twins, a new dormitory wing with 2 4-bedded rooms and yet another dorm – this one with AC – sleeping 6. There is a second communal kitchen (all accessories provided) and shared showers and toilets. Everything is neat and clean, all rooms come with mossie nets, desk fans and bed linen, and showers have both hot and cold running water. Free pancakes are offered poolside daily. Dinner is available at the popular Hippo's restaurant and bar with direct access from the garden. Fawlty Towers is quiet, secure, well run and tremendously convenient for the centre of Livingstone. They offer free transport and transfers to and from Victoria Falls border post daily and you can avoid paying Zambian entry visas if you book at least 24hrs in advance.

Dorm beds US$8 or US$10 AC, private/en-suite twins or dbls US$25/35 per room, camping US$5 with own tent, US$8 with tent hire. No children under 10.

🏠 **Jollyboys Backpackers** (8 chalets, 40 dorm beds, camping) 34 Kanyata Rd; 📞 324229; 📠 322086; email: jollybs@zamnet.zm; www.backpackzambia.com. In 2003, the ever-popular Jollyboys moved to new and improved premises to the west of Mosi-oa-Tunya Rd, just behind the museum, a 2min walk from the town centre. Owner-operated and managed by the friendly and helpful Kim and Sue, its reputation as the quintessential backpackers' lodge remains undimmed. The convenient purpose-built complex has 8 individual thatched chalets (6 dbl/twins and 2 dbl en suite) in the back garden where there is also ample camping space. The main facilities are set within a large, central thatched quadrangle, with the dorms, reception area and ablutions around the perimeter. 4 6-bed dorm rooms and one 16-bed dorm all share a well-sized toilet and shower block with endless hot water. In the middle of this 'quad' is a wonderful sunken lounge with fire pit and pillows — a perfect spot to chill out, read and meet fellow travellers. Above is a wooden deck from which you can see the spray from the falls. A pool table, table tennis and sitting area are also under cover looking out to an enticing rock swimming pool, lawns and gardens. Adjacent are the open-plan bar with satellite TV and the restaurant, where you can sip a cold beer (or several) and enjoy a home-cooked meal at reasonable prices. There's also a separate kitchen for those who wish to self-cater. Internet/email is on-site and they also have short and longterm baggage storage. Secure parking is part of the package and a laundry service is available. Kim and Sue offer friendly, first-hand advice on what to see and do, and can book any and all activities. There are free lifts to the falls at 10.00 daily. The atmosphere is relaxed and unpretentious, though sometimestoo abuzz with people to allow much peace and quiet All in all it's a fun place to stay. Book at least 2 days ahead to get your Zambian entry visa fees waived. *Chalets US$25 dbl/twin with shared ablutions, en-suite chalet with AC US$35, 4/8/16-bed dorm US$10/7/6 pp, camping US$4 pp per night.*

Beside the Zambezi: upriver

Livingstone's riverside lodges are for the most part spread along the shores of the Zambezi leading west from the town off Nakatindi Road. The lodges here are listed as if heading out of Livingstone.

🏠 **Sussi Lodge & Chuma House** (10 chalets, 2 luxury houses) 📞 324426; 📱 097 790726; 📱 097 840726; 📧 starofafrica@zm.celtelplus.com; www.star-of-africa.com. Zimbabwe reservations: 📞 +263 11 213345/13 45970; 📠 +263 13 42122; 📧 reservations@starofafrica@co.zw or sussi@telconet.co.zw. Built in 2001, this luxury lodge and nearby house is 10 mins' drive from Livingstone, also within the outer section of the Mosi-oa-Tunya National Park — at a highly prized site which, historically, was known as 'Fairyland'. The lodge's name has been taken from the 2 Zambian bearers who carried David Livingstone's body from Zambia to the British Embassy at Dar es Salaam: Sussi and Chuma.

If you've a yearning to act out a childhood fantasy of living in a tree house, this could be your chance. Set amongst the riverine forest, Sussi's large, almost circular chalets are set quite high up on raised wooden platforms, and command fabulous views over the Zambezi. Large glass doors form walls in themselves, folding out on to a sizeable balcony with comfortable wicker chairs. Furnishings are stylish and tasteful — lots of natural fabrics, woven matting on dark wooden floors, and a walk-in mosquito net around the bed(s) — while thoughtful touches include a fridge, a whistle and an umbrella. Each en-suite bathroom is open plan, housing a bath with a view; only the toilet is private.

Raised walkways connect the chalets to a large dbl-storey thatched boma, the repeated use of a circular design affording a sense of relaxation. Upstairs are the main dining, lounge and bar areas and meals may be taken with other guests, or individually, as you prefer. Downstairs you will find a gift shop and reading area, leading out to the swimming pool and further along to a deck with firepan, set on a sheltered bend of the river. There's even an elephant-viewing area overlooking a small waterhole. The reception building, at the entrance, has historical significance (and a preservation order),

17

though it has been extensively and thoughtfully refurbished. Activities currently include game drives at sunrise and sunset, a village tour, and visits to the falls and the museum.

US$300–365 pp sharing, inc all meals & 2 guided activities a day.

⌂ **Thorntree River Lodge** (7 cottages, 2 honeymoon suites) lodge ✆ 324480; bookings through Three Cities in South Africa: +27 31 310 6900; f +27 31 307 5247; e ceres@threecities.co.za. Thorntree is located 15km from the falls on private land within the broader confines of the national park, about 10 mins' drive from town along the Nakatindi Rd. It is clearly signposted to the left well before the national park exit gate, so if you get that far, turn back.

Accommodation is along the riverbank in brick under thatch cottages with electricity, en-suite bath, small riverside veranda and simple but attractive interiors. Each cottage also features an outdoor bath or shower, set in a private enclosure. 2 well-appointed honeymoon suites are raised on teak decking with open sides overlooking the river. There's a comfortable bar, lounge and dining area, with a riverside deck from which you can watch elephants moving between the islands in the Zambezi. A figure-of-8 swimming pool lies next to a thatched boma overlooking the waterhole where buffalo, elephants, hippo, waterbuck and bushbuck often come to drink — one of the advantages of being in the national park.

Set a little way along the river (though entirely separate from the lodge) is a thatched boma with ethnic decoration used for special functions and larger groups. This boma is the base for SafPar's elephant-back safaris (the only one in Zambia) and guests can meet their resident herd. In addition, they operate their own river cruises from the lodge, as well as offering other activities (see Safari Par Excellence page 468).

US$250 pp, inc FB, I daily activity (sunset cruise, game drive or falls tour), drinks (local beverages) & transfers, exc US$10 pp per day park fee. Drive-in rates for B&B & dinner, exc activities, are about half standard rates.

⌂ **The River Club** (10 luxury chalets) ✆/f 324457; m 097 892179; lodge e admin.trc@microlink.zm; for bookings and equiries contact Wilderness Safaris, e enquiry@wilderness.co.za; www.wilderness-safaris.com. Designed to reflect the colonial era, the River Club was opened in 1998, perched on a rise beside the Zambezi, next to Tongabezi. Guests are driven from town to a launch site upstream for the lodge, and then brought downriver by boat, a scenic

10min ride. The turn-off from Nakatindi Rd is signposted at the same junction as for Tongabezi.

Thatched, en-suite chalets are cleverly designed and constructed on stilts, amidst indigenous riverside trees. All are high up with stunning views, their entirely open fronts facing over the Zambezi below. 2 honeymoon suites have dbl beds, plus gardens with sun loungers in front; there is one wheelchair-friendly family room with dbl bed and 2 sgls; the other chalets have 2 sgls. All are large with good decoration, quality fabrics, canopied mosquito nets and many nice touches (like the claw-foot bathtubs). The beautifully polished floors tend to be slippery so be careful. Each is named after an explorer or colonial figure, like Stanley and Livingstone.

The main lodge building is also constructed in the colonial style with tin roof and wide verandas (which looks better than it sounds), boasting magnificent views of the river. Here you can sit and enjoy traditional high tea served each afternoon or watch the sun slip beneath the horizon with a cocktail in your hand. Inside are the reception, a small gift shop, cloakrooms, a formal dining room (with a magnificent teak table), a comfortable lounge, a massive dbl-sided fireplace and a well-stocked library, plus wireless internet connection. Antiques, colonial pictures and many decorator touches add to the lodge's Edwardian ambience. Meals are elegant affairs featuring pre-set dinner menus that change daily. The atmosphere, décor and service are reminiscent of a bygone era.

Overlooking the river is a stunning infinity swimming pool with rock fountain surrounded by patios and timber deck as well as plenty of sun loungers to soak up the sun, and over-sized umbrellas for shade. Walkways (illuminated at night) are set amongst the sweeping lawns, while palms, brightly coloured bougainvillea and gardens complete the picture. Croquet, boules and bush golf are on hand, and for the more active, a nature-walk/running track spans the 50-acre property that will soon feature an all-weather tennis court and maze. Included in the price is a choice of fishing, sundowner boat trips, game-park drives, museum and falls visits, and trips to local villages and schools, Stone Age sites and Livingstone town. A tented gazebo provides the perfect venue for riverside massages, which can be arranged at extra cost, and all other activities can be booked direct from the lodge. This exclusive and intimate lodge is set in a securely fenced compound which also has a heli-pad.

Rates pp per night sharing, all inclusive: Jan–14 Jun US$440, 15 Jun–Oct US$570, Nov–Dec US$440; sgl supplement US$125 per night. No bookings at the lodge; contact Wilderness Safaris or your agent.

⌂ **Tongabezi** (5 cottages, 5 houses) ☎ 324450/68, 323235; f 323224; e reservations@tongabezi.com; www.tongabezi.com. Set on a sweeping bend of the Zambezi, Tongabezi has set the region's standard for innovative camp design since it opened over a decade ago. It remains one of the most exclusive places to stay on the north side of the Zambezi, its setting matched by excellent service from a team of first-class local Zambian staff.

Beautiful thatched cottages overlook the river, 3 with king-size beds, the others twin; all are tastefully decorated and have large tiled en-suite bathrooms complete with river-view bathtubs, and their own private sitting area. Even more exclusive are the spacious houses: the Bird House, the Tree House, the Dog House or the Honeymoon House (once cited as 'worth getting married for'). Each is individually designed, with a king-size dbl bed, impressive en-suite bathrooms with inviting bathtubs and one side completely open to the river. Tucked away from the river in its own private enclosure is the Garden House with master bedroom, small twin room and living room ideal for families. Both cottages and houses are carefully secluded from their neighbours; all have the services of a private valet dedicated solely to looking after the guests in that cottage or house.

There is a lovely riverside thatched boma, shaded by ebony trees hung with trailing creepers, where you'll find the bar, dining room and a spacious lounge with fireplace and small library. In the evenings, everyone gathers for sundowners and hors d'ouevres that are served around a roaring campfire – a perfect vantage point to watch the sun slip into the horizon. The swimming pool is set against a rock wall, under a tumbling waterfall, while sun-loungers wait on a large wooden deck over the Zambezi. Meals are sumptuous affairs, served outdoors on the riverside deck, in the dining room, or even in the privacy of your own cottage. By special arrangement, couples can dine under the stars on Tongabezi's floating 'sampan' moored offshore, where each course is hand delivered by canoe – a romantic and memorable occasion.

The lodge's ethos is confirmed by its school, Tujatane, run for over 100 children of Tongabezi staff and from local villages. Visits to the school are popular, with many guests choosing to contribute to its upkeep and future development.

Guided sunrise and sunset boat trips from the lodge's own jetty, canoeing, birdwatching trips, fishing, game drives (to Mosi-oa-Tunya National Park), picnics on local Chundu island, village visits, shopping excursions, museum tours and gorge walks are all included (aside from national park and museum entrance fees, nominal at US$10 and US$5 pp, respectively). For the more energetic, mountain bikes are available to go and visit Simonga local village and explore the surrounding area. There are also options to sleep on Sindabezi, one of the islands in the river (see below), or to have a specially laid-on meal on Livingstone Island (see pages 454–5), beside the falls. These options are not included in the price and, like the lodge itself, should be booked well in advance.

Cottage US$365/440, house US$425/540 pp sharing, low/high season (Nov–May/Jun–Oct), 40% sgl supplement in high season; inc all meals, drinks & house wine (exc premium wines, champagne & liquours), laundry service, levies & all activities. No children under 7.

⌂ **Sindabezi Island** (5 chalets) contact via Tongabezi, above. Sindabezi Island is a short, 2km boat (or canoe) trip downstream from its parent lodge, Tongabezi. This small sandy island has just 5 thatched en-suite chalets, beautifully appointed with twin or dbl beds, and carefully spaced around the shores of the island for maximum privacy. A relaxed bar area with teak decking, surrounded by tall ebony trees, is the setting for sumptuous meals cooked by the island's own chef. It's all wonderfully private, an island hideaway with no electricity from which you can explore the river and surrounding islands with your own guide or simply relax and enjoy the beautiful setting. Elephants and hippos are frequent visitors, and game is often sighted on the banks of Zambezi National Park, a stone's throw away. Sindabezi is the closest you can come to being a castaway in luxurious comfort. Activities include canoeing, boating, walking, fishing and birdwatching, as well as all activities run at Tongabezi itself.

US$365/385, 4-night special rate US$274/337 pp per night, low/high season (Nov–May/Jun–Oct), inc meals, drinks, laundry, transfers to/from the island & all activities; 40% sgl supplement in high season. Four or more people booking together can reserve the whole island for their own exclusive use at no more than the pp rate.

17

⌂ **Tangala House** (sleeps up to 8) contact via Tongabezi, above, or direct: ben@tongabezi.com. Right on the Zambezi about 15km upstream of Victoria Falls and 1km from Tongabezi, this luxury private house is certainly worth considering for families, not least because it's well protected against insects, or for those seeking a greater degree of privacy and freedom than is possible in a lodge. Accommodation for 4–8 people is in 3 en-suite bedrooms with river views (one is a much larger master suite) and a 4th bedroom with a separate bathroom and garden view. Beautifully furnished and equipped living and dining areas lead out on to a large swimming pool overlooking the Zambezi, with views in both directions. The house is available either for rental only, or on a FB basis with food and drinks but without activitites, or on a fully inclusive basis serviced by Tongabezi with a chef, waiters, housekeeping staff, pool attendant, private guide and even a trained nanny, plus private use of vehicles and boats. On that basis all meals and drinks plus Tongabezi's river and land activities are included in the cost.
US$1200/day plus US$150 pp per day for food and drinks (US$75 per child under 14; activities extra (book through Tongabezi. Fully inc: US$600/455/445 pp for 4/6/8 sharing, minimum stay 3 nights

⌂ **Natural Mystic Lodge** (10 chalets) Nakatindi Rd; ✓f 324436; m 097 408024; e nmlodge@ zamnet.zm; www.naturalmysticlodge.com. Opened in 2002, Natural Mystic is 20km from Livingstone, but was up for sale in 2006.

The statue at the entrance to the lodge, of Namatama (Mother Earth) with her water pot, depicts the philosophy that underpins Natural Mystic, that the source of life comes from the earth. The low-lying, often wet site is crossed by a walkway with strategic points from which visitors can watch visiting hippos or the occasional elephant. 8 of the simple thatched chalets are grouped close together, 4 of them fronting the river, although the design means that you can only see the river if the front door is left open. The other 2 are set further back on the site. Some have bath and shower, others just a shower, and there's a small porch area by the door. With 2 dbl beds in each, they're quite cramped, but reasonably priced for a riverside location if you plan to spend most of your time out and about.

Right on the river is a large decked bar/restaurant area which is the lodge's best feature and is open to non-residents. Dinner costs US$10 pp,

sometimes accompanied by cultural dancing and marimba bands. There's also a small swimming pool, a curio shop and lounge with satellite television, plus an internet service. River cruises, game drives and other tours/activities can be organised direct at the lodge. *US150 per chalet (dbl), inc b/fast & transfers from Livingstone; reduced rates for Peace Corps and VSO volunteers.*

⌂ **Islands of Siankaba** (6 chalets, 1 honeymoon/VIP chalet) lodge ✓f 324490; m 097 791241; e siankaba@zamnet.zm; www.siankaba.com; reservations ✓f 01 260279; m 097 720530. One of the newer lodges on the Zambezi, Siankaba is a considerable 45km from Livingstone, down a 7km track through open bush, followed by a 5min boat ride. The mood is set as you leave the jetty with its small gift shop and chug along a peaceful back channel of the Zambezi before joining the main river. Shortly upstream, Siankaba lies on 2 separate islands. On one, spacious chalets nestle like bird hides among the trees that overhang the banks, their decks an ideal vantage point from which to watch the river in complete privacy. In contrast to the half-canvas walls and roof, everything about the accommodation oozes luxury and comfort. Polished teak furniture sits on polished teak floors, offset by thick oriental rugs. Stately comfortable beds with an integral ceiling fan are hung like 4-posters with pristine white mosquito nets, and good reading lights complement the otherwise subdued lighting. Set on a platform to the rear are a regal claw-footed bathtub and twin pedestal china basins with views towards the river, as well as a modern shower and separate toilet. Tucked discreetly away, a safe and fridge are almost incidental.

The 'Honeymoon/VIP chalet' has been designed for the discerning or romantic traveller in mind. It boasts its own garden decking with views across the Zambezi River and loungers provided in the shade of its pergola. Private meals are taken upon request for this chalet and set up on the decking overhanging the river and breakfast in bed is offered as standard. The chalet also contains a fully stocked mini bar, games compendium, specially designed 'his and hers' aromatherapy bathing products and private reference bookcase.

Raised walkways and swinging bridges lead to the adjacent island that serves at the epicentre of the camp. Here you'll find the spacious restaurant and comfortable bar/lounge area all very tasteful, with natural décor and tables out on the deck for alfresco dining. Among the trees nearby is a secluded pool with stylish sun-loungers, and running round the island is a 1.5km marked nature trail. In addition to this, activities include a sundowner cruise, birding and fishing excursions, and a trip via mokoro (local dug-out canoes exactly like those used by Dr Livingstone to travel the Zambezi River) among the islands. You can also do a village walk, which takes in a visit to the local school, with the return trip by mokoro. The school, Mandia, is a government-run establishment that is supported by a trust fund operated by the lodge as well as other community projects like tree planting and a clinic.

Siankaba is an exclusive lodge that offers considerable attention to detail and superb cuisine. *Sgl US$378/410, dbl US$310/392 pp, Honeymoon Suite US$ US$438/552 sgl US$365/460 dbl (Nov–May/Jun–Oct), inc drinks, transfers to/from Livingstone airport & activities; 5% discount for stays of 3 or more nights. Transfers to/from Victoria Falls & Kasane airport US$35 pp one way. Transfers for external activities US$20 pp return. No children under 12.*

⌂ **Royal Chundu Zambezi River Lodge** (10 chalets) Contact via South Africa, ☎ +27 13 744 9170; f +27 86 606 6944; m +27 83 456 4224; e royalchundu@netactive.co.za or reservations@royalchundu.com; www.royalchundu.com or www.royalchundu.co.za. At 60km from Livingstone, Royal Chundu Zambezi is the furthest lodge from town on the riverbank, and is about 11km off the main road on a well-maintained dirt road. The lodge offers luxury accommodation in en-suite chalets, and a range of activities both on-site and in the area. From the spacious main building, there's a walkway on to a deck overlooking the river; to the other side lies the swimming pool, a large outdoor jacuzzi and a thatched open-plan bar. Birdwatching is popular, with some 450 species found in the area. The lodge boasts a number of rarely seen bird species and specialises in guided fishing excursions especially for tiger fishing enthusiasts, suitable for novices or professionals. Guests can also enjoy river rafting, sunrise/sunset cruises, game viewing, island picnics, visits to a tribal village, elephant rides and microlight flights. If staying here, the best strategy is to plan a 'town' day of off-site activities, as going back and forth daily is impractical and takes up a lot of time. Royal Chundu is better as a 'get away from it all' destination rather than a base to explore the falls area. *US$400 pp per night with dinner, B&B. Transfers from airport US$60 return, max 7 people.*

⌂ **Kingfisher Houseboat** (16 beds) ☎ 322508, 323097, +267 71 516960; f 324081; e taonga@ zamnet.zm. A spacious houseboat, sleeping up to 16, cruises the Upper Zambezi waters, departing from the fishing village of Mambova some 14km beyond Kazungula (a good hour from Livingstone). From town, head upriver on Nakatindi Rd, take left turn at the signpost indicating the Kazungula border/ferry then right at sign for Mambova; follow the dirt track until you reach the river. The Kingfisher is ideal for groups or families seeking privacy and wanting to get away from the hustle and bustle of town, but is too far for participation in falls-based activities to be practical. Its upper deck features a dining area and bar, jacuzzi and plunge pool with ample seating and comfortable sun-beds to soak up the rays as you meander along the river. Downstairs are an open-plan kitchen, 3 toilets and showers and 8 twin-bedded berths. These are basic and small, with mattresses on the floor, in contrast to the more luxurious feel of the upper deck. Activities centre on the river and relaxation – the area is renowned for its scenic beauty, rich birdlife and good tiger fishing (tackle provided). Guided island walks and visits to nearby fishing villages are included in the price. The houseboat is accompanied by 2 tender boats, for hire at reasonable rates for daily excursions – ideal for keen fishermen. There's an onboard chef and menus can be adapted to suit your tastes. *US$80 pp per night FB, inc guided birdwatching, village & island excursions, fishing from the houseboat; exc transfers, alcohol, beverages & extended fishing trips. Minimum booking 4 guests. All-inc tour packages available.*

⌂ **Pride of the Zambezi** (5 staterooms, 1 honeymoon suite) ☎/f 324489; m 097 707829; e anglezam@zamnet.zm; www.zambezifishing.com. A luxury houseboat, the *Pride of the Zambezi* is a catamaran berthed at Mwandi on the Zambezi River, approximately 140km upstream of Livingstone on the Zambian side of the Caprivi floodplain. Although it's not practical as a base for exploring Livingstone or the falls, the *Pride of the Zambezi* offers a luxurious getaway, ideal for families or small groups. Accommodation is in luxury en-suite staterooms, and the bathrooms are bright, clean and amazingly spacious thanks to good design. The top deck houses the honeymoon suite, with king-size bed, built-in cupboards and en-suite bathroom. The suite is fully AC, with mosquito screens, an electronic safe and even complimentary dressing gowns and slippers. On the middle deck (also fully AC) is a lounge with wicker furniture and plasma TV/DVD player, plus a teak bar and a dining area that seats up to 16 guests. There's also a state-of-the-art kitchen and outdoor jacuzzi (cold water) for up to 10 people.

The staterooms are on the lower deck; all are en suite, AC and have electronic safes and wall-to-wall carpeting plus mosquito gauze. The boat even has a working crew of 5 (who have their own quarters): captain, host, chef and 2 deck hands.

This stretch of the Zambezi offers world-class fishing, and the boat serves as the base for Angle Zambia's fishing trips (with professional guides and equipment included, see page 455). Aside from fishing, activities on offer include birdwatching, village tours, mokoro trips and wave runner (only with guide). Island lunches and dinners can be provided if requested.

US$330 pp sharing , inc full board, local beverages, transfers from Livingstone airport, tender boats, guides, fishing equipment & tackle (lost/broken tackle to be paid for), plus 20 litres of fuel per tender boat per day. Extras: laundry, imported beers, wines & spirits. Transfers are provided to/from Livingstone airport.

Game Park, falls and gorge environs

The development by Sun International of a prime spot close to the falls has introduced a whole new style of accommodation to Livingstone. Other accommodation to the south of town has in recent years been augmented by lodges built away from the river, affording the advantages of open bush but without the high prices associated with a riverside location. Many of the following are actually much closer to the falls than those situated on the upper river to the west of Livingstone, and are listed as if heading south from Livingstone towards the falls, then out towards the gorges.

The Zambezi Waterfront (16 rooms, 20 tents on platforms, camping) Off Sichango Rd, near the Boat Club. Contact Safari Par Excellence, ℡ 320606/7; m 097 832906; f 320609; e waterfront@ safpar.com; www.safpar.net. This large and affordable riverside resort complex, within the unfenced area of Mosi-oa-Tunya National Park, incorporates a range of facilities on a beautiful spot, formerly known as the Makumbi launch site. To get here, leave Livingstone towards the falls on Mosi-oa-Tunya Rd, then turn right at the signpost by Tunya Lodge (Sichango Rd) towards the river and the national park. Secure and private, the complex has a stunning setting and is one of the best places around to view spectacular Zambezi sunsets.

The main thatch-and-pole building has a magnificent view over the river and contains the reception, booking office and a small souvenir shop. A spacious restaurant and teak bar (with satellite TV) both have plenty of seating indoors and out. Outside, amongst palm trees, is a lovely sunken pool surrounded by teak decking, where lounge chairs are set overlooking the river. Nearby, 8 large A-frame thatched chalets contain separate en-suite dbl or twin rooms, at ground level, with a patio and choice of river or garden views. The upper level comprises the larger executive suites with a queen bed, separate lounge area, good-size bathroom, and deck offering sweeping river views. Also up here are 3 spacious family rooms with 4 sgl beds and a deck, overlooking the garden. The rooms are all very comfortable, light and airy with teak furniture, quality fabrics and ethnic touches.

Beyond the main building is the Adventure Village which has a large natural-style rock pool, another bar and a thatched auditorium where daily activity briefings are given and rafting videos are shown in the evening accompanied by a barbecue. There are 20 permanent tents perched on wooden platforms along the river, each with 2 beds with all bedding and linen (or you can bring your own). Nearby ablutions are clean and spacious and contain flush toilets and hot and cold showers. Further along is a separate grassed camping area, with its own ablutions, barbecue and washing-up area, that can take about 60 campers.

The Waterfront is SafPar's one-stop-shop, where their own Adventure Centre booking office offers a full range of activities and excursions, many of which they operate themselves (see page 467). Among these are 2 boats offering river cruises directly from the Waterfront's own jetty. The Makumbi is the larger, more upmarket cruise boat offering b/fast, lunch, sunset or dinner cruises, while a smaller pontoon boat does the traditional booze-cruise route or caters for smaller groups. Both offer free snacks and unlimited drinks.

Chalet rooms pp sharing/sgl: river-view US$80/105, garden-view US$65/85, executive suite US$90/130; family room (4 people) US$180, Adventure village tent US$28/38 sharing/sgl, camping US$8 pp.

The Bushfront Lodge (13 chalets, camping) Zambia Reservations, ℡ 322446; f 321248; e bushfront@zamnet.zm; www.safpar.net. Formerly Nyala Lodge; now owned and operated by SafPar. Located about 5km from town near the entrance to

the Mosi-oa-Tunya National Park. From town, head towards the border and turn right at Tunya Lodge (Sichango Rd) heading towards the river and park entrance. the lodge is situated a few kilometres upriver from Victoria Falls, bordering the Mosi-oa-Tunya National Park. Chalets are all under African thatch, and each has an en-suite bathroom with 'waterfall' showers with potted plants and rock walls, from where water cascades off a small ledge that serves as the shower tap. There is also a private campsite with modern ablutions and a braai area, plus a restaurant and bar to relax in after a busy day doing all the activities in the Livingstone area, all of which can be booked at the lodge. Alternatively, clients can relax at the swimming pool. The main lodge area is well designed and maintained, and has satellite TV, a large bar/lounge and a restaurant. Meals are served daily and snacks are always available. Set amongst indigenous vegetation with abundant birdlife, the Bushfront has a bush-like feel and it's good value.
B&B US$65/80 pp sharing/sgl; packages and full board rates on request, children 3–11 pay 60%, over 12 full price; camping US$10 pp. Airport transfers: Livingstone US$16 pp, Victoria Falls US$31 pp.

🏠 **David Livingstone Safari Lodge** (72 rooms) ☏ +27 31 310 6900; f +27 31 307 5247; e ceres@threecities.co.za. This 4-star lodge, adjacent to The Waterfront on the banks of the Zambezi River, is currently under construction. When finished it will contain 72 river-facing rooms with a total of 144 beds, state-of-the-art conference facilities, a tropical pool with water feature, a restaurant and a bar. On offer will be daily river cruises aboard the newly built and specially designed 144-seater MV David Livingstone, as well as all the usual activities that can be booked via their in-house activity centre. At present the completion date is estimated at September 2007.
No rates yet available.

🏠 **Royal Livingstone** (173 rooms) Sun International Zambia, ☏ 321122; f 324 558; e sunintzam@zamnet.zm; www.suninternational.com; central reservations: P Bag 700 Sandton, 2146 South Africa; ☏ +27 11 780 7878; f +27 11 780 7061; www.suninternational.co.za. Opened by the president in July 2001, this opulent 5-star hotel situated in extensive grounds is owned by the South African Sun International group. If its broad, low, white frontage is rather disappointing at first glance, inside all is spacious and elegant, with an old-world attention to detail and service. Step outside on to extensive

verandas, where sweeping lawns lead to an unparalleled frontage along the Zambezi, the 'smoke' from the falls rising tantalisingly close. A 15min walk along the river brings you to the falls themselves via the direct access point that is the preserve of the 2 Sun International hotels, or visitors can be transported on one of the hotel's 'club cars' (golf cart style transport). The hotel is in the national park; zebras and giraffe are often seen grazing in the grounds.

All rooms have twin or king-size beds and are fitted with AC, satellite TV, radio, video, minibar, mini-safe and telephone; 2 rooms are fully equipped for the disabled. Tasteful and comfortable, but on the small side, each room has its own private balcony, and guests have the services of an individual butler. Should all this not be sufficient, there are also 4 suites.

Meals are served either in the excellent à la carte restaurant (see page 445), or outside on the veranda, while for a special occasion individual candle-lit dinners on the lawns can be arranged at extra cost. The long, wood-panelled bar has a relaxed, colonial air. Elsewhere on the property is an African boma, crafted in the traditional Zambian manner with seating for up to 350 people, with a smaller riverside boma adjacent for special functions (including weddings) and small groups. The grand swimming pool overlooks the Zambezi and is surrounded by sun-loungers. This is a great spot to relax, as are the massage tents along the river frontage (massages approximately US$65 pp; manicures, pedicures and facial treatments also available).

On the practical side, the concierge can organise your itinerary of activities, from white-water rafting to game drives.

Considerably more expensive than the adjacent Zambezi Sun, the Royal Livingstone caters for a very different market – those seeking traditional standards of décor and service in a truly gracious setting. It's Livingstone's equivalent of the Victoria Falls Hotel. If you'd like to indulge without the high price of accommodation, consider sundowners on their magnificent riverside deck or taking afternoon tea in the lounge; at about US$20 per person for tea. With a lovely selection of cakes and finger sandwiches on offer, it's highly civilised. Be warned that vervet monkeys are a nuisance at this hotel: they might try to steal food off your table or balcony. Don't approach the zebras in the grounds either.
US$517/542 sgl/dbl, inc b/fast.

⌂ **Zambezi Sun** (212 rooms) see the Royal Livingstone, above, for contact details. This is the lively 3-star sibling of the Royal Livingstone, and what a contrast. Crenellated walls are more reminiscent of a north African mosque than of southern Africa, their deep desert red contrasting with the Zambian sky. Vervet monkeys, the bane of the staff, cavort through the colourful grounds as if through a children's playground. Although it's close to the falls, there are no views of the river, though all the rooms have a balcony overlooking the extensive lawns. Well-designed, if rather compact, each has AC, satellite TV, safe, minibar and telephone, with a bath and shower in the en-suite bathroom. The rooms are very comfortable – the standard of a good international business hotel – but with considerably more flashes of ethnic colour and individuality.

In addition to the extensive buffet restaurant, there's a relaxed alfresco grill beside the pool that snakes through the grounds, or Squire's Grillhouse adjacent to the activity centre, or Fegos, a simpler Italian café. (You can always book into the posh restaurant next door if you want to feel more formal for a while.) The complex also includes a conference centre, a business centre and a children's club and playground. Ultimately, though, everything hinges on the location. Just a few hundred metres' walk from the lip of the falls and the curio market, and with unrestricted access, the hotel's position is unbeatable.

US$364/347 sharing/sgl, inc b/fast; all major credit cards accepted.

⌂ **Songwe Point Village** (8 thatched huts) ☏ 097 783053; e reservations@kwando.co.za; www.kwando.co.za. For an entirely different experience, Songwe Point Village, a joint venture between the local community and what is now Kwando Safaris, promises the cultural experience of staying in an African village-style setting with the service and comfort of a lodge. The 'village' is poised on the edge of one of the gorges downstream of the falls, 120m above the Zambezi between Rapids 10 and 12. It's a breathtaking location.

As the crow flies, it's only 5km downstream from the falls, but the road winding through the bush, past small villages and out to the gorge is a 30–45min drive. Accommodation is in comfortable, thatched huts built in the traditional style. Each has its own bathroom (showers, flush toilet and washbasin), and commanding views of the gorge. Accentuating the view, 3 huts also have bathtubs overlooking the gorge, and a communal shower and

bath facility is available for those that don't.

Zambian hosts welcome visitors into the 'village family' and explain local customs, beliefs and history of the area. Meals, served in the traditional style, allow guests to sample African cuisine like mealie meal and relish as well as standard fare, and are shared in a central thatched enclosure, called a Ntantaala. There is traditional singing and dancing in the evenings and guests are encouraged to participate if the mood strikes them. Everything tries hard to be authentic, right down to an ox-wagon journey to a small field museum displaying Stone Age artefacts, some more than 700,000 years old. It's the closest that the visitor can come to experiencing African culture first-hand, but with a higher level of comfort.

The area is steeped in archaeological history, and the emphasis is on sharing African culture with visitors. Guided visits are offered to early Stone Age sites, the 700-year old Mukuni village, the tree where David Livingstone first met the local chief, and various other local historical and cultural sites. The fine balance between authenticity and comfort is well executed and Songwe is ideal for those with a keen interest in experiencing African culture. If that is not your cup of tea, staying at one of the luxury riverside lodges may be better value for money, given that prices are comparable. Kwando Safaris also has 3 tented safari camps in Botswana's Okavango Delta (see page 170), linking up with Songwe Point Village to form a popular regional safari circuit.

US$350/475 pp sharing/sgl Apr–Jun & Nov, US$425/600 Jul–Oct, US$350 Dec–Mar, inc FB, all cultural activities, drinks, Zambezi River cruise, Mosi-oa-Tunya National Park visit & transfers.

⌂ **Taita Falcon Lodge** (6 chalets) ☎/f 321850; m +263 11 208387; e taita-falcon@zamnet.zm; www.taitafalcon.com or www.zambiatourism.com/taita. Perched atop the Batoka Gorge, this lodge overlooks Rapids 16 and 17, downstream of the falls. It is a 45min drive from Livingstone, along the road normally used to bring rafters back from the river. To get there, take the main road from town towards the falls, and then take the well-signposted left turning opposite the entrance to Zambezi Sun. From here it's about 11km of long, winding track through the Mukuni Village area. Near the end, you'll pass a turn on the right to Songwe Point. You'll want a 4x4 for this trip during the rains.

The lodge is named after a rare falcon that frequents cliffs and gorges, especially in the Zambezi Valley. Look for these especially in the evenings, perhaps trying to catch swallows or bats on the wing. Taita falcons are small (less than 30cm long) with cream to brown under parts – no bars or markings – and a strong, fast style of flight. This area is one of the best in Africa for spotting them. Verreaux's (black) eagles, peregrine falcons, and many other raptors and small birds are also resident.

Run by Faan and Anna-Marie Fourie, the lodge is a pleasant, friendly place surrounded by indigenous gardens. Its 6 comfortable, en-suite chalets, named after birds, are open-plan using stone, reeds and local furnishings throughout, and the ³/₄ walls, providing light and flow-through ventilation, can be raised to full height if preferred. The rustic chalets, with thatched ceiling with beams, mossie nets draped over beds and small patio in front, blend seamlessly with the natural bush environment 2 can be made up as family rooms, sleeping up to 5; the rest are dbls or trpls.

The camp is particularly notable for a lovely deck beside the bar, overlooking the gorges and river. Perched on the very edge of the gorge with the raging waters below, Taita's view is breathtaking to say the least. It's a great place to watch rafters from a very safe distance. Despite the fact that the chalets have been set back from the precipice, I'd be wary of letting children run wild here because of the cliffs nearby. The lodge's electricity is from a generator; it also has its own heli-pad, and there's a nice small pool for a dip, encompassed by a tiled patio with adjacent small lawn. Small pathways weave through the bush linking the chalets to the pool, bar and restaurant. The setting is casual and informal; the service friendly and personable.

Activities include guided bush and bird walks, village tours, hiking trails in and around the gorge (equipped hikers can do 2–3-day hikes), fishing and mountain biking. Taita Falcon's a good place if you want a remote spot away from it all, but if you want to pop in and out of the falls for activities, it can feel cut off from the epicentre of things. *Self-drive (dinner, B&B) US$145/110 pp sharing (US$172/110 sgl), high/low season (Apr–Oct/ Nov–Mar). All-inclusive (1–4-night stays, inc all meals & drinks, plus a range of tours & activities): US$345/288 pp sharing (US$414/288 sgl); extra nights US$288/252 (US$345/252 sgl). FB (all meals, airport transfers, guided bush & bird walks) US$260/216 pp sharing (US$312/216 sgl).*

⌂ **Maramba River Lodge** (9 chalets, 3 luxury safari tents, 12 standard safari tents, camping) ☏ 324189; f 323130; e maramba@zamnet.zm; www.maramba-

zambia.com. This well-established lodge and campsite, established in 1995, is located just 4km from the Victoria Falls (between the falls and Livingstone town) in the Mosi-oa-Tunya National Park. Situated on the banks of the Maramba River, it is a real oasis in the bush, with green lawns and mature trees, hippos, elephants and birds aplenty. The lodge is excellent for families and individuals, with an activity booking office, pool, kids' play area, craft shop, fully licensed bar, restaurant, braai stands and picnic tables. There are also 2 ablution blocks with hot showers for campers, and conference facilities for weddings and private parties.

There are 4 types of accommodation to choose from. The thatched chalets (2 twin-bedded, 1 dbl and 6 4-bedded family units) are bright and airy, and in a pretty location under the mopane and mahogany trees. Each is en suite and has treated mosquito nets, ceiling fans, safes and views over the Maramba River. The luxury (Landela) safari tents combine lodge comfort with the pleasures of camping. Each of the spacious beige tents is en suite (with tiled bathroom and open-air shower) and has handcrafted furniture. Small verandas and barbecue facilities are available outside. The standard green safari tents (10 twin-bed, 2 4-bed) are set under a thatched roof and are ideal for campers who do not own tents. Beds, chairs, clothes storage, electricity, barbecues and shared ablutions are provided. There's also plenty of space to pitch tents on the manicured lawns, and 2 ablution-blocks with hot showers and laundry facilities are on-site. *Chalets US$60/90/110/130, Landela safari tents US$60/90/110/130, standard safari tents US$30/40/55/70 sgl/dbl/trpl/qdpl pp sharing. Camping US$10 pp, US$3 per vehicle. No credit cards.*

⌂ **Stanley Safari Lodge** (4 chalets) ☏ +33 870 440693 (reservations), +260 97 848615 (lodge emergency no); f +206 3500259; e reservations@stanleysafaris.com; www.StanleySafaris.com. This Belgian-owned luxury lodge was opened in the autumn of 2002. To get there, turn off the main road to the falls almost opposite the Zambezi Sun and follow the signs for Lost Horizons. The turning is almost hidden, about 1km past Lost Horizons to the left; it's a sandy track for which a 4x4 is advisable.

The lodge is set behind a high electric fence, but once inside all is calm and spacious. Large, fairly formal gardens with a central pool face west with sweeping views down towards the Zambezi and the falls in the distance. Behind is the main building, a beautifully designed thatched affair with an open-aspect lounge, bar and dining area, and a 'map room' that deserves to be very popular with guests. Above is a further sitting area, while an innovative wine cellar on a mezzanine floor should be ready soon, allowing candle-lit wine tastings of a range of South African, French and Italian wines.

Stylish open 'cottages', each with a view, are built in a half-moon shape, with king-size or twin beds, a 'loo with a view' and an outside shower and bath. The honeymoon suite has its own plunge pool and fireplace, and those with children will love the family room, with a shallow paddling pool, and a bucket shower set outside around a tree, giving younger children the opportunity to experience in safety the fun of living in the bush. Throughout, the décor is both stylish and comfortable, with good use of wood, stone and natural fabrics, and plenty of space. There are plans to build a further 4 cottages, 2 with AC, plus a separate reception area with a curio shop.

Although visitors can expect to see the occasional elephant or kudu, and local activities can be arranged (including river rafting, bungee jumping, sunset cruises and elephant rides), for the most part this is a place to relax and unwind.
From US$220 pp sharing, FB, inc transfer from Livingstone.

✖ WHERE TO EAT

Take-aways and fast food There are several take-aways in town, including Wonderbake, the Hungry Lion on the corner and Exciting Biting down the street. For a few thousand kwacha, these serve the usual fare of pre-packaged chips, burgers, samosas, sandwiches and soft drinks. They are all in the centre of town, along Mosi-oa-Tunya Road.

If you prefer to sit down, then try the Eat Rite Snack Bar. Spacious and clean with ample seating, it has a good selection of cool drinks, cakes, pastries, fresh bread and baguettes, soft ice cream, meat pies, samosas, sandwiches and other staples to eat in or take away. Though often crowded, it's convenient, cheap and good. Several of the restaurants below also offer take-aways.

Restaurants For a long time most of Livingstone's better places to eat were in the upmarket lodges and hotels, which still remain fine choices. However, recently more dedicated restaurants have opened up, offering better variety (Indian, Chinese, seafood, etc) at fairly decent prices; this is just a selection. Don't expect to find *haute cuisine*, as food tends more towards standard pub fare and sustenance rather than fine dining. Here's a small selection of the current favourites, though it's also worth remembering restaurants in the other hotels and lodges which often cater to foreign tastes and have more to offer, albeit at higher prices.

✖ **African Visions Café** 125 Mosi-oa-Tunya Rd; ☎ 323668. This gift shop also doubles as a vegetarian restaurant with nice variety and daily specials, inc great lentil wraps, tostadas, salads, vegetable curries and freshly made fruit smoothies. The site has secure parking, plus a garden setting & playground for kids; funky, rustic and recommended.

✖ **Funky Munky Pizza Bistro** 214 Mosi-oa-Tunya Rd (within 217 area, a half block down from Fawlty Towers); ☎ 320120. Funky Monky serves great pizzas (eat in or take-away), salads, hot dogs, sandwiches, and a variety of low-priced snacks throughout the day. Its casual atmosphere makes it a good place to pop in for a quick bite or cool drink, or to start your day with a full English b/fast.
Open 07.30–20.30 daily.

✖ **Hippos** Behind Fawlty Towers; ☎ 323432. Hippos is a popular spot for visitors and local tour operators who come to unwind after a hard day's rafting, touring or guiding. There are signs for it at the corner of the Mosi-oa-Tunya and Kazungula roads. Hippos has undergone a complete refurbishment: it now has a bar with plasma screen satellite TV and tables set under a gigantic thached roof. Its atmosphere is unpretentious and friendly, and there are lots of choices on the menu catering for every taste (try the deep-fried mozzarella with blue cheese, or the crispy chicken wings).
Average costs: lunch US$10, dinner US$15.

✖ **Fez Bar** Kabompo Rd. From Mosi-oa-Tunya Rd, turn at the sign on to Kabompo Rd opposite Afric Trading, a block down from the Total service station. Fez Bar serves snacks, lunch and dinner daily, with standard meals of chicken, burgers, steaks and chips etc. It has a full bar and satellite TV, and is a popular hang-out in the evenings.

✗ **Laughing Dragon** John Hunt Way; \ 097 846919. Set behind the museum, Laughing Dragon serves authentic Szechuan Chinese food, has a full alcohol licence and will also do take-aways. Run by a family of Chinese origin, it has a detailed menu, though much depends on what ingredients are available for them to buy on the day in Livingstone. However, what they do cook is good, and the quantities are generous. Their chow mein is delicious, and one very reliable correspondent described their deep fried oyster mushrooms as 'too yummy for words'. Expect dinner with several dishes to share to be around US$8–10 each, which is good value for the quantity and quality of the food.
Open daily 11.00–23.00.

✗ **Ngolide Lodge's Indian Restaurant** One of the better places to eat in town is this small Indian restaurant, tucked away at the back of Ngolide Lodge. They boast a chef from Mumbai and offer a good variety of tasty Indian dishes – everything from *naan* bread to lamb curry – and you can also order take-away. A dinner for 2 with a couple of dishes to share, without drinks, averages about US$30. As it only has a few tables and is popular, do book in advance.

✗ **Ocean Basket** 82 Mosi-oa-Tunya Rd; tel: 321274; e oceanb@zamnet.zm. A branch of the South African chain, this fish restaurant is located in a restored historical building near the junction of Kazungula Rd. It opened in May 2002 to instant local acclaim – quite an accolade in a landlocked country. One shouldn't forget that the freshest seafood is invariably found closest to the ocean; but still, if you have a hankering for fish or prawns, this is the place. Set inside a large secure courtyard with sprawling lawn and ample parking, it offers dining either inside or out on the wide veranda. Staff are efficient and very friendly and the food, served in large frying pans, is good. Expect to pay anywhere between US$8 and US$15 pp for dinner.
Open daily 12.00–22.00.

✗ **Old Drift Restaurant and Bar** \ 323052; m 099 374308; e lrgccmarketing@microlink.zm. From the town centre, turn on to Akapelwa St, cross the railway line, turn left at the junction towards the police station and then immediate right. Follow the signs. À la carte restaurant and bar in the newly renovated, colonial-style clubhouse at the Livingstone Golf Club (see description under activities). Serves b/fast, lunch and dinner daily. Full English/continetal b/fasts cost around US$6.50/3; main meals (pizzas,

burgers, steaks, samosas) US$4–8. Dinners are more extravagant and consequently slightly more expensive. There are free snacks and happy hour prices 17.30–18.30 every Friday.

✗ **Rhapsody's** Located at the Falls Park Shopping Centre. Standard fare is on offer here: steaks, chicken, vegetarian dishes, salads, and a few oddities such as snails. Generally the food is good, but the service is very slow even when the place is empty.

✗ **Rite Pub & Grill** Mosi-oa-Tunya Rd. Diagonally opposite Barclays Bank, across from Mini Market, this is a pleasant enough place to stop for lunch, dinner or a drink. Individual booths with their own thatched roof are a bit on the dark side, but nevertheless cosy. A fairly standard menu includes pizzas (and chips) from US$1.30/Kw8,000 up to US$5/Kw25,000 for a large, and there's a full bar.

✗ **Royal Livingstone** Sun's flagship hotel has a fabulous restaurant with surprisingly reasonable prices, particularly when compared with the Zambezi Sun next door. It's not cheap but worth splashing out. The setting is lovely – old-world elegance and comfort – the service excellent, and the food certainly the best in town. Dinner costs from about US$30 each; lunch is about US$20, excluding drinks. The hotel also does a very genteel afternoon tea for about US$20, which includes lovely finger sandwiches and tea cakes, if you feel like a bit of refined luxury.

✗ **Squire's Grillhouse & Action Bar** Located behind the casino in The Falls (alongside the Zambezi Sun), right off Mosi-oa-Tunya Rd, Squire's is a South African restaurant chain serving decent but standard fare, mostly grilled meat, chicken and fish. It's not terribly cheap, for the quality and quantity provided, though they have a 'happy hour' in the early evening, and some lunch specials, which are better value. Its unprepossessing location is an obvious drawback, and there's noise from the road, but the service is friendly and efficient.
Open daily 11.00–22.00.

✗ **UTSAV Restaurant & Exciting Biting Takeaway** Mosi-oa-Tunya Rd; \ 322259. Opposite the post office, near Mini-Market, this is a small, family-run restaurant/take-away. It serves good curries, naan breads, samosas and tandoori chicken, and also pies. It is pleasantly air-conditioned, and usually has special meals designed to suit impecunious backpackers.
Open 10.00 until late.

✗ **Wonderbake** In the centre of town next to the Rite Pub & Grill. Serves fresh breads, samosas, drinks, chicken, cakes, sandwich rolls and ice cream. One of the few places in the area with wi-fi. A convenient location for a quick snack and a great spot to rendezvous with people.

✗ Zambezi Sun The buffet restaurant here is wide ranging with a good selection of grilled kebabs, burgers, omelettes to order, salads and desserts (though at US$25 pp for dinner it's not cheap). Alternatively, there's an alfresco grill located alongside the entertainment area at the pool, ideal for light lunches and snacks. It has a fun atmosphere, especially in the afternoons, and tables are set inside and out around a large pool. When there's live music, it's good value for an evening out, but don't expect cordon bleu standards. Within the same complex are Squire's (see above) and Fegos, a small Italian café serving coffees/teas, snacks and light lunches.

✗ The Zambezi Waterfront The magnificent setting of SafPar's riverside complex of the same name, down Sichango Rd near the entrance to the game park, makes this a great place to dine. You can enjoy b/fast, lunch or dinner (or a snack) overlooking the Zambezi at affordable prices. The food is good and plentiful with tasty chicken dishes, burgers and chips, soups, sandwiches and daily specials served by friendly staff. There is also a full bar. While it is out of town, it's the kind of place you might go for a meal and stay for hours to savour the riverside ambience.

✗ Zig Zag Industrial Rd; ☎ 322814; e zigzag@ zamnet.sm. Zig Zag is a welcome respite from the hustle and bustle of town. Look for the signpost indicating the turn. Large and inviting, with shady guava, lemon and mango trees, it's a popular place for coffee and cakes, lunch, or an evening meal. Tremazini – toasted filled pitta bread – makes a welcome change from the usual run of fast food, as do quiches, pasta, nachos and daily specials, all at reasonable prices. There's also a full children's menu, a range of desserts and milkshakes, and a fully licensed bar. The multi-purpose site was formerly a textile warehouse, and the space is being used to advantage. There's an enticing pool with grassy surround and a changing area for a nominal charge, and a children's play area, useful if you want to keep the kiddies entertained as you sip your cappuccino. There is also an interesting craft market in the warehouse itself.
Open daily 08.00–20.00.

NIGHTLIFE Livingstone's nightlife centres largely around dancing and drinking, although the bars at various restaurants (Hippos, The Waterfront, Sun Hotel, Zig Zag etc) offer a pleasant atmosphere if you simply want to relax and chat. Those wishing to dance and partake of the local nightlife should try Eat Rite's open-air disco on Kapondo Street, which moonlights as a nightclub – Steprite Sounds – on Fridays and Saturdays. Dress code is 'no shorts, no tropicals and no vests'. Ravestone, across the street, can also be a fun spot where you can shoot a round of pool as well. The New Fairmount Hotel has a popular disco/dance club (and casino), generally jam-packed on weekend nights. In all of these places, the music is loud, you can dance until you drop and, because they can become very rowdy later in the evenings, it's advisable to venture out in a group.

The Fez Bar (see pages 444–5) on Kabombo Road is a lively venue most nights – a favourite hang-out for local expatriates blowing off steam after a tough day looking after visitors.

SHOPPING Keep in mind when paying by credit card that you'll usually be charged 3–5% commission. Be sure to enquire, prior to using your card, about any commission charges.

Food and drink There is no shortage of grocers and shops in Livingstone and you can find most things, though you may have to visit several shops, and imported gourmet items are harder to come by and expensive. The Spar Super Store (*Falls Park Shopping Centre*) is definitely the best choice: clean, bright and well-stocked with local and imported produce (from gourmet cheeses to rice-wine vinegar), it has made grocery shopping in Livingstone far easier. Mini Market (*Mosi-oa-Tunya Road;* ☎ 320633) across from the post office stocks a good supply of fresh fruits and vegetables in addition to all the basics like eggs, milk, cheese, chickens, meats and dry goods. Shoprite (*Kapondo Street*) is a large South African supermarket chain with a wider variety of goods, but often at higher prices and with some past the expiry date – and parking is a nightmare. Furthermore, their fruit and vegetables are not very fresh since most have travelled up from South Africa via Lusaka and down to Livingstone. Spar is a better option for a big shop; if you're buying fruits and vegetables only, try the Zambian open-air markets or wheelbarrow marketeers. Positioned around town, these have fresh tomatoes, onions and other basic fruits and vegetables, and are generally cheaper. Further down the road, by Nanoo's, is Tunya Meats & Deli with a selection of meats, poultry and pork, and biltong. Shopper's Butchery (*John Hunt Way*), behind the post office, is also a good choice for meat, and Wonderbake sells lovely fresh-baked bread and staples. For speciality and hard-to-find items, try the new Spar or Sun International Warehouse (*2652 Linda Road;* ☎ *324290*), off Mosi-oa-Tunya Road in the industrial area, beyond Zig Zag, which stocks a wide range of imported goods – from wines and spirits to meat and dairy produce and many canned goods – all highly priced in US$ and some only in bulk.

Souvenirs and curios If you like bargaining and have lots of patience, try the Curio and Craft Market in Mukuni Park, where local artisans, craftsmen and carvers sell their wares. They have a great selection of wooden carvings and crafts, but expect to be bombarded with vendors vying for your attention and business.

Similarly, there is the larger curio market at the Zambian side of the falls (beside the Falls Museum) with a wider selection of items and even more aggressive salesmen. It can be fun if you have time and enjoy haggling over prices, but frustrating if you are in a hurry. Failing those, one of the following might suit you much better:

African Visions 125 Mosi-oa-Tunya Rd; ☎ 323668; e katkalai@yahoo.uk. 2 blocks down from Ocean Basket, opposite 217 in a historical railway house, you'll recognise this shop by its distinctive burglar bars of African faces at the entrance gate. Alongside a good selection of textiles, baskets, jewellery, artefacts and many Zambian-produced souvenirs you'll find a well-stocked bookshop, selling mainly secondhand books, and a small café that serves filter coffee, milkshakes, homemade cakes, vegetarian meals and light snacks. The playground in the garden provides a welcome diversion for children, giving parents a chance to relax or browse.

The Hammerkop's Nest Mosi-oa-Tunya Rd; ☎ 323466. Opposite Barclays Bank, this spacious shop has a wide range of crafts, gifts and curios, including textiles, stationery, jewellery, basketware, some safari wear, hats and home accessories. Its central location makes it ideal for those without much time to spare.

Kubu Crafts 133 Mosi-oa-Tunya Rd; ☎ 324093; e kubucrafts@zamnet.zm. The main shop is located in a renovated historical railway house in the 217 area; you can't miss the delightful flying hippo at the entrance. It is well stocked with everything from furniture, wrought-iron fittings and jewellery to textiles, paintings by local artists, glass and beautiful handmade cards. You are bound to find something

you like here. Kubu manufactures its own teak furniture (having outfitted many of the local lodges) and has seemingly endless stock, so allow plenty of time for browsing. Nice things don't come cheap here, but there is something for everyone and the friendly staff can arrange to ship your purchases back home. Throughout the day, Kubu serves tea/coffee and delicious homemade cakes in their pleasant garden; this alone is worth a visit. Kubu also has several smaller outlets, at the airport and Sun's activity centre, as well as a newly opened shop at Falls Park Shopping Centre.

The Shop that Thunders Between the curio market and Field Museum on the Zambian side of the falls; e theshopthatthunders@zamnet.zm. This shop stocks the usual collection of souvenirs and memorabilia — wall hangings, basket ware, carvings, postcards and gifts. It's convenient if you are at the falls and doesn't involve the haggling required at the adjacent curio market. They also sell cool drinks and snacks.

The Whole in the Wall 217 area, next to Fawlty Towers; ☎ 324189; e tambao@zamnet.zm. This small but well outfitted shop has a good variety of fun and innovative locally produced souvenirs, tending towards smaller and easy-to-carry items like wire animals, key chains, postcards, maps, T-shirts, handicrafts and gifts.

17

Zig Zag Craft Market Industrial Rd; ✆ 322814; ;
e zigzag@zamnet.zm. Within Zig Zag's multi-
purpose complex (see page 434) is a dedicated
shopping area selling a range of locally produced
crafts, curios, textiles and souvenirs.

Other supplies For cosmetics, toiletries or medicines there are three good **pharmacies** with a selection of items as well as insect repellents, suncreams, medical supplies, baby supplies, batteries, film and more. Each has a trained pharmacist, who can also offer advice on medications and fill prescriptions. Otherwise, the Spar Super Store in the new Falls Shopping Centre and Shoprite in the centre of town sell a variety of beauty products and the basics. The pharmacies are:

L F Moore Chemists Akapelwa St; ✆/f 321640.
Located across from the High Court and bus
depot, L F Moore was established in 1936 and is
a Livingstone institution. It remains one of the
best-stocked chemists in town and with friendly,
helpful service; they will go out of their way to
assist you.
*Open Mon–Fri 08.00–12.30 & 14.00–18.00, Sat
08.00–13.00, Sun/public holidays 09.30–12.30.*
Link Pharmacy In the new Falls Park Shopping

Centre next to the Spar. Well-stocked chemist; if they
don't have it, they can usually get it for you from
their Lusaka store.
*Open Mon–Fri 09.00–18.00, Sat 09.00–17.00, Sun
09.00–13.00.*
Musamu Chemist ✆ 323226, after hours ✆ 095
832197. Located next to Capital Theatre on Mosi-oa-
Tunya Rd by Wonderbake.
*Open Mon–Fri 08.30–19.00, Sat 08.30–16.00, Sun
09.00–13.00.*

You can pick up **clothing essentials** at the Pep store on Mosi-oa-Tunya Road, almost opposite Zambia National Commercial Bank, or at Power Sales, a few doors down from the same bank, though you'll need to be selective. For more fashionable wear try the clothing stores at the new Falls Park Shopping Centre or at the Sun Hotel, though these will be pricer. The Hammerkop's Nest (see above), next to Capital Theatre, has a small selection of safari wear – mainly hats, shirts and shorts as well as African-style tops. For shoes, try Bata, next to AutoWorld by Barclays Bank, though both the selection and sizes are rather limited.

Despite its shortcomings on high fashion, Livingstone is a great place to find African wear – brightly coloured shirts, skirts and dresses, some complete with matching caps or headscarves – and garments can often be made to order with a few days' notice. *Chitenge*, the colourful lengths of traditional African cloth, can be found at most of the small Indian shops on the main road and on Kuta Way, one block down, parallel to the main road or at any of the local African markets. Alternatively, take a trip to the large, busy and colourful Maramba Market where these vivid fabrics are on sale amid a multitude of stalls selling almost everything you can imagine. For the widest selection of ready-made clothing at reasonable prices, check out the Mukamba Boutique and Tailoring (*John Hunt Way, off Airport Rd: turn by Barclays Bank, go up one block and turn right*), who also have their own tailor.

Emma's Tailoring (*Mosi-oa-Tunya Rd*), on the right a block past 217, can tailor-make anything from clothing to tablecloths, quickly and affordably. Bring your own fabric (bought at a local market or an Indian shop in town) or choose one of hers.

For **dry cleaning or laundry**, try Sun International's warehouse (see above; ✆ 320134, f416927). Clothing is returned within 24 hours and a same-day service is offered for items delivered by 10.00.

For **books** the newly opened Bookworld (*Falls Park Shopping Centre*; ✆ 321414) has the best stock in Livingstone and also sells stationery, games and the like. Otherwise try African Visions (*Mosi-oa-Tunya Rd*), near 217 area. They sell a good selection of new and secondhand books at reasonable prices. Jollyboys (see page 435) has a book-exchange system, as do many of the accommodations in town.

Alternatively, curio shops like Kubu Crafts (see page 447) stock wildlife reference books and regional travel guides, as does the Livingstone Trading Company shop at the Zambezi Sun (see page 442).

Current magazines may be harder to come by. Your best bet is at the new Spar at Falls Park Shopping Centre or Shoprite in town (though be warned, magazines are expensive). Be sure to check the issue date: magazines sold here tend to be several months old. Oddly the street vendors in front of the Capital Theatre often have more recent ones and at much lower prices, but this is very hit-or-miss.

Basic **camera supplies** can be found at L F Moore Chemists (see above), but a better bet is the Konica Film Centre on the main road or Kodak Express (\ *320241*) with two locations (*Liso House, next to Finance Bank; Falls Park Shopping Centre*). Konica does one-hour photo processing, enlargements and passport photos, and stocks film, photo albums and related supplies. There's also the HK Photo Studio (*Mosi-oa-Tunya Rd*), next to Mo-Money, which sells Agfa film, and Kodak Express (Liso House, Mosi-oa-Tunya Rd); both will process film, the latter in an hour.

For cassette tapes of popular **music**, including many African selections, try the open-air market at the bottom of Kapondo Street (called 'Zimbabwe' or Central market). They have a wide selection of cheap (probably bootlegged) cassette tapes (and DVDs and videos too). Follow your ears for blaring music and you'll find a kiosk selling tapes!

For **photocopying** and **stationery** needs, your best choices are Reprographix or The Print Shop, across the street from each other on Mosi-oa-Tunya Road just before Liso House, though many shops offer copying services as well.

If you have **computer** trouble, Falcon Technologies (*Linda Road past Zig Zag; tel 322676 or 097 747707;* e *support@mosinet.zm*) offers repair and service and also sells new and used computers.

BANKS AND MONEY Livingstone has several major banks and various bureaux de change dotted throughout town. There are also freelance 'money changers' around Eat Rite and at the border. Unless you are very savvy or desperate, avoid the money changers. They always take advantage of unsuspecting (and even suspicious) tourists by short-changing them somehow.

You can also change money at many of the lodges and hotels. This is the least favourable exchange rate, but most convenient method. There's an ATM at Barclays Bank, but don't rely on it to have money when you want it.

The major banks are situated around the post office area, parallel to the main road. Most open Monday to Friday 08.00–14.00, but get there early if you want to avoid long queues.

$ **Barclays Bank** \ 32114/5 or 324196; f 322317
$ **Zambia National Commercial Bank** \ 321901, 320171 or 320995; f 320182

$ **Standard Chartered Bank** \ 321743 or 321745; f 321721

Of these, Zambia National Commercial Bank is our favourite with its spacious air-conditioned interior and more private exchange facilities. Barclays tends to be the most crowded with slowest service, and money is doled out in front of the watchful eyes of everyone else, yet it is the only bank to offer Visa facilities. Barclays also has a small branch at Sun's resort complex.

Alternatively the larger bureaux de change, many of which are close to or opposite, Barclays Bank, include:

$ **Falls Bureau de Change** In the post office complex, next to Zamtel Telecom Centre; \ 322088.

Open Mon–Fri 09.00–13.00 & 14.00–17.00, Sat 09.00–13.00.

$ **Mo-Money** Ground floor, Stanley House, on the main road by the Capital Theatre; ✆ 323431. Consistently has the best rates in town and does not charge commission. Accepts travellers' cheques or cash,

and can even do cash advances on your Visa card. *Open Mon–Fri 08.00–17.00, Sat/Sun 09.00–13.00.*
$ **Southend Bureau de Change** Liso House; ✆ 320241/320773; f 322128

COMMUNICATIONS

Internet Internet cafés have cropped up all around town, including the new one at Falls Park Shopping Centre. While rates are low and comparable, the standard of computers, speed and service varies widely, so it's best to enquire before you log on. Virtually all lodges and accommodation offer some kind of internet access; these seem to be most geared to tourists and offer helpful service, better facilities and more reliable connections, though note that high-speed service has yet to come to Livingstone.

🌐 **Cyber Post** Mosi-oa-Tunya Rd; ✆ 321338 or 324440/1; e cyberpost@zamnet.zm. Just south of the turn-off to Nakatindi Rd, next to the Livingstone Adventure Centre, this was Livingstone's first internet café and has maintained consistently good service.

Rates are Kw300 per min. They also have local and international phone and fax facilities at competitive rates.
Open Mon–Fri 7.00–17.00, Sat/Sun 09.00–12.00.

Post and courier You can't miss the Livingstone post office (✆ *321400; open Mon–Fri 08.00–17.00, Sat 08.00–13.00*) in the centre of town in a sprawling complex of banks and shops, adjacent to the main road. The post office is also the agent for Western Union.

The best way to send mail quickly within Zambia is via EMS (Expedited Mail Service), a reasonably priced service where letters are hand delivered (no postbox mail). It is also available to overseas destinations and is generally less expensive than a courier company. For express mail services, there are several choices, some of which also offer phone, fax and internet as well. With any you can send letters, parcels and small packets to destinations within Zambia and worldwide. This is costly but reliable. If you need important documents sent from overseas, DHL or FedEx is the quickest way to be assured of them reaching you safely. Packages take about a week from Europe or the USA.

Western Union/Federal Express Mosi-oa-Tunya Rd; ✆ 322742. Next to Hammerkop's, this is the agent for FedEx and ships documents and parcels worldwide.
DHL Mosi-oa-Tunya House; ✆ 320044. Located in the centre of town in the big high-rise building on the bottom floor.

Professional Packaging & Freight Services ✆ 322925 or 097 783034; f 324264. If express mail is too expensive, you can have items packed and sent from here at generally cheaper freight rates.

Telephone and fax If you need to make phone calls or send/receive faxes, and can't do so where you are staying, then the obvious choices, open throughout the day, are listed under *Internet*, above. Each has local and international telephone and fax facilities at competitive prices, though calling overseas is not cheap from anywhere in Zambia.

Alternatively, Zamtel's Public Telecommunications Centre (*open Mon–Fri 08.00–13.00 & 14.00–17.30, Sat 08.00–12.30, though hours can be erratic*) is conveniently next to the post office in a modular trailer. Phone calls within Livingstone are about US$0.20 per minute, but about US$1.20 per minute to elsewhere in Zambia.

International calls to Europe, USA and Australia average about US$15 for three minutes. They also offer a fax service but this is not always reliable. Strangely,

Zamtel has no incoming public telephone line to inquire about faxes or other information, so you need to go there personally. On the other side of the post office, adjacent to the postboxes, is a small office offering international phone and fax. They are open throughout the day, and tend to keep more reliable hours than Zamtel. You will find many such venues dotted around town.

MEDICAL EMERGENCIES Medical facilities are limited in Livingstone, and the local hospitals are not up to the standard of those in the developed world, but there are options should you need medical assistance. Specialty Emergency Services (SES; ↘ 322330; emergency control centre 01 2733027; e med@zamnet.zm) has a base here staffed with South African-trained paramedics. SES operates a well-equipped ambulance service and is quick to respond to medical emergencies. Its office is on the corner of Likute and Obote roads; turn left on to Obote and SES is two blocks up on the left side; it is well signposted. SES also handles all aspects of medical evacuation, if necessary, although this can take time. It's advisable to keep your health insurance and emergency contact details with you. Most tour operators, activities and upmarket accommodation include SES medi-evac coverage in their rates, and Sun hotels have a mini-clinic with nurse for their own guests. In any case it's a good idea to have your medical insurance and emergency contact details on hand in case of emergency. Costs for ambulance service and local medical help are reasonable, but medi-evac costs run extremely high.

The options for medical assistance are as follows:

✚ **Med Prof** (2623 Mosi-oa-Tunya Road; ↘ 321023; m 096-688209 (also for emergencies); f 321024; email medprofzambia@yahoo.co.uk) A newly opened clinic, clean and well-equipped, and professionally run by Dr Andre Hattigh. It is the same clinic used by SES. Conveniently located on the main road, just past New Fairmount Hotel as you head out of town, on the right side (look for the sign). The facilities are bright, clean and tidy with comfortable, spacious waiting rooms. The clinic seems to be the best equipped in Livingstone, with a laboratory that does malaria tests, a large diagnosis room, comprehensive ICU and waiting and examination rooms, bathrooms etc. This should be the first clinic you come to; the others in town don't come up to quite the same standard.

✚ **Dr Shafik's Clinic & Surgery** ↘ 321130 (24hrs), m 097 784804

✚ **Health Point (Dr Shanks)** office ↘ 322170; m 095 794888; e shanks@zamnet.zm

✚ **Southern Medical Centre** ↘ 323547, 323786 or 095 797577; e southmed@zamtel.zm

For pharmacies, see page 448.

TRAVEL AGENCY For international airline tickets and fares, your best choice is Southend Travel (*Liso House, and Falls Park Shopping Centre;* ↘ 320773, 320241 or 322128; e southend@zamnet.zm; open Mon–Fri 08.00–17.00 exc 12.30–14.00; Sat 08.00 –12.30), next to Finance Bank along Mosi-oa-Tunya Road. They are agents for 20 different airlines and are able to advise on special air fares. They can book Nationwide, British Airways and SAA flights in and out of Livingstone and other regional or international destinations. Keep in mind when paying by credit card you'll be charged 3% commission.

CAR REPAIRS The two best workshops in town are Foley's Africa (*Industrial Rd;* ↘f320888; e foleys@zamnet.zm), near Bundu Adventures, catering for Land Rovers; and Bennett Engineering (↘f 321611; e bqes@zamnet.zm) opposite the new Falls Park Shopping Centre, who service most of the tour-operator vehicles in town. Although both are generally very busy, they are your best bet for more serious problems and employ the most qualified mechanics. For more basic repairs, contact Fallsway Motors (↘ 321049) at the corner of Nakatindi Road, or

Channa's Motors (✆ *320468*) on the main road just across the railway line. Their facilities are somewhat limited and service can be slow but they can often help get you moving again, barring major problems. For punctures and tyre repairs try the Total fuel station, on the right side of Mosi-oa-Tunya Road as you head up towards the centre of town, or Zambezi Tyre Centre (✆ *324405;* f *324406;* e *zambezityres@zamnet.zm*) on Industrial Road, who sell new tyres at good prices and offer a full range of tyre services from wheel balancing to retreads. If it's parts or vehicle accessories that you need, the most central place is Auto World (✆ *320264;* f *320265;* e *autoworld@zamtel.zm*) next to Barclays Bank.

WHAT TO SEE AND DO The falls area has been a major crossroads for travellers for the past 100 years. From the early missionaries and traders, to the backpackers, overland trucks and package tourists of the last few decades – virtually everyone passing through the region from overseas has stopped here. Recently this has created a thriving tourism industry and, apart from simply marvelling at one of the world's greatest waterfalls, there are now lots of ways to occupy yourself. Some are easily booked after you arrive; one or two are better pre-arranged.

The past decade has witnessed a huge shift in the area's atmosphere. Visitors used to be from southern Africa, with perhaps the odd intrepid backpacker and the fortunate few who could afford an upmarket safari. Now the sheer volume of visitors to the falls has increased massively. This increase, especially noticeable in the proportion of younger visitors, has fuelled the rise of more active, adventurous pursuits like white-water rafting, bungee jumping, river-boarding and other thrill-based pastimes.

A genteel cocktail at the Victoria Falls Hotel is no longer the high point of a visit for most people. You are more likely to return home with vivid memories of the adrenaline rush of shooting rapids in a raft, or the buzz of accelerating head-first towards the Zambezi with only a piece of elastic to save you.

For contact details of operators running the activities listed below, see page 467.

The falls The falls are 1,688m wide and average just over 100m in height. Around 550 million litres (750 million at peak) cascades over the lip every minute, making this one of the world's greatest waterfalls.

Closer inspection shows that this immense curtain of water is interrupted by gaps, where small islands stand on the lip of the falls. These effectively split the falls into smaller waterfalls, which are known as (from west to east) the Devil's Cataract, the Main Falls, the Horseshoe Falls, the Rainbow Falls and the Eastern Cataract.

Around the falls is a genuinely important and interesting rainforest, with plant species (especially ferns) rarely found elsewhere in Zimbabwe or Zambia. These are sustained by the clouds of spray, which blanket the immediate vicinity of the falls. You'll also find various monkeys and baboons, whilst the lush canopy shelters Livingstone's lourie amongst other birds.

The flow, and hence the spray, is greatest just after the end of the rainy season – around March or April, depending upon the rains. It then decreases gradually until about December, when the rains in western Zambia will start to replenish the river. During low water, a light raincoat (available for rent!) is very useful for wandering between the viewpoints on the Zimbabwean side, though it's not necessary in Zambia. However, in high water a raincoat is largely ineffective as the spray blows all around and soaks you in seconds. Anything that you want to keep dry must be wrapped in several layers of plastic or, even better, zip-lock plastic bags.

The falls never seem the same twice, so try to visit several times, under different light conditions. At sunrise, both Danger Point and Knife-edge Point are fascinating – position yourself carefully to see your shadow in the mists, with three concentric rainbows appearing as halos. (Photographers will find polarising filters invaluable in capturing the rainbows on film, as the light from the rainbows at any time of day is polarised.)

Moonlight is another fascinating time, when the falls take on an ethereal glow and the waters blend into one smooth mass which seems frozen over the rocks.

On the Zambian side, viewing the falls could not be easier. Simply follow the signs and your nose along the paths from in front of the Field Museum and curio stalls. Entrance is US$10 per person, and the gate is open 06.00–18.00 daily and in the evenings on full-moon. One track leads upstream for a while. For photographers, this is best explored in the early morning (good for photographers as the sun is still behind you and illuminates the falls) or in the late afternoon when you may catch a stunning sunset.

If you visit when the river is at its lowest, towards the end of the dry season, then the channels on the Zambian side may have dried up. While the falls will be less spectacular then, their fascinating geology, normally obscured by spray, is revealed. Every season brings a reason to visit the falls: low water presents a good opportunity to view the rocks, gorge and interesting geology. In recent years, the diversion of water to generate power has been curtailed so the flow of water is more constant with generally some water flowing over the edge on the Zambian side.

The main path leads along the cliff opposite the falls, then across the swaying knife-edge bridge, via scenic points, photo stops and a good vantage point from which to watch bungee jumpers. This finishes at the farthest west of the Zambian viewpoints.

A third path descends right down to the water's edge at the Boiling Pot, which is used as a raft launch-site during the main rafting season. It is a beautiful (but steep) hike down first navigating big cement steps, then through palm-fringed forest and finally scrambling over boulders, but well worth the long, hot climb back as long as you have good footwear. Take a picnic and relax by the river if you've time (and if you notice a smell of urine, it's probably from the monkeys!).

Viewing the falls by moonlight is not restricted, though elephants wander about occasionally and it is best not to go alone. If you can visit during a full moon then watch for a lunar rainbow, an amazing sight.

While the falls can easily be explored on your own, most tour operators offer excellent guided tours of the falls (both Zimbabwe and Zambia sides) and the surrounding area, either stand-alone or in combination with historical, cultural, game viewing and other sightseeing tours. These are highly informative with professional guides offering detailed explanations of the formation of the falls and gorges, the river, local history and flora and fauna. Tours cost around US$25–40 per person, including entrance fees.

From the Zimbabwean side, viewing the falls is more regulated. There is now a small ticket booth and display at the entrance gate to the falls, which is a few hundred metres from the Zimbabwean border post. Tickets are valid for the whole day, so you can return for no extra cost during the same day.

Technically this area is within the Victoria Falls National Park – and you will find a map of the paths at the entrance. Start at the western end, by Livingstone's statue – inscribed with 'Explorer, Missionary and Liberator', and overlooking the Devil's Cataract.

Visiting the viewpoints in order, next is the Cataract View. If water levels are low, and the spray not too strong, after clambering down quite a steep stairway you will be greeted by views along the canyon of the falls. Climbing back up, wander from one viewpoint to the next, eastwards, and you will eventually reach the slippery-smooth rocks at Danger Point.

Few of these viewpoints have anything more than brushwood fences and low railings to guard the edges – so going close to the edge is not for those with vertigo. Viewing the falls by moonlight is possible by special arrangement.

Livingstone Island Livingstone Island lies in the middle of the great waterfall, and is the island from which Dr Livingstone first viewed the falls. Trips are run exclusively by Tongabezi (see page 437) between July and March (subject to water levels), with guests transferred to the island from the Royal Livingstone launch site by boat. There you'll have the opportunity to take in the scene – gazing over the edge, perhaps taking a thrilling dip in the Devil's Pool right on the falls edge, and having a gourmet meal in an exclusive setting. Several trips are offered daily; choose either morning (called 'breezer'), gourmet lunch or afternoon tea and cocktails. When the water's at its lowest, around October and November, you can sometimes walk across the top of the falls to the island, climbing over rocks, exploring pot-holes and crossing small streams along the way. Strictly speaking, it is not permitted for safety reasons and to keep people from trespassing on the island. More than likely, you will be turned back and prohibited from accessing the island. You also run the added risk of being stuck on top of the falls, should water levels unexpectedly rise. If you do go, be aware of the risks, proceed cautiously, stay along the falls' edge and respect the privacy of the island
Prices inc transfers & park fees. Breezer (full English b/fast) US$45; lunch US$90; afternoon tea US$70 (inc traditional high tea and a full bar with hors d'oeuvres).

River cruises Floating on the Upper Zambezi with a glass in one hand, and a pair of binoculars in the other, is still a pleasant way to watch the sun go down, even if nowadays the river is full of booze-cruise boats operating round the clock (you can choose from breakfast, lunch, sunset or dinner cruises!), and sometimes all congregating close together. On the Zambian side, surely the most elegant and leisurely way to experience the river is aboard the *African Queen*, an old-style double-decker riverboat complete with gleaming brass that cruises regally upriver from its dock on the aptly named Royal Mile (the name is derived directly from royalty, in fact, for it was from here that George VI and his entourage took a launch on to the river during their visit in 1947). In the rarified atmosphere on board, guests sip cocktails or soft drinks to the rhythmic accompaniment of xylophones, or *marimba*, sounding the vessel's imminent departure. As the boat makes her stately way upstream, you take a gentle look around the Zambezi's islands, surrounded by national parks on both sides of the river. You may well spot the odd hippo, crocodile, or elephant – or even, if you're very lucky, a white rhino – not to mention numerous birds. Such luxury doesn't come cheap, but the price is inclusive of drinks and a substantial finger buffet and is good value. Lunches and dinners are also of a high standard, giving a memorable and unique dining experience.

Smaller craft ply the same route, of course. On the Zambian side, these are organised by Victoria Falls River Safaris, Safari Par Excellence, Bwaato Adventures and Taonga Safaris, the last three the most popular with backpackers, boasting all you can drink. (SafPar and Bwaato also have offices on the Zimbabwean side.) These used to be strictly at sundown, and the drinks were free. Now, sadly, booze cruise boats operate round the clock and they are often less generous – with drinks bought from a bar on board. However, you can still take a gentle look around the Zambezi's islands, surrounded by national parks on both sides of the river. Away from the crowded waters near the falls, Wild Side Tours & Safaris offers a more serene alternative, 25km upstream. Here you can cruise in solitude, taking in the scenery, prolific birdlife and wildlife along the banks of the Zambezi National Park. Hippos, elephants and crocodiles are commonly seen as well as waterbuck, bushbuck and even buffalo. Victoria Falls River Safaris operate several propeller-free aluminium safari boats in and around the falls and on the Upper Zambezi for game viewing, also with small groups (up to eight people per boat). Choose from three 2½-hour cruises daily (morning and sunset cruises for US$55, and lunch cruise at US$60).

On the Zambian side these are organised by Safari Par Excellence, Bwaato Adventures and Taonga Safaris.

In Zimbabwe, boats leave from several different jetties and there is also a range of trips to choose from – from upmarket cruises to more basic ones. On both sides, book in advance, either direct or through one of the agents in town, who can advise what will best suit you, and will also arrange for you to be picked up about half an hour before the cruise. For contact details, see page 467.

African Queen US$44 pp b/fast, 2hr lunch or sunset cruise, inc drinks & canapés. Wild Side US$35 pp for sunset or coffee cruise inc drinks & snacks. Others US$20–40 pp.

Fishing excursions Among the angling fraternity, the Zambezi River is synonymous with great fishing for prized tiger fish and Zambezi bream. If you dream of hooking a 'tiger' then a memorable day on the river with a knowledgeable guide leading you to the finest fishing spot can help make it come true. Angle Zambia (see page 467) with excellent local knowledge and friendly, personalised service is highly recommended. Owner-operated by Gerard and Viv Simpson, they run half- and full-day fishing trips in the Upper Zambezi waters, about 30km from Livingstone. Catering to both novice and experienced anglers as well as fly fishermen, Angle Zambia is well-outfitted, with three 6m aluminium boats complete with fish finders, sunshades and radio communications to their base. Trips are fully inclusive of fishing equipment, tackle, boat hire, fuel, transfers, qualified guide and refreshments. The company can also arrange multi-day fishing excursions to Mwandi (about 200km upriver), location of their *Pride of the Zambezi* houseboat (see pages 439–40), for world-class angling during the prime fishing season, which runs from Junr to September.

US$98/110 half/full day inc lunch; multi-day trips upon request.

Birding Birdwatching isn't normally regarded as an adrenaline sport, but with the outstanding avifauna to be found in and around the falls, serious 'twitchers' (as keen birdwatchers are known) might disagree.

Even the casual visitor with little interest will often see fish eagles, Egyptian geese, lots of kingfishers, numerous different bee-eaters, ibis (including sacred), and various other storks, egrets and herons. Meanwhile, avid twitchers will be seeking the more elusive birds like Taita falcon, as they occur only rarely and the Batoka Gorge is certainly one of the best sites to look for them. Rock pratincoles have almost as restricted a distribution (just following the Zambezi), but can often be seen here balancing on boulders by the water's edge and hawking for insects, while African skimmers can be found nesting upon sandy shores of islands. Look in the riverine forest around the falls and you may spot a collared palm thrush rummaging around, and again these are really quite rare birds recorded in only a few areas.

In contrast, African finfoot occur throughout the subcontinent, but are always shy. They prefer slow water, overhung with leafy branches, and they find the upper sections of the Zambezi perfect, so are often seen there if you look when it's quiet.

Bob Stjernstedt, known locally as 'Bob the Birder' (e *bob@zamnet.zm; www.zambiatourism.com/birdingwithbob*), is one of Zambia's leading ornithologists.

He is based in Livingstone and leads guided birdwatching excursions in the area for US$50/100 per half/full day.

Museums Given its fascinating history, it is no surprise that Livingstone has several good museums. The main Livingstone Museum is the most important of these, and certainly one of the best in the country.

Livingstone Museum In a prime position on the crest of Mosi-oa-Tunya Road, in the middle of town, Livingstone's main museum (*adult/child US$5/1; open 09.00–16.30 daily*) has undergone extensive renovation. There are exhibits on the Stone Age, and features on Zambian culture, politics, history, animals and traditional village life in the area. There is also a unique collection of Livingstone's personal possessions and the museum often has special exhibits, of which the witchcraft one is especially interesting, if somewhat hair-raising. Sculpture and paintings by Zambian artists are also displayed and available for sale.

The staff are friendly and knowledgeable and guided tours are included. It is well worth a visit, if only to familiarise yourself with the area and culture. There is also an excellent large relief map depicting the falls and gorges, which puts everything into good perspective.

Railway Museum Unconfirmed reports suggest that this specialist museum (\ *321820, 323452;* f *324509;* e *nhccsowe@zamnet.zm; US$3; open daily 08.30–16.00*) has burned down. In the hope that this is not the case, or that it will be rebuilt, this entry has been left. The museum is situated about 1km along Chishimba Falls Road, towards the southwest side of town. There's a collection of beautifully preserved old steam locomotives and memorabilia, including a working 1922 10th Class 156 out of Glasgow that is occasionally given an airing, to the delight of local children; and displays on railway history – appropriate for a town where the railway was built in 1905. Even if you're not a railway enthusiast, it's worth popping in if you've half an hour or so, if only to climb into the cab of the working steam engine (it's all very hands-on) or to come face to face with a real 'Thomas the Tank Engine'.

Field Museum Much smaller than the main museum in town, the Field Museum (*adult/child US$5/1*) is next to the curio stands by the border and concentrates on the origin of the falls, and the development of man in the area. Snacks and cold drinks are available in the shop next door.

Handicrafts

Craft markets Just inside the Zambian border, next to the Field Museum, is an outstanding curio stand. The carvers and traders come mostly from Mukuni village, though the goods come from as far as the Democratic Republic of Congo and Malawi. Mukuni Park, in the centre of town (see page 447), has a similar area of curio vendors. Both are excellent places to buy wood and stone carvings, handicrafts, chessboards, masks, drums, malachite bangles, baskets and the like. There are usually about 20 or 30 individual traders, laying their wares out separately. All compete with one another and vie for your business. The best buys are makenge baskets (these come exclusively from Zambia's western province), malachite and heavy wood carvings: hippos, elephants, rhinos, giraffes and smaller statues, often made out of excellent-quality, heavy wood. However, you should consider the ethics of encouraging any further exploitation of hardwoods. Note, too, that some wooden items, especially wooden salad bowls and tall giraffes, are prone to cracking once you get them home due to changes in climate and that very rarely are 'antiques' sold at craft markets anything other than fakes. Unless you have the expertise to tell the difference, it's better to buy such artefacts from a reputable shop in town.

The curio market is a place to bargain hard, and you can expect to hear all sorts of prefabricated stories as to why you should pay more. When you start to pay, you will realise how sophisticated the traders are about their currency conversions, reminding you to double-check any exchange rates. Traders will accept most currencies and sometimes credit cards.

Victoria Falls Craft Village Behind the main post office on Livingstone Way, this is Zimbabwe's more regulated answer to Zambia's curio stalls. Amongst this complex are well-built curio shops, and other traders lay their wares out on the surrounding ground. Within the shops you'll find some excellent pieces; if you are shopping for high-quality pieces of art, then this may be the place for you. Alternatively, try the Elephant's Walk Shopping Complex with tribal dancers in front and interesting shops set around an inner courtyard where you can browse in peace or enjoy tea and cake on the patio. Here you will find African art, safari wear, teak furniture, wildlife products, clothing and much more. But if you're simply seeking good-value curios then look to the carvers and vendors outside, who will bargain hard for your business. Zimbabwe's currency regulations means that they can only accept Zimbabwe dollars for payment. The large, newly built Landela complex, along the main road on the upper part of town, also has a multitude of shops chock full of every imaginable handicraft and souvenir, as well as clothing, music, books and pottery, sunglasses, and restaurants or take-aways.

Crocodile Park Just to the south of Livingstone, the Crocodile Park (\ 321733; entry US$7; open all year) offers the opportunity to see some huge crocs at close quarters – from behind the safety of a chain-link fence or from covered walkways – and to get some great photographs. Well-informed and friendly guides offer explanations about behaviour and the history of the animals, and feeding times (usually early afternoon) are posted at the entrance. The park has a valuable educational role, with visiting groups from local schools and the wider community learning about these dangerous creatures, and in many cases developing a new-found respect for them. Picnic tables are set in the landscaped grounds.

The adjacent 'reptile park' features some of Zambia's snakes, housed in glass cages. It, hopefully, will be your only chance to see Africa's most dangerous snakes – black mamba, cobra, puff adder – up close and personal; you can even hold the 'safe' snakes to get a feel for them. There is also an activity centre here where visitors can book any of a wide range of activities or go on one of Gwembe's game drives in the Mosi-oa-Tunya National Park (in which case you get free entrance to the Crocodile Park).

Victoria Falls Crocodile Park On the Zimbabwean side, outside of Victoria Falls town before the entrance to Zambezi National Park, is another crocodile park that also has a few lions, a leopard, duikers and ostriches. A visit to the Victoria Falls Crocodile Museum (US$5; open all year) makes for a memorable excursion for young and old alike. Set among shady trees and lush tropical gardens are several ponds containing crocs of various ages and sizes, the smallest of which (less than a year old) visitors may hold during a guided tour – and find out just how strong even a baby croc is. The complex has several walkways and bridges leading this way and that – to the restaurant, over small manmade streams and pools filled with lurking crocs, to the large lion enclosure or game cages, to the small auditorium and back to the entrance where there is also a gift shop. The big cats, all grown orphans and raised in captivity, are housed in fenced enclosures but are about as close as you'll safely come to a face-to-face encounter with big predators.

Victoria Falls Aquarium Rather surprisingly, Victoria Falls town is home to Africa's largest freshwater aquarium, including some 62 different species of fish plucked from the middle Zambezi and displayed in settings to mirror their natural habitats, as well as a 200,000-litre main exhibition tank full of 'big fish'. If you thought fish were boring, a visit here, costing just US$5, will set you straight. Informative guides will regale with you with surprisingly fascinating fish facts. Did you know that the Zambezi River – with its varied eco-systems – contains over half of Africa's freshwater fish? The aquarium is professionally run by an expert ichthyologist (someone who studies fish) and is not only very interesting but educational as well. While keen anglers will undoubtedly be in their element here, the aquarium is great family fun and well worth a visit during your stay. It's located on the falls road at the top of the Landela complex, across and down from the Wimpy. You can't miss its big sign in front.

Golf Golf enthusiasts can tee off at Elephant Hills Hotel's 18-hole course along the Zambezi on the Zimbabwean side, where amidst warthogs, baboon and impala you can play a leisurely 9 or 18 holes. Elephants also frequent the grounds while the occasional lion sauntering across the fairway quickly turns golf into an adrenalin sport. The setting is lovely and the cost very reasonable. Golf clubs and caddies are available for hire. From Livingstone, Bushtracks offers golf excursions inclusive of transfers (excluding visa) costing US$42 for nine holes and US$52 for 18.

On the Zambian side, the Livingstone Royal Golf and Country Club (\f 323052; m 099 374308; e lrgccmarketing@microlink.zm), established in 1908, was once a popular social and sports club (complete with tennis and lawn bowling). It remains a national monument and is the second-oldest golf club in Zambia. To get to the club from the centre of town, turn on to Akapelwa Street,

THE LIVINGSTONE GOLF CLUB

The end of June 2006 marked the official re-opening of the Livingstone Golf Club, one of the oldest clubs in Africa and a Zambian National Heritage Monument. For years, golf was limited to the Elephant Hills course in Zimbabwe, as Livingstone's golf course and facilities had fallen into a state of disrepair. But golf has now returned to Livingstone. The course and clubhouse have undergone a total renovation, breathing new life into a club that was once visited by royalty and was the site of many tournaments. The first nine holes of this par-72, 6,205m parkland type golf course have been entirely re-landscaped, the fairways and greens replanted with Bermuda and Hybrid Bermuda grass, respectively. The entire property has been fenced, and landscaping work continues with improvements slated for the back nine. Players, visitors, members and non members all welcome to play a round of golf on the newly refurbished front nine holes, enjoy a meal in the beautiful clubhouse, or simply relax, drink in hand, on its sweeping veranda. The clubhouse itself was renovated with great care to preserve its teak woodwork and many historical features, and the result speaks for itself – a stunning colonial-style clubhouse with restaurant and bar, in a genteel setting in the heart of Livingstone. Further renovations on the cards include refurbishing the back nine holes, converting the old manager's house to a gym and fitness centre, renovating the old bowling green and building a swimming pool, tennis and squash courts. For the kids there are a trampoline, boules and a wooden climbing frame with swings.

In Livingstone's heyday, the golf club was the epicentre of the city's social life and activities. By the looks of things it will soon be that again. Golf lessons and club hire (left- and right-handed) are available.

cross the railway line, turn left at the junction towards the central police station, and then immediately right. Follow the signs.

Massages and pampering When you are exhausted from all the sightseeing, shopping and other diversions, relief is only a phone call away. If your idea of the ultimate massage is in a billowing white tent on the banks of the Zambezi with spray from the falls and hippos as backdrop, then the Royal Livingstone Hotel is the place to go. Its Royal Salon (⊙ *321121–7, ext 2546; open 10.00–19.00 daily*) offers riverside massages (Swedish, aromatherapy, sportsman's, Zambian Ukuchina and more) in stylish tented gazebos, each with one side open to the river and two massage beds. A trained masseuse offers what has to be one of the world's most scenic ways to unwind, though such divine pampering isn't cheap: expect to pay upwards of US$65 per person for an hour. Also available within the salon itself are all the usual spa services: manicures, pedicures, facials, waxing, basic hair care and beauty products, all catering to foreign visitors and priced accordingly.

In Victoria Falls, Spa Hair and Beauty (⊙ *+263 11 200 466 or 13 44275/9, ext 6023*) offers similar services with convenient locations inside the Kingdom Hotel, Elephant Hills Hotel and Victoria Falls Hotel.

Sightseeing, cultural and historical tours There are many companies offering guided sightseeing tours around Livingstone, including visits to traditional villages, local markets, museums, the falls, game park and historical sites. If you are staying in one of the lodges, sightseeing tours for guests using their own guides and vehicles are generally included. Bushtracks, Wild Side Tours & Safaris and Bwaato Adventures are popular operators on the Livingstone side, although there are many other operators as well. Of these, Wild Side is run by people who have lived in Livingstone for years, and who understand the place well; it can personalise tours to suit individual requirements. Bwaato Adventures, operating here for many years, is also well positioned, while Bushtracks is larger, based at Sun International's activity centre and with set trips aimed primarily at Sun's clientele and incentive groups. In all cases, trips are professionally run with competent guides. Most tours can be either stand-alone or in combination with others. Wild Side's 'Livingstone Tour & Surrounding Areas' costs US$65 per person (half-day, including entrance fees and refreshments) or US$110 (full day, including lunch). Options for speciality tours may include the following:

Village visits To the east of the falls is Mukuni village, a settlement of over 6,000 Leva people. An organised tour here will give you a glimpse of how local people live and work in a traditional setting along with informative explanations. You can visit local huts, view villagers at work, watch curio making and even sample traditional beer and food. However, Mukuni village, with its close proximity to the falls and popularity with tour operators, relies heavily on the tourist trade, so tends towards a commercial, rather than authentic, feel, with often relentless though friendly pressure to buy curios made there. Further afield is Songwe village, about a 40-minute drive through the bush, and less commercial as it receives fewer tourists. The Livingstone Quad Company (Batoka Sky) offers guided quad-bike excursions to outlying villages and the bush. If your heart is set on a more remote village off the beaten path and you have the time, Bwaato Adventures offer a day trip some 45km upriver to one of the rural villages along the Zambezi.
Bwaato Adventures Village Tour US$70 inc transfers, lunch & refreshments. Bushtracks Mukuni Village Tour US$26. Livingstone Quad Bike Company village & bush tour US$90/105/115 for 1¹/₂/3hrs.

Museum tours Guided tours will also take you to visit Livingstone's museums – the Livingstone Museum or the Railway Museum, or both. Although you can readily visit on your own, an organised tour is an easy alternative with transfer included, especially as part of a full day's sightseeing trip.
One-hour tours, inc entry fees & transfers, from US$15 pp with Bwaato Adventures, up to US$26 with Bushtracks.

Market tours Livingstone has many colourful local markets, of which Maramba Market is the largest and the most fascinating. At the heart of Livingstone's community, it offers everything from fresh produce to secondhand clothes (called *salaula*), from hand-fashioned metal pots to live chickens, from *chitenges* (the traditional African cloth) to hand-crafted wood furniture and more.
Makora Quest US$15 pp (1hr); Bwaato Adventures City and Market Tour US$15 pp (2hrs); Bushtracks US$26 pp.

Historical tour of Livingstone Livingstone, the capital of Northern Rhodesia from 1907 to 1935, has a fascinating history marked by many old historical buildings and accented by colourful characters, intriguing tales and a once-vibrant social life. A guided historical tour through town – on foot and by vehicle – will trace the town's history from frontier town to modern-day tourist capital, including the first hospital, school, library, churches, sports clubs, shopping districts, hotel and other historical sites.
Bushtracks US$26 pp; UTC 2¹/₂hr city tour inc market and museum US$25 pp.

Thrills and spills The falls area is indisputably *the* adventure capital of southern Africa. There is an amazing and seemingly endless variety of ways to get your shot of adrenaline: white-water rafting, canoeing, bungee jumping, kayaking, abseiling, gorge swinging, river boarding or simply a flight over the falls.

None comes cheaply. Most are in the US$50–150 range per activity, which adds up quickly. If you wish to do multiple activities, check out the many combination packages on offer. These can be slightly cheaper than booking individually. There are also choices of operator for most of these, so if you book locally, shop around to find something that suits you before you decide. Prices won't vary much, but you will find the true range of what's available. Whatever you plan, expect to sign an indemnity form before your activity starts.

On the Zambian side, construction has been under way on two gorge lifts, a funicular-style railway at Rapid 23 and a single cable car at Rapid 25, to bring clients out of the gorge after rafting trips, with the cost to be included in the activity price. The race is on to see which of these is operational first.

Flight of Angels Named after Livingstone's famous comment, 'Flight of Angels' describes any sightseeing trip over the falls by small aircraft, microlight, helicopter or ultra-light aircraft. This is a good way to get a feel for the geography of the area, and is worthwhile if you really want to appreciate the falls. If you're arriving from Kasane, or leaving for there, consider combining a sightseeing flight and a flight transfer. Otherwise any of these trips can be readily booked by agents in the area, including:

Light aircraft Surely the most novel is United Air Charters' daily scenic flights over the falls in a 1940s two-seater de Havilland Tiger Moth, departing from Livingstone's airport. The vintage biplane with its open cockpit offers a single passenger an 'Out of Africa' experience, complete with leather flying helmet, goggles and wind in the hair. The flights provide stunning views of the falls and take visitors upstream over the Mosi-oa-Tunya National Park for game viewing. Unlike in a microlight, cameras can be readily taken along. Meanwhile, if you prefer something more conventional, Livingstone Air Safaris offers scenic flights over the falls in a light aircraft. Tour operators in Victoria Falls offer comparable flights in light aircraft using the small runway near the town (not the main airport). *UAC's Tiger Moth: US$100/160 pp for 20/30 mins, inc transfers & tea/coffee. Livingstone Air Safaris US$75 pp.*

Microlight This is a totally different experience from a light aircraft: essentially sightseeing from a propeller-powered armchair 500m above the ground. It is only available on the Zambian side and is operated by Batoka Sky out of their Maramba Aerodrome. Like the Tiger Moth, microlights take only two people: one pilot, one passenger. Because the passenger sits next to the propeller, cameras cannot be carried for safety reasons. However, you can arrange to be photographed, or even pictured on video, above the falls from a camera fixed to the wing. This is the closest you can come to soaring like a bird over the falls.

The microlights are affected by the slightest turbulence, so when you book a flight in advance, it's best to specify early morning or late afternoon, when conditions are ideal. Transport between the Maramba Aerodrome (about a five-minute drive from the border) and Livingstone or Victoria Falls border is provided. *US$80 pp for 15 mins inc circuits over the falls and a flip over the game park; US$140 for 30 mins, inc safari flight up-river.*

Ultra-light Another way to get a bird's-eye view of the falls is from an ultra-light (which feels like a cross between a microlight and small plane). As with the microlight, you are completely exposed, with the wind in your hair, and they take only one passenger at a time. The craft flies more like a small plane but it's much quieter and you can take your camera with you; the lack of confines makes for good photographic opportunities.

These trips are based out of the Victoria Falls main airport (look for them on the tarmac if you fly in here) and run by Bush Birds Flying Safaris. Being so far out of town does make them slightly inconvenient, but they are the closest alternative to a microlight on the Zimbabwean side. On balance, the microlight is more fun, though you do get a nice view of the gorges as you fly up to the falls. *US$100/150 pp for 35/55 mins.*

Helicopter This is the most expensive way to see the falls, but it is tremendous fun. United Air Charters takes passengers in four- or five-seater helicopters from their aptly named Baobab Ridge just south of town. A 15-minute trip takes in the falls and the national park, or for 30 minutes you will fly over the gorges below the falls as well (you can even stop in the gorge for a one- or two-hour picnic, at extra cost). Alternatively, if you plan to raft, river-board or ride a jet boat, you can get an exhilarating lift out of the gorge by helicopter – at extra cost of course, but including a scenic flight over the falls and Zambezi gorges. Batoka Sky, based at the Maramba Aerodrome, use a five-seat Squirrel helicopter, which is designed to give all passengers a good view. The front seats are on a first-come, first-served basis. *Flights typically US$95/190 pp for 15/30 minutes, inc transfers from either Livingstone or Victoria Falls.*

Bungee jumping There's only one company organising bungee jumping: Vic Falls Bungi, an offshoot of the original pioneers from New Zealand, Kiwi Extreme. You jump from the middle of the main bridge between Zambia and Zimbabwe, where the Zambezi is 111m below you. It is among the highest commercial bungee jumps in the world, and not for the nervous. Alternatively, 'tandem' bungee jumps are possible for two people.

17

You can book in advance, through any of the agencies or directly with Vic Falls Bungi (✆ 324231; f 324157; e bungee@zamnet.zm; www.shearwateradventures.com), or simply turn up at the bridge and pay there. Hours are 9.00–17.00, though at high water they begin at 10.00 due to spray from the falls. Digital pictures (US$10) and videos (US$40) of your jump are available, and there is often a '2 for 1' promotion whereby clients who purchase video or merchandise to the value of US$40 qualify for a complimentary second jump, with the footage added to their tape at no extra cost. *US$90 for 1 jump (no refund if you change your mind); tandem jump US$130. Minimum age 14, but under-18s require attendance of parent or guardian and their signature on the indemnity form. Minimum/maximum client weight 40/140kg (88/308lb).*

Bridge walks There's no one better positioned to show you the ins and outs – no, make that ups and downs – of the Victoria Falls Bridge than the bungee folks, whose intimate bridge knowledge will not only fascinate you but have you clambering around and underneath the bridge like a monkey. Vic Falls Bungi now offers bridge tours in which, with safety harness on and accompanied by guide, you have the opportunity to explore its superstructure while hearing all about the bridge's construction and riveting history. While not as adrenalin-charged as bungee jumping, it's still bound to get your heart beating as you navigate your way around the bridge 111m above the Zambezi.

Abseiling, high-wiring and gorge swing A very popular addition to the adventure menu is the Zambezi swing, a cable swing set across the gorge which, together with a 90m-high cable slide (flying fox), abseiling and 'rap' jumps (rappelling forwards) down the side of the gorge, offers daring fun for all ages. These are currently offered only by Abseil Zambia at the top of the fifth gorge on the Zambian side.

The swing is a fixed 135m cable spanning the gorge. Participants are harnessed to ropes attached to the cable's sliding pulley and, after stepping off the cliff face, experience a heart-stopping 53m, three-second free-fall, followed by an exhilarating pendulum-like swing across the gorge, accelerating up to 140km/h (with a pull of roughly 2.5 times gravity) for some two minutes before being lowered to the ground. Described by participants as 'even more thrilling than bungee jumping', it's definitely not for the faint-hearted, though participants as young as eight and as old as 76 have braved it. It's even possible to try it out in tandem.

A slightly tamer alternative is the high wire or flying fox, set on another static cable stretched across the gorge. With harness and pulley, you leap off a platform and 'fly' (slide) across the gorge some 90m above the ground. It can be done in either a sitting or a flying position, and is suitable for children.

For more thrills, there are abseiling (rappelling: lowering yourself down a cliff face with a rope while facing inwards) and rap-jumping (facing and jumping forwards), down a 45m cliff at the edge of the gorge.

Except for the flying fox, be prepared to hike some 30 minutes out of the gorge after each go.

A full day's activity allows you to go up, down and over the gorge to your heart's content. Lunch, beer and cool drinks are included and sundowners are offered. Videos or floppy disks of your activities are available at extra cost. It's also possible to spend just a half day, or to do any activities on their own.

The site is 5km from the falls. If you're driving yourself, turn off the main road to the falls just before the Zambezi Sun, and follow the signposts.
US$95/85 pp for a full/half day, inc insurance, transfers, Zambian day visa & meals. Gorge swing only: US$60/50 dbl/sgl. Flying fox or cable slide only: US$30. Open from 08.00.

Upper Zambezi canoeing Canoeing down the Upper Zambezi is a cool occupation on hot days, and the best way to explore the upper river, its islands and channels. Zimbabwe's Zambezi National Park stretches all along the western shore providing ample opportunity for game viewing, while lodges, farms, villages and bush dot the Zambian side as you head downstream to the upper reaches of the Mosi-oa-Tunya National Park. The silence of canoes makes them ideal for floating up to antelope drinking, elephants feeding or crocodiles basking. Birdlife is prolific – you may hear the cry of the African fish eagle or see pied kingfishers hover and dive. Hippos provide the excitement, and are treated with respect and given lots of space.

There is a variety of options available, from half-day to full-day excursions, combo canoeing and game drives, and even overnight camping trips. You'll find any of them generally relaxing, although paddling becomes a bit more strenuous if it's windy. All canoe trips must be accompanied by a licensed river guide. Canoes range from two-seater open-decked kayaks to inflatable 'crocodiles'.

There are some sections of choppy water if you'd like a little more excitement, though it's possible to avoid most of these easily if you wish. Trips concentrating on these are sometimes sold as white-water kayaking – which shouldn't be confused with the white-water rafting beneath the falls (see below).

For those who'd like the experience but don't want to paddle, canoe operators also run guided 'float' trips on the Upper Zambezi. Participants can paddle when they feel like it or simply float downstream on a raft.

No prior canoeing experience is necessary, and once you are used to the water, the better guides will encourage you to concentrate on the wildlife. Lunch is typically served on an island. Trips on the Zambian side have long been run by Makora Quest and Chundukwa Adventure Trails; both are owner-operated and run by very experienced guides.

Larger entrants on the Zambian side include Bundu Adventures and Safari Par Excellence, both of whom also run float trips using rafts. SafPar offers an Elephant Encounter trip combining a half-day canoeing safari, riverside brunch and an opportunity to interact with their elephants used for elephant-back safaris. Both offer a 'River & Rhino' combo, with a half-day's canoeing (or floating) followed by lunch and a drive in the game park.

US$85/105 for half/full day, with lunch. SafPar also operates overnight trips with the evening spent under the stars on an island for US$140.

White-water rafting The Zambezi below the falls is one of the world's most renowned stretches of white water. It was the venue for the 1995 World Rafting Championships, and rafting is now very big business here, with keen competition for tourist dollars. (About 50,000 people now go down the river every year, paying about US$80–100 each. You can do the sums.)

Experienced rafters grade rivers from I to VI, according to difficulty. Elsewhere in the world, a normal view of this scale would be:

- Class I   No rapids, flat water.
- Class II   Easy rapids, a float trip. No rafting experience required.
- Class III   Intermediate to advanced rapids. No rafting experience required.
- Class IV   Very difficult rapids. Prior rafting experience highly recommended. No children.
- Class V   For experts only. High chance of flips or swims. No children or beginners.
- Class VI   Impossible to run.

The rapids below the falls are mostly graded IV and V. This isn't surprising when you realise that all the water coming slowly down the Zambezi's 1.7km width is being squeezed through rocky gorges that are often just 50–60m wide.

Fortunately for the rafting companies, most of the rapids here may be very large, but the vast majority of them are not 'technical' to run. This means that they don't need skill to manoeuvre the boat while it is within the rapids, they just require the rafts to be positioned properly before entering each rapid. Hence, despite the grading of these rapids, they allow absolute beginners into virtually all of the rafts.

High or low water, and which side of the river? Rafting is offered from both sides of the river by a wide range of companies. Some operate from both sides, like SafPar. The Zambian side offers a far more spectacular entry, just at the base of the falls, whereas on the Zimbabwean side you miss this entirely and start off at Rapid 4.

During high water this might be partially obscured by spray, but you should try to go from the Zambian side during low-water months (roughly August to January) so as not to miss such a stunning place to start below the falls. These low-water months are probably the best time to experience the Zambezi's full glory, as then its waves and troughs (or 'drops') are more pronounced.

In high-water months (February to July), only half-day trips are offered. These start below Rapid 9 on both sides. Note that when the river is highest its rapids may seem less dramatic, but it is probably more dangerous, due to the strong whirlpools and undercurrents. At that time, the water is sometimes too high and rafting should then be stopped until it recedes to a safer level.

The trips A typical rafting trip will start with a briefing, covering safety/health issues, giving the plan for the day and answering any questions. Once you reach the 'put-in' at the river, you will be given a short safety/practice session to familiarise yourself with the raft and techniques that will be used to run the rapids. Half-day trips will run about half of the rapids, but a full day is needed to get through all the rapids from 1 to 23. Lunch and cool drinks are included

Note that the climb up and out of the gorge at the end can be steep and tiring, especially in hot weather. Most companies offer a heli-raft combo, whereby you can opt to fly out instead at additional cost. Beyond the obvious advantage of 'taking the easy way out', the heli flight is an exhilarating end to an exciting day, zipping you out of the gorge with a bird's eye view of the rapids you've just run and the falls as well. On the Zambian side, though, the hike out will soon become a thing of the past once one of the new lift systems is in operation.

A trained river guide pilots every raft, but you need to decide whether you want to go in an oar boat or in a paddle boat. In an oar boat expect to cling on for dear life, and throw your weight around the raft on demand – but nothing more. Oar boats are generally easier and safer because you rely on the skills of the oarsmen to negotiate the rapids, and you can hang on to the raft at all times. Only occasionally will you have to 'highside' (throw your weight forward) when punching through a big wave.

In a paddle boat the participants provide the power by paddling, while a trained rafting guide positions the boat and yells out commands instructing you what to do. You'll have to listen, and also paddle like crazy through the rapids, remembering when and if you are supposed to be paddling. You can't just hang on! In paddle boats you are an active participant and thus are largely responsible for how successfully you run the rapids. The rafting guide calls commands and positions the boat, but then it's up to you. If your fellow paddlers are not up to it, then expect a difficult ride. Paddle boats have a higher tendency to flip and/or have 'swimmers' (someone thrown out of the boat).

Originally, only oar boats were run on the Zambezi. However nowadays paddleboats have become more popular as rafting companies compete to outdo each other in offering the most exciting rides. There is, of course, a very fine line between striving to be more exciting, and actually becoming more dangerous.

With either option, remember that people often fall out and rafts do capsize. Despite this, safety records are usually cited as excellent. Serious injuries are said to be uncommon and fatalities rare. (Curiously for an industry that claims such a good safety record, none of the larger companies seems to keep transparent records of injuries or fatalities.)

Rafting operators All rafting companies offer broadly similar experiences at prices that are invariably identical. To gain a competitive edge, some now offer freebies like dinner and sundowners in their prices, so it's well worth asking around and comparing what's included as this changes from time to time. For example, Raft Extreme and Safari Par Excellence currently include breakfast, lunch, sundowners and barbecue dinner in their rates. All offer videos and photos of your trip at additional cost.

Zambian operators include Bundu, Raft Extreme, Safari Par Excellence and Touch Adventure. The rapids are numbered from 1 to 23, starting from the Boiling Pot, so it's easy to make a rough comparison of the trips on offer.

In addition to day trips, there are four-day expeditions that go as far as the proposed Batoka Gorge dam site, while seven-day expeditions reach the mouth of the Matetsi River. These offer more than the adrenaline of white water, and are the best way of seeing the remote Batoka Gorge, though trips are few and far between. Adrift and Shearwater offer these longer trips from the Zimbabwean side.
Half/full-day trips approx US$85/95 pp, inc transfers & Zambian visa as well as b/fast & snacks or lunch and cool drinks.

River-boarding For a more up-close and personal encounter with the Zambezi rapids, adrenaline junkies can try their hand at river-boarding (also known as boogie-boarding). Bundu and Safari Par Excellence offer daily trips down the Zambezi from Zambia.

After donning your flippers, lifejacket and helmet, you and your foam board (the size of a small surfboard) will have an opportunity to 'surf' the big waves of the Zambezi, after being taught basic skills in a calmer section of the river. A raft accompanies each trip and takes you downstream to the best spots of the day. Here you can try your hand at finding the best 'standing waves' where you can stay still and surf as the water rushes beneath you. Experts can stand, but most will surf on their stomachs.

Thrilling for the fit who swim strongly, but not for the faint of heart. Trips are fully inclusive of transfers, Zambia day visa, a light breakfast, lunch and sundowners.
US$125 pp, fully inc.

White-water kayaking Yet another option for white-water enthusiasts is tandem kayaking in the gorge in Topolino Duo Kayaks. Trips are run by Bundu and Safari Par Excellence, in conjunction with their rafting trips for logistics and safety. A qualified kayaker-guide sits in the back, piloting and manoeuvring the kayak through rapids, while you sit in front and assist with paddle power. Kayaking experience is not necessary, but you should be a confident swimmer. Kayaks, smaller and lighter than rafts, may capsize in bigger rapids. Although your guide will attempt to right it by executing an 'Eskimo roll', failing this be prepared to swim the rest of the rapid (together with your guide). For experienced kayakers,

Kayak-the-Zambezi in Livingstone offers one-day trips below the falls and fully outfitted multi-day expeditions by special arrangement. (For further information, see list of operators, page 467.)
SafPar: tandem kayaking US$135 pp full day, inc transfers, visas & lunch.

Jet boats Jet-Extreme, on the Zambian side, runs 30-minute jet-boat trips between rapids 23 and 27. These promise a thrilling ride, zipping up and down rapids at breakneck speeds, screaming past gorge walls and spinning on flat water. A similar operation is run by Shearwater on the other side of the river. They have been widely criticised as noisy and damaging to the river's tranquil ambience, but are nevertheless highly popular with thrill-seekers, and fun for all. Readers should, however, think twice about these allegations before embarking on such a trip, *US$60 for 30 min.*

Horseriding Riding along the Zambezi and through the bush is a wonderful way to experience nature up close. You can choose from rides as short as a couple of hours to half- and full-day trips with lunch along the river and/or through the bush. Operators offering horse-back safaris in the falls area are Chundukwa Adventure Trails, in Zambia, and Zambezi Horse Trails, in Zimbabwe. Both offer guided trips for all levels in the bush: day trips for novices in search of game, as well as longer sojourns with fully catered overnight camps (or optional lodge stays) for more experienced riders.

Would-be polocross players are invited to watch and, if experienced, join in with local teams playing at Chundukwa on Thursday and Sunday afternoons (from about April through September).
Chundukwa Adventure Trails: 1¹/₂/2¹/₂hr ride US$35/45, half day without/with lunch US$65/70, full day with lunch & drinks US$90.

The Lion Encounter Safari Par Excellence offers a 'Lion Encounter' tour at the Masuwe Estate. There are two morning trips and two afternoon trips, lasting about 1¹/₂ hours, every day of the year. Guests are picked up from their lodge and transferred to the estate, where they are given a short talk on conservation and safety, and then taken to meet the lions and their handlers. The safari trail itself leads through the bush and valley of the Masuwe River, where you'll have the chance to see elephants, kudu, leopards and (hopefully) lions. It's a great opportunity to take some memorable photos. Contact Safpar for current rates.

Elephant riding SafPar's Zambezi Elephant Trails, based at Thorntree River Lodge on the Zambezi River, offer the only elephant-back safaris in Zambia. Here you and your 'Nduna' (the elephant pilot) will ride majestic African elephants – through the bush and along the river – in the upper reaches of the Mosi-oa-Tunya National Park, where you may encounter wild elephants, buffalo, bushbuck or small game.

The Elephant Company in Victoria Falls offer morning, lunchtime or afternoon elephant-back safaris. They are only 15 minutes' drive from Victoria Falls, at the Nakavango Estate adjacent to Zambezi National Park. Here you will ride African elephants through the bush accompanied by the professional guide on foot. There is game in the area – including kudu, buffalo, bushbuck and impala – which are sometimes seen.

All the elephants were originally orphaned and raised on family farms, and so are comfortable around people, and they are shown great respect and sensitivity. You will have a chance to feed them and interact with them close up – an unforgettable and moving experience. You will also hear about elephant issues and conservation efforts in Africa. Advance booking is absolutely essential if you have your heart set on this very popular activity!

SafPar charge US$110 half day, plus US$10 park fees, inc transfers & either b/fast, brunch or sundowners & snacks.

Quad bikes Another recent addition to the activity menu is guided quad-bike (four-wheeled motorbike) excursions operated by the Livingstone Quad Company, a joint venture between Batoka Sky and Voyagers. Options include the 'eco-trail' at 'Batoka Land' (starting at Maramba Aerodrome), consisting of 42 acres in and around the unfenced portion of the national park, or venturing out into the bush to explore African villages and the landscape by the Zambezi gorges. This is a fun and leisurely way to explore the bush at your own pace, on your own all-terrain vehicle. No experience is required; quad bikes are easy to operate and participants are given an introduction and a chance to practise before heading out on the trail of their choice. All trips are accompanied by a qualified guide.

US$55 for 1¹/₂hrs at Batoka Land; village & bush tours US$90/105/115 for 1¹/₂/2/3hrs; inc refreshments & transfers. Other destinations & tailor-made trips also available.

LIVINGSTONE TOUR OPERATORS
This list focuses on companies that run the specified activities, and don't merely act as booking agents, although note that all operators are able to book any activity:

Abseil Africa Zambia aka The Zambezi Swing Fawlty Towers; ☏ 03 321188 or +263 11 213835, 213837; e theswing@zamnet.zm; www.thezambeziswing.com. Activities at their site atop the fifth gorge on the Zambian side, some 5km from the Falls.

African Extreme/Vic Falls Bungi MOT Rd, ☏ 03 324156 (town), 324231 (bridge), +263 11 407696; e bungee@zamnet.zm, www.shearwateradventures.com.

African Queen ☏ 03 321513; m +263 11 417953; e african.queen@thevictoriafalls.co.zm, www.theafricanqueen.co.za.

Angle Zambia ☏/f 03 324489; m 097 707829; e anglezam@zamnet.zm; www.zambezifishing.com. Recommended. Also operate Pride of the Zambezi — see write-up.

Batoka Sky Maramba Aerodrome, off Sichango Rd; ☏ 03 320058; m +263 11 409578; e freedom@zamnet.zm; www.batokasky.com. Turn off MOT Rd at the signpost by Tunya Lodge. Microlights and helicopters for scenic flights over the Falls; game viewing from aerodrome

Bundu Adventures 699 Industrial Road, off MOT Rd; ☏ 03 324407; e zambezi@zamnet.zm; www.bundu-adventures.com. Near the railway crossing — look for the sign. Rafting, riverboarding and canoeing.

Bushtracks Africa ☏ 03 323232; e victoriafalls@bushtracksafrica.com; www.bushtracksafrica.com. Signposted from MOT Rd, Bushtracks is located in a stand-alone complex down past the railway station, just where the railway line crosses the road. One of the best, most reliable companies in Livingstone.

Bwaato Adventures ☏ 03 324106; e bwaato@zamnet.zm

Chundukwa Adventure Trails ☏ 03 324006; e chundukwa@zamnet.zm

Gwembe Safaris ☏/f 03 324470; e gwemsaf@zamnet.zm. Booking agents and tour operators, and owners of the Crocodile Park.

Jet Extreme ☏ 03 321375; e jetx@zamnet.zm or jetextremereservations@zamnet.zm. New-Zealand-style jet-boat trips in the gorge.

Kayak-the-Zambezi Livingstone Adventure Centre; ☏ 03 322089; e kayak@thezambezi.com or sventhunderlord@yahoo.com. For novice and experienced kayakers.

Livingstone Quad Bike Company Maramba Aerodrome, off Sichango Rd; ☏ 03 320058; f 03 324071; m +263 11 409578; e freedom@zamnet.zm; www.batokasky.com. Quad-bike excursions.

Makora Quest 131MOT Rd; ☏/f 03 320732; e quest@zamnet.zm; www.wildsidesafaris.com. One of Livingstone's top canoe operators, with extensive local knowledge and friendly service.

Nomad African Travel Zambia ☏/f 03 322769; m 097 846164, 755429; e nomad@microlink.zm; skype: nomadzambia; www.nomadafricantravel.co.uk. Safari and tour operators.

Raft Extreme 2 Maambo Way; ☏ 03 324024, 323929; ☏/f 03 322370; e grotto@zamnet.zm;

www.raftextreme.com. Caters predominantly for white-water rafting groups, with bookings from individuals if there's space.

Safari Par Excellence Zambezi Waterfront and Sun's Activity Centre; ☎ 03 321629; m +263 11 218654; e safpar@zamnet.zm; www.safpar.com, www.zambezisafari.com. One of Livingstone's larger tourism enterprises, 'SafPar' is a one-stop shop for everything you need.

Taonga Safaris Sichangoa Rd, ☎/f 03 322508 or 324081 or 097 795535; e taonga@zamnet.zm; www.thezambezi.com/taonga. On the riverbank next to the Boat Club (off Mosi-oa-Tunya Rd at the Tunya Lodge). Catering mainly to backpackers.

Touch Adventure 2586 Chitimukulu Rd, two blocks off the Nakatindi (Kazungula) Rd turn-off; ☎ 03 321111, +263 13 40073–5; ☎/f +263 13 40075; m +263 11 209 746; e info@ touchadventure.com, res@touchadventure.com; www.touchadventure.com. Rafting company and tour operator

United Air Charters ☎/f 03 323095; e uac@microlink.zm; www.uaczam.com. Relatively new company operatING a fleet of helicopters and a 1940s' Tiger Moth biplane for scenic flights and charters from its base on Baobab Ridge, to the east of Mosi-oa-Tunya Rd

UTC 360s MOT Rd next to Heritage House; ☎ 03 324413; e utczam@zamnet.zm; www.utctravelplanner.com. Part of a larger group; guided tours and transfers .

Victoria Falls River Safaris ☎/f +263 3 32358; m +263 11 418 858; e riversafaris@ zamnet.zm. Aluminium 'safari' boats with shade. Can go far beyond the reach of conventional craft.

Wild Side Tours & Safaris 131 MOT Rd, ☎/f 03 320732; e wild@zamnet.zm; www.wildsidesafaris.com. Located in a restored railway house in the 217 Area; look for the big 'i' sign indicating tourist information. Owner operated, and one of Livingstone's long-time tour companies.

Appendix I

WILDLIFE GUIDE

This wildlife guide is designed in a manner that should allow you to name most large mammals that you are likely to see in Botswana. For much more detailed information, see *Southern African Wildlife: A Visitor's Guide* by Mike Unwin, also published by Bradt Travel Guides. Less common species are featured under the heading ***Similar species*** beneath the animal to which they are most closely allied, or bear the strongest resemblance.

CATS AND DOGS

Lion (*Panthera leo* Shoulder height 100–120cm. Weight 150–220kg) Africa's largest predator, the lion, is the animal that everybody hopes to see on safari. It is a sociable creature, living in prides of five to over 20 animals and defending a territory of between 20 and 200km². Lions often hunt at night, and their favoured prey is large or medium antelope such as wildebeest and impala. Most of the hunting is done by females, but dominant males normally feed first after a kill. Rivalry between males is intense and take-over battles are frequently fought to the death, so two or more males often form a coalition. Young males are forced out of their home pride at three years of age, and cubs are usually killed after a successful take-over.

When not feeding or fighting, lions are remarkably indolent – they spend up to 23 hours of any given day at rest – so the anticipation of a lion sighting is often more exciting than the real thing. Lions naturally occur in any habitat, except desert or rainforest. They once ranged across much of the Old World, but these days they are all but restricted to the larger conservation areas in sub-Saharan Africa (one residual population exists in India).

Lions occur throughout Botswana, and are very common in the main northern areas of Chobe, Linyanti–Kwando and the Okavango. They also range across the Kalahari, in the Nxai/Makgadikgadi areas and the Central Kalahari Game Reserve, though the relative scarcity of prey leads to small, dissociated pride structures which have vast territories.

In the northern reserves, where food is plentiful, the converse is the case. Large prides are the norm and some, like those currently around North Gate and Savuti, have become so big that they make a speciality of killing young and juvenile elephants in order to have enough meat to go around. Even visiting these prolific reserves for just a few days, you're unlikely not to see at least some lions!

Leopard (*Panthera pardus* Shoulder height 70cm. Weight 60–80kg) The powerful leopard is the most solitary and secretive of Africa's big cats. It hunts at night, using stealth and power, often getting to within 5m of its intended prey before pouncing. If there are hyenas and lions around then leopards habitually move their kills up into trees to safeguard them. The leopard can be distinguished from the cheetah by its rosette-like spots, lack of black 'tearmarks' and more compact, low-slung, powerful build.

The leopard is the most common of Africa's large felines. Some of Botswana's bush is perfect for leopard, which like plenty of thickets, cover and big trees. The riverine woodlands found throughout the Chobe, Linyanti–Kwando and Okavango areas are firm favourites with them. Here they're quite often seen by sharp-eyed observers who scan low-hanging branches for these lounging felines. Meanwhile drives around dusk and early evening in the private concessions will sometimes yield good sightings of leopard going out on hunting forays as the light fades. Remarkably, leopard often seem unperturbed by the presence of a vehicle and spotlight, and will often continue whatever they are doing regardless of an audience. Watching a leopard stalk is captivating viewing.

Leopard are very adaptable. There are many records of individuals living for years undetected in close proximity to humans, for example in the suburbs of major African cities like Nairobi, where they prey on domestic dogs. Given this, it's no surprise that they're also found throughout the Kalahari, though in lower densities commensurate with the relative lack of prey.

Cheetah (*Acynonix jubatus* Shoulder height 70–80cm. Weight 50–60kg) This remarkable spotted cat has a greyhound-like build, and is capable of running at 70km/h in bursts, making it the world's fastest land animal. Despite superficial similarities, you can easily tell a cheetah from a leopard by the former's simple spots, disproportionately small head, streamlined build, diagnostic black tearmarks, and preference for relatively open habitats. It is often seen pacing the plains restlessly, either on its own or in a small family group

consisting of a mother and her offspring. Diurnal hunters, cheetah favour the cooler hours of the day to hunt smaller antelope like springbok, steenbok and duiker; plus young wildebeest, tsessebe and zebra, and also warthog, large birds, and small mammals such as scrub hares.

Given that cheetah never occur in high densities, Botswana is a better place than most to see them. In areas of dense game, they often lose their prey to lion or spotted hyena, so the relative scarcity of competition in areas like Nxai, Makgadigadi and the Central Kalahari make these ideal. These also harbour large populations of springbok – a cheetah's ideal prey – and their ability to go for long periods without water gives them flexibility to move far from waterholes. Although cheetah are often thought of as animals of the open savannah, they do need some cover from which to sprint – so the Kalahari's thin scrub is ideal for them.

Having said that, all of my sightings of cheetah in Botswana have been in some of the central Okavango's areas of densest game – on Mboma Island and in the Mombo Concession! Looking through the sightings records at the camps, it's certainly notable that many of these cats move further into the Delta as the waters recede, and then move back out into the surrounding Kalahari to avoid the floods.

Estimates suggest that there are about 4,000–6,000 cheetah left in southern Africa, plus a few in Iran, Pakistan and the Near East. (They did occur throughout India, but are now extinct there.) Scientists, noting an amazing lack of genetic diversity amongst all living cheetah, have suggested that the species must have gone through a 'genetic bottleneck' in the past – thus perhaps all living cheetah are descended from one female. This goes some way to explaining why they are very susceptible to disease.

Serval *(Felis serval* Shoulder height 60cm. Weight 9–18kg) This long-legged cat is the tallest of Africa's 'small cats'. It has a similar build to a leopard, but black-on-gold spots giving way to streaking near the head. Seldom seen, it is widespread and quite common in moist grassland, reedbeds and riverine habitats throughout Africa, including northern Botswana. It's largely absent from the drier areas of the Kalahari.

Serval do particularly well in wetter areas where there is lots of long grass – and are common throughout the Okavango and Linyanti–Kwando area. Although they're relatively rarely seen, there have been consistent reports of good sightings from night drives along the channel from Savuti Camp. Serval prey on mice, rats, small mammals, birds, snakes, lizards and will sometimes even take fish or the young of small antelope. They use their big ears to locate their prey precisely by sound, and their long legs to see over tall grass, and to help them jump high as they pounce.

Caracal *(Felis caracal* Shoulder height 40cm. Weight 15–20kg) Smaller but heavier than the serval, caracal resemble European lynx, with their uniform tan coat and tufted ears. They are

solitary, mainly nocturnal hunters which feed on birds, small antelope and young livestock. Caracal are remarkable hunters for their size, and will often take prey as large as, or even larger than, they are. Their style is very much like small leopards; they normally stalk their prey as closely as possible, before springing with surprise. They also take many of the same species, even caching their prey in trees to return and feed later, and can be quite acrobatic hunters: they have been known to bat birds out of the air as they fly.

Caracal occur throughout sub-Saharan Africa, easily adapting to a variety of environments. They're found throughout Botswana and whilst night drives in the early evening provide your best chance of a glimpse of them, they're still very rarely seen.

Similar species The smaller **African wild cat** *(Felis sylvestris)* ranges from the Mediterranean to the Cape of Good Hope, and is similar in appearance to the domestic tabby cat. It has a ringed tail, a reddish-brown tinge to the back of its ears and an unspotted torso – which should preclude confusion with the even smaller **small spotted cat** *(Felis nigripes)*, a relatively rare resident of the central and southern Kalahari which has a more distinctively marked coat. Both species are generally solitary and nocturnal, often utilising burrows or termite mounds as daytime shelters. They prey upon reptiles, amphibians and birds as well as small mammals.

Wild dog *(Lycaon pictus* Shoulder height 70cm. Weight 25kg) Also known as the painted hunting dog, the wild dog is distinguished from other African dogs by its large size and mottled black, brown and cream coat. Highly sociable, living in packs of up to 20 animals, wild dogs are ferocious hunters that literally tear apart their prey on the run. The most endangered of Africa's great predators, they are now threatened with extinction. This is the result both of relentless persecution by farmers, who often view the dogs as dangerous vermin, and of their susceptibility to diseases spread by domestic dogs. Wild dogs are now extinct in many areas where they were formerly abundant, like the Serengeti, and they are common nowhere. The global population of fewer than 3,000 is concentrated in southern Tanzania, Zambia, Zimbabwe, Botswana, South Africa and Namibia.

Wild dogs prefer open savannah with only sparse tree cover, if any, and packs have enormous territories, typically covering 400km² or more. They travel huge distances in search of prey, so few parks are large enough to contain them. Northern Botswana has one of the healthiest and most prolific populations in Africa, and Botswana is the best place on the continent to see them. These range right across Chobe, the Kwando–Linyanti and Okavango areas, and spreading out beyond these into Namibia and the northwest areas of the Kalahari.

They generally den around July to early October, and this is the only time when you can be fairly sure of seeing them in any given area. Sometimes they'll den in the same area for several years running, whilst at other times they'll change from year to year. For the best chances of seeing them – and a possibility of following a pack as they hunt (an amazing, exhilarating experience), choose a mainly dry reserve with plenty of open ground. Make sure that off-road driving is permitted, or you'll never be able to follow them, and ideally night drives should be allowed. Selinda, southern Kwando, Kwara and Vumbura would all currently be high on my list – and I've seen dogs in all of these. Better still, ask someone who knows the Delta and the reserves well where specific packs have denned the previous season, and go there.

Given that dogs will take most antelope and always run down their prey, the only strategy that their prey can adopt to avoid death is to run as far, and as fast, as they can. They will do this as soon as they realise that dogs are in the area. Thus if you ever see game seriously sprinting with a purpose, and just not stopping, then look hard: maybe there's a pack of dogs behind them!

Black-backed jackal (*Canis mesomelas* Shoulder height 35–45cm. Weight 8–12kg) The black-backed jackal is an opportunistic feeder capable of adapting to most habitats. Most often seen singly or in pairs at dusk or dawn, it is ochre in colour with a prominent black saddle flecked by a varying amount of white or gold. It is probably the most frequently observed small predator in Africa south of the Zambezi, and its eerie call is a characteristic sound of the bush at night. It is found throughout Botswana, with the exception of the far north of the country around the Chobe and Linyanti–Kwando, and is fairly common in the drier areas of the Kalahari.

Side-striped jackal (*Canis adustus* Shoulder height 35–40cm. Weight 8–12kg) Despite its prevalence in other areas of Africa, the side-striped jackal is common nowhere in Botswana. It occurs in the far north of the country, including Chobe, the Linyanti–Kwando area and the Okavango. It is about the same size as the previous species, but greyish in colour, with an indistinct pale horizontal stripe on each flank and often a white-tipped tail. These jackals are also usually seen singly or in pairs, at dusk or dawn. Both the side-striped and the black-backed jackal are opportunistic feeders, taking rats, mice, birds, insects, carrion, wild fruits and even termites.

Bat-eared fox (*Otocyon megalotis* Shoulder height 30–35cm. Weight 3–5kg) This endearing small, silver-grey insectivore is unmistakable, with its huge ears and black eye-mask. It can be found throughout Botswana, anywhere that the harvester termite (*Hodotermes mossambicus*) occurs. The best areas are usually short grass plains that receive relatively low rainfall – Savuti Marsh is certainly a favourite habitat.

It is mostly nocturnal, but can sometimes be seen in pairs or small family groups during the cooler hours of the day, usually in dry open country. It digs well, and will often 'listen' to the ground (its ears operating like a radio-dish) whilst wandering around, before stopping to dig with its forepaws. As well as termites, bat-eared foxes will eat lizards, gerbils, small birds, scorpions, beetle larvae and other insects.

Insect populations vary with the seasons and bat-eared foxes will move with them, but when conditions allow, some areas will have very high densities of individuals.

Similar species The **Cape fox** (*Vulpes chama*) is an infrequently seen dry-country predator which occurs throughout central and western Botswana, but is absent from Chobe and the north side of the Okavango. The Cape fox lacks the prominent ears and mask of the bat-eared fox, and its coat is a uniform sandy-grey colour. I once had a Cape fox approach me cautiously, after dusk, whilst camping in Namibia's Namib-Naukluft Park, but have never seen another.

Spotted hyena (*Crocuta crocuta* Shoulder height 85cm. Weight 70kg) Hyenas are characterised by their bulky build, sloping back (lower hindquarters), rough brownish coat, powerful jaws and dog-like expression. Contrary to popular myth, spotted hyenas are not exclusively scavengers; they are also adept hunters, which hunt in groups and kill animals as large as wildebeests. Nor are they hermaphroditic, an ancient belief that stems from the false scrotum and penis covering the female hyena's vagina. Sociable animals, hyenas live in loosely structured clans of about ten animals, led by females, who are stronger and larger than males, and based in a communal den.

Hyenas utilise their kills far better than most predators, digesting the bones, skin and even teeth of antelope. This results in the distinctive white colour attained by their faeces when dry – which is an easily identified sign of them living in an area.

The spotted hyena is the largest hyena, identified by its light-brown, blotchily spotted coat. It is found throughout most of Botswana, only absent from the eastern areas around Ghanzi, and perhaps the country's furthest southern edge. They are a common predator throughout the north, and will frequently scavenge around camps and campsites at night. Savuti's campsite was, for years, completely plagued by them, whilst few camps in the Delta are without a story of hyena breaking into kitchens or eating their way through larders.

Although mainly nocturnal, spotted hyenas can often be seen around dusk and dawn, and their distinctive, whooping calls are one of the most wonderful, yet spine-chilling, sounds of the African night.

Brown hyena (*Hyena brunnea* Shoulder height 75–85cm. Weight 40–47kg) This secretive, apparently solitary hyena occurs in the most arid parts of Namibia, and throughout Botswana; it is absent only from the far north. It is unmistakable with a shaggy, dark brown coat – not unlike a large, long-haired German shepherd dog – with faint black stripes and sloping back. In contrast to the spotted hyena, brown hyenas do tend to scavenge rather than hunt, and are generally solitary whilst doing so.

They are the dominant carnivore in the drier areas of the Namib and Kalahari, where clans (typically containing two to ten animals) will defend enormous territories against neighbouring clans. Individuals normally forage on their own and will eat whatever they can, from small birds and mammals to the remains of kill, as well as fruit and vegetables. They can go without water for long periods in the Kalahari, gaining moisture from tsama melons as well as their other food.

Brown hyena are very rarely seen on game drives, although in the last few years researchers based at Jack's Camp have habituated a small clan of hyena to their presence – making this probably the best place in Africa to see them. See *The clans of Makgadikgadi* on page 397 for more information on brown hyena.

Aardwolf (*Proteles cristatus* Shoulder height 45–50cm. Weight 7–11g) With a tawny brown coat and dark, vertical stripes, this insectivorous hyena is not much bigger than a jackal and occurs in low numbers in most parts of Botswana. It is active mainly at night, gathering harvester termites (specifically those of the genus *Trinervitermes*), its principle food, with its wide, sticky tongue. These termites live underground (not in castle-like termite mounds) and come out at night to cut grass and drag it back down with them. Occasionally the aardwolf will also take other insects, mice, birds and carrion.

Thus open grassland or lightly wooded areas form the typical habitat for aardwolves, which can sometimes be spotted around dusk, dawn or on very overcast days, especially during the colder months. The *Trinervitermes* termites often thrive on overgrazed land, which means that aardwolf are often more common on farmland than in national parks. I don't know of anywhere in central or northern Botswana where they're seen frequently.

Chacma baboon (*Papio cynocephalus ursinus* Shoulder height 50–75cm. Weight 25–45kg) This powerful terrestrial primate, distinguished from any other monkey by its much larger size, inverted-U-shaped tail and distinctive dog-like head, is fascinating to watch from a behavioural perspective. It lives in large troops that boast a complex, rigid social structure characterised by a matriarchal lineage and plenty of inter-troop movement by males seeking social dominance. Omnivorous and at home in almost any habitat, the baboon is the most widespread primate in Africa, frequently seen in most of Botswana. The centre of the Kalahari (including the CKGR) is the only area from which they are absent.

There are three African races, regarded by some authorities as full species. The chacma baboon (*P. c. ursinus*) is grey, and confined largely to areas south of the Zambezi. The yellow baboon (*P. c. cynocephalus*) is the yellow-brown race occurring in Zambia, northern Mozambique, Malawi, southern and eastern Tanzania and eastern Kenya. The olive or anubis baboon (*P. c. anubis*) is a hairy green-to-brown baboon found in Ethiopia, Uganda, northern Tanzania and Kenya.

With a highly organised defence system, the only predator that seriously affects them is the leopard, which will try to pick them off at night whilst they are roosting in trees or cliffs. Campers in Chobe and Moremi should treat these animals with respect; long exposure to humans has taught them to steal, and not to be afraid.

Vervet monkey (*Cercopithecus aethiops* Length (excluding tail) 40–55cm. Weight 4–6kg) Also known as the green or grivet monkey, the vervet is probably the world's most numerous monkey and certainly the most common and widespread representative of the *Cercopithecus* guenons, a taxonomically controversial genus associated with African forests. An atypical guenon in that it inhabits savannah and woodland rather than true forest, the vervet spends a high proportion of its time on the ground. It occurs throughout the northern and eastern parts of the country, but is absent from the drier areas of central, western and southern Botswana. Vervets like belts of tall trees with thick vegetation within easy reach of water, and much of northern Chobe, the Kwando–Linyanti area and the Okavango is ideal for them.

The vervet's light grey coat, black face and white forehead band are distinctive – as are the male's garish blue genitals. Vervet monkeys live in troops averaging about 25 animals; they are active during the day and roost in trees at night. They eat mainly fruit and vegetables, though are opportunistic and will take insects and young birds, and even raid tents at campsites (usually where ill-informed visitors have previously tempted them into human contact by offering food).

Lesser bushbaby (*Galago senegalensis* Length (without tail) 17cm. Weight 150g) The lesser bushbaby is the most widespread and common member of a group of small and generally indistinguishable nocturnal primates, distantly related to the lemurs of Madagascar. In Botswana they occur throughout the northern half of the country, including Nxai and Makgadikgadi.

More often heard than seen, the lesser bushbaby can sometimes be picked out by tracing a cry to a tree and shining a torch into the branches; its eyes reflect as two red dots. These eyes are designed to function in what we would describe as total darkness, and they feed on insects – some of which are caught in the air by jumping – and also eating sap from trees, especially acacia gum.

They inhabit wooded areas, and prefer acacia trees or riverine forests. I remember being startled by a small family of bushbabies once; they raced through the trees above us, bouncing from branch to branch whilst chattering and screaming out of all proportion to their size.

LARGE ANTELOPE

Sable antelope (*Hippotragus niger* Shoulder height 135cm. Weight 230kg) The striking male sable is jet-black with a distinct white face, underbelly and rump, and long decurved horns – a strong contender for the title of Africa's most beautiful antelope. The female is chestnut brown and has shorter horns, whilst the young are a lighter red-brown colour. Sable are found throughout the wetter areas of southern and eastern Africa, but are common nowhere.

In Botswana they occur in the north of Botswana, as far west as the central Okavango. The Chobe riverfront is a good place to look for them, usually between the Kasane and Chobe Game Lodge as there's a herd that frequently comes down to drink there. Similarly, they're occasionally seen near the Kwando and Linyanti rivers. They're not common in the Delta region, but are seen periodically. Good sightings have recently been recorded around the Gomoti River (near Starling's Camp), and in NG20 and NG21. The Vumbura Concession (NG22) probably offers the highest density of sable in the Delta, whilst they're generally absent from NG26, NG27, NG30 and further west.

Sable are normally seen in small herds: either bachelor herds of males, or breeding herds of females and young, which are often accompanied by the dominant bull in that territory. The breeding females give birth around February or March; the calves remain hidden, away from the herd, for their first few weeks. Sable are mostly grazers, though will browse, especially when food is scarce. They need to drink at least every other day, and seem especially fond of low-lying dewy vleis in wetter areas.

Roan antelope (*Hippotragus equinus* Shoulder height 120–150cm. Weight 250–300kg) This handsome horse-like antelope is uniform fawn-grey with a pale belly, short decurved horns and a light mane. It could be mistaken for the female sable antelope, but this has a well-defined white belly, and lacks the roan's distinctive black-and-white facial markings. The roan is a relatively rare antelope; common almost nowhere in Africa (Malawi's Nyika Plateau being the obvious exception to this rule). In Botswana, small groups of roan are found in the Chobe and Kwando–Linyanti areas, and occasionally some will wander as far as the drier parts of the Okavango Delta – but they're always something of a rarity.

A1

Ngwezumba Pans is probably the best location to search for them, but they're not seen regularly even there.

Roan need lots of space if they are to thrive and breed; they don't generally do well where game densities are high. This alone precludes them from success in most of the Delta. Game farms prize them as one of the most valuable antelope. They need access to drinking water, but are well adapted to subsist on relatively high plateaux with poor soils.

Oryx or gemsbok (*Oryx gazella* Shoulder height 120cm. Weight 230kg)

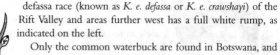

This is the quintessential desert antelope, unmistakable with its ash-grey coat, bold black facial marks and flank strip, and unique long, straight horns. Of the three races of oryx in Africa, the gemsbok is the largest and most striking. It occurs throughout the Kalahari and Namib and is widespread all over central and western Botswana. They are the dominant large antelope in the CKGR, where they can be seen in large numbers during the early months of the year.

As you might expect, gemsbok are very adaptable. They range widely and are found in areas of dunes, alkaline pans, open savannah and even woodlands. Along with the much smaller springbok, they can sometimes even be seen tracking across open plains with only dust-devils and mirages for company. Gemsbok can endure extremes of temperature, helped by specially adapted blood capillaries in their nasal passages that can cool their blood before it reaches their brains. Thus although their body temperature can rise by up to 6°C, their brains remain cool and they survive. They do not need drinking water and will eat wild melons and dig for roots, bulbs and tubers when grazing or browsing becomes difficult.

Waterbuck (*Kobus ellipsiprymnus* Shoulder height 130cm. Weight 250–270kg)

The waterbuck is easily recognised by its shaggy brown coat and the male's large, lyre-shaped horns. The common race of southern Africa (*K. e. ellipsiprymnus*) and areas east of the Rift Valley has a distinctive white ring around its rump, seen on the right of the sketch. The defassa race (known as *K. e. defassa* or *K. e. crawshayi*) of the Rift Valley and areas further west has a full white rump, as indicated on the left.

Only the common waterbuck are found in Botswana, and they're restricted to the Chobe, Kwando–Linyanti and eastern sides of the Delta. Favourite areas include the northern side of the Linyanti Concession (NG15), and also Vumbura (NG22), but they're relatively uncommon elsewhere. They certainly used to occur at Savuti when the channel flowed, but they deserted the area when the marsh dried up.

Waterbuck need to drink very regularly, so usually stay within a few kilometres of water, where they like to graze on short, nutritious grasses. At night they may take cover in adjacent woodlands. It is often asserted that waterbuck flesh is oily and smelly, which may discourage predators.

Blue wildebeest (*Connochaetes taurinus* Shoulder height 130–150cm. Weight 180–250kg)

This ungainly antelope, also called the brindled gnu, is easily identified by its dark coat and bovine appearance. The superficially similar buffalo is far more heavily built. When they have enough space and conditions are right, blue wildebeest can multiply rapidly and form immense herds – as perhaps a million do for their annual migration from Tanzania's Serengeti Plains into Kenya's Masai Mara.

In Botswana during the middle of the 20th century they were probably the most numerous large herbivore, forming herds estimated at a quarter of a million individuals. Although they are still found throughout Botswana, these numbers have reduced drastically. (See *Fauna* in *Chapter 16, The Central Kalahari*, pages 407–8, for further discussion of this.)

Wildebeest are best adapted to take large mouthfuls of short, nutritious grasses, and they need access to drinking water every two or three days. This limits them to remain relatively close to a source of water, and if that dries up they will journey as far as necessary to find another.

Hartebeest (*Alcelaphus buselaphus* Shoulder height 125cm. Weight 120–150kg) Hartebeests are ungainly antelopes, readily identified by the combination of large shoulders, a sloping back, a glossy, red-brown coat and smallish horns in both sexes. Numerous subspecies are recognised, all of which are generally seen in small family groups in reasonably open country. Though once hartebeest were found from the Mediterranean to the Cape, only isolated populations still survive.

The only one native to Botswana is the red hartebeest, which is found throughout the arid central, southern and western areas of the country. They can be seen in Nxai and Makgadikgadi, and they're one of the more numerous large mammals in the CKGR. Hartebeest may occur in the drier, southwestern corners of the Delta, or in the drier parts of southern Chobe, but I've no records of them being seen in either location.

Hartebeests are more or less exclusively grazers, and although they like access to water they will eat melons, tubers and rhizomes when necessary. In the central Kalahari they'll range widely, often with wildebeest, following thunderstorms in search of fresh, green shoots.

Tsessebe (*Damaliscus lunatus* Shoulder height 120cm. Weight 125–140kg) Tsessebe are basically a slightly smaller, darker version of hartebeest, coloured red-brown with an almost purple sheen, though their lower legs are distinctly paler. (A closely related subspecies is known as topi in east Africa.) They look similar in profile or at a distance, although often in the field you can make a good guess from the environment which antelope you're looking at long before you're close enough to examine its colouring.

Tsessebe are found in northern Botswana, and are one of the most common antelope in some parts of the Okavango Delta. (One study claimed 70% of lion kills in the Delta are tsessebe.)

Its favourite habitat is open grassland, where it is a selective grazer, eating the younger, more nutritious grasses. This makes it efficient in pastures where some grasses are old and some fresh, or in more broken country, but less efficient than, say, wildebeest where the pasture is uniformly short, good grass. The tsessebe is one of the fastest antelope species, and jumps very well.

Kudu (*Tragelaphus strepsiceros* Shoulder height 140–155cm. Weight 180–250kg) The kudu (or, more properly, the greater kudu) is the most frequently observed member of the genus *Tragelaphus*. These medium-sized to large antelopes are characterised by their grey-brown coats and up to ten stripes on each side. The male has magnificent double-spiralled corkscrew horns. Occurring throughout Mozambique, Zimbabwe, Zambia and Namibia, kudu are found all over Botswana with the exception of the Kgalagadi Transfrontier Park, in the extreme southwest.

Kudu are particularly common in the well-wooded areas of Chobe, the Kwando–Linyanti area and the Okavango, though they also occur throughout the drier areas of the Kalahari. They are browsers that thrive in areas with mixed tree savannah and thickets, and the males will sometimes use their horns to pull down the lower branches of trees to eat.

Wherever they occur, kudu are normally seen in small herds, consisting of a couple of females and their offspring, usually accompanied by a male. Otherwise the males occur either singly, or in small bachelor groups.

Sitatunga (*Tragelaphus spekei* Shoulder height 85–90cm. Weight 105–115kg) This semi-aquatic antelope is a widespread but infrequently observed inhabitant of west and central African papyrus swamps, from the Okavango in Botswana to the Sudd in Sudan. In Botswana they're concentrated in the Okavango – which has a strong population – though they're also seen periodically in the Kwando–Linyanti and Chobe systems. The best places to go and spot them are the deep-water areas with plenty of papyrus, including Moremi and NG21, 22, 23, 24 and 25.

Because of their preferred habitat, sitatunga are elusive and seldom seen, even in areas where they are relatively common. They are also less easy to hunt/poach than many other species, although they are exceedingly vulnerable to habitat destruction. Sitatunga are noted for an ability to submerse themselves completely, with just their nostrils showing, when pursued by a predator.

Eland (*Taurotragus oryx* Shoulder height 150–175cm. Weight 450–900kg) Africa's largest antelope, the eland is light brown in colour, sometimes with a few faint white vertical stripes. Relatively short horns and a large dewlap accentuate its somewhat bovine appearance. It was once widely distributed in eastern and southern Africa, though the population has now been severely depleted. Small herds of eland frequent grasslands and light woodlands, often fleeing at the slightest provocation. (They have long been hunted for their excellent meat, so perhaps this is not surprising.)

Eland are very rare in the Okavango area and although they probably occur throughout Chobe, they are seldom seen. Better areas to see them are in the Kalahari's salt pans or, better still, the central Kalahari. They are opportunist browsers and grazers, eating fruit, berries, seed pods and leaves as well as green grass after the rains, and roots and tubers when times are lean.

They run slowly, though can trot for great distances and jump exceedingly well. Eland have a very special significance for the San people – illustrated by the highlight of the famous 'van der Post panel' at the Tsodilo Hills (see pages 353–4), which is a painting of a particularly magnificent eland bull.

MEDIUM AND SMALL ANTELOPE

Bushbuck (*Tragelaphus scriptus* Shoulder height 70–80cm. Weight 30–45kg) This attractive antelope, a member of the same genus as the kudu, is widespread throughout Africa and shows great regional variation in its colouring. (The animals found in sub-saharan Africa are often claimed to be a subspecies, the 'Chobe bushbuck' – though it seems likely that they're simply a colour variation of the main species.)

They occur in forest and riverine woodland, where they are normally seen singly or in pairs. The male is dark brown or chestnut, while the much smaller female is generally a pale reddish brown. The male has relatively small, straight horns and both sexes are marked with white spots and sometimes stripes, though the stripes are often indistinct.

Bushbuck tend to be secretive and very skittish, except when used to people, when they relax and become almost tame. They depend on cover and camouflage to avoid predators, and are often found in the thick, herby vegetation around rivers – and are the only solitary antelope in Africa which do not defend a territory. They will freeze if disturbed, before dashing off into the undergrowth. Bushbuck are both browsers and grazers, choosing the more succulent grass shoots, fruit and flowers. In Botswana they have a limited distribution around the Okavango, beside the Kwando–Linyanti and the Chobe. Look for them slowly picking their way through the thick bush near the water. (Serondella used to be a favourite spot, and the island on which Kwetsani stands had several fairly relaxed resident pairs when I last visited.)

Impala (*Aepeceros melampus* Shoulder height 90cm. Weight 45kg) This slender, handsome antelope is superficially similar to the springbok, but in fact belongs to its own separate family. Chestnut in colour, and lighter underneath than above, the impala has diagnostic black and white stripes running down its rump and tail, and the male has large lyre-shaped horns. The impala is one of the most widespread and successful antelope species in eastern and southern Africa. It is often the most common antelope in wooded savannah habitats, including most of Chobe and the drier, more forested parts of the Okavango Delta – though is rarely seen west of the Okavango, or south of Nxai Pan. Although they can survive without drinking, impala prefer to live near water and are largely absent from the Kalahari.

As expected of such a successful species, it both grazes and browses, depending on what fodder is available. Despite some people's tendency to overlook them as common, take a close look and you'll realise that they're exceptionally beautiful animals. Socially you'll normally see large herds of females and young, lorded over by a dominant male, and small bachelor groups of males.

Springbok (*Antidorcas marsupilis* Shoulder height 60cm. Weight 20–25kg) Springbok are graceful herbivores, similar in size to impala, which generally occur in large herds. Visitors from east Africa, noticing their passing resemblance to Thomson's gazelle (*Gazella thomsonii*), will not be surprised that they're southern Africa's only member of the gazelle family.

Even from a distance, springbok are unlikely to be confused with anything else; their finely marked short coats have fawn-brown upper parts and a white belly, separated by a dark brown band. Springbok favour dry, open country, preferring plains or savannah, and avoiding thick woodlands and mountains. They can subsist without water for long periods, provided that there is moisture (minimum of 10%) in the vegetation that they graze or browse.

Since springbok are more dependent on food than water, they congregate in huge numbers during the rains on areas where they can find fresh, green shoots – like the pans of the CKGR. In contrast, during the dry season they spread out across the vast arid parks of the Kalahari. This is exactly the opposite pattern to that followed by most water-dependent antelope, which typically congregate during the dry season (around rivers to remaining pans), whilst spreading out during the rains. This explains why the Kalahari's game is at its densest during the rains, whereas the game in Chobe and the Okavango is at its most prolific during the dry season.

Springbok occur throughout central and southern Botswana, where they are usually the most common small antelope by far; they number in the thousands in Nxai, Makgadikgadi and the CKGR.

Reedbuck (*Redunca arundinum* Shoulder height 80–90cm. Weight 45–65kg) Sometimes referred to as the southern reedbuck (as distinct from mountain and Bohor reedbucks, found further east), these delicate antelope are uniformly fawn or grey in colour, and lighter below than above. They are generally found in reedbeds and tall grasslands, often beside rivers, and are easily identified by their loud, whistling alarm call and distinctive bounding running style.

In Botswana they are only found where there is close access to water in the north: in northern Chobe, the Kwando–Linyanti region, and throughout the Delta. They live in monogamous pairs that defend a territory. You'll often see just a pair together, and they have a distinctive rocking gate as they take flight by bounding away through tall reedbeds.

Klipspringer (*Oreotragus oreotragus* Shoulder height 60cm. Weight 13kg) The klipspringer is a strongly built little antelope, normally seen in pairs, and easily identified by its dark, bristly grey-yellow coat, slightly speckled appearance and unique habitat preference. Klipspringer means 'rockjumper' in Afrikaans and it is an apt name for an antelope which occurs exclusively in mountainous areas and rocky outcrops, from Cape Town to the Red Sea. Klipspringers are mainly browsers, though they do eat a little new grass. When spotted they will freeze, or bound at great speed across the steepest of slopes.

Though often thought to be absent from all but the extreme southeast corner of Botswana, there were several reliable reports of sightings on Qumxhwaa Hill, near Savuti Marsh, at the end of the 1970s. Given that they only live in rocky hills and kopjes, and that most of Botswana is amazingly flat (or gently rolling at best), it's no surprise that only the odd isolated population exists. It's the same in other parts of their range. I've no reports of them at the Tsodilo Hills, but it would be a perfect habitat for them!

Red lechwe (*Kobus leche* Shoulder height 90–100cm. Weight 80–100kg) Red lechwe are sturdy, shaggy antelope with a chestnut-red coat, paler underneath than on top, and beautiful lyre-shaped horns. They need dry land on which to rest, but otherwise are adapted for life in the seasonal floodplains that border lakes and rivers. They will spend much of their time grazing on grasses and sedges, standing in water if necessary. Their hooves are splayed, adapted to bounding through their muddy environment when fleeing from the lion, hyena and wild dog that hunt them, making them the most aquatic of antelope after sitatunga.

Lechwe reach the southern limit of their distribution in the Okavango and Linyanti areas. They are also found in the DRC, Angola, Namibia's Caprivi Strip, and in Zambia, their stronghold. Wherever they occur, the males are generally larger and darker than the females. When conditions are right, they can be found in huge numbers, and they are the most numerous antelope in the shallow-water environments of the Delta.

Puku (*Kobus vardonii* Shoulder height 80cm. Weight 60–75kg) Easily confused with the lechwe at a glance, the puku has an orange-red colour overall, which is lighter underneath than above. Its legs are uniformly red, and its tail is a lighter yellow. Puku are smaller and slightly shaggier than lechwe, and the males have smaller, stouter, lyre-shaped horns when compared with the lechwe.

Puku are found all over eastern and central Africa, and are one of the most common antelopes in Zambia. Typically they inhabit open areas near rivers and marshes, though in Zambia are found in a wide variety of habitats. In Botswana their distribution is restricted to the floodplain areas of the Chobe riverfront, and often virtually the only place that you'll see them is the aptly named Puku Flats, just west of Chobe Game Lodge and east of the of campsite at Serondella.

Steenbok (*Raphicerus cempestris* Shoulder height 50cm. Weight 11kg) This rather nondescript small antelope has red-brown upper parts and clear white underparts, and the male has short straight horns. It is one of the most commonly observed small antelope, especially on farmland; if you see antelope fleeing from you across grassland, then it is likely to be a steenbok. Like most other small antelopes, the steenbok is normally encountered singly or in pairs and tends to 'freeze' when disturbed, before taking flight.

A1

Similar species The **Oribi** (*Ourebia ourebi*) is a relatively widespread but generally uncommon antelope, which occurs in very localised areas throughout sub-Saharan Africa. It is usually found only in large, open stretches of dry grassland, where there are also patches of taller grass for cover. It looks much like a steenbok but stands about 10cm higher at the shoulder and has an altogether more upright bearing. In Botswana it is thought to occur in Chobe, and specifically in the Ngwezumba Pans area – although sightings of it even there are not common. **Sharpe's grysbok** (*Raphicerus sharpei*) is similar in size and appearance, though it has a distinctive white-flecked coat. It occurs alongside the steenbok in the far northeastern corner of Botswana, around northern Chobe and the Kasane area, but is almost entirely nocturnal in its habits and so very seldom seen.

Common duiker (*Sylvicapra grimmia* Shoulder height 50cm. Weight 20kg) This anomalous duiker holds itself more like a steenbok or grysbok and is the only member of its (large) family to occur outside of forests. Generally grey in colour, the common duiker can most easily be separated from other small antelopes by the black tuft of hair that sticks up between its horns. It occurs throughout Botswana, and across virtually the whole of southern Africa, with the exception of the Namib Desert. Common duikers tolerate most habitats except for true forest and very open country, and are tolerant of nearby human settlements. They are opportunist feeders, taking fruit, seeds and leaves, as well as crops, small reptiles and amphibians. Despite its widespread occurrence, duiker are relatively rarely seen.

OTHER LARGE HERBIVORES
African elephant (*Loxodonta africana* Shoulder height 2.3–3.4m. Weight up to 6,000kg) The world's largest land animal, the African elephant is intelligent, social and often very entertaining to watch. Female elephants live in closely knit clans in which the eldest female

plays matriarch over her sisters, daughters and granddaughters. Their life spans are comparable with those of humans, and mother-daughter bonds are strong and may last for up to 50 years. Males generally leave the family group at around 12 years to roam singly or form bachelor herds. Under normal circumstances, elephants range widely in search of food and water, but when concentrated populations are forced to live in conservation areas their habit of uprooting trees can cause serious environmental damage.

Elephants are widespread and common in habitats ranging from the deserts to rainforest; but they require trees and access to drinking water. They are very common in the north of Botswana.

The Chobe, Kwando–Linyanti and Okavango areas have one of Africa's strongest populations of elephants. During the rains, from December onwards, these disperse in the interior of the country, into the vast expanses of mopane forest and into the drier areas of the northern Kalahari. They split up into smaller family groups and spread out as they can then find water all over the place (the clay pans of the mopane woodlands are especially valuable as sources).

Despite their range having become more restricted by human expansion over the years, individuals will often wander widely, turning up in locations from which they have been absent for years.

However, as the dry season progresses and the waterholes dry up, they gradually coalesce into larger herds, and head for the permanent sources: the rivers and the Delta. Thus by September and October you can normally see huge herds of elephants along the Chobe, Kwando and Linyanti rivers. The number and size of herds in the Okavango increases also.

In many areas elephants have no natural predators (the huge prides of lion in the Savuti and North Gate areas are an exception to this rule); they are generally constrained by lack of suitable habitat (ie: trees and water) and by man. Thus in many confined national parks in southern Africa, there are programmes to cull elephants to restrict their numbers. This is controversial, even amongst ardent conservationists. Botswana has no such policy. The result, some argue, is an over-population of elephants here, and the severe environmental degradation to be seen around the riverfront in Chobe, where the riverine forests have been decimated. Whilst not denying the observation, it's well worth remembering that there was a sawmill in this area, and extensive logging during the 1930s and early 1940s – so humans should take part of the blame for this.

Black rhinoceros (*Diceros bicornis* Shoulder height 160cm. Weight 1,000kg) This is the more widespread of Africa's two rhino species, an imposing and rather temperamental creature. Black rhino were once found all over northern Botswana, but were thought to have been poached to extinction in Botswana, whilst becoming highly endangered in many other countries within their range.

Black rhino exploit a wide range of habitats from dense woodlands and bush, and are generally solitary animals. They can survive without drinking for four to five days. However, their territorial behaviour and regular patterns of movement make them an easy target for poachers. Black rhino can be very aggressive when disturbed and will charge with minimal provocation. Their hearing and sense of smell are acute, whilst their eyesight is poor (so they often miss if you keep a low profile and don't move).

Now, following the successful reintroduction of white rhino to Chief's Island, there are plans to reintroduce black rhino here also. The environment is very suitable, and the island is effectively isolated within a large area devoted to wildlife; so it is hoped that poaching them from here would be difficult. Watch this space, and see the comments on page 269; and if you want to help with this work, then see *Giving something back* on pages 39–40.

White rhinoceros (*Ceratotherium simum* Shoulder height 180cm. Weight 1,500–2,000kg)
The white rhino is in fact no paler in colour than the black rhino – the 'white' derives from
the Afrikaans *weit* (wide) and refers to its flattened mouth, an ideal shape for cropping grass.
This is the best way to tell the two rhino species apart, since the mouth of the black rhino, a
browser in most parts of its range, is more rounded with a hooked upper lip. (Note
that there is *no colour difference at all* between these two species of rhino; 'white' and
'black' are *not* literal descriptions.)

Unlike their smaller cousins, white rhino are generally placid grazing
animals which are very rarely aggressive. They prefer open grassy plains
and are often seen in small groups. In the accounts of the first trips across
Africa by the early white explorers, rhino were found (and shot) in huge
numbers.

As with the black rhino, hunting and poaching reduced the population of
African white rhinos drastically, reaching a crisis in the 1980s, when only a
few South African reserves remained with really strong populations (notably Umfolozi and
Hluhluwe). Amongst other countries, Zimbabwe retained remnants whilst Botswana,
Zambia and others were effectively poached out.

Since then those parks which effectively saved the species have been used as reservoirs, to
slowly re-populate a few protected areas. Recently some have been reintroduced into the
Chief's Island area of Moremi, with encouraging success. It's hoped that this will continue,
and that once again Botswana will be able to boast at least one area where rhino are prolific.

Hippopotamus (*Hippopotamus amphibius* Shoulder height 150cm. Weight 2,000kg)
Characteristic of Africa's large rivers and lakes, this large, lumbering animal spends most of
the day submerged but emerges at night to graze. Strongly territorial, herds of ten or more
animals are presided over by a dominant male who will readily defend his patriarchy to the
death. Hippos are abundant in most protected rivers and water bodies and are still quite
common outside of reserves.

They are widely credited with killing more people than any other African mammal. They
are clearly very, very dangerous – but I know of no statistics to support this, and many reliable
sources suggest that crocodile, elephant and lion could all vie for this dubious title. So, whilst
undoubtedly dangerous, perhaps they don't quite deserve their reputation.

In Botswana you'll find hippo in good numbers in all of the major river systems: Chobe,
Kwando–Linyanti and the Okavango. It'd be difficult to go on safari in any of the wetter areas
of northern Botswana without seeing large numbers of hippo.

Buffalo (*Syncerus caffer* Shoulder height 140cm. Weight 700kg) Frequently and erroneously
referred to as a water buffalo (which is actually an Asian species), the Cape, or African, buffalo
is a distinctive, highly social, ox-like animal that lives as part of a herd. It prefers well-watered
savannah, though also occurs in forested areas. Buffalo are primarily grazers and need regular
access to water, where they swim readily. Lion often follow herds of buffalo, their favourite
prey.

Huge herds are generally fairly peaceful, and experienced guides will often
walk straight through them on walking safaris.
However, small bachelor herds, and especially single
old bulls, can be very nervous and aggressive. They
have a reputation for charging at the slightest
provocation, often in the midst of thick bush, and are
exceedingly dangerous when wounded.

Buffalo smell and hear well, but it's often claimed that they
have poor eyesight. This isn't true, though when encountered
during a walking safari, if you keep still and the wind is right
they won't be able to discern your presence.

Common and widespread in sub-Saharan Africa, in Botswana the buffalo is limited to the north of the country, largely by the absence of sufficient water in the rest of the country. Their annual movements mirror those of elephants in general terms. During the rains, from December onwards, they disperse into the mopane forests and into the drier areas of the northern Kalahari, splitting up into smaller groups and spreading out.

However, as the dry season progresses, they gather together into larger herds, and congregate near permanent sources of water: along the Chobe, Kwando and Linyanti rivers, and throughout the Okavango Delta. Then you'll see them in most reserves with water, though the open plains of NG23 (Duba Plains) seem to have particularly high concentrations of buffalo.

Giraffe (*Giraffa camelopardis* Shoulder height 250–350cm. Weight 1,000–1,400kg) The world's tallest and longest-necked land animal, a fully grown giraffe can measure up to 5.5m high. Quite unmistakable, giraffe live in loosely structured herds of up to 15 head, though herd members often disperse, when they are seen singly or in smaller groups. Formerly distributed throughout eastern and southern Africa, in Botswana these great browsers are now found only in the centre and north of the country. The CKGR has a very healthy population, as do Makgadikgadi and Nxai, and they are also found through the Chobe, Kwando–Linyanti and Okavango areas.

Giraffe are adapted to browse vegetation that is beyond the reach of all the other large herbivores, with the exception of elephant. They prefer *Acacia* and *Combretum* species, and a 45cm tongue ensures that they can extract the leaves from the most thorny of branches.

Burchell's zebra (*Equus burchelli* Shoulder height 130cm. Weight 300–340kg) Also known as common or plains zebra, this attractive striped horse is common and widespread throughout most of eastern and southern Africa, where it is often seen in large herds alongside wildebeest. There are many subspecies of zebra in Africa, and most southern races, including those in Botswana, have paler brownish 'shadow stripes' between the bold black stripes (which are present in all races).

Zebra are common in most conservation areas, from northern South Africa, Namibia and all the way up to the southeast of Ethiopia. In Botswana they occur in Makgadikgadi, Nxai and to the north– but I don't believe that they still occur within the CKGR. If the rains have been good in the Makgadikgadi Pans area, then during the first few months of the year you can witness huge herds of zebra roaming across the open plains in search of the freshest new grass.

Warthog (*Phacochoreus africanus* Shoulder height 60–70cm. Weight up to 100kg) This widespread and often conspicuously abundant resident of the African savannah is grey in colour with a thin covering of hairs, wart-like bumps on its face, and rather large, upward-curving tusks. Africa's only diurnal swine, the warthog is often seen in family groups, trotting around with its tail raised stiffly (a diagnostic trait) and a determinedly nonchalant air.

They occur throughout Botswana with the exception of the far south, although they don't usually fare well near settlements, as they are very susceptible to subsistence hunting/poaching. Wherever they occur, you'll often see them grazing beside the road, on bended knee.

Similar species Bulkier, hairier and browner, the **bushpig** (*Potomochoerus larvatus*) only occurs in the wetter areas of northern Botswana – northern Chobe, the Kwando–Linyanti and the Okavango. Like the warthog, they don't survive well near settlements: they damage crops and so are persistently hunted. That said, even where they do occur, they are rarely seen due to their nocturnal habits and preference for living in dense vegetation.

SMALL MAMMALS

African civet (*Civettictis civetta* Shoulder height 40cm. Weight 10–15kg) This bulky, long-haired, rather feline creature of the African night is primarily carnivorous, feeding on small animals and carrion, but will also eat fruit. It has a similarly coloured coat to a leopard, which is densely blotched with large black spots becoming stripes towards the head. Civets are  widespread and common throughout a band across northern Botswana, including Chobe, the Kwando–Linyanti and Okavango areas. They occur in many habitats, and make frequent cameo appearances on night drives.

Note that although they are occasionally referred to as 'civet cats', this is misleading. They are more closely related to the mongooses than the felines.

Similar species The **small-spotted genet** (*Genetta genetta*) and **large-spotted genet** (*Genetta tigrina*) are two members of a large group of similar small predators found in Botswana. As even experts often can't tell the various species apart without examining their skins by hand, precise identification of genets is difficult. All the genets are slender and rather feline in appearance (though they are *not* cats), with a grey to gold-brown coat marked with black spots (perhaps combining into short bars) and a long ringed tail.

You're most likely to see genets on nocturnal game drives or occasionally scavenging around game reserve lodges. The small-spotted genet is found all over Botswana, whereas its larger cousin is thought to be restricted to the northern areas of Chobe, Kwando–Linyanti and Okavango. Genets are excellent climbers and opportunists, eating fruit, small birds, termites and even scorpions.

Banded mongoose (*Mungos mungo* Shoulder height 20cm. Weight around 1kg) The banded mongoose is probably the most commonly observed member of a group of small, slender, terrestrial carnivores. Uniform dark grey-brown except for a dozen black stripes across its back, it is a diurnal mongoose occurring in playful family groups, or troops, in most habitats throughout northern and northwestern  Botswana. It feeds on insects, scorpions, amphibians, reptiles and even carrion and bird's eggs, and can move through the bush at quite a pace.

Similar species Another six or so mongoose species occur in Botswana. Some are social and gather in troops; others are solitary. Several are too scarce and nocturnal to be seen by most visitors.

The water or **marsh mongoose** (*Atilax paludinosus*) is large, normally solitary and has a very scruffy brown coat; it's widespread in the Chobe, Kwando–Linyanti and Okavango regions.

The **white-tailed mongoose** (*Ichneumia albicauda*), or white-tailed ichneumon, is a solitary, large brown mongoose with long, coarse, woolly hair. It is nocturnal and easily identified by its bushy white tail if seen crossing roads at night. It has a similar distribution, where it can also be found in a few cattle-ranching areas, where it eats the beetle-grubs found in manure.

The **slender mongoose** (*Galerella sanguinea*) is also widespread throughout Botswana where there is lots of cover for it. It, too, is solitary, but it is very much smaller (shoulder height 10cm) and has a uniform brown or reddish coat and blackish tail tip. Its tail is held up when it runs.

The **large grey mongoose** (*Herpestes ichneumon*), also called the Egyptian mongoose, is a large mongoose with coarse, grey-speckled body hair, black lower legs and feet, and a black tip to its tail. It's found in the same northern areas of Botswana, but is common nowhere. It is generally diurnal and is either solitary, or lives in pairs. Large grey mongooses eat small rodents, reptiles, birds and also snakes, generally killing rather than scavenging.

A1

Selous's mongoose (*Paracynictis selousi*) is smaller, with fine, speckled grey fur, and a white tip at the end of its tail. It likes open country and woodlands, occurring in many areas of northern and the further eastern areas of Botswana. It is nocturnal and solitary, eating mainly insects, grubs, small reptiles and amphibians. It seems especially fond of the larvae of dung beetles, and so is sometime found in cattle country.

The **yellow mongoose** (*Cynitis penicillata*) is a small, sociable mongoose with a tawny or yellow coat, and is commonly found across most of Botswana – even in the drier areas of the central Kalahari. It normally forages alone and is easily identified by the white tip on the end of its tail.

Finally, **the dwarf mongoose** (*Helogate parvula*) is a diminutive (shoulder height 7cm), highly sociable light-brown mongoose often seen in the vicinity of the termite mounds where it nests. This is Africa's smallest carnivore, occurring in a higher density than any other. It is widespread throughout the Chobe, Kwando–Linyanti and Okavango areas, and often seen. Groups of 20–30 are not unknown, consisting of a breeding pair and subordinate others. These inquisitive little animals can be very entertaining to watch.

Meerkat or suricate (*Suricata suricatta* Shoulder height 25–35cm. Weight 650–950g)

Found throughout central and southwest Botswana, and much of neighbouring Namibia, meerkats are absent from Makgadikgadi and further north. The best places to see them are the CKGR and further towards the southwest corner of Botswana (eg: the KD1 concession, south of Ghanzi, and the Kgalagadi Transfrontier Park).

These small animals are sandy to silvery-grey in colour, with dark bands running across their backs. They are exclusively diurnal and have a distinctive habit of sitting upright on their hind legs. They do this when they first emerge in the morning, to sun themselves, and throughout the day.

Living in complex social groups, meerkats are usually seen scratching around for insects, beetles and small reptiles in dry, open, grassy areas. Whilst the rest forage, one or two of the group will use the highest mound around as a sentry-post – looking out for predators using their remarkable eyesight. Meerkats' social behaviour is very complex: they squeak constantly to communicate and even use different alarm calls for different types of predators. Because of their photogenic poses and fascinating social behaviour, they have been the subject of several successful television documentaries filmed in the southern Kalahari.

Honey badger (*Mellivora capensis* Shoulder height 30cm. Weight 12kg)

Also known as the ratel, the honey badger is black with a puppyish face and grey-white back. It is an opportunistic feeder best known for its allegedly symbiotic relationship with a bird called the honeyguide which leads it to beehives, waits for it to tear them open, then feeds on the scraps. The honey badger is among the most widespread of African carnivores, and also amongst the most powerful and aggressive for its size. It occurs all over Botswana, but is thinly distributed and infrequently seen, except when it has lost its fear of people and started to scavenge from safari camps.

Similar species Other mustelids occurring in the region include the **striped polecat** (*Ictonyx striatus*), a common but rarely seen nocturnal creature with black underparts and a bushy white back.

Cape clawless otter (*Aonyx capensis* Shoulder height 20–30cm. Weight 3–5kg)

This is the larger of the two species of otter that occur in southern Africa. It has a chocolate-brown coat with a pale cream-to-white chin and throat. In Botswana, it is restricted to the northern river systems of Chobe, Kwando–Linyanti and the Okavango (it's not found in broad, tropical rivers like the Zambezi), though will occasionally move away from there, across dry land, in search of other pools and waterways.

Cape clawless otters are active mostly around dusk and dawn, although they will sometimes be seen in broad daylight or at night. Rough skin on their paws gives excellent grip, and with this they prey mostly on frogs and fish. They'll also take freshwater mussels, and will use rocks to help them crack these open.

Although very shy (they'll usually flee when approached by a boat or people), they're delightful to watch, seeming very playful, with a variety of aquatic acrobatics, and cleaning their face and paws scrupulously after every meal. Visiting Botswana, you're most likely to see otters in the shallow floodplain areas of the Okavango when on a quiet mokoro trip.

Similar species The smaller **spotted-necked otter** (*Lutra maculicollis*) is darker with light white spots on its throat – though difficult to distinguish from its larger cousin unless you're familiar with them both. Their distribution and habits are similar to the Cape clawless, though they are more diurnal, and more tied to bodies of water.

Aardvark (*Orycteropus afer* Shoulder height 60cm. Weight up to 70kg) This singularly bizarre nocturnal insectivore is unmistakable with its long snout, huge ears and powerful legs, adapted to dig up the nests of termites, on which it feeds. Aardvarks occur throughout southern Africa, except the driest western areas of the Namib. Though their distinctive three-toed tracks are often seen, and they are not uncommon animals, sightings of them are rare.

Aardvarks prefer areas of grassland and sparse scrub, rather than dense woodlands, so much of Botswana's bush suits them well. You're most likely to see them on a late-night game drive, and many guides say that they are seen more often during the rainy season, from December to March.

Pangolin (*Manis temmincki* Total length 70–100cm. Weight 8–15kg) Sharing the aardvaak's diet of termites and ants, the pangolin is another very unusual nocturnal insectivore, with distinctive armour plating and a tendency to roll up in a ball when disturbed. (Then it can swipe its tail from side to side, inflicting serious damage on its aggressor.) Sometimes known as Temminck's pangolins, or scaly anteaters, these strange animals walk on their hindlegs, using their tail and front legs for balance. They are both nocturnal and rare, and their distribution is uncertain, although they are thought to occur throughout Botswana. Sightings are exceedingly rare; thus an average of three sightings of pangolin per year in NG31 Reserve counts as a remarkably prolific record by the standards of most areas in Africa!

In some areas further south, particularly Zimbabwe, local custom is to make a present of any pangolin found to the paramount chief (often taken to mean the president). This has caused great damage to their population.

Porcupine (*Hystrix africaeaustralis* Total length 80–100cm. Weight 15–25kg) This is the largest rodent found in the region, and occurs all over southern Africa, except for the western reaches of the Namib Desert. It easily identified by its black-and-white-striped quills, generally black hair, and shambolic gait. If heard in the dark, then the rustle of its foraging is augmented by the slight rattle of its quills. These drop off fairly regularly, and are often found in the bush.

The porcupine's diet is varied, and they are fairly opportunistic when it comes to food. Roots and tubers are favourites, as is the bark of certain trees; they will also eat meat and small reptiles or birds if they have the chance. You're most likely to see porcupines on night drives, as individuals, pairs or small family groups.

Similar species Also spiky, the **Southern African hedgehog** (*Erinaceus frontalis*) has been recorded in eastern and southeastern areas of Botswana, though it is small and nocturnal, so rarely seen even where it does occur. Hedgehogs are about 20cm long (much smaller than porcupines), omnivorous and uncommon.

Rock hyrax (*Procavia capensis* Shoulder height 35–30cm. Weight 4kg) Rodent-like in appearance, hyraxes (also known as dassies) are claimed to be the closest living relative of elephants. The rock hyrax and similar **yellow-spotted rock hyrax** (*Heterohyrax brucei*) are often seen sunning themselves in rocky habitats, and become tame when used to people.

They are social animals, living in large groups, and are largely herbivores, eating leaves, grasses and fruits. Where you see lots of dassies, watch out for black eagles and other raptors which prey extensively on them. In Botswana they're restricted to the southeast of the country, although places like the Tsodilo Hills would seem an ideal habitat for them.

Scrub hare (*Lepus saxatilis* Shoulder height 45–60cm. Weight 1–4.5kg) This is the largest and most common African hare or rabbit, occurring everywhere in Botswana. In some areas a short walk at dusk or after nightfall might reveal three or four scrub hares. They tend to freeze when disturbed.

Similar species Very similar, the **Cape hare** (*Lepus capensis*) has been recorded in Botswana, both in the southwest and in an area to the north of the great salt pans. However, distinguishing between these two similar species at night, when they are most likely to be seen, would be very difficult.

Ground squirrel (*Xerus inauris* Shoulder height 20–30cm. Weight 400–700g) This terrestrial rodent is common in the more arid parts of Botswana, including the central Kalahari, and southeastern areas. The ground squirrel is grey to grey-brown with a prominent white eye ring and silver-black tail. Within its range, it might be confused with the meerkat, which also spends much time on its hind legs. Unlike the meerkat, the ground squirrels has a characteristic squirrel mannerism of holding food in its forepaws.

The ground squirrel is a social animal; large groups share one communal burrow. It can often be spotted searching for vegetation, seeds, roots and small insects, whilst holding its tail aloft as a sunshade.

Bush squirrel (*Paraxerus cepapi* Total length 35cm. Weight 100–250g) This common rodent is a uniform grey or buff colour, with a long tail that is furry but not bushy. It's widely distributed all over southern and east Africa, and occurs throughout northern Botswana in most woodland habitats, although not wet evergreen or montane forests. Bush squirrels are so numerous in mopane woodlands that it can be difficult to avoid seeing it, hence its other common name, the mopane squirrel.

Bush squirrels live alone, in pairs or in small groups, usually nesting in a drey of dry leaves, in a hole in a tree. They are diurnal and venture to the ground to feed on seeds, fruit, nuts, vegetable matter and small insects. When alarmed they often bolt up the nearest tree, keeping on the side of the trunk away from the threat, out of sight as much as possible. If they can find a safe vantage point with a view of the threat, then they'll sometimes make a loud clicking alarm call.

Appendix 2

LANGUAGE *Based on an original compiled by Phil Deutschle*

Setswana is the national language of Botswana, while English is the official language. In practice this means that though many people speak other languages at home, most will be able to converse in Setswana. English will be spoken by those who have been to school, or who have been outside the country. This means most people, with the exception of the older generation in rural areas.

Learning to speak a little Setswana is easy and, even in educated circles, trying to speak a few words of the language will mark you out as showing respect for the country's culture. It will open many doors, and will really make a difference to how you are received. Carry the most important phrases on a slip of paper, and practise whenever you can.

PRONUNCIATION The only difficult sound in Setswana is the g, pronounced like ch in the Scottish 'loch' or German 'Ich'. If you have trouble with that, just say the g like an ordinary h. The r is often rolled, especially if it's written 'rr'. Vowels are pronounced as follows:

a	like a in China
e	like ay in day
i	like ee in see
o	like o in go
u	like oo in too

GREETINGS Greetings are relatively easy to master, as you can practise them with everyone you meet. They'll also get you instant results; using them is almost guaranteed to bring a smile to the face of those you greet – whilst sending out the message that you're not an arrogant foreigner who can't be bothered to learn a word of Setswana. So even if you never learn anything else in Setswana – do learn the basic greetings and it'll make your trip so much easier and more pleasant.

English	Setswana
Words in underlined italics are optional	
Hello (literally 'Greetings Sir/Madam')	*Dumela Rra/Mma*
How did you rise?	*O tsogile jang?*
I have risen *well*	*Ke tsogile sentle*
How did you spend the day?	*O tlhotse jang?*
I spent the day *well*	*Ke tlhotse sentle*
How are you? (Informal)	*O kae?*
I'm fine (Literally, 'I'm here')	*Ke teng*
It's OK	*Go siame*
I am going	*Ke a tsamaya*
Stay well (said to someone staying)	*Sala sentle*

489

| Go well (said to someone going) | *Tsamaya sentle* |
| Sleep well | *Robala sentle* |

BASIC PHRASES

What's your name? (formal)	*Leina la gago ke mang?*
My name is . . .	*Leina la me ke . . .*
Who are you? (informal)	*O mang?*
I'm . . .	*Ke . . .*
Where are you from? or	
Where are you coming from?	*O tswa kee?*
I'm (coming) from . . .	*Ke tswa kwa . . .*
Yes	*Ee*
No	*Nnyaa*
I don't know *Setswana*	*Ga ke itse Setswana*
What is this in *Setswana*?	*Se ke eng ka Setswana?*
How goes it?	*Wa reng?*
It goes OK	*Ga ke bue*
Thank you	*Ke aleboga, Ke itumetse* (lit 'I am happy')
What's the time?	*Nako ke mang?*
Excuse me!	*Sorry!*
I'm asking for money/tobacco	*Ke kopa madi/motsoko*
I have no money/tobacco	*Ga ke na madi/motsoko*

NUMBERS Unusually, numbers are said in English.

SHOPPING

Where's the shop?	*Shopo e kae?*
What do you want?	*O batla eng?*
I want . . .	*Ke batla/kopa . . .*
There is none	*Ga go na*
How much?	*Ke bokae?*
It's expensive/cheap	*Go a tura/tshipi*
sugar	*sukiri*
mealie meal	*dupr*
tea	*tee/*
coffee	*kofee*
meat	*Fnama*
milk	*mashi*
water	*metse*

TRAVELLING PHRASES

Where are you going?	*O ya kae?*
I'm going to . . .	*Ke ya . . .*
Where are you coming from?	*O tswa kae?*
I'm coming from . . .	*Ke tswa kwa . . .*
Far/near	*Kgakala/gaufi*
I'm satisfied (regarding food)	*Ke kgotshe*
It tastes good	*Go monate*
Men/Women (written on toilets)	*Banna/Basadi*
What do you do? (your job)	*O dira eng?*

Appendix 3

FURTHER INFORMATION

BOOKS

Coffee-table picture books

Chobe: Africa's Untamed Wilderness by Daryl and Sharna Balfour. Southern Books, Johannesburg, 1997. An almost day-by-day account of a year that this renowned couple spent in Chobe and Selinda. Good pictures and a readable diary-format style give a fair picture of the changing seasons and the wildlife.

The Lion Children by Angus, Maisie and Travers McNeice. Orion Books Ltd, London, 2001. Taken from the UK to live in the Okavango (around NG34) by their parents, who moved there to research lions, this an entertaining scrapbook written by the children about life in the bush. Whilst basically a children's book, it's a lot of fun to read and occasionally quite insightful.

The Miracle Rivers: The Okavango and Chobe of Botswana by Peter and Beverly Pickford. Southern Books, Johannesburg, 1999. A coffee-table book with some colour plates and grainy black-and-white shots. Text is a mixture of quotes and travelogue with attention (and almost homage) paid to various hunting operations.

Okavango: Africa's Last Eden by Frans Lanting. Published in 1993 by Chronicle Books, San Francisco, 1993. Probably the ultimate in coffee-table books includes minimal text but many impressive and beautiful images that were originally commissioned for *National Geographic* magazine.

Okavango: Africa's Wetland Wilderness by Adrian Bailey. Struik Publishers, Cape Town, 1998. Bright colour plates and an informative text make this a good coffee-table overview of the Delta.

Okavango: Jewel of the Kalahari by Karen Ross. BBC Enterprises Ltd, London, 1987. Written by Karen Ross in parallel with her research for a short series of films, produced by Partridge Films for the BBC. The film series is stunning, and certainly raised the UK's awareness of the Okavango Delta considerably when it was first shown. The book's also first-class. Its photography is good, though not exceptional, but the depth of its text raises it well above the normal standard of coffee-table books. Though perhaps slightly dated now, it's still well worth getting hold of.

Running Wild: Dispelling the Myths of the African Wild Dog. Text by John McNutt and Lesley Boggs Ross; photography by Hélène Heldring and Dave Hamman. Southern Books, Johannesburg, 1996. Some beautiful pictures of dogs in the Delta (the 'Mombo Pack' in the early 1990s) plus informative text about their behaviour and group dynamics – put into the context of observations made throughout northern Botswana.

Savuti: The Vanishing River by Clive Walker. Southern Books, Johannesburg, 1991. Using many simple line drawings, and just a sprinkling of generally impressive photographs, this is less pictorial than most coffee-table books. It concentrates mainly on Walker's personal experiences in Savuti, where he spent time with Lloyd Wilmot, amongst others, and witnessed the final drying out of the Savuti Channel. It's a good read, though too large to easily travel with.

The Swamp Book: A View of the Okavango by Bob Forester, Mike Murray-Hudson and Lance Cherry. Southern Books, Johannesburg, 1989. This interesting and quirky coffee-table book includes highly readable sections on the Okavango Delta and some of its more common flora and fauna, as well as comments on a few interesting historical accounts of travel there. Photographs include several taken underwater.

Botswana Notes and Records

The Botswana Society (see page 41) has published an annual journal, *Botswana Note and Records*, since 1969. It contains 'scientific, and semi-scientific articles and notes, written by amateur as well as professional experts on subjects of permanent interest relating to Botswana'. This is an amazing archive of reliable information, which I've only scratched the surface of here – it's a real treasure trove for anyone interested in Botswana. During my researches I've read many articles and made reference to some of them, including the main ones, which are mentioned here:

An Assessment of the Impact of Fences on Large Herbivore Biomass in the Kalahari by D T & J E Williamson. Volume 13 (1981), pages 107–10.

The Caves of Ngamiland: An Interim Report on Explorations and Fieldwork 1972–74 by H J Cooke and T Baillieul. Volume 6 (1974), pages 147–56.

A Chronology of Major Events Relating to the Central Kalahari Game Reserve by Robert Hitchcock. Volume 31 (1999), pages 105–17.

Clan size of Spotted Hyenas in the Savuti Region of Chobe National Park, Botswana by Dr S M Cooper. Volume 21 (1989), pages 121–33.

The Climate of Botswana in Histograms by J Andringa. Volume 16 (1984), pages 117–26.

A Comment on Kalahari Wildlife and the Khukhe Fence by Alec Campbell. Volume 13 (1981), pages 111–18.

The Depression Rock Shelter Site, Tsodilo Hills by L H Robbins and A C Campbell. Volume 20 (1989), pages 1–3.

Discovery and Exploration of Two New Caves in the Northwest District by Ron Ritter and Paul Mann. Volume 27 (1995), pages 1–12.

Discovery and Preliminary Exploration of a New Cave in the Gcwihaba Valley by R C Ritter and R A Garner. Volume 26 (1994), pages 55–65.

Excavations at the Tsodilo Hills Rhino Cave by L H Robbins, M L Murphy, A C Campbell and G A Brook. Volume 28 (1996), pages 23–45.

Franz or Klikko, the Wild Dancing Bushmen: A Case Study in Khoisan Stereotyping by Q N Parsons. Volume 20 (1989), pages 71–6.

Further Exploration and Resurvey of !WaDoum Cave by P M Mann and R C Ritter. Volume 27 (1995), pages 13–20.

The Middle Stone Age of Kudiakam Pan by Lawrence H Robbins. Volume 20 (1989), pages 41–50.

Modelling of Surface Outflow from the Okavango Delta by A Gieske. Volume 28 (1996), pages 165–92.

New Locality Record for the Klipspinger by P C Viljoen. Volume 12 (1980), page 169.

A Preliminary Report on the Number, Distribution and Movement of Elephants in the Chobe National Park with Notes on Browse Utilisation by M W L Sommerlatte. Volume 7 (1975), pages 121–9.

Putting the Bushmen on the Map of Botswana by Cornelius VanderPost. Volume 32 (2000), pages 107–15.

Resurvey of Gcwihaba Cave and Exploration of the Aha Sinkhole Caves by R A Garner and R C Ritter. Volume 26 (1994), pages 183–8.

The Riddle of the Stone Walls by Alec Campbell. Volume 23 (1991), pages 243–50.

Some Edible Wild Cucumbers of Botswana by Audrey Renew. Volume 1 (1968), pages 5–8.

Some Notes on the Colonial Era History of the Central Kalahari Game Reserve Region by Jeff Ramsay. Volume 20 (1989), pages 91–4.

A Terminal Pleistocene Assemblage from Drotsky's Cave, Western Ngamiland by J E Yellen, A S Brooks, R Stuckenrath and R Welbourne. Volume 19 (1987), pages 1–6.

Field guides

Newman's Birds of Southern Africa by Kenneth Newman. Struik Publishers, South Africa. This has been re-published numerous times since its first edition in 1988 and has become the standard field guide to birds in southern Africa, south of the Kunene and Zambezi rivers. It also covers most species found in Zambia.

Birds of Botswana by Kenneth Newman. Southern Books, South Africa, 1990. Although the text is dedicated to Botswana, the cost of this book is likely to steer most ordinary birders towards the more general southern African text above.

Common Wild Flowers of the Okavango Delta by Veronica Roodt. Shell Oil Botswana, Gaborone, 1998. The second book in Shell's 'Field Guide' series is a little more specialist than the first book on trees, but still manages to comment on diverse topics from the formulae for gunpowder to the treatment of scorpion stings. It's well worth getting.

The Safari Companion by Richard Estes. Russell Friedman Books, South Africa, 1993 (co-published Tutorial Press, Zimbabwe and Chelsea Green Publishing, Vermont).. Whilst slightly too thick to be an ideal travelling companion, this is a real treasure-chest of information on animal behaviour. It covers all the main animal species found in mainland Africa, from duikers and dwarf antelope to cats, dogs and the great apes. For each it includes a brief description of its social systems and forms of communication, with helpful outlines of body postures and diagrams to explain typical forms of behaviour. If you've longed to decipher the language of animals, and have the time to stop and watch rather than simply tick game off a list, then you must bring this book.

Southern African Wildlife: A Visitor's Guide by Mike Unwin. Bradt Travel Guides, UK, 2003. A compact single-volume guide to the habitats, identification and behavioural characteristics of the region's wildlife. A well-written text, which includes sections on tracks and signs, is matched by exceptionally good photographs.

Trees and Shrubs of the Okavango Delta by Veronica Roodt. Shell Oil Botswana, Gaborone, 1998. This first book in Shell Publication's 'Field Guide' series isn't just about trees or shrubs, and doesn't restrict its comments rigidly to the Okavango – but it is a masterpiece. Veronica Roodt has lived and worked in Moremi for many years, researching the plants of the area. This book is ostensibly just a field guide to slightly over 60 of the more common trees and shrubs in the area, but in reality it's a fascinating treatise on the insects and animals associated with all of them, plus the medicinal uses and local superstitions attached to each. It's well worth buying a copy as soon as you get to Botswana, even if you're not that interested in trees; it reads very well!

Trees of Southern Africa by Keith Coates Palgrave, R B Drummond and Eugene John Moll. Struik, Cape Town, 3rd edition 2003. The definitive guide to the region's trees is a must have for natural history buffs.

Other useful guides

African Adventurer's Guide to Botswana by Mike Main. New Holland, UK, 2001. Mike Main is a leading authority on all things to do with Botswana, and especially its wilder areas. This book builds on the earlier *Visitor's Guide to Botswana*. It features route descriptions for some very offbeat 4x4 trips, including a few GPS points and schematic maps of the routes.

African Rock Art: Painting and Engraving on Stone by Alec Campbell and David Coulson. Abrams, New York, 2001. Campbell's informative text underpins some stunning photography, making this so much more than a coffee-table book.

Cry of the Kalahari by Mark and Delia Owens. Mariner Books, 1992. A highly personal account of the authors' seven years in the Kalahari, during which time they set up a conservation project.

Discovering Southern Africa by T V Bulpin. Discovering Southern Africa Productions, South Africa (distributed by Book Sales). Part guidebook and part history book, this covers mainly South Africa but also extends into Namibia and Zimbabwe. A weighty tome with useful background views and information, written from a South African perspective.

An Explorer's Handbook: Travel, Survival and Bush Cookery by Christina Dodwell. Hodder and Stoughton, London, 1984.. Over 170 pages of practical and amusing anecdotes, including chapters on 'unusual eatables', 'building an open fire' and 'tested exits from tight corners'. Practical advice for both possible and most unlikely eventualities – and it's a great read.

The Guide to Botswana by Alec Campbell. Winchester Press, Johannesburg, first published 1968. Alec Campbell is perhaps the leading authority on Botswana's natural areas and history, having not only lived in Botswana for most of his life, but also held posts as the Director of National Parks and later as the Director of the National Museum of Botswana. There were several very substantial editions to this early guide which give insights into what Botswana was like decades ago. It's also fascinating to contrast and compare his guides with more contemporary guidebooks.

Kalahari: Life's Variety in Dune and Delta by Mike Main. Macmillan, UK, 1988.

Life and Work of Thomas Baines by Jane Carruthers & Marion Arnold. Fernwood Press, South Africa, 1995, reprinted 1996.

The Lost World of the Kalahari by Laurens van der Post. First published Hogarth Press, 1958, subsequently many reprints by Penguin. Laurens van der Post's classic account of how he journeyed into the heart of the Kalahari Desert in search of a 'pure' Bushman group – eventually found at the Tsodilo Hills. His almost mystical description of the Bushmen is fascinating, so long as you can cope with the rather dated, turgid prose. You then need to read Robert J Gordon's very different book, *The Bushman Myth* (see below), to put it in perspective.

Top Birding Spots of Southern Africa compiled by Hugh Chittenden. Southern Book Publishers, South Africa, 1992. This useful, practical book details about 400 sites for keen birdwatchers, listing local specialities and endemic species with a checklist of key species for each site. Some of its simple maps are now out of date, though I'm not aware of it being reprinted in the last decade.

Historical interest

Africa: A Biography of the Continent by John Reader. Penguin Books, London, 1997. Over 700 pages of highly readable history, interwoven with facts and statistics, to make a remarkable overview of Africa's past. Given that Botswana's boundaries were imposed from Europe, its history must be looked at from a pan-African context to be understood. This book can show you that wider view; it is compelling and essential reading. (Chapters 41 and 42 deal with the early settlers in the Cape, and are largely devoted to the Lozi people.)

The Archaeology of Botswana edited by Paul Lane, Andrew Reid and Alinah Segobya. Co-published by The Botswana Society, PO Box 71, Gaborone, Botswana, 1998. This is a detailed and academic overview of the archaeology of Botswana, as well as how archaeology has progressed in the country to date. It's an excellent reference, but not a light read.

Botswana: The Road to Independence by Peter Fawcus and Alan Tilbury. Co published Botswana Society, Gaborone, 2000. The authors of this were two of Britain's most senior administrators during the final decade that led to Botswana's independence. Their book paints a rare picture (quite densely packed with detail) of a country's smooth transition from a colonial protectorate to an independent state – and has a particularly interesting foreword by Sir Ketumile Masire, one of Botswana's former presidents.

The Bushman Myth: The Making of a Namibian Underclass by Robert J Gordon. Westview Press, Colorado and Oxford, 1992. If you, like me, had accepted the received wisdom that Bushmen are the last descendants of Stone Age man, pushed to living in splendid isolation in the Kalahari, then you must read this. It places the Bushmen in an accurate historical context and deconstructs many of the myths we have created about them. Despite being mainly based on facts about the San in Namibia, it's still well worth reading for an understanding of their position in contemporary Botswana.

Explorations in South-west Africa by Thomas Baines. London, 1864. Although linked more with the countries further east, the travels of Baines, as he accompanied Livingstone and others, makes good reading and is well illustrated by the author.

Lake Ngami and the River Okavango by Charles John Andersson. Originally published late 1850s; republished as a facsimile reprint by Struik, Cape Town, 1967. Records Namibia and Botswana in the 1850s through the eyes of one of the first traders and hunters in the area.

The Mammals of South West Africa by G C Shortridge. London, 1934. This is more of historical interest than a practical field guide.

Serowe: Village of the Rain Wind by Bessie Head offers a fascinating collection of oral-history transcripts, recording villagers' memories of their past, and especially the deeds of their enlightened leaders, Khama the Great, who ruled from 1875 to 1923, Tshekedi Khama (1926–59), his son from a late second marriage, and finally Sir Seretse Khama, Khama's grandson, by his first-born son Segkoma II (1923–25), who became first president of the independent Botswana.

Travels and Researches in South Africa by David Livingstone, 1857. This classic is fascinating reading, over a century after it was written.

Health

Bugs, Bites & Bowels by Dr Jane Wilson-Howarth. Cadogan Books, London, 2006. An amusing and erudite overview, small enough to take with you, of the hazards of tropical travel.

Your Child Abroad: A Travel Health Guide by Dr Jane Wilson-Howarth and Dr Matthew Ellis. Bradt Travel Guides, UK, 2004. Full of practical first-hand advice from two leading medical experts. An indispensable guide if you plan to travel abroad with young children.

Novels

Head, Bessie *Maru* Heinemann, 1995. The uplifting story of a Mawarwa orphan's experiences of racial prejudice at a time when the Bushmen were treated as slaves by the dominant peoples of Botswana.

McCall-Smith, Alexander *The No 1 Ladies' Detective Agency* Abacus, 2003. Mma Precious Ramotswe and her detective agency have been taken to the hearts of readers worldwide, but her roots are firmly in Gaborone. McCall-Smith's gently humorous tales, of which this is the first, are set in the context of modern-day Botswana, and will enrich even the shortest visit to the country.

USEFUL WEBSITES A selection of the web's most interesting resources on Botswana might include, in alphabetical order:

www.advertiser.bw is a site full of commercial and classified advertisements, as found in the *Botswana Advertiser* paper. If you want to buy or sell something in Botswana, or check the latest TV schedules, try here.

www.bidpa.bw is home for the Botswana Institute for Development Policy Analysis (BIDPA). It's a fairly slow-loading, dry NGO site but includes some quite detailed papers on Botswana economic development.

www.botswana-travel-guide.com/bradt_guide.asp is an on-line, searchable version of this book.

www.cbnrm.bw is the home page of the Community Based Natural Resource Management Support Programme in Botswana. This is an extensive site used as a noticeboard for communities involved in managing areas. It has lots of information about concessions and community developments, if you're prepared to spend time digging through it, and some real gems.

www.chobeguide.com is a fairly impressive and fast-loading directory for the Chobe area – though judging by the inclusion of the long-closed Lloyd's Camp in Savuti, not everything here is up to date.

www.columbia.edu/cu/lweb/indiv/africa/cuvl/Botswana.html is the Botswana page of Columbia University's Department of African Studies. It's a good starting place for information with basic summaries and lots of good links.

http://dmoz.org/Regional/Africa/Botswana is the Open Directory Project's page on Botswana, which leads to a number of useful links. (The home page, dmoz.org, is a useful starting point for links to information on any country.)

www.expertafrica.com is the home page for Expert Africa, run by the author. UK residents can order maps from here, and in there are Google maps featuring many locations within Botswana.

www.info.bw is a fast-loading site from one of the country's main ISPs. It includes a listing of virtually every Botswana website (no comments, just an alphabetical list), a useful page of links to the media on the web, and even weather forecasts for Botswana's various towns.

www.gov.bw is the home page of Botswana's government. It has links to a huge variety of sites from the official tourist information site (which is good) to the various government departments. If you want to email a minister, download the latest customs regulations or read the latest budget speech – this is the place.

www.mindspring.com/~okavango is a site by the Okavango researcher, John Bock, which focuses on the peoples of the Okavango area – though it also includes numerous links to other sites of interest concerning Botswana.

www.newafrica.com/history is a general pan-African site, with good coverage of Botswana's history.

www.okavango-delta.net is a small site with a useful links page, a few photos, a couple of scanned-in maps and a little general information.

www.stud.ntnu.no/~skjetnep/opwt is the site of the Okavango People's Wildlife Trust, an organisation representing some of the Okavango's local communities.

www-sul.stanford.edu/depts/ssrg/africa/bots.html has a long page of links to sites relating to Botswana – some useful, others not – but is a useful starting point if you're surfing around seeking information.

http://ubh.tripod.com/bw/bhp1.htm is run by a part of the University of Botswana and includes an impressive section on Botswana's history written by Neil Parsons. This links to a number of other relevant web pages covering many topics, from tourism and the media, to history, geography and Botswana's literature. (The university's official site, www.ub.bw, has much less of interest!)

Newspapers on the web

www.gazette.bw is home to the *Botswana Gazette*, an independent paper which is updated every Wednesday. Sadly, the site is limited and there is not yet a proper archive of past editions (though clearly one has been started).

www.gov.bw/cgi-bin/news.cgi is home to the online version of the *Daily News*, the free, government-sponsored paper. There's a good archive going back to the start of January 1999.

www.mmegi.bw has an online version of the substantial *Mmegi* weekly newspaper which only finally started cataloguing articles regularly in April 2002.

Index

Page numbers in bold indicate major entries; those in italic indicate maps or charts.

aardvark 487
aardwolf 474
abseiling, Victoria Falls 462
Abu Camp 294–7
acacia woodland 56
accommodation
    general remarks 135
    see also under individual places
age regiments 8, **38**
agriculture 17
    early 4, 5
Aha Hills 329, 345, 355–61, *357*, **363**
AIDS 16, 17, 19, 109
air travel 68, **74–6**, 133
    flight companies 172–3
    flights over Victoria Falls 460–1
    to/from Kasane 179
    to/from Livingstone 426–7
    to/from Maun 147–8
alcohol 134–5, **136**, 161
alcoholism 27
ANC 14, 15
ancestor worship 32, 34
Andersson, Charles John 128–9, 273, 344
Anglo-Boer War 12
Angola 225
animal orphanage, Francistown 41
animals *see* game; wildlife
antelope 57, **475–81**
anthrax 111
anthropology 20
apartheid 12, 14, 405
archaeology 3, 5, 6, 20
    Kubu Island 389
    Tsodilo Hills 6, 23, **346–7**
area, of Botswana 2
arrest, threat of 114–15
ATM machines 92
Audi Camp **156**, 159

Babolaongwe people 33
baboon 474
Baby Huey 217
Back to the Bridge Backpackers 156
backpacking trips
    camping equipment for 122–4
    cost 89–90
    organising 83
Baines, Thomas 379
Baines' Baobabs 365, 373–5, **379–80**
Baines' Camp 318, **320**
Bakalahari Schwelle 45
Bakalanga people 32–3
Bakgalagadi people 27
Bakgwatheng people 33
Bakwena people 9
Balozi people 30
Bamangwato people 7–9, 12, 38–40
Bana ba Letsatsi 150
Bangologa people 33

banks 92
    Kasane 184
    Livingstone 449–50
    Maun 163
Banoka people 31
Bantu-speaking people 3, 4, **5–6**, 23, **30–3**, 345
Baobab Safari Lodge 209
baobabs 373–5, 379–80, 382, 391, 395
Basarwa people 28
basket-making 32, 137
Basubiya people 30–1, 191
Batawana people 241, 344
Bathoen, Chief 11
Batswana people *see* Tswana
Bayei people 30, 31, 167, 191, 326
Bechuanaland, British Protectorate of 7, **9–12**, 38–9, 405
Bechuanaland Democratic Party (BDP) 13
Bechuanaland People's Party 12
bed & breakfast 155
beef production 17, 58, 159
beer 136
Bekwena people 344
beliefs, traditional 34
bibliography 491–5
bicycle hire 429
bilharzia 110
binoculars 98
birdlife 59, 62
    best season for 71
    flamingos 388
    kori bustard 218
    ostriches 399
    whydahs 376
blue wildebeest 476–7
boating **128–30**, 187–8, 258–9
Bodumatau Lagoon 261, 262
Boers 7, 9, 10, 11, 12
booking offices, national parks 138
bookshops 162, 185, 448
booze cruises, Upper Zambezi 454
border posts 76–7
Boro River 165, 166, 265, 305, 307, 318, 319
Boteti River 49, 196, 368, 369, 380, 381, 395, 396
Botswana Congress Party (BCP) 16
Botswana Defence Force (BDF) 14, 16, 66, 186
Botswana Democratic Party (BDP) 12–13, 14–15, 16
Botswana Independence Party 12
Botswana National Front (BNF) 14–15, 16
Botswana People's Party 12
Botswana Society, The 41
breakdowns, vehicle 119–20
bribery 115

British Protectorate of Bechuanaland
    see Bechuanaland
British South Africa Company 10–11
brood parasites 376
budgeting 78, **88–92**
buffalo 57, 58, 126–7, **483–4**
bungee-jumping, Victoria Falls 461–2
bus travel 133–4
    to/from Kasane 177–9
    to/from Livingstone 427–8
    to/from Maun 148
bush
    camping in 121–4
    walking in 125–8
bushbaby 475
bushbuck 478–9
Bushfront Lodge 440–1
Bushmen **21**, 23, **27**, 28, 191, 213, 345, 356, 421

cable swing, Victoria Falls 462
Camp Kalahari 394
Camp Moremi **255–6**, 280
Camp Okavango 280–1, **282–3**
Camp Okuti 256
Campbell, Alec 31, 217, 344, 389
camping 121–4
    equipment 93–4, **122–4**
camps
    fly-camps 298
    general remarks 135
campsites
    booking in national parks 87, 138
    choosing a site 121–2
canoeing, Upper Zambezi 463
Cape Colony 6, 7, 9, 10
Caprivi Strip 15, 225, 329, 334
car hire *see* vehicle hire
caracal 471
Carr, Norman 63
catfish 339
cattle fences 58, 59, 382, 403, 408
caves
    Gcwihaba Caverns 355–6, 361, *362*
    Waxhu Caves 363
CDW *see* collision damage waiver
Central Kalahari Game Reserve 70, *404*, **405–20**, *412–13*
    San communities in 27, 28–9, 405, **406**
Chamberlain, Joseph 11
channels, vegetation 57
Chapman, James 213, 379
Chapman's Baobab 395
charities 40
cheetah 57, **470**
Chief's Camp **266–71**, 309
Chief's Island 52, 241, 244, 246, 267, 306
Chitabe Camp 314–17
Chitabe Trails Camp 317

Chobe Chilwero Lodge 189
Chobe Forest Reserve 191, 204, 207, **209–11**
Chobe Game Lodge 203–4
Chobe Marina Lodge 181
Chobe National Park 174, **191–223**, *192–3*
Chobe River 58, 186, 191, 205, 211
Chobe riverfront 70, 191, **198–205**, *200*
Chobe Safari Lodge 180–1
Chobe Savannah Lodge 188, **204**
Chobe Snake Park 187
Chobe Society, The 41
cholera 100
Christianity 9, 34
civet 485
click languages 21, 22
climate 2, **52–3**, 67
clothing 92–3
  offensive **38**, 115
  on walking safaris 126
collision damage waiver 85–6
communications 139–40
Community Area (NG24) 289–90
Community Based Natural Resource Management (CBNRM) 64
community concessions *see* concessions
community-run projects 131
concessions, private and community **64**, 231, 285
conservation 41, **62–6**, 205
consulates *see* embassies and consulates
Costa, Lilian 150
craft markets, Livingstone/Victoria Falls 456–7
credit cards 92
Crocodile Camp 156–7
Crocodile Farm, Maun 164–5
Crocodile Park, Livingstone 457
crocodiles 130, 164–5, 333, 398, 457
cultural sensitivity 22, 37–9
culture, traditional 9, 29, **38–9**
curios **137**, 161–2, 447–8, 456–7
currency 2, 88, 91–2
Cusack, Emily 150
customs, Setswana 9
customs regulations 143

Damara molerat 411
dambo 55
David Livingstone Safari Lodge 441
Davis, Professor Ronald 23
De Beers 10, 13, 17
De Klerk, F W 15
Debswana 17, 403
Deception Pan 419
Deception Valley 406, 415, 418, **419–20**
Deception Valley Lodge 415–16
deep vein thrombosis *see* DVT
Delta Camp 303, 304, **305**
dengue fever 109
dentists 103–4
dialling codes, international 2, 140
diamonds 27, 28, 45, 381
  mining 10, 13, 16, **17–18**, 403
diarrhoea 108–9
Difaqane Wars 6–7
digital photography 96–7
diphtheria 100
diplomatic missions, Botswanan 73–4
disabled travellers 112–13
Dobetsaa Pans 258
Drifters Safaris 158
drink 136

driving 68, **117–21**, 130, 134
  near game 121, 208, 210
  techniques, 4x4 118–21
  through private concessions 231
Drotsky's Cabins 334
Drotsky's Caverns *see* Gcwihaba Caverns
drugs 115
drunk driving 134–5
dry season 52–3, **67**
Duba Plains Camp 288–9
Duba Plains Concession 284–9
duiker 481
Duma Tau Camp 230
DVT 104–5

Eagle Island Camp 303, **308–9**
economy 2, 13, **16–18**
ecotourism 18
education 7–8, 19, **37**, 150
eland 478
elections, general 13–16
electricity 2, **142**
elephant 57, 58, **481–2**
  Abu Camp 296–7
  Baby Huey 217
  driving near 121, 208, **210**
  facing a charge 127, **210**
  Grey Matters 321, 322
elephant-back safaris 295–7, 466–7
email 140, 450
embassies and consulates 142–3
  see also diplomatic missions, Botswanan
emergency services 140
emigration 9
entry fees, national parks 138–9
entry requirements 73–4
equipment hire 162–3
etiquette 22, 37–9
  on walking safaris 126
Etsha 6 289, **342–3**
Etsha 13 339
Etsha villages 341
evergreen forest 56–7
exchange rates 2, 88–9
expatriates 33
exports 17, 143

fault lines 46–9, *47*, *48*
fauna *see* game; species by name; wildlife
Fawcus, Peter 12
Fawlty Towers Lodge & Backpackers 434
fax 140, 450
ferries, Kazungula 175, 177
field guides 62, 493
film 96–7
fires, camp 122
fishing, Zambezi 455
flag 2
flamingos 388
flights
  over Okavango Delta 166
  over Victoria Falls 460–1
  see also air travel
floodplains, vegetation 57
floods, Okavango Delta 69, *69*, 305
flora 53–7, *54*
fly-in safaris
  costs 78, 90–1
  organising and booking 77–82
  suggested itineraries 82–3
folklore, Tsodilo Hills 346
food 135–6
  shopping for **137**, 161, 185, 446–7
  storage 106

Footsteps across the Delta 284
footwear 93
forests, vegetation 55–7
fox 472–3
Francistown
  animal orphanage 41
  driving to/from Kasane 175
  driving to/from Maun 148
fuel 117, 134
further reading 491–5

Gabasadi Island 391, **395**
Gaborone 12, 13, 15
  links with Maun 147
  population 2
game
  best season for viewing 68–71
  danger to campers from 124
  danger when boating 129–30
  driving near 121, 208, 210
  face-to-face encounters 126
  migrations **58–9**, 196, 225
  reserves 64
  see also species by name; wildlife
Gana people 27
garages
  Kasane 185
  Livingstone 451–2
  Maun 163–4
Garden Lodge 182
Gchoha Hills 46
Gcodikwe Lagoon **259**, 278, 279, 281
Gcwihaba Caverns 355–6, 361, *362*
Gcwihaba Hills 329, **355–63**
GDP 2, 17, 19, 20
gemsbok *see* oryx
genet 485
genetic research 22–3
geology 43–52
German-Herero War 32
Germany, colonisation 10, 32
getting around 67–8, **133–5**
getting there 74–7
  by air 74–6
  overland 76–7
Ghanzi 12, 76
Ghoha Gate 207, 208
Ghoha Hills 206, 209
Gidikwe Sand Ridge 46
giraffe 484
giving something back 39–40
global positioning system *see* GPS
Goaxhlo Island and Pan 257
Gobabis 76
gold mining 10, 11
golf 458–9
Gomoti River 244, 314, 315, 324, 325
Gondwanaland 43–5
Gordon, Robert 23, 353
GPS x, 95–7
grass seeds, driving through **119–20**, 350, 360
Great Rift Valley 46, 226
Great Salt Pans 43, 365–403, *366–7*
  flora and fauna 368–72
  geology 49
Great Zimbabwe dynasty 389
Green's Baobab 395
greetings 37–8, 489–90
Grey Matters 321, 322
Gubanare Camp 311
Gubanare Concession 309–14
Gubatsaa Hills 212, 215
Gudigwa 276
guesthouses
  general remarks 135
  see also under individual places

guides
  Tsodilo rock art 352
  walking 73, **125–6**
Guma Island Lodge 340, **341**
Guma Lagoon 339–42, *342*
Guma Lagoon Camp 341–2
Gumare 48–9, **343**
Gunn's Bushcamp 308
Gunn's Camp 307–8
Gutsha Pan 391
Gweta 391, **401**
Gweta Restcamp 401
Gwi people 27

Habu 343
Hailey, Lord 13
Hambukushu people 30–2, 191, 346, 351
handicrafts 32, **137**, 161–2, 447–8, 456–7
handshaking 38
hare 383, 488
hartebeest 59, **477**
Head, Bessie 7, **40**
health 99–113
  see also hospitals
heatstroke 107
helicopter trips, Victoria Falls 461
hepatitis 100, 109–10
Hereros *see* Ovaherero people
hippopotamus 128, **483**
  danger when boating 129–30
  hunting 31
history 3–16
  early peoples 3–6
  early settlers 8–9
  independence 13
  modern 12–16
  the Protectorate 9–12
  Tswana 6–8
hitchhiking 134–5
HIV 16, 17, 109
honey badger 195, 486
honorary consuls 142–3
horse-riding safaris 297–8, 312–14, 466
hospitals **103–4**, 164, 185, 451
host communities 131
hotels
  general remarks 135
  see also under individual places
Hottentot Venus 24
hunter-gatherers 4–5, 22, 23, 24, **25**
hunting 62, 63, **64–5**
  San methods 26
  Hwange National Park 195, 217
hyena 57, 397, **473**
hygiene 106, 130

Ichingo Chobe River Lodge 189
Ichobezi (safari boat) 189
Ihaha Public Campsite **202–3**, 206
Ikoga Gate 338
immunisations 99–100
impala 479
Impalila Island 188–90
Impalila Island Lodge 189–90
imports 17, 143
independence 13
industrial relations 18
infant mortality 2
inflation 16, 88
initiation ceremonies 8, 9, **38**
insects
  bites 106–7
  danger to campers 124
  Kalahari 370–2
insurance
  travel 99
  vehicle 85–6

international organisations 143
internet **140**, 163, 184, 450
investment, foreign 18
Iron Age 4–6
Island Safari Lodge 157–8
Islands of Siankaba 438–9
itineraries
  fly-in 82–3
  self-drive 86–7
ivory trade 8–9

Jacana Camp 290, 292, **294**
jackal 472
Jack's Camp 372, 383, **391–4**
Jameson Raid 11–12
Jao Camp 292
Jao Reserve 290–4
Jao River 241, 244, 265
Jedibe Camp 289
jet boats, Upper Zambezi 466
Johannesburg, as gateway 74–5, 147
Jollyboys Backpackers 435
Jwaneng 17

Kachikau 207
Kagalagari people 33
Kalahari Conservation Society 41
Kalahari Desert 5, 20
  Central Kalahari Game Reserve *404*, **405–20**
  geology of 45–9
  Great Salt Pans area 365–403
  Northwest area 329, **345–63**
  San communities 20, 24, 25, 27, 28
Kalahari sandveld 56
Kalahari Surf Club 402
Kanana Camp 299, 300, 301, **302**
Kariba weed (*Salvinia molesta*) 205
Kasane **175–88**, *176*, *178*
  accommodation 180–4
  driving to Savuti from 205–9
  getting there and away 175–9
  safari operators 186–7
  services 184–5
  what to see and do 187–8
  where to eat and drink 184
Kasikili Island *see* Sedudu Island
Katima Mulilo 30, 177, 205
Kavimba 207
kayaking, white-water 465–6
Kazikini Campsite **174**, 326
Kazungula 76, 175, 177
Kgama-Kgama Pan 365, 373, 378–9, *378*
Khama the Great, King 7, 9, 10, 11, 38–9
Khama, Lt-General Seretse Ian **15–16**, 141
Khama, Seretse *see* Seretse Khama
Khama, Tshedeki *see* Tshekedi Khama
Khoe people **4–5**, 21, **30**
Khoisan peoples 3, 4–6, 20–4, 29–30
  languages 35–6
Khumaga Campsite 400
Khwai Community Concessions 276
Khwai Gate *see* North Gate
Khwai River 215, 232–3, 244, 248–52
Khwai River Lodge **250**, 276
kimberlite pipes **45**, 381
Kingfisher Houseboat 439
King's Den 188, **204**
King's Pool Camp 229
Kiri fly-camp 313–14
klipspringer 480
Koanaka Hills 355
kori bustard 218
Krokovango Crocodile Farm, Shakawe 333

Kubu Island 381, 382, 386, 388, **389–90**
Kubu Lodge 183
Kudiakam Pan 365, 373, **379–80**
kudu 477–8
Kudumane 9
Kujwana Camp 313
Kukome Island 381, **390**
Kung! San 24
Kunyere Fault 49
Kwando Concession (NG14) 70, *224*, 225–6, **237–9**
Kwando River 45, 47, 59, 225, 237–8
Kwara Camp 279
Kwara Reserve (NG20) 276–80
Kwena people 7
Kwetsani Camp 290, 291, 292, **293–4**

Lagoon Camp 238–9
lagoons, vegetation 57
Land Rovers
  backed-up hire of 85
  spares 117
languages 2, **34–6**
  click 21, 22
  research 20, **21–2**
  Setswana 30, 34, **489–90**
  Sotho 33
law, traditional 39
Lebala 237
Lebala Camp 238–9
lechwe 480–1
leopard 57, 127–8, **469–70**
Leopard Pan 416
Leroo-La-Tau Lodge **399–400**, 415, 416
Leshoma 14
Letiahau Valley 419
Letlhakane 17, 403
Liambezi, Lake 207, 209, **211**, 225
life expectancy 2, 17, 19
Limpopo River 10, 45
Linyanti Campsite 222, **223**, 231
Linyanti Concession (NG15) 70, 222, *224*, 225, **226–30**
Linyanti River 47, 48–9, 59, 62, 194, 208, 211, 222–3, 225, 226
Linyanti Swamps 211, 212, 215, 225, 226, 230
Linyanti Tented Camp 222, **229**
Linyanti–Gumare Fault 48–9, 226
lion 57, 127, 398, 403, 466, **469**
literacy 19
Little Kwara Camp 280
Little Mombo Camp 270–1
Little Vumbura Camp 287–8
Livingstone **421–67**, *422*, *424*, *430–1*
  accommodation 429–44
  airport 426
  getting there and away 426–7
  services 446–52
  tour operators based in 467
  what to see and do 452–67
  where to eat 444–6
Livingstone, David 7, 9, **10**, 191, 198, 213, 241, 344, 421, 423
Livingstone, Mary 9
Livingstone Golf Club 458
Livingstone Island 454–5
Livingstone Museum 456
Lloyd's Camp 213, 217, 218
Lobatse 12
Lobengula 10
local payments 131
lodges
  general remarks 135
London Missionary Society 9, 11
long-haul flights 104–5

Luangwa 46
Lusaka, as gateway 76

Mababe Depression 212, 215, 225, 365
Mababe Gate 174, 221, 252
Mababe Village 174, 206, 221
Mabele 206, 207
Macatoo Camp 294, **298**
Machaba Camp 276
Mafikeng 13
Magwegqana Spillway *see* Selinda Spillway
Magwikhwe Sand Ridge 46, 174, 194, 212, 215, 220–1, 252
Mahango National Park 77, 336
Maherero, Samuel 32
Main, Mike 22, 43, 58, 95, 213, 215
Makgadikgadi Camp 372, **395**
Makgadikgadi, Lake 45–6, *46*, 194, 225, 368, 373, 395
Makgadikgadi Pans 45, 70, 365, 372, **380–95**
Makgadikgadi Pans National Park 365, *392–3*, **395–403**
Makoba Woods Campsite 354
Makuni village 459
Makwena Camp 290
malaria 109
   prophylaxis 100–1
Malatso Campsite 354–5
Mamili National Park 225
mammals *see* wildlife
Mamuno 76
Mankwe Bush Lodge 174, **327**
Mankwe Reserve 326–7
maps **94–5**, 143, 149
   Department of Survey and Mapping 143, 149
Maqwee Gate *see* South Gate
Maramba River Lodge 443
Marshall, John 24, 25
Masire, Sir Kentumile 12, 13, **14–15**
massages 459
Masuwe Estate 466
Matetsi River 423
Matswere Scout Post 410, 416, 419, 420
Maun *146*, **147–73**, *152–3*, *157*
   accommodation 150–9
   climate 53
   getting around 149–50
   getting there and away 147–8, 173–4
   safari operators 168–72
   services 161–4
   what to see and do 164–7
   where to eat 159–60
Maun Educational Park 164
Maun Lodge **151**, 159
Maun Rest Camp 158
Maun Sports Complex 165
Mbiroba Camp 331, **332**, 333
Mboma Island 253, **258**
Mboroga River 315
media 140–2
medical kit 103
meerkat 486
melons 382
Meno A Kwena Lodge 398–9
mephato *see* age regiments
microlight trips, Victoria Falls 461
mineral deposits **17–18**, 28, 29, 45, 380–1
miombo woodland 55
missionaries 7, **9**, 32
Mmatshumo Village 390
Mmusi, Peter 15

Moanachira River 244, 255, 281
mobile safaris 83–4, 90
Moeng College of higher education 8
Moffat, Robert 9
Mogae, Festus **15–16**, 28
Mohembo 77, 329, 331, **333**, *335*
Moklowane Camp 313
Mokoba Camp 236
mokoro 31, **128–9**
   budget trips 321–2
   trips 165–6, 258–9
Mombo Camp 264, **266–71**, 309
money 88–92
mongoose 485–6
monitor lizard 300
monkey 474
Mopane Tongue 241, 244, **248–63**
   accommodation 250–1, 255–9, 261
   flora and fauna 249–50
   getting there and away 251–3, 259–60, 261–3
mopane woodland 54
Mopipi 391, 402
Moremi Game Reserve 70, 173–4, 221, **241–63**, *242–3*
   flora and fauna 41, **244–5**, 246
   private areas of (NG28) 264–71
   private reserves around 273–327
   regulations 248
   when and how to visit 245–6
Mosi-oa-Tunya National Park 422
mosquitoes 100, 106–7, 111
Motopi **402–3**, 411, 414, 418
Motopi Pan 418
motor boats **129**, 187–8
Motsentsela Tree Lodge 151, 154
Motswiri Camp 230, 235, **236**
Mowana Safari Lodge 182
Muchenje Safari Lodge 209–11
mud, driving in 120
Mugabe, Robert 14
Muyongo, Mishake 15

Namibia 15, 225
   as entry point 76–7, 177, 204–5, 333
   San communities 24
   and Sedudu Island 15, **186**
Nantanga Pans 206
Nata 175, 365, **385**, 388
Nata Lodge 385, **386**, 388, 389
Nata River 365, 368, 382, 384, 386, 388
Nata Sanctuary 365, 372, 385, **388–9**
national anthem 2
national parks 64, 138
   booking and entry fees 64, **138–9**
Natural Mystic Lodge 438
navigation **94–7**, 117–18
Ndebele people 421
newspapers 141, 496
NG12 – Gudigwa 276
NG14 – Kwando Concession 237–9
NG15 – Linyanti Concession 226–30
NG16 – Selinda Concession 230–6
NG18 and NG19 – Khwai Community Concessions 276
NG20 – Kwara Reserve 276–80
NG21 – Xugana, Camp Okavango and Shinde 280–4
NG22 and NG23 – Vumbura and Duba Plains 284–9
NG24 – Community Area 289–90
NG25 – Joa, Kwetsani, Jacana and Tubu Camps 290–4
NG26 – Abu Camp and Macatoo 294–9
NG27A – Pom Pom, Kanana and Nxabega 299–303

NG27B – Delta, Oddballs, Gunn's and Eagle Island 303–9
NG28 – Xigera, Mombo and Chief's Camp **264–71**, 309
NG29 and NG30 – Gubanare and Xudum 309–14
NG31 – Chitabe and Sandibe 314–18
NG32 – Stanley's and Baines' Camp 318–22
NG33 – Sankuyo Tswaragano Community Trust 322–3
NG34 – Sankuyo Community Trust and Starling's Camp 323–6
NG43 – Mankwe 326–7
Ngami, Lake 9, 46, 49, 128–9, 241, **344–5**
Ngamiland 64
Ngoma 77, 177, 198, **204–5**, 206, 209
Ngoni people 6
Ngwaketse people 7
Ngwato dynasty 7–8
Ngwezumba Pans 194, 206, **211–12**
Nhabe Museum, Maun 166
nightlife 161, 446
Nile River 9
Njuca Hills Campsite 400
Nkomo, Joshua 14
Nogatsaa 206, 212
Nogatsaa Pans 194
Nokaneng 77, **343**
North Gate 246, *247*, **248–52**
   getting there and away 251–3, 259, 262
North Gate (Khwai) Campsite 251
Nqoga River 241, 244, 305
Ntwala 190
Ntwetwe Pan 365, 372, 380, 381, **391–5**, *392–3*
Nxabega Camp 299, 300–1, **302–3**
Nxai Pan 70, 196, 365, 373, 375, 378, *378*
Nxai Pans National Park 365, **373–80**, *374*
   accommodation 377
   flora and fauna 373–6
Nxamaseri 336–7
Nxamaseri Lodge 337
Nxunxutsha Pan 206

Oddballs Palm Island Luxury Lodge 303, 304, **307**
Okavango Delta 15, 43, 70, 225–6, **241–345**
   annual flood 69, *69*, 305
   flights over 166
   formation of *48*, 49–52
   Moremi Game Reserve 241–63
Okavango Kopano Mokoro Community Trust (OKMCT) 166
Okavango Panhandle 49, 51, 226, 232, *328*, **329–38**
   private areas of Moremi 264–71
   private reserves around Moremi **273–327**, *274–5*
   vegetation 57
   Western fringes 338–45
Okavango River 15, 45, 49, 59, 62, 225–6, 329–30, 336
Okavango River Lodge 155, **158–9**
Okavango Wildlife Society 41
Orange River 45
Orapa 13, 17, 365, 381, 391, **403**
oryx 476
ostriches 399
otter 486–7
Ovaherero people 32, 344, 356
Ovambanderu people 32

overheating, vehicle 120
overland routes 76–7
Owens, Mark and Delia 58, 406

packing 92–4
Palapye 7, 33
Pandametenga 76, 177
pangolin 487
Panhandle 49, 51, 226, 232, *328*, **329–38**
  accommodation 332, 334–6, 337, 338
  Eastern 331–3
  flora and fauna 330–1
  getting around 331
  getting there and away 331–2, 333
  Western 333–8
pans 55
papyrus 262
  swamps 263
Parakarunga 207
Passarge Pan 418
Passarge Valley 416–17
permits, national parks 138–9
pharmacies **105**, 164, 448
Phofu dynasty 6
Phokoje Pan 418
photography **96–8**
  best season for 71–2
  sensitivity about **38–9**, 97, 115
  supplies 164, 449
  wildlife 63
phrases 489–90
Phukwi Pan 418
Piper's Pan 418, *419*
Planet Baobab 401–2
Plumtree 76
poachers 63, **66**
police 114
polio 100
politics 13–16
Pom Pom Camp 299, 300, 302, **304**
population 2, **19**
porcupine 487–8
postal services **139**, 185
  Livingstone 450
  Maun 163
poverty 18
press 140–1
prices 88–92
  flights 75, 76, 426
  in rural communities 131
  safaris 73, 89–91
  seasonal variation 73, 246
Pride of the Zambezi (houseboat) 439–40
private concessions *see* concessions
public holidays 2, **137–8**
puku 481
push-starts, vehicle 120

Qua Ledibe 253
quad bike excursions 467
Qwapu fly-camp 313–14

rabies 100, 110
radio 141
rafting, white-water 463–5
rail travel 133, 428
Railway Museum, Livingstone 456
rain-making 32
rainfall 52–3
Rakops **402**, 409, 410, 414, **420**
Ramokgwebane 76
Rann's Camp 311
Reader, John 6, 24, 43
red lechwe 480–1
reedbuck 480

refugees
  Namibian 15
  Zimbabwean 14, 16
religion 2, 9, **34**
resettlement policies 28–9
responsible tourism 65, **130–1**
restaurants
  general remarks 136
  see also under individual places
rhinoceros 41, 57, 127, 195–6, **482–3**
Rhodes, Cecil John **10–11**, 12
Rhodesia 11, 14
riding *see* horse-riding
Riley's Hotel, Maun **154**, 159
River Club, The 436–7
river-boarding, Zambezi rapids 465
riverine forest 56–7
rivers, driving across 121
road travel *see* bus travel; driving;
  hitchhiking; self-driving trips; taxis;
  vehicle hire
roads 118–21, 134
roan antelope 475–6
rock hyrax 488
rock paintings 3, 213
  Tsodilo Hills 3, 345, **352–4**
rocky terrain, driving in 120
Royal Chundu Zambezi River Lodge 439
Royal Livingstone 441
rubbish 131

sable antelope 475–6
safari operators
  Kasane 186–7
  Livingstone 467
  Maun 168–72
  offices outside Botswana 79
safaris
  budgeting for 78, 89–91
  elephant-back 295–7, 466–7
  fly-in 77–82, 90–1
  horse-riding 297–8, 312–14, 466
  mobile 83–4, 90
  organising and booking 77–88
  self-drive 68, 84–8, 90
  walking 72–3, **125–8**, 236, 284, 326
safety 113–15
  boating 129–30
  camping 124
  driving at night 118
  in Great Salt Pans 385
  hitchhiking 135
  safari camps 295
  vehicle breakdown 119–20
  walking in the bush 125–8
salt pans 49, 55, 365–403
San Camp 394–5
San Pan 418
San people 3, 4, **20–9**, 213, 345, 346, 355, 391, 421
  political representation of 26–7
San village, Tsodilo Hills 351–2
sand, driving in 119
Sandenberg, Peter 65
Sandibe Camp 314–18
Sandvelt Tongue 309
Sankuyo Tswaragano Community
  Trust 174, **322–6**
Sankuyo Village 174
Santantadibe River 165, 166, 315, 318, 319
Santawani Safari Lodge 262, **322–3**
Savute Elephant Camp 219
Savute Safari Lodge 219–20
Savuti 194, **212–20**, *214*
Savuti Camp (NG15) 220, **230**
Savuti Campsite 218–19

Savuti Channel 194, 196, **212–15**, 217, 225, 226, 231
Savuti Marsh 191, 194, 212, 215, 220
schistosomiasis 110
scorpions 107, 124
seasons 67–73
Sebele, Chief 11
Sechele, King 7
Sedia Hotel, Maun **154–5**, 159
Sedudu Island 15, **186**
Sedudu Lodge 181
Segkoma I, Chief 7
Segkoma II, King **7**, 9
Sehithwa 329, 332, **343**
self-driving trips
  best season for 68
  cost 84–5, 90
  organising and booking 84–6, 87–8
  suggested itineraries 86–7
Selinda Camp 230, **235**
Selinda Concession (NG16) *224*, 225–6, **230–6**
Selinda Spillway 48, 225, 226, 230, 236
Selous, Frederick Courtney 213
Semetsi Camp 308
Sepupa 330, **337–8**
Sepupa Swamp Stop 338
Seretse Khama 7, 8, 12, **13–14**
Serondela Campsite **203**, 206
Seronga 221, 330, 331, **332**, 338
Serowe 7, **40**
serval 471
Seseke 177
Setata Veterinary Fence Gate 343
Setswana
  customs 9
  language 30, 34, 489–90
sexually transmitted diseases 109
Shaka, Zulu leader 6, 7
Shakawe 77, 329, 330, 332, **333**, *335*
Shakawe Lodge 334–6
Shandereka Cultural Village 326
Shinde Camp 280–2, **283–4**
shopping
  for food and drink 137, 446–7
  for souvenirs and curios 137, 447–8
  in Kasane 185
  in Livingstone 446–9
  in Maun 161–3
Shorobe 173–4, 263
Shoshong 7, 9
sightseeing tours, Livingstone area 459–60
Sindabezi Island 437
sink holes 363
Sitatunga 478
Sitatunga Camp 159
slavery 6–7, 23–4
sleeping bags 123
sleeping sickness 110–11
snakes 124, 128, 187
  bites 107–8
social system, San 25–6
soft drinks 136
Songwe Point Village 442, 459
Sotho language 33
South Africa, as entry point 77
South Gate 260–3
  flora and fauna 260–1
  getting there and away 253, 259–60, 261–3
South Gate Campsite 261
Southern Africa Customs Union 13, 17
Southern African Development
  Community 17

Southern African Development
  Coordination Conference
  (SADCC) 14
souvenirs **137**, 161–2, 185, 447–8,
  456–7
Sowa Pan Mine 390
spare parts, vehicle **117**, 163–4, 185,
  451–2
spiders 107, 124
spring hares 383
springbok 479–80
squirrel 488
Squirrel Valley Camp 354
Stanley Safari Lodge 443–4
Stanley's Camp 318, **320**
star-gazing 277–8
Starling's Camp 174, 323, **326**
steenbok 481
Stone Age 4–5, 347, 379, 391
stoves, camping 123
street children 150
Sua Pan 365, 372, 380, 381, **386–90**,
  387
sunburn 107
Sunday Pan 416
suricate *see* meerkat
Survival International 27, 28
Susi Lodge & Chuma House 435–6
Swakopmund 32
swamp forest 57

Taita Falcon Lodge 442–3
Tati 12
Tau Pan 418
taxis
  Livingstone 428
  Maun 149
Tchinga 194, 206, 212
teak forests 55–6
telephone services **140**
  Livingstone 450–1
  Maun 185
television 141–2
telex 140
temperance 11, 38
temperatures 52–3
tents 122, 123
termites 371
tetanus 100
Thabatshukudu Village 390
Thamalakane Fault 49, 225
Thamalakane River 49
Thaoge River 244, 305
Thebe River Camping 182
theft 114
Third Bridge 257, 258, 260, 261
Thithaba Island 389
Thorn Tree Lodge 436
Tilbury, Alan 12
time zone 2
tipping 91
Tokaleya people 421
Tongabezi 437
Tongala House 438
topography 43
torches 123–4
Toro Safari Lodge 182–3
Toromoja 4
Toteng 344
tour operators 79–82
  Kasane 186–7
  Livingstone 467
  Maun 167–72
  see also safari operators; travel agents

tourism 16, 29, **65**
  high-revenue, low-volume policy
    63, 138, 191
  levels of **18**, 191
  responsible 65, **130–1**
  sustainable 63, 64
tourist board offices 74, 425
Toutswe 5
tracks, animal 59, 60–1
traders 8–9
trance dancing, San 26
Trans-Kalahari Highway 76
Transvaal 9, 11
travel *see* air travel; bus travel; getting
  around; getting there; rail travel;
  road travel
travel agents
  Kasane 186
  Livingstone 451
  Maun 167
travel clinics 101–3
travellers' cheques 91–2
tribes 19–20
Trotha, General von 32
trypanosomiasis 110–11
Tsaro Elephant Lodge **250–1**, 276
Tsau 343
tsessebe 477
tsetse fly 110–11
Tshekedi Khama 7–8, 12
Tshukumutshu 352
Tshwagong 389
Tshwene Camp 236
Tsodilo Hills 329, *335*, **345–55**, *348*
  rock paintings 3, 347, **352–4**
  trails 352–4
Tsumkwe 24, 77
Tswana people **6–8**, 9, 11, 12, 30, 34,
  40, 405–6
Tswapong Hills 6
tuberculosis 100
Tubu Tree Camp 290–2, **294**
Tuli 12
typhoid 100

Uitlanders 11
ultra-light trips, Victoria Falls 461
unemployment 14, 16
Union of South Africa 12

vaccinations *see* immunisations
van der Post, Laurens 24, 346, 353–4
vegetation **53–7**, *54*, 68
vehicle breakdowns 117, 119–20
vehicle hire **84–6**
  Kasane 179
  Livingstone 429
  Maun 149
Victoria, Lake 4
Victoria, Queen 11, 39
Victoria Falls 46–7, 421–5, *424*, **452–4**
  activities around 460–7
  airport 75, 461
  bridge 462
Victoria Falls Aquarium 458
Victoria Falls Crocodile Park 457
Victoria Falls National Park 453
villages, traditional 167, 174, 326,
  351–2, 459
visas 73, 425
Vumbura Concession 284–9
Vumbura Plains Camp 288

wages 18

walking
  in the bush 125–8
  safaris **72–3**, **125–8**, 236, 284, 326
  trails 125
  trails camps 236
warthog 484
water
  containers 124
  drinking 19, **106**, 136–7
  driving through 121
Water Lily Lodge 181
Waterberg 32, 344
waterbuck 476
waterlilies 277
Waxhu caves 363
websites 495–6
weights and measures 2
wet season 52–3, **67**
what to take 92–8
wheelchair access 112–13
when to go 67–73
white Botswanans 33
white-water kayaking 465–6
white-water rafting 463–5
whydahs 376
wild dog 57, 262, 323, **471–2**
wildebeest 59, **476–7**
wildlife 57–62, **469–88**
  best season for 68–71
  conservation 41, **62–6**, 403
  danger to campers 124
  see also birdlife; game; species by
    name
wildlife management areas 64
Williams, Ruth 8, 12
Wilmot, Lloyd 213, 218
Windhoek 32, 76, 147–8
Witwatersrand 10, 11
women travellers 113–14, **115**, 135

Xade 29, 406
Xai Xai 356, 359, 360
Xakanaxa Camp 256
Xakanaxa Campsite 256–7
Xakanaxa Lagoon 246, **253–60**, *254*,
  281
Xaro Lodge 334
Xau, Lake 59, 365, 391
Xigera Camp **264–6**, 309
Xudum Camp 311–12
Xudum Concession 309–14
Xugana Island Lodge 280–1, **282**
Xwaraga Campsite **400**, 415, 416

Zambezi Express (train) 428
Zambezi River 45, 46–7, 49, 421, *422*,
  423
  activities on 455, 460, 463–6
  cruises 454–5
  Victoria Falls 421–5
Zambezi Sun 442
Zambezi Waterfront 440
Zambia 9, **421–67**
  as entry point 76, 177
zebra 59, **484**
Zepa Camp 264, 266
Zhu bushmen 3
Zibadianja Lagoon 212, 215, 226, 232,
  233
Zibalianja Camp 230, **235–6**
Zimbabwe 14, 16, 421, 425, 426,
  453–4, 457
  as entry point 76, 175, 177
Zweizwe 194